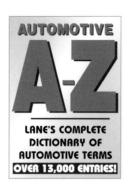

AUTOMOTIVE A-Z

LANE'S COMPLETE
DICTIONARY OF
AUTOMOTIVE TERMS

OVER 13,000 ENTRIES!

I dedicate this book to Val, my wife and co-driver, and to my children Paul, Phillip and Charlotte
for their constant encouragement.

First published in 2002 by Veloce Publishing Ltd., 33, Trinity Street, Dorchester DT1 1TT, England. Fax: 01305 268864/e-mail: info@veloce.co.uk/website:
www.veloce.co.uk
ISBN: 1-901295-92-3/UPC: 36847-00192-6
© 2002 Keith Lane and Veloce Publishing Ltd

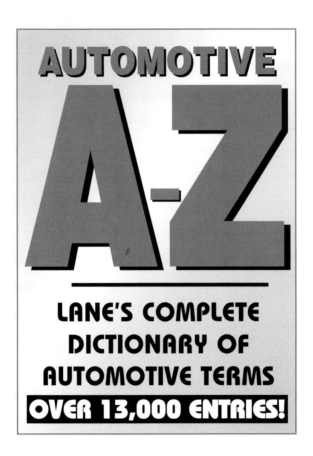

AUTOMOTIVE A-Z

LANE'S COMPLETE DICTIONARY OF AUTOMOTIVE TERMS

OVER 13,000 ENTRIES!

Keith Lane

VELOCE PUBLISHING
THE PUBLISHER OF FINE AUTOMOTIVE BOOKS

CONTENTS

Introduction
& Preface

Back in the days of The Jackson Five it may have been as simple as 1-2-3 but in the world of today's mysterious motoring jargon ABC could probably stand for just about anything, and let's face it, would you know what? What about ASC, BAS, or CBC come to mention it? Thought not.

But the simple fact is that these days manufacturers use these terms all the time. Most now quote the power output of their engines as PS, and not simply because they forgot to mention it the first time round.

Do you understand what these terms really mean or do you simply smile and nod when your colleagues are banging on about bobtailing and bunnyhopping when your knowledge of modern terminology really only extends as far as ABS?

Isn't it all getting just a little OTT?

But despite the fact that very few people are able to wade through this quagmire of inexplicable gibberish, it remains the case that glossy brochures are littered with it as the manufacturers try to bamboozle you with science and, time and again, if its got RSW and TPC you'll buy it.

Well now, finally, you too can understand exactly what that pushy salesman is harping on about. It may be ACE but now you can decide for yourself whether you really need it.

This essential dictionary finally unravels all those automotive buzzwords in a definitive layman's guide. If you drive any type of vehicle or just want to keep up with the latest developments, this dictionary will keep you one step ahead of the pack, so you'll know why those dampers are filled with gas even if your gas-filled salesman doesn't.

What this dictionary is not, is a list of vehicle manufacturers, nor is it a list of model names nor model numbers nor designations of vehicles. This dictionary does contain many vehicle component names, however it does not attempt to go into such technical detail that a doctorate in automobile engineering would be necessary to understand a definition.

One of the many features of this dictionary is to seek to put a name to letters commonly used as an abbreviation. For example the manufacturer denoted by the initials BMW is well known but only by those initials, this dictionary seeks to give the original or full name to such an organisation.

Although unusual for a dictionary, there is a large section of numbered entries here. The normal convention for dealing with a numbered entry would be to convert it into a word and incorporate it generally. Unfortunately in the subject areas of driving and vehicles that may not be possible because of the style of some abbreviations in use. For example, the requirement may be to find what '4L' means, or even '4LLc'. Of course these are not words at all, but as abbreviations they certainly have a meaning. Following convention, all the numbered entries have been listed before the letter A, whilst the few Greek letters in common use are listed in the appendix.

While researching this dictionary many initialled entries were observed in many different formats. For example, ac, a.c., a/c, a-c, AC, A.C., A/C, and A-C, were observed in various publications and all denoting air conditioning. In some cases if a format is observed to be most common, then this has been used. Wherever a variety of styles has been seen without a common trend then for simplicity preference has been given here to using the lower case format in the simplest form observed.

Some organisations known primarily by initials sometimes have a stop between each letter and sometimes do not, and in many other cases other abbreviations may be written with and without stops, for example ADI and A.D.I. For standardisation and to follow the most modern trend, no stops have been used at all. However, in some cases organisations may use a specific style, *e.g.* 'RoSPA', in all of these cases respect has been given to the official style where one exists.

It appears that hyphens are used almost at random by many authors and publishers. Many of the entries in this dictionary are actually two words used together to give a new meaning, for example: 'blow-out'. If such entries have been observed in publication with and without a hyphen then the hyphens have been discarded wherever possible.

Some headwords may remain as two separate words or they may have become combined as one new word. For example 'airbag' is now commonly in print as one word whereas 'air cleaner' remains as two words. It would appear that there may be a gradual evolution towards combining two separate words into one with time and usage.

Many of the definitions have a subsequent definition, *i.e.* where an abbreviation is expanded to give its full wording this may then have been used elsewhere as a headword thereby providing additional definition. For example, ABC is defined as 'active body control'. This definition then becomes a new headword to give the definition 'an active suspension system that … ' etc. Similarly, sometimes within a definition, a word or phrase is used which is defined elsewhere.

An objective of any dictionary is to remove inconsistencies, this has been a major function here too. Which is correct when the clutch is transmitting power: clutch in, or, clutch out? A perceived answer in some cases may depend upon the area in which the reader lives. Similarly, some other parts or techniques or terms may have two or more names, and where feasible all names have been accorded their own headword, this results in different headwords having similar definitions.

Conversely one headword may have several definitions. Where the meanings are similar the definitions are listed under the one headword. However, where the definitions differ significantly the headword is repeated for each definition.

As this dictionary will be used by drivers in many different countries, some of whom drive on the left and others on the right, the words left and right are not normally used in relation to vehicles, manoeuvres, or junctions where confusion could arise. Instead, the terms nearside and offside are used to enable the book to be equally readable to all.

Some of the definitions are of legal terms as used in Acts and Regulations from various countries. For the sake of brevity and simplicity some of these legal definitions are paraphrased to remove legal jargon and clauses, to make them easier to read and understand.

A function of this dictionary is to list in print as much new technology as was available at the time of publication. However, new technology is developing in vehicles at as fast a pace as in any other field. The editor shall therefore remain grateful to readers and particularly to manufacturers for their suggestions enabling extension of this work in future editions. All comments including those regarding any errors or omissions will be greatly appreciated, and possibly incorporated into future editions.

Comments should be sent to: automotive_az@hotmail.com

DISCLAIMER

This book contains descriptions of many techniques and procedures, some of which should NOT be attempted without the guidance of a specialist instructor in a suitable vehicle in a suitable place, and which must NOT be attempted in a public place or on a public road. Such techniques could cause injury or death to a driver, passenger, or any person nearby, or damage to a vehicle or to the environment. The author and publisher cannot be held liable for the actions of any person following or attempting to follow any of the techniques described.

Visit us on the web –
veloce.co.uk
velocebooks.com

NUMERICAL TERMS

0 – 60, a measure of acceleration performance, the time taken to accelerate from rest to 100 km/h (62.137 mph).

$^1/_4$ bumper, a style of bumper mounted around the 4 corners of a vehicle only, leaving the centre of the front and rear unprotected, typically on some classic sports cars.

$^1/_4$ elliptic spring, half of a semielliptic leaf spring, typically mounted longitudinally and cantilevered such that all leaves are rigidly attached to the chassis with the axle at the sprung end.

$^1/_4$ floating axle, an axle drive shaft which transmits torque to a wheel, and at its outer end it also supports and restrains the wheel vertically and laterally.

$^1/_4$ light, a small triangular side window at the leading edge of the front door abutting the A pillar and typically swivelling on a vertical axis to open, occasionally abutting the C pillar.

$^1/_4$ mile, USA, a distance of 1,320 feet (402.3 metres) along a straight test track used to measure the acceleration performance of a vehicle from rest in terms of the minimum time taken for travel and the vehicle speed at the end point.

$^1/_4$ panel, the rear side section of a bodyshell including the C pillar.

$^1/_4$ to 3, the modern pattern for holding the steering wheel giving maximum control, having the left hand at 9 o'clock and the right hand at 3 o'clock, the standard hold.

$^1/_4$ turn fastener, a button shaped positive locking quick release device, for retaining engine covers etc.

$^1/_4$ window, USA, $^1/_4$ light.

$^1/_2$ cab, a bus or lorry having a drivers compartment on 1 side of the vehicle only, typically on older buses.

$^1/_2$ change, to change a $^1/_2$ gear up or down on a transmission having a splitter.

$^1/_2$ cloverleaf, a grade separated junction where a road crosses a motorway or similar, using 1 overbridge and where 2 link roads turn through 180° or more; see appendices.

$^1/_2$ diamond, a grade separated restricted access junction having 1 bridge over or under the main road but only 1 pair of sliproads to/from the lesser roads, typically used to match traffic demand or where space is minimal; named from the resulting plan shape; see appendices.

$^1/_2$ gear, a splitter system having $^1/_2$ gears between each primary gear.

$^1/_2$ inch rule, the maximum distance a window should be opened in any high risk stationary traffic situation to avoid risk of personal attack or theft; also named 1 cm rule.

$^1/_2$ lane straddle, the position of an emergency vehicle when straddling the centre of a 2 way road whilst in emergency driving mode, allowing the driver maximum visibility ahead and maximum visibility to oncoming drivers.

$^1/_2$ lock, the angle of the front wheels when they have slewed approximately $^1/_2$ the angle between straight and full lock to either the left or right.

$^1/_2$ shaft, the shaft that transmits the drive from the differential to the wheel, the driving axle at 1 side.

$^1/_2$ shift, to change a $^1/_2$ gear up or down on a transmission having a splitter.

$^1/_2$ split, to change a $^1/_2$ gear up or down on a transmission having a splitter.

$^1/_2$ track, a tracklaying vehicle so designed and constructed that its weight is transmitted to the road surface by a combination of wheels and continuous tracks whereby the weight transmitted to the road surface by the tracks is not less than $^1/_2$ the weight of the vehicle, (C&U); typically of military origin.

$^3/_4$ floating axle, an axle drive shaft which transmits torque to a wheel, and at its outer end it also restrains the wheel laterally, but it does not transmit any vertical load.

$^3/_4$ rule, an allowance to reduce lateness on standard sections of a road rally which exceed 4 miles (6.4 km) in length, which allows *e.g.* a 12 minute section to be completed in 9 minutes but not less.

1, see also: A, B, C, category, child, class, cylinder, D, dog leg, Euro, formula, Highway, HORT, L, lane, LL, Route, see, stage, STGO, T, Thatcham, tier.

1, 1st gear, a gear which gives a low ratio of road speed to engine speed, such that it gives the highest torque so is used for moving off, hill starts, and climbing very steep hills; on an automatic gear selector it restricts automatic selection by the gearbox to the lowest forward gear only.

1 armed bandit, CB jargon, a petrol pump or fuel pump.

1 bell, part of the bus conductor to driver bell code: stop when safe.

1 box, a car body style without externally obvious divisions between engine and passenger compartments.

1 cm rule, the maximum distance a window should be opened in any high risk stationary traffic situation to avoid risk of personal attack or theft; also named $^1/_2$ inch rule.

1 cyl, an engine having a single cylinder and piston.

1st cylinder, the reference cylinder in an engine upon which the timings of the other cylinders follow, usually the cylinder on the crankshaft furthest from the flywheel.

1 for the road, a suggestion of 1 additional alcoholic drink just before leaving to drive, obsolete since the advent of drink driving legislation.

1L, a rally pace note, an easy bend to the left through about 20°.

1 lane bridge, a narrow bridge having sufficient width only for traffic to flow in 1 direction, typically marked with signs stating which direction has priority.

1 off, a concept car of which only a single example is made.

1 off, a hybrid or kit car of which there is no closely similar vehicle.

1P, Australia, a parking area having a 1 hour time limit.

1st party, the insurance company.

1 piece rim, a wheel rim and disc manufactured as 1 piece.

1 point steering, a steering system at the front of some heavy trailers where the front axle pivots on a turntable.

1 point turn, to perform a U turn with any vehicle, to turn a vehicle around through 180° to face in the opposite direction in 1 continuous forwards movement.

1R, a rally pace note, an easy bend to the right through about 20°.

1 star, a quality of leaded petrol with a rating of 87 to 90 octane.

1v, a carburettor with a single venturi.

1+V, a composite transmission system having a manual 1st gear and a CVT system for higher gearing.

1 way clutch, a clutch which transmits power in 1 direction only and freewheels to prevent power being transmitted in the other direction.

1 way street, a road where traffic is permitted to travel in 1 direction only, first used in London in 1617 when 17 streets were restricted.

1.3 %, the angle of downwards alignment of the top of the horizontal cutoff of an asymmetrical dipped headlight beam on a vehicle where the headlamp centre is not more than 850 mm from the ground.

$1^1/_2$ cab, club cab, a single cab on a pickup having an extended area behind the front seats for storage of small items.

2, see also: 3+, 4x, 6x, 8x, 10 to, blues, braking, child, class, D, Euro, formula, H, invalid, L, lane, LL, M5x, see 1, stage, STGO, T, Thatcham, WW.

2, 2nd gear from lowest, on an automatic gear selector it restricts automatic selection by the gearbox to the 2 lowest forward gears only.

2, 2wd, referring to a selector position on a manually lockable fwh.

2.0 %, the angle of downwards alignment of the top of the horizontal cutoff of an asymmetrical dipped headlight beam, on a vehicle where the headlamp centre is more than 850 mm from the ground.

2+2, a sports car or coupé with 2 normal seats at the front but seats sized only for 2 small children at the rear.

2+2, a combination of a 2 axle tractive unit with a tandem semitrailer.

2+3, a combination of a 2 axle tractive unit with a triaxle semitrailer.

2-3, a selection range on an automatic gearbox selector, the transmission will start the vehicle moving in 2nd gear and not use any gears higher than 3rd gear.

2-4, a selection range on an automatic gearbox selector, the transmission will start the vehicle moving in 2nd gear and not use any gears higher than 4th gear.

2-5, a selection range on an automatic gearbox selector, the transmission will start the vehicle moving in 2nd gear and not use any gears higher than 5th gear, on a 5 speed auto it is the equivalent to selecting D.

2 axle dolly, a short trailer comprising only an A frame drawbar with 2 axles and carrying a 5th wheel coupling, to enable a semitrailer to be drawn by a rigid lorry or by other vehicles, *e.g.* an agricultural tractor.

2 barrel, a carburettor with 2 throttle valves, operating simultaneously or sequentially.

2 bells, part of the bus conductor to driver bell code: move off when safe.

2 box, a modern design of car having the engine in the first box at the front, and the passenger compartment comprises the second box.

2 bridge roundabout, a grade separated junction on 2 levels where the main carriageway passes under or over 2 bridges carrying part of a large roundabout, and the roundabout is connected to the main carriageway by 4 sliproads, typical of many junctions between a motorway and a main road; see appendices.

2 cycle engine, USA, 2 stroke engine.

2 cyl, an engine having 2 cylinders and pistons.

2d, a 2 door car.

2H, a selectable gear range on a 4wd vehicle, it transmits the drive to 2 wheels only using high (normal) range.

2L, a rally pace note, a fast bend to the left through about 30°.

2 lane highway, USA, a single carriageway road carrying 2 way traffic.

2+ lane, a lane on a multilane road reserved for

vehicles transporting 2 or more occupants.

2 line brakes, an air brake system comprising a service line using a yellow hose, and an emergency line using a red hose.

2P, Australia, a parking area having a 2 hour time limit.

2 part adhesive, a glue supplied in 2 parts, a resin and an accelerator which are mixed only just before application.

2nd party, the insured driver or vehicle.

2 pedal drive, a vehicle with automatic transmission.

2 piece wheel, a wheel consisting of a separate rim and spider (or disc) which are bolted together.

2 plus 2, a sports car or coupé with 2 normal seats at the front but seats sized only for 2 small children at the rear.

2 point belt, a seat belt being a lap strap only and having 2 fixing points, often fitted to the centre of the rear seat.

2 point steering, the conventional Ackermann steering system in which each steered wheel slews around its own pivot.

2 point turn, to turn a vehicle around to face the opposite direction within the width of the road using 2 shunts: the first shunt is to reverse on full lock to at least 90° across the road, then drive forwards to complete the turn; similar manoeuvres on a narrower road involving a greater number of shunts will result in 4, 6, 8, etc. point turns, most useful if starting from the wrong side of the road.

2 point turn, USA, to turn a vehicle around to face the opposite direction, by either: driving into a 90° opening on the left, or reversing into a 90° opening on the right, then reversing or driving back onto the road.

2 pot, brake calipers having 2 cylinders.

2R, a rally pace note, a fast bend to the right through about 30°.

2 seater, typically a sports car seating only 2 persons.

2 second rule, a primary safety rule requiring the maintenance of a minimum time interval of 2 seconds between the rear of the vehicle ahead and the front of your vehicle, and which should be lengthened by additional seconds in high risk conditions, a basic defensive principle important at all speeds above 15 km/h (10 mph); see also: 3 second, 4 second.

2 speed, a vehicle with only 2 forward gears, typically only veteran vehicles.

2 speed, a function of some minor controls, *e.g.* fan or wipers in operating at selectable speeds.

2 speed axle, a drive axle incorporating either: 2 crownwheels and 2 pinions with different ratios and a selector mechanism, or more usually, a planetary gear system allowing selection of 2 gear ranges.

2 star, a quality of leaded petrol with a rating of 91 to 93 octane.

2nd steer, the second axle of a vehicle with 2 or more steering axles.

2 stroke cycle, an engine operating cycle where each piston moves up and down once per cycle, each movement from top to bottom is the power and exhaust stroke, and from bottom to top is the induction and compression stroke.

2 stroke engine, a simple engine operating on the 2 stroke cycle, requiring lubricated fuel, and where movement of the piston passing the port acts as a valve.

2 stroke fuel, fuel that contains lubricating oil in the proportion 100:4 fuel to oil ratio, for lubrication of some engine parts just before combustion.

2 tone, a bodywork paint scheme comprising 2 complementary colours, 1 painted below the waistline and a lighter shade above, typically on some classic cars.

2 tone horn, a horn system on an emergency vehicle comprising 2 trumpets each emitting a different note, each horn is sounded alternately at approximately 1 second frequency; see also: twin air horn.

2 turn door locks, a feature sometimes with central locking whereby only the drivers door is unlocked when the key is first turned in that lock to provide extra security, until a second turn of the key which then unlocks the other doors.

2 up, the condition when a motorcyclist is carrying a passenger.

2v, a carburettor with twin venturi.

2+V, a composite transmission system having 2 manual gears for 1st and 2nd and a CVT system for higher gearing.

2 valve, a typical engine having 2 valves per cylinder, 1 inlet and 1 exhaust.

2 way, a cab to cab radio on a specific frequency.

2 way cat, a catalytic converter usually containing platinum and rhodium to oxidise HC and NO_x in the exhaust gas of diesel engines.

2 way road, a single carriageway road carrying traffic in both directions without physical separation between opposing traffic flows.

2 way traffic, a road carrying traffic moving in opposite directions.

2 way turning lane, USA, a single lane marked along the centre of a multilane road for use by traffic from both directions before turning to their offside across oncoming traffic, and as an acceleration lane for drivers entering traffic from the far side of the street; usually marked with yellow lines along both sides of the lane.

2wd, 2 wheel drive.

2 wheel drive, a vehicle in which the engine drives only the 2 front wheels or only the 2 rear wheels.

2 wheeler, any motorcycle or bicycle.

3, see also: A, child, class, D, dot, Euro, FA, formula, invalid, L, lane, LL, PI, RA, stage,

STGO, T, Thatcham.

3, 3rd gear from lowest, on a 3 speed transmission it is the highest gear; on an automatic gear selector it restricts automatic selection by the gearbox to the 3 lowest forward gears only.

3+2, a combination of a 3 axle tractive unit coupled to a tandem axle semitrailer.

3+3, a combination of a 3 axle tractive unit coupled to a triaxle semitrailer.

3 and 9 hand position, the standard hold on the steering wheel in which the right hand holds at 3 o'clock and the left hand at 9 o'clock, the modern hold for maximum control.

3 arm junction, see: 3 leg junction.

3 axle, a tractive unit or rigid vehicle having 3 axles.

3 bells, part of the bus conductor to driver bell code: the bus is full.

3 box, a traditional design of car, the engine in the first box at the front, the passenger compartment is the second box, and a luggage box at the rear; a typical saloon car.

3 cyl, an engine having 3 cylinders and pistons.

3d, a 3 door car, 1 each side plus a rear door.

3E's, engineering, education, enforcement.

3 in a bed, the condition when 3 vehicles on a motorway or similar road are abreast of each other for some time; a high risk situation as the risk of an incident is increased but the number of escape routes are reduced.

3L, a rally pace note, a mid bend to the left through about 45°.

3 lane road, a road carrying 1 lane at each side for each direction and a central overtaking lane that may be available to both directions or may give priority to 1 direction of traffic flow.

3 leg junction, T junction, Y junction.

3 level diamond, USA, a symmetrical grade separated junction on 3 levels where 2 freeways cross in a city centre where space is scarce, having centrally a signal controlled square gyratory system connected by 8 sliproads to/from the freeways, *e.g.* the junction of the I29 with the US77; see appendices.

3 level roundabout, a symmetrical grade separated junction on 3 levels where 2 motorways cross, the roundabout being at ground level connected by 8 sliproads to/from the motorways, 1 motorway is above and 1 motorway is below the roundabout, *e.g.* the junction of the M1 with the M62 in Yorkshire; see appendices.

3 line brakes, an air brake system comprising a service line using a yellow hose, an emergency line using a red hose, and an auxiliary line using a blue hose.

3 litre car, a utopian car which will have a fuel consumption a low as 3 litres/100 km for general use.

3rd motion shaft, the gearbox output shaft.

3+O, a 3 speed gearbox with overdrive, *i.e.* an electrically selected 4th gear.

3 on the tree, a 3 speed column change gear selector.

3 over 3, a single H gear selector layout having 3 basic gear selector positions plus reverse, it uses additional range change and splitter switches to allow selection of 6 or 12 gears or other numerical possibilities.

3rd party, any claimant on an insurance policy that is not the insurance company nor the insured driver or vehicle owner.

3 pedal car, a car having a standard clutch pedal and a manual gearbox.

3 piece wheel, a forged alloy wheel having a spider or disc and a rim which is split around the well to aid tyre removal and replacement, common on lorries and buses in countries where the driver must repair his own punctures.

3 ply road, a single track road surfaced only where the tyres run, thereby having 2 strips of hard surface with a strip of grass or similar along the centre.

3 point belt, a seatbelt having lap and diagonal straps hence 3 fixing points, standard for most car passenger seats, invented by Nils Bohlin in 1955, Sweden, developed by Volvo.

3 point coupling, a coupling commonly used to mount and suspend implements at the rear of agricultural tractors.

3 point turn, to turn a vehicle around to face the opposite direction within the width of the road, using forward and reverse gears and efficient steering, and using 3 shunts: the first shunt being forwards to a position approximately 90° across the road; similar manoeuvres on narrower roads involving a greater number of shunts will result in 5, 7, 9, etc. point turns; see also: hammerhead.

3 port engine, a traditional 2 stroke engine having an inlet port from the atmosphere, the transfer port from the crankcase to the combustion chamber, and the exhaust port.

3R, a rally pace note, a mid bend to the right through about 45°.

3 seater, a lorry or truck cab having 3 seats.

3 second rule, an enhanced version of the 2 second rule, used when it is prudent to increase safety margins, *e.g.* at higher speeds, and at night.

3 speed, a vehicle with only 3 forward gears, in some classic cars and still used in some automatics.

3 star, a quality of leaded petrol with a rating of 94 to 96 octane.

3v, 3 valves, an engine having 3 valves per cylinder, usually 2 inlet and 1 exhaust but can be found contrary.

3 way cat, 3 way catalyst.

3 way catalyst, a catalytic converter usually containing platinum, palladium, and rhodium to oxidise HC, CO, and NO_x in the exhaust gas of petrol engines.

3 way junction, T junction, Y junction.

3 way roundabout, a roundabout having only 3 routes to/from the junction.

3 way stop, an intersection of 2 roads where all 3 approaches are terminated by a stop line and/ or a stop sign such that no road has priority.
3 way tipper, the ability to tip rearwards or off the left or right sides of a lorry or dump truck.
3 wheeled motorcycle, a motor cycle having 3 wheels, not including a 2 wheeled motorcycle with a sidecar attached, (C&U).
3 wheeler, a small lightweight car with either 1 wheel at the front and 2 at the rear, or with 2 wheels at the front and 1 at the rear.
4, see also: 2-, 6x, 8x, 10x, 12x, A, active, child, class, D, dot, Euro, FA, flat, FM, full time, H, I, L, LL, M, part time, permanent, QA, QM, RA, real time, RM, SAT, square, stage, Torque, TT, V, X.
4, 4th gear from lowest, on a 4 speed transmission it is the highest gear; on an automatic gear selector it restricts automatic selection by the gearbox to the 4 lowest forward gears only.
4, 4wd, referring to a selector position on a manually lockable fwh.
4 arm junction, see: 4 leg junction.
4 arm wheel nut wrench, 4 way spider.
4 axle, a drawbar trailer with 2 axles at the rear and 2 axles connected to a steering mechanism at the front.
4 axle, an articulated lorry comprising a 2 axle tractive unit with a tandem axle semitrailer.
4 banger, USA, a 4 cylinder inline engine.
4 barrel, a carburettor with 4 throttle valves, effectively 4 carburettors in a single assembly, or 2 twin carburettors depending upon sequencing of the throttle valves.
4 bells, part of the bus conductor to driver bell code: emergency on the bus.
4 beside 4, a double H gear selector layout having the appearance of H-H to provide selection of 8 or 16 gears, also 2 reverses and 1 or more crawlers, the ranges are selected by knocking the gear lever left or right in the neutral position to switch between low and high ranges.
4 bolt mains, a crankshaft main bearing cap secured by 4 bolts, typically in high performance engines.
4 by 4, 4x4.
4 channel antilock brakes, an ABS system having speed sensors on all 4 wheels, standard on modern vehicles.
4 cycle, 4 stroke Otto cycle.
4 cyl, an engine having 4 cylinders and pistons.
4d, a 4 door car, *i.e.* 2 each side.
4ECT, 4 speed electronically controlled automatic transmission.
4ECT-i, 4 speed electronically controlled automatic transmission with intelligence.
4H, a selectable gear range on a 4wd vehicle, it transmits the drive to all 4 wheels using high (normal) range.
4HLc, a selectable gear range on a 4wd vehicle, it transmits the drive to all 4 wheels using high (normal) range, and locks the centre

differential but not the axle differentials.
4 in line, a vehicle with 4 separate wheels spaced almost equally on 1 axle using 4 stub axles, typically on a semitrailer, generally obsolete due to poor stability.
4L, a selectable gear range on a 4wd vehicle, it transmits the drive to all 4 wheels using the low range of gears.
4L, a rally pace note, a medium bend to the left through about 60°.
4 legger, a 2 axle rigid lorry or tractive unit.
4 leg junction, a cross roads or a 4 way roundabout.
4 level interchange, typically a braid junction, a symmetrical grade separated junction on 4 levels between roads at 90° to each other and which allows all vehicles to move freely from any road to any other excepting a return to the route of origin, all link roads turn through 90° and are fed from sliproads on the nearside only.
4 level stack, USA, 4 level interchange, a braid junction.
4 link suspension, a rear suspension layout in which each wheel is guided by 2 control arms, 1 mounted longitudinally, the other transversely, used for irs and on live rear axles.
4LLc, a selectable gear range on a 4wd vehicle, it transmits the drive to all 4 wheels using the low range of gears, and locks the centre differential but not the axle differentials.
4L's, look, lower, left, leave.
4+O, a 4 speed gearbox with overdrive, *i.e.* an electrically selected 5th gear, sometimes also having overdrive on 3rd gear giving 6 gears.
4 on the floor, a 4 speed gear selector lever mounted conventionally on the floor of a car.
4 over 4, a single H gear selector layout having 4 basic gear selector positions plus reverse and sometimes a crawler, it uses additional range change and splitter switches to allow selection of 8 or 16 gears or other numerical possibilities.
4 point belt, a seatbelt system comprising a lap strap with a single 2 part buckle and 2 parallel shoulder straps, having 4 anchorage points and a central latching mechanism, used in competition vehicles.
4 point belt, a crisscross seatbelt having regular 3 point lap and diagonal belts plus an extra diagonal belt across the chest in the opposite direction.
4 point turn, to turn a vehicle around to face the opposite direction, using reverse & forward gears and efficient steering, using 4 shunts, the first shunt being reverse.
4 pot, a 4 cylinder engine.
4 pot, a 4 cylinder brake caliper unit.
4R, a rally pace note, a medium bend to the right through about 60°.
4 seater, a small saloon, a coupé, or a large sports car, etc. seating only 4 persons.
4 second rule, an enhanced version of the 2 second rule, used when it is prudent to increase safety margins, *e.g.* on a wet road, or

when being tailgated.

4 speed, a vehicle with 4 forward gears, generally obsolete in most manual transmission production cars, but common in many automatics.

4 speed electronically controlled automatic transmission, a computer controlled automatic transmission where a transmission computer controls the hydraulic shift pressure, developed by Toyota.

4 speed electronically controlled automatic transmission with intelligence, a computer controlled automatic transmission where the transmission computer networks with the engine computer to precisely control hydraulic shift pressure and automatically adjusts for transmission wear over time, developed by Toyota.

4ss, a 4 speed sequential shift gearbox.

4 star, a quality of leaded petrol with a rating of 97 to 99 octane.

4 stroke cycle, the Otto cycle, an engine operating sequence where each piston moves up and down twice giving 2 rotations of the crankshaft for each cycle, each piston movement from bottom to top or vice-versa being a stroke, the 4 strokes being: 1 induction, 2 compression, 3 power, 4 exhaust.

4 stroke engine, a petrol or diesel engine operating on the Otto cycle where each piston moves up and down twice giving 2 rotations of the crankshaft to complete each cycle.

4 stroking, a fault condition in a 2 stroke engine which is only firing on each alternate cycle.

4v, an engine having 4 valves per cylinder, 2 inlet and 2 exhaust.

4WAL, 4 wheel antilock brakes, ABS brakes operating on all 4 wheels.

4 way junction, a cross roads or a 4 way roundabout.

4 way lug wrench, USA, 4 way spider.

4 way roundabout, a roundabout having 4 routes to/from the junction, *i.e.* in the place of a crossroads.

4 way spider, a wheel nut wrench having a socket on each of 4 arms in the form of a cross.

4 way stop, an intersection of 2 roads where all 4 approaches are terminated by a stop line and/ or a stop sign such that no road has priority.

4 way wheel, a steering wheel which can easily be adjusted fore and aft for reach and up and down for height or rake.

4wd, 4 wheel drive.

4WDemand, a system which allows the driver to select between 2wd and 4wd while the vehicle is in motion, automatically locking the front hubs at speeds up to 80 km/h (50 mph), developed by Toyota.

4 wheel, a light truck with 1 front axle and 1 rear axle.

4 wheel alignment, the alignment of the tracking angle of the rear wheels in addition to the tracking angle of the front wheels on all vehicles excepting those having a live rear axle, and the relationship between axles to eliminate crabbing.

4 wheel drift, a controlled 4 wheel skid having a small slip angle whilst negotiating a long bend at speed and under power, during which the cornering forces slightly exceed the limit of maximum adhesion of the tyres but in which the car is in a balanced understeer and oversteer condition, a racing and rallying technique.

4 wheel drive, a 4 wheel vehicle in which the engine drives all 4 wheels.

4 wheeling, driving off-road in a 4x4 vehicle.

4 wheel skid, a condition when all the wheels of a vehicle lock or suffer significant sideslip; in a straight line typically caused by braking harshly; in a bend typically caused by entering too fast; in all cases steering and braking performance are lost and it has the potential to develop into a spin.

4 wheel steering, a 4 wheel vehicle where all 4 wheels may steer, the rear may steer either in the same or opposite direction to the front and may be dependant upon speed or driver selection; see also: active, passive.

4ws, 4 wheel steering.

4W's, weather, weight, width, winches.

4x2, a 4 wheel vehicle with drive to either 2 front or 2 rear wheels only.

4x4, a 4 wheel vehicle with drive to all 4 wheels.

4x4x4, a 4 wheel vehicle having 4wd and 4ws.

5, see also: 2-, A, class, dot, Euro, FA, FM, L, LL, M, QA, QM, RA, RM, SAT, sliding, V.

5, 5th gear from lowest, on a 5 speed transmission it is the highest gear.

5 axle, an articulated lorry having a 2 axle tractive unit with a triaxle semitrailer.

5 axle, an articulated lorry having a 3 axle tractive unit with a tandem axle semitrailer.

5 cyl, an engine having 5 cylinders and pistons.

5d, a 5 door car, *i.e.* 2 each side and a rear door.

5L, a rally pace note, a sharp bend to the left through about 75°.

5 link suspension, a rear suspension layout in which each wheel is guided by 2 trailing links, 2 transverse links, and a common track rod, used for independent suspension and for live rear axles.

5 point belt, a seat belt system comprising a lap strap, a crotch strap, and 2 shoulder straps, having 5 fixing points and a central latching mechanism, used in competition vehicles.

5 point turn, to turn a vehicle around to face the opposite direction within the width of the road, using forward & reverse gears and efficient steering, using 5 shunts, the first shunt being forwards.

5 point walkaround, an introduction of the purchaser to a car by the car salesman, explaining its major features.

5R, a rally pace note, a sharp bend to the right

through about 75°.

5 seater, a typical car seating 5 persons.

5 speed, a vehicle with 5 forward gears, normal in most manual transmission production cars and small lorries, becoming common in automatics.

5ss, a 5 speed sequential shift gearbox.

5 star, a quality of leaded petrol with a rating of 100 to 102 octane.

5v, 5 valves, a cylinder head having 5 valves per cylinder, usually 3 inlet and 2 exhaust, but can be found contrary.

5v, 5 volts, an electronically controlled supply voltage to the instrument panel and gauges on many vehicles.

5 way roundabout, a roundabout having 5 routes to/from the junction.

5 way stop, an intersection of several roads where all 5 approaches are terminated by a stop line and/or a stop sign such that no road has priority.

5ᵗʰ wheel, the coupling device on a tractive unit, for coupling with the kingpin of a semitrailer.

5ᵗʰ wheel, a test or measuring wheel, an additional wheel of bicycle size attached to the rear of a vehicle being performance tested, and which is connected to accurate speed measuring equipment.

5ᵗʰ wheel travel trailer, USA, a large mobile home constructed in a semitrailer, coupled to a pickup using a 5ᵗʰ wheel coupling.

6, see also: 8x, 10x, Chinese, class, flat, FM, M, QM, RM, SAT, straight, V.

6, 6ᵗʰ gear from lowest, on a 6 speed transmission it is the highest gear.

6, a 6 cylinder engine.

6 axle, an articulated lorry having a 3 axle tractive unit with a triaxle semitrailer.

6 cyl, an engine having 6 cylinders and pistons.

6d, a 6 door car, typically an estate or a 4x4 off-road car with 2 doors each side, a tailgate and an opening rear window.

6 jet, a fuel injection nozzle delivering simultaneously 6 sprays of atomised fuel.

6 legger, a common rigid truck or a tractive unit and some buses and coaches with 1 steering axle at the front and 2 load carrying axles at the rear.

6 light saloon, a car having 3 windows at each side, in the front doors, in the rear doors, and a small triangular window to the rear of the rear door.

6 point belt, a seat belt system comprising a lap strap, 2 leg straps, and 2 shoulder straps, having 6 fixing points and a central latching mechanism, used in competition vehicles.

6 pot, a 6 cylinder engine.

6 ramp junction, USA, a partial cloverleaf junction in a confined city centre or where freeways intersect at acute angles, typically having 2 exit ramps and 4 entry ramps.

6 seater, typically a mini MPV seating 6 persons.

6 speed, a vehicle with 6 forward gears, in many high performance cars, also common in many buses and small lorries.

6ss, a 6 speed sequential shift gearbox.

6v, 6 volts, an electrical system based upon a 6 volt battery, generally obsolete since the 1960s.

6 way roundabout, a roundabout having 6 routes to/from the junction.

6 way spider, a wheel nut wrench having a socket on each of 6 arms all at 90° in 3 dimensions from a central point.

6 wheel drive, a 3 axle vehicle having drive to all 3 axles.

6 wheel, a common rigid truck or a tractive unit and some buses and coaches with 1 steering axle at the front and 2 load carrying axles at the rear.

6 wheeler, USA, a 4x2 light truck with twin rear wheels.

6 wheel steering, a 3 axle vehicle in which all 3 axles steer, typically axles 1 and 2 steer normally and the rear axle steers in the opposite direction.

6x2, a 6 wheeled vehicle having drive to the rear 2 wheels only.

6x2, a 6 wheeled vehicle having drive to the first rear axle only.

6x4, a 6 wheeled vehicle having drive to the rear 4 wheels only.

6x6, a 6 wheeled vehicle having drive to all 6 wheels.

6x6x6, a 6 wheeled vehicle having 6wd and 6ws.

7, see also: class, QM, RM.

7, 7ᵗʰ gear from lowest.

7 pin plug/socket, a common electrical plug and socket to connect between towing vehicle and trailer.

7 seater, typically a luxury MPV only seating 7 persons.

7ss, a 7 speed sequential shift gearbox.

7 way connector, a common electrical plug and socket to connect between towing vehicle and trailer.

8, see also: flat, rigid, straight, twin steer, V, W.

8, 8ᵗʰ gear from lowest, on an 8 speed transmission it is the highest gear.

8, an 8 cylinder engine.

8, see: rigid 8, twin steer 8.

8 cyl, an engine having 8 cylinders and pistons.

8 in line, an axle on a low loader trailer comprising 4 stub axles and each stub axle carrying a pair of wheels; typically there may be 3 or 4 such axles on the trailer.

8 legger, a rigid lorry having 2 steering axles at the front and 2 load carrying axles at the rear, formally common for brewery delivery now common as a bulk tipper.

8 pot, an 8 cylinder engine.

8 pot, an 8 cylinder brake caliper unit.

8's, CB jargon, best wishes.

8 seater, a typical MPV seating 8 persons.

8 speed, a gearbox having 4 primary gears in

each of 2 ranges, *i.e.* 4 low range and 4 high range; it will also have 1 or 2 reverse gears, and it may have 1 or 2 crawler gears.

8 track, a type of music cassette having an endless tape loop, common in 1960s cars.

8v, 8 valves, a conventional 4 cylinder engine with 1 inlet valve and 1 exhaust valve per cylinder.

8 wheeler, a tractive unit having 4 axles, 1 or 2 axles may steer, depending upon configuration, often used for oversized loads.

8 wheeler, occasionally, an 8 legger rigid lorry.

8x2, an 8 wheeled 4 axle vehicle having drive only to the 3rd or to the 4th axle.

8x4, an 8 wheeled vehicle having drive to the rear 4 wheels only.

8x6, an 8 wheeled vehicle having drive to the rear 6 wheels only.

8x8, an 8 wheeled vehicle having drive to all 8 wheels.

8x8, a tractor gear selector system having 4 gears in each of 2 ranges plus a forward/reverse selector resulting in 8 forward gears and 8 reverse gears.

9 o'clock 3 o'clock, see: 3 and 9 hand position.

9 speed, a gearbox having 1 crawler gear plus 4 primary gears in each of 2 ranges, *i.e.* 4 low range and 4 high range, or having a splitter; also having 1 or 2 reverse gears.

10, see also: V.

10–1, CB jargon, reception is weak or fading out.

10–10, CB jargon, signing off.

10 cyl, an engine having 10 cylinders and pistons.

10 speed, a gearbox having 5 primary gears in each of 2 ranges, *i.e.* 5 low range and 5 high range; it will also have 1 or 2 reverse gears.

10 to 2, an older pattern for holding the steering wheel, having the left hand at 10 o'clock and the right hand at 2 o'clock, now generally superseded by the standard hold at $^1/_4$ to 3.

10 wheeler, USA, a 6x4 rigid truck, the count is of the tyres on twin wheels.

10x4, a 10 wheeled vehicle with drive to 4 wheels only, usually on the 3rd and 4th axles, with the 1st, 2nd, and 5th axles steering; typically a mobile crane.

10x6, a 10 wheeled vehicle with drive to the rear 6 wheels only.

11 metres, CB jargon, the CB radio band.

12, see also: V, W.

12 car event, a mini navigational road rally in which a maximum of 12 cars take part, performed under strict MSA rules by members of an official motor club but not requiring a competition licence.

12 cyl, an engine having 12 cylinders and pistons.

12 o'clock position, the position of the offside hand at the top of the steering wheel whilst reversing in a straight line and the driver is turned to look directly through the rear window.

12 point, a bihexagon socket or ring spanner, *i.e.* 2 concentric hexagons being 30° apart, for ease and speed of use.

12 speed, a gearbox having 4 primary gears and a twin splitter, *i.e.* having 2 splits on each gear, thereby giving $^1/_3$ gears, thereby giving 12 one-third gears; also 3 reverse gears.

12v, 12 valves, a 4 cylinder engine with 2 inlet valves and 1 exhaust valve per cylinder (usually, but can be found contrary).

12v, 12 valves, a 6 cylinder engine having 2 valves per cylinder.

12v, 12 volts, an electrical system based upon a 12 volt battery, standard in production cars.

12x4, a tractor gear selector system having 3 gears plus reverse in each of 4 ranges resulting in 12 forward gears and 4 reverse gears.

12x12, a tractor gear selector system having 4 gears in each of 3 ranges plus a forward/reverse selector resulting in 12 forward gears and 12 reverse gears.

13 speed, a gearbox having 1 crawler plus 4 primary gears in each of 2 ranges, *i.e.* 4 low range and 4 high range, the high range having a splitter giving 8 half gears in that range; also 1 or 2 reverse gears.

13 way connector, a modern electrical plug and socket to connect between towing vehicle and trailer.

14 speed, a gearbox having 2 crawler gears plus 3 primary gears in each of 2 ranges, *i.e.* 3 low range and 3 high range, all 6 having a splitter giving 12 half gears; also 2 reverse gears.

14 wheeler, USA, a 4x2 tractive unit with a tandem axle semitrailer, the count is of the tyres on twin wheels.

15 speed, a gearbox having 5 primary gears in each of 2 ranges, *i.e.* 5 low range and 5 high range, plus 5 gears in a deep reduction range; also 3 reverse gears.

16, see also: W, X.

16 cyl, an engine having 16 cylinders and pistons.

16 speed, a gearbox having 4 primary gears in each of 2 ranges, *i.e.* 4 low range and 4 high range, all 8 having a splitter giving 16 half gears; it may also have 2 crawler gears, also 2 reverse gears.

16v, 16 valves, a conventional 4 cylinder engine but having 2 inlet valves and 2 exhaust valves per cylinder.

18 speed, a gearbox having 2 crawler gears plus 4 primary gears in each of 2 ranges, *i.e.* 4 low range and 4 high range, all 8 having a splitter giving 16 half gears; also 2 reverse gears.

18 wheeler, USA, a 6x4 tractive unit with a tandem axle semitrailer, the count is of the tyres on twin wheels.

18x6, a tractor gear selector system having 3 gears plus reverse in each of 6 ranges resulting in 18 forward gears and 6 reverse gears.

14

20v, 20 valves, a 4 cylinder engine with 3 inlet valves and 2 exhaust valves per cylinder (usually, but can be found contrary).

20v, 20 valves, a 5 cylinder engine with 2 inlet and 2 exhaust valves per cylinder.

24v, 24 volts, an electrical system based upon 2 x 12 volt batteries in series, standard on buses, lorries, and military vehicles.

30 – 0, the braking distance and/or time required to stop from 30 mph on a dry level road without locking the wheels, measured from the instant the brakes are applied, *i.e.* not including thinking, reaction, or brake lag times/distances.

32 speed, a gearbox on a tractor having 32 forward gears based upon a 4 speed gearbox with 4 ranges including hare and tortoise, all split; also 8 reverse gears.

42v, 42 volts, a new standard voltage for all vehicles.

49 state car, USA, a car meeting emission standards in all states except those of California.

50-50 split, a common arrangement in a 4wd where equal power is delivered to the front and rear wheels; other splits are common on awd cars.

54 speed, a gearbox on a fastrac tractor having 54 forward gears based upon a 3 speed gearbox with 9 ranges including hare and tortoise, all split; also having 18 reverse gears.

60 – 0, the braking distance and/or time required to stop from 100 km/h (62.137 mph) on a dry level road without locking the wheels, measured from the instant the brakes are applied, *i.e.* not including thinking, reaction, or brake lag times/distances.

85M, see: M85.

85th percentile, the speed up to which 85 % of vehicles travel, or may be expected to travel, in free flow wet surface conditions on each specific length of road; the figure is used for planning speed limits.

88's, CB jargon, very best wishes.

90 left, a rallying pace note denoting a sharp right-angle corner to the left.

90 right, a rallying pace note denoting a sharp right-angle corner to the right.

100 – 0, the braking distance and/or time required to stop from 100 km/h (62.137 mph) on a dry level road without locking the wheels, measured from the instant the brakes are applied, *i.e.* not including thinking, reaction, or brake lag times/distances.

134a, a refrigerant gas used in most modern vehicle ac systems.

180 spin, see: forward, reverse.

180 turn, USA, see: handbrake turn.

Visit us on the web –

veloce.co.uk
velocebooks.com

A

a, the symbol for acceleration.
A, Accelerate, the last phase of the IPSGA mnemonic.
A, ampere, a measure of electrical current flow.
A, Europe, a driving licence category for light motorcycles having an engine size exceeding 125 cc or a power output exceeding 11 Kw (14.6 bhp).
A, USA, a driving license and vehicle category: any combination of motor vehicles with a GVWR exceeding 26,000 lbs (11.8 tonnes), towing a trailer exceeding 10,000 lbs (4.5 tonnes); a CDL is required; not including motorcycles.
A, USA, the tire temperature code denoting a high standard, moulded into the tire sidewall.
A, USA, the tire traction code denoting high braking performance on a wet surface, moulded into the tire sidewall.
A, Austria, international vehicle distinguishing sign, see appendices.
A, a hire car size and price category for cars based upon their floor pan; a small car often designated supermini, *e.g.* Mercedes A-class, or Peugeot 206 sized.
A, a write-off category in which the car is seriously damaged, *e.g.* burned out, such that no parts are reusable and the complete vehicle must be crushed.
A, automatic, a gear mode selector position on a vehicle having both manual and automatic modes of transmission operation.
A, referring to insurance sub grouping, standard security requirements.
A1, a European driving licence category for light motorcycles having an engine size not exceeding 125 cc and a power output not exceeding 11 Kw (14.6 bhp).
A2 tire, an earthmoving or off-road tyre, typically greater than 16.00 size.
A3, a 3 speed automatic gearbox.
A4, a 4 speed automatic gearbox.
A4L, a 4 speed automatic gearbox also having high and low range gearing.
A4x2, a 4 speed automatic gearbox also having high and low range gearing.
A5, a 5 speed automatic gearbox.
A arm, a component of a suspension on a rigid axle where the axle is located by trailing arms and the A arm gives lateral stability to the suspension.
A arm, USA, wishbone.

A arms, double wishbone suspension.
A band, a VED category within which vehicles emitting up to 150 g/km of CO_2 are charged.
A bar, a style of front bumper resembling a letter A with a flattened top, typically on 4x4 vehicles.
A bracket, a suspension system for a rigid axle.
A frame, a chassis in the form of a letter A, typically on simple trailers where the hitch is at the apex of the converging chassis rails.
A frame, a triangular towing device that can be clamped to the front of a vehicle to tow it driverless behind another, the steering performs by transverse force on the caster angle of the steering mechanism.
A frame drawbar, a hinged triangular framework at the front of a full trailer with which it is coupled.
A frame drawbar trailer, a trailer having 2 axle sets including a steering mechanism, a full trailer.
A frame trailer, a trailer having either a turntable or Ackerman steering at its front axle(s).
A framing, the action of towing a car driverless as a trailer with all wheels on the road surface using an A frame.
A pillar, the angled roof support pillars at each side of the front windscreen.
A post, A pillar.
A road, part of a primary route, a main road linking large towns.
A segment car, a size category for cars based upon their floor pan; a very small car, mini sized.
A thread, any external thread.
A trailer, the first trailer of a road train, the pup.
AA, Automobile Association, UK and many other countries.
AA, USA, the tire temperature code denoting the highest standard, moulded into the tire sidewall.
AAA, American Automobile Association.
AAA, Association Auxiliere de l'Automobile, provides a statistical service to the French motor industry, closely allied to CCFA.
AAA, Australian Automobile Association.
AAA, Automobile Association of America.
AAAFTS, American Automobile Association Foundation for Traffic Safety.

16

a/a/c, automatic air conditioning, *i.e.* climate control.
AADF, annual average daily flow.
AADT, annual average daily traffic.
AAFRSR, Automobile Association Foundation for Road Safety Research, USA.
AAHF, average annual hourly flow.
AALA, American Automobile Labelling Act 1994, regulations which require vehicle manufacturers to state content details for cars and trucks.
AAM, Alliance of Automobile Manufactures, USA.
AAMA, American Automobile Manufacturers Association, but representing only GM, Ford and DaimlerChrysler, formerly MVMA.
AAMVA, American Association of Motor Vehicle Administrators.
AAR, automatic air recirculation.
AASHTO, American Association of State and Highway Transportation Officials.
AAWF, average annual weekly flow.
a/b, airbag.
ABA, American Bus Association.
abandon, the act of an owner discarding a vehicle with no intention of removing it to a suitable location.
abandon, the act of parking a vehicle badly such that part of it is more than approximately 30 cm (1 foot) from the road edge.
abandon, the act of leaving a broken down vehicle in its driving position, a long distance from the road edge.
abandon, the act of leaving a stolen vehicle anywhere.
ABC, active body control.
ABD, Association of British Drivers.
ABD, automatic brake differential system.
abdc, after bottom dead centre.
abeam, the situation where 2 vehicles are alongside each other facing in the same or opposite directions, where the B pillars are exactly level; see also: abreast.
ABI, Association of British Insurers.
aboard, to be in a bus.
abrasive, small, hard, sharp cornered, fragments of natural or synthetic material that will scratch or wear another material.
abreast, a situation where 2 vehicles are side by side and facing in the same direction; see also: abeam.
ABS, antiblockier system, German, antilock braking system.
absolute prohibition, a mandatory command, as at a traffic signal, or at a prohibitory or obligatory sign.
ABS override, a switch for the driver to disable the ABS system when on some soft surfaces on which it could be an advantage to lock the wheels to cause the wheels to plough in deep to assist stopping, *e.g.* soft sand or deep gravel.
ac, air conditioning.
ac, alternating current.

AC, Auto Carrier, the original name for the oldest independent car manufacturer in Britain.
ACAP, Associação do Comércio Automovóvel de Portugal.
ACC, accelerate, a marking on a cruise control switch.
ACC, adaptive cruise control.
ACC, automated cruise control.
ACC, automatic climate control.
accelerate, to increase speed, or to gain velocity.
acceleration, the rate of change of velocity, measured in distance per second per second, m/s^2.
acceleration lane, an additional lane along the nearside of a major road, or before the merging lane on a motorway, to facilitate vehicles increasing speed to that of others on the main carriageway before merging.
acceleration performance, the rate at which a vehicle will accelerate compared with a measured standard distance or time, or compared with another vehicle.
acceleration sense, a drivers ability to judge the road conditions with forward planning for subtle, delicate and precise control of the accelerator relevant to the actual and potential hazards, to smoothly and gradually increase or decrease the accelerator so as to avoid braking, it is a significant part of defensive and advanced driving.
acceleration skid control, a traction control system that prevents the wheels from spinning during acceleration, developed by Mercedes.
acceleration skid reduction, a microprocessor based system which provides an improvement in traction when moving off and accelerating on slippery surfaces by reducing engine output to electronically limit acceleration if wheelspin from both drive wheels is detected, developed by Mercedes.
acceleration zone, the part of the acceleration lane on which a driver accelerates before merging.
accelerator, a primary control, a pedal operated by the drivers right foot which controls the flow of air into the engine, hence controls engine speed and power output.
accelerator balance, to use exactly the amount of power required to maintain a constant speed in a bend or other situation.
accelerator interlock, a connection between the accelerator pedal and the automatic transmission to prevent a gear being selected at high revs.
accelerator jet, a nozzle in a carburettor that supplies additional fuel whilst the accelerator pedal is increasingly depressed.
accelerator pedal, the foot operated pedal by which the driver controls the operation of the throttle valve, or controls the ECU to influence engine speed.
accelerator pump, part of a carburettor, a small pump which enriches the fuel-air mixture

- **AAA** -

during increasing depression of the accelerator pedal.

accelerometer, an instrument which measures the rate of acceleration of a vehicle, either instantaneously or averaged over a set distance or time.

access land, areas of open moor and mountain which are open to the public for walking whilst prohibited to 4wd vehicles, under the CRoW Act 2000.

accessories, items of equipment which may be fitted to a vehicle to enhance comfort or other parameter.

accessories, additional items of equipment which may be used with a basic tool.

access road, an exclusive route to a specific facility.

access road, a residential road with footways that may serve up to approximately 300 dwellings; see also: minor, major.

access tunnel, the part of an access road that runs in a tunnel.

accident, a rare, random, multifactor event in which 1 or more road users fail to cope with their environment and which then results in an occurrence when owing to the presence of a mechanically propelled vehicle, damage is caused to a vehicle other than that mechanically propelled vehicle or a trailer drawn by it, or to any person other than the driver, or to any animal, or to any property constructed on, or fixed to, or growing in, or otherwise forming part of the land on which the road in question is situated, or on the land adjacent to such land, (RTA).

accident avoidance, a range of techniques each of which if used will significantly reduce the risk of collision, *e.g.* maintaining a safety zone, long braking, maintaining escape routes.

accident data recorder, a microprocessor fitted to some production cars that continuously records data at 500 Hz from many sensors on a vehicle and re-records over unwanted earlier data after a short interval such that it stores data for 30 seconds before a collision and for 15 seconds afterwards.

accident migration, the change in the location of collisions sometimes caused by engineering improvements at a black spot.

accident transfer, a change in the type of collision recorded at a site caused by engineering improvements.

accident triangle, warning triangle.

accommodation road, a route for the private use of persons with an interest in the land to which it leads, and which may also carry public rights; typically created to link fields separated by a canal or railway; see also: occupation.

accordion bus, articulated bus.

accumulated lateness, the total time behind the planned time schedule of an individual crew in road rally navigation.

accumulator, a device that stores hydraulic pressure, *e.g.* part of the suspension of some

vehicles.

accumulator, battery, secondary cell, an archaic name.

ACCUS, Automobile Competition Committee for the United States.

ace, CB jargon, a user with a high opinion of himself.

ACE, active cornering enhancement.

ACEA, Association des Constructors Européens d'Automobiles, European Automobile Manufacturers Association.

acetylene, a gas used as the fuel for a naked flame carriage lamp, typical on vehicles between 1900 and 1915.

acetylene, a gas used with oxygen for welding body parts, especially for small repairs.

ACFO, Association of Car Fleet Operators, UK.

Ackermann, Rudolf Ackermann, the patentee of a steering principle in 1818, still used on all vehicles, based on geometric principles that all wheels must describe different circles around a common centre, hence the wheel on the inside of a curve must turn a greater angle than the wheel on the outside of the curve.

AcL, a rally pace note, acute left bend exceeding 150°.

ACORD, Automotive Consortium on Recycling and Disposal, UK.

ACPO, Association of Chief Police Officers, UK.

AcR, a rally pace note, acute right bend exceeding 150°.

ACS, automatic clutch system.

activated carbon canister, carbon canister.

active 4 wheel steer, a facility where all of the wheels of a vehicle are connected to the steering mechanism, in some cases the rear steering may be speed sensitive, or may be controlled separately by the driver such that the vehicle may turn sharper corners, or in some cases the vehicle may be able to crab manoeuvre.

active accident avoidance, the use of any of a series of predevised strategies to actively avoid being hit by another vehicle approaching from any direction in any traffic situation when a collision is imminent.

active body control, an active suspension system that constantly electronically adjusts the suspension hydraulics to eliminate or reduce the body roll on bends and eliminate or reduce pitch and dive when accelerating and braking, originally devised by Citroën, developed by Mercedes.

active braking time, the time taken for a vehicle to stop from a specific speed, timed from the instant the brakes are applied, *i.e.* excluding thinking, reaction, and brake lag times.

active collision, a collision where a driver makes a statement that includes "I hit …".

active cornering enhancement, a microprocessor system that recognises different road surfaces; when the vehicle enters a bend on a road it stiffens the suspension, whilst on rough tracks it allows the suspension to absorb bumps with maximum suspension travel, developed by Landrover.

active differential, a differential which is controlled hydraulically by electronics to allow only a specific difference in wheel speeds.

active driver assist, a system that analyses drivers intended behaviour, issues warnings to the driver, and helps the car to react in evasive manoeuvres.

active driver assist, a system using 2 video cameras linked to a microprocessor to create a 3 dimensional image to recognise approaching hazards that may become close to the front or sides of the car, and reduce the speed of the vehicle and sound an alarm to the driver, developed by Subaru.

active handling, an electronic stability control, coordinating ECU and ABS and TC to reduce the power and apply the brakes to 1 or more wheels, developed by GM.

active head restraint, a head restraint which automatically pivots to meet the drivers head on rear impact to reduce the effect of whiplash.

active noise system, a noise counteraction system which measures noise near to the drivers head and produces matching counter-frequencies to cancel the noise as much as possible.

active safety equipment, safety equipment which will respond to a signal, *e.g.* air bags or ABS.

active safety measure, see: primary safety measure.

active service system, a system whereby the vehicle will inform when it is time for a service, by calculating the service interval according to the driving style and usage, developed by Mercedes.

active skid control, a system that recognises oversteer and understeer skids and reduces power and applies the brake to 1 wheel, developed by BMW.

active steering, a system under development that will work with ACC, where the vehicle is able to steer automatically, either by magnetic sensors beneath a vehicle signalling to a microprocessor that controls the steering to follow magnets beneath the road surface, or by a video camera and microprocessor controlling the steering to remain between 2 lane lines.

active suspension, electronic control of the suspension by hydraulics or by control of the dampers to improve stability, roadholding, and comfort, by reducing roll, dive and rise.

active TRAC, a traction control system using sensors at all four wheels to monitor a loss of traction and which controls brake and accelerator to reduce wheelspin and transfer torque to the wheel with the most traction, developed by Toyota.

active vehicle, a vehicle which is moving or of which the engine is running, hence has the ability to change speed and position and influence the course of another.

active ventilation, ventilation within the driver and passenger seats to maintain a comfortable seat temperature.

active vibration isolation, engine mountings which act like loudspeakers to emit anti-noise vibrations in the opposite phase to those produced by the engine, cancelling vibration and noise.

actual hazard, any situation that will cause a driver to change speed or direction.

actual power , the power delivered at the wheels of a vehicle, *i.e.* engine horsepower minus losses in the transmission.

actuator, part of a control system, an output device or transducer that converts electric or hydraulic or pneumatic energy into mechanical movement.

ACU, Auto Cycle Union, UK.

acute, a rallying pace note indicating a very sharp bend to the left or right through more than 150°.

AD, adaptive damping.

ADA, active driver assist.

ADA, Advanced Drivers Association, UK.

ADAC, Allgemeine Deutsche Automobilclub, German, motoring organisation.

adaptive airbags, airbags which inflate to match the amount of restraint required, triggered by sensors that measure the size and position of each occupant, and the severity of impact in the collision.

adaptive cruise control, a system that automatically keeps a safe distance from the vehicle ahead by radar and control of the accelerator and brake, normally maintaining a 2 second interval, the system will brake at up to 0.3 g, but will not detect stationary objects in the path of the car, developed by Mercedes, Fiat, and Nissan, first in production by Jaguar.

adaptive damping, suspension dampers that have a variable rate, controlled electronically to reduce dive and rise, developed by Jaguar.

adaptive gearbox system, a system that recognises a drivers driving style with inputs from many relevant factors to determine the best choice of gear, automatically compensating for normal, winter, hill starts, hill descents, and bends, developed by BMW.

adaptive headlamps, headlamps that automatically track the steering angle and react to the direction of travel, developed by Citroën, also by Mercedes.

adaptive light control, headlamps having moving segments that angle the beam of light to follow the course of the road, developed by BMW.

adaptive pneumatic damping, gas filled suspension dampers that have a variable rate controlled electronically to reduce dive, rise, and roll, developed by Mercedes.

adaptive restraint technology system, a

system which recognises the positions of the driver and front passenger and their relevant distance from the steering wheel and dashboard using a pair of OSS devices, and triggers the airbags to suit the space available, developed by Jaguar.

adaptor, a device which allows the connection of 2 parts which would otherwise be incompatible.

adaptor plate, a plate used to link incompatible parts, *e.g.* to fit a different engine to a gearbox.

additive, a substance that is added to another to enhance the properties of the host substance.

ADED, Association of Driver Educators for the Disabled, USA.

ADEFA, Asociacion de Fabricas de Automotores, Argentina.

ADEPD, Association of Driver Educators for People with Disabilities, UK.

ADF, Automotive Distribution Federation, formerly MFA, UK.

adhesion, the force of the static friction between the tyres and the road surface.

adhesion, the capability of a lubricant to remain in contact with a metal surface.

adhesion utilisation, the sequence in which the front and rear wheels will lock under certain braking conditions; to meet EC requirements the front must lock before the rear.

adhesive, a substance used to bond 2 solids so they can be used as a single piece.

adhesive weight, a lead balance weight designed to be fitted to an alloy wheel using an adhesive backing.

ADI, Approved Driving Instructor, UK.

ADINJC, Approved Driving Instructors National Joint Council, UK.

adjust, to move parts of a component or system to a specified relationship or dimension or pressure.

adjustable spanner, wrench.

adjuster, a part of a device enabling a change in position to be effected.

adjustment, a necessary change in relationship, to alter the position, clearance, or fit.

ADN, Yemen, international vehicle distinguishing sign, see appendices.

adopted road, a road for which the local authority accept responsibility for maintenance at public expense.

ADR, accident data recorder.

ADR, Article Dangereu de Routière, European designation for Dangerous Goods by Road, divided into 7 sub classes depending upon the type of substance.

ADR, Australian Design Rules, equivalent to UK Type Approval.

ADS, advance direction sign.

ADS, automatic debiting system.

adsorb, a very thin layer of one material on the surface of another.

ADTA, Australian Driver Trainers Association.

ADTSEA, American Driver and Traffic Safety Education Association.

advance, to move ahead, to bring forwards in time the operation of a function, *e.g.* to advance the ignition timing is to cause it to happen earlier within the cycle.

advanced driver, a person who practices the art of driving to a high standard, driving which is safe, systematic, smooth, and progressive, using the skills of intuition, consistency, precision, flexibility, and concentration endurance, he will have undergone a period of advanced training.

advanced driving, the art of driving to a high standard, driving which is safe, systematic, smooth, and progressive, using the skills of intuition, consistency, precision, flexibility, and concentration endurance, it requires advanced training to achieve.

advanced driving test, a test of a drivers ability to a much higher standard than a learner test; conducted by several organisations.

advanced stability and traction control, a system that recognises oversteer and understeer skids and reduces power and applies the brake to 1 wheel, developed by Volvo.

advanced stop line, a stop line for cyclists waiting at traffic signals where there is a cycle reservoir, positioned so cyclists can wait at red lights ahead of other vehicles which wait at the first stop line.

advanced techniques, controlling a vehicle with a high degree of skill, especially with regard to smoothness and vehicle sympathy, achieved by specific training.

advection fog, fog caused by the slow movement of moist air over a cold surface, common near the coast in winter.

adverse camber, a road surface condition where the outer radius of a curve is at a lower height than the inner radius such that lateral force on the tyres is increased leading to significant reduction in stability.

advisory speed limit, a maximum speed limit sign that is not mandatory, typically on a rectangular panel or some matrix signs.

AE, Authorised Examiner, a person permitted to conduct and supervise roadworthiness tests for the VI, UK.

AE, rear overhang, the distance from the rearmost point to the centreline of the rear axle.

A&E, accident and emergency, part of the information on a road sign leading to a hospital showing that the hospital has these facilities.

AERA, Automotive Engine Rebuilders Association, USA.

aerial, a radio antenna.

aerodynamic coefficient, relating to a retarding force or drag on a vehicle as it moves along pushing air aside.

aerodynamic drag, wind resistance, expressed by a measurement of coefficient of drag, Cd, a lower number means a vehicle passes through wind more efficiently resulting in better fuel economy and lower wind noise.

aerodynamic lift, a force acting on the body of a vehicle or a part caused by airflow, causing the body to rise on the suspension resulting in loss of stability, it can be designed as negative lift *i.e.* to create a downforce to increase stability.

aerodynamics, the effect of airflow over the vehicle at speed, especially with respect to wind resistance or drag.

aerofoil, aircraft style wings at the front and rear of a racing car to increase downforce and stability, first used in F1 in 1968, now named airfoil.

aeroscreen, the very small windscreen on some sports and racing cars, sometimes a separate left and right pair, sometimes hinged to lay flat.

aerosol, a container designed to dispense its contents usually as a fine mist aided by a propellant gas.

AET, advanced emissions test.

AETR rules, a European agreement concerning the work of crews of vehicles engaged in international transport, especially drivers hours and rest periods in specified countries outside the EU.

AF, across the flats, the diametrical measurement between opposite faces of the hexagon of a nut or bolt, the measurement used for sizing metric spanners and some imperial sizes.

AF, air-fuel mixture.

AFG, Afghanistan, international vehicle distinguishing sign, see appendices.

AFQUAD, European Quadricycle Association.

after bottom dead centre, the crankshaft rotational position after a piston has passed the bottom of its stroke, after the start of the compression stroke or exhaust stroke.

afterburner, a system of injecting more fuel and air into the burning exhaust of a jet powered dragster or speed record attempt car powered by a jet engine.

aftercooler, a device to cool induction air after compression by a supercharger or turbocharger, before induction to the cylinders.

aftercooling, a system of removing excess heat from a hot engine when it is stopped; a thermostat controls a secondary electrical coolant pump which continues to circulate hot coolant from the engine through the radiator where the cooling fan also operates.

aftercooling pump, a secondary coolant pump which circulates hot coolant through the radiator after the engine is stopped.

aftermarket, vehicle accessories that do not need to be fitted by the manufacturer.

after sales, a quality of service expected from a dealer selling a new vehicle.

after top dead centre, the crankshaft rotational position after a piston has passed the top of its stroke, after the start of the induction stroke or power stroke.

AG, a tyre design for agricultural vehicles.

AGA, Association Generale Automobile, France, the organisers of the first nationally agreed series of road signs.

agency driver, a lorry or coach driver who is supplied by an organisation to drive vehicles for another organisation.

agreed value, the value of a classic car as valued by an appropriate club for insurance purposes.

agressivity, an inverse quality of the structure of a car bonnet in reducing injury to a pedestrian during a collision.

agricultural tractor, a mechanically propelled vehicle having wheels and tyres suitable for driving on earth and similar surfaces, and which may be constructed or adapted to carry a load, draw a trailer, or may be fitted with machinery for loading bulk materials, excavating, or for other industrial purposes.

agricultural trailed appliance, a trailer which is an implement constructed or adapted for use off roads for the purpose of agriculture, horticulture, or forestry, (C&U).

agricultural trailed appliance conveyor, an agricultural trailer which has an unladen weight not exceeding 510 kg, has pneumatic tyres, and is designed and constructed for the purpose of conveying an agricultural, horticultural, or forestry implement, (C&U).

AGS, adaptive gearbox system.

AGS, automatic gear selection.

AGT, automated guided transit.

Ah, ampere hour.

AH, active handling.

AHAI, Association of the Hungarian Automotive Industry.

ahap, as high as possible.

ahara, as high as reasonably achievable.

AHRA, American Hot Rod Association.

AH rim, a design of wheel rim used only with a specific tyre having run-flat capability.

ahead, a direction with which to follow a road where the course steered at a junction is not straight, but there is no overall change in heading, *e.g.* at a roundabout.

AHR, active head restraint.

AIA, Automobile Importers of America.

AIACR, Association Internationale des Automobile Clubs Reconnus, now superseded by the FIA.

AIADA, American International Automobile Dealers Association.

AIAG, Automotive Industry Action Group, USA.

AIAM, Association of Indian Automobile Manufacturers.

AIAM, Association of International Automobile Manufacturers, USA.

AIA-SAP, Automotive Industry Association of Czechoslovakia.

AIA-ZAP, Automotive Industry Association of Slovakia.

AICA, Automotive Industry Certification

Association, UK.
AIMA, Associação dos Industriais de Montagem de Automóveis, Portugal.
aimer, USA, a headlamp beamsetter.
aim high, to look to the distance whilst driving, typically at least 12 seconds ahead in all driving conditions, as part of a scanning routine.
AIMS, Association of Independent Motor Stores, UK.
air, a mixture of nitrogen, oxygen, and other gases as in the atmosphere.
air, a component of air-fuel mixture.
air, a fluid used as a compressed gas for inflating pneumatic tyres, operating air brakes, etc.
airbag, a srs or secondary safety restraint which will explosively inflate in 25 milliseconds in serious frontal collisions to protect the occupants; European driver size 60 litres, passenger 80 litres, USA driver 75 litres, passenger 140 litres, lorry driver size 70 litres, additional side airbags and side curtains are sometimes fitted.
airbag trigger, Hamlin switch.
air bleed valve, a valve for eliminating air from high points within a cooling system.
airbrake, a braking system using an engine driven air compressor to store air in tanks which is released by a valve connected to the footbrake pedal to operate the wheel brakes.
airbrush, a tool used to paint detailed murals etc. onto vehicles using compressed air and a very fine nozzle.
air cleaner, a device on the engine air intake that prevents dust and dirt entering the engine.
aircompressor, an auxiliary device connected to a vehicle engine to produce compressed air for use in a vehicle braking system, or to inflate tyres etc.
aircon, air conditioning.
air conditioning, a system of cooling and sometimes cleaning and/or drying air before delivering it to the cabin, using a refrigeration system incorporating a compressor driven by the engine to chill the air and to supply it to the vehicle occupants.
air cooled engine, an engine which is cooled directly by ambient air, where the cooling air passes directly over fins on the cylinders and cylinder head, without the need for a water jacket and radiator.
air dam, a device at the lower front of a car to restrict air from passing beneath a car, it may improve roadholding at higher speeds.
air deflector, a wedge shaped structure on a lorry cab roof to deflect wind over the trailer to reduce wind resistance.
air down, to reduce air pressure in tyres to approximately $^1/_2$ the on-road pressure for specific situations, e.g. mud, soft sand, etc.
aire, French, a rest area on an autoroute.
air filter, a device on the engine air intake that prevents dust and dirt entering the engine.

airflow, the passage of air over a moving vehicle.
airfoil, aircraft style wings at the front and rear of a racing car to increase downforce and stability, first used in F1 in 1968, originally named aerofoil.
air-fuel mixture, the air and fuel mixed by the carburettor or fuel injection system and vaporized, usually at the stoichiometric ratio or as it exists before ignition.
air-fuel ratio, the stoichiometric ratio of air and fuel to achieve full combustion, for petrol this is 14.7:1 i.e. 14.7 parts of air to 1 part of petrol by weight; for diesel this is 18.0:1 i.e. 18 parts of air to 1 part of diesel by weight.
air gap, a small space between parts, usually those related magnetically or electrically, e.g. as in the alternator, or in the sparkplug.
air horn, a device emitting a loud noise as a warning instrument, powered by compressed air.
air horn, the tubular passage in a carburettor housing the choke valve.
air injection system, an exhaust emission control system that injects air into the exhaust system to complete all combustion of unburned hydrocarbons and carbon monoxide and reduce nitrogen oxides.
air jack, a device for lifting a car, a wide fabric balloon powered by the exhaust or from an air compressor, typically used off road on soft surfaces.
airline, the hose used to inflate the tyres of a vehicle.
airline, the suzies and piping that conduct air to the brakes of a trailer.
air locker, an air operated locking differential, having a remote control system allowing the driver to lock the axle shafts together to increase traction on slippery surfaces.
air over hydraulic, a braking system where the brakes are operated hydraulically with power assistance from a compressed air system, typically on small commercial vehicles.
air pollution, the contamination of air by any natural or manufactured pollutant, e.g. smoke, gas, dust.
air portable general purpose, a military designation for lightweight vehicles, typically 4x4, occasionally amphibians, but all easily transportable by aircraft.
air pressure, the amount of air inside a tyre, vessel, or system pressing outwards on each unit of area, typically expressed in psi or kPa; 1 psi = 6.9 kPa.
air pump, a device for compressing air for its use elsewhere, usually driven by the engine, sometimes electrically.
air scoop, a device designed to allow easy access for induction air assisted by the forward motion of a vehicle, especially at speed.
air seat, a lorry drivers or passengers seat having in-built air suspension.
AIRSO, Association of Industrial Road Safety

Officers, UK.

air spring, a rubber chamber inflated with compressed air mounted between the wheel and chassis as part of an air suspension system, becoming common on heavy vehicles and on some cars.

air suspended cab, a lorry cab which is suspended above the chassis using compressed air for suspension for increased comfort.

air suspension, a vehicle suspension system using compressed air in chambers between the wheels and chassis, replacing steel springs with a cushion of air, to give an even road height and a smoother ride; also used for cab suspension above the chassis.

air tank, a reservoir containing compressed air, typically on lorries and buses to operate air brakes.

air tap, a valve used to close an airline before uncoupling a trailer, and to open the line after recoupling.

air vent, a device that admits air to a closed system to prevent a vacuum forming in a fluid system or reservoir.

aisle, a roadway in a carpark between the rows of parking bays.

AIT, Alliance Internationale de Tourisme.

AKI, antiknock index.

AL, abnormal load.

AL, Albania, international vehicle distinguishing sign, see appendices.

alap, as low as possible.

alara, as low as reasonably achievable.

alarm, a vehicle theft protection system.

ALC, adaptive light control.

alcodiesel, a biofuel diesel made from an alcohol typically derived from vegetation.

alcofuel, alcohol fuel.

alcohol, ethyl alcohol, ethanol, a hydrocarbon, the active component of beers, wines and spirits, a sedative beverage, it slows drivers reactions whilst giving a sense of well-being.

alcohol, methyl alcohol, methanol, a hydrocarbon, sometimes used as a fuel, sometimes used for cleaning parts, a constituent of windscreen wash.

alcohol fuel, any of: ethanol, methanol, ethanol-methanol blends, ethanol-gasoline blends, or methanol-gasoline blends, mixed in various proportions.

aldc, USA, after lower dead centre, abdc.

alfin, light alloy fins bonded to a steel base as in some air cooled engines and some brake drums.

alfresco driving, to drive any open top car with the hood down or removed.

ALI, additional liability insurance, additional insurance to hire car insurance to provide cover against the high value of possible claims.

alight, to get out from or get down from a vehicle.

align, relating to the angular arrangement of parts that should have a definite relationship.

alignment, the geometric course of a road; see:

horizontal, vertical.

alignment, the lateral and vertical angles at which each headlamp emits a beam of light.

alignment, the mechanical relationship between timing marks on gears, sprockets, and other parts that must be properly arranged when the engine is assembled.

alignment, the angles at which each wheel should be adjusted, any of the: caster angles, camber angles, or tracking angles, *i.e.* the toe in or toe out of wheels, in order to maintain the specifications engineered by the vehicle manufacturer for optimum performance of the steering and suspension.

alkaline cell, a battery containing dilute potassium hydroxide instead of acid.

Allen key, a tool made from hexagonal rod, for turning screws with a female hexagonal socket.

Allen screw, a screw or bolt having an axial hexagonal socket in its head.

Allen wrench, Allen key.

alley, a narrow street between and/or behind buildings, typically the road extends to the walls of the buildings without a separate footway.

alley, USA, a narrow road having a speed limit of 15 mph (24 km/h).

alleyway, alley.

alligator clip, a spring clip connected to the end of a wire for making a temporary electrical connection, *e.g.* for circuit testing or on jump leads.

all indirect gearbox, a gearbox in which none of the forward gears has a 1:1 ratio.

all out braking, the maximum braking performance possible at that time allowing for the surface conditions, tyres, and suspension.

alloy, a combination of 2 or more elements to produce a metal with qualities suitable for a specific purpose.

alloys, road wheels made from an aluminium-magnesium alloy, much lighter than steel wheels.

all purpose road, any road other than a special road, *i.e.* a road which is not restricted by a special road order, and which is open to all types of traffic.

all road, a hybrid tyre designed to give reasonable performance off-road and on a highway.

all season tyre, winter tyre, mud & snow tyre, a tyre that is designed for general use on wet and dry roads having a tread and compound giving reasonable friction in snow and mud.

all terrain tyre, a tyre designed primarily for off-road use on mud and rock etc.

all terrain vehicle, a vehicle designed for off-road use, having 4wd, appropriate gear ratios, all terrain tyres, long suspension travel, and typically with many additional features.

all way stop, an intersection of several roads where all approaches are terminated by a stop line and/or a stop sign such that no road has priority.

23

all weather tourer, a convertible or cabriolet where all side windows are of glass.

all weather tyre, all season tyre.

all wheel drive, usually referring to a saloon car or high performance sports car where the power from the engine is directed to all 4 wheels, *i.e.* a 4x4 but without specific off road ability, sometimes it may imply a 6x6 etc, first used in 1902.

ally, aluminium.

alm, alarm.

alphanumeric tire, USA, a tire sizing system based upon the load carrying capacity of the tire related to its overall size, and indicated by a system of letters from the smallest at A progressing sequentially to N the largest, in current use since 1968.

alpine window, a long narrow window in the curved edge of a vehicle roof above a side window, typically on some mpv and minibuses.

ALR, automatic locking retractor.

ALS, automatic levelling system.

alternating current, an electric current that flows alternately in each direction for a fraction of a second, the output of an alternator, it has to be rectified before it can be stored in a battery.

alternative fuel, a range of non-fossil fuels such as alcohols, especially ethanol and methanol.

alternator, an electrical generator that uses magnetism to convert mechanical energy into electrical energy for powering circuits in a vehicle, very efficient, giving an ac output.

alterpower, a system where the load is disconnected from the alternator when at full throttle to maximise power to the road wheels.

altimeter, an instrument that displays the actual height above sea level, typically on off-road vehicles.

altitude power loss, the loss of engine power due to decreased air density, thus warmer, lighter, rarefied, or humid air decreases engine output; typically 1 % reduction in power is lost for each 100 metres increase in altitude.

aluminium, a metallic element, lightweight but soft, usually alloyed to improve its properties, sometimes used as sheets for body panels, used as an alloy for wheels, engine blocks, cylinder heads, and other parts.

aluminium block, an engine cylinder block cast from aluminium and usually having cast iron liners or sleeves within the bores.

aluminiumised, a part covered with a very thin layer of aluminium for a hard corrosion resistant coating, typically on valves.

aluzinc, an alloy of aluminium and zinc, sometimes used as a thin coating on steel to prevent rusting.

AMA, American Motorcycle Association.

AMA, Automobile Manufacturers Association, USA.

amateur built vehicle, a hybrid or kit car constructed by an individual from a variety of parts from either donor vehicles, a kit, or self manufactured.

amber, a colour between yellow and orange, used as a world standard for a phase of traffic lights, for vehicle direction indicators, and for warning beacons etc.

amber arrow, USA, an illuminated traffic signal indicating a protected turning period is ending and drivers must be ready to obey the next signal.

amber gambler, a driver who runs an amber traffic signal and drives on when there was ample time to stop before the red light.

amber hazard posts, delineator posts having an amber reflector which mark the central reservation of motorways and dual carriageways.

amber studs, cats eyes or reflective studs which mark the central reservation of motorways and dual carriageways.

ambient temperature, the temperature of the air surrounding a vehicle, before being inducted to the engine or supplied to the passenger compartment.

ambulance, see: motor ambulance.

ambuscade, the location of a hidden radar speed trap or hidden speed camera.

AMC, American Motors Corporation.

American Association of State Highway Transportation Officials, the organisation responsible for maintaining interstate and US highways.

AMG, Aufrecht Melcher Grossastach, named from Hans-Werner Aufrecht and Erhard Melcher of Grossastach, producer of racing engines and conversions, now owned by DaimlerChrysler.

AMIA, Asocicion Mexicana de la Industria Automotriz, Mexico.

ammeter, an instrument displaying the instantaneous rate at which current is flowing, typically measuring current flow into or out from the battery, reading in amps.

amp, ampere.

ampere, the unit of electrical current, symbol I, a flow of 6.24×10^{18} electrons per second, in a 12 volt system 1 amp will produce 12 watts of power, $I = W/v$, also $I = v/R$.

ampere hour, the capacity of a battery, indicating its potential power output.

ampere hour capacity, the numerical capacity of a battery, based upon the current a fully charged battery can deliver continuously for 20 hours without any cell voltage dropping below 1.75 volts.

amphetamine, a drug that should not be used by drivers, often contained in dieting pills.

amphib, amphibian.

amphibian, a car that is specially designed or subsequently modified to self propel itself across the surface of deep water.

amplitude, the absolute maximum value of a waveform representing voltage, current, sound, or other variable quantity.

amtrac, an amphibious tractor.

AMVIR, Association of Motor Vehicle Importers Representatives, Greece.

anaerobic sealant, a material that cures or hardens only without air, when squeezed tightly between 2 surfaces as a gasket material.

analogue gauge, any gauge with a pointer or needle.

analogue instruments, an instrument that indicates a numerical figure by use of a pointer against a fixed scale.

analyser, a device used to check the internal function of a system or component.

anchor, brake.

anchorage, a fixing point on a stress bearing part of a vehicle body, for the termination of a seat belt.

ancillary, any component external to the engine but which is vital to either the engine or the vehicle, and which is driven by and consumes power from the engine during its operation, *e.g.* fuel pump, cooling pump, alternator, power steering pump.

AND, Andorra, international vehicle distinguishing sign, see appendices.

ANFAC, Asociacion Espanola de Fabricantes de Automoviles y Camiones, Spain.

ANFAVEA, Associação Nacional de Veículos Automotores, Brazil.

ANFIA, Associazione Nazionale Fra Industrie Automobilistiche, Italy

angle of approach, the maximum gradient at the front of a vehicle that may be approached and climbed from a level surface, without any part of the vehicle contacting the surface.

angle of departure, the maximum gradient at the rear of a vehicle that may be climbed in reverse from a level surface, without any part of the vehicle contacting the surface.

angle of tilt, an angle at which any vehicle may lean, but if exceeded will result in the vehicle rolling onto its side; for tall vehicles the angle is small.

angle parking, herringbone parking.

annual average daily traffic, the total volume of traffic passing a point or length of road in both directions for one year divided by the number of days in the year.

annular gear, a gear in the form of a cylinder or ring with teeth on the inside.

anode, a positive electrode.

anodise, an oxide coating on aluminium, it can be natural or brightly coloured.

ANPR, automatic number plate reader.

ANS, active noise system.

ANS, anti-noise system.

ANSI, American National Standards Institute.

antenna, a radio aerial.

antibackfire valve, a valve in an air injection system that prevents backfire through the exhaust during deceleration.

antiburst lock, a design of door closing mechanism on modern vehicles that prevents a door from opening during a collision.

antichip coating, a thick resilient coating between the primer and top coat of paint to protect the bodywork from stone chip damage, especially to the bonnet.

anticipation, the ability to recognise situations before they develop, to recognise what is unseen, *i.e.* that another driver is going to perform an action before it commences.

anticorrosive paint, paint containing lead chromate or zinc chromate or similar to protect steel surfaces against rust.

antidazzle mirror, a dipping mirror having a sheet of glass in front of the mirror such that the mirror may be angled downwards to reduce dazzle, but as the mirror angle changes a weak reflection remains from the glass.

antidive suspension, a front suspension arrangement designed to reduce dive when braking, typically by angling the pivots of a double wishbone system.

antidrum compound, a non-hardening bitumen coating applied to body panels to reduce noise.

antifogging liquid, a compound applied to the inside and outside of all glass to prevent moisture condensing on windows and mirrors.

antifreeze, a liquid that is added to the water in the cooling system of a vehicle to lower its freezing point, raise its boiling point, and prevent corrosion; usually MEG, MPG, or methanol is used; depending upon concentration freezing point can be as low as –97 °C, and boiling point up to +188 °C.

antifriction bearing, a bearing that supports its load on balls, rollers, or needles that are spaced between the journal and bearing surface.

antiknock, resistance to detonation or pinking in si engines, often achieved by electronics, earlier by addition of tetraethyl lead to fuel.

antiknock index, a measure of the antiknock properties of a petrol, the mathematical average of the MON and RON.

antilift suspension, a rear suspension designed to produce the minimum amount of lift due to apparent weight change during braking.

antilock brakes, a braking system designed to retain steering ability during harsh braking, where electronic sensors at each wheel activate the hydraulic system to release the brake pressure to 1 or more wheels just before each wheel is about to lock, to keep each wheel revolving so the wheels cannot become locked by the action of the driver, to allow some steering control during emergency braking and to prevent a brake induced skid; they are not antiskid brakes, a skid can still be developed, they will not shorten braking distances, the footbrake must NOT be pulsed manually, the brake should be held fully depressed until the emergency is resolved, developed by Bosch.

antilockout power door locks, a system which prevents the doors from being locked if the keys are in the ignition, developed by Toyota.

antimarten system, USA, physical barriers under and around an engine compartment to prevent entry of martens and other animals which may cause damage by chewing rubber and plastic components.

anti-noise system, a noise counteraction system which measures noise near to the drivers head and produces matching counter-frequencies to cancel the noise as much as possible.

antiperforation warranty, a guarantee that metal parts will not corrode sufficiently to create holes in the metal.

antique, USA, any vehicle constructed before 1925.

antiram post, a post sometimes positioned in commercial areas to prevent vehicles being driven through windows or doors to commit crime.

antiroll bar, a transverse spring bar between left and right suspension at front and/or rear of many vehicles, to reduce body roll.

antiseize compound, a coating on some surfaces especially on threads to prevent corrosion and seizing.

antishunt control, a system that automatically performs power changes, *i.e.* it matches engine speed to the drivetrain speed of the next selected gear before the clutch completes engagement, for smoother gearchanges, developed by Landrover.

antiskid brakes, see: antilock brakes.

antiskid surfacing, a road surface coating providing a high friction surface, typically calicined bauxite in a resin binder, usually coloured and laid in areas where drivers frequently brake hard on the approach to a hazard.

antislip regulation, a microprocessor controlled system that reduces the probability of a power–induced skid by detecting wheelspin and automatically reducing the engine power and/or applying the brake to one or more wheels, developed by Audi.

antispin system, a hydraulically controlled differential which is locked by a system of friction discs to reduce wheelspin at 1 wheel, developed by Mercedes.

antisquat suspension, rear suspension designed to resist squat under hard acceleration, typically by using a trailing arm system.

antisubmarine seats, a seat base design, preventing the occupant from slipping beneath the seatbelt in a severe collision.

antisway bar, USA, antiroll bar.

anti-theft device, any mechanical, electrical, or electronic device that will reduce the risk of a vehicle being stolen.

anti-trap, electric windows with a sensor preventing injury if the window is closed whilst fingers etc. are obstructing closure.

antivibration mounting, a rubber or plastic bushing for mounting the engine or transmission, to reduce noise and vibration being passed to the chassis or body.

antiwaxing, a property of some diesel fuels designed for use in cold climates to prevent wax from precipitating and blocking lines and the fuel filter.

antiwaxing fluid, an additive for diesel fuel to prevent the paraffinic hydrocarbons in diesel fuel from precipitating as wax and blocking the fuel lines and filter in cold weather.

antiwear additive, an additive for mixing with unleaded petrol which usually contains either manganese, phosphorus, potassium, or sodium compounds as alternatives to lead to protect the engine exhaust valve seats from excessive wear.

antiwhiplash head restraint, a head restraint which automatically pivots to meet the drivers head on rear impact to reduce the effect of whiplash.

ANWB, Royal Dutch Touring Club.

AOH, air over hydraulic.

APC, armoured personnel carrier.

apex, see: double, early, late, long, short.

apex, on a public road, the point on the inside of a bend where an arc of maximum radius between start and finish of the bend on ones own side of the road only, touches the road edge or centre line; see also: double.

apex, on a race circuit, the point on the inside of a bend where an arc of maximum radius between entry and exit touches the kerb; see also: double.

apex area, the portion of a bend between entry and exit transitions where the steering angle is held constant whilst the wheels follow the ideal line.

apex seal, a straight metal seal along each of the 3 ridges of the epitrochoidal rotor in a Wankel and similar rotary engines to retain compression; for the same purpose as a piston ring in a reciprocating engine.

APGP, air portable general purpose.

API, American Petroleum Institute, an organisation that sets international standards for oil qualities.

APIA, Association of Automotive Manufacturers and Importers, Romania.

apparent weight transfer, the effect of inertia on a vehicle causing the nose to dip whilst braking and to rise when accelerating, and the body to roll laterally when cornering, such that the centre of weight of the vehicle appears to move.

appliance, a fire services vehicle.

appliance operator, CB jargon, a user not familiar with his set.

application pressure gauge, an instrument which informs the driver of a vehicle having air brakes the pressure which is being applied to the brakes at any instant.

apply the brake, to operate the footbrake or handbrake.

approach angle, the maximum gradient at the front of a vehicle that may be approached and climbed from a level surface, without any part of the vehicle contacting the surface.

approach lights, remote control operation of the parking lights, interior lights, and security or doorstep lights, developed by Volvo.

approach road, the road leading towards a motorway, comprising the acceleration lane and sliproad.

Approved Driving Instructor, UK, a person who is registered with the DSA and holds a licence entitling him/her to teach driving for money or moneys worth.

approved route, USA, a route across a limited use area which is at least 2 feet (600 mm) wide and showing significant evidence of prior vehicle use.

apron, hard shoulder.

APTA, American Public Transit Association.

aquachannel tyre, a tyre tread having a very wide central channel for water dispersal, and which may remove up to 10 litres of water per second at motorway speeds.

aqua pan, a skidpan which functions using water without an oil or lubricant, typically requiring the use of slick tyres on the training vehicles, but on which vehicles will not slide at slow speeds.

aquaplane, a condition which occurs when the speed of the vehicle is greater than the ability of the tyre tread to remove the water from between the tyre and the road, the tyre rides up on a thin layer of water thereby having no direct contact with the road surface thereby suffering a severe loss of steering and braking ability; see also: visco.

aquatread, a tyre primarily designed to give good traction on wet roads.

AR, all roads, a road rallying pace note meaning the clue may be in any direction.

aramid, a synthetic fabric used in the construction of some tyres that by weight is stronger than steel.

ARB, Air Resources Board, the body responsible for regulating vehicle emissions in California.

arc, the effect of an electrical current jumping across an air gap, especially in a sparkplug.

ARCADY, assessment of roundabout capacity and delay.

arch, wheel arch, the bodywork around a wheel cutout.

arch bridge, a bridge passing over a road to support a structure typically a railway line, which is supported by 1 or several arches, usually made from brick or stone.

arch bridge, a road bridge where the road surface is supported by 1 or several arches, usually made from stone.

arcing, a repetitive spark, sometimes crossing an insulator where it is not desirable.

ARDS, Association of Racing Drivers Schools, UK.

area familiarisation, an act by a driver in making a reconnaissance of a route or area before the occasion on which it is to be driven.

area licence, a permit to drive within a controlled zone, typically a city centre, paid on a daily or annual basis.

ARG, autonomous route guidance.

argon, an inert gas used to fill most bulbs typically available as replacements in most vehicles, having a shorter life than krypton filled originals.

arm, an approach/departure road to/from a junction, more usually named leg.

ARM, Armenia, international vehicle distinguishing sign, see appendices.

armature, a part rotated within a magnetic field to produce an electric current.

Armco barrier, a safety barrier formed from a strip of corrugated steel on short posts.

armoured personnel carrier, a military wheeled or tracklaying vehicle encased in armour plate.

armoured vehicle, a wheeled or tracklaying vehicle protected by armour plate, used for combat security.

armour plate, thick steel alloy plating on some military and VIP vehicles designed to withstand attack by bullets and explosive devices, usually including special window glass.

armrest, an upholstered projection on the inside of some doors and sometimes between the seats to support a persons arm.

arm restraint, physical protection for a drivers arms in the event of a rollover, especially in an open car.

arm signal, any of 7 different signals given physically by a driver or rider to other road users or to a police officer controlling traffic, to describe the intentions of the driver, generally obsolete except the straight ahead signal.

armstrong, any steering system without power assistance.

arrester bed, the area of soft sand or loose gravel at the end of an escape lane, which is designed to safely stop an out of control vehicle suffering brake failure on a long downhill gradient by bogging down the wheels.

arrowhead, the visual limit point created by a bend where the left and right road edges appear to meet, *i.e.* the visual shape of the apparently converging road edges.

arterial road, a high volume trunk road or main road, typically connecting major towns.

artic, articulated.

articulated, connected by joints to allow pivoting.

articulated bus, a bus so constructed that it can be divided into 2 or more parts, each of which are vehicles and 1 of which is a motor vehicle, connected by a pivoting joint such that when following a curved course the longitudinal axes of each section are not congruent, and passengers carried by it can at all times pass from any part to another, (C&U).

articulated lorry, a vehicle in 2 or more sections, *e.g.* a tractive unit and semitrailer connected by a pivoting joint such that when following a curved course the longitudinal axes of each section are not congruent.

articulated steering, a vehicle having all axles which are rigid and non-steering, but having a chassis that hinges near the centre allowing the vehicle to bend, usually controlled by hydraulic ram power steering, typically on construction plant but on some road vehicles.

articulated truck, a lorry having rigid axles and which steers by articulation of the chassis, typically used for earthmoving, not usually used on a road.

articulated truck, USA, articulated lorry.

articulated vehicle, a heavy motor car or motor car with trailer so attached that part of the trailer is superimposed upon the drawing vehicle and not less than 20 % of the weight of the load is borne by the drawing vehicle, (RTA).

articulation, see: axle articulation.

artillery wheels, a wheel having wooden spokes, on some veteran vehicles.

ARTS, adaptive restraint technology system.

ARV, armed response vehicle.

AS, active steering.

AS, active suspension.

ASA, Bundesverband der Hersteller und Importeure von Automobil-Service Austustungen.

asbestos, a fibrous silicate incombustible mineral formerly a major constituent of brake pads, brake shoes, and clutch friction facing, now prohibited from use due to health risks.

ASBS, antiskid braking system.

ASC, acceleration skid control.

ASC, active skid control.

ASC, anti shunt control.

ASCE, American Society of Civil Engineers.

ASC+T, active skid control plus traction control.

ASD, automatic slipcontrol differential.

ASE, active safety equipment.

ash frame, a vehicle chassis or body framework constructed of wood cut from a tree of the ash family due to its desirable properties.

asl, advanced stop line.

ASME, American Society of Mechanical Engineers.

aspect ratio, the relative height of a tyre sidewall from the bead seat to the tread compared to the section width as a percentage, and which can range from approximately 35 on a low profile tyre to 82 which is the maximum for a radial.

asperities, the microscopic imperfections in smooth surfaces, *e.g.* bearings.

asphalt, a bituminous pitch occurring naturally, mixed with sand or gravel for surfacing roads.

asphaltic concrete, a common road surface material comprising small stones bound by a black petroleum based substance, commonly known as tarmac.

aspiration, the drawing in of air or air-fuel

mixture by the induction stroke of the piston.

ASR, acceleration skid control.

ASR, acceleration skid reduction.

ASR, antislip regulation.

ASR, antispin regulation.

ASR, automatic suspension regulator.

ASS, antispin system.

assemble, to construct or put together.

assembly, a component made from assembled pieces.

assessment licence, a temporary licence issued to a person following a period of unfitness on medical grounds, which requires the display of L plates and which allows the person to retrain, practice, and take an assessment test with a medical examiner before the reissue of a full licence.

assist grip, USA, a grab handle mounted on the inside of a vehicle which provides a convenient place to hold and obtain leverage for entering and exiting the vehicle.

ASSYST, active service system.

AST, advanced stability and traction control.

ASTM, American Society for Testing and Materials.

As tronic, a semiautomatic gearbox having no clutch, and which communicates with the ECU, developed by Iveco trucks.

asymmetrically split, a rear seat that is not split symmetrically, typically split 60/40 enabling long items to be carried with 1 or 2 rear passengers.

asymmetric headlight, a modern style of headlight beam with a flat cut off at the top and an angled kickup to the nearside.

asymmetric power distribution, the deliberately unequal distribution of torque between front and rear axles in a 4x4, it can be variable using a d-pump and wet clutch, or at a specific percentage using a planetary differential; either front or rear may be designed to transmit the greater power.

asymmetric rim, a wheel having the well located closer to 1 rim than the other, usually outboard.

asymmetric tread, a tyre tread where the pattern of the grooves vary across its width to provide an optimum of wet and dry ride and handling characteristics, typically the outer tread and shoulder are designed for cornering, the crown zone for precise steering control, and the inner tread and shoulder for traction and braking, rotation is critical in 1 direction only and the tyres must not be rotated between axle positions.

at, automatic transmission.

A/T, all terrain, a tyre designed primarily for off road use, having a tread suitable for rock, mud, and road surfaces.

ATA, American Trucking Association.

ATA, Associazione Tecnica Dell'Automobile.

atdc, after top dead centre.

ATDO, Association of Track Day Organisers, UK.

– AAA –

atf, automatic transmission fluid.
at grade, any junction, pedestrian crossing, or railway level crossing which is level with the road surface, *i.e.* not above or below a road.
at grade crossing, USA, a railway level crossing.
atmos, atmospheric, normally aspirated, an engine without assistance from a supercharger or turbocharger.
atmospheric pressure, the weight of the atmospheric air per unit area, standard at sea level is 101 kPa (14.7 psi) absolute.
atomise, to spray fuel through a nozzle or jet so the liquid is broken into a fine mist.
ATRA, Advanced Transit Association, USA.
at rest, a vehicle which is stationary.
ATSSA, American Traffic Safety Services Association.
attendant parking, a parking area supervised by an attendant; see: valet.
attended, a vehicle condition when the driver is in or near the vehicle.
attention span, the duration of time that a driver, especially a learner driver can concentrate on a specific task before a change of circumstances is required, typically limited to about 20 minutes.
at the wheel, to be driving a vehicle.
at the wheel, to be sitting in the driving seat.
attitude, behaviour reflecting a way of thinking.
attitude, the position of a vehicle relative to a specific direction.
attraction signing, private and supplemental signs featuring logos or verbal messages indicating tourist attractions, food, fuel, and rest locations.
attrition, rubbing, wearing down by abrasion.
ATV, all terrain vehicle, typically a 4x4 jeep.
ATV, all terrain vehicle, sometimes relating to a motor tricycle or quadricycle having seating and controls similar to that of a motorcycle.
auberge, French, a roadside inn.
auction, a place where vehicles are sold to the person offering the highest bid.
audc, USA, after upper dead centre, atdc.
AUDI, Association of United Driving Instructors, UK.
Audi, AudiWerke GmbH originally, then merged to form Auto Union, then merged with NSU to form Audi AG, a german car manufacturer.
AUS, Australia, international vehicle distinguishing sign, see appendices.
ausfahrt, German, motorway exit.
aut, automatic, referring to automatic descent speed control, a hydraulic retarder control system on some lorries and buses using electronics to control hydraulics to maintain a constant speed during a long descent.
authorised dealer, a company selling and/or servicing a particular make of vehicle, and having an agreement with the manufacturer.
AUTIG, Autoreservedels - og Tilbehors

foreningen I Danmark.
auto, automatic.
auto, motor car.
autobahn, Austrian motorway.
autobahn, German motorway.
autobahn, Swiss motorway.
auto box, automatic gearbox.
auto cancelling, a function of the direction indicator switch and mechanism such that the indicators will automatically switch off as the steering wheel returns to a straight position.
autocar, motorcar, archaic name.
autoclutch, a transmission system having a manual gearbox and dry clutch but where operation of the clutch is controlled electronically.
autocross, motor racing in specially prepared cars on a variety of surfaces including clean tarmac, shale, and loose gravel within each lap of a course.
autocross, motor racing on unsurfaced roads or cross-country.
autocross, USA, auto test, a driving competition conducted on a firm surface off the public road, typically in a closed large carpark, where each vehicle must complete a series of accurate manoeuvres around a predefined course against the clock.
autocycle, a bicycle to which a small motor has been fitted.
auto dipping, an automatic dipping rear view mirror.
autodrome, a motorsport or driver training venue, typically converted from a disused aerodrome or airport.
autogas, LPG propane gas supplied for use in vehicles.
auto hood, a convertible car where the task of removing or replacing the roof is performed electrically or hydraulically controlled from a dashboard switch.
auto hubs, automatic locking front hubs.
auto-ignition, the spontaneous ignition of air-fuel mixture in an internal combustion engine, as required at injection in a diesel engine, but a fault condition in an si engine.
autojumble, a market where vehicle parts, especially second hand, can be bought and sold, typically at a 1 day motoring event.
auto loop, a 1 way road system with separate entry and exit, used for drive-in facilities, *e.g.* a drive-through fast-food, or within a wildlife park etc.
auto lube, an automatic lubrication system for suspension and steering systems controlled from a central point.
automated cruise control, a microprocessor based system that uses radar to lock-on to the vehicle ahead to keep a constant distance, accelerating and braking as necessary.
automated transmission, a system which combines the convenience of an automatic transmission with the control of a manual transmission, and which has a clutch and gear

29

selector but in which the clutch is electronically controlled; see also: automatic.

automatic, a term applied to devices that are self moving or self regulating.

automatic advance control, a device operated by the inlet manifold vacuum that automatically adjusts the advance of the ignition spark timing by rotation of part of the distributor.

automatic air recirculation, a system where outside air quality is measured by a sensor and a microprocessor determines when to admit fresh air or when to recirculate, to reduce pollutants entering a car, developed by BMW.

automatic box, automatic gearbox.

automatic brake differential system, a system that will recognise oversteer and understeer skids and apply the brake to 1 wheel to control the situation, developed by Porsche.

automatic choke, a device that automatically adjusts the choke valve to match engine temperature.

automatic closing system, a system of electronics that will close all windows and sunroof and lock all doors when signalled, see also: power closing.

automatic cushion restraint, an obsolete alternative to a seatbelt, comprising a cushion held against the occupants chest by a hinged arm.

automatic debiting system, a system of charging a toll automatically from a vehicle without requiring the vehicle to stop, for toll charging on motorways, town centres, tunnels, bridges, and carparks, etc.

automatic gearbox, a gearbox that changes gear automatically without driver input when moving, according to designed parameters, usually the power is input from a torque converter effectively giving an automatic clutch.

automatic gearbox, for the purposes of a driving test in any EU member state: a vehicle with a gearchange effected by use only of the accelerator or brake.

automatic levelling system, a suspension system which adjusts the front and rear ride heights to compensate for the weight and seating position of each passenger.

automatic locking front hubs, front wheel hubs that will automatically select either lock or free when 4wd is selected or disengaged, so the front axle and transmission will transmit power when required and will freewheel when 2wd is selected, on some 4wd vehicles.

automatic locking retractor, a seatbelt function that makes it possible to secure a child seat by pulling the shoulder belt all the way out then allowing it to retract to the desired length, then pressing down firmly on the child seat as the belt retracts to buckle the child seat securely in place.

automatic number plate reader, a portable roadside smart camera having character recognition software which reads the registration plate of each approaching vehicle and checks using a direct link to the DVLC computer if VED has been paid, and if not, automatically issues legal proceedings.

automatic seatbelt, USA, a seatbelt which is permanently fastened at all anchorages but where 2 of the anchorages are either on the door or on a rail along the door frame such that when the door is open the seatbelt moves to allow the person in and out of the seat.

automatic slipcontrol differential, a differential which will self control automatically to lock when there is a more than a small difference in wheel speed between the 2 wheels.

automatic speed control, cruise control.

automatic stability control & traction, a system that recognises oversteer and understeer skids and reduces power and applies the brake to 1 wheel, it also prevents the rear wheels from spinning on a slippery surface to ensure a safe grip when starting or accelerating in a bend, developed by BMW.

automatic suspension regulator, a traction control system developed by Renault.

automatic transmission, a gearbox needing no driver input whilst the vehicle is moving, it changes gear automatically meeting the manufacturers determined parameters, the system normally having a torque converter instead of a clutch; see also: automated.

automatic transmission fluid, a type of gear oil for automatic gearboxes and for some high performance gearboxes.

automatic transmission shift lock, a safety device which requires that the ignition is on and the brake pedal is depressed before the transmission lever can be moved out of P, to prevent inadvertent selection of D or R, and unintentional acceleration.

automatic vehicle, a vehicle having an automatic gearbox.

automatic wear adjuster, a mechanical device that responds to wear in the brakes or clutch and makes automatic adjustments.

automobile, a land vehicle running on at least 4 complete wheels, of which at least 2 are used for steering and at least 2 for propulsion; USA, car.

automobile association, any major motoring association that offers services to its members; individual or related organisations exist in many countries worldwide.

automobilia, collectable artefacts related to vehicles and motoring.

automotive, relating to motor vehicles.

automotive air pollution, vaporized unburned fuel and products of combustion, mainly carbon monoxide CO, hydrocarbons HC, nitrogen oxides NO_x, sulphur oxides SO_x, and particulates.

automotive electrician, a person who repairs electrical faults on vehicles and/or installs electrical accessories.

automotive emissions, vaporized unburned fuel and products of combustion, mainly carbon monoxide CO, hydrocarbons HC, nitrogen oxides NO_x, sulphur oxides SO_x, and particulates.

automotive engineering, the design and manufacture of vehicles.

autonomous route guidance, a route planning and navigation system having a digitised road map within the receiver, using origin and destination driver inputs and satellite navigation to direct the driver using visual or spoken instructions; see also: DRG, pre-trip.

auto-on/auto-off headlamps, a system which detects the amount of daylight and automatically turns the headlamps on or off as required, it also automatically turns the lights off when the key is removed and the driver's door is opened to provide an added level of convenience, safety and security.

Autopar, a trade name used by DaimlerChrysler for its spare parts.

autopatrol, a grader used when repairing the surface of unmetalled roads.

autopilot, a mental condition when a driver has mentally switched off and is not concentrating on the surrounding driving conditions.

autopista, Spanish motorway.

autoporto, Italian motorway services.

autorail, a vehicle with retractable flanged wheels having the ability to drive along railway lines in addition to tyres for road use.

auto rickshaw, a 3 wheeled taxi, the front resembling a motorcycle, the rear having a covered bench seat, common in many Asian countries, often nicknamed tuk-tuk from the exhaust note.

autoroute, Belgian motorway.

autoroute, French motorway.

autoroutes a peàge, French toll motorway.

Autoshift, a semiautomatic gear selector system using a clutch pedal for starting and stopping only, and with the gear selector on the steering column.

autostick, a semiautomatic gearbox having manual gear selection but without a clutch pedal.

auto stop, a function of some hybrid electric vehicles, whereby the ic engine automatically shuts down when not used, *e.g.* when stationary at traffic signals.

autostrada, Italian motorway.

Auto Telligent EPS, a clutchless version of Telligent EPS semiautomatic gear system, offering automatic gear selection or manual override, developed by Mercedes trucks.

auto test, a driving competition conducted on a firm surface off the public road, typically in a closed large carpark, where each vehicle must complete a series of accurate manoeuvres around a predefined course against the clock.

Autotrac, electronic remote selection of 2wd/4wd and H/L ratios or automatic 4x4, the automatic mode operates in 2wd until sensors detect slip, then torque is directed to the wheels with the most traction, developed by GM.

autovia, Spanish dual carriageway.

auto wipers, a system which automatically controls the speed of the windscreen wipers dependent upon the quantity of rainfall, developed by Mercedes.

auxiliary, any additional or subsidiary or supplementary parts or system.

auxiliary brake, an additional means of applying the brakes on some buses and lorries with full air brakes in addition to the service and emergency brakes, controlled by the footbrake pedal, using a blue hose if coupled to a trailer.

auxiliary brake light, an additional brake light, typically mounted at eye level.

auxiliary control, each of the secondary controls, *e.g.* horn, indicators, lights, wipers.

auxiliary driving lamp, an additional lamp that enhances high beam visibility, used only in pairs.

auxiliary gearbox, an addition to a gearbox to provide extra ranges or splits between gears.

auxiliary lane, a lengthened parallel merging lane to allow greater than a normal distance for traffic to merge onto the main carriageway of a motorway, typically where a high number of lorries are common, sometimes continuing between interchanges where there is a heavy traffic demand

AV, active ventilation.

AV, automatic variable transmission.

Ave, Avenue, a road name designation.

avenue, a road lined with 1 or several species of tree planted at regular intervals; a high capacity avenue is typically named a boulevard.

avenue, USA, a road running perpendicular from the main road.

average speed, the distance travelled divided by the time taken, commonly in units of km/h, mph, or m/s.

AVI, active vibration isolation.

AVI, automatic vehicle identification.

AVL, automatic vehicle location.

avoidance strategy, procedures or techniques used to reduce the risk of a collision, a function of defensive driving.

AVRO, Association of Vehicle Recovery Operators, UK.

a/w, alloy wheels.

awa, antiwear additive.

awareness, to know where all nearby road users are and where they are going, knowing what is happening on all sides of the vehicle at all times.

awd, all wheel drive.

AWDC, All Wheel Drive Club, a competitive organisation for owners of 4x4 vehicles, UK.

awg, American wire gauge, a sizing system for wire and metal sheet.

AWLREM, Association of Webbing Load

Restraint Equipment Manufacturers, UK.

axis, the centreline of a symmetrical part.

axis, a horizontal transverse line midway between the first and last axles in any group or set of axles.

axle, 1 or more fixed or rotating shafts or spindles in the same axial line forming the centre of rotation to which 1 or more wheels are fastened.

axle, see: $^1/_4$ floating, $^3/_4$ floating, fully floating, semifloating.

axle alignment, the alignment of a rear live axle with respect to the longitudinal centreline of the vehicle.

axle articulation, the length (height) of travel of a suspension, a desirable quality to prevent cross axling situations.

axle interspace, in the case of a full trailer, the longitudinal distance between the centre of the front axle set and the centre of the rear axle set, (C&U).

axle interspace, in the case of a semitrailer, the longitudinal distance between the kingpin and the centre of the axle or the centre of the group of axles, (C&U).

axle loading, the total load transmitted to the ground through the wheels by the load the axle is carrying plus the weight of the wheels and axle itself.

axle ratio, the final drive reduction gear ratio in the drive axle, expressed as the number of times the propshaft rotates to turn the axle shaft 1 rotation.

axle set, a number of closely spaced axles which share the load at that part of the vehicle, see: single, tandem, triaxle.

axle spacing, the distance between the axles of a vehicle, especially the distance between the

axles on a tandem or triaxle system as it is a factor in calculating the gross load.

axle stand, a 3 legged device incrementally height adjustable, for supporting a raised vehicle before working underneath, normally used in pairs.

axle tramp, a bouncing reaction sometimes occurring when climbing a steep hard surface using a lot of power in a low gear, especially with leaf spring suspension; also named bouncing.

axle travel, axle articulation.

axle view, the view through the space beneath a vehicles' bodywork, to see what is beyond it as a function of advanced or defensive driving, most prominent when the vehicle is cresting, but it is a most valuable observation below every parked vehicle.

axle weight, the weight transmitted to the ground by the wheels of that axle.

axle weight limit, a limit imposed on a section of road that prohibits use by any vehicle having an axle loading exceeding that weight.

axle wind-up, the stress on a 4x4 vehicle without a centre differential or with the differential locked, or on a multidrive axle system with the interaxle differential locked, when wheels are travelling unequal distances in a curve or unequal speeds as in a lead/lag situation, resulting in wheel slip.

axle wind-up, the axial rotation of the axle casing under torsional load and periodic sudden release resulting in a bounce of the wheel when climbing a steep hard surface using a lot of power, especially with leaf springs; commonly named axle tramp.

AZ, Azerbaijan, international vehicle distinguishing sign, see appendices.

B

B, Belgium, international vehicle distinguishing sign, see appendices.

B, bias belt construction, a designation within a tyre size coding indicating the tyre is not a radial or crossply.

B, blue, black, or brown, the colour of roads to be used at that point in road rally navigation as marked on an OS map.

B, brake, a marking moulded into the brake pedal rubber of many vehicles especially buses and lorries.

B, brake, a selector button on a Geartronic gearlever that will instruct the automatic gearbox to select the best gear for high revs for engine braking during a descent.

B, Brake, a phase of the IPBGA mnemonic.

B, a hire car size and price category for cars based upon their floor pan; a small car designed to seat 4 with some comfort, *e.g.* Ford Focus, or Peugeot 306 sized.

B, Europe, a driving licence category for motor vehicles with a MAM not exceeding 3,500 kg and having not more than 8 passenger seats, and permitting drawing of a trailer up to 750 kg, or combinations of towing vehicles in category B with a trailer where the MAM of the combination does not exceed 3,500 kg and the MAM of the trailer does not exceed the kerbweight of the towing vehicle.

B, USA, a driving license and vehicle category: any single motor vehicle with a GVWR exceeding 26,000 lbs (11.8 tonnes) or any such vehicle towing another not exceeding 10,000 lbs (4.5 tonnes); a CDL is required; not including motorcycles.

B, USA, the tire temperature code denoting a satisfactory standard above the lowest, moulded into the tire sidewall.

B, USA, the tire traction code denoting average braking performance on a wet surface, moulded into the tire sidewall.

B, a write-off category in which the car cannot be put back on the road but can be used as a donor car to yield spare parts for other vehicles; typically where the bodyshell is seriously lozenged.

B, the driving licence category for cars in many countries.

B1, a European driving licence category for motor tricycles and quadricycles having a design speed exceeding 50 km/h, and an unladen weight not exceeding 550 kg.

B automatic, a European driving licence category for cars in category B but where the vehicle is fitted with automatic transmission.

B band, a VED category within which vehicles emitting between 151 and 165 g/km of CO_2 are charged.

B double, double bottom.

B flange, a style of wheel rim flange, the part of the wheel rim against which the tyre locates, used only on smaller vehicles.

B pillar, on a car, the roof and door frame support pillar just behind the driver, where the front seat belt anchorages are usually located.

B post, B pillar.

B road, a secondary route, a minor route less important than an A road.

B segment car, a size category for cars based upon their floor pan; a small car but larger than a mini.

B thread, any internal thread.

B trailer, the second trailer of a road train.

B train, a type of roadtrain, a tractive unit hauling 2 or more semitrailers, the rear of every semitrailer except the last is constructed with a 5th wheel coupling over the rear wheels to couple with the kingpin of the next semitrailer; if only 2 trailers it is named a B double.

BA, brake assist.

BA, British Association.

babbitt, an alloy used for lining bearings, which consists of tin, antimony, copper and other metals.

BABFO, British Association of Bio Fuels and Oils.

baby seat, a child safety seat in 6 sizes for children from birth to age 11, see: stage 1, to stage 4.

BAC, blood alcohol concentration.

back, to reverse.

back axle, rear axle.

backbone chassis, a chassis formed from a single central structure, typically tubular or tuboid, but sometimes of rectangular section.

back door, CB jargon, the vehicle behind you.

backfire, an explosion in the carburettor caused when the air-fuel mixture is ignited by still-burning exhaust gas at the gas-exchange tdc.

backfire, an explosion in the exhaust caused by the ignition of unburned air-fuel mixture which is ignited via faulty seating or timing of the exhaust valve.

backhoe, a multipurpose industrial vehicle similar to an agricultural tractor, fitted at the rear with a hydraulic arm and bucket for excavating earth, and usually at the front a loading bucket.

back in, to reverse into a garage or parking space.

back in, to reverse off a road.

backing, the action of reversing.

backing up, the action of reversing.

backlash, freeplay, clearance, a specific space between 2 moving components when 1 is moved back and forth, *e.g.* between 2 meshing gearwheels.

backlite, USA, rear window.

backload, a load carried by a lorry for a third party to a convenient location to prevent returning unloaded after dropping the primary load.

backmarker, the vehicle at the tail end of a line of moving vehicles.

back on, to reverse onto a trailer.

back out, to reverse from a garage or parking space.

back out, to reverse onto a road.

backplate, a strong steel plate at the axle end that carries the brake operating mechanism.

backpressure, pressure created in the exhaust system of a running engine as exhaust gas flows through.

backrest, the near vertical portion of any vehicle seat.

back seat, the rearmost row of seats in a vehicle.

backseat driver, any passenger openly criticising or giving unwanted advice to a driver.

back side, CB jargon, a return trip.

backslide, a rear wheel skid.

back stroke, CB jargon, a return trip.

backup, to drive in reverse gear.

backup alarm, USA, reversing horn.

backup lamp, USA, reversing lamp.

bad egg smell, a smell from the exhaust of hydrogen sulphide, H_2S, similar to rotten eggs, typically caused by a car having a cat and a carburettor, such that there is no feedback from an oxygen sensor to weaken the mixture.

badge bar, a bar fitted on the front of vehicles to display motoring and other enamelled badges, now generally out of fashion.

badge engineering, the selling of similar models under the names of different manufacturers when they are working in association, when the only significant difference between vehicles may be the badge affixed to each vehicle.

baffle, metal plates constructed inside an exhaust silencer to reduce exhaust noise by absorption and reflection.

baffle, metal plates in fuel tanks and oil reservoirs to restrict fluid movement when accelerating, braking, and cornering.

bag, the rubber air cylinder on an air suspension unit.

bail bond, an insurance document recommended or required before entry by vehicle into some countries.

Bailey bridge, Sir D. Bailey, designer of a temporary beam bridge constructed from a lattice of steel in 1940, usually installed by the military, many continue in use after many years.

Baja, a small town in southern California, famous for hosting the Baja 500 and 1,000 mile (1,600 km) cross country races.

Baja 500, a 500 mile (800 km) cross country race in the southern Californian desert.

bakkie, South Africa, pickup truck.

balaclava, a fireproof hood worn by competition drivers underneath a crash helmet, made from nomex.

balance, see: static balance, dynamic balance.

balanced agricultural trailer, an agricultural trailer the whole of the weight of which is borne by its own wheels, (C&U); see also: unbalanced.

balanced throttle, delicate skilful use of the accelerator to maintain a constant speed through a hazard, to balance all the physical forces acting on the vehicle.

balance patch, a factory fitted patch vulcanised to the inside of a new tyre carcass to restore the dynamic balance of a tyre that would otherwise be outside the limits of quality control.

balancer, a machine that balances a wheel and tyre assembly, usually with microprocessor control.

balancer pipe, exhaust piping between 2 parts of a twin exhaust system.

balancer shafts, counter-rotating shafts, usually revolving at double the crankshaft speed, to reduce engine vibration.

balance weight, a small lead weight fitted to a wheel rim to correct static or dynamic imbalance in a wheel and tyre assembly.

balancing the accelerator, using exactly the amount of power required to maintain a constant speed in a bend or other situation.

balancing the clutch, controlling exactly a clutch pressure to maintain a specific clutch slip such that a vehicle is held stationary on a gradient using the clutch and accelerator only; not recommended for longer than a few moments.

balancing the throttle, balancing the accelerator.

bald, the condition of a tyre having less than the legal minimum depth of tread, especially if any of the original channels and grooves are not visible.

ball and nut steering, recirculating ball.

ballast, weight which is added to increase traction in special circumstances, in the case of a tractor either external steel weights are suspended or a substance is injected into the pneumatic tyres, in the case of a locomotive either concrete blocks or a water filled tank are carried; see also: dry, liquid.

ballast resistor, an electrical resistor in the ignition circuit to assist starting.

ball bearing, an antifriction bearing constructed with a row of caged balls between the inner and outer race.

ball joint, a ball and socket joint giving good flexibility within a range of movement, used for steering and suspension joints.

balloon tyre, a tyre designed for off-road floatation for use on sand or mud etc, typically of wide section having a large footprint without significant shoulders and designed to be inflated only to a low air pressure.

ballotini, very small reflecting glass beads as incorporated in road marking paint to cause it to be reflective.

BAMA, British Automobile Manufacturers Association, USA.

banana marking, a ghost island or ladder marking marked along the centre of a road around a bend to create additional separation between opposing traffic.

banded wheel, a steel wheel which has been cut around the circumference of the well and a strip of steel welded into place to widen the distance between the rims.

banger, an old car in poor condition.

banger, USA, preceded by a number, an engine having that number of cylinders.

banger racing, racing of elv cars on a small oval gravel circuit where vehicle contact is encouraged.

banjo, a type of hose joint where the connection is at 90° to a pipe.

banking, superelevation, the transverse slope of a road or race circuit around a bend.

BAPPCO, British Automotive Parts Promotion Council.

bar, a unit of pressure, 1 bar = 100 kPa, 14.5 psi.

bar, each of many transverse or angled blocks of tread where each extends from the crown to the shoulder of a tyre.

barium sulphate, a fine powder added dry into tractor tyres as ballast to increase traction in specific conditions.

bar tread, a tyre having a tread comprising transverse lateral bars at 90° to the centreline, used primarily for off road driving especially in mud, favoured by the military for general use.

barbiturate, a drug that should not be used by drivers, often contained in sleeping tablets.

BARC, British Automobile Racing Club.

barn door, the large hinged rear panel on a tipper lorry.

barrel, a unit of measure of oil or fuel, 1 barrel = 159 litres.

barrel, an engine cylinder.

barrel, the throttle bores in a carburettor.

barrelling, to drive at a high speed.

barrel spring, a shape of coil spring where the coils at the centre are of a wider diameter than those at the ends, to allow compression to a very short length.

barrier, safety barrier.

barrier cream, a preparation recommended for coating the hands before working on vehicles to reduce soiling and to reduce the risk of developing allergic reactions to vehicle fluids.

barrow, a 2 wheeled cart pushed manually, typically by street vendors.

BARS, British Association of Rally Schools.

BAS, brake assist system.

bascule bridge, a lifting bridge distinguished by a parallelogram system of links which raise the carriageway.

base circle, the low part of a cam on a camshaft, opposite from the lobe.

base coat, the final coloured coat of paint which is to be covered with a layer of clear lacquer.

base coat, the first coating of paint, *i.e.* the primer on bare metal.

base kerbweight, the kerbweight of the base model of a range of vehicles, before installation of accessories and auxiliaries.

base weight distribution, the comparison of the distribution of the front/rear axle weights when the vehicle is at its kerbweight.

basic price, the minimum list price of a new vehicle to which must be added the cost of registration, number plates, delivery, etc.

basic speed law, California, a rule that prohibits driving faster than is safe for the present conditions regardless of the posted speed limit.

Battenberg, the large scale blue and yellow checked livery on some police vehicles.

battery, a lead acid secondary cell for storing chemical energy that can be released as electrical power.

battery acid, a liquid mixture of 40 % sulphuric acid and 60 % water to form an efficient electrolyte.

battery box heater, a heater to keep the battery warm for maximum efficiency when operating in very cold climates, typically on a bus or lorry where the battery is remote from the engine.

battery capacity test, a test made with a high power resistor to discharge the battery at 3 times its ampere hour rating for 15 seconds, if a 12 v battery remains at or above 9.6 volts it is satisfactory.

battery cell, each of a series of battery elements containing the electrolytic plates immersed in electrolyte, it has an rd of 1.265 and a voltage of 2.1 volts when fully charged.

battery charge indicator, an instrument that displays the state of charge of a battery.

battery charger, an electrical device to re-charge a vehicle battery from mains power.

battery charging, restoring the chemical energy to a battery by forcing an electrical current in the reverse direction so as to reverse the chemical reaction between plates and electrolyte.

battery cut off key, a safety device to manually disconnect the battery, required on some competition cars, sometimes also used as an anti-theft device.

battery fluid, the battery electrolyte, usually acid, but sometimes alkali.

battery master switch, battery cut off key.

battery post, battery terminal.

battery rundown protection, a system that senses low residual capacity of a battery and will automatically start the engine of the vehicle to recharge the battery before the remaining charge becomes too low.

battery terminal, a soft metal projection on the battery to which the electrical cable is clamped.

battery tester, a capacity tester, a device that imposes an electrical load on the battery and interprets the residual voltage in terms of condition.

battery tester, a voltmeter, an instrument that displays the voltage of the battery.

battery tester, an hydrometer, an instrument that shows the rd of the electrolyte.

battery wear, the shedding and sedimentation of the active material especially from the positive cell plates thereby reducing the effective area, capacity, and life.

baulk, a heavy piece of timber used to secure a load on the bed of a lorry.

baulk, a hindrance, to be slowed or stopped by other traffic, *e.g.* to follow behind a slow vehicle uphill.

baulk, a hindrance due to the vehicle design, *e.g.* by a sluggish gear selector system.

bay, a marked area in a carpark within which to park a car.

bay, a marked area of road where parking or loading is permitted, but usually with restrictions, and typically marked with white, yellow, or red lines.

bayonet cap, the cylindrical base of a light bulb having 2 pins that locate in J shaped spring slots.

bayonet socket, a socket for receiving a bayonet cap bulb.

bbdc, before bottom dead centre.

BBPG, British Bus Preservation Group.

BBT, Byways and Bridleways Trust, a registered charity having an interest in the rights and laws pertaining to such highways, UK.

BCC, Bus & Coach Council, UK.

BCWMA, British Car Wash Manufacturers Association.

BD, Bangladesh, international vehicle distinguishing sign, see appendices.

bdc, bottom dead centre.

BDS, Barbados, international vehicle distinguishing sign, see appendices.

BDS, British Driving Society, an organisation concerned with driving of horse drawn carriages.

bdy, body.

B+E, a European driving licence category for a vehicle in category B when drawing a trailer, but where the combination thus formed is not in category B.

beach buggy, a hybrid or kit car, usually having wide wheels, a fibreglass convertible body, and reasonable off-road ability.

beacon, a lamp with a rotating reflector that causes a flash in every direction, having a blue lens for emergency vehicles, a green lens for doctors and paramedics, and an amber lens for road works, slow vehicles and recovery vehicles.

bead, an inextensible hoop of high tensile steel wires around the seating area of a tyre which anchor the plies and conforms to the rim seat to secure the tyre onto the wheel rim to form a mechanical joint to transmit the forces of steering, traction, and braking, and forms an airtight seal.

bead lock wheel, a wheel having an internal ring with which to clamp each tyre bead to the bead seat enabling a large tyre to be operated at very low pressure without risk of unseating the bead.

bead seat, the inner ledge portion of the wheel rim adjacent to the flange, where the tyre bead rests.

beam, the rays of light emitted from a headlamp.

beam axle, an axle that is rigid along its length, not having independent suspension.

beam bridge, a bridge where the road surface is supported on steel or concrete beams between supports.

beam deflectors, small lenses affixed to the headlamp glass that convert part of the beam to dip from left to right when a rhd vehicle is being driven in a lhd country, or vice-versa.

beamsetter, optical beam setter, a device to check the angle of headlamp beams, especially whilst adjustment is made.

bean store, CB jargon, a café.

bear, CB jargon, the police.

bear, followed by left or right, a navigational directive to veer positively through a small angle to take a side road, *i.e.* a similar angle to that taken when leaving a motorway or freeway along a deceleration lane; see also: fork.

bear bait, CB jargon, to commit a traffic offence.

bear bite, CB jargon, a speeding ticket.

bear den, CB jargon, a police station.

bearing, a part that transmits a load to a support with the minimum of friction between the moving parts.

bearing cap, a device to hold a bearing in place.

bearing clearance, the space between a shaft and a bearing that is supporting it.

bearing crush, the slight additional height manufactured into each half of main and big end bearings to ensure complete contact with the bearing bore on assembly.

bearing groove, a channel in the surface of a bearing to distribute oil.

bearing oil clearance, the space purposely provided between shaft and bearing for oil to flow.

bearing prelubricator, a system of supplying lubricating oil around the lubricated parts of an engine before it is started.

bearing puller, a tool designed to remove a bearing from its housing.

bearing spin, a bearing failure where the bearing seizes to the shaft but the outer rotates in its housing.

bear off, to leave a main road at a slight angle, *e.g.* a similar angle to that taken when leaving a motorway or freeway along a deceleration lane; see also: fork.

bears lair, CB jargon, a police station.

bear trap, the location of a radar speed trap.

beast, a vehicle having high acceleration performance.

beater, USA, a banger, a well worn car that is still usable.

beavertail, a flatbed lorry where the deck area behind the rear wheels is fixed at a downwards angle, especially when designed for the recovery of other vehicles.

bed, the load carrying surface of a pickup, lorry, or trailer.

bed-in, to wear in, to deliberately create a small amount of wear so parts are a better fit, *e.g.* to bed-in new brake pads to a worn brake disc having slight ridges.

bedliner, a 1 piece plastic lining to protect the bed of a pickup.

bee sting aerial, a short straight non-telescopic radio aerial.

beef up, to modify or uprate part of a vehicle to improve strength or performance etc.

beeline, USA, a freeway taking a direct route, especially to or through a city centre.

Beemer, BMW.

before bottom dead centre, the crankshaft rotational position before a piston arrives at the bottom of its stroke, before the end of the induction stroke or power stroke.

before top dead centre, the crankshaft rotational position before a piston arrives at the top of its stroke, before the end of the compression stroke or exhaust stroke.

BEG, British Engines Group.

Belgian pavé, a road surface constructed with cobbles, especially when each cobble is in the design of a truncated pyramid, typically 200 mm deep and 100 to 150 mm square.

Belisha, Sir Leslie Hore-Belisha, former Minister for Transport, introduced an improved system of marking for pedestrian crossings, including the Belisha beacon, in 1934.

Belisha beacon, an amber globe mounted on top of a pole to assist visibility of each zebra crossing, introduced by Sir Leslie Hore-Belisha in 1934.

bell code, a system of communication from a bus conductor to the driver, having a code using 1, 2, 3, or 4 rings of a bell.

bell housing, a conical casing between engine and gearbox, which houses the flywheel and clutch or the torque converter.

bellmouth, a pair of buildouts constructed at a junction to visually show that the character of a side road is different from that on the main road.

bells, CB jargon, hours, the time of day.

belly out, to become grounded on a crest.

bellybutton, the nickname for the Beetle in Mexico, everybody has one.

belt, see: fan belt, V belt, poly V belt, timing belt.

belt, a rubber coated layer of cords in a tyre between the body plies and the tread, that determines the tyre diameter and stabilises the tread by resisting deformation during cornering, braking, acceleration, and centrifugal forces due to high rotational speeds; made from: aramid, fibreglass, nylon, polyester, rayon, steel, or other fabrics.

belt deflection, the amount of lateral movement in a fanbelt depending upon its tension.

belt drive, a system for transmitting power from 1 shaft to another using a drive belt.

belted bias tyre, bias belted tyre.

belt force limiter, a device on some seatbelts that allows a small amount of elasticity from the fixing during a collision, to reduce injuries.

beltline, USA, waistline, an imaginary horizontal line along the sides of the passenger compartment of a car at the widest point, typically just below the door handles, sometimes emphasized by a chrome or plastic rubbing strip.

Beltline, the beltway encircling Raleigh, North Carolina.

Belt Parkway, the beltway encircling New York City.

belt retractor, a device which maintains an appropriate seatbelt tension against the wearer, and automatically rewinds a seat belt onto its reel when not in use.

belt tension, the tightness of a drive belt.

belt transmission, CVT transmission.

belt up, to secure the seatbelt around the person.

belt wrench, a tool having a flexible strap which is locked to the length required for gripping and turning large round or irregular shaped objects, especially for unscrewing an oil filter.

beltway, USA, a ringroad or major freeway encircling a city.

BEN, Motor & Allied Trades Benevolent Fund, UK.

bench seat, a seat with no contours for individual passenger comfort, usually seating more than 2 passengers, sometimes a combined seat for driver and front passengers.

bend, a length of road where its course changes direction.
bendi bus, articulated bus.
bending my ears, CB jargon, a bidding request.
bending my windows, CB jargon, a message received clearly.
Bendix, a helical gear and spring system that causes the starter motor pinion to be thrown into mesh with the starter ring when the starter motor is activated.
bent, a vehicle with crash damage.
Benz, Carl Benz, builder of a petrol engined car in 1885, and the first production car for sale in 1888.
benzene, a constituent of petrol typically amounting to 2 %, carcinogenic hence harmful as a liquid and vapour.
benzodiazapine, a drug that should not be used by drivers, often contained in tranquillisers.
benzol, unrefined benzene used as a fuel or mixed with other fuels.
BER, Belarus, international vehicle distinguishing sign, see appendices.
Berlin cushion, a speed cushion having a castellated top surface.
berline, a veteran luxury car having very small windows.
berm, the raised edges of a rough track that have not been compressed or eroded by tyres.
Bernoulli principle, the phenomena that causes a reduction in pressure when a the speed of a fluid increases, as in a carburettor choke and in the airflow between vehicles during overtaking.
berth, a parking space.
be seen, the art of ensuring ones own vehicle is as visible as possible to others, *e.g.* not to linger in the blind spot of another driver.
bevel gear, a conical shaped gear wheel, used for transmission of power between shafts that are not parallel, typically through 90° as in a crownwheel and pinion, or the planetary gears of the differential.
bezel, a circular surround or rim for a dashboard instrument, or around a headlamp, usually chromium plated.
BG, Bulgaria, international vehicle distinguishing sign, see appendices.
BH, Belize, international vehicle distinguishing sign, see appendices.
bhp, brake horse power, 1 bhp equals raising 550 foot-pounds per second, also equal to 745.7 watts, 1 bhp = torque x rpm/5252 when torque is measured in foot-pounds, see also PS.
bias belted tyre, a type of tyre construction having diagonal plies laid at angles of about 30° to 40° relative to the tyre centreline as a crossply tyre, and having 2 or more circumferential plies under the tread as a radial tyre.
bias ply tyre, crossply tyre.
bias valve, a control that allows the driver to adjust the proportion of brake pressure to the

rear wheels; for competition use only.
bib, USA, nose protector.
Bibendum, the name of Michelin man, registered in 1898.
Bicycle Union, the organisation responsible for placing the first road signs at the top of steep hills around UK in 1879.
bidet, a dealer term for a rear wash/wipe system.
biffabout, runabout.
bifuel, a vehicle fuel system which can operate on either of 2 different fuels and change between them whist in motion but which cannot operate on both simultaneously; typically running on petrol or gas, the gas is usually either LPG or CNG; see also: dual fuel.
bifurcation arrow, South Africa, divergence arrow.
big block, USA, a large engine, generally exceeding 400 cu.ins (6,500 cc), although some at only 366 cu.ins (6,000 cc) are included.
big boy, any large vehicle.
big brother, CB jargon, the Home Office or other ministry
big circle, CB jargon, the M25 London orbital motorway.
big dummy, CB jargon, a truck driver.
big end, the crankshaft end of the connecting rod.
big end bearing, the bearing within the big end of the connecting rod, bearing upon a crankpin on the crankshaft.
big end journal, a crankpin on the crankshaft, on which the big end of the con rod bears.
big inch, USA, a large engine, typically exceeding 250 cu.ins, (4,000 cc).
big Jim, a device for opening door locks without a key, a thin flexible metal strip with a hook at its lower end, it is inserted between the window glass and frame in order to pull and release the lock mechanism.
big slab, CB jargon, a motorway.
big smoke, CB jargon, the capital city.
big wheels, CB jargon, a lorry.
BIH, Bosnia and Herzegovina, international vehicle distinguishing sign, see appendices.
bihexagon, a spanner or socket having 12 internal angles to facilitate fitting onto and turning hexagonal nuts and bolts.
BIL, Bilimportorenes Landsforening, Norway.
BIL, Bilindustriforeningen, Association of Swedish Automotive Manufacturers and Wholesalers.
bill of lading, the document which shows the cost of a vehicle, or the value of its load or freight.
bimetal, a thermostatic element constructed from 2 metals with different rates of thermal expansion such that a change in temperature produces a bending or distortion of the element which is measured or directly acts on some other part.
bimetallic corrosion, galvanic corrosion suffered by 2 different metals in contact,

usually aided by moisture.
BIMTA, British Independent Motor Traders Association.
bin lorry, refuse vehicle.
binding brakes, unwanted rubbing of the brake pad or shoe surface against the disc or drum, typically caused by seizure of a mechanism.
binding clutch, a situation when the clutch drive plate does not clear from the flywheel when the pedal is pressed out, often because of excessive friction on the splines, usually caused by a trace of rust.
binnacle, the instrument panel or housing.
biodiesel, a diesel fuel produced from vegetable matter which is a replaceable and sustainable source, typically made from rapeseed oil and oils from other plants.
biofuel, a fuel produced from vegetable matter, typically based upon an alcohol or oil taken from some plants, *e.g.* rapeseed.
birdcage, CB jargon, an airport.
birdcage chassis, a chassis constructed in a complex pattern of fine gauge tubing, typically in some high performance sports cars.
Birfield joint, Rzeppa cvj.
bit, a small interchangeable tool fitted to a handle for turning screws.
BITER, British Institute of Traffic Education Research.
biting point, to control the clutch pedal pressure such that the clutch pressure plate just causes the clutch drive plate to start to transmit power from the engine to the wheels.
bitumen, a naturally occurring dark hydrocarbon mineral, often used as approximately 10 % of a mixture with sand and gravel to make a road surface.
bitumen, Australia, a tarred road.
bituminised road, a road having a metalled surface of tarmac or similar.
BL, British Leyland.
black and white, USA, a police patrol car.
black and white diagonal flag, a flag to communicate with racing drivers, warning of unsportsmanlike behaviour.
black box, any electronic or microprocessor control unit, *e.g.* the ECU.
black bulb, a bulb glass which has become blackened internally due to deposition of metal vapour, an indication that the filament is near the end of its life.
black cab, a style of taxi having a purpose built body, typically seating 6 passengers.
black chromium, a black electrolytic coating on some metals for aesthetic decoration.
black death, engine seizure, occurring when engine lubricating oil suddenly changes its structure under high temperatures and harsh operating conditions to form a thick black sticky tar-like substance which blocks the oil galleries and starves the bearings of lubrication; typically occurring if engine oil is not changed at the recommended interval.

black flag, a flag to communicate with racing drivers displaying a car number in white, meaning the driver must stop at the pit and report to clerk of the course for a stop-go penalty or disqualification.
black flag with red spot, a flag to communicate with racing drivers, it also shows the car number in white, meaning a mechanical failure, the driver must pit.
black ice, clear ice, glazed ice, a condition where water has frozen without entrapping air bubbles hence the ice is clear and gives an optical illusion to a driver that the road surface is merely wet, it usually creates less tyre noise.
Black Maria, a large police vehicle having high security for transporting prisoners, named after a black woman Maria Lee who frequently helped police escort persons to jail in Boston USA.
black panel, a small black area with a white number on a motorway sign, normally in the bottom left corner enumerating the specific motorway junction being approached.
black sign, a rectangular sign displaying an advisory route for lorries.
black smoke, smoke emitted from the exhaust when the air-fuel ratio is too high, hence the fuel is not fully burned causing soot.
blackspot, a specific location where more than an average number of collisions occur.
blacktop, a road surfaced with asphalt or tarmacadam.
blacktop cowboy, USA, truck driver.
blackwall tyre, a tyre without a whitewall, white lettering, or other colouring in the sidewall.
bladder, a plastic coating applied directly to the inner surface of a fuel tank to prevent further corrosion of the tank.
bladder, a rubberised bag inserted into a fuel tank to contain the fuel to prevent further corrosion of the tank.
blade, each rotating member of a fan or pump.
blade, a windscreen wiper blade.
blade, the tip of a screwdriver or cutting tool.
blade connector, a male electrical connector, a spade connector, often as a fixed part of an electrical device to which the female wire terminal is mated.
blade fuse, an electrical fuse common in modern production vehicles, having 2 flat blade contact areas, each amperage value is colour coded.
blade plates, a pair of back to back registration plates fitted longitudinally on the front mudguard of a motorcycle showing to the left and right; not permitted on modern motorcycles for safety.
blade rubber, the rubber windscreen wiper strip as fitted to the arm of the wiper.
blanking plug, a rubber or plastic plug for sealing manufactured holes in body panels.
blaster, an antihijack security device whereby gas is released from nozzles at each side of a

– BBB –

car over a spark such that a fireball issues from both sides of the car.

bldc, USA, before lower dead centre, bbdc.

bleed, to physically remove air from a fluid system, especially from brake hydraulics or fuel or cooling systems.

bleed, a harmful practice of releasing air from a hot tyre in the mistaken belief that the pressure is higher than required.

bleeper breaker, CB jargon, a CB user having a set which transmits a bleep when the transmit button is released.

blind alley, cul-de-sac, a road leading to a dead end.

blind bend, a bend, especially when sharp, where visual sight lines are very short due to the presence of obstructions, *e.g.* tall walls close to the road edge.

blind corner, a corner especially at a junction where visual sight lines are very short due to the presence of obstructions, *e.g.* tall walls close to the road edge, or to the road layout, *e.g.* a corner much sharper than 90°.

blind crest, a crest where the visual sight lines are very short due to the vertical alignment of the road changing severely.

blind intersection, USA, an intersection where a driver does not have visibility for 100 feet (30 m) in each direction when 100 feet (30 m) before the junction.

blind junction, a junction where visual sight lines are very short due to the presence of obstructions, *e.g.* tall walls close to the road edge, or to the road layout, *e.g.* emerging from a junction on the inside of a bend.

blindspot, an area at each side and behind a vehicle which cannot be seen by a driver whilst facing forward and looking in any mirror, typically the angle measured from ahead between 90° and 135° over the left and right shoulders of the driver.

blindspot, an area into which there is no direct vision due to an obstruction, typically each area obstructed by a window pillar and other bodywork.

blindspot mirror, an additional small mirror affixed on or near a door mirror and angled to give a wide angle of vision to reduce the angular size of a blindspot.

blinker, Australia, direction indicator.

blinker, USA, a traffic control signal which includes a flashing light or phase.

blip, a very short operation of the accelerator to briefly rev the engine.

blister, a bubble in paintwork, sometimes caused by rust penetrating a panel.

blister, a raised area on the surface of a tyre, typically caused by penetration of air into the carcass and separation within the plies; it is potentially dangerous as it is likely to result in a blowout.

BLM, Bureau of Land Management, USA, the organisation which regulates use of public land by vehicles.

BLMC, British Leyland Motor Corporation.

block, cylinder block, a large metal casting with cavities machined into it, the principal component of many engines.

block, an individual section of tread separated from adjacent blocks by grooves to the left and/ or right and by channels or sipes ahead and behind.

block change, the deliberate omission of unnecessary intermediate gearchanging in any vehicle, *e.g.* selecting from 2 to 4 to 6, or from 5 to 3, whenever conditions are favourable, most common when downshifting.

block vehicle, the first vehicle encountered at the rear of a mobile lane closure, having an impact cushion on its rear to reduce the effect of a collision.

blood alcohol concentration, the proportion of alcohol in a persons blood, measured as milligrams of alcohol in millilitres of blood, most countries permit up to 50 mg/100 ml before prosecution.

bloom, an unwanted haze on paintwork typically caused by moisture when the paint was applied.

blow, the rupture of an electrical fuse, caused by a fault.

blowback, backfire through the carburettor caused by excessive gas exchange overlap.

blowby, leakage of compressed air-fuel mixture and combustion gas through the piston rings into the crankcase.

blowdown, a vehicle retarding system using engine braking by decompressing the cylinder directly after compression, preventing the compressed air from driving the piston, used on lorries, developed by Mack.

blower, a supercharger.

blower, a turbocharger.

blower, the heating and ventilation fan.

blowing, the effect of exhaust gas leaking from any point in the exhaust except exiting the tailpipe.

blowing through, the action of driving at speed through an intersection marked by stop signs; see also: jumping, running.

blown engine, an engine fitted with a supercharger or a turbocharger.

blown engine, an engine that has suffered a catastrophic failure of internal parts.

blowout, a rapid rupture of a tyre with a loud bang, rare with modern tyres, sometimes occurring when the tyre has become severely overheated, or when a tube tyre has become excessively worn through the carcass.

blow over, a respray, typically of low quality, usually a single coat of paint with little preparation.

blue badge scheme, a European and USA wide standard scheme allowing parking concessions for disabled drivers or passengers, replacing the orange badge scheme as from 1 April 2000.

blue book, the book of motor sport rules

40

published by the RAC MSA.

blue book, USA, a regularly updated listing of car values based on age and condition.

blue bulb, a headlamp bulb containing a mixture of halogen and xenon gas which may give 30 % greater light output compared with halogen only.

blue circular sign, generally an obligatory traffic sign, a sign giving a positive instruction which is legally enforced.

blue curb, USA, a painted marking denoting a restriction from parking except for disabled drivers only, provided a disabled placard is displayed or the vehicle displays disabled veteran license plates.

blue flag, a flag carried on the front offside of the lead vehicle of a military convoy.

blue flag, a flag to communicate with racing drivers, meaning a faster car is close behind, if waved the driver must give way.

blue headlamp, a blue filter fitted over the offside headlamp of the lead vehicle of a military convoy.

blue hose, UK, the air hose supplying the auxiliary brake system on the coupling to a trailer.

blue hose, USA, the air hose supplying the service brake system on the coupling to a trailer.

blue light, CB jargon, a police vehicle.

blue light vehicle, any emergency vehicle.

blue metal, broken blue stone used for making roads.

blue panel, a small blue area on a larger sign of a different colour showing the route to a specific motorway.

blueprinting, the construction of an engine using parts that are machined to an exact dimension for optimum performance within the standard tolerance of dimensions.

blue road, a motorway in road rally navigation, as marked on OS maps.

blue smoke, smoke emitted from the exhaust when lubricating oil is burned, *e.g.* when the piston rings or cylinder bores are badly worn.

blue square, a sign depicting loading is permitted but not parking.

blues and 2s, the blue lights and 2-tone siren or other siren of an emergency vehicle.

bluing, a blue tinted oxide layer that appears on a chrome exhaust after being subject to high temperatures.

blunt end, the rear of a vehicle.

BMC, British Motor Corporation.

bmep, brake mean effective pressure.

BMIHT, British Motor Industry Heritage Trust.

BMMC, British Motorsport Marshals Club.

bmpr, bumper.

BMW, Bayerische Motorenwerke, German, Bavarian Engine Works, a vehicle manufacturer.

bnt, bonnet.

board, to get into a vehicle.

boat, byway open to all traffic.

boat tail, a fashion on some vintage cars where the rear bodywork resembled the front of a boat.

boat trailer, a trailer designed to transport a boat on a cradle mounting that permits launching of the boat from the rear of the trailer.

bobtail, any hardtop car that has been cut down behind the driver to resemble a truck cab pickup.

bobtailing, driving a tractive unit without a trailer.

bodge, a repair performed without an appropriate degree of accuracy, care, or quality, typically rushed and performed without proper tools or materials.

body, the part of a vehicle that houses the occupants or the load.

bodybuilder, USA, coachbuilder.

body flex, the lack of rigidity in the chassis of any vehicle, excessive flex reduces stability.

body in white, USA, an unpainted bodyshell without any bolt-on components.

body jack, a hydraulic device to push or pull crash damaged areas to their original position or shape.

body lead, an alloy of lead and tin used to fill joint seams between body panels to achieve a smooth finish.

body repair, any repair to vehicle bodywork caused by crash damage or corrosion.

body roll, the lean of a vehicle due to centrifugal force when cornering.

body styling kit, a package of cosmetic body parts, *e.g.* air dam or spoiler, that can be bolted on to change the aesthetic appearance.

bodyshell, a 1 piece framework of welded panels including floor and roof, to which all other panels, doors etc. are fastened.

bodyshop, a workshop specialising in the repair of vehicle bodywork.

body tub, USA, the bodyshell without any bolt-on parts.

bodywork, the external panels of a vehicle in contact with the external air stream, which display its function or having aesthetic qualities.

bogged, bogged down.

bogged down, the condition when 1 or more wheels of a vehicle have sunk into a soft surface, *e.g.* mud, sand, snow, etc. such that there is greater drag than traction and the vehicle is not capable of propelling itself.

bogie, an assembly of 2 or more axles with a common suspension.

Bohlin, Nils Bohlin, inventor of the 3 point seatbelt in 1955.

boil, a condition of the engine coolant if certain fault conditions arise.

boiling over, a condition when the engine cooling system malfunctions, typically caused by a fault in the cooling system, insufficient coolant, loss of coolant pressurisation, high ambient temperature, or the wrong coolant with a low boiling point.

BOL, Bolivia, international vehicle distinguishing sign, see appendices.

bollard, a wide post at the roadside, especially on a traffic island, often made from plastic, sometimes illuminated, usually displaying a sign.

bolster, each vertical steel post, as used to restrain logs on a logging trailer.

bolt, a mechanical device to connect 2 parts, usually made from metal with a male helical thread at 1 end.

bond, to permanently join parts using an adhesive.

bonnet, the body panel covering an engine on a front engined car.

bonnet, the body panel covering a front luggage area on a rear engined or mid engined car.

bonnet badge, an emblem positioned centrally on the leading edge of the bonnet identifying the manufacturer, sometimes also the model.

bonnet hump, a raised part of the bonnet, to allow clearance for an enlarged or modified engine or auxiliaries.

bonnet liner, sound absorbing foam or fibre material affixed to the underside of the bonnet to absorb and reduce engine noise.

bonnet pin, a positive locking quick release pin, for retaining engine covers etc.

bonnet spring, a positive locking quick release device, for retaining engine covers etc.

bonnet stay, a metal rod which holds the bonnet in its open position.

Bonneville Salt Flats, the Great Salt Lake Desert in Utah on the border with Nevada USA, the site of many land speed world records.

boom, Australia, a barrier that drops in a vertical arc to stop traffic, e.g. at a railway level crossing.

boom barrier, a barrier that is lowered across a road in a vertical arc to stop traffic, typically at railway level crossings.

boost, to boost charge a battery, to impose a relatively high terminal voltage to force a high current to flow into the battery to charge the battery rapidly; the battery must be disconnected to prevent the high voltage destroying the vehicle electrics and electronics.

boost gauge, an instrument showing the air or air-fuel pressure in the inlet manifold.

boost pressure, the pressure in the intake manifold while the turbocharger or supercharger is operating.

booster battery, a high capacity battery briefly connected in parallel with a weak battery to give extra power to start an engine.

booster cable, a pair of jump leads.

booster cushion, a firm cushion on which children sit whilst travelling in a car such that they may safely wear an adult seatbelt.

boot, Denver boot, a wheel clamp.

boot, gaiter.

boot, the area for holding luggage in a car, normally accessed externally via the bootlid at the rear, but in some rear-engined cars the boot may be at the front.

boot, USA, the covering over a folded soft top on a cabriolet, either flexible or a solid panel over a well.

bootlegger turn, the technique of inducing a controlled 180° spin at speed as an emergency escape manoeuvre, i.e. a 1 point U turn on a narrow road, performed by: braking hard from high speed to encourage a rear wheel skid, when at 50 km/h (30 mph) the steering is turned rapidly to initiate a U turn whilst continuing to brake hard, as the vehicle turns countersteer and accelerate; it is ideally suited to a rwd car that will naturally oversteer, some cars may need application of the parking brake thereby converting the manoeuvre into a handbrake turn, CAUTION, if attempted in a pickup, suv, 4x4, or similar the car may roll, i.e. only possible in a car having a low centre of gravity.

bootlid, an opening panel providing access to the boot.

BORC, British Off Road Championship.

BORDA, British Off Road Driving Association, the representative body for off-road driver training organisations.

bore, an engine cylinder, or any cylindrical hole.

bore, the diameter of an engine cylinder, or of any cylindrical hole.

bore, the measured diameter of any hole, especially that of an engine cylinder.

bore, the process of accurately machining a hole, especially for an engine cylinder.

bore out, to increase the cylinder diameter by accurately boring it to a larger size, thereby increasing the engine size and requiring larger size pistons etc.

bore x stroke, the critical engine dimensions, the means of determining engine size from the actual dimensions when the area of the bore x the stroke is multiplied by the number of cylinders, also a means of assessing some characteristics from the ratio of the dimensions.

boss, an enlarged area or knob at the end of a shaft, especially the centre of the steering wheel.

BOSS, British Oil Security Syndicate, an organisation which exists to reduce the incidence of pump and run by measures such as NPR systems.

botch, a repair performed without an appropriate degree of accuracy, care, or quality, typically rushed and performed without proper tools or materials.

bottle jack, a hydraulic jack, the body often resembling the shape of a bottle.

bottleneck, a traffic situation where the carrying capacity of a road is significantly reduced at some point, it may at times cause a tailback.

bottle shop, CB jargon, a pub.

bottom dead centre, the crankshaft position at 180° when a piston is exactly at the bottom of its stroke, between the induction stroke and compression stroke, or between the power stroke and exhaust stroke.

bottom dump, a trailer which unloads through doors in its underside.

bottom end, the crankshaft and all main and crankpin bearings.

bottom end torque, torque produced whilst an engine is running at low revs.

bottom gear, the lowest gear on a gear selector system which gives maximum torque but minimum speed, sometimes below the numbered gears, 1st gear on cars, low 1st on many 4x4 vehicles, low crawler or LL1 on many lorries.

bottom hose, the hose carrying cooled coolant from the radiator to the engine.

bottoming, the momentary condition of the chassis as it hits the suspension bump stop at the chassis's lowest limit of travel, *i.e.* the wheel and suspension has reached the top limit of its travel with respect to the chassis.

bottom of the shop, CB jargon, channel 1.

boulevard, a multilane avenue, an aesthetically pleasing tree-lined high capacity road, typically an urban dual carriageway having trees along the sides and median.

bounce, a basic test of a damper, performed by rapidly pressing down on each corner of a vehicle in turn and noting any continued oscillation.

bounce, a means of manhandling a disabled vehicle sideways by several persons by bouncing the body on its suspension and manually pushing sideways when the body is at its highest point and tyre friction is minimal.

bounce, an effect sometimes created at the inlet and exhaust valves when the engine runs at high revs and the valves rebound from their seat.

bounce, an occurrence when driving on a tyre that is statically imbalanced, *i.e.* having a heavy or light area centrally across the tread causing the suspension to oscillate at speed, usually most noticeable above 60 km/h (40 mph).

bounce, the action of persons applying additional weight synchronised to suspension travel in order to extract a bogged or cross-axled vehicle.

bounce, the relative motion between the wheels and the chassis when a vehicle is travelling at speed on a rough surface including potholed tarmac, such that for part of the time the tyres may exert very little frictional contact with the surface.

bounce around, CB jargon, the return leg of a trip.

bouncing, the reaction sometimes of the suspension of a vehicle when climbing a steep

hard surface using a lot of power in a low gear, especially with leaf spring suspension, caused by axle wind-up.

bow, the front of a vehicle.

bow wave, a significant wave generated by the front of a vehicle when wading through deep water too quickly.

Bowden cable, a spring steel wire closely encased in a helical casing, typically used for the accelerator cable, clutch cable, handbrake cable, and others.

bowser, a fuel tanker for refuelling military or road construction vehicles.

bowser, a water tanker for road construction purposes, especially for dust suppression or grading operations.

Bowser, Sylvanus F Bowser, inventor of fuel measuring and dispensing pumps in 1885, and an improved version of pump for motor spirit in 1905.

box, exhaust silencer.

box, gearbox.

box, the load carrying area of a pickup.

box junction, an area of road surface painted with criss-cross yellow lines on which drivers must not stop, except when waiting to turn into a junction to the offside, *i.e.* drivers must not enter the box junction unless their exit is clear.

box section, square or rectangular tubing or a similar fabrication made from folded steel sheet, typically as part of a chassis where high strength and rigidity is required.

box spanner, a device to turn nuts or bolts etc, made from hexagonal tubing to allow access into a deep recess.

box trailer, a small lightweight trailer for general use, typically having low sides with an open top.

box trailer, a trailer having a body in the form of an enclosed box, usually with rear doors.

box van, a van having the goods body in the form of a simple box, usually with rear doors.

box wrench, box spanner.

boxed in, to be prevented from leaving a parking space by other vehicles badly or wrongly positioned.

boxed in, to be temporarily prevented from overtaking on a motorway by a long stream of traffic in the overtaking lane, typically caused by poor anticipation.

boxed in, to have no escape route available to avoid an impending collision from any direction.

boxed in, to have no escape route available when suffering road rage or being attacked.

boxer, an engine layout with pistons on opposing sides of the crankshaft, also referred to as a flat 4, flat 6, or flat 8.

boy racer, any person who considers themselves a fast driver, but without recognising that they lack some skills.

BPA, British Parking Association.

BR, Brazil, international vehicle distinguishing sign, see appendices.

bra, nose bra.

brace, a reinforcing part between 2 parts.

bracket, a protruding support for a part, typically made from metal strip.

braid, a woven wire covering over a hose, usually tightly woven stainless steel wire, covering brake hoses, fuel lines, etc. for high performance systems.

braid, a feature of an entrance sliproad and an exit sliproad in crossing each other at a slight angle with grade separation, where junctions are closely spaced.

braid junction, a symmetrical grade separated junction on 4 levels between roads at 90° to each other and which allows all vehicles to move freely from any road to any other excepting a return to the route of origin, all link roads turn through 90° and are fed from sliproads on the nearside only, *e.g.* the junction of the M4 with the M5 near Bristol; the name is derived from the resulting plan shape, sometimes named a petal junction; see appendices.

brake, a device that applies friction to a surface to slow it, stop it, or hold it stationary; a device that that slows or stops the rotation of the wheels, so tyre friction slows or stops the vehicle.

brake adjuster, a mechanism in drum brakes with which the distance between brake shoes and drum surface can be varied to allow for wear.

brake assist system, a system where a microprocessor measures the speed of the drivers foot lifting off the accelerator and depressing the brake pedal and calculates the level of emergency and increases the brake pressure as necessary, developed by Mercedes.

brake balance, a function of a braking system in not exhibiting brake pull.

brake balance control system, a braking system where the driver can adjust the percentage of front/rear brake pressure dependant upon the road surface, controlled by a linked pair of master cylinders connected to a single servo unit; not for road use.

brake bleeding kit, a tool comprising a set of parts to enable efficient removal of air from the hydraulic braking system, or to assist in replacing the brake fluid.

brake booster, a device and control system that will rapidly increase brake pressure according to the demands of BAS.

brake cable, a steel wire cable system typically used for the handbrake in most modern cars, and for parking brakes on light trailers.

brake caliper, an assembly fitted astride a wheel brake disc and holding the brake pistons, brake pads, etc.

brake cylinder, wheel cylinder.

brake disc, a circular steel disc that is attached to a wheel and against which the brake pads generate friction when brake pressure is applied.

brake dive, the action of inertia in compressing the front suspension when the brakes are applied due to apparent weight transfer.

brake drum, a cylinder attached to a wheel and against which the brake shoes generate friction when brake pressure is applied.

braked trailer, a trailer fitted with a braking system.

brake fade, the effect of prolonged use of the brake causing the brakes to become very hot causing a chemical change to the brake linings resulting in loss of braking performance, especially with drum brakes.

brake failure, complete or partial failure of a braking system, or failure of 1 of 2 or more circuits within a system such that the brakes fail to operate on some or all wheels.

brake fluid, a liquid having good hydraulic properties and which should have a minimum boiling point of 180 °C, usually polyglycol, but silicone is also used in high performance vehicles; see: dot 3 to dot 5.1.

brake fluid recirculation, a system that constantly recirculates the brake fluid through the caliper to eliminate heat buildup in the piston to prevent the fluid boiling in the caliper, for high performance vehicles.

brake hard, to apply maximum or near maximum brake pressure.

brake horsepower, power developed by an engine as measured by the force applied to a friction brake or dynamometer, 1 bhp equals raising 550 foot-pounds per second, also equal to 745.7 watts, see also PS.

brake hose, flexible high pressure tubing used to transmit hydraulic brake pressure to the wheels as the suspension oscillates.

brake induced skid, a skid caused by the driver operating the footbrake, such that there is greater friction exerted in the brakes than the friction present between the tyres and the road surface.

brake lag distance, the distance travelled by a vehicle fitted with air brakes after operation of the brake pedal and before the brakes start to operate, typically about 12 metres at 80 km/h (40 feet at 50 mph) due to the time taken for the air to flow through the lines; a factor in the total stopping distance.

brake lag time, the interval of time which passes before air brakes start to operate after operation of the brake pedal, typically about $1/2$ second due to the time taken for the air to flow through the lines.

brake lamp, a red lamp used to indicate to other road users to the rear of the vehicle that its driver is applying the service brake, *i.e.* footbrake, it may sometimes be activated by the application of a retarder, (C&U).

brake line, brake pipe.

brake lining, the thin sheet of friction material bonded or riveted to a brake shoe or brake pad.

brake lining sensor, a sensor in some brake pads that will send a signal to light a panel indicator to warn that the brake pads have reached the end of their life.

brake mean effective pressure, the pressure due to combustion acting on the top of the engine piston which would result in a given power output if there were no losses due to friction or driving engine accessories.

brake modulation, the technique by which a driver achieves threshold braking as the surface changes along the stopping distance such that the driver varies the pressure on the footbrake pedal for maximum braking performance.

brake pad, a device made from high friction material, designed to grip in pairs on each side of the brake disk when brake pressure is applied.

brake pad wear indicator, brake lining sensor.

brake pedal, the primary control operated by the drivers foot in order to operate the service brake system.

brake pipe, small diameter steel or cupronickel tubing that carries hydraulic pressure from the master cylinder to the brake hose and wheels.

brake pressure sensor, an instrument that measures the brake pressure and sends a signal to the VSC or other microprocessors for comparison with rate of deceleration.

brake proportioning valve, an automatic load sensing proportioning and bypass valve which varies the pressure to the rear axle or trailer to match the load carried by the vehicle.

brake puck, USA, brake pad.

brake pull, a fault within the braking system such that the braking effect is unevenly balanced on each side of the vehicle causing the vehicle to veer left or right when the brakes are applied.

brake reaction time, the interval between the instant a driver recognises the need to brake, and the instant that the driver actually starts to apply the brake.

brake rotor, USA, brake disc.

brake servo, a device to increase brake pressure, powered by the vacuum generated in the intake manifold or by a vacuum pump, to add safety and reduce driver fatigue.

brake sfc, brake specific fuel consumption.

brake shoe, a fabrication having a thin layer of high friction material, designed to move outwards to grip the inside of the brake drum when brake pressure is applied.

brake specific fuel consumption, the measure of the fuel efficiency of an engine at full load at a range of engine speeds, measured on a dynamometer in kilograms of fuel per hour per unit of power, usually in kg/PS.hour.

brake steer overlap, to brake whilst steering, commonly because braking has not ended before steering into a bend commences, a bad technique that can lead to skidding.

brake steering, a means of turning a tracklaying vehicle by braking either track

individually to slow or stop that track, whilst the other track continues to drive; see also: differential steering.

brake swept area, the total friction area of the discs and drums at all wheels which is swept by brake lining material, including both sides of a disc.

brake swept area per tonne, a relative quotient to assess braking performance, the higher the figure the better the braking performance.

brake test, see: moving, static.

brake test, an operational test of the brakes of a vehicle to ascertain balance and efficiency.

brake test, a test of the frictional characteristics of a road surface, achieved by applying the brakes progressively and noting the retardation available, especially on a road surface that is suspected of having a poor surface, e.g. ice.

brake test, an event induced to a tailgating driver by a tailgated driver, when the leading driver brakes suddenly and hard causing the tailgating driver to immediately brake very hard to avoid a collision.

brake torquing, the technique used for achieving maximum acceleration in a vehicle having a torque converter: firmly left foot brake, select D, then raise the rev's to the torque converter stall speed, then release the footbrake; the technique also overcomes turbo lag if a turbocharger is fitted.

braking, see: ABS, active, all out, cadence, comfort, degressive, dragging, dynamic, emergency stop, engine, feathering, grenading, harsh, independent, integrated, left foot, long, minimum, overrun, power, progressive, pulse, regenerative, relevant, rhythmic, secondary, squeeze, stab, threshold, trail.

braking, the action of operating the service brake to control the speed of a vehicle.

braking distance, the distance taken for a moving vehicle to stop on a clean dry level road providing the vehicle is mechanically sound, not including perception distance, reaction distance, or brake lag distance, i.e. measured from the moment the brake is applied; the actual distance increases with the square of the speed of the vehicle, and is further increased when any factor e.g. road surface or vehicle suspension is not in the ideal condition.

braking efficiency, the maximum braking force capable of being developed by the brakes of a vehicle, expressed as a percentage of the weight of the vehicle including any persons or load carried on the vehicle, (C&U).

braking for 2, long braking, early gentle braking when being tailgated with an eye on the mirror to ensure the driver behind does not cause a shunt.

braking performance, the rate at which a vehicle or a tyre will brake to stop compared with a measured standard distance or time.

45

braking point, the latest point some distance before a bend where braking should start, on roads and race circuits.
braking ratio, the proportion of braking force performed by each axle.
braking system, all of the equipment on a vehicle associated with the operation of any brake.
braking systems, see: auxiliary, emergency, footbrake, handbrake, parking, retarder, secondary, service.
branch connection, USA, link road, a connection between 2 freeways.
branch road, a lateral subdivision of a road perpendicular to the main road.
Brantz, a trip computer which records distances to 10 metres, used when route planning and setting some types of rally.
brass, an alloy of copper and zinc which resists corrosion and is a good electrical conductor, used in some high current circuits, for hydraulic brake connections, and sometimes for decorative parts.
braze, to repair a vehicle part by soldering with brass or hard solder.
BRC, British Rally Championship.
BRDC, British Racing Drivers Club.
break, CB jargon, to call a station.
breakaway, the point when a lateral force exceeds tyre friction such that a steering induced skid or speed induced skid commences.
breakaway angle, the angular difference between a planned course and the actual course taken during a skid, the sideslip angle.
breakaway switch, a safety device that automatically operates the brakes of a trailer if the hitch uncouples.
break break, CB jargon, a changeover in conversation directed then at another user.
breakdown, a condition when a vehicle suffers any mechanical or electrical failure that prevents onward travel.
breakdown service, a service to effect roadside repairs to a vehicle or to take it to be repaired.
breakdown truck, a vehicle equipped to tow, winch, or transport disabled vehicles, or fitted as a mobile workshop to effect roadside repairs.
breaker, CB jargon, a CB user.
breaker break, CB jargon, a user wanting to get onto a channel.
breaker cam, the distributor shaft cam, having the same number of lobes as the engine has cylinders.
breakerless ignition, any of many varieties of electronic or transistorised ignition systems based upon a pulse generator which feeds the ignition coil.
breaker points, the contact points which provide pulses of current to the ignition circuit, obsolete, not on modern vehicles.
breakers yard, scrapyard, a place where

crashed or end of life vehicles are dismantled to recover any useable parts.
break in, USA, run in.
breaking, the action of dismantling a crashed or end of life vehicle to salvage and sell useable parts.
breaking in, running in.
breakity break, CB jargon, a user wanting to get onto a channel.
break time, the duration of time that the contact breaker points are open.
breathalyse, to use a device to measure the proportion of alcohol in a persons exhaled breath.
breathalyser, a device with which to measure the level of alcohol in breath, formerly by blowing through a tube with reagent crystals, now read electronically.
breather, a venting tube, *e.g.* from the crankcase to the air inlet.
breathing capacity, the volume of air that enters the cylinder during each induction phase, typically having a volumetric efficiency of less than 80 %.
breath screening test, a test conducted using an electronic alcohol measuring device or a tube containing crystals which is blown into by the subject as an initial method of measuring breath alcohol level, to determine the need for an evidential breath test.
breath test, breathalyser test, see also: breath screening, evidential, passive.
BRF, British Roads Federation.
brg, bearing.
brg, British Racing Green, a dark green colour.
brick carrier, a lorry specially designed for the carriage of bricks or concrete blocks, usually having a self-loading crane, sometimes having rws.
brick road, a road surfaced with bricks made from baked clay, *i.e.* similar to cobbles.
Brickyard, the first purpose built racing circuit in USA at Indianapolis in 1911, a 4.023 km (2.5 mile) oval banked track surfaced with 3.5 million bricks.
bridge, a structure to carry a road over a physical feature, or to carry others over a road.
bridge, see: arch, Bailey, bascule beam, cable stayed, cantilever, chain, humpback, lifting, packhorse, pontoon, suspension, swing, transporter, vertical lifting, viaduct.
bridge bashing, the act of inadvertently colliding with a low bridge, with the top of a lorry, van, or bus etc.
bridle path, bridleway.
bridle road, bridleway.
bridleway, a way normally intended for use on horseback, pedal cycle, or on foot only, motor vehicles may be permitted on a definitive bridleway.
brim the tank, to fill the fuel tank fully to the top of the filler neck, typically done at the start and end of a period when fuel consumption is to be measured.

bring it back, CB jargon, end of transmission and awaiting a reply.
BriSCA, British Stock Car Association.
Brit disc, a vignette purchased by operators of foreign commercial vehicles in order to use roads in Britain.
British Association, a series of small screw thread sizes formerly used for electrical connections and small precision equipment, superseded by metric.
British racing green, a dark green colour, part of an obsolete colour code used to identify the nationality of racing cars at international events.
British standard fine, a screw thread based upon imperial dimensions where the spanner size is related to the thread diameter, obsolete since metrication.
British standard Whitworth, a screw thread based upon imperial dimensions where the spanner size is related to the thread diameter and the width across the flats of the nut is double the thread diameter, obsolete since metrication.
British touring car championship, a race series where cars are limited to 2,000 cc engine size and must use a standard production bodyshell, run over 26 rounds at 13 venues.
British truck racing championship, a race series for tractive units over 13 rounds in 2 classes of truck.
BRMA, British Rubber Manufacturers Association.
BRN, Bahrain, international vehicle distinguishing sign, see appendices.
broken back, an optical illusion which may occur where horizontal and vertical curves change but their starts of each do not coincide with each other, *e.g.* a bend starting on the middle of a crest, a type of location where the accident rate is known to be higher.
broken yellow line, a central road marking used alongside a white marking in some countries denoting an approach to a solid yellow line which prohibits crossing of the line
bronze, an alloy of copper and tin, sometimes including zinc, nickel, or lead.
Brooklands, an oval banked racing circuit in Surrey, built in 1907.
broom wagon, the course closing car, sweeper car.
brougham, a large chauffeur-driven veteran car, typically in the style of an early taxi where the driver is exposed to the weather and the passengers ride in a closed saloon.
brown bottles, CB jargon, beer.
brown bottle shop, CB jargon, a pub.
brown road, a B class road in road rally navigation, as marked on an OS map.
brown sign, a rectangular direction or information sign for the benefit of tourists.
BRS, British Road Services.
BRSCC, British Racing and Sports Car Club.
BRU, Brunei, international vehicle

distinguishing sign, see appendices.
brush, a block of conducting substance, usually carbon based, that maintains electrical contact with a rotating surface, used in alternators and starter motors etc.
brush guard, USA, tubular steel or similar framework, which may reduce the damage to the front bodywork and lights of a vehicle caused by bushes and low branches etc. during cross country driving.
brush spring, a light spring that holds the electrical brush in contact with the slip ring or commutator at a constant pressure.
BS, Bahamas, international vehicle distinguishing sign, see appendices.
BS, Brooklands Society, UK.
b/sd, bodyside.
BSF, British standard fine.
BSFC, brake specific fuel consumption.
BSI, British Standards Institution.
BSM, British School of Motoring.
BSW, British standard Whitworth.
BTCC, British Touring Car Championship.
btdc, before top dead centre.
BTPA, British Tractor Pullers Association.
BTRA, British Truck Racing Association.
BTRC, British Truck Racing Championship.
BTS, British Trolleybus Society.
bubble car, usually a type of 3 wheeler car having only 2 seats, with a rounded canopy or rounded body, mostly post war classics.
buck, a full size clay model of a new body design, now superseded by CAD.
bucket headlamp, a headlamp mounted external to bodywork and having a spheroidal housing, typically above the front wing, typically on vintage and early classic cars.
bucket seat, a seat which extends the base and the backrest around the driver to give total support especially when cornering, used in most motor sports.
bucket tyres, tyres having tread in the form of tall lateral scoop shaped ridges for high speed performance in mud, sand, and on water.
buckled, a disc or wheel where some points on its circumference do not rotate through the same point, they have an axial component as they rotate.
buckle up, USA, to secure the seatbelt around the person.
budc, USA, before upper dead centre, btdc.
Budd mounting, a common securing device for twin wheels comprising an inner sleeve nut and an outer cap nut.
buff, to polish a surface, either by hand or with a power tool.
buff, to remove part of the tread of a tyre before racing on road tyres, for greater stability.
buffer lane, a lane on a high level bridge that is kept empty of traffic during strong crosswinds to allow for vehicles that are blown off course from the adjacent lane.
buffet, an uncomfortable pulsing wind sometimes experienced when driving quickly

with the windows open or with the hood down.

buffet, the effect of turbulence generated by a large vehicle affecting another that is overtaking, especially when there is a strong crosswind.

Bugatti axle, a front suspension system in which the leaf springs pass through the tubular axle.

bug shield, an aerodynamic strip on a bonnet designed to deflect air and insects over the windscreen to reduce the effect of squashed insects hindering visibility.

buggy, a small open top car, typically a beach buggy, hybrid, or kit car; originally a 4 wheeled horse-drawn cart for carrying people.

BUI, US Virgin Islands, international vehicle distinguishing sign, see appendices.

build quality, a qualitative measure of the workmanship and materials in the construction of a vehicle.

buildout, a physical obstruction extending into 1 side of a carriageway, created as part of a traffic calming scheme to narrow the road, sometimes forming a crossing point for pedestrians.

built-up area, an area where there is direct access to residential and/or commercial property at the roadside, usually having street lighting and normally having a lower speed limit.

bulb, a glass enclosure carrying a wire filament that emits light when an electrical current flows through it.

bulb failure warning, a system that checks specific lamps on a vehicle and gives an alarm to the driver if a bulb is not able to function.

bulb kit, a set of bulbs containing one of each type for a specific vehicle, carriage is a legal requirement in some vehicles in many countries.

bulge, the result of air seeping between the layers of a tyre carcass and causing a blister.

bulk carrier, a lorry for the transport of bulk loads, usually with a tipping mechanism.

bulk haulage, any material that will assume the shape of its container and which is loaded into a lorry without being boxed, bagged, hand loaded, or palletised, *e.g.* sand, coal, grain, turnips.

bulker, bulk carrier, typically a tipping lorry body for the transport of bulk loads.

bulkhead, a panel separating different compartments of a vehicle, *e.g.* the engine from the saloon.

bull bar, tubular steel or similar framework fitted across the front of a vehicle which may reduce the damage to the front bodywork and lights of a vehicle during a collision.

bulldozer, a tracklaying vehicle fitted with a steel plate at the front for pushing excavated materials.

bull low, USA, a very low gear in some older 4 speed lorries, typically used only for hill starts.

bummer, a low 2 wheeled dolly for carrying or dragging logs.

bump, a sudden horizontal jolt, as a result of a minor collision.

bump, a sudden vertical jolt, caused by a significant defect on the road surface.

bumper, strong bodywork across the front and rear of a vehicle to protect the body panels from minor collision damage.

bumper bar, a tubular or rectangular bar across the front or rear of a vehicle to protect against minor collision damage.

bumper blade, a bumper bar constructed of flat or C shaped steel strip.

bumper iron, a bumper mounting bracket.

bumper to bumper, a visually endless queue of stationary traffic.

bumping out, the first action of panel beating in returning a crash damaged panel to its original shape.

bump start, to start the engine of a vehicle which has a flat battery by pushing the vehicle, or allowing it to roll downhill, or in some cases to tow with another vehicle, until it is moving above 10 km/h (6 mph), then whilst using 2nd gear the clutch is rapidly let in so inertia from the wheels turns the engine to start it, not possible with automatic transmissions.

bump steer, the effect on the steering mechanism of any vehicle caused when the suspension for a front wheel is deflected up or down, resulting in a slight deviation from its steered course.

bump stop, a rubber buffer to prevent mechanical shock when a suspension reaches the top of its travel.

bump stroke, jounce, the upward travel of a wheel and suspension; see also: rebound.

bumpy, a road having an uneven surface due to many bumps or potholes.

bunch, a collective noun for a number of vehicles in a close group; also clot, cluster, platoon.

bunkering, to refuel a lorry or coach.

bunny hopping, to perform clutchless split gearchanges with a splitter, a skilled technique using the accelerator to match the engine revs to the roadspeed, and rapid movement of the gearlever from gear to neutral to the same primary gear.

BUR, Myanmar, international vehicle distinguishing sign, see appendices.

burn, chemical erosion, *e.g.* to exhaust valves and seats.

burn, electrical erosion, *e.g.* to sparkplug electrodes.

burn, to consume fuel.

burned out, the condition of an electrical device that is no longer serviceable, normally due to an electrical fault.

burned out, the condition of a clutch when there is insufficient friction material remaining on the clutch drive plate such that it is no longer serviceable and the vehicle cannot be driven.

burning rubber, the action of deliberately causing wheelspin.
burning rubber, the action of driving quickly.
burning the clutch, slipping the clutch for an excessive distance, causing excessive heat and wear to the clutch drive plate such that its life is severely shortened.
burnish, to polish by rubbing, especially of metal parts.
burnout, the action of spinning the driving wheels, having locked the non-driving wheels to prevent the vehicle moving, to heat the tyres to increase friction, performed by drag racers.
burnup, to accelerate quickly with the wheels spinning, often producing smoke from the tyres.
burr walnut, a wood veneer that is aesthetically pleasing, used for the surface of dashboards and other internal trim in luxury cars.
burst, USA, a punctured tyre.
bury the needle, to drive at speed such that the speedometer reads beyond the highest marked figure, and on some models the needle may then disappear behind the instrument facing.
bus, omnibus, a motor vehicle which is constructed or adapted to carry more than 8 seated passengers in addition to the driver, (C&U).
bus, see also: accordion, articulated, bendi, coach, crew, duo, fully built, guided, gyro, historic, kneeling, lowbridge, macro, mega, micro, midi, mini, omni, overland, service, tour, trailer, trolley, vestibule, walking.
bus advance area, an area on approach to a junction where buses have priority over all other traffic in all lanes, controlled by a pre-signal.
bus lane, an area of road that is reserved for buses, or sometimes buses and other specified vehicles.
bus lay-by, a bus stop positioned off the side of the carriageway to allow the free flow of other traffic when a bus stops.
bus link, a road for the use of buses only.
bus station, a place having a restricted roadway and organised interchange facilities between buses and passengers, typically in a town centre.
bus stop, a place at the side of a road where buses halt to allow passengers to alight or board.
bus stop clearway, a clearway which permits buses to stop during the hours of operation of the clearway.

bush, a sleeve placed in a bore to act as a bearing surface, made from metal, nylon, rubber, ptfe, etc.
BUSK, Belt Up School Kids, a transport safety pressure group, UK.
busman, the driver of a bus.
bustleback, USA, notchback.
busway, a specific route for buses which is physically segregated from other traffic, sometimes using a bus guidance system.
butane, a liquefied petroleum gas sometimes used as a vehicle fuel but not in cold climates as it vaporises at –2 °C.
butterfly doors, doors that are hinged at the front edge behind the front wheel, but when opening move upwards and outwards, *i.e.* a cross between a conventional door and a scissor door.
butterfly fastener, a positive locking quick release device, for retaining engine covers etc.
butterfly nut, a nut with 2 small lugs designed to be tightened and released by finger pressure.
butterfly valve, a pivoted disc to regulate air flow through the carburettor.
buttonhook ramp, USA, a J shaped sliproad which connects the main highway to a frontage or access road.
BVRLA, British Vehicle Rental and Leasing Association.
bw, USA, a blackwall tire.
BY, Belarus, international vehicle distinguishing sign, see appendices.
bypass, a road which enables through traffic to avoid an urban area through which it would otherwise have to pass.
bypass, a separate passage which permits a liquid, gas, or electric current to take a different path from normal.
bypass filter, an oil filtering system where only about 5 % to 10 % of the oil is filtered at each pass and returns to the sump, the oil flow to the bearings is unfiltered; see also: full flow.
bypass valve, a valve that opens to allow a fluid to take a different route, in the oil system a valve that opens to allow oil to flow past the filter when it is clogged.
byroad, a minor road.
byway, a minor highway, minor road, or a track which has been defined as a byway but may or may not be used by motor vehicles.
byway open to all traffic, a minor unsurfaced or unsealed highway which has been defined as a byway having vehicular rights; physical progress may only be possible in a 4x4.

C

c, cold, the engine temperature required before some engine adjustments may be made.

C, carbon.

C, Celsius, or Centigrade, a measurement of temperature.

C, comfort, a basic car model specification.

C, comfort mode, referring to ABC active suspension, it allows the driver to select comfort to allow some body roll.

C, commercial, an API oil classification for an oil suitable for diesel engines.

C, coupé, a car body style.

C, a hire car size and price category for cars based upon their floor pan; a small family car to seat 5 with some comfort, e.g. Audi A4, or Ford Mondeo sized.

C, Europe, an LGV driving licence category for rigid lorries over 3.5 tonnes, and permitting drawing of a trailer up to 750 kg MAM.

C, USA, a driving license and vehicle category: any motor vehicle with a GVWR exceeding 16,000 lbs (7.25 tonnes) but not exceeding 26,000 lbs (11.8 tonnes) or any such vehicle towing another not exceeding 10,000 lbs (4.5 tonnes); any vehicle designed to transport 16 or more persons, or used in the transportation of hazardous materials; not including motorcycles.

C, crawler, a very low gear on many lorries and some buses.

C, USA, the tire temperature code denoting the lowest satisfactory standard, moulded into the tire sidewall.

C, USA, the tire traction code denoting low braking performance on a wet surface, moulded into the tire sidewall.

C, a write-off category in which the cost of repair to the damaged car exceeds 60 % of the trade value of the car, but if repaired and checked by an alignment specialist a pass will be entered on the VCAR register.

C, Cuba, international vehicle distinguishing sign, see appendices.

C1, a European MGV driving licence category for lorries 3.5 tonnes to 7.5 tonnes, and permitting drawing of a trailer up to 750 kg MAM.

C1+E, a European MGV driving licence category for lorries 3.5 tonnes to 7.5 tonnes with a trailer over 750 kg, total weight not to exceed 8.25 tonnes (12 tonnes if a driving licence was issued after 1 January 1997).

C1+E MTV, the European minimum specification of a driving test vehicle that may be used for driving licence category C1+E; a vehicle of minimum 4 tonnes MAM and capable of a speed of 80 km/h (50 mph), with a trailer of minimum 2 tonnes MAM, and not less than 8 m overall length.

C1 MTV, the European minimum specification of a driving test vehicle that may be used for driving licence category C1; a vehicle of minimum 4 tonnes MAM and capable of a speed of 80 km/h (50 mph).

C band, a VED category within which vehicles emitting between 166 and 185 g/km of CO_2 are charged.

C cab, the visual shape of the doorless or windowless access aperture in the cab side of some veteran goods vehicles.

C+E, a European LGV driving licence category for articulated lorries over 3.5 tonnes MAM with a trailer over 750 kg.

C+E MTV, the European minimum specification of a driving test vehicle that may be used for driving licence category C+E; either: an artic of minimum 18 tonnes, minimum 12 m overall length, or: a drawbar outfit being a category C vehicle with a trailer 4 m minimum platform length and trailer minimum 4 tonnes MAM, with a combined weight of 18 tonnes minimum and a combined length 12 m minimum, either vehicle being capable of a speed of 80 km/h (50 mph).

C MTV, the European minimum specification of a driving test vehicle that may be used for driving licence category C; a vehicle of minimum 10 tonnes MAM and capable of a speed of 80 km/h (50 mph), minimum 7 m long, excluding tractive units.

C pillar, the 3rd side pillar, at the rear of the rear seats on most cars, supporting the roof, sometimes a wide panel.

C road, a minor road, usually unclassified or where its route number is not published on maps.

C segment car, a size category for cars based upon their floor pan; a small family car to seat 5 with some comfort.

C&U, Construction and Use Regulations, UK and many other countries.

CA, Consumers Association, UK.

CA, Countryside Act 1968, in which byways replaced RUPPs but with downgrading on grounds of suitability, UK.

CA, the length of a load carrying area forwards from the centreline of the rear axle to the rear of the cab.

CAAI, Chinese Association of Automobile Industry.

CAAM, China Association of Automobile Manufacturers.

cab, taxi, named from taxicab, from hackney cab, from hackney cabriolet.

cab, the housing for the driver and controls in a van, bus, lorry, etc.

cabbie, taxi driver.

cabbing, the action of spending a night sleeping in the sleeper cab of a lorry.

cab driver, taxi driver.

cabin, the passenger compartment of a car.

cabin drill, cockpit checks, part of the drivers pre-driving checks, to check: the doors, handbrake, seat, backrest, mirrors, seatbelt, tell-tale lights, and footbrake.

cable, a linear metallic device for conducting electricity, usually consisting of many strands for flexibility, and covered with insulating material.

cable, a linear metallic device usually consisting of many strands for flexibility, for applying physical tension, *e.g.* for operating the hand brake.

cable brake, mechanically operated brakes using a system of cables and levers; common on many vintage and pre-war classic cars to facilitate four wheel braking; now only for handbrakes and light trailers.

cable clamp, a device for connecting a cable to its terminal, especially for each battery cable to the battery terminal.

cable operated, any device functioning through tension in a cable, *e.g.* a cable operated clutch or gearshift.

cable shift, a vehicle in which the mechanical linkage between the gear lever and gearbox is performed by cables.

cable stayed bridge, a bridge with one or several towers each supporting many cables that support the road surface.

cabman, the driver of a hackney carriage.

cabotage, the point to point transportation of property or passengers.

cabover, a design where the cab of a lorry is over the engine, current European style to reduce the length of a lorry; abbreviated coe; see also: conventional.

cabover camper, USA, a demountable mobile home designed to be transported on the bed of a dual wheel pickup truck, having additional volume which overhangs the cab.

cabrio, cabriolet.

cabriolet, a luxury open top car having a removable roof, or a roof which can be folded away.

cab suspension, an independent secondary suspension system by which a lorry cab is suspended above the chassis of the lorry for additional driver comfort.

cab tilt, the operating switches or levers which enable the cab of a lorry to be tilted forwards for engine access.

cab to cab, a 2-way radio link on a specific frequency.

cac, charge air cooling.

CACIS, continuous ac ignition system.

CAD, computer aided design.

CADD, Campaign Against Drinking and Driving, a pressure group, UK.

cadence braking, an emergency braking technique performed by rapidly manually pulsing the footbrake fully on and off, in order to steer whilst braking on a slippery surface; the technique must NOT be used on any vehicle fitted with ABS, the technique has been superseded by the facility of ABS.

cadmium, a metallic element, used as a coating on steel to prevent rusting.

CAFE, USA, corporate average fuel economy.

caffeine, a stimulant, usually found significantly in coffee and in some soft drinks, it helps to reduce tiredness if taken during frequent breaks in a long journey, 120 mg taken before a short sleep may temporarily remove drowsiness.

CAG, computer aided gearshift.

calcium, a metallic element, used as a base for some grease, especially between slow moving parts.

calcium chloride, a solution in water pumped into tractor tyres as ballast to increase traction in specific conditions; desirable due to its high rd and low freezing point.

calibrate, to determine an exact value, to reset the initial setting of a device or measuring equipment to its designed setting.

calliper, part of the braking system that holds and operates the brake pads.

Cal-look, California looking, an infinite range of minor bodywork modifications to change the aesthetic appearance of a car, typically removing chrome trim and painting in a very bright or striking colour.

cam, a rotating lobe used to change rotary motion into reciprocating motion.

CAM, Cameroon, international vehicle distinguishing sign, see appendices.

cam and lever, a type of steering box in which a conical peg on a lever engages in a helical groove on a shaft.

cam and peg, a type of steering box in which a conical peg on a lever engages in a helically cut groove in a wide cylindrical shaft.

cam and roller, a type of steering box in which a tapered disc or a set of discs or rollers engage in a helically cut tapered groove on a cylindrical shaft.

cam angle, dwell angle.

cam belt, camshaft timing belt.

camber, see: camber angle.

camber, the lateral slope or curve of a normal road surface, where the crown of the road is higher than the edges on both sides for water drainage, normally having a crossfall of 2.5 % from the crown or central reservation to the road edge.

camber angle, the slight tilt of the wheels on independent suspension where the tops of the wheels are not the same distance apart as the track width; see: negative, neutral, positive.

cambered axle, a front axle which is curved upwards in the centre, on some veteran vehicles .

camber thrust, a cornering force generated by the camber of the wheel.

camel, a dealer term for a car with an odd and undesirable specification.

camelback, uncured retread rubber shaped to fit over a tyre carcass for retreading a tyre.

Camel trophy, a severe cross country expedition run in a different country each year from 1980 to 1998 using 4x4 vehicles.

camera car, a police car fitted with a video camera and video recording equipment.

cam follower, a device that rolls or slides on the cam lobe surface to create reciprocating motion.

cam handbrake, a vertical handbrake lever without a release button and having a cam in its operating mechanism, it is pushed forwards for release and pulled back to secure, typically used by some disabled drivers.

cam heel, the low area on the cam, the base circle.

cam lobe, the high point on the cam, the part which operates the valve.

camloc fastener, a positive locking quick release device, for retaining engine covers etc.

camper, USA, a demountable structure designed to be transported by pickup, and which provides facilities for living accommodation.

campervan, a motor vehicle adapted, modified, or specially designed and constructed to provide living accommodation.

camping trailer, a trailer having an integral tent such that when erected the trailer forms a specific platform within the tent.

cam profile, the physical shape of the cam including the heel and the height and width of the lobe, such that it determines the timing, rate, duration, and height of valve lift.

camp trailer, USA, a vehicle not exceeding 16 feet (4.88 m) long which provides facilities for living accommodation or recreational purposes.

camshaft, a shaft having a series of cams at intervals along its length, for operating the engine valve mechanisms.

camshaft drive gear, a gear on the crankshaft to drive the camshaft gear.

camshaft gear, a gear on the camshaft enabling it to be driven at half the speed of the crankshaft.

camshaft position sensor, a magnetic sensor that provides the ECU with a signal to identify the exact position of each piston.

camshaft timing, the physical rotational relationship between the camshaft and crankshaft to determine the exact timing for valve operation with respect to piston position.

camshaft timing belt, a toothed belt driven by a sprocket wheel on the crankshaft that drives another sprocket wheel on the camshaft for accurate timing of the cams in opening the valves.

CAN, computer area network, a databus in-vehicle communication system.

candela, the basic unit of luminous intensity by which the brightness of vehicle lights may be measured.

candidate, a person taking a driving test.

candles, CB jargon, years.

candy paint, custom paintwork using a translucent colour over a base coat of a slightly different colour.

canopy, a rounded roof and window unit, typically on bubble cars.

cantilever bridge, a bridge where the road surface is supported on steel or concrete cantilevers.

cantilever spring, a quarter elliptic spring mounted to the chassis by its stiffest point, to reduce the unsprung weight, generally not a modern system.

canvas top, soft top, hood, a fabric roof, especially if made from duck or other natural fabric.

cap, a cover, usually round, *e.g.* hub cap, petrol cap, radiator cap.

capability, a quality of the performance of a driver including his/her vision, reaction times, and degree of skill.

capability, a quality of the performance of a vehicle including acceleration performance, braking performance, and steering performance.

capacitor, an electrical device containing 2 conductors insulated from each other to hold an electrical charge, to provide capacitance in a circuit, to block the flow of dc, to prevent arcing, and to amplify the primary ignition pulse.

capacitor discharge ignition, an ignition system that stores primary energy in a capacitor and releases it to the ignition coil when the contact points open.

capacity, the ability to hold, the volume of a container of fluids, *i.e.* the volume taken by liquid in a fuel tank or in a cooling system when it is full.

capacity, the measure of engine size as the sum of the fluid displaced by every piston moving from bdc to tdc, measured in litres.

capacity, the volume of a fluid handled by a device in a unit of time.

capacity, the maximum number of vehicles that can pass along a road in a unit of time, typically limited by junctions and other features.

capacity mass ratio, a vehicle acceleration performance figure comparing engine size with vehicle weight, typically measured in litres/tonne.

Cape to Cape, a long distance route from the North Cape of Norway to Cape Town in South Africa, total length 17,000 km (10,600 miles).

Capital Beltway, the I495, the major freeway encircling Washington DC, having a circumference of 64.13 miles (103.2 km).

cap nut, dome nut, a nut having a cover over its outer end, typically chromium plated.

captains chair, driver or passenger seats that resemble armchairs with armrests, usually they also swivel to face the rear.

cap tarp, a top tarpaulin fitted over other tarpaulins, especially where there is a lengthwise join in the lower layer.

car, motorcar.

car, a motor vehicle constructed or adapted for the carriage of passengers and their effects but which is not a goods vehicle; having no more than 9 seats including the driver, has 4 or more wheels, and has a maximum laden weight not exceeding 3.5 tonnes, (MV(DL) regulations); first constructed by Jean-Joseph Etienne Lenoir, Belgium, in 1862, and driven 18 km from Paris to Joinville-le-Pont in 1863.

CAR, consider all roads, when searching for a clue to a route in road rally navigation.

car ambulance, a short trailer having a crane or a spectacle lift, towed behind a vehicle as a device for towing a broken down vehicle by lifting and supporting 2 of its wheels.

caravan, a convoy of vehicles, a line of vehicles travelling together from origin to destination.

caravan, a trailer fitted with living accommodation, constructed as a mobile home.

caravan, USA, a covered truck or lorry.

caravanette, a motor vehicle the size of a minibus constructed or adapted with living accommodation for use as a small mobile home, originally named a caravette.

caravanning, the act of travelling with or living in a caravan, especially for a holiday.

caravan park, a high quality caravan site having quality amenities and/or landscaped surroundings.

caravan registration and identification scheme, an electronic tagging system where a microchip holding the VIN is concealed within the vehicle.

caravanserai, a service area or truckstop in southeast Europe – Middle East – southern Asia.

caravan site, a place where caravans may be parked for use as living accommodation, typically having appropriate amenities.

caravette, a vehicle the size of a minibus constructed or adapted with living accommodation for use as a small mobile home.

carb, carburettor.

car banging, the creation of a fake collision in order to defraud insurance companies by using fake repair bills.

car benefit tax, a tax that drivers of company cars pay for the benefit of private usage, calculated for petrol fuelled cars at 15 % of the list price of the car, plus a surcharge which increases with CO_2 emissions up to a maximum of 35 % of the list price.

carbide lamp, a type of lamp commonly fitted to vehicles until approximately 1905, burning acetylene gas generated by dripping water onto calcium carbide.

car bomb, a terrorist bomb concealed within or under a parked vehicle.

carbon, a non-metallic element with many uses; alloyed with iron to produce a range of steels with different qualities, added as a powder to resist UV degradation, used as a fibre for lightweight body panels, used in some greases, sometimes as a black deposit left on internal engine parts by combustion when it is sometimes named coke.

carbon black, a fine powder added to tyre rubber to resist degradation by sunlight.

carbon brush, a rod made from compressed carbon, used as an electrical connection to the rotating circuit in an alternator or starter motor etc.

carbon canister, a container in the evaporative control system to trap fuel vapour while the engine is not running, to prevent fuel vapour from reaching the atmosphere.

carbon core leads, ht sparkplug leads in which the conductor is in the form of a fibre impregnated with powdered carbon or graphite, inevitably having a high resistance and relatively short life of approximately 50,000 km (30,000 miles); see also: copper.

carbon deposit, the residue from burnt gasses inside the combustion chamber, if the accumulation becomes excessive it will reduce engine efficiency, also named coke.

carbon dioxide, CO_2, an asphyxiating gas created by combustion of fuel, having a density of about 1.5 times that of air.

carbon fibre, fibres made from carbon, each thinner than hair but 5 times stronger than steel, usually made into lightweight panels and structures by bonding in polyester or epoxy resins.

carbon leads, carbon core leads.

carbon monoxide, CO, a very poisonous gas, created during combustion of fuel and resulting from incomplete combustion due to insufficient oxygen.

carbon tax, a tax on a vehicle based upon the CO_2 exhaust emissions of a vehicle, measured in g/km.

car boot sale, a market at which participants sell unwanted possessions from the boots of their cars.

car broker, a person or organisation selling new cars with a significant discount below the standard price.

carburation, the process of vaporising fuel and mixing it with air in the carburettor.

carburetor, USA, carburettor.

carburetted, having a carburettor.

carburettor, a device that vaporises fuel and mixes it with air in an exact ratio and at a controlled rate before the mixture is supplied to the intake manifold.

carburettor engine, a petrol engine fitted with a carburettor.

carburettor icing, ice formation internally and externally within and around the choke body due to the temperature drop created by evaporation of petrol, common at temperatures between −5 °C and +12 °C especially if the throttle is at or near idle and when humidity is above 60 %; it will seriously alter the shape of the venturi and restrict air flow hence reduce efficiency of the carburettor thereby reducing engine power, and may cause an engine to cease running.

carburettor throat, the barrel, venturi, the main air passage through the carburettor at the point where its diameter is reduced.

car burglar, a person who steals from cars.

car care, the preservation of the bodywork and upholstery of a vehicle.

car care product, an article or substance used for cleaning or polishing the bodywork, or cleaning the upholstery of a vehicle.

carcass, casing, the body of a tyre, especially the plies of fabric or metal wire within a tyre that give strength and shape to the tyre.

car cloning, to change the VIN and registration numbers on a stolen vehicle to match those on a fraudulently obtained duplicate registration document belonging to another vehicle of the same make, model, and colour, so the vehicle can be sold with apparently genuine documents, sometimes done after importing a non-type approved vehicle; see also: clone plates.

car coat, a short heavy coat, typically worn in cold climates before cars were commonly fitted with an efficient heater.

car combination, a passenger car with a trailer.

car cover, a shaped fabric cover to protect a car from dust or weather.

car creeper, a low framework having small wheels to support a person whilst lying on their back and enable them to position and work under a vehicle.

car crime, crime related to vehicles, especially theft of, or from, a vehicle.

cardan joint, a simple universal joint having 2 yokes connected by a spider, typically at each end of a vehicle propeller shaft.

car derived van, a goods vehicle derivative of a passenger vehicle, *i.e.* a van built upon the floorpan of a car, and which has a maximum laden weight not exceeding 2,000 kg.

Cardington, the training centre for driving test examiners, named after the village of its location in Bedfordshire, UK.

Cardington test, an advanced driving test, a qualifying test for driving examiners also available to ADI's, UK.

car dipping, theft of personal items from a car whilst the driver is in slow moving or stationary traffic.

card parking, a zone where parking is permitted provided a parking card is correctly displayed.

CARE, Consortium for Automotive Recycling, UK.

careen, to turn a vehicle onto its side for repair of the underside, using a special device clamped to the wheel hubs.

careen, USA, to follow an erratic course, to swerve about.

career, to follow an erratic course, a condition when there is little or no accurate control over speed or steering.

careless driving, an act committed by the driver of a mechanically propelled vehicle on a road or other public place when driving without due care and attention for other persons using the road, (RTA), UK.

car ferry, a ferry capable of carrying cars and usually larger vehicles.

car following theory, a mathematical model of the interactions between vehicles in terms of relative speed, absolute speed, separation, and vehicle length.

cargo, USA, goods carried in a motor vehicle.

car hop, USA, a waiter at a drive in restaurant.

car jacker, a thief who targets stationary or moving vehicles whilst occupied by the driver, to steel the contents or the vehicle.

car jacking, to steal a vehicle by ejecting the driver, or to force the driver to follow directions.

car key, a mechanical or electronic instrument that locks and unlocks doors, boot, ignition, fuel filler, etc.

carload, a quantity of goods that can be carried in a car.

car mat, removable rubber carpets for the floor of a car.

carnet de passage, the paperwork for goods transported internationally, and as a temporary import/export for vehicles.

carom, a collision in which a vehicle sideswipes another and bounces off.

car parc, the total number of cars and light vehicles in use in a country; see also: vehicle.

carpark, a place where cars and similar vehicles are permitted to park, sometimes for a fee, sometimes restrictions on type of user may apply.

carpark rash, small dents and scratches in the side of a car caused by careless opening of the doors of adjacent cars, common where parking spaces are narrow.

car phone, a cellular telephone where part or all of the circuitry is permanently installed in the vehicle.

car polish, polish formulated to give good performance on the bodywork of a car.

carpool lane, a multi-occupancy lane, for use only by vehicles carrying 2 or more persons, typically marked by yellow lines.

carport, a vehicle shelter having a roof and open sides.

car pound, a secure enclosure to which illegally parked cars are officially removed and retained until redeemed.

car radio, a radio receiver where the circuitry is permanently installed in a vehicle.

carriage, a horsedrawn passenger carrying vehicle, usually enclosed.

carriage, the conveying of goods or persons.

carriageway, a road or part of a road having a surface intended for frequent use by vehicular traffic.

carrier, a person engaged in the transportation of passengers or property by land, sea, or air.

carryall, USA, a vehicle having the rear seats arranged longitudinally along both sides allowing some goods to be carried on the floor between the facing seats.

carrying capacity, the quantity of persons or load which can be carried by a vehicle.

car salesman, a person who earns his income by selling cars, typically most earnings are from commission on sales.

car sickness, nausea resulting from acceleratory movement, especially by jerky movements initiated by the driver.

car size, see: group, segment.

CARSP, Canadian Association of Road Safety Professionals.

car sponge, a large synthetic sponge typically used for cleaning car bodywork.

car supermarket, a car dealer selling large numbers of nearly new cars, typically ex-rental and ex-company cars.

car supermart, a car supermarket.

cart, a 2 or 4 wheeled wooden vehicle drawn by 1 or several horses, smaller versions may be pushed by hand.

CART, Championship Auto Racing Teams, USA.

car tax, tax added to the purchase price of a new car.

car tax, VED.

car theft index, a listing of cars and their risk of being stolen, compiled by the Home Office, UK; see also: NCSR.

car thief, a person who steals cars.

car transporter, a lorry or trailer specially designed to carry cars.

cart spring, a leaf spring, semielliptic spring, becoming obsolete on modern vehicles.

cart track, a route having an unmetalled surface, typically passable only by 4x4 vehicles.

cartwheel, the action of a crashing vehicle when turning end over end.

car tyre, see: tyre.

car ute, USA, a utility vehicle or mpv based upon the floorpan of a car; see also: truck ute

carvac, a battery operated miniature vacuum cleaner for vehicles.

car wash, a place where the bodywork of a vehicle is cleaned, typically by machine.

car wash, a substance added to water to form a cleaning agent with which to wash car bodywork, typically containing detergent and wax.

car wax, a wax polish formulated to give good performance on the bodywork of a car.

CAS, Centre for Auto Safety, USA.

casing, a cover that extends all around a piece of equipment, e.g. the rear axle casing.

casing, USA, carcass.

cast, the production of a metal part by pouring molten metal into a mould, e.g. to cast an alloy wheel.

castellated nut, a nut with machined recesses in its non-bearing face, and which is locked in position by a split pin.

cast iron, a metallic alloy of iron with 1.8 % to 4.5 % carbon, used for engine blocks and piston rings.

castor action, castor torque.

castor angle, the longitudinal angle between the line extending the steering pivot axis and a vertical line through the centre of the wheel, it is normally positive to maintain directional control, improper caster angle can cause the steering to pull to 1 side; see: negative, neutral, positive.

castor length, the longitudinal distance along the road surface between the line extending the steering pivot axis and the vertical line through the centre of the wheel; the end of the steering pivot line is always designed to be ahead of the wheel centre on road vehicles.

castor torque, the force that causes the front wheels to self straighten after cornering.

castor wobble, a type of wheel shimmy typically noticed on a beam axle system on rough roads.

casualty, any person killed or injured in a road traffic accident.

cat, catalytic converter.

cat, computer aided technology.

catalyst, a substance that influences a chemical reaction without itself becoming consumed by the reaction, typically platinum, palladium, and rhodium are used as catalysts in an exhaust system.

catalyst, accelerator, a chemical substance added to a resin and some paints to speed the setting process.

catalyst coating, the thin layer of catalysing metals within the body of a cat.

catalytic contamination, irreversible damage to the catalysing metals resulting in degradation of performance caused by a reaction with chemicals which should not be passing through the system, e.g. leaded petrol.

catalytic converter, a vessel in the exhaust system containing catalysts: platinum, palladium, and rhodium; platinum and palladium convert harmful exhaust gasses by further oxidation of carbon monoxide and unburned hydrocarbons into water and carbon dioxide, and rhodium reduces the nitrogen oxides into nitrogen and oxygen.

cat and mouse engine, scissor engine, a type of rotary engine typified by the Tschudi engine which is an analogue of the reciprocating piston engine except the pistons travel in a circular motion.

cataphoretic coating, a coating for a car body or chassis applied with an electrical charge to encourage adhesion.

category A, a European driving licence category for light motorcycles having an engine size exceeding 125 cc or a power output exceeding 11 Kw (14.6 bhp).

category A1, a European driving licence category for light motorcycles having an engine size not exceeding 125 cc and a power output not exceeding 11 Kw (14.6 bhp).

category B, a European driving licence category for motor vehicles with a MAM not exceeding 3,500 kg and having not more than 8 passenger seats, and permitting drawing of a trailer up to 750 kg, or combinations of towing vehicles in category B with a trailer where the MAM of the combination does not exceed 3,500 kg and the MAM of the trailer does not exceed the kerbweight of the towing vehicle.

category B1, a European driving licence category for motor tricycles and quadricycles having a design speed exceeding 50 km/h, and an unladen weight not exceeding 550 kg.

category B automatic, a European driving licence category for cars in category B but where the vehicle is fitted with automatic transmission.

category B+E, a European driving licence category for a vehicle in category B when drawing a trailer, but where the combination thus formed is not in category B.

category C, a European LGV driving licence category for rigid lorries over 3.5 tonnes, and permitting drawing of a trailer up to 750 kg MAM.

category C1, a European MGV driving licence category for lorries 3.5 tonnes to 7.5 tonnes, and permitting drawing of a trailer up to 750 kg MAM.

category C1+E, a European MGV driving licence category for lorries 3.5 tonnes to 7.5 tonnes with a trailer over 750 kg, total weight not to exceed 8.25 tonnes (12 tonnes if a driving licence was issued after 1 January 1997).

category C1+E MTV, the European minimum specification of a driving test vehicle that may be used for driving licence category C1+E; a vehicle of minimum 4 tonnes MAM and capable of speed of 80 km/h (50 mph), with a trailer of minimum 2 tonnes MAM, and 8 m overall length.

category C1 MTV, the European minimum specification of a driving test vehicle that may be used for driving licence category C1; a vehicle of minimum 4 tonnes MAM and capable of a speed of 80 km/h (50 mph).

category C+E, a European LGV driving licence category for articulated lorries over 3.5 tonnes with a trailer over 750 kg.

category C+E MTV, the European minimum specification of a driving test vehicle that may be used for driving licence category C+E; either: an artic of minimum 18 tonnes, minimum 12 m overall length, or: a drawbar outfit being a category C vehicle with a trailer 4 m minimum platform length and trailer minimum 4 tonnes MAM, with a combined weight of 18 tonnes minimum and a combined length 12 m minimum, either vehicle being capable of a speed of 80 km/h (50 mph).

category C MTV, the European minimum specification of a driving test vehicle that may be used for driving licence category C; a vehicle of minimum 10 tonnes MAM and capable of a speed of 80 km/h (50 mph), minimum 7 m long, excluding tractive units.

category D, a European driving licence category for any bus having more than 8 passenger seats, and permitting drawing of a trailer up to 750 kg MAM.

category D1, a European driving licence category for minibuses having between 9 and 16 passenger seats, and permitting drawing of a trailer up to 750 kg MAM.

category D1+E, a European driving licence category for minibuses drawing a trailer where the minibus is in subcategory D1 and its trailer has a MAM exceeding 750 kg, provided that the MAM of the combination thus formed does not exceed 12,000 kg and the MAM of the trailer does not exceed the kerbweight of the minibus.

category D+E, a European driving licence category for any bus having more than 8 passenger seats, and permitting drawing of a trailer exceeding 750 kg MAM.

category F, a driving licence category for agricultural tractors.

category G, a driving licence category for road rollers.

category H, a driving licence category for tracklaying vehicles.

category K, a driving licence category for pedestrian controlled vehicles, *i.e.* where the driver is not seated but walks with the vehicle to operate it, *e.g.* some mowing machines and road rollers.

category P, a driving licence category for mopeds.

caterpillar track, an endless wide band of steel links passing longitudinally beneath all the wheels on each side of a tracklaying vehicle for travel on rough or soft ground.

cathode, a negative electrode.

catnap, a short sleep of approximately

15 minutes, strongly recommended for any driver feeling sleepy.

CATS, computer active technology suspension.

cat's eye, a colour coded reflective road stud bonded onto or partly recessed into the road surface; the reflectors may be: red, green, white, amber, or yellow, to give information to a driver at night.

cattle float, a lorry designed to transport cattle, sheep, and other animals.

cattle grid, a transverse series of spaced metal bars across the road acting as the carriageway surface over a void, to permit the passage of vehicles but prevent animals from straying.

cattle guard, USA, cattle grid.

cattle stop, New Zealand, cattle grid.

catwalk, a walkway along the top of a lorry body, *e.g.* above a tanker, for access to check levels, or to cover the load.

catwalk, the platform behind a tractive cab for access to suzies etc.

causeway, a raised road, track, or path across low or wet ground or across water, and which in some cases may sometimes become submerged during high tide.

causing danger to other road users, an act committed by a person who, intentionally and without lawful authority or reasonable cause, causes anything to be on or over a road, or, interferes with a motor vehicle, trailer, or cycle, or, interferes directly or indirectly with traffic equipment, (RTA), UK.

causing death by dangerous driving, an act committed by a driver who causes the death of another person by driving a mechanically propelled vehicle dangerously on a road or other public place, (RTA), UK.

caution, a rallying pace note drawing attention to a severe hazard, *e.g.* a significant yump.

cavalcade, a procession of vehicles, sometimes slowly, sometimes the vehicles are specially prepared for a specific display.

caveat emptor, Latin, let the buyer beware, a sellers disclaimer that a vehicle is sold with undescribed faults and that the purchaser is responsible if dissatisfied.

cb, contact breaker.

CB, citizens band, a radio communications system consisting of 80 channels on which all users can talk to each other.

CBC, cornering brake control.

cbe, cab behind engine.

CBI, Confederation of British Industry.

CBT, compulsory basic training.

cc, cold cranking, a battery rating in terms of current output when the battery is very cold.

cc, cubic capacity.

cc, cubic centimetres, the total volume of the displacement of the engine pistons in all cylinders measured in cubic centimetres.

CC, Chrysler Corporation.

CC, climate control.

CC, cruise control.

ccc, course closing car.

CCC, Camping and Caravanning Club, UK.

CCC, Classic Car Club, UK.

CCCA, Classic Car Club of America.

ccd, combustion chamber deposits.

CCFA, Comité des Constructeurs Français d'Automobiles, it represents the 2 major French car manufacturers PSA Peugeot Citroën and Renault.

cc-ing, the method of measuring the volume of the compression chamber when the piston is at tdc with the valves closed using a burette of light liquid, for the purpose of establishing the compression ratio of a modified engine.

CCMC, Committee of Common Market Automobile Constructors, superseded by ACEA.

CCMTA, Canadian Council of Motor Transport Administrators.

CCR, California Code of Regulations, typically the most strict in the world.

CCTA, Consumer Credit and Trade Association, UK.

ccv, closed crankcase ventilation.

ccv, cross country vehicle.

cd, candela.

cd, coded.

Cd, coefficient of drag.

CD, compact disc, used to store music, video, or mapping software.

cdi, capacitor discharge ignition.

cdl, centre differential lock.

CDL, USA, commercial drivers license.

CDN, Canada, international vehicle distinguishing sign, see appendices.

CDP, USA, commercial driving permit.

CDV, car derived van.

CDV, closed delivery vehicle.

CDW, collision damage waver.

CE, the total length of the load carrying area on a lorry bed.

C+E, a European LGV driving licence category for articulated lorries over 3.5 tonnes with a trailer over 750 kg.

CEES, California Exhaust Emission Standards, typically the most strict in the world.

cell, each compartment in a battery containing positive and negative plates suspended in electrolyte, a fully charged cell has a voltage of 2.1 volts, 6 cells form a 12 volt battery, 12 cells form a 24 volt battery.

cellulose, a material used for making sponges and cloths for cleaning a vehicle bodywork, and a base for some paints.

C+E MTV, the European minimum specification of a driving test vehicle that may be used for driving licence category C+E; either: an artic of minimum 18 tonnes, minimum 12 m overall length, or: a drawbar outfit being a category C vehicle with a trailer 4 m minimum platform length and trailer minimum 4 tonnes MAM, with a combined weight of 18 tonnes minimum and a combined length 12 m minimum, either vehicle being capable of a speed of 80 km/h (50 mph).

centimetre, a unit of length equal to 10 mm.

centistokes, a measure of the kinematic viscosity of oils; named after Sir G G Stokes.

central accelerator, a pedal layout on some vehicles before standardisation in the 1950s; where the accelerator was in the centre with the footbrake on the right.

central chassis lubrication, a system whereby many vehicle parts can be grease lubricated via a series of pipes from 1 point.

central gearchange, a common arrangement where the gearlever is positioned in the centre of the vehicle floor.

central locking, a system in which the operation of a key in one door will electrically lock or unlock all doors simultaneously, in some cases it may lock all doors but only unlock one door; the system may also be operated remotely by a plipper.

central locking hub, a Rudge hub, wheel, and nut, designed to facilitate a rapid wheel change.

central refuge, an island between lanes where pedestrians may wait when crossing a road.

central reservation, a median strip, a strip of land, usually planted, between road carriageways on which traffic moves in opposite directions.

centre, a point in a central position, the middle point or line or plane.

centre axle trailer, a simple trailer with 1 or several axles close coupled and located near to its centre and without any inbuilt steering mechanism.

centre cab, a lorry having a single seat cab positioned on the centreline of the vehicle.

centre console, the dashboard area between the front seats.

centre differential, a differential in a 4wd transmission on the output from the gearbox where the drive is divided between front and rear axles, to allow each axle to turn at differing speeds when steering a curved course.

centre differential lock, a system for locking the centre differential, thereby causing the drive to be delivered equally to front and rear axles, to increase traction on a poor surface.

centre drive, an engine crankshaft design where the power is driven from a point at the centre of the crankshaft, between the crankpins, to reduce rotational twisting of a long crankshaft.

centre electrode, the electrode running axially inside the centre of a sparkplug.

Centre for Auto Safety, USA, a watchdog for safety standards.

centre gear, sun gear.

centreline, an imaginary line or vertical plane passing longitudinally through the centre of a vehicle.

centreline, a broken white line consisting of a short stripe and a long gap, used to mark the centre of a road where there are no significant permanent hazards.

centre of gravity, the fixed point within a vehicle through which the resultant force of gravitational attraction acts.

centre of inertia, the fixed point within a vehicle that moves as though the total mass of the vehicle existed at that point, and all external forces are applied at that point.

centre of mass, see: centre of inertia.

centre of weight, a point within a vehicle at which its weight appears to be centred at any instant, and which appears to move around the vehicle due to the effects of inertia acting upon the suspension, during apparent weight transfer.

centre opening doors, a style of door on the side of some cars, a conventional door ahead combined with a suicide door behind, closing without a B pillar.

centre pillar, B pillar.

centre point steering, a wheel geometry layout having significant offset such that the steering axis is aligned with the wheel axis and the crown of the tyre.

centre routier, French, a truckstop and general services.

centre terminal, a spring loaded carbon brush in the centre of the distributor cap that feeds the high voltage to the rotor arm.

centre tunnel, the transmission tunnel, or a dummy transmission tunnel in a fwd car designed only to add strength to the floor and bodyshell.

Centrex, the RTITB Driver Training Centre in Shropshire, UK.

centrifugal advance, a rotating weight mechanism in some distributors using centrifugal force to vary the ignition timing as engine speed varies, obsolete on modern engines.

centrifugal clutch, a clutch in which pressure is exerted on the drive plate only above a specific speed of rotation, so the clutch automatically engages and disengages with respect to engine speed.

centrifugal force, the imaginary force implied by the inertia of a vehicle being reluctant to follow a curved path; see: centripetal.

centrifugal governor, a device which controls speed by means of a centrifugal force, *e.g.* in some automatic transmissions.

centrifugal oil filter, a filter which removes particles from oil by centrifugal force created by spinning the oil at speed in a rotating element.

centrifugal pump, a pump having a rotating impeller that operates by spinning rapidly, *e.g.* a water pump.

centrifugal weight, a weight in a controlling device which is displaced by centrifugal force and causes the operation of other linkages.

centripetal force, the force towards the centre of an arc created by the tyres and other parts when a vehicle follows a curved path.

ceramic, a non-metallic material made at high temperature, used for insulators, filters, and the honeycomb within the catalytic converter.

ceramic brake discs, brake discs made from ceramic material to reduce brake fade during repeated hard use.

ceramic coated exhaust, an exhaust system where all the internal surfaces except the cat are coated with ceramic material to smooth and insulate the gas flow, to increase power and reduce engine bay and cabin temperatures.

certificate of conformity, a document certifying that a vehicle has been modified or adapted and that the vehicle complies with the relevant safety regulations.

certificate of conformity, a document given with a new car proving it is built to EC safety and environmental standards, required when registering a car at a VRO.

certificate of initial fitness, a document issued by the VI certifying that a new or newly built or imported vehicle is fit for service, due to it not otherwise requiring a MOT certificate.

certificate of professional competence, a qualification that must be held by operators of buses and lorries, or by at least 1 member of the staff in each such organisation.

certificate of temporary exemption, a certificate permitting the temporary use of an unlicenced vehicle, *e.g.* when travelling to a port for export.

cetane, an alkane hydrocarbon, a substance that ignites very easily, used in standardizing ratings of diesel fuel.

cetane index, a quality of a diesel fuel based upon density and boiling point, the number is typically in the range 45 to 52.

cetane number, an index number indicating the ignition quality of a diesel fuel, the higher the number the greater the tendency of a fuel to support self ignition; it is measured by comparing the diesel fuel to a percentage by volume of cetane in a blend with methyl naphthalene, the number is typically in the range of 48 to 55.

Cf, coefficient of friction.

CFC, chlorofluorocarbon.

CFC free air conditioning, a vehicle air conditioning system that uses R134a refrigerant instead of freon or other CFC based chemicals.

ch, coupler height.

ch, French, cheval, from cheval vapour, metric horsepower, see: PS.

CH, cab height above the chassis height.

CH, Switzerland, international vehicle distinguishing sign, see appendices.

chain, an obsolete measure of distance, equal to 66 feet (20.1168 metres).

chain, a series of metal links, often arranged such that they may drive and be driven by a sprocket wheel, in some engines for driving the camshaft.

chainage, a distance measured in any units but typically metres from a fixed reference point, often measured along a long tape measure, *e.g.* in measuring a site after a collision.

chain bridge, a suspension bridge in which the primary support between the towers is a series of chain links.

chain drive, a form of power transmission using a chain passing between sprocket wheels.

chain hoist, a lifting device for raising and lowering heavy objects, *e.g.* removing or replacing an engine.

chain tensioner, a jockey wheel and/or spring system fitted to stabilise a chain and maintain the correct tension.

chain wrench, a tool having a chain which is locked to the length required for gripping and turning large round or irregular shaped objects, especially for unscrewing an oil filter.

chalk gun, a device used to fire a pellet of chalk onto the surface of a test track at the commencement of braking, when testing the braking performance of a vehicle or tyres.

chalking, disintegration of a painted bodywork due to weathering and lack of maintenance.

chalk test, a trial and error method of finding the correct tyre pressure for each tyre when the figure is not known, usually due to a change of tyre size: to draw a transverse chalk line across the tread of each tyre then drive a short distance on a straight dry road then check the wear on the chalk which is a magnification of wear to the rubber, the pressure is adjusted and the test repeated until the chalk wears evenly across its width.

chamber, a wide part in a system through which any fluid passes or is held.

chamber, the combustion chamber of any engine, especially when it is not cylindrical, *e.g.* in a Wankel engine.

chameleon, a car finished in several shades of a similar colour due to poor colour matching when partially resprayed after accident damage.

chamois leather, a large thin sheet of soft leather, used for drying bodywork and glass after washing a vehicle.

champion, the driver who has surpassed all rivals in a series of races, rallies, or other competitions.

championship, a contest for the position of champion over other competitors.

changeable message sign, a portable variable message sign.

change down, to select a lower gear.

change gear, to select a different gear.

change the oil, to replace the oil, typically the engine oil, with fresh new oil of the correct grade.

change up, to select a higher gear.

channel, each of the transverse or diagonal slots in a tyre tread to allow water dispersal to the sides of the tyre.

channelled, the condition of a vehicle body where it has been lowered on the chassis rails.

channellisation, the separation or regulation of conflicting traffic movements into definite paths of travel by use of painted road markings or physical structures, to facilitate the safe and orderly movement of vehicles and pedestrians.

channel master, CB jargon, a breaker monopolising or controlling a channel.

channel section, a metal section having a U profile, common for many chassis members.

Chapman strut, a suspension unit of similar construction to a MacPherson strut but without the facility for steering, sometimes used at the rear of cars.

charabanc, a veteran motor coach, typically without side glazing and having a fabric folding or solid roof.

character line, a longitudinal ridge along the side of a car bodywork for aesthetic appearance and for noise reduction by reducing panel vibration.

charcoal canister, a container in the evaporative control system to trap fuel vapour while the engine is not running, to prevent fuel vapour from reaching the atmosphere.

charge, the quantity of air-fuel mixture supplied to a cylinder for combustion.

charge, the specific quantity of power available from a battery.

charge, to charge a battery, to convert electrical energy into chemical energy in a battery by forcing a current through the battery.

charge air, the quantity of induction air supplied to a cylinder of a diesel engine.

charge air cooling, a system of cooling supercharged or turbocharged air before induction to increase power by use of an intercooler.

charge changing, the process by which the exhaust gasses are removed and a fresh charge of air-fuel mixture enters through the transfer port in a 2 stroke engine.

charge indicator light, a small light on a dashboard that illuminates when the battery is not being charged.

charge losses, the part of the fresh charge in a 2 stroke engine that is lost with the exhaust during the charge changing process.

charger, battery charger.

charging current, the electric current forced through the cells of a battery whilst a battery charger is operating.

charging efficiency, the mass of charge retained in the cylinder of a 2 stroke engine divided by the actual swept volume.

charging rate, the rate at which a charging current flows from the alternator or generator though a battery; see: boost, float, trickle, maintenance.

charging stroke, induction stroke.

chart, tachograph chart, a circular paper disc inserted into a tachograph which automatically records on it drivers hours, rest periods, speed, distance, time, and other vehicle operating parameters.

chassis, the framework to which the suspension, engine, transmission, body, etc. of a vehicle are fastened.

chassis cab, a vehicle with no bodywork,

having drivers controls, power train, and rolling chassis only, allowing the body to be constructed by the purchaser, typically a bus chassis as delivered to a coachworks.

chassis dynamometer, a power absorbing device that measures the power output of a vehicle at the drive wheels, typically measuring in units of PS.

chassis frame, a pair of longitudinal side members joined by a number of crossmembers, to which the suspension, transmission, and body, etc, are attached.

chassis number, VIN number, the manufacturers 17 digit code that individually identifies every vehicle and some of its specifications.

chassis section, a box section or channel section forming part of the chassis.

chassis set, the balance of the chassis at any moment, referring especially to the control of the centre of weight of a racing car.

chauffeur, driver, a driver who provides safe smooth punctual transportation as part of a quality service, especially the driver of a limousine and typically uniformed; from French, fire lighter, referring to steam powered vehicles and hot tube ignition systems.

chauffeur mentality, an attitude of some VIP drivers in not being prepared to suffer some damage to their own car in order to effect an escape with their VIP from an attacker.

check point, a location on a road where police, customs, Ministry of Transport officials, etc. may stop all vehicles or some at random to check documentation, load, loading, drivers hours, the vehicle, legality, etc. or to conduct a survey.

check point, a point on a rally at which all vehicles must stop, *e.g.* to record a stage timing.

check test, a test approximately every 4 years for ADI's during which his/her quality of teaching is assessed.

check the oil, to inspect the oil level with respect to the manufacturers recommendations.

check the plugs, to inspect the sparkplug gaps and readjust or replace as necessary.

check the tyres, to inspect the tyres for cuts, bulges, damage, tread depth, and physically test the air pressure in each tyre and adjusting the pressure as necessary.

check valve, a 1 way valve that allows passage of a fluid in one direction only.

Chelsea tractor, a 4x4 off-road vehicle purchased for highway use only, named from a residential district in London, UK.

chemical energy, the potential energy released by a chemical reaction; when fuel energy is converted into energy of forward motion diesel and petrol engines are typically between 21 % and 28 % efficient, the remainder is wasted as heat and exhaust.

chequered flag, a flag to communicate with racing drivers, meaning winner or end of race.

cherished number, a registration plate that is desirable because of a short or distinctive series of characters.

cherry condition, USA, mint condition, perfect condition.

cherry picker, a vehicle having a hydraulically raisable platform to enable workmen to reach and maintain street lights etc.

cherry stones, organic material used with walnut shells in small fragments which are air-blast as a mild abrasive for removing carbon deposits when rebuilding an engine, but without causing damage to metal parts.

cheval vapeur, French, horse steam, metric horsepower, see: PS.

chevron, a V shape painted between solid or broken lane separation lines to mark a non-driving area, usually where lanes merge or diverge.

chevron, an angled shape painted on a sharp deviation sign marking the location of a sharp bend to the left or right and showing the direction, as a supplement to standard delineators.

chevron, an inverted letter V shape painted in the centre of a driving lane to assist drivers to maintain a safety gap.

chicane, on a race circuit, a close series of significant bends, esses, the surface may also be reduced in width rendering overtaking impossible.

chicane, on a road, a horizontal traffic deflector created with a pair of alternate build outs narrowing the road on both sides alternately to create a triple bend, typically as part of a traffic calming scheme.

chicken coop, CB jargon, a truck inspection station.

childproof lock, a tamperproof lock which when set enables the rear doors of a car to be opened only from the outside.

child restraint seat, USA, child safety seat.

child restraint system, a child safety seat in 6 sizes for children from birth to age 11; see: stage 1, to stage 4.

child safety seat stage 1, a size of child car safety seat for a child up to 10 kg, birth to 9 months, rearwards facing, used in the front or rear secured by existing seat belts.

child safety seat stage 1-2, a size of child car safety seat for a child up to 18 kg, birth to 4 years, forwards or rearwards facing, used in the front or rear secured by existing seat belts.

child safety seat stage 2, a size of child car safety seat for a child 9 kg to 18 kg, 6 months to 4 years, forwards facing, used in the front or rear secured by existing seat belts.

child safety seat stage 2-4, a size of child car safety seat for a child 9 kg to 36 kg, 6 months to 11 years, forwards facing, converts into a booster seat, used in the front or rear secured by existing seat belts.

child safety seat stage 3, a size of child car safety seat for a child 9 kg to 25 kg, 6 months to 6 years, forwards facing, used in the front or rear secured by existing seat belts.

child safety seat stage 4, a size of child car safety seat for a child 15 kg to 36 kg, 4 years to 11 years, forwards facing, used in the front or rear secured by existing seat belts.

child seat, see: child safety seat.

Chinese 6, a vehicle having 2 steering axles at the front and 1 load carrying axle at the rear, sometimes used for small mobile cranes, also some coaches.

chip, a small pit in paintwork commonly along the leading edge of the bonnet, damage made by the impact of a small stone, typically caused by driving too close to vehicles ahead.

chip, an electronic device, a processor, an integral part of many electronic circuits in a vehicle.

chipping, replacing the engine management processor chip with another chip giving enhanced characteristics.

chip seal, a structure of road surface created by a layer of stone chippings laid over a thin layer of hot tar.

chirp, USA, the noise made by a tire when driving around a bend on a paved road with the differential locked.

chlorofluorocarbon, freon 12, a chemical formerly used in vehicle air conditioning systems.

chock, a block of wood usually cut at an angle, placed against the wheel of a vehicle to prevent movement during repairs.

chock a block, CB jargon, all channels are in use.

chocolate, a sweet snack believed to aid concentration, if eaten before driving it may significantly reduce the risk of a driver having a collision.

choke, a narrowed section within a carburettor that increases the speed of the air hence reduces the pressure, thereby sucking fuel vapour from the jet into the partial vacuum.

choke knob, a small handle on the dashboard of some cars having a carburettor, normally pulled a short distance to operate the choke valve when the engine is cold, not on modern vehicles.

choker, USA, a buildout on both sides of the road.

choke valve, a butterfly valve within the carburettor that reduces the airflow whilst increasing the partial vacuum to increase fuel delivery from the jet, thereby increasing the richness of the mixture for cold starting, on some vehicles it was manually operated on others it was automatic, not on modern vehicles.

chopped wheel, a lightened flywheel.

chop top, a saloon or similar car which has been made into a convertible.

Christmas tree, a vehicle displaying a large number of additional lights, especially small coloured lamps on the front.

chrm, chromium plate.

chrome nickel, an alloy of chromium and nickel, sometimes used as the wire core in high performance ignition leads.

chrome plated ring, a piston ring where the cylinder wall face is plated with hard chromium.

chromium, a metallic element used as an alloy with steel and other metals, often electro-plated to give a reflective surface.

chromium molybdenum , a high strength steel alloy used for manufacturing some tools and specialist vehicle parts.

chromium plate, a metallic surface coated with a thin layer of chromium for aesthetic purposes, also for wear and corrosion resistance normally resulting in a mirror-like finish; usually electroplated onto nickel plate on copper plate on a base metal.

chromoly, an alloy of chromium, molybdenum, and steel.

chuck hole, USA, pothole.

chuckwagen, an old vehicle or trailer converted into a mobile café for the purpose of food preparation and sale, typically parked indefinitely at 1 roadside location.

ci, coil ignition system.

ci, cu.ins.

CI, cetane index.

CI, compression ignition.

CI, Ivory Coast, international vehicle distinguishing sign, see appendices.

cid, cubic inch displacement, the measure of engine size in USA.

CIE, Commission Internationale de l'Éclairage, International Commission on Highway Lighting.

CIECA, Commission Internationale des Examens D'Conduite Automobile, International Driving Tests Committee.

CIF, certificate of initial fitness.

CIF, cost, insurance, and freight, the combined values of which are used to determine the gross value of a vehicle for import tax purposes when a car is imported.

cigarette lighter, a small removable electric heater having an element that glows red hot when actuated.

cih, cam in head, an engine in which the camshaft is in the cylinder head.

CIMAC, Conseil International des Machines de Combustion, International Council on Combustion Engines.

circle, roundabout.

circlip, a C shaped retaining ring made from spring steel, with a pair of eyes at the ends so it can be gripped with circlip pliers, specifically designed for either an internal or an external slot, made in a range of sizes.

circuit, racing circuit.

circuit, the complete path of an electric current from its source including its return path.

circuit breaker, an electrical protection device that is resettable, it will protect parts of a

circuit from electrical overcurrent damage.

circuit-closed tell-tale, a visual or auditory signal indicating that a device has been switched on, but not indicating whether it is operating correctly or not, (C&U).

circuit diagram, a pictorial representation showing the complete wiring system for a specific vehicle or type.

circuit tester, a test lamp or multimeter.

circular herringbone, in road rally navigation, a herringbone diagram drawn as a circle, on which the navigator has additionally to decipher the start and direction.

circular route, any journey from an origin to a destination and returning to the origin, by which the return route is not along the outward route; see also: linear.

circulating carriageway, the road surface that passes around a roundabout.

circulation map, a map showing traffic routes and the measures for traffic regulation, indicating the roads for use by certain classes of traffic, the location of traffic control stations, and the directions in which traffic may move.

cis, continuous injection system, a type of fuel injection.

CIT, Chartered Institute of Transport, UK.

CIT, Commission for Integrated Transport, UK.

city car, a small car, typically group A or smaller, designed primarily for town use.

city diesel, a highly refined ultra low sulphur diesel fuel having less than 0.003 % (30 ppm) m/m sulphur content, which will give less soot particles when burnt; this may be compared with 0.03 % (300 ppm) in standard diesel or 0.5 % (5,000 ppm) sulphur in low grade diesel in some countries.

city limit, the edge of a town or city, typically the point where a speed limit may change.

city mode, a selectable mode on some automated manual transmissions such that all gearchanges are performed automatically.

city plan, a large scale map of a city naming all streets.

cl, central locking.

Cl, Close, a road name designation.

Cl, coefficient of lift.

CL, comfort luxe, a car model superior to L but below that of GL.

CL, Sri Lanka, international vehicle distinguishing sign, see appendices.

clamp, a device which may be applied to the wheel of a car as a penalty for not complying with parking restrictions, it renders the car immovable until a fine has been paid for its removal.

clamshell bonnet, a bonnet that is hinged at its front edge.

clapped out, worn out, a vehicle or engine at the end of its life.

Clara position, centre lane residents association, a derogatory name applied to a driver who is unnecessarily hogging the centre

lane and causing an obstruction to others.
class 1, UK, a certified high level of driving
ability taught and tested by the police.
class 1, UK, a vehicle classification for MOT
testing purposes, a moped.
class 1, UK, an obsolete driving licence
category that referred to an articulated vehicle,
now categorised as C+E.
class 2, UK, a vehicle classification for MOT
testing purposes, a motorcycle.
class 2, UK, an obsolete driving licence
category that referred to a rigid lorry with 3 or
more axles, now categorised as C.
class 3, UK, a vehicle classification for MOT
testing purposes, a 3 wheeled vehicle not more
than 450 kg unladen, excluding a motorcycle
with a sidecar.
class 3, UK, an obsolete driving licence
category that referred to a rigid lorry with only
2 axles, now categorised as C.
class 4, UK, a vehicle classification for MOT
testing purposes, a car, taxi, minibus or
ambulance having up to 12 passenger seats,
goods vehicles not exceeding 3,000 kg DGW,
motor caravans, and dual purpose vehicles.
class 5, UK, a vehicle classification for MOT
testing purposes, a passenger carrying vehicle
having more than 16 passenger seats.
class 6, UK, a vehicle classification for MOT
testing purposes, a goods vehicle exceeding
3,500 kg DGW.
class 7, UK, a vehicle classification for MOT
testing purposes, a goods vehicle between
3,000 and 3,500 kg DGW.
class A, USA, any combination of motor
vehicles with a GVWR exceeding 26,000 lbs
(11.8 tonnes), towing a trailer exceeding
10,000 lbs (4.5 tonnes); a CDL is required; not
including motorcycles.
class A thread, any external thread.
class B, USA, any single motor vehicle with a
GVWR exceeding 26,000 lbs (11.8 tonnes) or
any such vehicle towing another not exceeding
10,000 lbs (4.5 tonnes); a CDL is required; not
including motorcycles.
class B thread, any internal thread.
class C, USA, any motor vehicle with a
GVWR exceeding 16,000 lbs (7.25 tonnes) but
not exceeding 26,000 lbs (11.8 tonnes) or any
such vehicle towing another not exceeding
10,000 lbs (4.5 tonnes); any vehicle used to
transport 16 or more persons, or used in the
transportation of hazardous materials; not
including motorcycles.
class D, USA, cars and any motor vehicle with
a GVWR not exceeding 16,000 lbs (7.25
tonnes) except those vehicles requiring a class
A, B, C, L, or M, license.
classic, any vehicle built after 1st January 1930
and more than 25 years old; see also: pre-war,
WW2, post-war.
classic, USA, specific vehicles built during the
years 1925 to 1948 inclusive.
classified ad, a small advertisement in a

newspaper describing a car, or sometimes parts,
for sale.
classified road, UK, a highway which is of
importance to the movement of traffic and
which is in either class I, II, or III; the classes
of which generally coincide with the A, B, and
C prefix in the national road numbering system
.
class L , USA, any motor driven cycle with less
than 150 cc displacement.
class M, USA, any motorcycle or motor driven
cycle.
clay model, a traditional mockup of a new or
revised body design sculpted in clay before the
prototype is built, now superseded by computer
design, CAD.
CLCCR, Committee de Liaison de la
Construction de Carrosseries et de Remorque.
clean, a vehicle which is mechanically sound,
and which has a current MOT certificate,
complete documentation, and a neat and tidy
interior.
clean air, the condition when there is no
vehicle ahead, especially on a racing circuit
when there is no turbulence from a vehicle
ahead; see also: dirty air.
clean gearchange, a neat powerchange made
without clutch slip or clutch drag.
clearance, the space needed between 2 moving
parts or between a moving part and a stationary
part.
clearance circle, the diameter of the turning
circle of a vehicle measured at the most
extreme point on the body when making a 360°
turn.
clearance lights, USA, continental lights.
clearance period, the period between
conflicting green traffic signals at a junction,
normally 5 seconds total duration consisting of
3 seconds of amber after a green followed by
2 seconds of red and amber before the other
green light.
clearance volume, the volume that remains
above the piston at tdc.
clear ice, black ice, glazed ice.
clearway, a major road having signs that
prohibit stopping, waiting, parking, loading,
and setting down passengers, but without road
edge markings.
CLEDIPA, Committee de Liaison European de
la Distribution Independante de Pieces de
Rechange et Equipements pour Automobiles,
Liaison Committee of EEC Automobile Parts
Wholesalers.
CLEPA, Comite de Liaison de la Construction
d'Equipement et des Pieces d'Automobile, now
European Association of Automotive Suppliers.
clerk of the course, the judges secretary at a
motor racing event.
clicks, kilometres, a measure of distance;
verbal only.
clicks, kilometres per hour, a measure of speed;
verbal only.
climate control, air conditioning taken to a

high level of sophistication; the system maintains the temperature to within 1 °C and in some systems temperature variations are possible for each occupant, it automatically switches to recirculation of air if sensors detect high levels of pollutants, usually having pollen and charcoal filters.

climate responsive, a vehicle system responding to changes of climate for engine control or passenger comfort.

climatic chamber, a test chamber which can produce various extremes of temperature, humidity, etc, to test a car during its design stage.

climbing ability, gradeability.

climbing lane, an additional lane on the nearside on an uphill gradient, normally without a minimum speed limit, to allow faster traffic to overtake on the offside, originally named crawler lane.

climbing power, the power required to climb a specific gradient at a specific speed, measured in kW as a function of force x speed; equal to the vehicle mass x gravitational acceleration x the sine of the angle of the gradient x speed.

climbing resistance, the force required to move a vehicle up a gradient, measured in Newtons with respect to the vehicle mass x gravitational acceleration x the sine of the angle of the gradient.

clipping point, the apex on the inside of a bend on a race circuit where the tyres may clip or run onto the kerb.

clock, an instrument displaying the exact time.

clock, odometer, milometer, a distance measuring device showing the total distance the vehicle has covered in its life, measuring in either km or miles.

c/lock, central locking.

clocked, a measured speed.

clocked, a measured time.

clocked, a vehicle on which the odometer reading has been tampered with such to reduce the measured figure.

clocking, the act of changing the display on an odometer to show a lower mileage to increase the value of a vehicle.

clock up, to travel a distance of.

clogged, an obstruction of debris in the route a fluid normally takes.

clone plates, false registration plates fitted illegally to misrepresent the ownership of a vehicle, the registration copied from a similar make, model, and colour of car; typically done to avoid legal proceedings by a person expecting to be photographed by speed cameras; see also: car cloning.

Close, a road which is closed at 1 end.

close convoy, a protective arrangement of vehicles in close formation around a host vehicle whilst travelling.

close coupled, in relation to wheels on the same side of a trailer, fitted so that at all times while the trailer is in motion they remain

parallel to the longitudinal axis of the trailer, and the distance between the centres of their respective areas of contact with the road surface does not exceed 1 metre, (C&U).

close coupled trailer, a simple trailer having more than 1 axle, but where all axles are grouped at a point near the centre, such that trailer does not have any steering mechanism other than the pivot at the coupling.

closed car, a car having a fixed roof.

closed crankcase ventilation system, the system whereby crankcase vapours are directed to the air intake to be consumed during combustion to reduce pollution.

closed delivery vehicle, a van not having any side windows to the rear of the drivers seat and without rear visibility via an internal mirror.

closed loop, an electronic signal operating a device from which it receives feedback, *e.g,* the signal from the lambda sensor in an exhaust which influences the ECU in controlling the stoichiometric air-fuel ratio.

closed van, closed delivery vehicle.

closely spaced, in the case of 2 axles, that they are spaced at a distance apart of not less than 1.02 m, and not more than 2.5 m; or in the case of 3 axles that the outermost axles are spaced not more than 3.25 m apart and none of the axles has a plated weight exceeding 7.5 tonnes, (C&U).

close ratio, a transmission with some or all of the gear ratios mathematically closer than normal, especially for competitions.

closing distance, the distance travelled by an oncoming vehicle whilst an overtaking manoeuvre is being performed.

closing gap, a reducing longitudinal space between 2 vehicles moving in the same direction, and which implies that the following vehicle is very likely to change lanes and overtake the leading vehicle especially on a multilane road.

closing speed, the sum of the speeds of opposing traffic.

clot, a cluster of moving traffic, typically all having slowed to overtake a police car travelling at the speed limit on a motorway with a very small speed differential.

clothoid bend, the geometric shape of a typical bend having a transitional entry where the radius increases, an apex area of constant radius, and a transitional exit where the radius decreases.

cloth upholstery, vehicle seating etc. covered in fabric.

cloud point, the low temperature at which diesel fuel tends to thicken due to crystallisation of wax, and become cloudy.

cloverleaf, a symmetrical grade-separated junction on 2 levels between roads at 90° to each other and which allows all vehicles to move freely from any road to any other excepting a return to the route of origin, 4 link roads turn through 90° and the other 4 link

---

roads turn through 270° all having bends to the nearside only and are fed from sliproads on the nearside only; the name is derived from the resulting plan shape; see appendices.

cloverleaf loop, a curved link road between 2 parts of a junction where the link road turns through 270°.

clth, cloth upholstery.

clubcab, $1^1/_2$ cab, a single cab on a pickup having an extended area within the cab behind the front seats for storage of small items.

cluesheet, a list of information required on a road rally to locate typically 30 route checks.

clunker, Australia & USA, banger, an old car in poor condition.

cluster, a collective noun for a number of vehicles in a close group; also bunch, clot, platoon.

clutch, a device allowing smooth connection and disconnection of rotating shafts by means of variable axial pressure between a disc of friction material and a steel disc, fitted between the engine and gearbox.

clutch abuse, any action which will unnecessarily shorten the life of a clutch, *e.g.* excessive slipping of the clutch, dragging the clutch, slipping the clutch whilst driving in a mid gear instead of changing down, holding the vehicle stationary on an uphill gradient especially at traffic signals, attempting to creep forwards in stationary traffic, letting the clutch in suddenly causing a shock to the transmission, riding the clutch.

clutch aligning tool, a tool used to ensure the clutch drive plate is aligned concentrically with the pressure plate, between the pressure plate and the flywheel on reassembly of the unit.

clutch balance, to manually set and control exactly, a clutch pressure to maintain a specific clutch slip such that a vehicle is held stationary on a gradient using the clutch and accelerator only; not recommended for longer than a few moments.

clutch binding, a condition when the clutch drive plate does not clear from the flywheel when the pedal is pressed out, usually because of excessive friction on the drive plate splines, usually caused by a trace of rust or sometimes by oil.

clutch biting, to manually set and control exactly a clutch position and pressure such that the clutch pressure plate causes the clutch drive plate to start to transmit power from the engine.

clutch brake, a device for slowing the clutch and gearbox input shaft to enable easier selection of 1st gear on some lorries with constant mesh gears.

clutch cable, an operating mechanism between pedal and clutch on many small vehicles.

clutch drag, an abuse of the clutch when the driver selects a lower gear without using the accelerator to raise the revs, such that the engine speed is relatively less than the road speed, such that the clutch pressure plate is rotating significantly slower than the clutch drive plate, such that the clutch raises the engine speed or slows the vehicle, thereby creating wear to the clutch drive plate.

clutch drag, the action of the clutch not fully disengaging when the pedal is fully depressed, caused either by wear or contamination of the lining or splines.

clutch drive plate, a disc coated with friction material on its 2 faces, and having internal splines to transmit drive to the gearbox input shaft; it is sandwiched under driver controlled pressure between the clutch pressure plate and the flywheel.

clutch foot, the drivers left foot.

clutch fork, the clutch operating lever which has a forked end to operate the release bearing.

clutch friction plate, clutch drive plate.

clutch housing, bell housing.

clutch in, the condition when the clutch is engaged, when the clutch pedal is released, *i.e.* when the foot is removed from the pedal, hence the vehicle speed is under direct control of the accelerator.

clutch judder, a fault condition in which the clutch does not take up the drive smoothly, sometimes caused by excessive play in transmission mountings or insufficient free movement of the clutch outer cable.

clutchless, a vehicle without a manual clutch, usually having a torque converter in the transmission.

clutchless gearchange, to change gear without using the clutch pedal, a skilled technique using the accelerator to match the engine revs to the roadspeed; with a splitter gearbox splits may also be performed by use of the accelerator only; see: snatch change.

clutch lining, friction material bonded or riveted to both faces of the clutch drive plate.

clutch out, the condition when the clutch is out of engagement, when the clutch pedal is depressed, *i.e.* the pedal is pushed to the floor, hence there is no drive from the engine to the wheels.

clutch pedal, the lever with which the driver operates the clutch with his/her left foot.

clutch plate, see: clutch drive plate, clutch pressure plate.

clutch pressure plate, a device that exerts pressure on the clutch drive plate typically with a diaphragm spring when the clutch pedal is released, to hold the drive plate against the flywheel in order to transmit power to the gearbox.

clutch release bearing, the thrust bearing operated by the clutch fork and which acts upon the springs to release the pressure from the pressure plate.

clutch shaft, the first motion shaft.

clutch slip, a condition when the clutch pressure plate exerts insufficient pressure on the clutch drive plate, such that it does not transmit all the power from the engine; this may be controlled manually but will also occur when the clutch drive plate is worn to the end of its life.

clutch spring, a diaphragm spring usually, or a series of coil springs, that applies pressure the drive plate.

clutch start-cancel switch, USA, a safety device in a manual transmission vehicle which prevents the starter motor from engaging unless the clutch is depressed.

clutch stop, clutch brake.

cm, centimetre, a unit of length equal to 10 mm.

cm³, cubic centimetres, the total volume of the displacement of the engine pistons in all cylinders measured in cubic centimetres.

CMA, Canadian Motorcycle Association.

C-matic transmission, a semiautomatic transmission developed by Citroën.

CMS, changeable message sign.

C MTV, the European minimum specification of a driving test vehicle that may be used for driving licence category C; a vehicle of minimum 10 tonnes MAM and capable of a speed of 80 km/h (50 mph), minimum 7 m long, excluding tractive units.

CMVMA, Canadian Motor Vehicles Manufacturers Association.

CMVSS, Canadian Motor Vehicle Safety Standards.

CN, cetane number.

CNDA, Cherished Number Dealers Association, UK.

CNG, compressed natural gas, a hydrocarbon gas principally methane, stored under very high pressure, a fuel having an equivalent octane rating of 113 but only about 78 % the energy of petrol per litre.

CNPA, Conseil National des Professions de l'Automobile, French retail motor industry association.

co, coupler offset.

CO, carbon monoxide.

CO, Columbia, international vehicle distinguishing sign, see appendices.

CO₂, carbon dioxide.

CO₂ mass emission, the minimum quantity of carbon dioxide gas discharged as a pollutant from a particular vehicle with a specific engine, measured in grams per kilometre, g/km; a small car emits approximately 150 g/km CO_2.

coach, a luxurious passenger carrying vehicle originally pulled by a team of horses, see: motor.

coach, to subtly teach a person to a high standard of driving.

coachbuilder, a company specialising in the construction of special bodies for various motor vehicles, mostly buses, sometimes vans or lorries, or sometimes cars, *e.g.* limousines.

coachbuilt, a vehicle body which is individually built by craftsmen.

coachlining, long thin lines painted by hand, typically a border around each panel on a vehicle body.

coachwork, the internal trim and upholstery, and external bodywork of any vehicle, especially if it has been specially prepared, *e.g.* painted to a standard above that of production manufacturing.

coaming, a raised lip around the edge of the bed of a flatbed lorry or trailer.

Coanda effect, the tendency for airflow over a vehicle to attach itself to and follow the shape of the bodywork.

coast, to freewheel, to travel in neutral at any speed, a very dangerous practice especially downhill or whilst slowing.

coast, to freewheel, to travel with the clutch depressed other than at a very slow speed; or to travel with the clutch depressed for a considerable distance, a very dangerous practice especially downhill or whilst slowing.

coastdown, USA, the procedure before stopping the engine in any vehicle fitted with a turbocharger, to let the engine idle for at least 1 minute to allow the turbo to cool before stopping the engine to prevent possible turbo seizure.

coat, a thin layer of substance covering a surface, *e.g.* a layer of grease or paint.

coated ring, a piston ring with its cylinder wall face coated with ferrous oxide, soft phosphate, or tin, for oil retention.

cobbles, stones of a uniform size approximately 100 mm across, originally used to surface roads, sometimes slippery when wet.

cockpit, the drivers volume within a vehicle, including the seat, controls, and instruments.

cockpit checks, part of the pre-driving checks, to check: the doors, handbrake, seat, backrest, mirrors, seatbelt, tell-tale lights, and footbrake.

cockpit padding, non-structural parts placed within the cockpit for the purpose of improving driver comfort and safety.

cocoon, safety zone.

CODE, College of Driver Education, UK.

code board, in road rallying, a small hidden card bearing a written word to be noted as proof of visiting a location.

co-driver, a second driver or assistant required for some oversize loads.

co-driver, a second driver allowing alternation of duty for long distance travel.

co-driver, a navigator on a rally.

co-driver, an instructor for some specialist advanced driver training.

coe, cab over engine.

COE, Certificate of Entitlement, a requirement to enable vehicle ownership in Singapore.

coefficient of drag, a dimensionless ratio equal to the resistance of the vehicle body moving through the atmosphere divided by the resistance of a flat area of identical frontal silhouette but with no axial length moving through the atmosphere at the same speed.

coefficient of friction, a dimensionless ratio equal to the friction force required to slide a body across a surface divided by the perpendicular force holding the body to the surface.

coefficient of lift, a dimensionless ratio equal to the reduction in weight acting on the suspension caused by airflow over the body divided by the force propelling the vehicle when travelling at speed, usually measured separately at each of the front and rear axles; in vehicles fitted with airfoils the lift is negative to provide downforce to increase stability.

COF, Coach Operators Federation, UK.

coffee, a stimulant providing it contains caffeine, it helps to reduce tiredness if taken during frequent breaks in a long journey.

cog, a tooth on a gear wheel.

cog swapping, changing gear.

COIF, conditions of initial fitness.

coil, a transformer used to step up from 12 volts to over 30,000 volts to fire the sparkplugs.

coil ignition system, an ignition system having an ignition coil to create the high voltage necessary to fire the sparkplugs.

coil over oil , a concentric coil spring and damper suspension assembly, typically a MacPherson strut unit.

coil robbing, an effect occurring sometimes when trying to start a si engine with a weak battery, such that the voltage drop caused by the starter motor severely reduces the current through the ignition coil.

coil spring, a steel alloy rod in the form of a helix having elastic properties, often used for vehicle suspension and other parts.

coke, a build-up of carbon in the cylinder head and valve stems.

coked up, a condition when the combustion chamber and related areas are covered with a thick deposit of carbon.

col, colour.

cold condensate corrosion, a condition that may develop inside an exhaust system if a vehicle is driven only for short journeys, resulting in rapid corrosion of the exhaust by acidic compounds, especially at the last silencer box.

cold cranking rate, a battery rating, indicating the ability of a cold battery to crank an engine, there are 2 ratings in use: the number of amps a 12 v battery can deliver for 30 seconds at –18 °C (0 °F) without the voltage falling below 7.2 volts; or, the number of amps a 12 v battery can deliver for 30 seconds at –29 °C (–20 °F) without the voltage falling below 6.0 volts.

cold galvanising, the coating of bare metal with zinc or certain other metallic based paints.

cold inflation pressure, the amount of air pressure in a tyre measured at ambient temperature.

cold sparkplug, a sparkplug designed for high compression and high performance engines which run hot, specified in order to dissipate heat rapidly to avoid pre-ignition.

cold start, a mixture containing ethoxyethane in an aerosol, squirted into the air intake of an engine to assist starting, especially in cold weather.

cold start, to start an engine that is at ambient temperature, especially in cool or cold climates.

cold start enrichment, the addition of extra fuel to the combustion mixture when starting a cold engine to allow for incomplete vaporization or condensation of some fuel, such that the vaporized fuel will have the correct stoichiometric ratio.

cold welding, the process of repairing a crack in a casting by drilling perpendicular to the crack and tapping the hole and using a stud and nut to clamp it together.

col kyd, colour keyed, see: colour coordinated.

collapsible spare tire, USA, a lightweight temporary spare wheel and tyre which is carried deflated in order to take less storage space in a car, and which requires inflation before use.

collapsible steering column, the ability of a steering column to fold or telescope during a frontal collision, to reduce driver injury.

collapsing pedals, a safety feature to reduce injury to feet and legs in a collision, developed by GM.

collar, a ring below the head of a gear lever, lifted to open the gate to select reverse on many vehicles.

collector distributor, each 1 way road running parallel to a motorway or similar which provides access to/from more than 1 sliproad, collecting traffic from sliproads and main carriageways, and distributing traffic back to other carriageways and sliproads, *e.g.* the junction where the M61, M62, A580, and A666 all meet near Manchester.

collector road, a road which distributes access traffic within a large residential development, linking to an arterial or main road.

collectors car, any car that is notable by its rarity, typically a classic, vintage, or veteran car.

collet, a small removable collar split in 2 parts, *e.g.* holding the valve spring to the valve stem.

collision, a violent impact of a vehicle with another vehicle, object, or person.

collision avoidance, a range of techniques each of which if used will significantly reduce the risk of collision, *e.g.* maintaining a safety zone, long braking, maintaining escape routes.

collision damage waver, additional insurance to hire car insurance covering the loss of, or damage to, a hire vehicle.

collision data recorder, accident data recorder.

colour blindness, the inability of a driver to perceive 1 or more colours.

colour chart, a pictorial listing of exact colours with their names and code for matching paint to bodywork.

colour coat, the coat of paint which gives the

final colour.

colour code, a system of identifying vehicle wiring by using wires with insulation in a variety of different colours, each colour representing a different circuit.

colour coordinated, to colour match some vehicle parts, *e.g.* bumpers or door mirror housings to the same colour as the car body.

coloured curb, USA, a painted curb using a colour code to denote special rules for stopping, standing, waiting, parking, loading, unloading, and for parking by disabled drivers; see: blue, green, red, white, yellow.

colour keyed, colour coordinated.

colour vision, the ability of a driver to perceive the full normal spectrum of colours, a legal requirement only for drivers of vehicles exceeding 3.5 tonnes MAM.

column change, a gear lever that is mounted on the steering column.

column shift, column change.

combat vehicle, a vehicle with or without armour or armament designed for specific functions in combat.

combi, combination, a dual purpose passenger and freight version of a light commercial vehicle, *i.e.* a car derived van having windows and seats in the rear.

combination, a car drawing a trailer.

combination, a motorcycle coupled to a sidecar.

combination, a rigid lorry drawing 1 or more trailers.

combination, a tractive unit and semitrailer.

combination spanner, a tool for turning nuts etc. having open jaws at 1 end, and a ring spanner to fit the same size at the other end.

combined cycle, the fuel consumption of a vehicle measured by laboratory tests on a rolling road, averaging the consumption obtained by the urban test cycle and the extra urban test cycle, weighted by the distances covered during each test.

combined lamps, lamps having a common housing and bulb but with individual lenses, *e.g.* tail lamp and registration lamp, (C&U).

combustible mixture, a mixture of fuel and oxygen that will readily burn.

combustion, rapid burning of air and fuel vapour in the combustion chamber.

combustion chamber, the space between the cylinder head and the piston where the fuel is burned.

combustion efficiency, the ratio of heat actually produced by combustion, to the heat that would be released if combustion was perfect.

combustion knock, a condition in si engines whereby there is unwanted rapid combustion of the last part of the charge before ignition by the flamefront, resulting in a characteristic noise.

combustion pressure, the pressure created during the combustion of the air-fuel mixture, expressed as the MEP.

combustion speed, the speed of the flame front as it travels through the combustion mixture, typically at a speed of 20 m/s to 40 m/s, and is fastest in a weak mixture.

come on, CB jargon, talk back to me.

come to rest, to cease moving.

comfort braking, deceleration at any rate less than 0.20 g, *i.e.* less than 1.96 m/s^2, that is to stop from 50 km/h in not less than 48 metres (from 30 mph in not less than 160 feet).

coming around on you, USA, a vehicle which is oversteering.

coming out of the windows, CB jargon, a message received clearly.

commentary drive, to drive whilst giving a full commentary, to remark on all that is seen, thought, anticipated, and the control of the vehicle; typically performed by an instructor, by a trainee to increase concentration, or by a person undergoing an advanced driving test.

commercial drivers license, USA, a license which authorizes the holder to drive any vehicle having a GVWR exceeding 26,000 lbs (11.8 tonnes), operate tanker vehicles, drive vehicles with air brakes, vehicles carrying passengers, vehicles carrying hazardous materials, and towing of a trailer exceeding 10,000 lbs (4.5 tonnes).

commercial driving permit, USA, a special permit issued by the office of the Secretary of State to a commercial motor vehicle driver who has had more than 3 but fewer than 5 minor moving traffic violations, and which allows driving only during specified times along specified routes for work purposes.

commercial vehicle, a vehicle used by any organisation or business for any purpose to earn, either directly or indirectly, revenue or advantage for the organisation.

common rail, a fuel injection common pressure chamber in the form of a tube, that supplies fuel at a constant pressure at up to 1,400 bar to each electronically controlled injection nozzle.

communal parking, an off-street parking area designed to serve the residents of a community not having a parking space within their own curtilage.

communication, the various methods of signalling between drivers, including: direction indicators, arm signals, brake lights, reversing lights, hazard lights, eye contact, horn, vehicle position, vehicle speed.

Community Directive, followed by a number, a directive adopted by the Council or the Commission of the European Communities.

commutator, part of an armature consisting of a series of insulated copper sectors that conduct the current to the brushes within a starter motor or dynamo.

commute, daily travel between home and work using any mechanical means of transport.

commuter parking, parking intended to be used by drivers parking near their place of work, and where the vehicle typically remains unused during the working day.

compact, USA, a small saloon car having 100 to 110 cubic feet (2.831 to 3.115 m³) of passenger and luggage space.

company car, a car provided by an employer to an employee for work and/or for private use; those typically used by salesmen are often named a repmobile.

compass, an instrument having a permanent magnet and a calibrated scale so the navigator can determine the direction in which the vehicle is heading.

compensator, equaliser.

compensatory rest, when referring to EC drivers hours, a rest period that must be taken in 1 continuous block of time to catch up on reduced daily or weekly rest, such that it is added to another rest of 8 or more hours.

competition car, a vehicle specially constructed, adapted, modified, or prepared for performing in a specific type of race, rally, hill climb, or trial etc.

competitive safari, a type of off-road or cross country competition having special stages at least 1 mile (1.6 km) in length that must be completed to a maximum and minimum target time but with and average speed less than 40 mph (64 km/h), typically for 4x4 vehicles.

competitive section, part of a road rally, see: regularity, standard.

competitor, a person driving or taking part in a motor race or time trial event, etc.

complete interchange, USA, a full junction.

complete wheel, a wheel, valve, and inflated tyre.

compliance, the resiliency designed into suspension which allows a wheel to move upwards and slightly rearwards when striking a bump.

component, part of an assembly or unit which may be individually identified.

composite headlamp, a headlamp having a separate replaceable bulb, although the lens and reflector may be separate units or combined.

composite test cycle, a method of measuring the fuel consumption of a car by taking the fuel consumption at several speeds and combining the consumption as following: (0.5@ urban + 0.25@ 90 km/h + 0.25@ 120 km/h).

composite trailer, a semitrailer coupled to a converter dolly hence having the appearance and performance of a full trailer.

compound, the composition of tyre rubber, referring to tyre tread material, a hard compound gives a long life and reasonable friction, whereas a soft compound gives maximum friction but a short life.

compound carburettor, a multichoke carburettor fitted to a single port.

compound glass, laminated glass.

compound shift, a gearchange in a lorry or bus that involves movement of the splitter switch or range change switch and the gear lever, e.g.

6 hi to 7 lo.

comprehensive insurance, insurance covering most risks, including claims from a 3rd party and claims where the damage was caused by the action of the 2nd party, i.e. the insured driver.

compressed natural gas, methane, a hydrocarbon, a fuel having an equivalent octane rating exceeding 120 but only about 78 % the energy of petrol per litre, it can be produced from renewable sources.

compression, the squeezing of a gas into a smaller space by the piston before ignition, this increases the temperature and density of the gas.

compression gauge, an instrument with which to measure the compression ratio in each cylinder of an engine to aid fault diagnosis.

compression ignition, an engine in which the ignition of the air-fuel mixture is effected solely by the temperature rise caused by the compression of the air.

compression ignition engine, a diesel engine, in which the ignition of the air-fuel mixture is solely by the heat generated by its compression.

compression leakage, loss of compression pressure due to escape of gases through either piston rings, valves, or cylinder head gasket.

compression pressure, the pressure in the combustion chamber at the end of the compression stroke.

compression ratio, the ratio of the volumes of the cylinder, and combustion chamber, i.e. the volume at bdc compared to the volume at tdc; the volume at tdc is considered as 1 unit; a typical petrol engine has a compression ratio of 9:1, a typical diesel engine has a compression ratio of 22:1.

compression release, a retarding system to maximise engine braking by decompressing the cylinder directly after compression, preventing the compressed air from driving the piston, used on lorries, developed by Mack.

compression retarder, a system on some lorries and buses that changes the engine valve timing to have the effect of converting the engine into an air compressor, to control the speed of the vehicle during a long descent, e.g. a Jake brake.

compression ring, the top ring or rings on a piston, designed to prevent blowby.

compression stroke, the piston movement from bdc to tdc with inlet and exhaust valves closed, to compress the air-fuel mixture.

compression tester, a diagnostic gauge that measures cylinder pressure during engine cranking, hence the efficiency of each cylinder.

compression volume, the volume of the cylinder and combustion chamber when at bdc divided by the volume at tdc.

compressor, a machine which increases the pressure of air or gas.

comp safari, competitive safari.

compulsory basic training, a compulsory training course for riders of motorcycles before being allowed to ride on the road.

computer active technology suspension, a system that automatically stiffens the suspension when driving hard, developed by Jaguar.

computer aided design, a modern method of designing all aspects of a car, making obsolete the requirement to sculpt a clay model.

computer aided gearshift, a semiautomatic gear selector system which informs the driver when to change gear, and requiring the operation of the clutch only for starting and stopping, developed by Scania.

computer aided technology, any type of modern technology which employs a chip to process information, present a readout, or control a function.

computer area network, a databus vehicle communication system having a central microprocessor that communicates with many local microprocessors around the vehicle, such that the whole vehicle can be wired with just 4 wires.

computer test, a test of knowledge of driving rules for the safe and correct driving of a motor vehicle, to pass the test is the minimum acceptable standard of proficiency, performed using a computer; the test being a theory part of a driving test.

concealable lamp, a retractable lamp, capable of being partly or completely hidden when not in use, usually by displacement of the lamp, (C&U).

concentration endurance, the ability of a driver to mentally focus and concentrate for extended periods, a component of advanced driving.

concept car, a car produced by major car manufacturers for international motor shows displaying very futuristic ideas not yet in production.

concours d'élégance, a show or competition where vehicles are assessed on their aesthetic appearance.

concrete safety shape barrier, New Jersey barrier.

condensation, the change of state of a gas or vapour to a liquid, as on the cylinder walls of a cold engine hence requiring a richer fuel mixture.

condensation, the change of state of water vapour to liquid, as moisture on the inside or outside of windows, rendering driving dangerous.

condenser, capacitor.

conditional safety, the result of reduced physiological stress that vehicle occupants are subject to from reduced vibration, noise, and climatic conditions, a branch of primary safety.

conductor, any metal or material that allows the easy flow of electrical current or heat.

cone, a hollow conical rubber or plastic shape of various heights from $^1/_4$ m to $1^1/_2$ m, usually orange with a retroreflective band and deformable if driven over, used to mark the edge of the carriageway at temporary hazards, *e.g.* roadworks etc.

cone clutch, a part of the synchronising mechanism in a synchromesh gearbox.

conflict, the occurrence of a near-miss in which there is no collision, loss, or injury, but where a change in speed and/or direction by 1 or more road users is necessary to avoid the potential collision.

conflict point, a location where flows of traffic meet or cross, hence a potential site for a collision; a crossroads may have 24 conflict points whereas a roundabout may have only 4.

confliction parking, to park on a road opposite or almost opposite another vehicle or obstruction such that the road is unreasonably narrowed causing a hindrance to the flow of traffic; sometimes misnamed double parking.

congestion, the impedance vehicles impose upon each other when traffic flow is close to the carrying capacity of a road network, an unwanted and/or abnormal accumulation of traffic that is unevenly distributed in space and time.

congestion charging, the levying of a fee for using roads within parts of a city or routes which are heavily trafficked, in an attempt to reduce traffic and congestion.

conk out, to breakdown.

connecting rod, the rod that connects piston to the crankshaft, the little end is connected to the piston and the big end is connected to the crankshaft, often named con rod.

connection, USA, link road, a ramp between 2 freeways.

con rod, connecting rod, the link between the piston and the crankshaft, with little end and big end bearings.

con rod bearings, connecting rod bearings, with the little end having a sleeve bearing and the big end usually having a split insert bearing.

con rod cap, connecting rod bearing cap, the big end journal having a cap to allow fitting of a split bearing.

con rod journal, connecting rod journal, the part of the crankshaft to which the connecting rod is attached, also named big end journal.

cons, console.

considerate, thoughtful allowance made for other road users.

consistency, for a driver to be true to the recommended system of vehicle control, rarely making errors.

console, the drivers instrument and switch panel on the dashboard.

constant mesh, a gearbox without synchromesh, requiring the driver to double-declutch for all gearchanges, an obsolete system.

constant regenerative trap, a chamber in the exhaust system to filter and re-burn particulates from the exhaust of diesel vehicles to reduce pollution, developed by Volvo.

constant speed test , a method of measuring the fuel consumption of a car at 120 km/h, (74.56 mph) on a test track with no traffic, starting with a warm engine and maintaining a constant speed, it gives a figure intended to be representative of motorway driving.

constant speed test , a method of measuring the fuel consumption of a car at 90 km/h, (55.92 mph) on a test track with no traffic, starting with a warm engine and maintaining a constant speed, it gives a very optimistic figure that will not be equalled in normal driving.

constant velocity joint, a joint on the front axle of fwd and 4wd vehicles that allows the drive shaft to transmit power whilst the front wheel is steering.

construction, USA, road works.

Construction and Use Regulations, legal regulations defining the construction dimensions and methods, and the style of use of all vehicles, with regard to safety, UK and other countries.

consumption, the rate of consuming, especially fuel or oil etc, measured in various units of volume, distance, or time, *e.g.* 15 km/litre, or, 0.5 litre per week.

contact patch, the footprint of a tyre.

contact points, a pair of electrical contacts in a distributor that switch the primary current through the ignition coil, obsolete on modern vehicles.

contaminant, any substance which is unwanted in any location, a fluid that will cause harm to other substances or processes, *e.g.* water or dirt in fuel or oil, water or air in hydraulic fluid, ions or cations in battery fluid, lead in the cat.

continental fuse, an electrical fuse type previously common in vehicles, almost cylindrical with a conical connection at each end.

continental lamp, a lamp fitted near to the extreme outer edges and as close as possible to the top of the vehicle and intended to indicate clearly the vehicle's overall width, this lamp is intended for certain vehicles and trailers to complement the vehicle's front and rear position lamps by drawing particular attention to its bulk.

continuity, an uninterrupted flow of current in an electrical circuit.

continuous ac ignition system, an ignition system having a high frequency ac spark that continues throughout the power stroke and which reduces sparkplug erosion.

continuous fuel injection system, a single point fuel injection system where the fuel is injected in varying quantities into the inlet manifold, not pulsed to meet the needs of each cylinder.

continuously variable transmission, a transmission system without gear wheels but utilising 2 V pulleys that have a controlled variable distance between their faces such that as 1 gap widens the other decreases so giving a variable radius to the V belt, so giving an infinitely variable number of gears though a gear spread of approximately 6:1.

Conti tyre system, a wheel and tyre design having rim flanges turned inwards to the wheel centre and a dedicated tyre seated on the inner surfaces such that the tyre has significant run-flat capability, developed by Continental.

contraflow, a situation on a dual carriageway or motorway where traffic is temporarily diverted onto the other carriageway to flow contrary to the normal direction, creating a 2 way traffic flow on that carriageway.

contraflow bus lane, a bus lane which operates in the opposite direction to other traffic in an otherwise 1 way street.

contre pente, a raised portion adjacent to the rim bead seat intended to restrain a partially deflated tyre so the bead may not suddenly move into the well whilst cornering, to prevent loss of control.

control, a physical skill enabling the driver to have maximum feel for the vehicle at all times, knowing how the vehicle will handle in any situation by understanding its capabilities and limitations.

control, any device that will regulate the functioning of a system, operated either by the driver by pedal, wheel, switch, or lever, or operating automatically.

control arm, USA, a wishbone or an A arm a part of the suspension system designed to precisely control wheel movement.

control box, a unit containing relays or voltage regulator.

control cable, a cable from a drivers control to a device it operates, *e.g.* heater.

controlled access highway, a highway which may be entered and exited only at specific points.

controlled crossing, a pedestrian crossing controlled by traffic signals, police officer, traffic warden, or a school crossing patrol.

controlled crossing, a railway level crossing controlled by traffic signals or an attendant, and which may have full, half, or no barrier, or sometimes gates.

controlled junction, a junction controlled by traffic signals or a police officer.

controlled parking zone, an area of a town having a uniform set of parking rules including hours of operation, which are specified on entry to the zone but which may not be displayed on any other signs within the zone.

controller, an electronic control module.

control safety, any system that assists the driver in avoiding an actual hazard, *e.g.* ABS.

control stalk, a lever projecting from the steering column just below the steering wheel

– cCc –

with which to operate various secondary
controls, *e.g.* direction indicators.
control tower, a floor mounted gear selector
lever for an automatic transmission.
control unit, electronic control unit.
conv, convertible.
conventional, a lorry or tractive unit with the
engine and bonnet ahead of the driver, T cab,
current USA style; see also: cabover.
conventional fuel, petrol or diesel fuels, but
not gas or electric.
conventional highway, a highway without
control of access and which may or may not be
divided.
conventionally aspirated, an engine without a
turbocharger or a supercharger.
conventional spare wheel, a spare wheel and
tyre of the same width and diameter as the 4
road wheels.
conversion kit, a kit of parts required to
improve or change a system, *e.g.* to replace a
dynamo with an alternator.
converter dolly, a short trailer which is
designed to support the front of a semitrailer to
enable it to move without any part of its weight
being directly superimposed on the drawing
vehicle, (C&U), comprising only an A frame
drawbar with 1 or 2 axles carrying a 5th wheel
coupling to enable a semitrailer to be drawn by
a rigid lorry or an agricultural tractor etc.
converter gear, converter dolly.
convertible, an open top car having a
removable roof, or a roof which can be folded
away.
convertible sedan, USA, a convertible having
wind-down glass side windows.
convex, curving outwards, as part of the
external surface of a sphere, the normal shape
for all vehicle external mirrors.
convex mirror, a mirror with a curved surface,
giving a wide angle of view; see also: multivex.
convey, to transport or carry goods or
passengers.
conveyance, any mechanically propelled
vehicle constructed or adapted for the carriage
of a person by land, water, or air.
convoi exceptionnel, French, oversized load.
convoy, a procession of at least 6 vehicles
travelling in line together from a common
origin to destination, sometimes escorted.
CoO, cost of ownership.
coolant, a liquid designed to remove surplus
heat from an engine, usually MEG, MPG, or
methanol is added to the water in the cooling
system of a vehicle to lower its freezing point
and raise its boiling point and prevent
corrosion; depending upon concentration these
can be as low as –53 °C, and up to +188 °C.
coolant expansion tank, a reservoir to collect
engine coolant when the liquid expands, and to
supply coolant to the cooling system.
coolant level indicator, a panel indicator lamp
which illuminates to give a warning when the
volume of coolant is below the minimum level.

coolant pump, water pump.
coolant temperature sensor, a thermistor that
sends a continuous signal to a gauge or to the
ECU.
cooling fan, a fan which pulls air through the
radiator of a liquid cooled engine.
cooling fins, metal strips cast or bonded onto a
surface in order to increase the surface area for
heat dissipation.
cooling system, the system that removes
surplus heat from an engine by circulating air
or liquid past parts of the engine, in the case of
liquid this circulates in a sealed system through
the engine and radiator assisted by a pump and
controlled by a thermostat.
cooling system pressure tester, a diagnostic
device to pressurise the cooling system to
detect any pressure loss.
COP, Europe, conformity of production, a
certification process to check the quality of
type approved vehicles to ensure they conform
with ECWVTA, LVA, VLV, or other
certification.
cop car, police car.
copper, a metallic element, a good electrical
conductor, normally used in vehicle wiring,
usually alloyed for other rigid electrical parts,
often used in engine bearings.
copper leads, sparkplug hv leads in which the
conductor is in the form of a copper wire
having a low resistance and relatively long life;
see also: carbon core.
cop shop, CB jargon, a police station.
copy?, CB jargon, did you hear me?
copying the mail, CB jargon, listening but not
transmitting.
COR, Club Off Road, UK.
cords, the strands of material forming the body
or belt plies of a tyre, typically made from:
aramid, fibreglass; rayon, nylon, polyester, or
steel.
core, a central part which is totally enclosed,
e.g. the tyre valve core.
core plug, a pressed steel disc, for sealing the
ends of coolant passageways within the
cylinder block.
corner, a place where 2 streets or roads
intersect, typically at 90°.
cornering, the negotiation of a significant
bend, especially at speed.
cornering ability, a quality of the chassis,
steering, suspension and tyres of a vehicle in
negotiating a significant bend at speed whilst
remaining stable.
cornering ability, a quality with respect to the
turning circle of a vehicle, *i.e.* its ability to turn
around sharp corners.
cornering brake control, a microprocessor
controlled system that will apply greater brake
pressure to the front wheel on the outside of a
bend if a driver brakes whilst steering,
developed by BMW.
cornering force, the lateral frictional force,
centripetal force, generated by a cornering tyre,

opposite to centrifugal force.

corner steady, a jack support for the corner of a parked caravan.

cornflakes, large flakes of rust typically found to have developed beneath wet carpets.

coroners alley, the central overtaking lane on a 3 lane road where priority is equal in both directions, named from the prevalence of head-on collisions on such a road; also named suicide lane.

corporate average fuel economy, USA, the average fuel economy for each model of vehicle as stated by each manufacturer.

corporate trainer, a person who teaches the employees of an organisation advanced or defensive driving techniques.

corporate training, a driver training program delivered to employees of an organisation to reduce their risk of becoming involved in a collision, and to reduce other motoring costs.

corrected eyesight, eyesight that meets the statutory minimum with optical assistance.

corrosion, a chemical action by which most metals oxidise or decompose, resulting in significant loss of strength or loss of other desirable characteristics.

corrosion inhibitor, a substance which prevents or reduces the rate of corrosion, *e.g.* an additive in an engine coolant.

corrugations, an uncomfortable surface condition on some tracks on sand and similar unpaved surfaces having endless transverse micro-ridges a few centimetres high caused by the resonance of vehicle suspension and causing significant vibration to vehicles passing over.

cost of ownership, the total of the fixed and variable costs of owning and operating a motor vehicle, including the costs of: depreciation, insurance, servicing, maintenance, road tax, fuel, parking fees, etc.

cost option, an accessory or optional extra not included in the price of a new car but which is available at additional cost.

Cotal gearbox, an electrically operated pre-selector gearbox.

cotter pin, split pin.

countdown marker, a rectangular sign in various colours depending upon the location, displaying 3 or 2 or 1 coloured diagonal bars indicating 300 yards, 200 yards, 100 yards, (270 m, 180 m, 90 m) respectively to a junction or hazard.

counterflow, a cylinder head with inlet and exhaust manifolds on the same side.

countershaft, USA, layshaft.

countersteer, to steer secondly in the opposite direction to initial steering, typically the action of regaining a straight line after an emergency lane change.

countersteer, to steer in the opposite direction to which the vehicle is yawing when attempting to correct and recover from a rear wheel skid.

countersteer, with regard to a cycle, to initially steer in the opposite direction to an intended turn to cause the bike to lean over sufficiently for the required turn.

counterweight, a weight on a crankshaft opposite each con rod journal, to reduce vibration and bearing wear.

country of final destination, the country to which a grey import or a parallel import is imported.

country mile, an inaccurate or unmeasured distance.

country road, a road that is not built-up on either side and is not a motorway, typically having countryside on both sides.

coupé, a cross between a saloon car and a sports car, having 2 doors, a fixed metal roof, a relatively powerful engine, but with very little space for rear passengers, often 2+2 configuration.

couple, to connect a trailer to a towing vehicle.

coupler, the socket at the front of a trailer A fame.

coupler height, the height of the centreline through a ball, or pintel coupling before a trailer is coupled.

coupler height, the height of the coupling surface of the 5th wheel before a semitrailer is coupled.

coupler offset, on a tractive unit, the horizontal distance ahead from the rear axle, or centre point of 2 or more axles, to the kingpin location in the 5th wheel.

coupling, hitch, a device to connect a trailer to a vehicle.

coupling capacity, the weight for which any coupling is rated as the maximum it can pull and/or carry.

course, a training course with which to learn how to drive a vehicle or a larger vehicle or learn how to improved or add to one's own level of driving ability, *e.g.* an advanced driving course.

course, the path of a vehicle as it moves along a road.

course, the route to be followed by a competitor.

course closing car, a vehicle that follows behind any rally and other event to collect any competitors that have crashed or broken down, often named sweeper car or broom wagon.

courtesy, to allow others to turn ahead of your vehicle when there is safe and suitable opportunity.

courtesy car, a car loaned to a customer whilst the customers car is being serviced or repaired.

courtesy light, the cabin interior light which illuminates automatically when a door is opened.

courtesy wave, a wave made in gratitude to another driver, usually by an extended hand, palm forward, fingers straight upwards, positioned just below the internal mirror for a couple of seconds where it can be seen by drivers in front or behind.

cover note, a temporary insurance document confirming: vehicle and driver details, degree of insurance cover, specifying the exact time of commencement of cover, and usually valid for a period of 14, 30, or 60 days.

cover the brakes, to position the right foot over the brake pedal, to reduce reaction time but without starting to press the pedal.

cover the clutch, to position the left foot over the clutch pedal, to reduce reaction time but without starting to press the pedal.

cover the horn, to place a finger directly on the horn control but without pressing, to reduce reaction time in high risk situations.

cowl, streamlined bodywork around a projecting part on an engine.

CPC, UK, Certificate of Professional Competence.

cpm, cost per mile, the operating cost of a vehicle including fixed and variable factors, assuming specific or average parameters.

CPT, Confederation of Passenger Transport, UK.

CPZ, controlled parking zone.

cr, compression ratio.

CR, climate responsive.

CR, Costa Rica, international vehicle distinguishing sign, see appendices.

CRA, Classic Rally Association, UK, organiser of international rallies.

crab manoeuvre, a control facility on some vehicles where the driver may steer the rear wheels the same direction as the front, so the vehicle will follow an angled course without turning, typically on some mobile cranes.

crabbing, the condition when the rear wheels of a vehicle with a live rear axle do not follow the line of the front wheels on a straight road, due to the rear axle not being at 90° to the centre line of the vehicle, see also: dog tracking.

crack on, to continue briskly on a journey.

crack on, to start a journey promptly.

crack the whip, the effect suffered by a trailer when the towing vehicle suddenly steers, *e.g.* makes a sudden lane change at speed, sometimes resulting in overturn of the trailer, and which increases in risk with the number of trailers such that the last trailer may very easily turn over.

crank, a device that converts reciprocating motion into rotary motion, or in some cases vice versa.

crankcase, the part of the engine in which the crankshaft rotates, usually including the sump.

crankcase breather, a pipe leading from the crankcase to the air inlet for combustion of fumes, or, on earlier vehicles directly to the road.

crankcase compression, in a 2 stroke engine, the initial compression of the air-fuel-oil mixture in the volume below the piston to enable the fresh charge to transfer to the cylinder.

crankcase dilution, dilution of the lubricating oil caused when the engine is cold and condensed petrol vapour is transmitted to the sump by blow-by.

crankcase emissions, pollutants entering the environment that originated in the crankcase.

crankcase ventilation, the removal of polluting gasses and vapours from the crankcase by air circulation into the air intake.

cranking, the action of the starter motor turning the crankshaft to start the engine, or attempting to start the engine.

cranking, the action of manually starting an engine with a starting handle.

cranking motor, USA, starter motor.

crankpin, a connecting rod journal on a crankshaft, commonly named big end journal.

crankshaft, a 1 piece steel casting or forging that is the main rotating member within the engine; having main journals and having offset journals to which the con rods are attached to convert the reciprocating motion of the pistons to rotary motion.

crankshaft journal, the part of the crankshaft that rotates in a main bearing.

crankshaft position sensor, a magnetic sensor that sends a signal to the ECU indicating crankshaft position and speed.

crankshaft pulley, a pulley on the non-drive end of the crankshaft that may drive the camshaft, alternator, water pump, or other auxiliaries, and may have sprockets or be grooved to drive a V belt or poly V belt.

crankshaft throw, the lateral distance between the centreline of the crankshaft and the centreline through a big end journal, half of the length of a piston stroke, sometimes named crank throw.

crank web, the angled part of a crankshaft between a main bearing journal and a big end journal.

crash, to collide with some object, person, or vehicle either on or off the road such that some damage is caused.

crash barrier, a safety barrier to prevent an out of control vehicle from travelling in an unwanted direction, *e.g.* down a steep embankment or crossing a central reservation.

crash box, crash gearbox.

crash course, intensive driving course.

crash cushion, impact attenuator.

crash data recorder, accident data recorder.

crasher, a competitive racing driver with a bad reputation resulting from frequently crashing off the track rather than finishing a race.

crash gearbox, a constant mesh gearbox, not having synchromesh, named from the noise made when the gears are not manually synchronised.

crash halt, a sudden stop by a vehicle.

crash helmet, headwear with a soft lining and a hard external shell to protect the wearer from head injury especially when riding a motorcycle, also used during most competitive

events in other vehicles, invented in 1904.
crashing, to drive quickly over a very rough surface such that the suspension bottoms or the wheels are not in permanent contact with the surface.
crash magnet, a driver involved in a disproportionately high number of collisions.
crash sensor, a deceleration sensor, typically a Hamlin switch, which triggers the air bags etc. when a specific rate and angle of deceleration occurs.
crash sensor safety, a system that recognises a sudden deceleration caused by a collision and activates the hazard lights, unlocks the central locking, and illuminates the interior lighting, developed by BMW.
crash stop, an emergency stop to avoid a crash.
crash stop, crash halt.
crash test, a controlled test in which a vehicle is propelled into another, or into a fixed object, in order to make a series of measurements including the amount of deformation to parts of the vehicle, see: NCAP.
crash the lights, to continue driving at speed through a red traffic signal.
crawler, a slow moving vehicle.
crawler, a tracklaying vehicle, a vehicle in which the wheels bear on an endless belt of linked segments, *e.g.* a bulldozer.
crawler gear, a very low gear or a range of very low gears, sometimes marked C or LL on many lorries and some buses, used for hill starts when fully loaded.
crawler lane, climbing lane.
CRD, common rail diesel.
crease, a fold in bodywork as the result of collision damage.
creep, the tendency of a vehicle with an automatic transmission to transmit a little power and start to move when D or R is selected without use of the accelerator, caused by the torque converter transmitting some power.
creeper, a low trolley enabling a mechanic to move and work under a vehicle.
creeper, an ultra low gear or range of gears selectable on some tractors typically denoted by a symbol of a snail, where the road speed at maximum revs may be as low as 0.36 km/h, or 100 mm/second (0.23 mph, or 4 inches per second).
creeper, USA, crawler gear.
CRER, Community Recording Equipment Regulation, 1970, Europe.
crest, the ridge along the outermost part of a screw thread.
crest, the top of a significant rise in the road surface, a place where a road crosses a ridge or sometimes 1 of several, or the top of a hill.
cresting, the action of approaching a crest on a road where sight lines become short.
cresting, the action of driving over a severe off-road crest where there is a probability of

grounding.
crew, any person including the driver carried in any competing vehicle.
crew bus, a dual purpose light commercial vehicle designed to carry a team of workmen and tools or equipment, having a 2nd row of seats behind the driver, and the rear being a van or pickup body.
crew cab, a commercial vehicle with an additional row of seats behind the front seats, sometimes named double cab, common on a USA style pickup.
crimp, a method of affixing terminals to wires by compression effecting a cold weld.
CRIS, Caravan Registration and Identification Scheme, UK.
crisscross belt, a 4 point seatbelt having regular 3 point lap and diagonal belts plus an extra diagonal belt across the chest in the opposite direction.
critical gap, the gap between a driver and the nearest oncoming vehicle that the driver will accept to initiate a turning or crossing manoeuvre 50 % of the time it is presented, measured in seconds.
critical speed, the speed of rotation at which a wheel or shaft becomes dynamically unstable due to resonance with the natural frequencies of vibration of the wheel.
critical speed, the speed of traffic at maximum highway capacity.
CrMo, chromium molybdenum.
CRO, coloured roads only, a road rallying note indicating the next clue lies along a classified road as marked on an OS map, *i.e.* white roads will not be used.
crock, a worn out vehicle, or a broken down vehicle.
crocodile clip, a spring clip connected to the end of a wire for making a temporary electrical connection, *e.g.* for circuit testing or on jump leads.
crocodiled, a dealer term for car upholstery that has been chewed up by a dog.
cross, to turn off a main road into a road to the offside across the front of oncoming traffic.
cross axle, the effect sometimes on rough ground when 2 diagonally opposite wheels have reached the top limit of suspension travel, and the other 2 diagonally opposite wheels have reached the bottom limit of suspension travel such that those wheels are tending to lift from the surface and lose traction.
cross axle diff lock, a device to lock an axle differential to increase traction on slippery surfaces.
cross country, to drive across land without evidence of previous passage of vehicles.
cross country, to drive on a track with an unmetalled surface.
cross country vehicle, an off-road vehicle, generally a 4x4.
cross counts, the number of times, usually up to 255 each second, that the exhaust oxygen

sensor voltage crosses the reference voltage of 0.45 volts.

cross differential lock, cross axle differential lock.

crossfall, the average camber between the road crown and road edge, typically a gradient of 2.5 % for water drainage.

crossfire injection, on some V engines, a fuel injection system where some of the cylinders injected are on the opposite side from the injection pump.

crossfiring, the firing of the wrong sparkplug, usually caused by damaged cable insulation or a faulty distributor cap or rotor.

crossflow, a cylinder head having inlet and exhaust manifolds on opposite sides.

crossflow radiator, a radiator in which the flow of coolant is side to side, to allow a reduction in bonnet height.

crosshead, a type of screwdriver with a 4 point cross forged into the tip with a specific axial angle at the centre, or a corresponding screw head.

crossing, an at grade location where a footpath crosses a road.

crossing, an at grade location where a railway line crosses a road.

crossing, an at grade location where roads cross.

cross intersection, cross roads, a 4 leg or 4 way junction.

crossmember, any structural component mounted transversely.

crossply tyre, a type of tyre construction having layers of cords running diagonally across the carcass, resulting in stiff side walls, becoming obsolete.

crossroads, a road junction where 2 roads cross or intersect, a 4 leg or 4 way junction, typically at 90°, and where 1 road may be designated priority over the other.

cross section, an imaginary view of any part if it were to be cut through any plane.

cross shaft, USA, the output shaft from a steering gearbox which turns the drop arm.

cross slope, a lateral gradient driven across when neither climbing nor descending a hillside, such that 1 side of the vehicle is higher then the other; if the cross slope exceeds the manufacturers recommendation the vehicle will roll over onto its side.

cross spoke wheel, an alloy wheel having an appearance to imitate a steel wire spoked wheel.

cross spring, a single transverse leaf spring used for the front suspension on some veteran and vintage cars.

cross thread, to screw together any parts such that the axes of male and female parts are not congruent, hence to damage the threads.

crossview, a view at an angle sideways, *e.g.* through a gap in a hedge, which provides advance information regarding other traffic flows, *e.g.* when approaching a junction or bend.

crosswalk, Australia, a pedestrian crossing.

crosswalk, USA, that part of the pavement (road) where at a junction the sidewalk lines would extend across the street and are areas set aside for pedestrians to cross the road with priority, sometimes marked by white lines and/ or controlled by traffic signals.

crosswind, a significant wind blowing on the side of a vehicle that may cause directional instability or may cause a tall vehicle to capsize.

CRoW, UK, Countryside and Rights of Way Act 2000.

crown, the centre of the road, especially where a significant camber raises the centre above the edges.

crown, the centreline through the tread of a tyre around its circumference.

crown, the top of a piston.

crowned rumble strip, a cross between a speed hump and a rumble strip created by replacing a lateral strip of road surface with several lines of cobbles extending up to 40 mm above the road surface.

crownwheel, a gearwheel with teeth set at 90° to its plane and which meshes with a smaller pinion gear at 90°, *e.g.* as the propeller shaft meets the rear axle.

crownwheel and pinion, a pair of gears used where a significant gear reduction is required, also where 2 shafts meet at 90°, *e.g.* as the propeller shaft meets the rear axle.

CRS, USA, child restraint seat, child safety seat.

CRT, constant regenerative trap.

crude oil, a dark liquid that occurs naturally under the ground, typically formed over a period of 200 million years.

cruise, to drive around without a precise destination or route.

cruise, to drive at any reasonably constant speed, either slow or fast.

cruise control, an electronic system with which to maintain a constant vehicle speed without the use of the accelerator pedal, regardless of changes in gradient, having controls for setting the speed on a steering column stalk.

cruiser, USA, police car.

cruise speed, the speed calculated to be an efficient speed for a long distance journey, allowing for fuel consumption and cost, drivers hours limits, and trip time.

cruising speed, a high speed at which a car can be driven constantly without strain, damage, overheating, etc. previously some margin below maximum speed but modern cars will typically cruise at maximum speed.

crumple zone, an area at the front of a car that is designed to deform to absorb the energy of a collision, so the passenger compartment remains intact during a frontal collision, also a zone at the rear.

crusher, a hydraulically operated machine designed to crush scrap cars to small cubes for recycling.

crv, compact recreational vehicle.

CSI, Commission Sportive Internationale, a subsidiary body within the FIA.

CSMA, Civil Service Motoring Association, UK.

CSS, crash sensor safety.

CSSA, Chambre Syndicale Suisse de L'Automobile et Branches Annexes, Switzerland.

csu, compact sport utility.

CT, a type of tyre having significant run-flat capability.

CT, community transport.

CTA, Community Transport Association, UK.

CTAA, Community Transport Association of America.

CTE, UK, Certificate of Temporary Exemption.

CTI, car theft index.

ctr, centre.

ctrls, controls.

CTS, Conti tyre system.

C&U, Construction and Use Regulations.

cubby, a receptacle for storing small items.

cubes, USA, cu.ins.

cubic capacity, the volume of an enclosed space, the swept volume of all cylinders in an engine, measured in cm³, cc, litres, or cu.ins.

cubic centimetre, a measure of volume and engine capacity, 1,000 cc = 1 litre.

cubic inch, the volume of a 1 inch cube, the measure of engine capacity in USA, 1 cu.ins = 16.387 cc.

cubs, CB jargon, non-traffic police.

CUEES, Car User Entrapment Extrication Society, UK.

Cugnot, Nicolas Joseph Cugnot, France, the maker of the first power driven vehicle in 1769.

cu.ins, cubic inch, the unit of engine size in USA, 1 cu.ins = 16.387 cc.

cul-de-sac, French, bottom of the bag, the only route out is the same as the route in, a local road open at 1 end only with provision for turning around; see: dead end.

culvert, a lateral underground channel carrying water beneath a road.

CUR, UK, Road Vehicles (Construction & Use) Regulations 1986.

curb, USA, kerb.

curb weight, USA, kerbweight, the weight of a vehicle with all fluids and fuel at maximum levels, including spare wheel and tools, but without the driver, load, or passengers.

cure, the gaining of strength by a resin at the conclusion of the chemical reaction after the resin sets and hardens.

current, the flow of electrons along a conductor, see: ampere.

curtain, a flexible material often on lorry sides for load protection, moveable as a curtain, and fastened and tensioned at the ends and bottom.

curtain airbag, an airbag that inflates downwards from the edges of a rooflining in severe side-impact collisions, to protect the head of each occupant during the collision.

curtain buckle, a device to provide vertical tension to a curtain side, many are used along the lower edge of the curtain.

curtain side, a type of lorry or trailer where the load is protected by flexible material on lorry sides, moveable as a curtain, and fastened and tensioned at the ends and bottom.

curve, a gentle bend, a bend where fixed-grip steering is used.

custom, a vehicle or part specifically designed and constructed or modified or painted to meet the requirements of the owner, typically for aesthetic purposes.

custom car, a car with significantly modified bodywork which may even be dysfunctional but designed to draw visual attention, typically painted a striking colour scheme, sometimes having a modified interior, engine, suspension, etc.

cut across, to pass closely across the front of another vehicle causing that driver to slow down.

cut and shut, a vehicle constructed by joining the undamaged front and rear halves of 2 damaged cars that are prepared and welded together; safe only if completed professionally.

cut in, the action of trailer wheels in following a smaller radius than those of the towing vehicle, especially those on a semitrailer at sharp corners and at slow speeds.

cut in, to move to a lane on the nearside after overtaking without leaving a safe space behind, especially if causing the overtaken vehicle to slow down.

cut it fine, to arrive on time but with no safety margin.

cutoff, the upper limit of illumination emitted by an asymmetrical dipped headlight beam.

cut out, a circuit breaker, a re-settable automatic electrical overload protector.

cut out, a driveability condition in a running engine, a temporary complete loss of power at irregular intervals.

cut out, a relay in a dynamo charging circuit that prevents the dynamo draining the battery at low revs and when parked.

cut out, outtrack, the action of semitrailer wheels in following a wider radius than those of the tractive unit on a moderate curve at speed, due to the effect of centrifugal force on the trailer.

cut-out box, USA, fuse block.

cutting a corner, to steer an incorrect line at a junction or bend, to go across the corner not around it, such that the inside wheels are not on the correct part of the road.

cutting compound, a paintwork polishing paste, a very fine abrasive designed to remove the top surface of the paint and create a new gloss surface.

cutting line, a series of lines established by the manufacturer where a crash damaged part my be cut out and replaced without reducing mechanical strength of the chassis or bodywork.

cutting torch, an oxyacetylene gas torch for cutting steel, used for dismantling vehicles or removing large sections for repair.

cut up, to cause unwarranted disruption to the passage of another vehicle.

cv, French, cheval vapour, horse sweat, metric horsepower, see: PS.

CV, a tyre design for commercial vehicles including buses and lorries.

CVBB, Commercial Vehicle Bodybuilders, UK.

cvj, constant velocity joint.

CVM, Company of Veteran Motorists, UK, now renamed GEM.

CVMA, Commercial Vehicle Manufacturers Association, UK.

CVRTC, Commercial Vehicle Road Transport Club, UK.

cvt, continuously variable transmission.

cwt, hundredweight, an imperial unit of weight equivalent to 0.05 ton, (50.8 kg), formally used to indicate the carrying capacity of some goods vehicles, obsolete.

Cx, coefficient of drag, usually abbreviated Cd.

CY, Cyprus, international vehicle distinguishing sign, see appendices.

cycle, a bicycle, typically having 2 wheels and propelled manually with pedals.

cycle, a series of repeating events, *e.g.* the Otto cycle.

cycle car, an early lightweight car having a maximum weight of $7^{1}/_{2}$ cwt unladen.

cycleguard, a mudguard mounted on the suspension such that as the wheel oscillates vertically the cycleguard remains a constant distance from the tyre, and over a front wheel it turns as the wheel steers, typically on an open wheel sports car.

cycle lane, a longitudinal division of a carriageway, along the nearside edge, which is reserved for cyclists, either permanently or with conditions, on which it is prohibited to drive or park.

cycle reservoir, the area between a stop line for vehicles and an advanced stop line for cyclists at some traffic signals.

cycle rickshaw, a hooded manually pedalled tricycle for the carriage of goods or 2 passengers, common in many Asian countries, named from Japanese jinrikisha.

cycle slip, a short dedicated cycle lane to enable cyclists to bypass chicanes, pinch points, gateways, etc, to avoid conflict with other traffic.

cycle time, the duration of time taken for a set of traffic signals to show each phase through each stage in sequence.

cycle track, a way which is part of a highway over which the public have right of way on pedal cycles, except for pedal cycles which are motor vehicles, with or without the right of way on foot.

cyclist, a person riding a pedal cycle.

cyclone, a series of static blades within some air filters that spin the induction air to cause some of the dust to gather in a dust bowl, to lengthen the service interval of the filter.

cyclone chamber, a device which separates oil vapour from air by centrifugal action, to return the oil to the sump to reduce oil consumption and reduce emissions, developed by Landrover.

cyl, cylinder.

cylinder, a round or tubular chamber, especially the circular bore in an engine block in which a piston reciprocates.

cylinder 1, the reference cylinder in an engine, upon which the timings of the other cylinders follow, usually the cylinder on the crankshaft furthest from the flywheel.

cylinder bank, any single row of cylinders in a H, V, W, or X engine.

cylinder barrel, a tubular unit having a cylinder bore internally and cooling fins externally, fitted between the crankcase and the cylinder head.

cylinder block, usually a metallic casting with a bore for each piston, the basic framework of an engine, to which most other parts are attached.

cylinder displacement, the volume swept by a piston between tdc and bdc.

cylinder head, a metallic casting forming part of the combustion chamber, machined to house the engine valves and their operating mechanism, sparkplugs and/or injectors, and carries part of the cooling system.

cylinder head gasket, a gasket located between the cylinders and the cylinder head to prevent leaks of compression and coolant, typically of copper sheet with folded edges.

cylinder liner, a replaceable sleeve set into the cylinder block to form a bore, usually a steel sleeve in alloy castings.

cylinder sleeve, a replaceable liner set into the cylinder block to form a bore, usually a steel liner in alloy castings.

CZ, Czech Republic, international vehicle distinguishing sign, see appendices.

D

D, diagonal construction, crossply, a designation within a tyre size coding.

D, diesel.

D, diesel, an oil approved for use by CCMC in diesel engines.

D, drive, on an automatic gearbox it allows automatic selection by the gearbox of the best forward gear to match road speed and the power demand from the driver.

D, down, on a road rally typically a lower spot height.

D, dysgwr, Welsh, learner, a plate bearing the letter D signifying the driver is a learner, permitted in Wales as an alternative to an L plate.

D, Germany, international vehicle distinguishing sign, see appendices.

D, a hire car size and price category for cars based upon their floor pan; a medium sized family car that will seat 5 with comfort, *e.g.* Audi A6, or BMW 5-series sized.

D, does not meet security requirements, referring to insurance sub grouping.

D, dynamo live, the terminal having the live output from the dynamo.

D, Europe, a driving licence category for any bus having more than 8 passenger seats, and permitting drawing of a trailer up to 750 kg MAM.

D, USA, a driving license and vehicle category for cars and any motor vehicle with a GVWR not exceeding 16,000 lbs (7.25 tonnes) except those vehicles requiring a class A, B, C, L, or M, license.

D, a write-off category in which the damage is confined to windows, locks, and/or bent panels, but where the car remains roadworthy, *e.g.* the state in which stolen cars are typically recovered after the insurer has paid out.

D1, a European driving licence category for minibuses having between 9 and 16 passenger seats, and permitting drawing of a trailer up to 750 kg MAM.

D1, the lowest drive gear on an automatic gearbox, it restricts automatic selection by the gearbox to the lowest forward gear only.

D1, dual single lane carriageways.

D1+E, a European driving licence category for minibuses drawing a trailer where the minibus is in subcategory D1 and its trailer has a MAM exceeding 750 kg, provided that the MAM of the combination thus formed does not exceed 12,000 kg and the MAM of the trailer does not exceed the kerbweight of the minibus.

D2, a drive mode on an automatic gearbox, it restricts automatic selection by the gearbox to the 2 lowest forward gears only.

D2, dual 2 lane carriageways.

D3, a drive mode on an automatic gearbox, it restricts automatic selection by the gearbox to the 3 lowest forward gears only.

D3, dual 3 lane carriageways.

D4, a drive mode on an automatic gearbox, it restricts automatic selection by the gearbox to the 4 lowest forward gears only, on a 4 speed system it is merely D.

D band, a VED category within which vehicles emitting over 185 g/km of CO_2 are charged.

D pillar, the rearmost side pillar joining the roof to the body on an estate car.

D segment car, a size category for cars based upon their floor pan; a medium sized family car that will seat 5 with comfort, a common size as a repmobile.

dab, a short operation of some controls, especially the footbrake or accelerator, usually causing jerky driving.

DAG, Drivers Action Group, a pressure group, UK.

dagmar, USA, each of a pair of large bullet shaped bumper protrusions, fashionable on some 1950s cars, named after a buxom TV personality.

daily checks, a sequence of checks to all critical vehicle systems typically prompted by the mnemonic POWER, for checks of petrol, oils, waters, electrics, rubbers.

daily driving, when referring to EC drivers hours, any period of 24 hours beginning when work starts, in which 9 hours may be spent driving, increased to 10 hours twice per week, with a 45 minute break after maximum $4^1/_2$ hours driving or multiples of 15 minute breaks totalling 45 minutes in the same period.

daily duty, when referring to domestic drivers hours, a driver must not be on duty for more than 11 hours per day.

daily rest period, when referring to EC drivers hours, a time of at least 1 hour when the driver is free to dispose of the time as wished, with a minimum of 11 consecutive hours daily rest, reducing to 9 hours on not more than 3 days in the week, providing equivalent rest is taken the following week.

Daimler, Gottlieb Daimler, the inventor of the first petrol engine in 1883, maker of the first prototype car by fixing an engine to a horse drawn carriage in 1886, and maker of the first 4 speed gearbox in 1889.

Dakar, the town in Senegal in west Africa where the annual Paris–Dakar rally finishes.

DAKS, Danske Automobil Komponentfabrikkers Sammenslutning, now AUTIG.

damage, see: direct, indirect, old, referred, secondary.

damage, to cause harm or injury less than complete destruction to a person or animal or property such that the health of a person or animal is impaired, or the value or usefulness of property is reduced.

damper, a device usually hydraulic that converts kinetic energy into thermal energy, typically mounted on the suspension between the wheel and chassis to prevent unwanted chassis/wheel oscillation after a deflection of the suspension, to increase safety and comfort, commonly misnamed shock absorber.

damping force, the amount of damping performed by a damper.

dangerous driving, an act committed by a driver if the way he drives falls below what would be expected of a competent driver, and, it would be obvious to a competent and careful driver that driving in that way would be dangerous, or, it would be obvious to a competent and careful driver that driving the vehicle in its current state would be dangerous, (RTA).

dangerous fault, a fault committed by a driver which directly impinges upon the safety of others.

dark adaptation, the adjustment of the eye to low levels of illumination which results in increased sensitivity to light.

DARR, digital accident research recorder.

dash, dashboard.

dash, to rush, to drive without thought for others.

dashboard, the panel on which drivers instruments are mounted; originally the wooden board at the front of a veteran car, named from the wooden panel on a horse drawn carriage which protected the driver from stones dashed up from the horses hooves.

dashboard warning indicator, see: tell-tale.

dashpot, a damper on a carburettor to reduce the rate the throttle valve is closed.

databus, a 2 core wiring loom around a vehicle carrying digital information and connecting all components.

data communication link, a connector on a vehicle by which a service bay diagnostic computer can communicate with the electronic modules on a vehicle.

data link connector, a connector on a vehicle by which a service bay diagnostic computer can communicate with the electronic modules on a vehicle.

day cab, a lorry cab without any sleeping accommodation.

daylighted, a bend where the elevated ground around the inside of a bend has been cut back to significantly improve sightlines across the bend.

daytime running lamp, a lamp facing in a forward direction used to make the vehicle more easily visible when driving during daytime, (C&U).

daytime running lights, a lighting system which activates the dip beam (on some models main beam) headlights at a reduced intensity during daylight to keep the car highly visible to other vehicles; on some models a dash-mounted sensor automatically switches between DRL's and the normal intensity low beams according to the lighting conditions, e.g. nighttime, or in a tunnel, etc see also: dim dip.

dazzle, the temporary saturation of a drivers eyes with an intense light or reflection such that other objects less bright cannot be seen.

dB, decibel, a measure of the amplitude of a sound level.

DBC, dynamic brake control.

dbw, drive by wire.

dc, direct current.

DC rim, drop centre rim.

DCL, data communication link.

DCS, detonation control system.

DDA, Disabled Drivers Association, UK.

DDE, digital diesel electronics.

DDMC, Disabled Drivers Motor Club, UK.

D+E, a European driving licence category for any bus having more than 8 passenger seats, and permitting drawing of a trailer exceeding 750 kg MAM.

de-activate, the action of the driver to be able to switch off the potential operation of some function, e.g. passenger air bag, or alarm system.

dead axle, a non-driven axle.

dead battery, a flat battery, a battery holding insufficient or no charge.

dead centre, the position of the crankshaft when the con rod little end, crankpin, and the main bearing are in line such that the turning force is zero, and occurs at $0°$ and $180°$ at the top and the bottom of each stroke.

dead end, not a through road, a local road open at 1 end only without special provision for turning around; see also: cul-de-sac.

dead ground, an area of road usually in the middle distance that is hidden from view in a dip, or beyond a crest, potentially containing unseen oncoming traffic.

dead man, a trailer brake operated from the lorry drivers seat.

dead pedal, a footrest for the left foot on many manual and automatic vehicles, to aid comfort and balance the driver, positioned to the left of the clutch.

dead stop, to cease movement.

on a vehicle.

dealer, a person who buys and sells vehicles for profit.

death driver, a driver responsible for a collision involving the death of a person.

death rattle, various sounds from an engine in poor condition indicating it is very likely to cease running at any moment.

death seat, the centre of the rear seat on a bus facing along the aisle.

death trap, a vehicle which is in a condition too dangerous to be used.

DEB, decompression engine brake.

de badge, the removal or non-fitting of all external identification regarding make, model, engine size, etc. from the rear of a car.

debus, to get out from, or to take equipment out from, a vehicle.

decal, decalcomania, a transfer or semitransparent design, wording, or logo on an adhesive plastic sheet applied to vehicle bodywork for aesthetic purposes.

decarbonise, the action of physically removing carbon deposits from combustion chamber surfaces.

decelerate, to reduce speed, or to lose velocity, typically by lifting off the accelerator.

deceleration, negative acceleration, to slow down.

deceleration fuel cutoff, the action of the ECU in stopping the fuel supply when the engine is at normal temperature, the throttle is closed, and the engine speed is above idle.

deceleration lane, an additional lane along the nearside of a major road, on a motorway after the diverging lane, to facilitate vehicles slowing after leaving a high speed road before a junction.

decelerometer, an instrument which measures deceleration, *i.e.* braking performance, typically used when performing a brake test on a vehicle which cannot be tested on a rolling road, *e.g.* typically vehicles having full time 4x4, or having a limited slip differential.

de chrome, the removal or non-fitting of all external identification regarding make, model, engine size, etc. from the rear of a car.

decision sight distance, the distance required for a driver to detect an unexpected or otherwise difficult to perceive information source or hazard in a roadway environment that may be visually cluttered, recognise the hazard or its threat potential, select an appropriate speed and course, and initiate and complete the required safety manoeuvre safely and efficiently.

deck, the floor or roadway of a bridge.

deck, the floor of each saloon in a bus.

deck, the goods carrying floor of a van, lorry, or trailer.

deckhand, warehouse staff who load and/or unload each lorry.

deck lid, USA, the engine cover on a rear engined car.

declamp, to remove a wheel clamp from a clamped vehicle.

declutch, the action of pressing the clutch pedal down, to press the clutch out of engagement, to disconnect the drive from the engine to the gearbox.

decoke, the action of physically removing carbon deposits from combustion chamber surfaces.

decompression engine brake, a retarding device that maximises engine braking by decompressing the cylinder directly after compression, thereby preventing the compressed air from driving the piston, used on lorries, developed by Mack.

decompression valve, a manually operated lever on older diesel lorries and buses which releases the compression in most cylinders to allow hand cranking and starting on 1 cylinder.

dedicated lane, a lane on a multilane road which is used by traffic going to a specific route only.

De Dion, an axle/suspension system comprising a driven axle but where the differential or transaxle is mounted on the chassis hence is a sprung weight and does not comprise part of the unsprung weight, also the drive shafts have uj's at each end to keep the wheels vertical to give satisfactory levels of handling and driveability; the actual arrangement of the suspension mechanism and springs can take many forms.

De Dion, Count Albert de Dion, France, designer of a rear axle suspension system in 1894 that continues as a current design.

de-energise, to deactivate, to prevent any movement or action.

deep layby, a longitudinal parking area off the side of the road but parallel to the road and separated from the carriageway by kerbing and access roads.

deep reduction, a range of very low ratio crawler gears, an addition to the transmission of some lorries, sometimes marked LL.

deer alert, an ultra-sound emitter mounted on the front of a vehicle in an attempt to warn animals of the approach of a vehicle by emitting a high-pitched noise.

defective eyesight, a person having a sight defect that prevents them from meeting the statutory minimum sight standards.

Defence School of Transport, each of several military driver training schools operated by the armed forces, UK.

defensive driver, a person who displays the art of controlling the space around his/her vehicle using fundamental principles combined with a planned system of driving, having the correct attitude and sufficient skill to control the vehicle with precision, driving with concentration, awareness, and anticipation, and always having an escape route.

defensive driving, the art of maintaining and defending (controlling) the space around your vehicle using a set of fundamental principles combined with a planned system of driving, having the correct attitude and sufficient skill to control the vehicle with precision, driving with concentration, awareness, and anticipation, and always having an escape route; if nothing enters the defended space it is impossible to have a collision.

definitive bridleway, a way normally intended for use on horseback, pedal cycle, or on foot only, although in some cases also carrying motor vehicle rights.

definitive footpath, a highway over which the public have right of way on foot, although in some cases also carrying motor vehicle rights; see also: footway, footpath.

definitive map and statement, the official record of all public rights of way available for inspection at county and district council offices, but not necessarily showing all unsurfaced rights of way, and some paths may also have vehicular rights; the map statement details the width and any gates etc.

deflated, the condition of a tyre containing less air than specified by the vehicle manufacturer.

deflation warning system, a system that will detect a pressure loss in a tyre and give a warning to the driver, using the ABS wheel sensors, developed by Dunlop.

deflection, the upwards movement of the suspension, the bump stroke.

deflection, see: tyre deflection.

deflection arrow, a curved arrow painted on a road surface showing where traffic may need to change position, typically where the number of lanes is reducing or when approaching an area where overtaking is prohibited.

deflection rate, spring rate.

deflector, an angled device above a lorry cab to direct airflow to reduce wind resistance from a bulky load or body.

defogger, USA, demister.

degrease, to remove oil, grease, or wax from a surface or part.

degressive braking, braking which begins with firm application of the brake pedal then progressively reduces in intensity until the vehicle is at the required speed or stationary; typically used to achieve a safe and controlled approach to hazards when no vehicle is initially close behind.

deice, to remove ice from vehicle windows, often by the use of ethylene glycol or alcohol, or with warm water.

deicer, a chemical substance used for removing ice from windows.

deicer, a mechanical tool used for removing ice from windows.

deionised water, water which has been chemically cleaned to remove all anions and cations, so it may be used to top-up batteries.

delaminate, the condition when the tread of a tyre separates internally from its carcass.

delay, the time lost while traffic is impeded by some element over which the driver has no control.

delayed prohibition notice, a legal restriction on the use of a vehicle but allowing 10 days for the repair of minor faults.

delineation, the system of marking the road surface, typically with painted lines but also with reflective studs, reflective hazard posts, and temporarily by lines of cones.

delineator, hazard post.

delivery, the discharging of a fluid, *e.g.* fuel into a tank.

delivery, the transportation of a new car from the factory to the dealer.

delivery mileage, the distance a vehicle is driven from leaving the production line, to storage, to docks, to a transporter, to a dealers yard, etc. typically up to 10 km (6 miles) but in special cases with prior arrangement it can be more.

delivery van, a small goods vehicle for local deliveries having a closed body, typically up to 3.5 tonnes.

delta link, a semi-independent rear suspension system comprising a transverse and a longitudinal arm on each side, on some fwd cars.

de luxe, a luxury model car, above a CL but below a GL.

demineralised water, deionised water.

demister, a system that will blow warmed or dried air onto the inside of a windscreen to remove or prevent condensation.

demonstration drive, a drive by an instructor to teach a driver by example a skill, technique, or procedure, usually with a full commentary throughout.

demonstration drive, a familiarisation and acceptance drive of a vehicle by a potential purchaser.

demonstrator, a vehicle used by a dealer for test drives by potential customers until it is a few months old.

demount, to remove from a rigid lorry the complete body of the goods container in order to take another.

demountable, the body of some lorries which are designed to be quickly removable for interchangeability, usually having hydraulics, some with inbuilt legs.

demountable flange, the removable rim held by a locking ring on a split rim wheel.

demountable pod containers, containers having hydraulic rams to enable self demounting from a flatbed and self lowering to ground level.

demountable rim, the removable wheel rim and locking ring on a split rim wheel.

denatured alcohol, USA, methylated spirit, a mixture of ethyl and methyl alcohols sometimes with colouring, used as a cleaning solvent, also as an antifreeze agent in windscreen washer fluid.

Denloc, a special wheel and tyre pairing having run-flat capability, developed by Dunlop, obsolete.

Denovo tyre, a special tyre fitted to a dedicated rim having run-flat capability, developed by Dunlop, obsolete.

de-NO$_x$, the action of a catalytic converter designed specifically to reduce nitrogen oxides in diesel exhausts when running on low sulphur fuel.

density, traffic density.

density, the degree of compactness of a substance, expressed as mass per unit volume, liquids and solids are often compared to water having a density of 1.

dent, a depression in a body panel which is the result of damage caused by an impact.

dent puller, a tool used to pull minor dents to their original shape.

Denver boot, a clamp which may be applied to the wheel of a car as a penalty for not complying with parking restrictions, it renders the car immovable until a fine has been paid, first used in Denver USA.

dépannage, French, any breakdown and repair service.

Department of Transport, Local Government and the Regions, UK, a ministerial body having many branches and agencies including the DVO which comprises: DVLA, DSA, VCA, and VI.

departure angle, the maximum gradient at the rear of a vehicle, that may be climbed in reverse from a level surface without any part of the vehicle contacting the surface.

dependant suspension, non-independent suspension, a suspension whereby any vertical movement of a wheel causes a reaction in the other wheel on the same axle which will result in changes of camber, toe, or tracking angles in the other wheel.

deposit, a coating on the surface of another, usually unwanted, especially in a hot water cooling system.

deposit, a layer of sediment in a tank, chamber, or fluid system

deposit, a sum of money paid initially as part payment for the purchase of a vehicle.

depreciation, the loss of value of a vehicle due to age and mileage, sometimes influenced by physical condition.

depth gauge, a post at the entrance to a ford which is calibrated to indicate the depth of the water.

depth perception, the ability to distinguish the relative distance of objects in visual space, used to interpret their motion over multiple observations.

de-rate, to restrict an engine to a lower output than the standard specification.

Dere Street, an ancient Roman road from York to Corbridge, UK.

DERF, Driver Education Research Foundation, UK.

derust, to remove rust from steel.

DERV, diesel engined road vehicle, originally; now used to imply white diesel.

design, an idea, concept, or plan, a scheme of lines or shapes.

designated country, any country which is deemed to have a driver testing system approximately equivalent to the quality of a UK driving test, including: all 15 EC countries plus Australia, Barbados, Canada, Cyprus, Gibraltar, Guernsey, Hong Kong, Iceland, Isle of Man, Japan, Jersey, Kenya, Liechtenstein, Malta, New Zealand, Norway, Singapore, South Africa, Switzerland, Virgin Islands, Zimbabwe.

designated road, a non-trunk road designated because of its importance.

designer, a person who conceives the plan of a technical specification in the construction of a vehicle; *e.g.* the suspension or transmission; see also: stylist.

design speed, the maximum safe speed that could be maintained over a length of road when the design conditions are met; for a recently constructed road the design speed will usually be well in excess of the imposed speed limit

design volume, the number of vehicles expected to use a highway in 1 hour, determined at the design stage before construction.

design weight, in relation to the gross weight, each axle weight or the train weight of a motor vehicle or trailer, the weight at or below which in the opinion of the Secretary of State or a person authorised in that behalf the vehicle could safely be driven on roads, (C&U).

desirable minimum stopping sight distance, a design consideration for a bend or other feature where forward visibility is interrupted, but having a greater safety margin over the SSD.

desire line, the ideal route favoured by pedestrians when crossing a road especially at a junction, and which is typically as straight and direct as possible to minimise time and energy regardless of traffic.

desmodronic, a system to mechanically close the cylinder valves without the need for springs, so allowing the engine to run to higher revs.

destination , the finishing point of a journey.

destination display, destination indicator.

destination indicator, a panel displaying externally from a bus the name of the destination or route the bus is taking.

detachable rim, a split rim, a wheel made in sections which can be dismantled to remove and fit a tyre, typically on lorries, agricultural, and industrial vehicles.

detector loop, a wide coil of wire buried in the road surface feeding to a microprocessor to recognise numbers of vehicles and vehicle types due to their magnetic footprint, typically placed on approach to traffic signals.

detent, a feature of a gear selector system that gives a good feel, reducing the possibility of wrong selection.

detent, a small depression in a shaft, rail, or rod into which a pawl or ball locates to provide a locking effect.

detergent oil, a lubricating oil with additives to keep impurities in suspension, to prevent the formation of sludge.

detonation, an uncontrolled secondary explosion in the combustion chamber occurring after the spark, resulting in spontaneous combustion of the remaining air-fuel mixture, also named pinking.

detonation control system, an electronic spark control system to prevent pinking.

detonation sensor, a device that recognises detonation and sends a signal to the ECU to reduce or eliminate its occurrence.

DETR, Department of Environment Transport and the Regions, now renamed DTLR, UK.

detune, to deliberately reduce the power output of an engine by changing part of its design.

DEUA, Diesel Engine Users Association, now IDGTE.

device, a mechanism, tool, or special equipment designed to serve a specific function.

dewaxed oil, a lubricating oil that has had a portion of its wax removed to improve some qualities.

DFC, diagnostic fault code.

dfv, double four valve, a vee engine configuration having dohc and 4 valves per cylinder.

DG, USA, diesel general, a lubricating oil for diesel engines.

DGSA, dangerous goods safety advisor.

DGW, UK, design gross weight.

dhaba, a truck stop in India and neighbouring countries.

dhc, drophead coupé.

Di, direct injection diesel engine.

DI, direct injection.

DI, driveability index.

DIA, Driving Instructors Association, UK.

diabetes, a medical condition that may prevent a person holding a driving licence due to the risk of losing consciousness whilst driving.

diagnose, to analyse the root cause of a problem or failure in any vehicle part.

diagnostic computer, a microprocessor based system used for diagnostic testing of a vehicle.

diagnostic connector, a connector on a vehicle by which a service bay diagnostic computer can communicate with the electronic modules on a vehicle.

diagnostic fault code, a numeric identifier for a fault condition identified by the vehicle on-board diagnostic system, to enable determination of the actual fault.

diagnostic testing, to examine a vehicle system to detect a fault, typically by means of a diagnostic computer.

diagnostic trouble code, USA, diagnostic fault code.

diagonal, USA, a tyre of crossply construction.

diagonal belt, a seat belt worn diagonally over the chest with no lap strap, on some older USA cars, not safe due to probability of submarining under the belt in a collision.

diagonal blocking, the principle of applying wheel chocks to the wheel diagonally opposite from that being raised from the road surface for a wheel change.

diagonal split brakes, a dual circuit braking system where each circuit operates a front and diagonally opposite rear wheel for reasonably balanced braking if a circuit should fail.

dials, the instruments on the instrument panel.

diameter, a straight line passing from side to side through the centre of a circle.

diamond honing, microscopic diagonal scratches that are applied to the bore of a cylinder to aid oil retention and reduce wear.

Diamond instructor, UK, a driving instructor who holds a diploma in driving instruction and has passed the Cardington special test at grade A.

diamond junction, a grade separated junction having 1 overbridge over or under the main road and staggered crossroads at each end of the bridge feeding to/from the sliproads and lesser roads; named from the resulting plan shape; see appendices.

diamond sign, road signs for the use of tram drivers.

Diamond test, UK, an advanced driving test administered by the DIA.

diaphragm, a thin sheet of flexible material, usually circular, to divide compartments and form part of the operating mechanism, *e.g.* in a fuel pump or some valves.

diaphragm spring, a spring in the form of a disc with internal radial sprung fingers, commonly used in clutches.

dickey seat, an additional seat in the rear of some vintage cars, when not in use it folds into the boot.

DID, direct injection diesel.

DID, driver information display.

Diesel, Rudolf Diesel, the inventor of the compression ignition internal combustion engine burning light oil, in 1893.

diesel clatter, a characteristic noise from many diesel engines, especially when starting from cold.

diesel cycle, an internal combustion engine operating cycle having 4 strokes: induction of air, compression of air, power, exhaust, where the fuel is injected at the end of the compression stroke and ignites due to the high temperature of the compressed air.

diesel engine, an internal combustion engine with a high compression ratio, burning oil instead of petrol, without a spark ignition system, the fuel burns due to the temperature created by high compression of air.

diesel fuel, a hydrocarbon, a light oil obtained by distillation from crude oil, the fraction of crude oil that distils after kerosene, typically in several qualities: ULSD containing less than 0.003 % m/m (30 ppm) sulphur; LSD having less than 0.03 % m/m (300 ppm) sulphur; and basic diesel (not available in Europe or USA) containing up to 0.5 % m/m (5,000 ppm) sulphur.

diesel index, an empirical expression for the correlation between the aniline number of a diesel fuel and its ignitability; a rating based on ignition qualities, high quality fuel has a high index number.

dieseling, the condition when a carburetted si engine runs on after the ignition is switched off; caused when fuel continues to be available and there is sufficient heat in the combustion chamber to ignite the air-fuel mixture.

diesel knock, a combustion knock caused by delayed ignition then a sudden high pressure explosion.

diesel oil, a heavy oil residue occasionally used as heating fuel, but not diesel fuel.

diff, differential.

differential, an arrangement of gears in the form of an epicyclic train usually within a drive axle or on the output of the gearbox, that allows the drive wheel on the outside of a bend to travel faster than the wheel on the inside of a bend whilst both transmitting equal power.

differential lock, a mechanism to lock a differential, thereby causing both wheels on an axle, or both outputs to 2 or more axles, to turn at the same speed, to increase traction on slippery surfaces.

differential steering, a mechanism for the steering of some tracklaying vehicles causing simultaneously 1 track to move rearwards and 1 track to drive forwards enabling the vehicle to turn on the spot; see also: brake steering.

diff lock, differential lock.

dig, digital.

digital, a microprocessor based data processing system.

digital, information displayed in the form of digits.

digital accident research recorder, a black box type of recorder linked to the airbag sensor, which measures and stores speed changes during a frontal collision, developed by Volvo.

digital diesel electronics, a microprocessor controlled system that determines the exact time to commence the fuel injection, the fuel volume, and the charge pressure, developed by BMW.

digital instruments, instruments that display a direct readout showing an exact figure.

digital motor electronics, the ECU, the microprocessor control of all major engine functions *e.g.* fuel injection, ignition, and auxiliary functions, developed by BMW.

digital tachograph, a microprocessor based tachograph that records driving hours, rest periods, speed, distance, time, and other

parameters onto a chip.

dim dip, a function of headlamps in fulfilling the role of daytime running lamps when the headlamp light output is electronically reduced to between 15 % and 30 % of normal intensity.

dimmer, USA, dipswitch.

dimmer control, a minor control on some vehicles by which the brightness of the instrument panel may be varied at night.

DIN, Deutsches Institüt für Normung, German Institute for Standardisation.

ding, a minor dent, including carpark rash.

dinge, a minor dent, including carpark rash.

dingy towing, USA, the action of towing a car driverless as a trailer with all wheels on the road surface using an A frame.

dinosaur juice, CB jargon, fuel.

diode, an electronic device that allows current to flow in 1 direction only, 6 are normally used to rectify the alternator output to dc.

dip, to switch the headlamps to low beam.

dip, dipped headlights only should be used in that location when on a road rally, known to be a PR sensitive area.

dip, a length of road having a surface several metres lower than the preceding length.

dip beam, dipped headlights.

Dip DI, Diploma in Driving Instruction, a UK qualification held by some driving instructors worldwide.

diplopia, double vision, a medical condition which prevents sufferers from driving due to confused observation.

dipped beam headlamp, a lamp used to illuminate the road ahead of the vehicle without causing undue dazzle or discomfort to road uses ahead.

dipped beam headlights, beams of light from the headlamps angled downwards between 0.5 % and 2.75 % such that the top of the beam typically strikes the road surface no more than 50 metres ahead (160 feet) so as not to dazzle drivers ahead.

dipper, dipswitch.

dipper bulb, a bulb having 2 filaments which are illuminated separately to give either of 2 beam patterns, developed by Osram in 1925.

dipping headlamps, headlamps which can alternately emit either of 2 light beams, first used by Morris in 1926.

dipping mirror, an internal mirror having a flat sheet of glass in front, such that the mirror may be angled downwards with a small lever leaving only a weak reflection from the clear glass.

dippy driver, a driver wrongly continuing to use dipped headlights on a clear road at night when mainbeam headlights should be used to advantage.

dipstick, a calibrated measuring rod for checking the level of fluids, *e.g.* the engine oil.

dipswitch, a switch used to alternate between the usage of main beam and dip beam of the headlamps to meet traffic conditions, normally at fingertip control near the steering wheel.

DiPTAC, Disabled Persons Transport Advisory Committee, UK.

dip the clutch, to depress fully the clutch pedal to disengage the engine from the transmission.

direct current, electric current that flows 1 one direction only.

direct damage, damage caused to a vehicle at the principle point of contact in a collision; see also: damage.

direct drive, a transmission mode where the engine, transmission, and propshaft all rotate at the same speed, typical of 4th gear on many rwd cars.

direct injection, a system by which the fuel is injected directly into the combustion chamber in petrol and diesel engines, the most efficient design but causing noise in a diesel engine.

directional sliproad, a sliproad which leaves from the side of the carriageway in the direction in which it turns, especially 1 that exits adjacent to the central reservation and continues turning to the offside to join a route in that direction.

directional stability, a resistance to unintentional yaw especially when due to some minor driver inputs, side winds, or longitudinal ridges in a road surface; a desirable design parameter of a vehicle especially at speed.

directional tyre, a tyre which is designed for maximum water dispersal or other specific purpose, having blocks and grooves which are angled backwards and outwards from the centre of the footprint, rotation arrows on each sidewall, and must be fitted so forward rotation is in the correct direction only; typically for high performance cars but also mud clearing tyres on 4x4 vehicles or a tractor.

direction indicator, an amber light near the each corner of a vehicle and sometimes on the sides, that flashes to indicate the drivers intention to change position in that direction.

direction indicator lamp, an amber lamp used to indicate to other road users that the driver intends to change direction to the right or to the left, (C&U).

direction of travel, the geographic direction in which a vehicle is or was moving, regardless of the direction it is facing.

direction sign, a road traffic sign, generally rectangular and with a background colour of either blue, green, white, black, yellow, or brown depending upon the type of route.

direct route, the shortest navigational distance between 2 places, but not necessarily the quickest.

dirt road, a road with a bare earth surface, usually loose but reasonably smooth.

dirt track, a dirt road with a poor surface, it may have deep ruts, holes, or other defects.

dirty air, very turbulent air directly behind a racing car or other high speed vehicle; see also: clean.

DIS, driver information system.

DIS, see: NDIS.

disabled, a driver having a specific medical condition such that they are permitted to drive only a vehicle with modified or adapted controls.

disabled, a driver or a passenger having a specific medical condition such that they are permitted parking concessions as afforded by the blue badge scheme.

disabled, a vehicle that cannot be driven due to breakdown or collision damage.

disc, a circular flat plate.

disc brake, a design of wheel brake having a disc that rotates with the wheel and which is retarded by friction pads that exert high pressure on both faces of the disc.

discharge, to take electrical power from a battery such that its reserve of power reduces.

discharge lamp, a device that emits light when a high voltage is applied to a gas in a glass enclosure, *e.g.* a xenon headlamp.

discharged battery, a flat battery having insufficient or no residual charge.

disc lock, a safety wheel nut.

disconnect, to remove a connection to a mechanical or electrical device, typically a hose or a wire.

disc wheel, a wheel in which a solid disc of material joins the hub to the rim.

disc zone, an area where free parking for a limited time is permitted provided the driver displays a parking disc, a cardboard clock face, to indicate the time of arrival.

disembark, to remove a vehicle from a ferry, ship, or aircraft.

disengage, to depress fully the clutch pedal, to press the clutch out, to cease transmission of power through the clutch.

disengage, to move the gear lever to select neutral.

dismantle, to separate the pieces of a unit, to disassemble the parts of an engine, transmission, or vehicle, etc.

displacement, the volume swept by a piston between bdc and tdc multiplied by the number of pistons.

disqualification, withdrawal of the privilege of holding a driving licence, an act performed by a court following a motoring conviction.

distilled water, water which has been condensed from steam thereby having no impurities, used to top-up batteries.

distinctive letters, the system of black letters used on a distinguishing sign to identify in which country a vehicle is registered, typically 1, 2, or 3 letters 80 mm (3.15 inches) tall on a 175 mm x 115 mm (6.9 inch x 4.5 inch) white oval plate displayed at the rear of a vehicle; see appendices.

distinguishing sign, the system of distinctive letters used to identify in which country a vehicle is registered, typically 1, 2, or 3 black letters 80 mm (3.15 inches) tall on a 175 mm x 115 mm (6.9 inch x 4.5 inch) white oval plate displayed at the rear of a vehicle; see appendices.

distributor, a rotary switch that distributes the high voltage to the sparkplugs at the correct time.

distributor cam, the cam within the distributor that opens and closes the contact points, and having as many lobes as the engine has cylinders.

distributor cap, a rigid component made from insulating material that holds the contacts for each sparkplug cable adjacent to the rotor arm round its radius.

distributorless ignition, an electronic ignition system having an ignition coil on top of each spark plug, or in some cases, two spark plugs share a coil, and where a sensor on the crankshaft sends a signal to the ECU which controls the ignition.

distributor points, a cam operated switch within the distributor body that switches the current through the ignition coil.

distributor road, see: district, local, primary, residential.

district distributor, a road which carries traffic between residential, commercial, and industrial areas of a town or city, forming the link between the primary network and local distributor roads within residential areas.

Distronic, a form of radar distance control linked to cruise control to maintain a safe separation between vehicles, developed by Mercedes.

ditch, a deep channel, near the side of many rural roads to carry rainwater.

ditch, to inadvertently drive off the edge of a road into deep water such that the vehicle sinks.

ditch, to abandon a vehicle other than to park it.

dive, the effect of inertia causing the front of the vehicle to dip whilst braking; opposite: pitch.

divergence arrow, an arrow painted on the road surface having 1 stem and 2 or more heads showing where traffic may diverge to take different routes.

diverge steering zone, the distance before an exit sliproad at which a driver starts to diverge from the motorway.

diverging, the dividing of a single stream of traffic into separate streams.

diverging lane, a lane or sliproad where traffic leaves the main carriageway at a slight angle before a junction.

diverging loop, a 90° curve at an at-grade junction facilitating a turn off a main road to the offside by leaving along a sliproad to the nearside which then loops around to approach the main carriageway at 90°, typically used where it would be dangerous for traffic to wait in the centre of the road before turning; see appendices.

diversion, an alternative route where a road or

a lane on a road is temporarily closed to traffic.

diversion sign, a yellow rectangular sign showing lane restrictions and other diversions, or a series of hollow or solid shapes directing traffic along the route of a diversion.

divert, to cause traffic to follow a different route.

diverter valve, a valve that diverts air out of an air-injection system during deceleration to prevent backfire and popping in the exhaust.

divided highway, USA, a highway divided into 2 separate carriageways by a median strip.

divided propshaft, a propeller shaft on a long vehicle, typically a lorry or bus, which is in sections, each section having bearings and cv joints.

divided road, USA, a dual carriageway, a road having a median strip with or without a physical barrier.

diy, do it yourself, a task that may be performed by a person without specific qualifications.

DK, Denmark, international vehicle distinguishing sign, see appendices.

DKW, Dampfkraftwagen, German, steam powered vehicle, a former manufacturer of steam and 2 stroke cars and lorries.

DL, de luxe.

DLC, data link connector.

dli, distributorless ignition system.

DME, digital motor electronics.

DMRB, Design Manual for Roads and Bridges, UK.

DM&S, definitive map and statement, UK.

DMSB, Deutscher Motor Sport Bund. German Motor Federation.

DMSSD, desirable minimum stopping sight distance.

DMU, Drivers Medical Unit, a department within the DVLA, UK.

DMV, Department of Motor Vehicles, a part of the Department of Transportation, USA.

doc, double overhead camshaft.

dock, a platform for loading or unloading lorries, especially at warehouses and supermarkets, where fork lifts may be driven directly into the rear of a lorry.

docking, the action of a lorry driver in reversing the lorry to the dock in preparation for loading or unloading.

dog clip, a safety fastener on a 5th wheel coupling that secures the kingpin release handle.

dog clutch, a simple shaft coupling having square projections on the end of 1 shaft that engage in square slots in the end of the other, coupling can only be performed if both are static or rotating at the same speed as no slip is possible.

dog kennel, the engine cover in a cabover lorry.

dog kennel, the sleeping area behind the front seats of a lorry sleeper cab.

dog leg, a sharp bend, a hairpin bend.

dog leg 1ˢᵗ, a gear selector layout where 1ˢᵗ gear is to the left and rearwards, with the next 4 gears following a normal H pattern, typically on some 5 speed vehicles especially where 1ˢᵗ is not expected to be greatly used.

dog tracking, a condition when the rear wheels of a vehicle do not follow the line of the front wheels on a straight road, due to faulty rear tracking on a vehicle with irs, see also: crabbing.

dog trailer, a trailer with a moveable front axle, *i.e.* having a turntable and 1 point steering.

dog trailer, the last trailer of a roadtrain.

dohc, double overhead camshaft.

dolly, 2 axle dolly.

dolly, car ambulance.

dolly, converter dolly.

dolly, jeep dolly.

dolly, towing implement.

dolly, trailing dolly.

dolly, wheel dolly.

dolly, USA, a mobile platform that rolls on castors or wheels used for moving loads.

dolly knot, a knot which will easily unfasten, used by lorry drivers to form a loop to enable efficient tensioning of a rope at every fixing point.

DOM, Dominican Republic, international vehicle distinguishing sign, see appendices.

dome light, USA, cabin light.

dome override, USA, a switch to control the cabin light.

domestic, USA, a vehicle manufactured in Canada, USA, or Mexico.

domestic drivers hours, rules relating to the number of hours that a driver may work and drive each day.

domestic driving limit, when referring to domestic drivers hours, a limit of 10 hours driving each day, excluding other daily duty.

dominate, to use an assertive road position and manner to remove confusion and prevent a situation developing where drivers may have a similar priority, especially when meeting head-on at a width restriction.

domino driving, a condition when a line of drivers are simultaneously tailgating each other in a chain.

donkey engine, an auxiliary engine on a lorry, sometimes on a semitrailer, *e.g.* to operate tipping hydraulics or an air compressor for loading.

donor car, a car from which major parts are taken, *e.g.* chassis or engine, to build a kit car or special.

donor vehicle, a vehicle from which parts are taken to be used in the repair of another of the same type.

don't be seen, CB jargon, don't get arrested.

don't feed the bears, CB jargon, don't get arrested.

doom blue, a dark blue, potentially the most difficult colour of car to re-sell, hence valued by car dealers less than other colours.

door, a hinged or moving panel allowing access or exit.

door, see: butterfly, double hinged, Dutch, folding, goose wing, gullwing, pillarless, scissor, sliding, suicide.

door alignment, the accuracy of fitting a door into its aperture.

door beam, side impact bar.

door gap, the gap around the external edge of a door between it and adjacent bodywork panels.

door handle, the interior or exterior handle with which to open a door.

door hinge, the part on which the door pivots as it opens and closes.

doorjamb decal, the decal detailing tyre pressures and sizes, normally located in the drivers door frame aperture near the door latch, or on the drivers door edge.

door latch, the part of the door lock which contacts the striker plate as the door closes and springs back when the door is fully shut to hold it in its closed position.

door lock, a mechanism for securing a door, usually operated by a key.

door mirror, a mirror mounted on the door near the A pillar, normally on both sides of the vehicle.

door pocket, a small receptacle where maps, books, or other documents may be stored, on the inside of the door near its lower edge.

door protector, a strip of plastic fitting vertically along the outer edge of a door to protect it from damage if opened carelessly against a vehicle, wall, or structure.

door rash, small dents and scratches in the side of a car caused by impact during careless opening of the doors of adjacent cars, common where parking spaces are narrow.

door seal, a weatherproof strip around the door aperture to form a seal and to reduce noise when the door is closed.

door skin, a large sheet of metal that forms the outer panel.

door stay, a device incorporated in the door check strap that holds the door in the open position to prevent it closing inadvertently.

doorstep lights, lights mounted in the bottom of the door mirrors to illuminate the ground outside the driver and passenger doors, developed by Volvo.

door trim, the internal door panel, normally upholstered.

door well, the cavity enclosed between the door frame, skin, trim, and containing the window winding mechanism.

Dormobile, a motorhome having a rear compartment for eating and sleeping, typically the size of a small minibus, sometimes having a rising roof.

dos-à-dos, a veteran coachwork style in which 2 rows of passengers sit back to back.

DoT, Department of Transport, now renamed DTLR, UK.

DOT, Department of Transportation, USA.

dot 3, a low grade glycol based brake fluid having a minimum dry boiling point of 205 °C and a wet boiling point of 140 °C when 2 % water has been absorbed.

dot 4, a commonly used borate ester based brake fluid having a minimum dry boiling point of 230 °C and a wet boiling point of 155 °C when 2 % water has been absorbed.

dot 5, a high performance silicone based violet coloured brake fluid which will not absorb water, having a minimum boiling point of 260 °C, but must not be mixed with dot 3, dot 4, or dot 5.1 fluids.

dot 5.1, a high performance borate ester based brake fluid with a minimum dry boiling point of 270 °C and a wet boiling point of 180 °C when 2 % water has been absorbed.

dot markings, a series of short lane markings used to direct a stream of traffic where it crosses other lanes at a shallow angle, *e.g.* joining a large roundabout or gyratory.

DOT markings, a code moulded into the sidewall of a tire signifying that the tire complies with USA DOT safety standards, and contains codes to denote the manufacturer, production plant, date of manufacture, and brand.

DOTFHA, Department of Transportation Federal Highway Administration, USA.

douane, French, customs point.

double, 2 of anything, *e.g.* 2 axles.

double, see: B double.

double acting, a damper in which both the upward and downward strokes are damped.

double apex, a bend on a road or race circuit, where the radius varies such that an arc of maximum radius touches the inside of the bend at 2 separate points, *i.e.* a long bend having a straighter section in the middle.

double back, to turn around and drive in the opposite direction.

double barrel carburettor, a carburettor having 2 separate venturi with a throttle valve in each.

double blank, a driver not concentrating on the other road users around his vehicle and hence not able to react quickly.

double bottom, a tractive unit hauling 2 semitrailers, the rear of the first semitrailer is constructed with a 5th wheel coupling over the rear wheels to couple with the kingpin of the second semitrailer; sometimes named a B train, a type of road train.

double bottom, Australia, a tractive unit hauling 2 semitrailers, the combination having a maximum overall length of 27.5 metres and a gross combination mass of 67.5 tonnes.

double cab, a misnomer, see: crew cab.

double cap nuts, a device consisting of an inner sleeve nut and an outer cap nut commonly used to mount twin wheels; also named Budd mounting.

double clutching, a misnomer, see: double declutching.

double deck, a bus having an additional saloon above the lower deck saloon, first constructed by Adams & Co of London in 1847.

double deck, a car transporter carrying cars on 2 levels.

double deck coach, a vehicle designed for long distance passenger travel with a high degree of comfort.

double declutching, the action of pressing the clutch out twice, a necessary technique if changing gear in a vehicle without synchromesh; to change to a lower gear: the clutch is pressed out whilst the accelerator raises the rev's as required to match the next gear to the road speed, neutral is selected, the clutch is let in keeping the rev's set constant to rotate the gears in the gearbox at the required speed, then the clutch is pressed out the second time and the gear is selected, finally the clutch is let in again still keeping the revs constant; to change to a higher gear: the clutch is pressed out whilst the accelerator reduces the rev's as required to match the next gear to the road speed, neutral is selected, the clutch is let in keeping the rev's set constant to rotate the gears in the gearbox at the required speed, then the clutch is pressed out the second time and the gear is selected, finally the clutch is let in again still keeping the revs constant.

double drive, a tractive unit or rigid lorry where both rear axles are driven, *e.g.* 6x4.

double filament bulb, a single glass envelope containing 2 separate filaments, in a headlamp they are arranged to each have a specific focus, in a tail lamp they are of different power to show as a position light and a brake light.

double footing, the technique of driving an automatic transmission using the accelerator and brake simultaneously with both feet, a useful technique when manoeuvring on steep or uneven surfaces, but unwanted in normal driving.

double H, a gear selector layout often used in vehicles with 8 or more gears, the ranges are selected by knocking the gear lever left or right in the neutral position to switch between low and high ranges; also named 4 beside 4.

double head, to have 2 locomotives pulling a very heavy load.

double hexagon socket, bihexagon, a 12 point socket or ring spanner.

double hinged door, a side door hinged on a parallelogram system of links to allow it to move outwards and forwards whilst only turning through a small angle, typically where the door is relatively wide.

double manned, the situation when 2 drivers are assigned to a lorry or coach, sometimes for long distance routes, or sometimes a mate to assist the driver.

double mini roundabout, a pair of mini roundabouts which are contiguous, having 2 central islands, and for some routes, the exit from 1 roundabout is directly an entry to the 2nd.

double overhead camshaft, an engine with 2 camshafts in each cylinder head, 1 camshaft operates the inlet valves and the other operates the exhaust valves.

double parking, to park on a road close to the side of another vehicle such that both are on the same side of the road, often performed by delivery van drivers, not an offence in itself but possibly an obstruction, sometimes a misnomer, see: confliction parking.

double pivot steering, the conventional Ackermann steering system in which each steered wheel slews around its own pivot.

double red lines, 2 red lines painted along the road edge that mark a red route and prohibit stopping 24 hours per day, 365 days per year, including prohibition from loading, waiting, parking, and picking up or setting down passengers.

double reduction gearing, a transmission system in which the ratio is reduced in 2 stages, typically having a main gearbox plus either a splitter, a range change, or hub reduction.

double road train, Australia, a combination vehicle typically comprising a tractive unit and semitrailer drawing a full trailer, or drawing another semitrailer using a dolly, having an overall length up to 36.5 metres long.

double trumpet, USA, a major freeway junction at which 2 roads crossing at 90° are joined indirectly by a pair of trumpet junctions, typically where a toll plaza is interposed between the 2 freeways.

double tube damper, a damper having 2 concentric tubes, 1 being the working cylinder and the other the reservoir, obsolete.

double vehicle ram, an emergency escape procedure used to escape from being boxed in by 2 attackers cars which are sideways across the road, the technique is similar to that for a single vehicle ram and involves stopping 10 metres before the attackers, selecting 1st gear and accelerating with maximum power and aiming to contact and push both ends of the attackers cars simultaneously in order to spin the attackers cars and force a path between them, this escape manoeuvre may not be possible in a small car; if performed in a vehicle having airbags the speed should not exceed 25 km/h (15 mph).

double wheel, twin wheel.

double white lines, a pair of longitudinal white lines marking the maximum limit of the position of a vehicle from the nearside; the lines must not be straddled or crossed except: to enter premises or a side road, to pass a stationary vehicle, or to overtake a pedal cycle, horse, or road maintenance vehicle but only if they are moving at less than 10 mph (16 km/h).

double wishbone, a suspension system where each wheel is supported by an upper and a lower pivoting triangular framework, typically

on sports and racing cars but also on some other vehicles.

double yellow lines, a central road marking used in many countries having generally the same meaning as double white lines, in some countries the yellow denotes the speed limit, in others that the road is 2 way with oncoming traffic.

double yellow lines, a road edge marking showing where parking and waiting restrictions exist, typically all day every day, but sometimes with exceptions.

doubling, a technique sometimes used enabling a second vehicle to follow along the nearside and half behind a vehicle turning to the offside at a T junction, so both may turn in little more than the time taken for 1 vehicle, especially in rush hour traffic.

doughnut, CB jargon, a roundabout.

doughnut, to perform a power turn through at least 360° around a point, sometimes many full rotations; the name is derived from the visual effect of the tyre marks deposited.

doughnut coupling, a flexible joint made from a reinforced rubber ring, sometimes used in a steering column.

dowel, a metal rod of specific dimensions inserted into 2 accurately machined holes to achieve an exact alignment between 2 parts.

downdraught carburettor, a carburettor having a vertical barrel.

downforce, the effect produced by airfoils at the front and/or rear of a high performance or racing car, to counteract lift and give greater tyre friction and stability.

downgear, USA, downshift, downchange, the selection of a lower gear.

downgrade, USA, a downhill gradient.

downgrade force, the force with which a vehicle will descend a gradient, measured in Newtons with respect to the vehicle mass x gravitational acceleration x the sine of the angle of the gradient.

downhill, to travel in a descending direction.

downhill start, to set a vehicle in motion on a downhill gradient by release of the footbrake whilst using an appropriate gear.

downpayment, an initial part payment for a vehicle.

downplating, certifying a goods vehicle at a lower gross weight when its maximum capacity is never required, in order to pay less VED.

downshift, the selection of a lower gear.

downshift inhibit, a feature of most automatic gearboxes such that a lower gear may be selected at any roadspeed but the actual engagement will not occur until roadspeed is reduced to be within the operating limits for that gear.

down split, to change down $\frac{1}{2}$ a gear using a splitter.

downtime, the period of time when a commercial vehicle is being serviced or repaired and is unable to earn revenue.

dp, dual pump, part of a power transmission system on some 4x4 vehicles.

DP, dual purpose, typically a van with additional seating and windows.

DPF, diesel particulate filter.

DPH, distance on a public highway, a note that on a road rally the mileage does not include that driven on private roads.

d-pump, dual pump, part of a power transmission system on some 4x4 vehicles.

DPV, dual purpose vehicle.

DQM, driver quality monitoring.

dr, door.

Dr, Drive, a road name designation.

drafting, USA, slipstreaming.

drag, a trailer that incorporates a steering mechanism within its front axle, when coupled the combination is commonly named wagon & drag.

drag, the resistance to movement of a vehicle caused by friction, principally wind resistance, but including tyre resistance and other frictional losses, but excluding the effects of gradients.

drag, USA, a main road or street.

drag coefficient, a measure of the quality of the aerodynamics of a vehicle body, the lower the figure the less the drag.

dragging the brakes, to maintain a light constant pressure on the footbrake, typically when adding slight assistance to engine braking during a long descent.

dragging the clutch, a condition when the driver selects a lower gear without using the accelerator to raise the rev's, such that the engine speed is relatively less than the road speed, such that the clutch pressure plate is rotating significantly slower than the clutch drive plate, such that as the clutch engages it raises the engine speed or slows the vehicle, thereby creating wear to the clutch drive plate.

dragging wagon, CB jargon, a wrecker tow truck.

drag link, the rod in a steering system which connects the idler arm with the steering arm.

dragons teeth, lane edge markings in the form of triangles pointing inwards from the lane edge, typically at changes of speed limit and gateways to attract a drivers attention.

drag power, the power required to overcome air resistance and rolling resistance, which increase exponentially with the roadspeed (windspeed), *e.g.* to double the roadspeed requires 4 times the power, measured in kW.

drag racing, a sprint race between 2 high performance cars, from stationary along a $^1/_4$ mile course.

dragster, a car designed to accelerate as rapidly as possible, some may achieve 0 to 100 km/h (0 to 62 mph) in one second, the usual target is a standing $^1/_4$ mile, not for road use.

dragstrip, a special twin tarmac strip where dragster cars race.

drain, to remove fluid from a system.

drain plug, a threaded plug at the lowest point in a fluid system, and which is removed to drain the fluid from the system, typically having a specially keyed head.

drain plug key, a special spanner or wrench that will mate with the drain plug in order to turn it.

drawbar, the projection at the front of a trailer enabling coupling to the rear of the towing vehicle.

drawbar horsepower, the horsepower available at the drawbar at the rear of a vehicle with which to pull the vehicle or trailer behind, *i.e.* after all losses in the drawing vehicle have been subtracted.

drawbar power, the product of drawbar pull multiplied by speed.

drawbar pull, the force with which a vehicle pulls on the drawbar behind it, measured in newtons N, and determined by the weight of the towing vehicle, the number of driven wheels, the characteristics of the tyres, and the surface conditions.

drawbar trailer, a trailer with inbuilt steering mechanism on the front axle, either Ackermann style or single point with a turntable; also named full trailer, commonly named wagon & drag.

drawbridge, a lift bridge or swing bridge.

drawer, drawbar trailer.

draw in, to arrive, especially by bus.

draw in, to move close to the roadside then stop.

dray, a cart without sides and a low bed constructed for heavy loads especially for delivery of beer barrels.

DRG, dynamic route guidance.

drift, a deliberate but mild rear wheel skid or 4 wheel skid controlled by the driver.

drift, a slight sideslip when cornering at speed, not noticed by the driver.

drift road, drove road.

driftway, bridleway, a highway over which the public have right of way on foot, on horseback, when leading horses, when driving animals, and in noted cases by motor vehicle.

drink driving, to drive after consuming alcohol, especially if the concentration within the body of the driver exceeds the legal limit.

drip moulding, a strip along the top of the door aperture to prevent rainwater from entering the cabin when the door is opened.

drip rail, USA, gutter, a rail along the sides of the roof to prevent rain entering the cabin.

drive, the means by which a machine is given motion or power.

drive, to operate the steering or speed controls of a vehicle.

drive, to travel in a vehicle.

drive, a pleasurable journey.

drive, a landscaped road.

drive, a private road to a house, sometimes very short.

drive, to herd animals on foot along a road.

DRIVE, Dedicated Road Infrastructure for Vehicle Safety in Europe.

driveability, a quality of an engine and fuel system in giving smooth delivery of power.

driveability, qualities that determine the pleasurable aspects of driving any vehicle, *e.g.* the design of the suspension.

driveability index, a quality of petrol volatility measured as demerits, *i.e.* a lower number gives higher driveability.

driveable, a track that is passable by vehicles.

driveable, a vehicle that may be moved under its own power.

driveable, a vehicle having a severe fault or damage or not meeting legal requirements, such that it should only be moved a short distance before repair.

drive-away, a vehicle crime in which a vehicle is taken by an opportunist, a joyrider, or stolen to order.

driveaxle, an axle that is driven by the engine.

drive belt, a belt that transmits motion from 1 shaft to another.

drive by, a crime performed by the driver or passenger in a vehicle whilst it is moving, *e.g.* a shooting.

drive by wire, a system of connecting any of the drivers controls to a sensor that signals to a microprocessor for accurate control of the vehicle, instead of a mechanical linkage; typically the accelerator operates a sensor that sends an electronic signal to the ECU which controls the engine speed and power.

drive chain, a chain that transmits motion from one shaft to another.

drive end, the specific end of a part *e.g.* alternator which is driven by the pulley.

drive gear, a gearwheel transmitting motion to a component.

drive handle, part of a tool having interchangeable bits.

drive in, a facility or function where drivers and passengers remain in the vehicle or are expected to arrive by car, but stay for some time, *e.g.* a drive in cinema.

drive layout, the transmission configuration in the chassis, resulting in *e.g.* rwd or 4x4 etc.

driveline, all of the complete power transmission systems from the engine pistons to the tyre tread.

drive module, an alternatively useable unit providing motive power in a hybrid vehicle having both electric and ic engines.

drive motor, an electric motor which drives an electric vehicle.

driven, an axle or wheel that transmits power from the engine.

driven, to be conveyed in a vehicle.

drive off, to set a vehicle in motion

drive off, a crime committed when a driver refuels a car then drives away without paying.

drive on, a ferry, ship, or aircraft onto which motor vehicles may be directly driven.

drive on, to continue a journey.

drive on, to restart a journey.

drive plate, on an automatic transmission, a light plate instead of a flywheel to which the torque converter is attached, it also carries the ring gear with which the starter motor engages.

drive pulley, a pulley which transmits motion to/from a drive belt.

driver, the person controlling the speed and/or the steering of a motor vehicle, including when broken down and under tow.

driver, a drive handle, especially when used in the style of a screwdriver.

driver, USA, each tyre on a drive axle.

driver, USA, an old car or pickup in good condition, maintained to high standards and typically used daily.

driver agency, an organisation that supplies van, lorry, or coach drivers to other organisations, either short or long term.

Driver and Vehicle Licensing Agency, a Government agency under the Department of Transport responsible for registering and licensing vehicles, and issuing licences to drivers, UK.

Driver and Vehicle Licensing Centre, the location of the DVLA, UK.

driver correction, teaching theoretical or practical driving skills or procedures to drivers who have committed serious traffic offences.

driver development, training to improve the standard of driving of an experienced driver, especially corporate drivers.

driver education, theoretical knowledge pertaining to driving taught in a classroom environment; see also: driver training.

driver error, a mistake made by a driver, usually not of significance if isolated but typically resulting in a collision if 2 or more drivers make mistakes at the same place and time.

driver improvement scheme, a driving theory session attended by drivers who have committed some categories of offence, instead of paying a fine.

driver information display, a dashboard mounted display panel operated by a right column stalk where the driver selects from a menu of information in the form of colour coded text or numeric messages and pictorial symbols, showing *e.g.* time, average speed, fuel consumption, vehicle fault analysis.

driver information system, a system that constantly monitors and displays all relevant fluid levels, pressures, and temperatures, especially those that are nearing a safe limit.

driver message centre, the dashboard instrument panel.

driver quality monitoring, an assessment of bus and coach drivers' safety and driving skills performed without the knowledge of the driver by an examiner purporting to be a passenger, for the purpose of defining further training requirements.

driver recognition program, a microprocessor based system that recognises the style of the driver and controls the engine and transmission to maximise that style coupled to economy and performance.

drivers information display, a digital display of information from the autocheck system and onboard computer, developed by Audi.

driver's license, USA, driving licence.

drivers side, offside.

driver status monitoring, a system using a video camera to monitor a drivers blink rate to warn against falling asleep, developed by Ford.

driver's test, USA, driving test.

driver trainer, a person who teaches, usually referring to teaching licensed drivers advanced or defensive techniques.

driver training, teaching theoretical or practical driving skills or procedures, usually referring to corporate advanced or defensive training.

driver training, USA, practical skills and procedures pertaining to driving taught in a vehicle; see also: driver education.

driver training regulations, the legal rules requiring that a driver of hazardous goods is given suitable training to cope with emergencies.

driver tuition, teaching theoretical or practical driving skills or procedures at any level but typically learner instruction.

drive safety, the result of harmonious suspension design in terms of wheel suspension, springing, steering, and braking that is reflected in optimum vehicle behaviour, a branch of primary safety.

driveshaft, the shaft that transmits the drive from the differential to the wheel, especially on a fwd or with irs.

drive shaft, USA, propeller shaft.

drive strain, the strain suffered by those drivetrain components between the transfer box and the tyres when any differential is locked, or within that part of the drivetrain of a part time 4x4 which does not have a centre differential.

drive thru, a facility where drivers and passengers remain in the vehicle whilst being attended to for a short period of time, *e.g.* a fast food outlet or ATM.

drive time, rush hour, the times of the day when many people are commuting by car.

drivetrain, all of the complete power transmission systems, from the engine pistons to the tyre tread.

driveway, a private road through a garden or park.

driveway, an unadopted paved area that provides access from a public road to garages and other parking spaces within the curtilage of an individual house.

drivewheel, any wheel that transmits driving power from the engine to the road.

driving, the action of providing motive power.

driving, to be at the controls of a vehicle for the purpose of controlling its movement, whether stationary or moving.

driving, travelling in a vehicle.

driving beam, the main beam, a lamp used to illuminate the road over a long distance ahead of the vehicle, (C&U).

driving conditions, the environment of a vehicle influenced by other traffic, the weather, and the roads.

driving consultant, a person who possesses specific qualifications and experience to analyse driver problems or teach specialist aspects of driving, *e.g.* advanced or defensive training.

driving fault, an error made by a driver; during a driving test categorised into either: minor, serious, or dangerous.

driving flair, all the skills of: intuition, consistency, precision, flexibility, and concentration endurance.

driving glasses, glasses usually having yellow or gold lenses to reduce UV light, but which must not be worn in bad weather, poor light, or darkness because they reduce visibility.

driving habit, the behaviour of an individual person in the way they control a vehicle, especially in the sequences used.

driving instruction, teaching theoretical or practical driving skills or procedures, usually referring to learner drivers in any size of vehicle.

driving instructor, a person who teaches driving, usually referring to teaching learner drivers in any size of vehicle.

driving lamp, a lamp designed to emit a long beam of light, *e.g.* main beam, or a spot lamp.

driving lane, USA, the nearside lane.

driving lesson, a period of instruction when learning takes place, *i.e.* a driver learns a new skill or procedure, or is given positive guidance in order to improve the performance of a previously learned skill or procedure.

driving licence, a licence issued permitting the driving of specific categories or types of vehicles, first issued in Paris on 14 August 1893, first in UK on 14 August 1903.

driving light, the light emitted by a driving lamp.

driving mirror, the main internal mirror in car.

driving plan, a systematic method of approach to any hazard using the sequence: mirror, signal, position, speed, gear, balance.

driving point, the condition when the clutch pressure plate exerts sufficient pressure on the clutch drive plate such that it transmits all the power from the engine with no slip.

driving position, the location of the drivers seat in a vehicle with respect to the chassis, *i.e.* the height from the road and distance ahead or behind the front wheels.

driving position, the position in which a driver sits whilst driving with respect to the adjustment of the seat base and backrest in relation to the primary controls.

driving road, drove road.

driving school, a business operating for the purpose of providing driving instruction.

Driving Standards Agency, the organisation responsible for administering driving tests and instructor licensing in UK.

driving standards observer, on a road rally a person checking compliance with rules enroute.

driving style, the manner in which an individual driver controls a vehicle, e.g. with regard to smoothness and use of the primary controls.

driving test, a test of competence to drive a motor vehicle, to pass the test is the minimum acceptable standard of proficiency, having theory and practical elements; introduced in Paris on 14 August 1893, in UK on 13 March 1935.

driving tutor, a person who teaches, usually referring to teaching others to become driving instructors.

driving with excess alcohol, an act committed by a person who is at the time of driving unfit through drink or drugs, or, has consumed so much alcohol that the proportion in his breath, blood, or urine at that time exceeds the prescribed limit, or, within 18 hours after that time fails to provide a specimen.

DRL, daytime running lights.

dromedary, a rigid goods vehicle fitted with a 5th wheel coupling behind the load area for drawing a semitrailer, a type of roadtrain.

drop, the place of delivery of a load or part of a load; or the load itself at the point of delivery.

drop back, to slow down slightly to increase the distance between ones vehicle and the vehicle ahead.

dropbox, USA, transfer gearbox.

drop centre axle, a beam axle which is lower than the wheel centres, typically the front axle of lorries.

dropdown handbrake, a handbrake with an additional pivot near its base, allowing the handle to be lowered after the brake is applied whilst keeping the brake applied, typically on vehicles where the handbrake is between the seat and the door to facilitate entrance and exit; see also: fly off.

dropframe, a lorry or trailer where the chassis and bed between the front and rear wheels are designed significantly lower than usual for the carriage of tall or heavy loads.

drophead, an open top car having a folding or removable hood.

drophead coupé, a luxurious open top 2 seater or 2+2, having a folding hood and wind-up windows.

drop kerb, a short length of kerb which has been lowered as a pavement crossing or to facilitate disabled persons to cross the road.

drop plate, a thick steel plate pre-drilled to allow a tow bar or hitch to be fastened at a variety of heights, typically at the rear of a 4x4.

dropside, the ability of the sides of a flatbed lorry to be individually hinged down for access to the load.

dropside tipper, the ability to tip rearwards or off the left or right sides of a lorry which also has hinged side panels.

drop the clutch, to let the clutch in very quickly, typically by sidesteping.

drop top, an open top car, a convertible having a folding or removable hood.

drove, past tense of drive.

drove road, an ancient route along which cattle and other animals were driven, i.e. herded on foot; some presently exist as roads or tracks, sometimes recognisable by being quite straight and having very wide verges.

drowsiness, the phase preceding falling asleep, if occurring whilst driving the drivers attention and concentration will be extremely low and reaction times very long leading to a significant increase in the risk of a crash unless the driver takes specific countermeasures.

DRP, driver recognition program.

DRP, dynamic rear proportioning.

drug, any substance used internally or externally as a medicine for a treatment, cure, or narcotic preparation, see: licit, prescribed, psychoactive.

drug driving, driving under the influence of any drug, whether licit, prescribed or psychoactive.

drugwipe, a portable instant test kit for drugs in drivers in which the sensor only has to touch the persons skin.

drum brake, a design of wheel brake having a short cylindrical surface that rotates with the wheel and which is retarded by friction shoes that exert high pressure outwards to the inner face of the drum.

dry ballast, finely powdered barium sulphate, inserted into tractor tyres to increase weight and traction in specific soil conditions; sometimes named lead after a brand name Ledballast; see also: liquid.

dry clutch, a conventional clutch in which a steel disc is faced with a high friction material and where the surfaces operate without lubricant or cooling.

dry engine, an engine without any fluids contained within, normally referring to the weight of a replacement engine for delivery purposes.

dry friction, the actual friction between 2 sliding surfaces when they are in direct contact and without any interposing substance which may reduce friction.

dry gas, Canada, gasoline or petrol having an alcohol additive to prevent water in the fuel from freezing in very cold climates.

dry ice, solid carbon dioxide, a substance which sublimes directly from solid to gas at $-78\ °C$, a short term refrigerant for cooling engines, radiators and cockpits of racing cars.

dry joint, a soldered electrical joint having a layer of flux trapped between the 2 metals such that visually it appears satisfactory but it does not conduct electricity.

dry liner, a cylinder liner or sleeve contacting totally with the cylinder bore such that there is no direct contact with the coolant.

dry miles, a statement or belief that a vehicle has only been used on dry roads in order to prevent damage by moisture, typically relating to specialist or classic restored vehicles.

dry steering, the action of turning the steering wheel whilst the vehicle is stationary, considered bad practice due to causing tyre scrub, strain to the steering mechanism, and buckling of a wheel or bending the steering if close to a kerb.

dry sump system, an engine where the hot oil is collected and delivered by a scavenge pump to a reservoir external to the engine before recirculation, *i.e.* the sump is not the main reservoir.

dry sump tank, the main reservoir for the lubricating oil in a dry sump system.

dry weight, the kerbweight of a vehicle minus the weight of all fluids.

DS, diesel severe, a lubricating oil for diesel engines operating under adverse or heavy duty conditions.

DS, direction sign, a sign which repeats information given on an ADS.

DSA, Driving Standards Agency, UK.

DSAA, Driving School Association of the Americas.

DSA ADI, Driving Standards Agency Approved Driving Instructor, UK.

DSC, dynamic stability control.

DSD, decision sight distance.

DSM, driver status monitoring.

DSO, driving standards observer, on a road rally a person checking compliance with rules enroute.

DSP, dynamic shift program.

DSP, dynamic stability program.

DST, Defence School of Transport, UK.

DTA, Drivers Technical Association, UK.

DTC, diagnostic trouble code.

DTC, UK, driving test centre.

DTLR, Department of Transport, Local Government and the Regions, a ministerial organisation which includes the DVO which comprises: DVLA, DSA, VCA, and VI, UK.

DTp, Department of Transport, now renamed DTLR, UK.

DTR, UK, Driver Training Regulations.

dual bed cat, a catalytic converter having only 2 catalysts, typically on a diesel engine.

dual cap nut, see: Budd mounting.

dual carriageway, a road constructed with physical segregation of opposing traffic, usually having at least 2 lanes in each direction.

dual circuit braking system, a braking system where 2 separate hydraulic circuits are used simultaneously to reduce the possibility of brake failure.

dual controls, some additional primary controls for the use of a driving instructor to maintain a safe control of the vehicle if a learner does not respond correctly, typically a footbrake and clutch.

dual exhaust, USA, twin exhaust.

dual fuel, a vehicle fuel system which can operate on either of 2 different fuels simultaneously, sometimes petrol and gas, or, in some cases 9 % to 15 % of gaseous fuel is added to diesel; the gas is usually either LPG or CNG, see also; bifuel.

dual ignition, an engine having 2 separate sparkplugs per cylinder fed by separate distributors.

dual ignition, twin ignition.

dualled, a former single carriageway converted into a dual carriageway.

dual line braking system, a braking system in which the towing vehicle and trailer are connected by 2 separate brake lines.

dual mode hybrid, a hybrid electric vehicle having both an ic engine and an electric motor(s) for direct motive power, switching between them to use either or both depending upon the situation and power requirements, and having an engine driven generator such that the engine can also recharge the batteries when power demand at the wheels is low; *i.e.* similar to a parallel hybrid plus a generator.

dual pump, part of a 4x4 power transmission system having 2 pumps controlling a multiplate wet clutch in the rear transaxle, such that provided there is no wheelslip the front axle drives normally as a 4x2 vehicle, but on sensing a difference in rotational speed between front and rear axles the multiplate clutch will lock the rear axle to the front thereby automatically engaging 4wd when required and disengaging it as soon as it is not required.

dual purpose tyres, tyres which are designed as a compromise between on-road and off-road use.

dual purpose vehicle, a mechanically propelled vehicle constructed or adapted for both passengers and goods, with a maximum unladen weight of 2,040 kg, and either: the driving power of the engine can be transmitted to all wheels; or, it is constructed with a rigid roof and behind the drivers seat there is at least 1 row of upholstered transverse seats, there are windows on the sides and rear, and the distance between the steering wheel and the backrest of the rearmost seats is not less than $^1/_3$ distance between the steering wheel and the rearmost part of the floor, (RTA).

dual range, a gear selector system having high and low ranges, thus doubling the number of gears.

duals, dual controls.

duals, USA, twin wheels.

dual spacing, the distance between the centrelines of the outer and inner twin wheels on a twin wheel hub.

dual steer straight, USA, a rigid lorry having 2 steering axles.

dual track vehicle, any vehicle having wheels which are separated laterally, *i.e.* a vehicle with wheels having a track width, *e.g.* a single axle trailer but not a motorcycle.

dual wheels, USA, twin wheels.

Dubonnet suspension, an independent front suspension system on some pre-war classic cars having a rigid beam axle and sprung kingpins and stub axles.

duck, waxed linen or cotton, traditionally used for the manufacture of a soft top hood or tonneau etc.

duct, a passage for ventilation.

duesy, USA, any desirable high quality vehicle, named from Deusenberg models renowned for quality.

due time, the time a crew are expected to arrive at a time control including accumulated lateness in road rally navigation.

DUI, USA, driving under the influence of alcohol and/or other drugs.

DUKW, duck, a 6 wheel amphibious military truck having a kerbweight of 7.5 tonnes and a mgw of 10 tonnes manufactured by GMC; the letters are a code for: year of design, utility/ amphibian, awd, tandem rear axle.

dumbbell junction, a grade separated junction having 1 overbridge over or under the main road and a roundabout at each end of the bridge feeding to/from 4 sliproads and the lesser roads; named from the resulting plan shape; see appendices.

dumb-iron, a chassis extension at each side of the front of a car to carry the front end of the leaf spring, on vintage and early classic cars.

dummy, a mannequin the size and weight of a person fitted with electronics to record decelerations, used when crash testing cars.

dummy motorcycle, any vehicle at nighttime having only nearside lamps illuminated, hence at risk from a head-on collision.

dummy transmission tunnel, a shape pressed into the floor of a fwd car to give strength to the floor and chassis, having a similar shape to a cover over the propeller shaft.

dump, the action of releasing air from an air suspension system to reduce the height of a suspension or to lift 1 axle from the road.

dumper, dump truck.

dump truck, a small construction vehicle for carrying earth etc. which normally discharges its load by gravity, usually having rws or articulated steering.

dune buggy, a hybrid or kit car designed for competitive off-road use, having a powerful engine, 4x4 or sometimes rwd transmission, wide wheels with tyres to match the terrain, and minimal bodywork, typically seating 1 or 2 persons.

Dunlop, John Boyd Dunlop, the patentee of a pneumatic tyre in 1888 but later invalidated as proved to be a copy of a patent by R W Thompson, London, in 1845.

dunnage, the packing material between parts of a load or between the load and the vehicle sides for stability.

duo-bus, a bus having dual power packs to enable operation primarily as an electric trolleybus powered from overhead wires, or off-wire using a diesel engine.

duplex chain, a chain with 2 rows of rollers, typically for some timing chains.

duplicate licence, a replacement driving licence that may be obtained for a fee if the original is lost, stolen, or destroyed, provided none of the licence holders details have changed or are incorrect.

Durashift, an EST automated gearchange system based upon a manual gearbox and dry clutch, but operated by paddles on the steering wheel and without a manual clutch pedal, developed by Ford.

durometer, a device for measuring the hardness of tyre rubber compound.

dust cap, valve cap.

dustcart, a vehicle used for collecting household refuse.

dust sheet, a sheet with which to cover a car when stored in a garage.

Dutch doors, a tailgate having twin half height doors, *e.g.* on the rear of some pickups and RVs.

duty exempt vehicle, any vehicle used on public roads for less than 6 miles (10 km) per week, and which only travels on roads between parts of the owners land, typically some agricultural vehicles and in some cases fishermen's tractors.

DVLA, Driver and Vehicle Licensing Agency, UK.

DVLC, Driver and Vehicle Licensing Centre, UK.

DVO, Driver Vehicle and Operating agencies, collectively the DVLA, DSA, VCA, and VI, each a part of the DTLR, UK.

dvr, driver's.

Dvr, driver.

DVR, traffic safety council, Germany.

DVS, vehicle stability control, a version developed by Daihatsu.

DWA, driving without awareness, driving without due care and attention.

dwell, the proportion of the time the ignition contact points are closed before being opened by the distributor cam.

dwell angle, the number of degrees between 0° and 90° on a 4 cylinder engine that the ignition contact points are closed before being opened by the distributor cam.

dwellmeter, an instrument used to measure dwell angle.

dwell time, the duration of time a bus is stationary at a bus stop.

dwell time, the duration of time travellers spend at a service area.

DWF, de-watering fluid, typically silicone

spray for removing moisture from damp hv electrics.

DWI, driving whilst intoxicated, USA.

DWS, deflation warning system.

DY, Benin, international vehicle distinguishing sign, see appendices.

Dynafleet, a corporate fleet communications system combining GSM mobile phone, GPS satellite positioning, and vehicle electronics to automatically send load status, delays, traffic holdups, and vehicle malfunction between operator and driver, developed by Volvo.

dynamic, relating to the application of forces on a moving vehicle.

dynamic balance, the condition when a rotating body does not produce any product of inertia other than around the centre of rotation, the state in which a tyre and wheel spin with all their weight distributed equally such that when rotated at speed there is neither bounce nor wobble.

dynamic brake control, a microprocessor based system that recognises the activation speed of the brake pedal and immediately applies maximum boost pressure when necessary, linking also to ABS, ASC+T, and DSC systems, developed by BMW.

dynamic braking, a system of electronic braking in which the retarding force is supplied by the same device that originally was the driving motor.

dynamic ignition timing, a method of checking and/or adjusting the ignition timing whilst the engine is running using a neon or xenon strobe light directed to read the engine timing marks.

dynamic imbalance, a tyre condition where the tyre may or may not be statically balanced but where a heavy or light area exists to the side of the crown of the tyre such that the centrifugal force during axial rotation causes an oscillating yaw of the wheel, named wobble.

dynamic rear proportioning, an automatic system which varies the brake pressure to the rear wheels before engaging the ABS.

dynamic route guidance, a route planning and navigation system having a digitised road map within the receiver, using origin and destination driver inputs and satellite navigation to direct the driver using visual or spoken instructions, with real-time traffic information, and which

will constantly recalculate enroute as conditions change; see also: ARG, pre-trip.

dynamics, the branch of applied mathematics which studies the way in which force produces motion.

dynamic seal, an oil seal between a moving and stationary part.

dynamic shift program, an intelligent automatic transmission, developed by Audi.

dynamic stability control, a microprocessor controlled system that unites signals from ABS, TC, CBC, steering angle sensor, yaw sensor, and transverse acceleration sensor, to prevent oversteer and understeer by controlling the ECU to reduce engine power and applying differing brake pressures to individual wheels to restore stability, developed by BMW and Jaguar.

dynamic stability program, an electronic gearchange system triggered by a paddle shift tiptronic system which ensures very smooth but rapid gearchanges in the style of a manual powerchange but performed by the ECU.

dynamic supercharging, low pressure supercharging of the induction air using the ram effect and a suitable nacelle.

dynamic visual acuity, the acuteness or clarity of vision of an object that has angular movement relative to the observer.

dynamo, an electrical generator that uses magnetism to convert mechanical energy into electrical energy for powering circuits in a vehicle, giving a dc output, superseded by an alternator in modern vehicles.

dynamometer, a machine which turns a roadwheel of a vehicle whilst having an instrument which measures the braking performance of the wheel, typically using a rolling road.

dynamometer, a power absorbing machine having an instrument that measures the power output of an engine, typically through the driving wheels using a rolling road.

dynamotor, a combined dynamo and starter motor as used on some vintage and early classic cars.

dynastarter, dynamotor.

DZ, Algeria, international vehicle distinguishing sign, see appendices.

dzus fastener, a positive locking quick release device, for retaining engine covers etc.

E

E, east.

E, economy gear, 5th gear, some early 5 speed gear selectors were marked: 1-2-3-4-E.

E, economy mode, referring to some automatic transmission, a switch to bias gear selection, *i.e.* it will change up into higher gears at lower rev's.

E, either leaded or unleaded is acceptable, referring to fuel type to use.

E, Electrics, a section of the POWER checks mnemonic.

E, España, Spain, international vehicle distinguishing sign, see appendices.

E, estate, a car body style.

E, exceeds security requirements, referring to insurance sub grouping.

E, extinguisher, marking the external operating button with which a marshal can operate the in-car extinguisher of a racing car.

E, a hire car size and price category for cars based upon their floor pan; a luxury car, *e.g.* Audi A8, or BMW 7-series, and usually estate versions of cars in group D.

E beam, the European standard headlamp asymmetric beam.

E box, any box of electronics or microprocessor system.

e mark, a vehicle part marked as approved to EEC standards, showing the letter e within a square followed by the number defining the country where certified, see appendices.

E mark, a vehicle part marked as approved to ECE standards, showing the letter E within a circle followed by the number defining the country where certified, see appendices.

e&oe, errors and omissions excepted.

E route, Euroroute.

E segment car, a size category for cars based upon their floor pan; estate versions of cars in group D.

e vehicle, electric vehicle, a vehicle driven by an electrical motor.

EAC, electronic accelerator control.

EAC valve, electronic air control valve.

EAE, energy absorbing engineering.

EAK, Kenya, international vehicle distinguishing sign, see appendices.

EAM, Engineering, Automotive and Minerals, a directorate of the DTI.

EAMA, Egyptian Automobile Manufacturers Association.

early apexing, the action of turning into a bend too early, reaching the inside edge before the apex such that additional steering has to be input before the exit of the bend; a common and unsafe cornering technique.

early decision, a principle of safe driving enabling early actions to be performed in order to be predictable to other road users.

early fuel evaporation system, a system that heats the inlet manifold by either the exhaust, coolant, or electrically, to warm the air fuel mixture to improve cold engine operation by reducing condensation, reducing the risk of carburettor icing, and reducing emissions.

earth, the electrical connection to the body or chassis of a vehicle.

earth mover, mechanical plant often used to excavate and transport earth to create road foundations.

earth strap, an uninsulated broad strip of braided wire which connects the battery to the chassis.

ear wigging, CB jargon, monitoring an ongoing conversation.

ease off, to slightly reduce the pressure on the accelerator pedal, to slow down slightly.

easing fluid, penetrating oil.

east, the direction 90° to the right of north.

eastbound, travelling towards the east.

easting, in navigation, the first half of a grid reference usually having 6 numbers in total, numbered from west to east from a reference point, enabling numerical identification of a location.

EAS valve, electric air switching valve.

easy chair, CB jargon, riding in the middle of a convoy.

Easytronic, an automated manual gear selector system allowing automatic or manual sequential selection, developed by GM.

EAT, Tanzania, international vehicle distinguishing sign, see appendices.

EAU, Uganda, international vehicle distinguishing sign, see appendices.

EAZ, Zanzibar, international vehicle distinguishing sign, see appendices.

EB, eastbound, to travel towards the east.

EBA, emergency brake assist.

EBD, electronic brake distribution.

EBD, electronic brakeforce distribution.

EBS, electronic braking system.

ec, exhaust valve closes, a valve timing specification relating to a specific number of

degrees atdc.
EC, Ecuador, international vehicle distinguishing sign, see appendices.
ECAS, electronically controlled air suspension.
ECC, electronic climate control.
ECC, evolutionary cruise control.
eccentric, an offset disc used to convert rotary motion to reciprocating motion.
EC directive, rules made by the European Parliament aimed at standardising or updating the national rules of the member states.
ECE test cycle, a 3 part test of automotive emissions for compliance with emission standards in Europe, and which simulates urban driving conditions using speeds less than 35 mph (56 km/h) and periods of idle.
ECF, European Caravan Federation.
echelon parking, herringbone parking.
ECI, electronically controlled injection.
ECM, electronic control module.
ECM, engine control module, USA, ECU.
ECMT, European Conference of Ministers of Transport, Paris.
ECN, excess charge notice.
Ecocard, a card bearing Ecopoint stamps which must be machine dated by all lorry drivers entering Austria.
econometer, an instrument showing instantaneous fuel consumption.
economical driving, a driving technique whereby less fuel is used, an advanced technique using distance observation, planning, and anticipation, linked to acceleration sense and feathering the accelerator.
economizer, a system that will weaken the air-fuel mixture when cruising at a constant speed to reduce fuel consumption.
economy gear, 5th gear, some early 5 speed gear selectors were marked: 1-2-3-4-E.
economy tuning, adjustment of the carburettor to give a weak air-fuel mixture.
Ecopoint, a road tax system for lorries crossing Austria, Ecopoint stamps must be purchased from UK DTLR in proportion to the lorry exhaust emission rating.
ECR, environmental car recycling.
EC rules, European regulations relating to the number of hours that a driver may drive and work each day and each week.
ECS, electronically controlled suspension.
ECS, engine control system.
ECT, electronically controlled transaxle.
ECT, engine coolant temperature.
ECU, electronic control unit.
ECU, engine control unit.
ECWVTA, European Community Whole Vehicle Type Approval, the full name for TA.
EDC, electronic damper control.
EDC, electronic diesel control.
edge line, a white line marking the edge of a road, typically used outside of built-up areas, sometimes differentiating between high risk and low risk stretches of road.
edgestrip, a surfaced area along the edge of

some roads, typically 1 m wide, of benefit to cyclists and for breakdowns etc.
EDL, electronic differential lock.
edm, electric door mirrors.
EDS, electronic differential locking system.
EDSA, European Driving Schools Association.
Edwardian car, a car constructed between 1 January 1905 and 6 May 1910, not old enough to compete in the annual London to Brighton Run, but constructed before the end of the reign of Edward VII.
EEA driving licence, European Economic Area driving licence, a driving licence issued in any of the 15 EC countries, plus Iceland, Liechtenstein, and Norway.
EEC, electronic engine control, USA, ECU.
EEE, engineering, education, enforcement.
EEV, enhanced environmentally friendly vehicle, an elev vehicle.
EFA, European Federation for Autoschools.
EFE, early fuel evaporation system.
effective observation, the action of keeping the eyes moving, observing systematically following a predetermined sequence, looking twice in every direction when emerging, and thinking about what is seen.
effective stroke, power stroke.
efficiency, the ratio between the energy input and the power output, most modern car engines have an efficiency of approximately 28 %, the rest of the energy being wasted through the radiator, exhaust, friction, and other losses.
efi, electronic fuel injection.
EFTE, European Federation for Transport and the Environment.
EGEA, European Garage Equipment Association.
egg crate grille, a radiator grille formed by lines of similar vertical and horizontal bars, approximately 50 mm (2 inches) apart.
EGO sensor, exhaust gas oxygen sensor, a lambda sensor.
EGOS, exhaust gas oxygen sensor, a lambda sensor.
egr, exhaust gas recirculation.
EHB, electro hydraulic brake.
ehdm, electric heated door mirrors.
EIN, engine identification number.
ejection, the situation when a vehicle occupant is propelled out from the crashing vehicle.
el, electric.
EL, a rally pace note, easy left bend through about 20°.
elastokinematics, the elastic and kinematic movements of a suspension system, especially to provide passive rear wheel steering for stability at speed.
ELB, electronically controlled braking system, typically for lorries and buses.
ELCODE, an electronic security key using an infrared system which operates the ignition and allows selective locking/unlocking of the doors, boot, windows and sunroof, developed by Mercedes.

electric, operated by or charged with electricity.
electric air switching valve, a valve in an emission control system which controls the airflow into the exhaust manifold.
electrical, relating to the nature of electricity.
electrical current, the flow of electrons along a conductor, measured in amperes.
electric car, a car whose motive force is an electric motor powered by a large bank of batteries; first devised by Sir David Salomons in 1874.
electric choke, a choke operating mechanism that uses an electric heater to simulate the engine normal warm-up rate.
electric fuel pump, a fuel pump that uses a motor or solenoid to deliver fuel to the engine.
electric ignition, the ignition of air-fuel mixture by high voltage spark.
electric ignition system, the system that supplies the hv spark for igniting the air-fuel mixture.
electricity, a flow of electric current which occurs when there is a difference in voltage in a system; the power supply for most devices on a vehicle.
electric mirror, a door mirror of which the alignments are adjusted by use of a switch inside the vehicle which operates motors and levers behind the mirror.
electric motor, a rotating machine powered by electricity.
electric roof, a power operated hood.
electric system, the system that stores electric power, conducts it to where it is required, allows switching and control, the devices that consume power, and the means of replenishing supply.
electric top, USA, a power hood.
electric windows, windows which are raised and lowered by electric motors.
electro, relating to or caused by electricity.
electrochemical cell, a cell within a vehicle battery that produces electric voltage and current by chemical action.
electrochemical corrosion, electrolytic corrosion.
electro coat dip, a corrosion inhibitor applied during manufacture whilst the body of the car is submerged in the inhibitor and electrically charged.
electrode, an electrical conductor through which current enters or leaves.
electrode gap, sparkplug gap.
electrohydraulic brake, a braking system using a microprocessor to calculate the brake pressure depending on driving conditions, developed by Mercedes.
electrohydraulic handbrake, a handbrake system operated electronically by a pushbutton on the dashboard.
electrolysis, decomposition of a substance by passing of an electric current through an electrolyte.

electrolyte, the liquid mixture of approximately 40 % sulphuric acid and 60 % distilled water in a lead-acid battery when fully charged.
electrolyte level, the height of the surface of electrolyte in cell.
electrolytic, relating to electrolysis or an electrolyte.
electrolytic corrosion, corrosion caused or accelerated by electrolytic action.
electromagnet, a device having a soft iron core surrounded by a coil of wire, it has little magnetism until an electric current flows in the coil then becomes highly magnetic.
electromagnetic clutch, a clutch which is operated electrically, typically that driving the ac compressor.
electromagnetic interference, energy transmitted from the hv ignition leads which may interfere with the ECU.
electromagnetic retarder, a device fitted on the propeller shaft of some lorries and buses to control the speed of the vehicle during a long descent by self generating a high current to create a powerful magnetic field which acts to reduce the speed of the propshaft.
electromechanical, any device that is controlled electrically to produce a mechanical output.
electron, a negatively charged particle that orbits the nucleus of an atom, when these are caused to move collectively a current flows.
electronic, a circuit that operates with a relatively small current.
electronic accelerator control, a system where the accelerator pedal is connected to an electronic sensor that sends a signal to the ECU.
electronic air control valve, a solenoid operated air gulp valve, developed by GM.
electronically controlled, controlled by means of electronics or a microprocessor.
electronic brake distribution, a system that varies the brake pressure to each wheel depending upon vehicle loading, wheelspeed, and yaw, at a level below that at which ABS operates, to reduce dive, developed by Audi.
electronic brakeforce distribution, a system that varies the brake pressure to each wheel depending upon vehicle loading, wheelspeed, and yaw, at a level below that at which ABS operates, to add stability, developed by Rover.
electronic braking system, a system that anticipates the drivers use of the footbrake and increases the initial brake pressure, developed by Renault.
electronic control unit, a control unit having a single function, *e.g.* controlling the engine temperature.
electronic convoy, electronic roadtrain.
electronic damper control, a microprocessor system that controls the suspension dampers to suit the varying road, load, and driving conditions, stiffening when accelerating,

braking, or steering, and softening when cruising, developed by BMW.

electronic diesel control, a system where the accelerator pedal operates a sensor that sends an electronic signal to control the engine speed.

electronic differential lock, a system that automatically engages the differential lock on the front axle when sensors dictate, to prevent a power induced skid at 1 wheel, developed by Audi.

electronic drawbar, electronic roadtrain.

electronic engine control, an engine management system controlling all major systems.

electronic fuel injection, a system that injects fuel into the intake manifold using an electronic device to control the fuel flow.

electronic hourglass, an electronic display at some pedestrian crossings where is shown a visual countdown to pedestrians of the time remaining before the signal will change to green.

electronic ignition, an ignition system that uses semiconductors as switches for reliability to control the ignition primary circuit, replacing mechanically operated contact points.

electronic navigator, trip computer.

electronic power shift, the second generation of semiautomatic gearbox systems using a standard clutch, developed by Mercedes trucks.

electronic power steering, a power steering system where the power assistance varies inversely with the road speed to give maximum assistance when manoeuvring and minimal assistance at high speed, developed by BMW.

electronic ride control, a microprocessor based system that controls the suspension, especially the air or gas dampers for optimum damping characteristics.

electronic road pricing, a system of charging by electronic means for the use of roads, typically in city centres but also other types of tolls.

electronic roadtrain, a system under development whereby lorries behind a lead lorry are linked electronically so all inputs by the lead driver are repeated in the following lorries so they may follow without need for a driver, under development by DaimlerChrysler.

electronics, electrical assemblies or circuits using semiconductors, *e.g.* transistors and diodes.

electronic shift transmission, an automated gearchange system based upon a manual gearbox and dry clutch, but operated by paddles on the steering wheel and without a manual clutch pedal, developed by Ford.

electronic spark advance, part of an ECU that controls the ignition timing and dwell angle.

electronic spark control, a detonation control system that signals the ECU to retard the ignition when detonation is sensed.

electronic spark timing, a system whereby engine speed, load and temperature are monitored by the ECU which provides an output to control spark timing for best control of economy and exhaust emissions.

electronic stability control, a stability enhancing system developed by Audi.

electronic stability programme, a microprocessor controlled system that unites signals from ABS, BAS, ASR, accelerometers on the longitudinal and lateral axis, and steering input, to reduce the risk of steering-induced skids by applying the brake to 1 wheel and instructing the ECU to reduce power, developed by Audi and Mercedes, also used by Ford.

electronic throttle control, a system where the accelerator pedal controls an electronic sensor that sends a signal to the ECU.

electronic toll collection, a system of charging a toll automatically by a transponder in conjunction with a smartcard in each vehicle without requiring the vehicle to stop, for toll charging on motorways, town centres, tunnels, bridges, and carparks, etc.

electronic traction control, see TC.

electronic traction support, a system which provides an improvement in traction when moving off and accelerating on slippery surfaces by applying the brake at the slipping wheel when wheelslip from 1 wheel is experienced, and which is active at speeds up to 80 km/h, developed by Mercedes.

electronic transmission controller, a system that allows a powershift system to make smooth upshifts or downshifts whilst transmitting power.

electronic unit injector, a system to give optimum performance and emissions control in diesel engines using a separate plunger pump for each cylinder, with injection pressures of up to 2,000 bar (30,000 psi) with ultra precise control of the injection timing, developed by Lucas.

electrophoretic dip, a corrosion inhibitor applied during manufacture whilst the body of the car is submerged in the inhibitor and electrically charged.

electropneumatic shift, the first generation of semiautomatic gear selector systems using a standard clutch, developed by Mercedes trucks in 1982.

electrostatic discharge sensitive, a solid state part, *e.g.* a chip, that is very easily damaged or destroyed by a discharge of static electricity.

electrostatic spraying, a coating applied whilst the car and spray nozzles electrically charged, for efficiency.

element, any substance made of only 1 type of atom.

element, a basic part of an assembly or unit.

element, an assembly of plate groups and separators in a battery cell.

element, the part of an electrical heater where the heat is generated due to current flow.

elev, extra low emission vehicle.

– EEE –

elk test, a manufacturers proving test, a sudden double swerve at speed, simulating an avoidance manoeuvre to miss a large animal or a load falling from a vehicle ahead; modern cars should retain a constant attitude to pass the test.

Elliot axle, a front axle design in which the ends of the axle are fork shaped to hold the kingpin.

ellipsoidal headlight, elliptical headlight.

elliptical headlight, an obsolete style of headlight beam having a bright central area without the sharp upper cut off associated with a modern headlight.

elongation, the result of a seatbelt operating successfully in a crash, when it is then longer than when installed with no residual elasticity and must be replaced.

ELR, emergency locking retractor.

elv, end of life vehicle.

EMA, Engine Manufacturers Association, USA.

Emancipation run, the annual London to Brighton run for veteran vehicles built before 31st December 1904, first run in 1896 to celebrate the repeal of the Locomotives Act.

embankment, a steep down-sloping surface along the edge of road, where an area of road is raised significantly above the natural ground level by terracing below the foundation to enable a road to cross a valley or depression in the ground with minimal change of gradient along the road surface.

embark, to put a vehicle on a ferry, ship, or aircraft.

embus, to get into, or to put equipment into a vehicle.

emerge, the action of leaving a minor road or private property in order to join or cross a main road.

emergency, see: traffic, vehicle.

emergency, a sudden unexpected occurrence resulting in a state of danger.

emergency brake, a backup braking system for vehicles with a full air system which will apply the brake automatically by spring force if the air pressure drops below a set point, using the red hose if coupled to a trailer.

emergency brake, a brake that can be set by hand and continues to hold until released, *e.g.* parking brake, handbrake.

emergency driving, the driving of an emergency vehicle in an urgent manner when the driver is responding to an emergency call, but not pursuit driving.

emergency flashers, hazard warning lights.

emergency inflator, an aerosol can containing a sealing compound and propellant gas to temporarily repair and inflate a punctured tyre.

emergency locking retractor, a device that allows the seatbelt to extend and retract with occupant movement yet which in an emergency locks the seatbelt retracting mechanism to allow the pretensioner to operate effectively.

emergency service, a service or organisation having vehicles permitted to use blue flashing lights and a siren, *i.e.* police, fire and rescue, ambulance, bomb disposal, coastguard, lifeboat service, mountain rescue, cave rescue, mine rescue, blood transfusion, forestry commission fire service, naval nuclear monitoring, and some military vehicles fulfilling the above functions.

emergency stop, a technique for stopping a vehicle as quickly as possible; in a vehicle with ABS fully depress the brake pedal followed immediately by depressing the clutch, with ABS some steering is possible and the footbrake should remain fully depressed until the emergency is resolved; in a vehicle without ABS use threshold braking and depress the clutch only at the last moment before stopping whilst steering a reasonably straight line; in both cases the brake should NOT be released or pumped.

emergency telephone, a free telephone for emergency use, usually spaced 1 mile (1.6 km) apart along each side of a motorway, and which are directly connected to the nearest police traffic control centre.

emergency triangle, a triangular shaped reflector with sides about 40 cm long and reflective edges about 4 cm wide, carriage is a legal requirement in many countries, to be displayed in case of breakdown or collision.

emergency vehicle, any vehicle permitted to use a blue identification beacon, typically: police, fire and rescue, ambulance, bomb disposal, coastguard, lifeboat service, mountain rescue, cave rescue, mine rescue, blood transfusion, forestry commission fire service, naval nuclear monitoring, and some military vehicles.

emergency windscreen, a sheet of clear plastic fitted in place of a broken windscreen.

emerging mirror, each of a pair of convex mirrors located on each front wing above the headlamp and angled such that the driver can see left and right around a blind corner when emerging.

emi, electro magnetic interference.

Emily, the affectionate name for the Spirit of Ecstasy, the Rolls Royce radiator mascot.

emission, the exhaust gas containing polluting gasses.

emission control, any device or modification added or designed into a vehicle for the purpose of reducing air pollution.

emissions default test, a basic emissions test applied to all petrol engined cars sold new in the UK from 1st August 1995, requiring that at idle it must not emit more than 0.5 % (5,000 ppm) CO_2 v/v, and in a speed range between 2,500 rpm and 3,000 rpm not emit more than 0.3 % CO_2 v/v or more than 0.02 % (200 ppm) v/v of hydrocarbons, and the air-fuel mixture in exhaust emissions must not vary by more than 0.03 of lambda.

102

emission standards, allowable emission levels, set by local, national, or international bodies.

EMS, engine management system.

EMU, engine management unit.

emulsion, a fine dispersion of 1 fluid in another where they will mix but will not fully combine or dissolve, *e.g.* water in oil creating a creamy mousse.

end float, endplay.

end of life vehicle, a vehicle that has reached the end of its useful life and is to be scraped as waste.

end on, the relative position of vehicles having a common longitudinal line, typically relating to relative positions during a front-rear or rear-rear collision.

endorsement, a note made legally on a driving licence showing that the holder has committed an offence, and giving details of the offence.

endorsement, USA, a permission granted by a licensing authority to applicants qualified by examination to drive specified vehicles.

endoscope, an instrument used to look into the interior of a chamber, *e.g.* to inspect the combustion chamber via the sparkplug hole.

end outline marker lamp, a lamp fitted near to the extreme outer edge and as close as possible to the top of the vehicle and intended to indicate clearly the vehicle's overall width, this lamp is intended for certain vehicles and trailers to complement the vehicle's front and rear position lamps by drawing particular attention to its bulk, showing white light to the front and red to the rear, fitting is optional for vehicles between 1.8 and 2.1 metres wide, and mandatory on vehicles exceeding 2.1 metres wide, (C&U), also named continental lamps.

endplay, the axial movement of a shaft or component permitted by a bearing clearance.

end to end, the relative position of vehicles having a common longitudinal line.

endurance brake, retarder.

endurance test, a test of a material, system, or vehicle over a long period.

enduro, a long distance race for vehicles designed to test endurance, when it is anticipated many will breakdown rather than finish, *e.g.* Le Mans 24 hour, or the Paris-Dakar rally.

energise, to activate a device causing it to operate.

energy, a measure of capacity to do work, measured in joules, J.

energy absorbing engineering, the internal design of a vehicle especially within the front of the chassis, such that it will deform gradually during a collision.

energy conversion, the changing of 1 form of energy into another so as to perform work, *e.g.* an ic engine converts the chemical energy in fuel to heat energy which creates pressure on the piston which then converts it to mechanical energy to cause the engine to run.

engage, to move the gear lever from neutral to select a gear.

engage, to partly or fully release the clutch pedal, to let the clutch in, to transmit power through the clutch.

engine, a machine that converts heat energy, electrical energy, or chemical energy, into mechanical energy.

engine, see also: 2 stroke, 4 stroke, air cooled, blown, carburettor, cat and mouse, compression ignition, diesel, donkey, dry, exchange, external combustion, F head, Federal, fire, flat, front, front mid, gas, gasoline, gas turbine, H, hc, heat, heavy duty, horizontal, horizontally opposed, I head, inclined, injected, inline, internal combustion, inverted, Junkers, L head, lean burn, liquid cooled, Mercier, mid, multivalve, opposed, oversquare, pancake, petrol, piston, precombustion, pushrod, quadrazontal, radial, Rajakaruna, rear, reciprocating, reconditioned, revolving block, rotary, rotary piston, scissor, Selwood, semidiesel, short, simple, single cylinder, square, square 4, steam, straight, stratified charge, Sulzer, supercharged, T head, traction, transverse, Tschudi, turbocharged, twin cam, undersquare, uniflow, unit, U, Unsin, V, variable compression, Virmel, W, Walter, Wankel, water cooled, wet, X.

engine adaptor, a device which allows a different engine to be fitted to an original gearbox.

engine analyser, a microprocessor based engine testing device which is connected to the diagnostic socket for the vehicle and which provides data on all aspects of the condition of an engine.

engine bay, the area that encloses the engine and auxiliaries.

engine block, a metallic casting with a bore for each piston, the basic framework of an engine to which most other parts are attached.

engine braking, the retarding effect provided by the engine compression during overrun, especially when the revs are just below the red line and which is enhanced in progressively lower gears, but operating only on the drive axle leading to potential instability especially on slippery surfaces.

engine capacity, the total volume swept by all pistons in the engine measured in litres.

engine check warning light, a tell-tale warning light that indicates a malfunction of an engine system.

engine compartment, engine bay.

engine control module, USA, the ECU.

engine control system, USA, the ECU.

engine control unit, a microprocessor which controls all engine operating parameters including ignition, fuel injection, exhaust emissions, and the immobiliser, also named EMU or EMS.

engine coolant, MEG or MPG or methanol, normally mixed with water; the mixture is used to fill the cooling system of a vehicle, to lower its freezing point, raise its boiling point, and prevent corrosion; depending upon concentration these can be as low as –53 °C, and up to +188 °C.

engine cooling, a system that prevents an engine from overheating and maintains a constant working temperature.

engine cover, the panel covering the engine in a rear engined car.

engine cradle, a subframe affixed to the body or chassis of the vehicle and onto which the engine is mounted.

engine cycle, the Otto cycle, or Diesel cycle.

engine damage, a severe reduction in the life of an engine caused by abuse, *e.g.* overrevving, or neglecting servicing.

engine displacement, USA, engine capacity, the volume swept by a piston between tdc and bdc multiplied by the number of pistons; it defines engine size and indicates potential engine power.

engine distillate, a heavy naptha-kerosene fluid having a low octane number, originally used as tractor fuel, generally obsolete.

engine dynamometer, a power absorbing device that measures the power output of an engine, it measures at the flywheel, usually measuring in hp, kW or PS.

engine efficiency, the ratio of energy supplied as fuel relative to the mechanical energy output at the crankshaft, typically only approximately 28 % for the best engines.

engineering, the constant evolution of vehicles for further increase in comfort, efficiency, and safety.

engineering, the improvements made to roads and networks to improve traffic flow and reduce accidents.

engineering education enforcement, the collective methods of reducing collisions by engineering work to improve road layouts, by educating drivers, and by enforcement of legal regulations.

engineering plant, moveable plant or equipment being a motor vehicle or trailer specially designed and constructed for the special purposes of engineering operations, and which cannot comply with all the requirements of C&U regulations; or a mobile crane which does not comply in all respects with the C&U regulations, (C&U).

engine hoist, a small crane, usually hydraulic with which to lift or replace an engine out from or into a vehicle.

engine hump, the cover over an engine inside a van or bus or lorry.

engine immobiliser, an electronic or mechanical device that will deliberately prevent the ECU from functioning, or to prevent the ignition circuit or fuel system from operating, other than by using the coded key or transponder for the vehicle.

engine knock, a condition in si engines

whereby there is unwanted rapid combustion of the last part of the charge before ignition by the flamefront.

engine layout, the basic arrangement of the cylinders and crankshaft, see: flat, horizontal, inline, inverted, opposed, pancake, quadrazontal, radial, square, straight, H, U, V, W, X.

engine layout, the position and alignment of an engine in a vehicle, either: front, mid, or rear location, and either: longitudinal or transverse aligned.

engine management system, the microchips which control all engine operating parameters for maximum efficiency, also named EMU or ECU.

engine management unit, the microchips which control all engine operating parameters for maximum efficiency, also named EMS or ECU.

engine map, a digital representation of interdependent qualities, specifically engine speed, load, and ignition timing, such that other operating parameters can be matched for maximum efficiency, power, and minimum exhaust emissions.

engine mount, each of several rubber or fluid-filled rubber vibration insulators which locate the engine and transmission in the frame of a vehicle.

engine noise, the amount of noise emitted by a running engine, but which varies with engine speed and load, typically measured a short distance from the exhaust.

engine oil, lubricating oil of a viscosity and a detergency designed for that specific engine type and which may be of monograde, multigrade, or synthetic.

engine overhaul, disassembly of an engine, regrinding the crankshaft and reboring the cylinders, replacement of other worn parts such that on reassembly all tolerances are as specified by the manufacturer.

engine performance, the output of an engine under various conditions, often as perceived by the driver.

engine power, the power available from the pistons to do work, measured at the crankshaft or flywheel in hp, kW, or PS.

engine protection, a system where the engine will de-rate itself or shut down if it senses a major defect.

engine size, see: engine displacement, cubic capacity.

engine speed, a measure of the rotational speed of the crankshaft, usually measured in revolutions per minute, rpm.

engine stand, a device for holding an engine at any angle to enable easy rebuilding.

engine starter, starter motor.

engine timing, relating to either: ignition, valve, or injection timing.

engine tuneup, to inspect, test, adjust, or replace components of an engine, to restore an

– EEE –

engine to its best possible performance.

enrichment, to add fuel to an air-fuel mixture, to reduce the stoichiometric ratio.

en route, on the way, in mid journey.

entry level, a basic model of car in any specific range without cost options or accessories.

entry licence, a prepaid permit to use roads in an ERP scheme, typically in a city centre.

entry sliproad, a road facilitating access to a motorway or similar road, the first section being the acceleration lane, the second section for merging.

entry speed, the speed of a vehicle entering a bend or hazard area.

envelope, the glass container of a light bulb.

envelope, the limits of the operating parameters of an engine with respect to engine speed, torque range, and power output, as affected by ambient air temperature, pressure, humidity, and altitude.

eo, exhaust valve opens, a valve timing specification relating to a specific number of degrees bbdc.

EOD, end of duty, a note written by hand onto a tachograph disc.

ep, extreme pressure.

EP, engine protection.

EPA, Environmental Protection Agency, USA, responsible for controlling levels of pollution.

EPA, European Pedestrians Association, The Hague.

EPA fuel economy, fuel economy tests in standard conditions simulating urban traffic, and simulating highway driving at 79.5 km/h (49.4 mph).

epicyclic gear, a system of gears in which 1 or more gears travel around the inside or outside of another gear whose axis is fixed, where some gears are in the form of rings with teeth inside.

epicyclic gearbox, a gearbox configuration in which some gears are in the form of rings with teeth inside, and the axis of some pinion gears travel around the ring as the gearwheel rotates, normally used in automatic transmissions.

epicyclic train, a combination of epicyclic gears.

epilepsy, a medical condition that normally prevents a person holding a driving licence due to the risk of losing consciousness whilst driving.

epitrochoidal rotor, the trianguloid rotor in a Wankel rotary engine, which performs the 4 Otto cycles in a continuous rotary motion.

ep oil, extreme pressure gear oil, a type normally specified for gearboxes and differentials, typically having compounds of sulphur and phosphorous which may have a corrosive effect on copper alloys.

epoxy resin, a polyether resin compound having separately a base and an accelerator that must be mixed to cause the resin to harden, it has a high strength and good adhesive properties.

EPS, electronic power shift.

EPS, electronic power steering.

EPS, electropneumatic shift.

equaliser, a bar that joins a pair of springs for equalisation of axle weight especially on tandem and triaxle trailers.

equaliser, a short bar that distributes braking force equally to both wheels from the handbrake.

equivalent lamps, a lamp having the same function as other authorized in the country in which the vehicle is registered, (C&U).

equivalent test speed, a calculated impact speed into a test barrier which would be required to cause the same degree of damage suffered by a crashed vehicle.

ER, a rally pace note, easy right bend through about 20°.

ERA, English Racing Automobiles; a racing car manufacturer.

erc, emission reduction credits.

ERC, electronic ride control.

ERF, Edwin Richard Foden, a lorry manufacturer.

ergomatic, a manufacturer designation implying ergonomic.

ergonomic, the layout of vehicle minor controls that are set out in a style for easy operation.

Ermine Street, an ancient Roman road from London to York.

ERP, electronic road pricing.

error, a drivers fault, the failure of a planned action to achieve the intended consequence, *e.g.* failing in observation of detail or failing to judge speed and distance of other traffic where the failed action has the potential to impinge upon the safety of others.

errors and omissions excepted, a disclaimer that the writer or publisher of an advertisement, brochure or specification does not accept any responsibility for any printed mistakes.

ES, El Salvador, international vehicle distinguishing sign, see appendices.

ESA, electronic spark advance.

ESC, electronic spark control.

ESC, electronic stability control.

ESC, European Stationary Cycle.

escape lane, a short exit road accessed by minimal steering terminating in an arrester bed which is designed to safely stop a lorry after suffering brake failure by bogging down the wheels, at the side of a long steep downhill gradient.

escape ramp, USA, escape lane.

escape road, escape lane.

escape route, a long space ahead of a driver that can be accelerated into with minimal steering in order to avoid a collision from another vehicle, a constant objective of a defensive driver.

escape route, a space longer than the queueing distance *i.e.* 8 metres minimum (25 feet), that can be used in stationary traffic to avoid road rage or being boxed in and suffering traffic conflicts.

escape route, see: primary, secondary.

escape voltage, the peak voltage from an ignition coil, usually around 30,000 volts but it can be up to 65,000 volts.

escort, a vehicle accompanying another, for safety, physical protection, security, or as a mark of status, performed by cars or often by 1 or several motorcyclists, leading and/or following.

ESD sensitive, electrostatic discharge sensitive.

ESP, electronic stability programme.

esr, electric sunroof.

esses, a series of sharp closely located bends or chicanes on a race track where overtaking is normally impossible, named after the letter S.

EST, electronic shift transmission.

EST, electronic spark timing.

EST, Estonia, international vehicle distinguishing sign, see appendices.

estate car, a car constructed to carry 4 or 5 persons, having folding rear seats and where the roof continues over the load area to vertical rear bodywork comprising 1 or 2 doors; originally designed as a utility vehicle for country houses for transport around their estate.

esv, experimental safety vehicle.

ESVA, European Secure Vehicle Alliance.

et, elapsed time, the time duration of 1 lap or of a standing $1/_4$ mile sprint etc.

ET, Egypt, international vehicle distinguishing sign, see appendices.

eta, estimated time of arrival.

ETA, Environmental Transport Association, UK.

etape, leg, part of a rally, a 1 day section.

ETBE, ethyl tertiary butyl ether.

ETC, electronic throttle control.

ETC, electronic toll collection.

ETC, electronic traction control.

ETC, electronic transmission controller.

ETC, European Transient Cycle.

etch, a system of chemically altering a small area of the glazed surface of glass to mark the registration or VIN of a vehicle onto each window to deter theft.

etching, degradation of a painted surface caused by bird droppings or industrial pollution etc.

etching primer, a special primer matched to a specific base metal, *e.g.* aluminium, zinc, etc. to ensure adhesion of paint.

ETH, Ethiopia, international vehicle distinguishing sign, see appendices.

ethanol, ethyl alcohol, a constituent of beer, wine, and spirits, sometimes blended with methanol or mixed in the proportion of up to 20 % with petrol for use as a fuel.

ether, an easily ignited hydrocarbon fuel sometimes dispensed from an aerosol to assist starting a cold engine.

ethoxyethane, ether, sometimes used to assist cold starting an engine, squirted from an aerosol into the air intake.

Ethyl, USA, gasoline to which ethylene dibromide, ethylene dichloride, tetraethyl lead, or other octane and knock resistant improvers have been added, a generic term for high octane petrol.

ethyl alcohol, see: ethanol.

ethylene glycol, a chemical used as the base for some types of engine coolant, MEG.

ethyl tertiary butyl ether, a substance sometimes used as a component in oxygenated fuel instead of methyl tertiary butyl ether, added at up to 15 % to reformed petrol as an octane booster, and to oxygenate the fuel.

ETL, electricity transmission line, a road rallying pace note giving directions with respect to overhead wires.

ETMRA, European Top Methanol Racer's Association.

EtOH, ethanol.

ETR, electronically tuned radio.

ETRTO, European Tyre and Rim Technical Organisation.

ETS, electronic traction support.

ETS, equivalent test speed.

ETSC, European Transport Safety Council.

EU driving cycle, a method of calculating typical fuel consumption for a vehicle, consisting of $1/_3$ city traffic driving and $2/_3$ out of town driving by distance.

EUI, electronic unit injector.

Euro 1, an emissions standard for lorry and bus diesel engines introduced in 1992 requiring that g/kWh emissions from these engines will not exceed: 4.5 CO, 1.1 HC, 8.0 NO_x, or 0.36 PM.

Euro 2, an emissions standard for lorry and bus diesel engines introduced in 1996 requiring that g/kWh emissions from these engines will not exceed: 4.0 CO, 1.1 HC, 7.0 NO_x, or 0.25 PM.

Euro 3, an emissions standard for lorry and bus diesel engines introduced in 1999 requiring that g/kWh emissions from these engines will not exceed: 2.1 CO, 0.66 HC, 5.0 NO_x, 0.10 PM, or 0.8 smoke.

Euro 4, an emissions standard for lorry and bus diesel engines introduced from 2005 requiring that g/kWh emissions from these engines will not exceed: 1.5 CO, 0.46 HC, 3.5 NO_x, 0.02 PM, or 0.5 smoke.

Euro 5, an emissions standard for lorry and bus diesel engines introduced from 2008 requiring that g/kWh emissions from these engines will not exceed: 1.5 CO, 0.46 HC, 2.0 NO_x, 0.02 PM, or 0.5 smoke.

Euroflag plate, a registration plate which incorporates before the first digit a blue panel showing the distinguishing letters of the European country of registration.

Euro I, an emissions standard for lorry and bus diesel engines introduced in 1992 requiring that g/kWh emissions from these engines will not exceed: 4.5 CO, 1.1 HC, 8.0 NO_x, or 0.36 PM.

Euro II, an emissions standard for lorry and

bus diesel engines introduced in 1996 requiring that g/kWh emissions from these engines will not exceed: 4.0 CO, 1.1 HC, 7.0 NO_x, or 0.25 PM.

Euro III, an emissions standard for lorry and bus diesel engines introduced in 1999 requiring that g/kWh emissions from these engines will not exceed: 2.1 CO, 0.66 HC, 5.0 NO_x, 0.10 PM, or 0.8 smoke.

Euro IV, an emissions standard for lorry and bus diesel engines introduced from 2005 requiring that g/kWh emissions from these engines will not exceed: 1.5 CO, 0.46 HC, 3.5 NO_x, 0.02 PM, or 0.5 smoke.

Euromix cycle, a standard fuel consumption test cycle covering open country roads and town driving.

EUROMOT, European Committee of Internal Combustion Engine.

Euro NCAP, new car assessment programme, evaluated by several European organisations.

European Automobile Manufacturers Association, ACEA, Association des Constructeurs Européens d'Automobiles.

Europeanized, an American car modified to suit European tastes.

European Stationary Cycle, an engine testing procedure to ensure that a diesel engine meets the Euro III standard.

European Transient Cycle, an engine testing procedure to ensure that a diesel engine meets the Euro III standard.

Europlate, a vehicle registration plate having a small blue panel on the left showing an EU flag and the distinctive letters of the country of registration, and which negates the need to display a separate distinguishing sign when in any European country.

eurorails, meat carrying rails conforming to safety requirements within a refrigerated lorry or trailer, which ensure the load does not move excessively to cause vehicle instability when steering or braking.

Euroroute, a major road within Europe which is designated an E number in addition to the national numbering system, *e.g.* the London to Leeds M1 is also designated E13.

Eurotronic, a semiautomatic gearbox having no clutch, and which communicates with the ECU, developed by Iveco trucks.

Euro V, an emissions standard for lorry and bus diesel engines introduced from 2008 requiring that g/kWh emissions from these engines will not exceed: 1.5 CO, 0.46 HC, 2.0 NO_x, 0.02 PM, or 0.5 smoke.

EU unified driving licence, a driving licence issued in any of the 15 countries in Europe where all vehicle categories are standardised.

ev, electric vehicle, a vehicle driven by an electrical motor.

EV, emergency vehicle.

EVA, Electric Vehicle Association.

evaporation, the changing of a liquid into a gas or vapour.

evaporative control system, a system that prevents escape of fuel vapour from the fuel tank by storing the vapour in a charcoal canister in the engine crankcase until the engine is started.

evaporative emission control system, a system of reducing evaporative emissions by means of a sealed fuel tank, a vapour-liquid separator, an activated carbon filter, valving, and a network of hoses.

evaporator, a heat exchanger in an ac system where the refrigerant evaporates internally and absorbs heat from air passing externally.

EVAP system, evaporative emission control system.

evc, exhaust valve closes.

evidential breath test, a test conducted using a machine which accurately measures the proportion of alcohol in a sample of breath and gives a reading which can be used as evidence in court.

evo, exhaust valve opens.

evolutionary cruise control, a vehicle system that communicates with traffic light signals ahead and which controls the approach speed of the vehicle to ensure arrival at the traffic lights when they are green to prevent unnecessary stopping, developed by Fiat.

EVSA, Electronic Vehicle Security Association, UK.

EVSC, external vehicle speed control.

ew, electric windows.

EWVTA, European Whole Vehicle Type Approval.

Ex, exhaust emission readings taken at the tail pipe.

examiner, a person who conducts driving tests for the issue of a driving licence or an advanced certificate.

examiner, a person who examines vehicles for roadworthiness for the issue of a certificate.

exc, excellent, an advertising abbreviation regarding the condition of a vehicle.

excess, a sum that is not covered by the insurance policy, such that in the event of a claim the policy holder must pay this sum.

excess charge notice, a notice given to a driver having overstayed parking or underpaid for parking, requiring payment of a fine.

excessive speed, exceeding a posted speed limit, see also: inappropriate speeding.

excessive wear and use, when related to a lease agreement, a specific standard for excessive wear and use including: missing parts, scratches, dents, mismatched or bald tires, cracked glass, ripped, burned, or torn interior and inoperable mechanical parts, such that at the end of the initial contract term, if the lessee does not purchase the vehicle, the lessee must either repair the excessive wear and usage or pay the lessor the estimated cost of repairs.

exchange engine, an overhauled replacement engine sold in part exchange for a worn but serviceable engine.

exchange licence, a replacement driving licence that may be obtained to add new categories to a full licence, remove out of date endorsements or suspension details, add or remove motorcycle entitlement, exchange an old style licence for a new one, or to change a foreign issued licence for a GB issued licence where the licence is from a designated country.

ex demonstrator, a car which was formerly used by a dealer as a demonstrator for potential customers.

executive car, a large luxury saloon car.

exempt crossing, USA, a railway level crossing at which drivers of buses and goods vehicles are exempt from the usual requirement to stop before proceeding over the crossing.

exempt vehicle, duty exempt vehicle.

exhaust, the expulsion of waste gasses after combustion.

exhaust backpressure, the pressure within the exhaust manifold created by the resistance to gas flow along the exhaust system.

exhaust brake, a method of restricting the exhaust to create a back pressure in the cylinders to retard lorries and buses; sometimes also used to stop the engine when parked.

exhaust emission, polluting products of combustion emitted into the atmosphere from the engine.

exhaust emission control, systems that will reduce the harmful exhaust emissions including: use of a catalytic converter, exhaust gas recirculation, and secondary air injection.

exhauster, an exhaust brake retarder.

exhaust gas, the burned and unburned gas, vapour, and smoke particulates that exist after combustion.

exhaust gas analyser, a measuring instrument that analyses gaseous products to determine the effectiveness of the combustion process and to warn when the amounts of pollutants in the exhaust gas exceed a pre-set limit; some may measure HC, CO, CO_2, O_2, NO_x.

exhaust gas oxygen sensor, a lambda sensor in the exhaust system made from zirconium dioxide with a thin layer of platinum, it measures residual oxygen in the exhaust gas and sends a signal to the ECU for accurate control of the air-fuel ratio.

exhaust gas recirculation, a recirculation system that recycles a small proportion of the inert exhaust gas into the air intake to lower the combustion temperature as an effective method of reducing nitrous oxide NO_x emissions by up to 60 %.

exhaust jacket, thermal insulation for the exhaust manifold to reduce under bonnet temperatures, increase performance, and reduce risk of fire or burns.

exhaust manifold, the pipework by which the exhaust leaves the cylinder head and is collected into the exhaust pipe.

exhaust muffler, USA, silencer, a chamber within an exhaust system designed to reduce the noise of the exhaust by reflection and absorption of sound waves.

exhaust note, the sound emitted from the exhaust tail pipe.

exhaust pipe, the pipework through which the exhaust travels from the exhaust manifold and between other devices or chambers in the exhaust system.

exhaust scrubber, catalytic converter.

exhaust side, the side of the engine on which the exhaust manifold is located on an inline crossflow engine.

exhaust stroke, the movement of the piston from bdc to tdc with the exhaust valve open, to allow the exhaust gasses to be expelled from the cylinder.

exhaust system, the complete system that collects and transports the exhaust gas and processes it to reduce pollutants and noise.

exhaust timing, an exhaust control system for 2 stroke engines to enhance low speed and mid speed power.

exhaust tuning, the design and fabrication of an exhaust pipe having a specific length and diameter such that maximum efficiency is achieved.

exhaust turbine, the primary side of a turbocharger that is driven by the engine exhaust.

exhaust valve, a valve that is open during the exhaust stroke to allow burned gasses to be expelled from the cylinder.

exhaust wrap, thermal insulation for the exhaust manifold to reduce under bonnet temperatures, increase performance, and reduce risk of fire or burns.

exit, a road leading off a motorway.

exit, the part of a road leading off a roundabout, gyratory, or other traffic system.

exit, a point on a race circuit where a bend finishes.

exit ramp, USA, exit sliproad, the deceleration lane off a motorway.

exit sliproad, a road facilitating exit from a motorway or similar road, the first section is for diverging from the main carriageway, the second section is for deceleration.

exit speed, the speed of a vehicle leaving a bend or other hazard or feature.

expander, the device in a drum brake which causes the shoes to move into contact with the drum.

expansion plug, core plug.

expansion stroke, power stroke.

expansion tank, a reservoir to collect engine coolant when the liquid expands and to supply coolant to the cooling system; occasionally fitted to a fuel tank.

experienced driver, a person having more than 4 years driving experience but without displaying greater expertise than a driver of only 4 years experience, typically displaying bad practices and habits.

experimental safety vehicle, a special vehicle

built for research and testing of safety features.

expert driver, a driver showing abilities in excess of those of an experienced driver, having some of the attributes of an advanced driver.

exploded diagram, a drawing or picture of any vehicle or assembly in which the component parts are drawn separated from each other but arranged to show their relationship to the whole; see also: phantom, sectional.

explosive fuel, any substance that combines with oxygen to produce explosion energy, including aluminium powder, paraffin wax, and diesel oil.

expressway, USA, a limited access divided multilane arterial highway having grade separated junctions, although in California some expressways are not divided and have at grade intersections controlled by traffic signals.

ex showroom, the price of a new vehicle as it is sold by a dealer, but excluding necessary extras, *e.g.* registration fees.

EXT, extrication / rescue vehicle.

extd, extended.

extended test, a driving test having double the duration of a standard test, a requirement often imposed by a court at the end of a period of disqualification before regaining a driving licence.

extension bar, part of a tool used with socket spanners between the handle and socket to reach a deeply recessed or confined nut or bolt.

exterior, a marking moulded into the sidewall of a directional tyre indicating the side of the tyre which must be fitted away from the vehicle.

exterior safety, an aspect of vehicle design, including exterior body shape and body deformation behaviour that will minimise severity of injury to pedestrians and riders in a collision, a branch of secondary safety.

external combustion engine, an engine where the fuel is burned external to the engine and an intermediate fluid carries the heat energy to the location where it is converted into motive power, typically a steam engine as developed from 1769 to the 1930s.

external mirror, any mirror located externally, typically a door mirror.

external vehicle speed control, an ISA microprocessor based in-vehicle system using satellite navigation equipment to know its exact location such that it will automatically control the speed of the vehicle when nearing a controlled speed limit zone, and prevent excess speed in the zone.

extras, accessories that may be fitted by the manufacturer, dealer, or owner.

extra urban test cycle, a laboratory test method of measuring fuel consumption on a rolling road, starting with a hot engine directly following an urban test, ambient air at 20 °C, simulating a series of accelerations, decelerations, and idling, half of the test is at 120 km/h (75 mph) and averaging 63 km/h (39 mph) over a distance of 7 km (4.3 miles).

extreme outer edge, on either side of the vehicle, the plane parallel to the median longitudinal plane of the vehicle and touching at its lateral outer edge, but excluding tyres near their point of contact with the ground, connections for tyre pressure gauges, rear view mirrors, and any side direction indicator lamps, end outline marker lamps, front and rear position lamps, parking lamps, side marker lamps, or retro reflectors, (C&U).

extreme pressure, a type of gear oil often used in gearboxes and differentials, sometimes having compounds of sulphur and phosphorous that may have a corrosive effect on copper alloys.

eye, a circular or oval hole in a part used for mechanical connection.

eye contact, the system of communication between 2 drivers when each is looking at the eyes of the other, typically used in congested traffic when a driver waiting to emerge seeks priority.

eyelash, a cosmetic part resembling a cap peak fitted above a headlamp, usually chromium plated.

eye mirror, a mirror sometimes fitted by a driving instructor, angled to observe the movement of the eyes of the learner driver.

F

f, front.
F, 4x4, a car chassis/body style.
F, a driving licence category for agricultural tractors.
F, Fahrenheit, an obsolete measure of temperature; to convert to Celsius subtract 32 then multiply by 5 and divide by 9.
F, field terminal, the input terminal to a dynamo.
F, France and territories, international vehicle distinguishing sign, see appendices.
F, friction.
F, a hire car size and price category for cars based upon their floor pan; executive cars and cars with automatic transmission.
F1, Formula 1.
F head, an ioe engine design having overhead valves for the inlet and side valves for the exhaust system.
F segment car, a size category for cars based upon their floor pan; executive cars typically with automatic transmission.
FA3, fwd automatic 3 speed transmission.
FA4, fwd automatic 4 speed transmission.
FA5, fwd automatic 5 speed transmission.
fabric, a material composed of natural or synthetic textile or fibres.
fabric body, lightweight bodywork made from waterproof fabric stretched over a wooden frame, a body construction method on some veteran and vintage cars.
fabric braced radial, a radial tyre having plies constructed from non-metallic fibres.
fabric hood, a soft top made from duck, a waxed linen or cotton.
facelift, minor styling modifications to a car model to improve its appearance in an attempt to boost sales at minimum cost.
facia, the dashboard or instrument panel; see also: fascia.
factory, CB jargon, the vehicle base depot.
fail, the result of a vehicle component being below the standard required to meet roadworthiness requirements.
fail, to perform part of a driving test below the standard required in order to pass.
failed, the condition of a component that ceases to function and causes a breakdown.
failed hillclimb, the safe procedure for self recovery in a manual 4x4 vehicle when attempting to climb a very steep off-road gradient such that the engine stalls or traction is

lost: footbrake firmly on, ignition off, select low range reverse gear, release the clutch, straighten the steering, check behind, gradually release the footbrake, (no feet in use), turn the ignition key to start a controlled descent.
failed hillclimb, the safe procedure for self recovery in an automatic 4x4 vehicle when attempting to climb a very steep off-road gradient such that traction is lost: footbrake firmly on, select low range reverse gear, straighten the steering, check behind, gradually release the footbrake to start a controlled descent.
failsafe brakes, an air brake system whereby loss of air pressure causes springs to apply the brakes.
fail safe lighting, a system that detects a bulb failure and switches on another adjacent bulb to counteract the defective lamp and warns the driver, developed by DaimlerChrysler.
fairing, a streamlined panel over a projecting part, sometimes for aesthetic purposes; see also: wheel fairing.
fairway, Australia, a road which is also used by a tram and where the tram has priority, typically marked with yellow lines either side of the tram tracks.
FAKRA, Fachnormenausschuss Kraftfahrzeugindustrie, German Motor Vehicle Authority for Standards.
fal, front axle maximum loading.
falling object protective structure, a structural framework above and around the driver on most industrial lifting vehicles, fork lifts, tractors, etc to protect in case of the load or other items falling.
fall off, to unintentionally leave the track of a racing circuit.
false overtaking, the situation when a leading racing driver catches up to and overtakes a slower car that is actually 1 or more laps behind.
false roundabout, a roundabout constructed where there is no junction, a means of restricting traffic speed by horizontal deflection, a method of traffic calming.
false start, an invalid or disallowed start in a race.
false start, the actions of a driver waiting to emerge at a junction who starts to accelerate, then changes his mind and stops again, common at busy roundabouts; it is very likely

to mislead the driver behind and result in a shunt.

family car, a car suitable for transporting a family, typically a 4 door saloon.

fan, an airscrew or paddlewheel designed to pull or push air through any cooling system or ventilation system, usually electrically powered, some may be mechanically driven by the engine by the fanbelt.

fanbelt, a belt having a rubber and fibre structure, usually V shaped or multi V, used to drive auxiliaries from the engine: cooling fan, water pump, alternator, pas pump, ac compressor, air compressor, etc.

fanning, the continual repeated operation and release of the footbrake on a vehicle having a full air brake system, which will deplete the reserve of air and cause brake failure.

fan pulley, the pulley on the hub of the cooling fan which is driven by the fanbelt.

FAP, particulate filter.

Farina, Pinin Farina, a notable car body stylist for Ferrari, Alfa Romeo, and others.

FARS, USA, fatal accident reporting system.

fas, facia.

fascia, USA, the vertical panels above the bumpers containing at the front the radiator grille and headlamps, and at the rear the taillamps and license plate; see also: facia.

fast, rapid, quick moving, capable of high speed.

fastard, a vehicle travelling significantly faster than other traffic.

fastback, a body style similar to a coupé but typically having a tailgate opening as a hatchback, but especially where the bodyline from the roof to bumper is very aerodynamic.

fast charger, a battery charger having a high output hence able to recharge a flat battery in a short time; in order to supply a high current it develops a higher voltage requiring disconnection of the battery to prevent damage to vehicle electronics.

fast idle, a higher than normal idle speed due to the operation of a choke, or when the ac compressor or other auxiliaries are running.

fast lane, a common misnomer, see: overtaking lane.

fast rack, a high geared string rack giving quick steering.

fast road, a road suitable for traffic to move at high speed.

fast steering, quick steering.

fast throttle control, a 2 stage accelerator response system using dbw, where the accelerator pedal has a short travel for good response when driving on roads, and a long travel when low range is selected for precise control on rough surfaces, developed by Land Rover.

fatal, an RTA in which a person dies within 30 days of the occurrence.

fatigue, a mental state when a driver is unable to concentrate, especially after driving for more than 2 hours, or driving with excessive noise or loud music, and common on any journey between midnight and 6 am.

fatigue, the effect on any vehicle part suffering mechanical failure due to excessive, sustained, or vibrational stresses.

fault, a defect inherent in a vehicle design, sometimes due to cost minimising in production.

fault, a defect which occurs whilst a vehicle is in use, causing a breakdown or a nuisance.

fault, an error made by a driver, categorised during a driving test into minor, serious, or dangerous.

fault code, diagnostic fault code.

fav, fun activity vehicle.

FB, footbridge, a reference in road rally navigation.

fbb, fully built bus.

FBHVC, Federation of British Historic Vehicle Clubs.

fc, fuel cell, a device that generates electricity by reaction of hydrogen and oxygen without heat.

FCAI, Federal Chamber of Automotive Industries, Australia.

fcv, fuel cell vehicle.

fdr, final drive ratio.

FDTA, Fleet Driver Training Association, UK.

fe, flywheel end.

feather, a tyre condition when each individual block of tread has a tapered surface, *i.e.* each block has worn more on 1 side than the other, typically the rear edge wears faster than the front edge, but sometimes the left or right edges wear faster due to the wrong tracking angle or due to cornering at high speeds.

feathered stop, the method of stopping a vehicle by feathering off the brake to create a soft stop over the last 10 metres (30 feet), *i.e.* so the vehicle rolls to a smooth halt with the brake released.

feathering off the brake, a braking technique that should be applied towards the end of all braking, whereby in the last 10 metres (30 feet) the brake pressure is smoothly reduced to the point where the vehicle rolls to a smooth halt with the brake released.

feathering on the brake, a braking technique that should be applied at commencement of all braking, whereby pressure is gradually increased such that a passenger cannot feel the start of braking.

feathering the accelerator, to drive such that changes in the rates of acceleration and deceleration are very smooth and progressive.

feathering the brake, feathering off the brake.

FEBIAC, Fédération Belge des Industries de L'Automobile et du Cycle 'réunies, Belgium.

Federal engine, an engine meeting USA Federal emission standards and certified by the EPA for use in any state except California.

Federalized version, USA, car that meets all emissions regulations in all states, as opposed to other versions for specific single state or export markets.

Federal test procedure, the method of testing automotive emissions by simulating typical driving conditions.

feedback, a sensation felt by the driver in feeling the effect of the road surface, especially through the steering wheel.

feedback, the situation in which part of an output signal or its result is returned to an input to assist regulate or control a vehicle system.

feedback carburettor, an electromechanical carburettor with a mixture solenoid controlled to adjust the air-fuel ratio for minimum exhaust emissions.

feeding in, to smoothly depress the accelerator to gradually increase power.

feed the bears, CB jargon, pay a fine.

feeler gauge, a tool consisting of several thin spring steel blades each of an exact thickness for measuring small gaps, *e.g.* the sparkplug electrode gap.

fei, fully electronic ignition.

fel, flywheel end left.

female, a part that fits around or encloses another.

fender, USA, wing, the bodywork over and around the area of each wheel to prevent mud from splashing.

fender bender, USA, a minor collision resulting in some damage to a vehicle.

fender flare, USA, spat, a wheel arch extension, a necessary fitment around a wheel arch over widened wheels.

fender skirt, USA, a removable panel covering the wheel cutout in the rear wing.

fend off position, the position in which an emergency or breakdown recovery vehicle should take when attending an incident on a motorway hard shoulder: to park about 15 metres (45 feet) behind the disabled vehicle with the front wheels turned to full lock away from the carriageway.

fer, flywheel end right.

FER, Federation of Engine Remanufacturers, UK.

Ferguson transmission, a transmission system using a viscous coupling differential and which supplies 37 % of the power to the front wheels and 63 % of the power to the rear wheels.

ferodo, asbestos based brake lining material developed by Herbert Frood in a 1908.

ferry, a boat or ship that caries vehicles across a river, lake, fiord, or sea, travelling back and forth on a regular schedule.

ferry lights, CB jargon, traffic lights, traffic control signals.

festoon bulb, a tubular light bulb having a conical cap at each end, commonly used for cabin and registration plate illumination.

fetch it back, CB jargon, end of my transmission, talk back to me.

fettle, the condition of a vehicle, *e.g.* in good fettle.

fettle, to repair a vehicle, typically a low quality or bodged repair, *i.e.* to fettle it.

FFM, Fédération Française de Motocyclisme, French Motorcycling Federation.

FFord, formula Ford.

FFÖ, Fachverband der Fahrzeugindustrie Österreichs, Austria.

FFR, fitted for radio.

FFVMA, Fire Fighting Vehicle Manufacturers Association, UK.

FH, fire hydrant, a sign which typically prohibits parking.

FHA, see: FHWA.

fhp, friction horsepower.

FHWA, Federal Highway Administration, USA.

fi, fuel injection.

FIA, Fédération Internationale de l'Automobile, Paris, the governing body responsible for international motorsport rules, also with an interest in road safety.

FIAA, Federation of International Automobile Associations.

Fiat, Fabbrica Italiana Automobili Torino, Italian Manufacturer of cars in Turin.

fibreglass, a material consisting of fine strands of glass matted or woven and bonded with a synthetic resin, used for the manufacture of grp bodywork and sometimes for repair of corroded bodywork.

fibre optics, the transmission of light along glass fibres, used in vehicles having a CAN system, potentially to be used for vehicle lighting.

FICC, Federation Internationale de Camping et de Caravanning.

fiddle brake, a handbrake lever that is used to individually select and brake just 1 rear wheel, or in some vehicles any of 4 selected wheels.

field coil, field winding.

field winding, a coil of insulated wire wound around an iron core that produces a magnetic field when current flows through it.

FIEV, Fédération des Industries des Equipements pour Véhicules, a French federation of 3 associations including SFEPA.

FIGIEFA, Federation Internationale des Grossistes Importateurs en Fourniture Automobiles.

filament, a thin tungsten wire in a bulb which becomes incandescent when a suitable current passes through it.

filler cap, a lid closing the wide pipe leading into the fuel tank, or, closing the aperture where engine oil is added.

filling station, a place at the side of a road where vehicles may refuel.

fill up, to refill the fuel tank.

filter, a screen or mesh through which a gas or a liquid passes to remove impurities, for cleaning air, fuel, oil, etc.

filter, a situation where 1 traffic flow joins another, sometimes bypassing traffic signals.

filter arrow, a traffic signal that permits traffic

to move in the direction of the arrow whilst other traffic is held by a stop signal.

filter lane, a lane to expedite merging by 2 streams of traffic, often bypassing a congested junction or traffic signals.

filter separator, a combination fuel filter and vapour separator between the fuel pump and carburettor on some vehicles.

FIM, Fédération Internationale de Motocyclisme, International Motorcycling Federation, Geneva.

fin, a vane or flat projecting plate designed to have a large surface area with minimum volume, such that a passage of air will remove heat from the internal body or fluid.

fin, a vertical plate at the rear of some vehicles, typically incorporated above the rear wings, designed to aid directional stability especially for high speed and record breaking attempts.

FIN, Finland, international vehicle distinguishing sign, see appendices.

final checks, Australia, shutdown checks.

final drive, a part of the transmission system, typically the crownwheel and pinion which gives the final gear reduction ratio to the wheels.

final drive ratio, the ratio between the rotational speed of the output of the gearbox and the rotational speed of the wheels.

fine, a monetary penalty imposed by a court on a driver who has been found guilty of violating the law.

finesse, the artful delicate precise manipulation of all of the controls as demonstrated by highly trained drivers.

fingerpost, a signpost which is positioned to point along the route to the named place, typically the sign has an arrowhead shaped end.

finger tight, tightened only with the fingers, without using any tool.

finish, the top coat of paint.

FIP, International Federation of Pedestrians, The Hague.

fire, the ignition of the air-fuel mixture causing the engine to run.

fire appliance, fire tender.

fire engine, a vehicle adapted or constructed for the purpose of attending and extinguishing fires.

fire extinguisher, a device with which to extinguish a small fire, it may be dry powder, halon, foam, water, or carbon dioxide, carriage is a legal requirement in some vehicles and in many countries.

fire lane, USA, a route frequently used by emergency vehicles and on which parking is prohibited.

fire path, a route for emergency vehicles only, to allow access into a bypassed or pedestrianised area.

fire protection system, a system to reduce the possibility of a vehicle catching fire after a collision by use of an inertia switch and a fuel stop valve.

fire tender, a vehicle adapted or constructed for the purpose of attending and extinguishing fires.

fire truck, USA, a vehicle adapted or constructed for the purpose of attending and extinguishing fires.

fire up, to start an engine.

firewall, the bulkhead between the engine and the passenger compartment.

firing, the action of a sparkplug in producing a spark.

firing order, the sequence in which the cylinders fire starting with cylinder 1; for many 4 cylinder engines this is: 1, 3, 4, 2, but many other permutations are possible especially for engines having more than 4 cylinders.

firing stroke, power stroke.

first aid kit, a small kit containing bandages and other medical aids, carriage is a legal requirement in some vehicles and in many countries.

first cylinder, the reference cylinder in an engine upon which the timings of the other cylinders follow, usually the cylinder on the crankshaft furthest from the flywheel.

first gear, a gear which gives a low ratio of road speed to engine speed, such that it gives the highest torque so is used for moving off, hill starts, and climbing very steep hills; on an automatic gear selector it restricts automatic selection by the gearbox to the lowest forward gear only.

first motion shaft, the input shaft by which power is transmitted from the clutch into the gearbox, usually the first shaft after the crankshaft.

first party, the insurance company.

first person, CB jargon, your name.

first used, in the case of a vehicle which is registered before being used, the date on which it was registered; or if used under a trade licence, or a vehicle belonging to the Crown and which was used for military purposes, or a vehicle which has been used on roads outside the country of registration before being imported, or a vehicle which has been used otherwise than on public roads before being registered, the date of manufacture of the vehicle, (C&U).

FISA, Fédération Internationale du Sport Automobile, Paris, the section of the Fédération Internationale de l'Autosport which is the world governing body responsible for motorsport.

fishtail, a condition when the rear of a rwd car oscillates from side to side under power.

fishtail, an effect resulting from over correction of a rear wheel skid when the rear swings to the opposite side, sometimes oscillating several times.

fishtail, a technique of deliberately pushing the rear of a target moving vehicle into a spin with the front of a pursuing vehicle by softly contacting the side of the rear wing of the target vehicle with the side of the front wing of the pursuing vehicle and pushing sideways then forwards with maximum power at approximately 50 km/h (30 mph), used by USA police to stop a violator, or as an emergency VIP protection procedure to escape from an attacker.

FISITA, Federation Internationale des Societes d'Ingeniurs de l'Automobile.

fit, to install.

fit, the shape or size of the space between 2 parts as they come together with varying degree of tightness.

fitted for radio, a military designation for a vehicle with additional necessary wiring.

fitting, a small part used to connect a hose to a pipe, or to connect pipes or hoses, especially in fuel or brake systems.

FIVA, Federation Internationale des Vehicules Anciens.

fixed drive, power transmission without a centre differential, *i.e.* having no differential action between front and rear axles; typical of part-time 4x4 vehicles.

fixed drive, relating to the drive axle of some early veteran cars constructed without an axle differential.

fixed grip steering, the action of using the standard grip to hold the steering wheel without moving the hands around it as if they were glued, for maximum steering control on slight bends and the best technique for all bends when roadspeed is in excess of 80 km/h (50 mph); often combined with single input steering.

fixed head, a hardtop version of a car commonly seen as a convertible.

fixed head, an early type of engine without a removable cylinder head, the bores being blind holes in the block.

fixed input steering, a misnomer when the phrases 'fixed grip' and 'single input' are combined.

fixed operating costs, the vehicle operating costs that are constant per month or year regardless of the distance a vehicle travels, *e.g.* insurance and road tax; see also: variable.

fixed penalty notice, a notice given to a driver having committed a minor offence and which results in a standard fine related to that offence being payable.

fixed penalty parking ticket, a notice affixed to a vehicle having committed a parking offence and which results in a standard fine related to that offence being payable.

FJI, Fiji, international vehicle distinguishing sign, see appendices.

fl, front left.

FL, fast left, a rally pace note describing a curve through about 30°.

FL, fork left, in road rally navigation a junction to the left through approximately 45°.

FL, Liechtenstein, international vehicle distinguishing sign, see appendices.

flag down, to gesture to an approaching driver to stop, usually by holding up or waving an arm.

flagship model, the most prestigious model in that range from that manufacturer.

flake, a condition when the adhesion of paint breaks down such that it peels off in thin slices.

flame front, the leading edge of the burning gas as the flame progresses through the air-fuel mixture.

flame glowplug, a diesel cold starting device that heats the intake air by burning a small quantity of fuel.

flame speed, the rate at which combustion progresses through a flammable mixture, typically at a speed of 20 m/s to 40 m/s, and is fastest in a weak mixture.

flame trap, a device that prevents the escape of ignited blowback gases in the hose from the crankcase to the air inlet.

flange, a projecting flat rim or collar.

flap, a lightweight piece of flat material which may flex along 1 fixed edge.

flare, a pyrotechnic designed to emit a bright light, sometimes used to mark an accident or to signal for help if broken down in remote areas of some countries.

flare, the shape of a part which is made wider than surrounding parts, *e.g.* the specially shaped end on rigid brake pipes, or widened wheel arches.

flash, a car distinctive by being ostentatious.

flash, to briefly switch the headlamps on then off.

flash, to use the direction indicators.

flashback, blowback.

flashed, to be photographed by a roadside speed camera or red-light camera.

flasher, the direction indicator switch.

flasher, the headlamp flashing switch.

flasher unit, the electronic unit which controls the flashing of the direction indicators or the hazard warning lamps.

flashing amber, a traffic signal showing when pedestrians crossing the road have priority, or at a junction when all drivers must slow down and give way.

flashover, hv current that short circuits at any point.

flashpoint, the minimum temperature at which vapour from any substance will ignite in air; for petrol vapour this is 49 °C.

flat, a rallying pace note informing the driver to keep the accelerator flat to the floor.

flat, flat tyre.

flat 4, an engine layout with 2 pistons horizontally opposed on each side of the crankshaft.

flat 6, an engine layout with 3 pistons horizontally opposed on each side of the crankshaft.

flat 8, an engine layout with 4 pistons horizontally opposed on each side of the crankshaft.

flat battery, a battery which holds little or no electrical charge, discharged.
flatbed lorry, a lorry on which the load carrying area is a flat platform.
flat bladed screwdriver, a typical screwdriver for slotted screws.
flat colour, a bodywork paint that is not metallic nor with other special effects.
flat cone, a traffic cone made from a flat triangle of plastic, and which can be driven over with no damage caused.
flat engine, an engine layout with pistons on opposing sides of the crankshaft, also named horizontal or boxer.
flat floor cab, any vehicle having an unobstructed floor to facilitate the driver to walk around when not driving, typically some lorries and tractors.
flathead, a cylinder head where its lower surface is flat except for its valves and seats.
flathead, an engine style where all the valves are mounted in the cylinder block, and the cylinder head has a flat surface except for the spark plug.
flat out, the condition when the accelerator is flat against the floor, *i.e.* at maximum power in any gear.
flat pente, a raised rib around the bead seat of a wheel, intended to retain the tyre bead of a deflated tyre to prevent the tyre from leaving the wheel when cornering.
flat power curve, a graph displaying the power output relative to engine revs where the curve is reasonably horizontal across most of its length indicating reasonably uniform power across a wide range of engine speeds.
flatshift, a gearchange performed whilst keeping the accelerator flat to the floor to enable some of the power lost during the gearchange to be recouped from the flywheel at the expense of the clutch, typically performed when performance testing a vehicle to show the lowest possible 0 – 100 km/h (0 to 62 mph) acceleration time.
flatspot, an area of a tyre where the tread has been worn away by a brake-induced skid.
flatspot, an area on a tyre that is not round, sometimes the effect of using a car that has been parked for a long time in cold weather.
flatspot, an engine speed at which there appears to be less power than expected.
flat torque curve, a graph displaying the engine torque relative to engine revs where the curve is reasonably horizontal across most of its length indicating reasonably uniform torque across a wide range of engine speeds.
flat twin, an engine layout having a single piston on each side of the crankshaft, horizontally opposed.
flat tyre, a deflated tyre or partially deflated tyre, typically due to a puncture.
fleet, a number of vehicles greater than 5 operated by an organisation.
fleet car, a company car, a vehicle which is

part of a fleet.
fleet sales, the sale of a number of vehicles by a manufacturer or dealer to an organisation, typically with a significant discount.
fleet trainer, a person who teaches advanced or defensive techniques to the drivers of an organisation having a fleet of vehicles.
fleet training, driver training delivered to employees of an organisation having a fleet of vehicles, consisting of theoretical and/or practical driving skills or procedures, usually advanced or defensive driving.
flex arm suspension, a design of rear axle having a torsionally flexible beam axle in line with the rear wheels and trailing links.
flexer, an articulated lorry or articulated bus.
flexibility, the ability to change driving styles to reflect the environment and the needs of passengers and other road users.
flexible, an operating characteristic of an engine in providing reasonable acceleration and torque at low engine revs.
flexible coupling, a method of joining shafts using a rubber block or disc, typically in the steering column.
flexible drive, a system of transmitting motion using a rotating cable in an outer sheath, *e.g.* a speedometer drive cable.
flex plate, drive plate.
f/lift, facelift.
flip flop, CB jargon, a return trip.
flip kit, a set of parts to facilitate lowering the rear suspension on a live axle vehicle by mounting the leaf spring under the axle instead of above.
flip top filler, a fuel filler cap that hinges closed on a spring clip, on some sports cars.
flivver, USA, a cheap car.
float, a negative quality of a vehicle in which it lacks directional stability and roadholding, especially at speed, originating from design of the steering and suspension.
float, a small vessel that floats and operates a needle valve to maintain a constant fuel level in a carburettor.
float, a vehicle typically a flat bed lorry which has been decorated for a specific occasion, *e.g.* a carnival.
floatation tyre, a large diameter tyre of very wide section typically with rounded shoulders, designed to have a very large footprint hence a very low ground pressure so it does not sink deeply into or compress soft ground, for agricultural and off-road vehicles.
float charge, a voltage of 13.2 volts applied to a 12 volt charged battery to counteract internal discharge.
floating, any part that is free to move within set limits, *e.g.* some brake calipers.
floating, the feel of the steering when there is relatively little weight on the front wheels due to the rear of a vehicle being severely overloaded.
floats, floatation tyres.

flooded, a situation when a road is covered with water across its whole width, making it difficult to assess water depth accurately.

flooded, a situation when there is too much fuel in the air-fuel mixture hence insufficient air for combustion, the carburettor, the inlet manifold, the cylinder, or the sparkplugs may become flooded.

flooded lead acid battery, a conventional battery of secondary cells containing a liquid electrolyte.

floodway, a length of road that is expected to be submerged by floodwater at times, sometimes with a strong cross current.

floor, a reasonably flat panel across the base of a vehicle.

floorboards, wooden planks used as the original flooring on many pre-war cars.

floor change, a typical gear lever mounted centrally on the floor.

floor mat, loose rubber or carpeting on the floor of a vehicle.

floor pan, the structural flooring of a car, part of the chassis, usually including the suspension mounts.

floor shift, USA, floor change, a typical gear lever mounted centrally on the floor.

flow, a traffic condition as a line of vehicles pass a point.

flow, a condition when a fluid or electricity passes through something.

flower car, a car in a funeral procession that is carrying only flowers.

flow meter, an instrument that measures and displays the amount of liquid passing through a system, typically measuring fuel consumption.

flow rate, the amount of fluid conveyed in a unit of time.

fluff stuff, CB jargon, snow.

fluid, any gas or liquid or mixtures of gases or of liquids.

fluid capacity, the amount of fluid used to fill a system.

fluid clutch, a type of fluid coupling, a fluid flywheel or torque converter.

fluid coupling, a means of transmitting power, a fluid flywheel or torque converter.

fluid drive, a fluid flywheel, hydraulic clutch, or torque converter.

fluid flywheel, an impeller that acts as a hydraulic pump to rotate a turbine when the rotational speed is sufficiently high, typically used between the engine and an automatic transmission instead of a clutch; generally superseded by a torque converter.

fluid friction, the situation where a fluid layer supports the load of a body.

fluorescent, a bright coating or coloured material used to increase visibility and safety in natural light.

flush, to clean a fluid system internally by washing all pipes and components with clean fluid or a special cleaner.

flushing oil, a high-detergent low-viscosity fluid used for cleaning oil galleries and other internal parts of engines.

flush median strip, a ghost island of extended length bounded by solid white lines used to separate opposing traffic on a wide multilane single carriageway road.

fly-drive, a holiday which includes a rental car for the duration.

flying kilometre, an average speed measured over a distance of exactly 1,000 metres, where all intentional acceleration is performed before entering the measured kilometre, and all slowing is performed after leaving the measured area.

flying lady, Emily, the Spirit of Ecstasy, the Rolls Royce radiator mascot.

flying mile, an average speed measured over a distance of exactly 1 mile, where all intentional acceleration is performed before entering the measured mile, and all slowing is performed after leaving the measured area.

flying overtake, an overtake in 2 way traffic performed without initially slowing to the speed of the vehicle overtaken.

flying start, a race starting method in which the starting point is passed at high speed with the cars in starting formation, typically led by a pace car.

fly-off handbrake, a handbrake that engages the ratchet when the button is pressed but will not engage the ratchet when not pressed, *i.e.* the opposite of a conventional handbrake; for rallying and other competitions; see also: drop down.

flyover, a grade separated road layout to carry 1 highway over another, with or without facilities for interchange, such that traffic crosses without interference to flow.

fly past, USA, flyover.

flywheel, a heavy disc connected to the crankshaft and rotating at the crankshaft speed to smooth power surges from the engine, it usually carries the clutch assembly and the ring gear for the starter motor.

flywheel magneto, a magneto mounted in the flywheel of some small engines.

FM, frequency modulated, a radio transmitting system.

FM4, fwd manual 4 speed transmission.

FM5, fwd manual 5 speed transmission.

FM6, fwd manual 6 speed transmission.

FMA, Federation du Materiel pour l'Automobile.

FMC, Ford Motor Company.

FML, a rally pace note, fast mid left bend through about 45°.

FMR, a rally pace note, fast mid right bend through about 45°.

FMSCI, Federation of Motor Sports Clubs of India.

FMVSS, Federal Motor Vehicle Safety Standard, USA.

FO, front overhang, the longitudinal distance from the centreline of the front axle to the foremost point.

foam, a formation of air bubbles in some oils, sometimes in the gearbox, final drive, or dampers.

FOF, front overhang to frame end, the distance from the centreline of the front axle to the front end of the chassis.

fog, a thick cloud of water droplets suspended in the atmosphere at ground level that reduce visibility to less than 100 metres.

fog code, a series of guidelines to maximise safety in fog: slow down to a speed such that stopping is possible in $^1/_2$ the distance seen to be clear, use dipped headlights and/or fog lights, don't follow tail lights, don't accelerate away from a tailgater, on a motorway vehicles over 3.5 tonnes use lane 1, light vehicles use lane 2, emergency vehicles use lane 3.

fog lamp, see: front fog lamp, rear fog lamp.

fog light, the illumination from a fog lamp.

fog line, an unbroken white line painted along the edges of a carriageway.

fold flat mirrors, door mirrors that will electrically fold back to the sides of the vehicle and re-set to their original position, to reduce the risk of damage when parking in narrow streets.

folding door, a door that folds as it opens, on most buses and some some tailgates.

folding gear lever, a gear lever that will fold down when not driving to facilitate cross cab movement of the driver in some sleeper cab lorries.

folding rear seat, a rear seat in an estate car or hatchback that will fold down into the footwell or into the side panel to give a larger loading area.

folding top, a rigid metal or similar roof of a convertible which can be folded away.

following position, the distance at which it is safe to follow a vehicle ahead and from where to plan overtaking the vehicle: 2 or more seconds behind its rear and close to the road centreline or sometimes close to the kerb for maximum visibility; see also: overtaking position.

follow me home, a personal safety function when the headlamp circuit is programmed to remain illuminated for up to 40 seconds after locking the vehicle.

follow the leader, a situation where a driver follows another into an overtake that may become a killer overtake.

Fomoco, Ford Motor Corporation.

footbrake, the pedal by which the driver operates the service brake, the primary brake on any vehicle.

footbrake modulation, the action of precisely varying the pressure on the footbrake, *e.g.* during threshold braking, or whilst feathering the brake.

footbridge, a structure which carries a footpath overhead a road or over some other feature.

foot cab, an agricultural tractor having a

reasonably flat floor but no cab.

foot operated parking brake, a system of operating the parking brake with the left foot and having a hand operated release on the dashboard or in the gear selector, instead of fitting a hand operated lever, common on luxury cars especially automatics.

footpath, a highway over which the public have right of way on foot only, not being a footway, and located away from a carriageway and not associated with a route for motor vehicles; see also: definitive, footway.

foot pedal, any lever operated by the foot.

footplate, the area on which the driver of a steam powered vehicle stands whilst driving.

foot pound, a measurement of torque, equal to 0.138 kg.m.

footprint, the area of a tyre tread that is in contact with the road or other surface, and which varies with tyre width, diameter, pressure, load, especially weight transfer associated with acceleration, braking, and cornering.

foot pump, a foot operated device to create compressed air with which to increase the pressure in a tyre.

footrest, an angled support for the left foot when not using the clutch and on automatics.

footstreet, a pedestrianised street.

foot valve, treadle valve.

footway, a part of a highway which also comprises a carriageway, over which the public has the right of way on foot only, and which is parallel with the carriageway and separated by a kerb or verge; see also: definitive, footpath.

footwell, the area around the drivers pedals, and a corresponding area on the passenger side.

FOPS, falling object protective structure.

FOR, Formula Off Road.

force, to act upon an object to make it move or to make a moving object change speed or direction, measured as mass x acceleration *i.e.* kg.m/s^2, in units of newton, N.

force bed, the action of rapidly bedding in brake pads by repeatedly braking to a hard stop, but which is likely to have undesirable consequences.

forced circulation, a cooling system having a pump to rapidly circulate the coolant.

forced downshift, USA, kickdown.

forced induction, the use of a supercharger or turbocharger to pressurise the induction system to force in a greater volume of air than would normally enter, hence allowing more fuel, to give greater power.

forced lubrication, a lubricating system having a pump to supply oil under pressure to bearings within the engine, géarbox, transfer box, or differential.

force fit, press fit.

force limiter, a system linked to the seatbelt pretensioners such that after deployment and a preset amount of force has been exerted, force limiters slowly release tension on the belt to

help absorb the energy of an impact.
forcible stop, the method used by USA police for halting the progress of a violator by using the fishtail technique.
ford, a place where a road crosses a shallow part of a river or stream, the river bed may or may not be prepared as a road surface.
fording, driving across a river at a suitable place; see also wading.
fording depth, the maximum depth at which a particular vehicle can operate in water; the depth may be briefly increased above the manufactures limit by raising the height of the air intake and disconnecting the fan.
Ford terminal, a type of connection to a battery terminal which is flat instead of round, used by Ford.
fore and aft, movement along the longitudinal axis of a vehicle, *e.g.* to adjust a seat forwards and rearwards.
forecourt, an area of a filling station where vehicles stop to refuel.
forecourt, an area where second-hand cars are displayed for resale.
forfeit, the situation when a vehicle is legally seized and disposed of and its value retained by a government agency.
forgiving, a vehicle characteristic suggesting it is easy to drive, *i.e.* mistakes in the use of the primary controls are easily rectified or absorbed by the vehicle, *e.g.* driving in the wrong gear.
forgiving, the nature of a roadside verge or structure in not causing greater loss of control or damage if a vehicle should run into this area.
fork, followed by left or right, a navigational directive describing a junction to the left or right through approximately 45°; see also: bear.
forklift truck, a vehicle for lifting and carrying goods short distances, usually by means of 2 forks lifting under a pallet, for loading and unloading lorries.
fork truck, forklift truck.
formula 1, a class of racing in which the car with driver and fuel weighs not less than 600 kg and is constructed to FIA regulations, with a 10 cylinder engine not exceeding 3,000 cc, a gearbox having between 4 and 7 gears, on a course where the number of laps will total 300 km, (188 miles), run over 17 races.
formula 2, a class of racing within the WRC for 2wd cars without a turbo.
formula 3, a class of racing car with an engine not exceeding 1,600 cc, run as separate national championships in each country.
formula 3000, a class of racing car constructed to FIA regulations with an engine not exceeding 3,000 cc.
formula First, a class of motor racing using low powered single seat racing car.
formula Ford, a class of racing car constructed using a 1,600 cc Ford engine and Ford road wheels.

formula V, a class of racing car constructed to FIA regulations with a Volkswagen 1,600 cc engine.
forward, drive, a gear selector mode marked as forward on some bus automatic transmission selector buttons.
forward 180 spin, see: bootlegger, handbrake turn.
forward control, a vehicle where the drivers seat is ahead of the front wheels of the vehicle, typical in buses, also in many lorries, and some minibuses and vans.
forward distance, on a rigid vehicle, the distance from the rear axis to the foremost point of the vehicle or its load if overhanging.
forward distance, on a full trailer, the distance from the rear axis to the foremost point of the trailer body or load, but excluding the drawbar.
forward overtaking sight distance, the sight distance required to permit a driver to complete a normal overtaking manoeuvre in the face of an oncoming vehicle, and includes: the perception reaction distance, the overtaking distance, the closing distance, and the safety distance.
forward side turn, a manoeuvre whereby the vehicle is driven forwards into a side road or opening then reversed whilst steering in the opposite direction onto the main road, potentially a dangerous manoeuvre; see also: reverse side turn.
forward spin, see: bootlegger, handbrake turn.
FOSA, Formula One Spectators Association, USA.
FOSD, forward overtaking sight distance.
Fosse Way, an ancient Roman road from Exeter to Lincoln, UK.
fossil fuel, any fuel which has formed naturally over about 300 million of years, including coal, crude oil, and gas; it also refers to fuels refined from these minerals.
foundation brakes, drum brakes.
founder, to become bogged down in mud.
founderous, a route which is out of repair, severely potholed or washed out; originally: a route which would be likely to bring a horse to its knees.
FPN, fixed penalty notice.
fps, fire protection system.
fr, front fitting radius.
fr, front right.
FR, Faeroe Islands, international vehicle distinguishing sign, see appendices.
FR, fast right, a rally pace note describing a curve through about 30°.
FR, fork right, in road rally navigation a junction to the right through approximately 45°.
fractional distillation, the process of separating crude oil into various components for producing petrol, diesel, and other fluids.
frame, the structural members of the body or chassis of a vehicle.
frame horns, USA, dumb-irons.

– F F F –

frameless, door windows which do not have a frame, they close against seals on the A pillar, B pillar, and roof edge.

franchised dealer, a dealer having a specific agreement with a manufacturer.

free, referring to manually lockable freewheeling front hubs on some 4wd vehicles, the unlocked position where the wheel is not driven by the axle.

freed up, an engine that has completed its running in period and where tight areas on bearings have worn away thereby reducing internal friction and producing full power.

free flow interchange, any junction where all crossing paths are grade separated, *e.g.* a braid junction.

free length, the length of a spring when no forces are exerted upon it.

free play, excessive movement in any part usually caused by wear beyond the life of a component, or maladjustment.

free play, lash, the amount of movement between gear teeth in a gear train.

free revving, an engine that responds rapidly to sudden increases in accelerator movement, assessed whilst not transmitting drive to the wheels.

free running, an axle that is not driven and does not steer.

free speed, the mean speed of single vehicles on a specific length of road when driven freely without traffic ahead.

free travel, the amount of movement between any 2 parts in a lever operated mechanism.

freeway, USA, a road which is free from encroaching properties and free from direct access to/from such premises, enabling a free flow of traffic and which is designed for high speeds; *i.e.* a multilane divided highway having grade separated junctions, and which may or may not be subject to a toll.

freewheel, to coast, to travel with the clutch depressed except the last few metres before stopping; a practice which saves nothing and which is potentially dangerous especially downhill or when stopping from speed.

freewheel, to coast, to select neutral whilst moving; a practice which saves nothing and which is potentially dangerous especially downhill or when stopping.

freewheel, a mechanism in the transmission of some vehicles which disconnects the drive when on overrun, but causing the loss of engine braking.

freewheeling hubs, front wheel hubs that may be selected to lock or free, either manually or on other vehicles automatically, when free the front transmission does not rotate when in 2wd, on some 4wd vehicles.

freewheeling steering lock, a security device that operates such that when the ignition key is removed the steering wheel will freely rotate rendering the vehicle undriveable, developed by VW.

freeze plug, USA, core plug.

French, a customising style whereby lights and other features are recessed into the bodywork down short tubes.

freon, R12, a halogenated hydrocarbon or CFC refrigerant used in older ac systems.

frequency, the number of completed cycles that occur in a period of time.

friction, the resistance to relative movement by 2 contacting surfaces; the action of an object rubbing against another resulting in heat; a force or load to be overcome or used; friction is very low in bearings; friction is designed to be driver controllable in brakes; in tyres friction is designed to be greater than the mass of the vehicle.

friction bearing, a bearing in which there is sliding contact between moving surfaces, *e.g.* sleeve bearings.

friction brake, a brake in which the resistance is provided by friction.

friction circle, the friction tradeoff of a tyre expressed as a percentage of g in each direction, resulting in an almost circular trace on a graph due to the compromise which exists between the vectors of the friction forces of steering and braking or accelerating, or a combination of forces.

friction clutch, a clutch in which torque is transmitted by pressure of the clutch faces on each other.

friction damper, a method of suspension damping using pressure between oscillating discs, typically on some vintage cars.

friction factor, friction force relative to normal force.

friction force, the amount of force with which the sliding motion of a body across a surface is resisted.

friction horsepower, power lost from the power train through friction.

friction lining, the thin sheet of friction material on brake pads, brake shoes, and the clutch drive plate.

friction plate, clutch drive plate.

friction power, the product of friction force multiplied by sliding speed.

friction tradeoff, the sharing of the tyre grip available between steering and accelerating or braking, *i.e.* if more of the available friction is used for braking less will be available for steering, as denoted by a friction circle.

front, the foremost part of a vehicle in the normal direction of motion.

frontage road, USA, a service road for access to shops, houses, etc, separated from but close and parallel to an arterial highway.

frontal area, the area of the silhouette of the vehicle as seen from the front, having a direct effect on power consumption at speed.

front axis, the front axle, or in the case of a vehicle having 2 or more steering front axles, a horizontal transverse line midway between the centres of the first and last axles in that group of axles.

front axle, the axle or stub axles to which the front wheels are attached.

front bumper, the bumper protecting the front of the vehicle.

front diff, the differential in the front axle of a 4x4 or awd vehicle.

front door, CB jargon, the vehicle at the front of a convoy.

front door, CB jargon, the vehicle directly ahead of you.

front end impact, a crash where the direct damage is at the front of the vehicle.

front end swing, the course followed by the front outside corner of a semitrailer beyond the course of the tractive unit, when turning a corner.

front engine, a vehicle engine and chassis layout where the engine is over or ahead of the front axle.

front fitting radius, a measurement in a horizontal arc from the kingpin in a 5th wheel coupling to the nearest point at the rear of a cab; any trailer having a greater diagonal measurement from the kingpin to a front corner cannot be coupled.

front fog lamp, a lamp used to improve the illumination of the road in case of fog, snowfall, or dust clouds, (C&U).

front mid engine, a vehicle having an engine located wholly behind the front axle but closer to the front axle than to the rear axle.

front overhang, New Zealand, the longitudinal distance that any part of a vehicle or its load extends forwards from the front edge of the drivers seat in its rearmost position.

front pillar, A pillar.

front pipe, the first section of the exhaust after the manifold.

front position lamp, a lamp used to indicate the presence and the width of the vehicle when viewed from the front, (C&U), formerly named side lights or parking lights.

front roll centre, the point at ground level or above on the longitudinal axis between the front wheels around which the vehicle body rolls due to centrifugal force on the body when cornering; the actual height of the roll centre depends upon suspension design; where the front roll centre is lower than the rear the vehicle will usually understeer.

front seat, a passenger seat alongside the driver.

front suspension, the assembly of levers and springs that support the body or chassis above the front wheels.

front trailing axle, a pusher axle, a non-driven load carrying axle closely ahead of a driven axle on a tractive unit, lorry, or bus, some may lift and/or steer; see also: rear trailing.

front trailing lift axle, a pusher axle, a non-driven load carrying axle closely ahead of a driven axle on a tractive unit, lorry, or bus, which may be raised from the road surface to

reduce costs when the vehicle is operated lightly loaded; see also: rear trailing.

front transaxle, a gearbox, final drive, and differential all contained within 1 casing, typical of a fwd car.

front wheel drive, a vehicle in which the engine drives the front wheels.

front wheel skid, the result when the front wheels of a vehicle lock, spin, or suffer significant sideslip, resulting in understeer, *i.e.* loss of steering control and reduced braking performance, or reduced acceleration performance; sometimes caused by harsh acceleration in a fwd, typically caused by brake steer overlap.

front wing, a body panel covering a front wheel.

frost, a coating of frozen moisture that can form a slippery surface on a road.

frosting, the theft of a car while the owner has left the engine idling to de-frost the windows outside his/her house.

frozen, USA, seized, a condition when a mechanical part which should normally move against another part becomes immovable, *e.g.* for a bearing to melt and weld within the engine, or for a nut to be rusted to a bolt.

frpl, full rated payload.

FRT, a marking on the sidewall of a tyre indicating that the tyre is not suitable for use on a driven axle.

fsh, full service history.

FT, front track width.

FTA, Freight Transport Association, UK.

FTA, USA, failure to appear, a traffic citation on a driving record.

FTC, fast throttle control.

ft lb, foot pound, a measurement of torque, equal to 0.138 kg.m.

FTP, Federal test procedure, any of a range of vehicle test procedures applied in USA, typically by FMVSS, especially for exhaust emissions.

FTP, USA, failure to pay, a traffic citation on a driving record.

FTWO, Functions of Traffic Wardens Order 1970, UK.

fuel, any combustible substance, usually a hydrocarbon, *e.g.* petrol, diesel, gas.

fuel additive, a substance added to fuel to improve a characteristic.

fuel cap, a removable cover over the aperture leading to the fuel tank.

fuel card, a credit card issued by a fuel management organisation.

fuel cell, an electrochemical device that converts chemical energy directly into electrical energy without high temperatures, such that fuel reacts with oxygen in an electrolyte to release electrons thereby producing electrical power; *i.e.* a chemical engine operating at ambient temperatures without undesirable emissions.

fuel cell catalyst, a substance such as platinum,

silver, or nickel from which the electrodes of a fuel cell are made and which speeds up the reaction of the cell.

fuel cell fuel, a substance that reacts with oxygen to create energy in a fuel cell.

fuel charge, the air-fuel mixture in the combustion chamber.

fuel consumption , the measurement of fuel consumed compared to distance travelled, typically measured as mpg, km/litre, or litres/100 km, manufacturers figures are standardised by measuring on the urban cycle, extra urban cycle, or combined cycle.

fuel cooler, a system which cools the surplus fuel returning to the tank from a fuel injection system to maintain a constant fuel temperature to improve performance and reduce emissions, developed by Landrover.

fuel duty, the taxes and VAT paid on petrol, diesel, and other fuels.

fuel efficiency, a measurement of the conversion of fuel energy into forward motion; diesel and petrol engines are usually between 21 % to 28 % efficiency, the remainder is wasted as heat and exhaust.

fuel energy density, the amount of energy contained within a specific weight of fuel, and which is different for each fuel type.

fuel expansion tank, a reservoir to collect fuel to prevent spillage when the liquid expands.

fuel filler flap, a small bodywork panel giving access to the fuel cap.

fuel filling breather, a valve that can be opened manually to allow faster refuelling with reduced likelihood of spillage.

fuel filter, a device to prevent particles of dirt in the fuel progressing into the engine, it may have a typical filter size of 100 microns.

fuel gauge, an instrument displaying the quantity of fuel remaining in the tank.

fuelie, USA, a car having fuel injection.

fuel induction, the system that supplies air-fuel mixture to the cylinders, usually either a carburettor or an injection system.

fuel injection, a system that sprays an exact quantity of fuel at high pressure through a fine nozzle to atomise it with air for combustion, sometimes it may be injected directly into the combustion chamber, or into a pre chamber, or sometimes into the intake manifold, sometimes having separate injector nozzles for each cylinder, first devised in 1902.

fuel injection safety switch, inertia fuel cut-off switch.

fuel injection system shut off switch, inertia fuel cut-off switch.

fuel injector, the device that sprays fuel under high pressure into the intake airflow or into the combustion chamber.

fuelled, a vehicle to which the fuel tank has been replenished.

fuel levy, a fund raised on the purchase of fuel which pays communally for third party insurance and medical treatment of casualties,

in many southern African countries.

fuel line, the piping through which the fuel flows between the fuel tank and the engine.

fuelling, the action of supplying with petrol, diesel, gas, etc, to fill or refill the fuel reservoir.

fuel mileage, fuel consumption.

fuel pressure gauge, an instrument displaying the instantaneous fuel pressure between the fuel pump and injectors, typically reading in bar or psi.

fuel pump, an electrical or mechanical pump that delivers fuel from the tank to the carburettor or injection system.

fuel pump shut-off switch, inertia fuel cut-off switch.

fuel rail, the manifold feeding the injectors in a fuel injection system.

fuel return line, the pipe which returns surplus fuel from the injectors to the tank.

fuel starvation, a fault condition when insufficient fuel is supplied to the engine such that it ceases to run, runs unevenly, or produces little power.

fuel system, the complete fuel storage, measuring, and delivery system, the tank, gauge, pipes, pump, filter, and carburettor or injection system.

fuel tank, the storage reservoir for fuel, usually having a gauge to display the contents.

fuel vapour, atomised air-fuel mixture ready for combustion.

fuel vapour, fumes in the atmosphere given off by fuel evaporating.

fuel vapour recovery system, evaporative control system.

fulcrum, the point around which a part pivots.

full air kit, a lorry having air suspension to all axles, air suspension to the cab, and an air suspended seat.

full air system, a braking system using an engine driven air compressor to store air in tanks which is released by a valve connected to the footbrake pedal to operate the wheel brakes.

full beam, main beam, a headlight beam that is not dipped.

full bore, full throttle, full power, to drive at maximum speed.

full circle, to make a U turn at a roundabout to return on the road of origin, potentially the safest and simplest way of turning a vehicle around, especially for a large vehicle.

full cog, a whole gearchange, not using the splitter.

full face helmet, a crash helmet with protection for the lower part of the face.

full flow oil filter, a filtering system that filters all of the oil before it is circulated around the engine; see also: bypass.

full harness, a seat belt system used in competition vehicles, it may be of 4 or 5 or 6 point fitting.

full junction, a grade separated junction having sufficient sliproads and link roads to offer a full permutation of links from any approach to any exit, but not necessarily a return to the route of origin; on maps the junction number is typically coloured black or blue; see also: restricted.

full leather upholstery, a car upholstery where not only the seats but all upholstered surfaces are covered with leather, *e.g.* door trim and rooflining.

full load, the engine condition when the accelerator is fully depressed.

full lock, the limit of the steering mechanism after slewing fully to the left or right.

full pelt, as fast as possible.

full profile, a crossply tyre having a sidewall height equalling the section width.

full profile, a radial tyre having a sidewall height 82 % of the section width.

full rated payload, the maximum weight which a vehicle may carry including a nominal allowance of 75 kg for the weight of the driver.

full seatbelt, a 3 point seatbelt.

full service history, documentary proof of all servicing and repairs to a vehicle.

full size car, USA, the largest standard car size, typically seating 6 persons.

full size spare, a spare wheel which is the same size as the road wheels, *i.e.* not a lightweight or emergency type.

full speed, at the rated maximum speed.

full stop, a complete cessation of movement.

full throttle, the condition when the throttle valve is fully open to allow maximum air into the intake system, when the accelerator pedal is pressed fully to the floor.

full throttle gear shift, a flatshift, a gearchange performed whilst keeping the accelerator flat to the floor to enable some of the power lost during the gearchange to be recouped from the flywheel at the expense of the clutch, typically performed when performance testing a vehicle to show the lowest possible 0 – 100 km/h (0 – 62 mph) acceleration time.

full tilt, at full speed.

full time 4wd, a 4wd vehicle with a centre differential allowing the driveline to divide power between front and rear axles.

full trailer, a trailer having axle sets at both the front and the rear, the foremost of which is steered by its drawbar having either Ackerman 2 point steering or a single point turntable; also named A frame drawbar trailer, or wagon & drag.

full up, a bus containing its maximum authorised number of passengers.

full up, a fuel tank which is completely full.

fully automatic, automatic.

fully built bus, a bus of which the chassis and body are constructed by a single manufacturer.

fully electronic ignition, a microprocessor

controlled ignition system having a distributorless mapped system with knock and dwell angle control, and digital idle stabilisation.

fully floating, a part that is free to rotate if it should want to, *i.e.* it has 2 bearing faces, *e.g.* the little end pin that connects the piston to the con rod.

fully floating axle, a live axle assembly where the axle driveshaft transmits torque only, all lateral and vertical forces are carried by the suspension.

fully fronted, an open top tourist bus having a windscreen for the upper saloon.

fully loaded, a car fitted with all available accessories.

fully locked, the action of locking all axle differentials and transmission differentials such that all wheels will rotate at the same speed for maximum traction on poor surfaces.

fumes, gas, smoke, or vapour, especially where unpleasant or polluting.

function back, a driver controlled signal to an automatic gearbox requesting a block change down.

function forward, a driver controlled signal to an automatic gearbox requesting a block change up.

funnel, a conical shaped vessel having a wide neck and a spout at the apex to aid pouring a fluid into a small opening.

funny car, a drag racing car having a lightweight fibreglass body styled to resemble a production car.

funny wagon, a custom built car with unusual features, *e.g.* hydraulically powered suspension enabling it to jump.

furniture, the traffic related and non-traffic related objects that are located near the roadside, *e.g.* lamp standards, road signs, telephone poles, mail boxes.

furniture van, a pantechnicon.

fuse, a thin wire of specific alloy that will rapidly melt if the flow of an electrical current is above its rating, thereby protecting the rest of the circuit from electrical damage.

fuse block, a panel that holds the fuses for many circuits on a vehicle.

fusee, USA, a pyrotechnic signal flare formally carried by lorry drivers.

fuse puller, a small tweezer-like tool for removing and inserting blade fuses.

fusible link, fuse.

FV, fire vehicle.

FVRA, Franchised Vehicle Retailers Association, UK.

fvt, family vehicle trial.

fwd, front wheel drive.

fwh, freewheeling hubs, either manual or automatic.

G

g, gram, a unit of mass, 1-thousandth of 1 kilogram, used when measuring rates of fuel consumption and quantities of pollutant gases.

g, gravity, a measure of the average natural rate of vertical acceleration on earth, to which horizontal accelerations can be compared, equal to 9.80665 m/s^2.

G, a driving licence category for road rollers, UK.

G, Gear, a phase of the IPSGA mnemonic.

G, general service, an oil approved for use by CCMC in si petrol engines.

G, a hire car size and price category for cars based upon their floor pan; mpv 8 seat capacity.

g sensor, an instrument that measures transverse acceleration and sends a signal to a display showing the lateral grip whilst negotiating a bend.

G coupling, a pintle hook.

G segment car, a size category for cars based upon their floor pan; mpv 8 seat capacity.

GAB, Gabon, international vehicle distinguishing sign, see appendices.

gage, USA, gauge.

gaiter, a rubber shroud around a moving part to keep dirt outside and lubrication inside, typically having concertina folds for articulation; originally a leather cover for a leaf spring.

gal, gallon, either an imperial gallon or a US gallon.

Galileo, a 2nd generation GPS using 24 satellites giving an accuracy to 2 metres and which will identify house numbers from a digital map

Galileo's law of inertia, the law that an object not subject to external forces remains at rest or moves with constant speed in a straight line; as Newton's 1st law.

gall, damage to metal surfaces resulting from friction and improper lubrication.

gallery, a main passageway within a wall or casting having many sub passageways, allowing distribution to many points , e.g. the main oil gallery within the cylinder block that carries the lubricating oil to all parts of the engine.

gallon, imperial gallon, a unit of capacity, 1 imp gallon = 4.54596 litres, 20.1 % larger than a US gallon.

gallon, US gallon, a unit of capacity, 1 US gallon = 3.78531 litres, only 83 % of an imperial gallon.

galvanised, steel which has a coating of zinc, a metal that does not react significantly with air, thereby preventing the steel from rusting.

gangway, the space provided for obtaining access from any entrance to the passengers' seats or from any such seat to an exit, but excluding a staircase, (C&U).

gap, the air space between 2 electrical parts, e.g. sparkplug electrode.

gap acceptance, the decision by a driver that there is sufficient time and/or distance before an approaching vehicle to allow safe performance of a desired crossing, turning, or merging manoeuvre.

gap judgement, the judgement of a driver of the time and/or distance before an approaching vehicle travelling in a lane which the driver desires to cross, turn, or merge into.

gapper, USA, feeler gauge.

gapping, accurately adjusting the electrode gap on a sparkplug for maximum power and efficiency.

gap search and acceptance zone, the zone on an acceleration lane from where a driver looks, evaluates, and decides on action to take for successful merging onto the main carriageway.

garage, a place close to or within a house where a car is stored.

garage, a place at the side of a road where vehicles may refuel, refreshments may also be available.

garage, a place where vehicles are serviced or repaired.

garage, a place where vehicles are sold.

gar'd, garaged, an advertising abbreviation.

GARO, Russian association for producers of garage equipment, specialised vehicles, and automotive repairs.

gas, a state of matter when it has no defied shape or volume, when the matter is above the temperatures of its freezing and boiling points.

gas, gasoline.

gas axe, an oxyacetylene welding or cutting torch.

gas burner, USA, a high performance vehicle running on standard petrol instead of alcohol or nitromethane, etc.

gas conversion, the converting of a petrol engined vehicle to enable it to operate as a bifuel, dual fuel, or gas fuelled vehicle.

gas damper, gas filled damper.

gas discharge lamp, production of light by high voltage in an envelope filled with a specific gas or vapour, typically mercury, neon, sodium, or xenon.

gas engine, an engine that uses LPG or CNG or other gas for fuel.

gas exchange tdc, the tdc position of the crankshaft when the exhaust valve and inlet valve are both open because the exhaust and inlet phases overlap some degrees.

gas filled damper, a hydraulic damper containing below the liquid a small flexible envelope of highly pressurised nitrogen gas, such that the nitrogen acts as a cushion allowing the damper to be made stiffer for improved stability but without increasing harshness.

gas filled shock absorber, gas filled damper.

gas flow, the movement of air-fuel mixture into, or exhaust gases out from, an engine.

gas fuel, any fuel which is wholly gaseous at 17.5 °C under a pressure of 1.013 bar absolute, (C&U).

gas generator, a device containing a pyrotechnic that explodes to produce sufficient gas to rapidly inflate an airbag if triggered by a sensor.

gas guzzler, a car that consumes a lot of fuel, often assumed of large cars manufactured in USA.

gasket, a layer of soft material clamped between 2 firm surfaces to form a seal, materials used include: paper, cork, rubber, copper, also synthetic materials, and those made from a paste.

gasohol, a blended oxygenated fuel made by mixing up to 20 % ethyl alcohol (ethanol) with 80 % unleaded petrol.

gas oil, any of a range of petroleum distillates including kerosene, diesel fuel, and light fuel oil.

gasolina, a mixture of petrol and alcohol.

gasoline, USA, petrol, a volatile flammable liquid hydrocarbon derived from crude oil.

gasoline direct injection, a petrol engine in which the fuel is injected directly into the cylinder instead of injecting into the manifold.

gasoline engine, an internal combustion engine that consumes a mixture of air and petrol vapour as fuel.

gas pedal, USA, accelerator pedal.

gas prop, a strut which supports the bonnet or tailgate and which uses compressed gas as a spring to support the weight.

gas pump, USA, petrol pump.

gasser, USA, a high performance vehicle running on standard petrol instead of alcohol or nitromethane, etc.

gas shock absorber, gas filled damper.

gassing, the release of oxygen and hydrogen from a lead acid battery that is being charged, due to electrolysis breaking down the water into its elements, the gassing is proportional to the charging current.

gas spring, a sphere containing pressurised nitrogen as used in hydrogas and hydropneumatic suspensions.

gas station, USA, filling station.

gas tank, USA, a vessel for the storage of fuel in a vehicle, it may be metal or plastic.

gas turbine engine, an engine formed by 2 turbines on 1 shaft separated by a combustion chamber; the compressor turbine compresses air into the combustion chamber where fuel is injected during continuous combustion, the exhaust gas drives the exhaust turbine which drives the compressor turbine, essentially a continuous process with only 1 moving part; only fitted into a few experimental vehicles as the turbine rotates at approximately 50,000 rpm and has a small speed range, common in aircraft.

gas welding, oxyacetylene welding.

gate, on a manual transmission, an arrangement of slots, typically based upon a H shape, into which the gear lever moves to select the required gear.

gate, on some automatic transmissions, the slightly zigzag path along the quadrant taken by the selector lever.

gate, headboard.

gated crossing, a railway level crossing having any type of gate or barrier.

gated road, a road having a gate across it, requiring manual opening and closing, typically where a minor rural road is unfenced through an area where livestock grazes.

gateway, a place where a road is narrowed for the purpose of slowing traffic as part of a traffic calming scheme or to slow traffic entering a lower speed limit, typically using tall vertical posts positioned close to the edge of the road and/or between lanes to increase the visual effect; typically narrowed to a width of 3.1 m per lane, or narrowed further for restricting wide vehicles.

gather speed, to increase speed, to accelerate gradually.

Gatso, Maurice Gatsonides, Dutch, the inventor of automatic traffic speed recording cameras, first used in 1957.

Gatso camera, a device that emits a radio or laser beam to measure the speed of a vehicle, and automatically photographs each vehicle exceeding a set speed, typically taking 2 photographs at 0.7 second interval.

gauge, a measuring tool having fixed dimensions.

gauge , an instrument for measuring *e.g.* temperature, pressure, or volume of a fluid.

gauge pressure, a pressure reading on a scale that ignores atmospheric pressure, *i.e.* 14.7 psi absolute is equal to 0 psi gauge.

GAWR, USA, gross axle weight rating.

GB, Great Britain, international vehicle distinguishing sign, see appendices.

GBA, Alderney, international vehicle distinguishing sign, see appendices.

GBG, Guernsey, international vehicle distinguishing sign, see appendices.

GBJ, Jersey, international vehicle distinguishing sign, see appendices.

GBM, Isle of Man, international vehicle distinguishing sign, see appendices.

GBW, guided busway.

GBZ, Gibraltar, international vehicle distinguishing sign, see appendices.

gc, good condition, an advertising abbreviation.

gc, ground clearance.

GCA, Guatemala, international vehicle distinguishing sign, see appendices.

GCM, Australia, gross combination mass.

GCW, UK, gross combination weight.

GCW, USA, gross combined weight.

GCWR, USA, gross combined weight rating.

GDI, gasoline direct injection.

GDL, gas discharge lighting.

GDL, USA, Graduated Driver License.

Gdns, Gardens, a road name designation.

GE, Georgia, international vehicle distinguishing sign, see appendices.

GEA, Garage Equipment Association, UK.

gear, a toothed wheel that meshes with another to transmit power from one shaft to another.

gear, preceded by a number, the number of that particular gear in a sequence from the lowest, or from the lowest in that range.

gear and go, a principle of advanced driving using block downchanges, whereby braking is continued without a downchange until the desired speed is reached followed by a single selective downchange, *i.e.* omitting intermediate gears before acceleration.

gearbox, a part of the transmission system which houses gears of different ratios that may be selected by the driver or automatically, such that the limited rev-range of an engine may drive a vehicle through a much wider range of roadspeeds with a different torque in each gear.

gearcase, gearbox.

gearchange, the process of changing gear.

gearchange cable, a cable that connects the gear lever to the selector mechanism in the gearbox, usually a pair of cables, becoming common on all types of vehicles.

gearchange pedal, a pedal pressed with the left foot and which sends a signal to the gearbox of a pre-selector system at the time the driver wants the system to change to the next pre-selected gear.

gear counter, a driver of an automatic transmission vehicle who habitually counts each gearchange to always be aware of the gear in use.

gear down, to select a lower gear.

gearing, the ratio or system of gears.

gear jammer, CB jargon, a truck driver.

gearknob, the handle at the top of the gearlever.

gearlever, the mechanical control used to select the chosen gear.

gearlinkage, the system of rods and/or cables that connect the gearlever to the selector mechanism in the gearbox.

gear oil, an oil designed to withstand the extreme pressures that occur between gear teeth.

gear pump, a rotary pump in the form of 2 meshing gearwheels which contrarotate so that fluid is entrained between the teeth and the casing on one side and discharged on the other, typically an oil pressure pump.

gear range, a group of consecutive gear ratios having a specific selector mechanism, *e.g.* low range.

gear range, the group of gears available when *e.g.* D is selected on an automatic transmission.

gear ratio, the number of revolutions of a driving gear required to turn the driven gear through 1 revolution, enumerated by the number of gear teeth on the driven gear divided by the number of teeth on the driving gear.

gears, gear wheels that may be moved in and out of mesh such that different ratios are selectable.

gear selection indicator, a visual display that informs a driver which gear is selected, typically on automatics and electronic gear selector systems.

gear selector, gearlever.

gearset, a train of 2 or more gears used to transmit power, and usually to change torque and rotational speed.

gearshift, USA, gearchange.

gearstick, USA, gearlever.

gear teeth, cogs, the projections on a gear wheel that mesh with cogs of another gear wheel.

gear tooth, cog, a projection on a gear wheel that meshes with cogs of another gear wheel.

gear train, a series of meshed gears that produce a specific ratio.

Geartronic, an automatic gear selector system with a manual override and without a clutch pedal, developed by Volvo.

gear up, to select a higher gear.

gearwheel, gear.

gel battery, a non-maintenance vehicle battery that contains an acid jelly not liquid, and which is sealed for life.

gel coat, the smooth outer layer of a grp panel, the first layer to be applied to the mould, typically self coloured.

GEM, Guild of Experienced Motorists, UK, formerly CVM.

Gemmer steering, cam and roller steering.

general service, a military classification for non-specialist vehicles.

generator, a device that uses magnetism to convert rotating mechanical energy into electrical energy; either a dynamo to produce dc, or an alternator to produce ac.

generator, USA, dynamo.

GEODESY, a dash-top system based on GPS technology to alert a driver when approaching an electronically mapped speed trap, and which can store the location of a newly found speed trap in its memory and transmit such locations into the central data bank.

geometric design, the arrangement of the visible elements of a road, including: alignment, gradient, sight distance, width, and cross slope.

geometry, the design, arrangement, or alignment of parts.

gerotor pump, rotor pump.

getaway car, a fast car for making an escape after committing a crime.

get in, to board a vehicle.

get off, to alight from a bus.

get on, to board a bus.

get out, to alight from a vehicle.

GH, Ghana, international vehicle distinguishing sign, see appendices.

Ghia, Giacinto Ghia, Italy, founder of a coachbuilding company in 1915 which has styled bodywork for many car manufacturers.

ghost island, an island painted on the road surface to separate traffic flows but without any raised kerb, the island may be bordered by a broken or solid line, and typically will contain hatching or chevrons.

ghost island merge, a multilane entry sliproad which is separated into individual lanes by a ghost island between each lane to cause each lane to merge separately, or sometimes which causes 1 lane to merge whilst the other continues into a lane gain.

ghost vehicle, a parked vehicle which contributes to a collision between others but subsequently moves away before investigation of the site.

GIEG, Groupe des Industries d'Equipement de Garage.

gifting, the theft of gifts and other loose items from unattended cars, typically by smashing a window.

GIT, goods in transit, a type of insurance cover.

give way, a requirement to let other traffic continue on a priority road before emerging from a lesser road.

give way line, a broken white line or a pair of broken white lines painted transversely across the road or sometimes at an angle, giving a mandatory instruction that traffic behind the line must give precedence to traffic on the other side of the line, although when it is observed safe there is no requirement to stop.

g/km, grams per kilometre.

GL, grand luxe, a model of car superior to a CL.

GL, grid line, a map referencing system in road rally navigation.

glad hand, the union device which connects an air hose to a trailer, sometimes incorporating an automatic shut off when disconnected.

glance, a collision where the side of a vehicle strikes a vehicle or object at a shallow angle.

glance, a very short look in a direction,

typically too short to accurately assess speed or distance of other traffic.

glare, intense light from a point close to the drivers line of sight which causes a reduction in visibility; see: physiological, psychological, veiling.

glare ice, USA, glazed ice

glass, a hard, brittle, transparent material, used to manufacture windscreens, windows, headlamp lenses, bulbs and fibres.

GLASS, Green Laning Association, an organisation for 4x4 and similar off-road users, UK.

glass fibre, very long thin glass filaments, often spun into thread or woven into fabric having a high tensile strength, used to produce a tough rigid material for vehicle bodies when bound in resin as grp.

glass reinforced plastic, a lightweight construction material for bodies of cars vans and lorries, usually made from glass fibre strands in polyester resin.

Glass's Guide, a frequently updated guide to second hand car prices, UK.

glass tampering detector, an element of some car alarms that will respond to glass being broken.

glaze, an unwanted very smooth finish that develops on cylinder walls.

glazed ice, black ice, clear ice.

glazing, glass fitted to a vehicle window frame.

GLi, a car having a grand luxe standard of trim and a fuel injected engine.

glide, to travel at very slow speed with the clutch depressed, retaining the last used gear, normally performed in the later stages of stopping, similar in effect to coasting but with no danger.

glide plate, a flat greased steel plate under the front of a semitrailer and around the kingpin, under which the tractive unit 5th wheel slides when coupling and uncoupling, and on which the trailer articulates.

global positioning system, a system that receives signals from 24 USA satellites orbiting the earth to accurately identify the exact location, speed, and heading of a GPS receiver.

gloss, a shine on a smooth surface.

glovebox, a container originally for holding the drivers gauntlets, now for holding any small items.

glowplug, a small powerful electrical heater fitted in each cylinder of most diesel engines to aid cold starting.

glowplug gasket, a captive ring shaped device which provides a seal between the glowplug and cylinder head, such that the glowplug is designed to be installed finger tight then turned $1/4$ turn only with a tool.

glow time, the duration of time when the glowplugs are heating, after which the engine may be cranked.

GLP, Canada, Graduated Licensing Program.

GLS, grand luxe special, a car having a grand

luxe standard of trim and special features common to only a small number of vehicles.

GLT, a car having a grand luxe standard of trim and a turbocharged engine.

GLT, guided light transit.

GLW, New Zealand, gross laden weight.

glycol, a substance added to cooling water to raise its boiling point and lower its freezing point, see: MEG, MPG.

GM, General Motors.

GMC, General Motors Corporation.

go cart, a miniature racing car with no body, small diameter tyres, no differential, but 1 or 2 engines, some may achieve speeds exceeding 160 km/h (100 mph).

Godspeed, an expression of good wishes to a person starting a journey.

goes like the clappers, a vehicle with significant acceleration performance.

go faster stripes, 2 broad contrasting stripes from front to rear over the roof of a car, typically a 1960s fashion; sometimes narrower stripes along the sides.

goggles, eye protection against wind, dust, dirt, and insects used when driving some cars with an aeroscreen or without a windscreen.

going breaker breaker, CB jargon, leaving the air.

going down, CB jargon, signing off the air.

go jack, a trolley with small castor wheels, designed to facilitate moving a car by lifting the tyre from the ground, sometimes 1 may be fitted under each wheel which allows a car to be pushed sideways into a storage area.

go juice, CB jargon, petrol or fuel.

go kart, go cart.

GoMW, Guild of Motoring Writers.

good lady, CB jargon, a female CB user.

goods vehicle, a mechanically propelled vehicle or a trailer constructed or adapted for the conveyance of goods or burden, (RTA).

go off, to start to set, the first of several stages when a body filler or resin changes from liquid to solid.

gooseneck, a hydroneck lowloader semitrailer.

gooseneck turn, a swan neck turn.

goose wing door, a single wide gullwing door serving the front and rear seats.

Go-Ped, a 2 wheeled vehicle, similar looking to a childs scooter, having an engine of approximately 20 cc powering the rear wheel, the vehicle is easily transportable in a car boot.

Gordon Bennett, James Gordon Bennett, USA, the founder of international car and air races to which his name was given to a cup, run annually from 1900 to 1905.

gore, the long narrow triangular ghost island area between the merge or divergence of 2 carriageways, especially on a motorway where a through carriageway and an entry or exit sliproad merge or diverge, normally chevron painted.

governor, a device which controls the occurrence of each gear change in an automatic transmission to match road speed and engine speed.

governor, a device which limits engine speed, either mechanically or electronically.

governor, a device which limits road speed, by sensing road speed and limiting fuel when the set speed is reached.

gp, general purpose, later phonetically transformed to Jeep when the vehicle was launched in 1940.

GP, Grand Prix, French, big prize.

gph, gallons per hour.

gph, graphite.

GPS, global positioning system.

GR, Greece, international vehicle distinguishing sign, see appendices.

GR, grid reference, a numerical means of determining an exact location in road rally navigation.

grab, the action of the brakes if they start to grip strongly as the pedal is initially depressed.

grabber, an electronic device used by a car thief which will read the signal from some plippers such that the signal can be used later to unlock the vehicle and disarm the alarm/immobilizer.

grab handle, a handle on the drawbar and/or each corner of a light trailer or caravan for manual manoeuvring.

grab handle, a handle usually placed above a door opening inside a vehicle to facilitate easy alighting.

grade, USA, gradient, hill.

gradeability, the performance of a vehicle stated as the maximum gradient it can climb at its GVW.

grade control, an exercise on a USA driving test whereby the candidate must park on a gradient with the front wheels turned in the appropriate direction and lodged against the curb.

grade crossing, USA, railway level crossing.

grader, a vehicle with a moveable blade between front and rear axles to smooth the foundations of a road, or to smooth the top surface of tracks with a loose surface, typically having a single front axle and drive to both rear axles.

grade separated junction, a road junction incorporating underpasses and/or flyovers such that traffic crosses at different levels without interference to flow.

grade separation, the carrying of 1 carriageway over or under another with or without facilities for interchange.

gradient, an inclined plane, a length of road that is not horizontal, significant gradients are usually marked with signs indicating the slope as a ratio or as a percentage.

graduated licensing, a system for phasing in of increasing driver privileges with age and experience, administered differently in various countries but generally starting with instructed or supervised learning, then unsupervised learning only in low risk situations, then unrestricted driving.

graduated tint, a tinted band across the upper edge of the windscreen to reduce glare, and where the tint at the lower edge of the band reduces gradually in strength.

graduated vehicle excise duty, a system of applying road tax based upon the CO_2 exhaust emissions, such that cars emitting greater CO_2 in terms of g/km pay greater road tax.

grain alcohol, ethanol, a constituent of beer, wine, and spirits, sometimes blended with methanol or petrol for use as fuel.

grams per kilometre, the units used to measure the CO_2 emissions from a vehicle, a small modern car may produce approximately 150 g/km of CO_2.

Grand Prix, any of several international motor racing events, especially F1; the first GP was run at Circuit de la Sarthe near Le Mans, France, in 1906.

grand tourer, originally an open top luxury car, now typically a high performance coupé built for speed and style.

grand touring, grand tourer.

grand touring, gran turismo.

Grand Trunk Road, National Highway 1, India, the road from Kabul, Afghanistan over the Khyber pass, through Lahore, Pakistan and across northern India through Delhi to Calcutta, 2,500 km (1,600 miles) in length.

granny lane, the nearside lane on a motorway or similar road, especially a crawler lane.

gran turismo, Italian, a high performance car, typically a coupé, built for comfort and speed.

graph, a pictorial representation of a series of numbers in the form of a line.

graphic plate, a registration plate incorporating an official emblem across the background, as used in USA and South Africa.

graphite, a type of carbon, an excellent dry lubricant for some parts, a constituent of some greases, especially for slow moving parts; also used in the form of fibres similar to fibreglass but stronger and lighter.

grasscrete, a surface prepared to support the passage or parking of vehicles, having a surface of grass and a subsurface of concrete blocks of which 53 % of their area comprises vertical pockets filled with soil.

grass heat shield, a heat shield fitted beneath a cat to reduce the risk of its heat igniting a fire when driving over long grass.

grasstrack, a type of racing in specially prepared cars on a grass surface.

grate, the feel and sound of a noisy gear selection made when the selected gears are not synchronised before meshing.

graunch, the feel and sound of a noisy gear selection made when the selected gears are not synchronised before meshing.

gravel, small stones used in surfacing roads, also used loosely to restrain racing cars that have left the circuit.

gravel crew, a non competing crew in a rally who drive the route to check the condition of stages and recommend tyre types.

gravel rash, bodywork damage caused by small stones hitting the front of the bonnet, each chipping the paint slightly; caused by habitually following too closely to vehicles ahead.

gravel trap, an area of gravel on the outside of racetrack bends to slow a car which has left the track.

gravity, a force acting upon every vehicle, attempting to cause acceleration or deceleration on a gradient, also the force that influences friction between the tyres and the surface.

gravity feed, a fuel supply system on motorcycles and vintage cars where the fuel tank is above the carburettor.

GRB, Groupe Rapporteurs Bruit, French vehicle noise control.

grease, a lubricant in the form of a solid dispersion in a thickening agent, *e.g.* oil thickened with a metallic soap.

grease cap, spindle cap.

grease gun, a tool with which to inject lubricating grease at high pressure into parts fitted with a receptive grease nipple.

grease nipple, a device through which grease is injected and which forms a seal to prevent entry of dirt.

greasy spoon, a transport café where standards of hygiene may be low.

Great North Road, the A1 road from London to Edinburgh, 650 km, (404 miles) in length.

greedy position, to drive along a road such that the offside of the vehicle is unusually close to, or slightly over, the road centre

green arc, a marking on a rev counter showing the most economical range of engine speeds at which that vehicle should be driven.

green arrow, an illuminated traffic signal having an obligatory function.

green arrow, USA, an illuminated traffic signal indicating a protected turn in the direction of the arrow.

green band, green arc.

green card, an international insurance document recommended to be carried when driving outside the country in which the vehicle is insured, and compulsory in some countries, a mandatory purchase for personal grey or parallel imports.

green cross code, UK, a set of rules for pedestrians to increase their level of safety when crossing a road.

green curb, a painted marking denoting parking is permitted for a restricted time only, as detailed on the curb or on an adjacent sign.

green diesel, ultra low sulphur diesel fuel having less than 0.003 % m/m, (30 ppm) sulphur.

green filter arrow, a traffic signal that permits traffic to move in the direction of the arrow whilst other traffic is held by a stop signal.

green flag, a flag carried on the rear offside of the last vehicle of a military convoy.

green flag, a flag with which to communicate with racing drivers, meaning end of a danger area previously signified by a yellow flag, or start of the warm-up lap.

green headlamp, a green filter fitted over the offside headlamp of the last vehicle of a military convoy.

greenhouse gas, carbon dioxide, emitted in quantity from vehicle exhausts and believed to influence the atmosphere and cause global warming.

green lane, an unsurfaced track typically with a grass surface which is normally classified as a highway.

green light, CB jargon, a clear road ahead.

green man, a symbol of a walking pedestrian illuminated green at some pedestrian crossings indicating to pedestrians when it is safe to cross the road.

green octagon, UK, an ADI licence, normally displayed in the nearside lower corner of the windscreen.

green panel, a small green area on a larger sign of a different colour showing the direction to a specific primary route.

green petrol, ultra low sulphur unleaded petrol having less than 0.003 % m/m, (30 ppm) sulphur.

green road, green lane, sometimes originally a drove road.

Green Road Code, UK, a set of rules and courtesies for users of green lanes, tracks, packhorse routes, trails, etc, including the 4 Ws.

green shield stamps, CB jargon, money.

green sign, a rectangular sign showing directions at a junction of primary routes.

green studs, cats eyes or reflective studs which mark the nearside edge of the main carriageway at lay-bys, side roads, and sliproads, and the offside edge of a carriageway at an offside turn off a dual carriageway.

green time, the duration of time which a green traffic signal shows to a specific traffic flow at a signal controlled junction.

green wave, a facility for emergency vehicles especially a fire tender, in creating a priority route through a network of traffic signals by bringing signals to green approximately 30 seconds before the emergency vehicle is due to arrive so traffic is cleared in addition to having a green priority; initiated at the fire station.

greenway, a motorway or similar road having wide verges and central reservation which are landscaped and planted.

grenade the brakes, USA, to panic brake, to stamp suddenly on the footbrake.

grey import, vehicles privately imported into a country because they are not available through main dealers and which require SVA.

gri, grille.

grid, an index system of numbered squares printed on a map as an aid to finding a location.

grid, an arrangement of town streets in a regular rectangular pattern.

grid, the designated starting positions painted on the surface of a race track.

grid girl, a female assistant that perform duties such as protecting racing drivers from the sun or rain before a race starts.

gridlock, a traffic jam that extends across a network of roads in a town or city.

grid reference, a numbering system enabling an exact location to be identified on a map.

grille, the mechanical protection for the radiator, often used by the manufacturer to carry a traditional styling belonging to that manufacturer.

grip, to hold firmly using friction; the adhesion between the tyre and the road surface.

grit, fine gravel often mixed with rocksalt for spreading on a snow covered road to assist traction.

gritter, a lorry which is used for the purpose of spreading grit and/or salt so as to avoid or reduce the effect of ice or snow on the road.

gritting trailer, a trailer which is used on a road for the purpose of spreading grit or other matter so as to avoid or reduce the effect of ice or snow on the road, (C&U).

GRM, Grands Randonneurs Motorisés, French off-road club.

grommet, a rubber or plastic ring located in a hole to protect a pipe or wiring as it passes through.

groove, the longitudinal space for water dispersal between 2 adjacent tyre tread ribs or blocks.

groove cracks, splits or cracks in the base of the grooves between tread ribs, typically on older tyres where the textile casing has lost its strength and where the rubber has aged and lost some suppleness.

grooved pavement, a road surface cut with numerous fine longitudinal slots for water drainage and to increase frictional resistance in a horizontal curve.

gross axle weight rating, USA, the maximum weight which any axle may transmit to the ground as specified by the manufacturer.

gross combination mass, Australia, the maximum permitted weight of a fully loaded road train.

gross combination weight, the total weight of a lorry and load, applying to an articulated vehicle and all vehicles that comprise a combination vehicle.

gross combined weight, USA, the total weight of a vehicle, including all its contents, plus the weight of a trailer and its entire contents, the GCW should not be allowed to exceed the gross combined weight rating GCWR.

gross combined weight rating, USA, the maximum recommended weight of a vehicle when towing a trailer, and is less than the sum of GVWR plus maximum trailer payload.

gross laden weight, New Zealand, the maximum permitted weight of a vehicle together with any load it is carrying, including any equipment and accessories.

gross power, engine power measured at the crankshaft before allowing for power losses due to necessary auxiliary equipment, *e.g.* coolant pump, alternator, etc. driven by the engine.

gross train weight, the total weight of vehicle and load, applying to articulated lorry and drawbar trailer combinations.

gross vehicle mass, Australia and New Zealand, the maximum permitted mass of a vehicle as specified by the manufacturer.

gross vehicle weight, the total weight of a lorry and load, applying to solo rigid vehicles and tractive units.

gross vehicle weight, USA, the sum of curb weight and payload.

gross vehicle weight rating, USA, the maximum allowable loaded vehicle weight, including the vehicle and its equipment, fluids and fuel, occupants and cargo.

gross weight, UK, in relation to a motor vehicle, the sum of all the weights transmitted to the road surface by all the wheels of the vehicle, (C&U).

gross weight, UK, in relation to a trailer, the sum of all the weights transmitted to the road surface by all the wheels of the trailer, and of any weight of the trailer imposed on the drawing vehicle, (C&U).

gross weight, New Zealand, the weight of a rigid or combination vehicle together with the load and including any equipment and accessories.

ground, the earth return path for electrical circuits where the current passes through a vehicle body.

ground, when referring to mechanical and lighting references, the surface on which the vehicle stands which should be substantially horizontal, (C&U).

ground clearance, the vertical distance between a flat surface and the lowest point on the underside of a vehicle when at its maximum kerbweight.

ground clearance control, a system for controlling the suspension height on a vehicle having hydropneumatic suspension which allows ground clearance to be varied by the driver.

ground clouds, CB jargon, fog.

grounded, the situation when a vehicle becomes immovable under its own power due to its underside resting heavily upon an uneven surface.

ground effect, the utilisation of under-vehicle aerodynamics to create a low pressure to suck a car down against the road surface at speed.

grounding, the situation when any part of the underside of a vehicle briefly strikes any surface.

group sub A, a hire car size and price category for cars based upon their floor pan; a very small car, *e.g.* the Mini, or Ford Ka sized.

group A, a hire car size and price category for cars based upon their floor pan; a small car often designated supermini, *e.g.* Mercedes A-class, or Peugeot 206 sized.

groupage, a mixed load on a lorry, *e.g.* individual different sized parcels from many customers.

group B, a hire car size and price category for cars based upon their floor pan; a small car designed to seat 4 with some comfort, *e.g.* Ford Focus, or Peugeot 306 sized.

group C, a hire car size and price category for cars based upon their floor pan; a small family car to seat 5 with some comfort, *e.g.* Audi A4, or Ford Mondeo sized.

group D, a hire car size and price category for cars based upon their floor pan; a medium sized family car that will seat 5 with comfort, *e.g.* Audi A6, or BMW 5-series sized.

group E, a hire car size and price category for cars based upon their floor pan; a luxury car, *e.g.* Audi A8, or BMW 7-series, and usually estate versions of cars in group D.

grouped lamps, lamps in a common housing but with individual lenses and bulbs, *e.g.* rear lamp cluster, (C&U).

group F, a hire car size and price category for cars based upon their floor pan; executive cars and cars with automatic transmission.

group G, a hire car size and price category for cars based upon their floor pan; mpv 8 seat capacity.

group M, a hire car size and price category for cars based upon their floor pan; luxury executive cars.

group W, a hire car price category for cars based upon their cost and performance; high power sports cars.

grown tyre, a used tyre which has slightly increased in size.

grp, glass reinforced plastic.

GRRF, Group of Rapporteurs on Wheels and Braking, French.

GRSA, Group of Rapporteurs on Safety Provisions on Motor Coaches and Buses, French.

grub screw, a small headless fully threaded screw.

GS, general service.

GS, grid square, a 1 km square as marked on an OS map in road rally navigation.

GSM, global system for mobile communications, a digital telephone system often used in vehicles to support other accessories, *e.g.* security features.

gsn, global satellite navigation system, a misnomer, see: GPS.

GT, Grand Trunk Road, India.

GT, gran turismo, Italian, suggesting a high performance luxury sports car or coupé, sometimes Anglicized by the misnomer grand touring.

GTi, grand touring injection, a car designation suggesting high performance having an injected engine; however, since mid 1990s all new cars have fuel injection.

GTO, gran turismo omologato.

GTR, Grand Trunk Road, India.

GTW, UK, gross train weight.

guarantee, warranty.

guard rail, a fence to restrict pedestrians from crossing a road in an unsafe place.

guard rail, USA, roadside safety barrier to restrain an out of control vehicle.

gudgeon pin, a tubular pin that locates the piston to the little end of the con rod.

guided bus, a bus having a pair of small horizontal jockey wheels ahead of the front wheels linked to the steering mechanism which will automatically steer the bus in a special narrow lane between raised kerbs.

guided light transit, a bus guidance system which uses a double flanged retractable wheel to engage in a central rail buried flush within the road surface for automatic steering, and which is retracted for manual steering off the guideway.

guideway, a route used by a guided bus or guided light transit bus.

guidosimplex, a transmission system having selectable manual and automatic modes, when automatic is selected the clutch pedal has no function whatsoever, in manual mode the clutch pedal must be operated for starting, stopping, and every gearchange.

gulley mount, a hidden mounting system for a car roof rack, accessed by removing the gulley covers to reveal the mounting points.

gullwing, doors that open in a vertical arc, hinged longitudinally along the roof centreline.

gulp valve, an antibackfire valve in an air injection system, it allows a sudden intake of air through the air intake during deceleration to prevent backfiring and popping in the exhaust.

gusher, an engine having faulty oil seals and which leaves a significant pool of oil below where the vehicle was parked; see also: leaker.

gutter, a shallow channel along the edge of a car roof to prevent rainwater entering an open door.

gutter, a shallow channel along the edge of most roads to carry rainwater.

gutter mount, the mounting system for a car roof rack on the roof gutter, on many modern cars this gutter may be within the vehicle door frame.

GUY, Guyana, international vehicle distinguishing sign, see appendices.

GVED, UK, graduated vehicle excise duty.

GV(PT)R, UK, Goods Vehicles (Plating and Testing) Regulations 1988.

GVM, Australia and New Zealand, gross vehicle mass.

GVW, UK, gross vehicle weight.

GVWR, USA, gross vehicle weight rating.

GW, give way, a specific junction in road rally navigation.

gyratory system, a complex junction consisting of 1 way links connected together to enable traffic to circulate along 1 or more links before exiting, *e.g.* some motorway junctions, a large roundabout, a magic roundabout, a system of linked roundabouts, or a grid network of 1 way roads forming a hub, sometimes part of an inner ring road.

gyrobus, a passenger carrying vehicle in which kinetic energy from braking or descending a hill is stored in a high speed horizontal flywheel beneath the floor and used to drive an electrical generator which supplies current to an electric motor to propel the vehicle.

H

h, hot, the engine temperature required before some engine adjustments may be made.

H, a driving licence category for tracklaying vehicles, UK.

H, an engine cylinder and crankshaft layout created by mating a pair of horizontal engines with 1 atop the other, the 2 crankshafts are connected by a gear drive to a common output shaft.

H, halogen, a prefix to a bulb designation indicating it contains a halogen gas, usually iodine vapour.

H, hard mode, referring to remote controlled variable dampers it allows the driver to select hard to match road surface and driving style.

H, hatchback, a car body style.

H, high pressure, a cover on a valve on ac piping marking that section of the system.

H, hill, referring to some automatic transmission, a command to the gearbox to demand higher engine rev's before changing up.

H, hold, referring to some automatic transmission, a command to the gearbox to hold the present gear, to prevent the gearbox from making frequent or unwanted changes whilst climbing or descending gradients.

H, horizontal grid line, a reference in road rally navigation.

H, hospital, a sign displaying information that the driver is in the locale of a hospital and the horn should not be used, or that the road is on a route leading to a hospital.

H, Hungary, international vehicle distinguishing sign, see appendices.

H, hydrogen.

H, the tyre speed rating code denoting a maximum design speed of 210 km/h (130 mph), moulded into the tyre sidewall.

H, see: single H, and double H.

H2, high range 2wd, a selectable gear range on a 4wd vehicle, it transmits the drive to only 2 wheels using the high range of gears.

H₂SO₄, sulphuric acid, a strong acid liquid, colourless, toxic, highly corrosive, normally used at 40 % concentration as electrolyte in batteries.

H4, high range 4wd, a selectable gear range on a 4wd vehicle, it transmits the drive to all 4 wheels using the high range of gears.

H16, an engine cylinder and crankshaft layout created by mating a pair of flat 8 cylinder engines with 1 atop the other, the 2 crankshafts are connected by a gear drive to a common output shaft.

H hump, a speed hump having lengthened approach and departure ramps matched to the track of larger vehicles, and a shorter section for smaller vehicles, for uniform speed control of all vehicles.

H pattern, the conventional gear selector layout on most manual transmission vehicles.

H tronic, a manual/automatic 4wd transmission system developed by Porsche for Hyundai.

HA, Highway Act, either 1835 or 1980, UK.

HA, Highways Agency, responsible for the condition of roads, UK.

HA, the height from the road surface to the top of the chassis.

hackney carriage, taxi; named from Hackney in London where horses were formerly pastured.

hairpin, a bend in a road where the direction of travel turns through 120° to 180°, usually associated with steep hills.

halation, dazzle created at night by light reflected from white parts of some traffic signs that can make adjacent detail difficult to discern.

halfcab, a bus or lorry having a drivers compartment on 1 side of the vehicle only, typically on older buses.

half change, to change ¹/₂ a gear up or down on a transmission having a splitter.

half cloverleaf, a grade separated junction where a road crosses a motorway or similar road using 1 overbridge and where 2 link roads turn through 180° or more; see appendices.

half diamond, a grade separated restricted access junction having 1 bridge over or under the main road but only 1 pair of sliproads to/ from the lesser roads, typically used to match traffic demand or where space is minimal; named from the resulting plan shape; see appendices.

half gear, a splitter system having ¹/₂ gears between each primary gear.

half inch rule, the maximum distance a window should be opened in any high risk stationary traffic situation to avoid risk of personal attack or theft; also named 1 cm rule.

half lock, the angle of the front wheels when they have slewed approximately ¹/₂ the angle between straight and full lock to either the left or right.

half shaft, the shaft that transmits the drive from the differential to the wheel, especially on a live axle.

half shift, to change $^1/_2$ a gear up or down on a transmission having a splitter.

half split, to change a $^1/_2$ gear up or down on a transmission having a splitter.

halftrack, a tracklaying vehicle so designed and constructed that its weight is transmitted to the road surface by a combination of wheels and continuous tracks whereby the weight transmitted to the road surface by the tracks is not less than $^1/_2$ the weight of the vehicle, (C&U); typically of military origin.

Hall effect sensor, Hall generator.

Hall generator, a pulse generator that responds to a rotating metallic disc with vanes and slots and which gives a signal that can be used by a microprocessor to recognise engine timing, engine speed, etc.

halobutyl rubber, a type of airtight rubber that is used as a thin layer on the inside of a tubeless tyre carcass for the purpose of holding air.

halogen, any of several specific gases, typically used in headlamps to improve some characteristics.

halogen bulb, a light bulb containing a halogen gas, usually iodine vapour, to improve brightness and extend its working life.

halt, a temporary stop on a journey.

halt, stop.

hamburger junction, a roundabout at which some routes have a shortcut directly across the centre when traffic is heavy, the whole junction controlled by part time traffic signals, the name is derived from the resulting plan shape which resembles a hot cross bun; see appendices.

Hamlin switch, a suspended mass inertial switch which responds to a significant impact and triggers the detonator to inflate an airbag, normally located in the centre console or floor tunnel, separate directional switches are fitted for the front airbags, side airbags, and curtain airbags.

hammer, CB jargon, accelerator pedal.

hammer down, CB jargon, to drive quickly.

hammerhead, a place at the end of a cul-de-sac where the road is widened to facilitate a 3 point turn.

hammerhead turn, a 3 point turn or similar performed at a location where a road is widened for the purpose, typically at the end of a cul-de-sac.

Hancock, Walter Hancock, builder of the first self-propelled steam driven omnibus, in London in 1831.

handball, to load or unload a lorry by hand.

handbook, a book supplied with a vehicle giving the operating and safety instructions, and some specifications.

handbrake, a parking brake operated by a hand lever which activates a friction device for locking the wheels to hold the vehicle stationary when stopped for more than a few seconds and before leaving a vehicle; it normally operates on the rear wheels, usually by Bowden cable but by air on larger vehicles.

handbrake lever, a hand operated control with which to set the parking brake for locking the wheels to hold the vehicle stationary, usually connected by Bowden cable but by air on larger vehicles.

handbrake turn, the technique of inducing a controlled 180° spin, a manoeuvre performed to turn a car in a long narrow space, executed at speed by operating the handbrake to create a rear wheel skid followed immediately by a large steering input such that the vehicle will yaw significantly, the manoeuvre is usually self limiting to about 180°, used by rally drivers and in some other competitions; CAUTION, if attempted in a pickup, suv, 4x4, or similar the car may roll, *i.e.* only possible in a car having a low centre of gravity.

handbrake warning light, a red tell-tale lamp on the dashboard indicating to the driver when the handbrake is applied.

handcart, a cart pushed or pulled manually.

hand crank, to start an engine manually by cranking with a starting handle.

hand cut, a method of creating a tread on a tyre by hand with a special tool to achieve a specific pattern, usually for racing.

handed, made to fit on a specific side, not interchangeable from left to right.

handle, CB jargon, a CB users nickname.

handling, the quality of the feel of the performance of the chassis, suspension, steering, and tyres.

handling skill, a level of proficiency in the control of a vehicle in various situations.

handover technique, a version of pull-push steering when approximately 180° of rotation of the steering wheel is anticipated and accomplished with a single hand movement, starting from the 3 and 9 position a left turn is performed by the left hand moving over the top of the wheel and gripping the wheel at 2 o'clock and pulling the wheel whilst the right hand slides on the rim remaining at 3 o'clock; typically used when speed around the corner is anticipated to be between 30 km/h and 80 km/h (between 20 mph and 50 mph).

hands free, a car phone having the microphone and speaker mounted in the vehicle.

handshaker, USA, a manual gearlever.

hand shuffle, USA, a version of the pull push steering technique in which the initial wheel movement is a push upwards.

hand signal, arm signal.

hands off, a stability test on a proving ground to confirm that a vehicle will run straight at speed, also performed on a banked circuit.

hand throttle, a hand operated accelerator, a misnomer, see: throttle.

hanger, a rubber or plastic strap or ring used as an antivibration support for an exhaust pipe.

hardback, a hardtop, a car body style having a complete metal roof as opposed to similar models having a softback.

hard on, a condition in the operation of the braking system when the driver exerts maximum pressure on the footbrake or handbrake.

hard shoulder, a margin with a firm surface contiguous along the nearside of lane 1 on a motorway and other busy roads, used for breakdowns and emergencies only.

hard solder, a copper-zinc or silver based alloy with a melting temperature above 450 °C.

hardstanding, a parking area surfaced with a hard material.

hard stop, hard braking from a high speed but without locking the wheels to generate significant heating of the brakes; an ill-advised procedure recommended by some to force-bed new brake pads to worn discs.

hardtop, a removable vehicle roof which is solid in structure.

hardtop, USA, a pillarless coupé.

hardtop convertible, USA, a sedan having a fixed roof disguised to give a misleading visual impression that it is a convertible.

hard trim, the exterior decoration on a car, especially all chromed and other bare metal parts.

hard up, when parking to be deliberately very close to another object.

Hardy Spicer uj, a Rzeppa constant velocity joint, commonly used in drive shafts.

hare, the highest range of gears on a tractor.

harmonic balancer, a vibration damper mounted just below the crankshaft and rotating at double crankshaft speed.

harmonic marking, the red spot on a tyre sidewall and a marking on a wheel rim, marked to facilitate match mounting to cancel tyre and wheel runout to minimise vibration.

harness, a seatbelt, usually in competitive vehicles having a 4, 5, or 6 point fixing.

harness, the wiring loom in a vehicle, the complete wiring system.

Harrah, Philip J Harrah, inventor of the hi-lift jack in USA in 1895.

harsh braking, to suddenly brake very hard, typically because of late application, usually due to poor observation, low concentration, or poor anticipation.

harvester, a vehicle designed for an agricultural purpose.

hat, Australia, a traffic safety cone.

hatch, hatchback.

hatchback, a car constructed to carry 4 or 5 persons, having a sloping rear that opens fully for carrying large items.

haul, to pull, or to carry a load.

haulage, the commercial transport of goods or materials by road.

haulier, a business that operates by transporting goods by road.

haul road, a road typically on a private site *e.g.* from a quarry, built to carry heavily loaded trucks at a good speed, normally having a gradient that does not exceed 17 %.

haulway, the surface used by heavy vehicles between a public road and a private commercial premises, typically quite short, *i.e.* the equivalent of a driveway from a road to a house.

hazard, any situation that may or will cause a driver to change speed or direction, a potential danger.

hazardous goods, a load or partial load on a vehicle that could cause danger to health or the environment or property if any of the material is released or burned etc.

hazard perception, the early recognition of hazards which many drivers do not see until too late to avoid, the product of the skills: anticipation, concentration, and observation.

hazard post, a short post at the side of a road having the appropriate reflectors on top: red at the nearside, white at the offside, amber on central reservations; to mark the edge of the road especially at night and to show the location of hazards, bends, steep drops etc.,

hazard warning line, a broken white line consisting of a long stripe and a short gap, used to mark the centre of a road where there are features generating a significant permanent hazard, *e.g.* a bend.

hazard warning sign, a road traffic sign, triangular with a red border and displaying a pictorial representation of the potential danger.

hazard warning signal, the simultaneous operation of all of a vehicle's direction indicator lamps to show that the vehicle temporarily constitutes a special danger to other road users, (C&U).

hazard warning switch, a switch usually marked with a red triangle that will operate the hazard flasher unit and give a hazard warning signal to others.

HAZCHEM, Europe, the system of marking all hazardous material whilst it is being transported, using a coded identification to distinguish the material, the nature of its hazard, and measures which must be taken by the emergency services if a spill or fire should occur.

HAZMAT, USA, hazardous material, any material which may pose an unreasonable risk to health, safety, property, or the environment during transportation.

hc, high compression.

hc, hydrocarbon.

HC, heading control.

HC, heavy combination, Australia, any single trailer combination exceeding 9 tonnes GVM.

hc engine, high camshaft engine.

HCV, heavy commercial vehicle.

HCVS, Historic Commercial Vehicle Society, UK.

hd, heavy duty.

HDC, hill descent control.

HDE, USA, heavy duty engine.

HDi, high pressure diesel injection.

hdtp, hardtop.

HDV, USA, heavy duty vehicle, exceeding 8,500 lb GVWR (3.85 tonnes).

head, cylinder head.

head and tail, the transport of an exceptional load in which 1 locomotive pulls at the front whilst another pushes from the rear, typically on a route with sharp bends.

headboard, a panel across the front end of a flatbed trailer or lorry, typically over 600 mm high and sufficiently strong to resist a force equal to $^1/_2$ the weight of the load to prevent the load from moving whilst braking.

header, an exhaust manifold made from separate tubes.

header bar, the foremost bar of a hood which attaches to the top of the windscreen.

header tank, a vessel containing coolant as part of the cooling system, typically of opaque plastic.

head gasket, cylinder head gasket.

heading, the direction in which a vehicle is facing at any moment.

heading angle, yaw angle.

heading control, a system using a video camera and microprocessor to recognise road markings and control an actuator to operate the steering automatically without driver input on a motorway.

headlamp, a lamp used to illuminate the road in front of a vehicle and which is not a front fog lamp, (C&U).

headlamp alignment, the angles at which each headlamp emits a beam of light.

headlamp assist, a system which automatically switches on the headlamps in dull weather and at night, developed by DaimlerChrysler.

headlamp converter, each of a pair of small lenses affixed to the headlamp glass that convert part of the beam to dip from left to right when a rhd vehicle is being driven in a lhd country, or vice-versa.

headlamp mask, each of a pair of small masks affixed to part of the headlamp glass that prevent the kickup part of the dip beam from dazzling oncoming drivers when a rhd vehicle is being driven in a lhd country, or vice-versa.

headlamp visor, a cosmetic part resembling a cap peak fitted above a headlamp, a 1960s fashion, usually chromium plated.

headlamp washer, a system that sprays a water based cleaning solution at high pressure onto the headlamps, often incorporating a wiper.

headlamp wiper, a device to wipe water and dirt from the headlamps, incorporating a washer system.

headlight, a bright beam of light projected forwards from the headlamp.

headlight flasher, a switch on a control stalk that enables the headlamps to be flashed briefly.

headlight levelling, an electrical system, sometimes automatic, that adjusts the alignment of the headlamp beam to compensate for varying load in the rear of a car or other vehicle.

headlight levelling control, a control typically a vertical thumbwheel marked 0-1-2-3 by which a driver may electrically adjust the levelling of the headlamp beams to compensate for the number of passengers and/or the load in the boot.

headlining, the covering over the inside of a car roof having sound absorbing and aesthetic properties.

head on, a situation where 2 moving vehicles approach front to front.

head on collision, a collision in which 2 moving vehicles meet front to front, typically the most severe of collisions.

headrest, a common misnomer, see: head restraint.

head restraint, a device on top of passenger seats designed for the prevention of whiplash injuries to the neck during collisions, providing each restraint is adjusted correctly.

headroom, the distance between the top of a persons head and the inside of a car roof.

headroom, the distance between the top of a vehicle and the underside of a bridge.

head up display, the projection of key readouts, *i.e.* the speedometer, tachometer, fuel level, all alarms, etc. onto the windscreen; originally developed for aircraft, now developed by Vauxhall.

headway, the distance between the front of a vehicle and the rear of the vehicle it is following whilst moving; it is usually considered as a time interval which should have a minimum of 2 seconds; see also: spacing.

headwind, wind blowing directly on the front of a vehicle, especially when it is strong.

hearse, a vehicle adapted to carry a coffin.

heart disorder, a medical condition that may prevent a person holding a driving licence due to the risk of losing consciousness whilst driving.

heat, a form of energy released by burning fuel.

heated front seats, seats with an electrical heating element in the fabric, to increase comfort before the cabin heater produces hot air.

heated rear window, a rear window fitted with an electrical heating element between the layers of glass or on the inside surface of the glass, or in some luxury saloons a hot air system, that will demist the inside and deice the outside.

heated steering wheel, an electrically heated wheel rim for added comfort in cold weather.

heated windscreen, a windscreen having an electrical element sandwiched between the layers of glass to facilitate demisting and deicing.

heat engine, any device which produces motive power from heat energy.

heater, a system for warming the interior of a vehicle.

heater fan, an electrical fan which pushes air from the heater into the vehicle, to facilitate heating and ventilation.

heater plug, glowplug.

heat exchanger, a device that transfers heat from 1 fluid to another, *e.g.* the radiator.

heat of compression, the temperature rise in air or the air-fuel mixture when compressed in the engine, in a diesel it is sufficient to cause combustion.

heat range, the index of the ability of a sparkplug to withstand thermal loads; see also: hot sparkplug, cold sparkplug.

heat riser, a flap in the exhaust manifold that diverts exhaust to heat the inlet manifold whilst an engine is cold.

heat shield, thermal insulation near the exhaust manifold to prevent heat spreading to surrounding items to reduce risk of fire or burns.

heat shroud, thermal insulation around individual items near the exhaust manifold to reduce risk of damage to wiring, fuel lines, hydraulics, etc.

heat sink, a metallic device for absorbing and dissipating heat from electronic components.

heat soak, a condition when heat spreads to an unwanted area, *e.g.* it may warm parts of the fuel system and cause a vapour lock.

heavy, the condition of any vehicle control, typically the steering or clutch, which is stiff to operate and which requires significant or increased effort from the driver.

heavy duty, a vehicle or part designed stronger to withstand hard use.

heavy duty engine, USA, an engine in a heavy duty vehicle.

heavy duty oil, lubricating oil with good oxidation stability, corrosion prevention, and detergent dispersant characteristics, used in high speed diesel and petrol engines under heavy duty service conditions.

heavy duty vehicle, USA, a vehicle at or exceeding 8,500 lb GVWR (3.85 tonnes).

heavy foot, a driver who is jerky with the accelerator, frequently alternating between accelerator and brake, an all or nothing style with no finesse, no feathering, and no acceleration sense.

heavy goods vehicle, a category of vehicle renamed LGV in UK, with a variety of defined weights in various countries, generally exceeding any figure in the range 4.5 to 25 tonnes.

heavy locomotive, a mechanically propelled vehicle not constructed itself to carry load other than equipment for propulsion, loose tools and loose equipment, with an unladen weight exceeding 11,690 kg, (RTA).

heavy motor car, a mechanically propelled vehicle, not being a locomotive, motor tractor or motor car, constructed itself to carry load or passengers where the unladen weight exceeds 2,540 kg, (C&U regulations).

heavy quadricycle, a microcar, a lightweight car having a kerbweight not exceeding 550 kg and an engine not exceeding 20 bhp or 15 kW, and in some countries a maximum speed not exceeding 50 km/h.

hedgehop, to rapidly alternate between the 2 lanes on a single carriageway road, typical of a driver wanting to overtake from a tailgating position but being too close and cannot see ahead.

hedgehopper, a driver making a series of unsuccessful attempts to overtake due to being too close to the vehicle ahead.

heel and toe, a technique for operating all 3 foot controls simultaneously; the right foot operates the brake and accelerator together in varying proportions by using the ball of the foot on the footbrake whilst flexing the ankle to enable the side of the toe or outside edge of the foot to operate the accelerator; a racing technique allowing braking whilst double declutching or braking during a power change; named in the 1920s when central accelerators were common and when the ball of the foot operated the footbrake and the heel operated the accelerator.

heel wear, USA, feathering of each block of tread on a tyre, where the trailing edge of each tread block typically wears at a faster rate than the leading edge.

HEGOS, heated exhaust gas oxygen sensor, a lambda sensor with electrical heating for a faster warmup.

HEI, high energy ignition.

HEI-EST, high energy ignition system with electronic spark timing.

height, a physical property of a vehicle created by its design and including the height of any load, for some vehicles it presents a physical prohibition in some places; see: overall height.

height adjustable headlights, electrically angled headlights enabling the driver to adjust the vertical alignment of the beam to allow for the weight in the rear of a vehicle.

height adjustable seat, a drivers seat the height of which may be varied to suit the size of the driver.

height adjustable wheel, a steering wheel the height of which may be varied to suit the size and comfort of the driver.

height corrector, an automatic levelling control in a hydropneumatic suspension system.

height limit, a limit imposed on a section of road that prohibits use by any vehicle exceeding that height.

Heim joint, a spherical or rose joint created by a sphere restrained by a ball race, used where high precision articulation without linear movement is required, typically in the suspension of racing cars.

helical gear, a gear wheel with teeth set oblique to the gear axis such that it mates smoothly with a similar gear on another shaft having an axis parallel to the first; see also: hypoid.

helical roundabout, a roundabout having lane markings which are not concentric but spiral outwards from the centre, so once ensconced in the correct lane that lane takes the driver to the required exit.

helical spring, a coil spring.

helicoil, a spiral insert to simulate the original female thread in a part where the thread has been damaged then tapped to a larger size, commonly used to replace sparkplug threads in an alloy cylinder head.

helix, a spiral along a cylinder, as a screw thread.

hell for leather, at maximum speed.

helmet connector, a special type of battery connector in the shape of an inverted cup which fits over a tapered terminal post and is secured with a self tapping screw driven vertically down into the top of the terminal, generally obsolete.

helper spring, an additional leaf or several which only carry any load when the primary leaf spring has deflected significantly, common on the rear axles of lorries.

hemi, hemispheric.

hemianopia, an eye defect where half the field of view is lost and which precludes a person from driving; a driver must have at least 120° of horizontal vision.

hemi engine, an engine having hemispherical shaped combustion chambers.

hemispheric head, a cylinder head machined to have hemispherical combustion chambers.

Henard, Monsieur Henard, the inventor of the roundabout in France in 1907, to replace crossroads and reduce traffic congestion.

HERO, Historic Endurance Rallying Organisation, UK organiser of international rallies.

herringbone, a diagram sometimes used for navigating in a road rally.

herringbone navigation, a method of defining a route in road rally navigation, where all roads not taken are marked either side of a straight line which is the route to be followed.

herringbone parking, a style of parking area where vehicles are parked at an angle to the access road, typically turning through 30° to 60°; see also: reverse herringbone.

hertz, the unit of measurement of frequency, measured in cycles per second.

hesitant, a characteristic of a novice driver lacking experience in observation, lacking recognition of speed and distance of approaching traffic, uncertain of the acceleration performance of the vehicle, and

untrained to make use of such performance.

hesitation, a momentary lack of response to operation of the accelerator.

hev, hybrid electric vehicle; see: dual mode, parallel, series.

hex, hexagon, having 6 sides or faces, the shape of many of the drive faces of many nuts and bolts, now often superseded by Torx and other shapes.

hexane, a hydrocarbon component of petrol.

HFC 134a, a refrigerant gas used in most modern vehicle ac systems.

hfs, heated front seats.

HGV, heavy goods vehicle, now renamed LGV large goods vehicle, UK.

hi, high.

HIAB, Hydrauliska Industri AB, Swedish, Hydraulic Industry Ltd, a major manufacturer of lorry mounted knuckle boom cranes.

hi beam, high beam, main beam, the normal driving beam from the headlamps.

hideaway wiper, a windscreen wiper having a parking position below the transparent bottom of the windscreen.

high altitude, an engine certified by the EPA to comply with emission standards for vehicles to be used above 1,219 metres, (4,000 feet).

highback seat, a seat in which the head restraint is a continuation of the backrest, typically used in competition vehicles.

highball, the practice by a salesman of deliberately over valuing a trade-in of a potential customer who is believed to be shopping around, then finding fault later and offering a lower value when they return.

high beam, main beam, the normal driving beam from the headlamps, a headlight beam that is not dipped.

high box, the high range of gears.

high camshaft engine, an engine in which the camshaft is located further from the crankshaft, just below the cylinder head facilitating shorter pushrods.

high centered, USA, grounded.

high centre rim, a wheel having a raised area around the circumference between the rims, the design of a CTS wheel.

high compression, a comparative term when comparing various engines, including comparing a modern engine with a much older design, or a diesel with a petrol engine.

high energy battery, a design of battery under development for electric cars using unconventional metals and electrolytes, *e.g.* nickel hydride, or liquid sulphur.

high energy coil, an ignition coil used in a high energy ignition system, typically producing 35,000 to 65,000 volts.

high energy fuel, a fuel that upon combustion provides greater energy than conventional carbonaceous fuels, but typically a hydrocarbon, *e.g.* methanol, typically for drag racing and other sports.

high energy ignition, an ignition system

capable of producing more than 35,000 volts.

higher rights, the rank order of highways, *i.e.* a carriageway has higher rights than a bridleway.

high floor coach, a highliner.

high gear, any gear such that the propshaft rotates at the same speed or faster than the engine.

high geared, a condition when a transmission system has a higher than usual or higher than expected gearing.

high gloss, a very shiny surface.

high intensity, a bright light, typically from a rear fog lamp which should only be used when visibility is less than 100 m.

high level brake lamp, a lamp which is mounted almost level with the roof of the car, so the light may be easily seen over or through intermediate cars; such lamps may reduce the risk of rear shunt collisions by over 50 %.

highlift truck, a lorry having a hydraulic mechanism designed to raise the goods container body to give direct access to service aircraft, typically raising by 6 metres.

highliner, a high floor coach, designed to provide superior views over vehicles and walls etc, for the passengers.

high mileage, a car that has covered more than an average of 24,000 km (15,000 miles) per year of age.

high occupancy vehicle, USA, a car containing a driver and at least 1 or 2 passengers, depending upon local regulations.

high occupancy vehicle lane, a lane on a multilane road reserved only for vehicles carrying at least 2 or 3 occupants, dependant upon local regulations; typically use of the lane is enforced during rush-hour periods.

high octane, a fuel with an octane number exceeding 96 therefore having good antiknock properties especially for use in high compression engines.

high performance, usually a vehicle having superior acceleration performance, it can also refer to braking performance or steering performance; typically a car having a power to weight ratio of less than 10 kg/kW, or a power density exceeding 100 kW/tonne.

high pressure, a fluid system having an operating pressure higher than others, *e.g.* some diesel fuel injection systems.

high pressure diesel injection, a diesel fuelled engine where the fuel is injected at a significantly higher pressure than other systems; the injection suffix is irrelevant as all diesels are fuel injected.

high reach safety headrests, headrests with a forward reach to reduce the risk of whiplash in a front-rear collision.

high resistance earth, an electrical fault resulting in loss of the normal return path for the current, sometimes finding an alternate path through other components, typically seen at the rear lamp clusters when the wrong lamp

illuminates.

high revs, an engine rotational speed near to its maximum limit.

high risk, a condition or action likely to result in a traffic violation or a collision.

high risk area, a situation or location with a high potential for a collision with any other road user, *e.g.* busy town centre.

high risk colour, a vehicle colour that may be difficult to see in some lighting conditions hence is involved in more than average collisions, *e.g.* beige, grey, black.

highroad, main road.

high side, the high pressure portion of an ac system, including the compressor, condenser, and expansion valve.

high side, USA, the outside of a bend.

high solar energy absorbing glass, glass which helps keep the vehicle's interior cooler and helps reduce interior window fogging.

high spec, a vehicle fitted with many optional extras for additional comfort, safety, styling, or performance.

high speed propshaft, a propeller shaft that rotates at engine crankshaft speed, typically on vehicles having a front mounted engine and a rear transaxle.

highstreet, the main route through a town or village centre, usually having the principal shopping area, or an original main route before through traffic was diverted.

high tensile, a steel alloy that is very strong in tension, typically having a yield strength of 50,000 to 100,000 psi, 3.4×10^8 to 6.9×10^8 newtons /m².

high tension, high voltage.

high violator, a driver who frequently commits a breach of traffic law and/or is involved in a disproportionately high number of collisions.

high voltage, usually 30,000 volts at the sparkplugs, on some vehicles up to 65,000 volts.

highway, see also: 2 lane, all purpose, avenue, bridleway, bus lane, busway, classified, controlled, conventional, cycle track, designated, divided, driftway, drive, driving, drove, footpath, footway, freeway, Inter American, interstate, Kings, lane, limited, Lincoln, MacArthur, Mexican, motorway, multilane, pan African, Panamericana, Pan American, primary, principle, public, Queens, quiet, radial, road, scenic, special, street, super, through, track, trail, Trans Canadian, trunk.

highway, UK, a way over which all members of the public have the right to pass and repass by foot, on horseback, or accompanied by a beast of burden or with cattle or with vehicles, and includes roads, byways, bridleways, and footpaths, each of which may have usage restrictions imposed; *i.e.* a highway is a route without reference to the right to use it.

highway, USA, any public road outside a city with a foundation and a hard surface, having at grade junctions and full access to/from adjacent premises.

Highway 1, Australia, the coastal highway almost encircling the country, 12,200 km (7,580 miles) in length from Cairns through Melbourne and Perth to Darwin.

Highway 1, India, GTR, the road from Kabul, Afghanistan over the Khyber pass, through Lahore, Pakistan and across northern India through Delhi to Calcutta, 2,500 km (1,600 miles) in length.

Highway 1, USA, the Pacific Coast highway connecting Canada to Mexico, 2,600 km, (1,625 miles) in length.

highway authority, the public body responsible for the maintenance of all highways in the area of its jurisdiction.

Highway Code, a book containing legal rules and advice on best practice in order to drive correctly; first published in France in 1921, first published in UK on 14 April 1931.

highway engineering, a branch of civil engineering dealing with highway planning, location, design, and maintenance.

highway hypnosis, a semi-alert state in which the driver continues to control the vehicle but is unable to react quickly to an emergency; caused by fatigue and/or inadequate visual scanning techniques, sometimes induced into a driver on roads having few features and little traffic, it typically leads to microsleep then sleep.

highway planting, vegetation placed for aesthetic, safety, environmental or erosion control purposes, especially to reduce adverse environmental impact.

highway status, UK, a classification of roads, including byways, bridleways, and footpaths, etc.

highway tire, USA, summer tire, a tyre designed for wet and dry weather use but not suitable for use on snow and ice.

hijack, to seize control of a vehicle in mid journey to steal the vehicle and/or the goods, or for the purpose of forcefully demanding transportation.

hi-lift, a mechanical lever ratchet tower jack, typically used on 4x4 vehicles, invented by Philip J Harrah, in USA in 1895.

hill, gradient.

hill climb, a high-speed trial up a hill usually with sharp bends on a private road having a hard surface, using sports or similar cars; the last on a public road in Britain was in 1925.

hill climb, a slow-speed distance trial up a steep slippery off-road surface passing numbered posts named gates, using specially constructed lightweight cars.

hill climbing power, climbing power.

hill descent control, a system providing electronic control of the engine speed and links the ETC and ABS systems to enable a 'feet off' safe descent of very steep slippery hills, the system maintains a target descent speed of less

than 9 km/h (5.5 mph), developed by Land Rover.

hillholder, a hill-starting device actuated by the clutch pedal, operated by depressing the footbrake, depressing the clutch, then releasing the footbrake, a hill start is then performed by raising the revs and engaging the clutch in the normal way, developed by Subaru.

hill stall recovery, the safe procedure for self recovery of a failed hill climb in a manual 4x4 vehicle when attempting to climb a very steep off-road gradient such that the engine stalls or traction is lost: footbrake firmly on, ignition off, select low range reverse gear, release the clutch, straighten the steering, check behind, gradually release the footbrake, (no feet in use), turn the ignition key to start a controlled descent.

hill start, to set a vehicle in motion on an uphill gradient, performed by accurate coordination of accelerator, clutch, and handbrake; there should not be any rearwards movement.

hinge bow, the hood support which carries the main pivot for the folding mechanism.

hinge pillar, the structural element forming the lower portion of the A pillar and which carries the front door hinges.

hip belt, lap strap.

hi perf, USA, high performance.

hi range, high range, the normal range of gears on a 4x4 compared with a low range.

hire car, a car available for self drive rental on a daily basis.

hired vehicle certificate, a document confirming ownership of the vehicle and granting permission for it to be used in another country, a legal requirement when crossing some international borders.

hire or reward, the systematic carrying of passengers for a fare beyond the bounds of social kindness, but excluding isolated occasions and social arrangements between friends to contribute towards the expenses of a journey, (PPVA).

hire purchase, a common and reliable method of purchasing a vehicle but where the vehicle remains the property of the finance company until the final payment is paid.

historic bus, any bus or coach more than 30 years old.

historic vehicle, any vehicle built before 31 December 1959.

hit and run, an accident causing damage, injury, or death where a driver fails to stop after the collision, or abandons the vehicle and absconds to avoid identification.

hitch, coupling, a device on a trailer drawbar with which to couple to its mating part on the towing vehicle.

hitch, to couple a trailer to a vehicle.

hitch ball, USA, towball.

hitchhike , to travel by begging free lifts in passing vehicles.

139

hitch weight, USA, tongue weight, noseweight.

hit the road, to depart.

hit the trail, USA, to depart.

hi vis, high visibility, usually referring to clothing worn by road workmen and some road users, typically a fluorescent material with retroreflective bands.

HK, Hong Kong, international vehicle distinguishing sign, see appendices.

HKJ, Jordan, international vehicle distinguishing sign, see appendices.

h/lamps, headlamps.

h/level, high level.

HMC, highly motorised country, typically USA, western Europe, and other developed countries.

HMMWV, high mobility multipurpose wheeled vehicle, a USA military specification.

hmsl, high mounted stop lamp.

HMSO, UK, Her Majesty's Stationary Office, publishers of books with Government authority, now renamed TSO.

HO, UK, Home Office, the Government department responsible for the police.

Hobbs meter, an instrument which records the total cumulative time that an engine has run, *e.g.* for a tractor running hours are a more useful guide to service intervals than mileage covered.

hodometer, odometer.

hodophobia, a fear of travel.

hold, a selection on an automatic gearbox when it is required to remain in the present gear, typically used when climbing or descending a hill to prevent the transmission from performing unwanted up and/or down changes.

holdback, a position, to maintain a vehicle separation at least 2 seconds behind the vehicle ahead and sufficiently to 1 side in order to have maximum visibility of the situation ahead of the other vehicle; and if the other vehicle should stop, to remain at least 10 metres behind for maximum view and minimum steering.

holdback, a strategy, to use the holdback position to gain maximum visibility and safety in advanced and defensive driving.

holding onto your mudflaps, CB jargon, driving close behind you.

holdup, a stationary queue of traffic, especially when it persists for some time.

homelink, a remote controlling system which stores the codes for remote controlled devices which can be activated at the push of a button from one unit permanently mounted in the vehicle's sun visor, overhead console, or mirror, to activate home lighting, garage doors, etc.

home test, UK, a driving test conducted in a category F, G, H, or K vehicle which may not be suitable to travel a long distance to a DTC, and where the driving test examiner travels to the home, workplace, or meeting place near where the vehicle is kept in order to conduct the driving test.

home zone, a pedestrian friendly area designed to improve the quality of life in residential streets.

homofocal headlamp, a headlamp having 2 reflectors of differing focal length.

homokinetic joint, cvj.

homologated, the acceptance that the construction of and modifications to a competition car are within the rules.

homologation, the acceptability of a car type or model in a class, such that it complies with all regulations, especially those concerned with safety.

homologation plate, a plate mounted on a vehicle displaying the VIN, engine model, transmission model, MGW, MTW, maximum front and rear axle loadings, technical specifications, paint code, equipment level, vehicle type, trim code, fabrication number, and interior trim code.

hone, to remove, clean, and smooth metal edges, especially rough edges on a casting.

honk, to sound the horn.

hood, a fabric roof on a convertible car.

hood, USA, the engine cover on a front engined car.

hood, a black tubular fabrication around a traffic signal lens to reduce interference by sunlight and to prevent drivers seeing an inappropriate signal.

hood rod, USA, bonnet stay.

hooking, kerb dragging.

hooking, the action of 2 traffic queues attempting to turn offside to offside and causing a mini-gridlock at a crossroads.

hooking, the theft of car ignition keys from the owners house where the keys are left near the door, by using a fishing rod or similar through the letter box to lift the keys.

hook loader, a lorry specially adapted to lift and transport demountable bodies that are handled by a hydraulic arm with a single hook that latches at the front of the demountable body.

Hook's joint, a simple universal joint having 2 yokes connected by a spider, typically at each end of a vehicle propeller shaft.

hook turn, Australia, a method of turning into a road to the offside but where the approach is made in the nearside lane, the procedure is typically used where trams run along the centre of streets and waiting traffic would block trams.

hookup, to couple a trailer to a vehicle.

hooped, USA, damaged or faulty, in need of immediate repair.

hoot, the sound made by a vehicle horn.

hooter, a vehicle horn.

hop up, USA, to increase performance of a production car by improving the acceleration, braking, or roadholding etc.

horizontal adjuster, the screw for adjusting

the sideways alignment of a headlamp.

horizontal alignment, the degree of curvature describing the geometry of a defined length of road as seen in plan view.

horizontal engine, any engine with a horizontal stroke, *i.e.* a flat engine.

horizontally opposed, an engine where the pistons are on opposite sides of the crankshaft; also named flat or boxer.

horn, the warning instrument, a device that emits a loud noise to inform other road users of ones presence, operated electrically or by air.

horn ready, a condition when the horn switch is covered by a finger in a recognised high risk situation to reduce driver reaction time.

horse box, a trailer for carrying 1 or 2 horses.

horsedrawn vehicle, a vehicle that is pulled by 1 or several horses, controlled by a driver on the vehicle.

horsepower, a measurement of the power produced by an engine, typically measured as brake horsepower on a dynamometer, 1 bhp equals raising 550 foot-pounds per second, considered originally to be the amount of work which could be performed endlessly by an average horse, also equal to 745.7 watts, see also: PS.

horsepower weight factor, USA, power to weight ratio.

HORT1, UK, Home Office Road Traffic 1, a document issued by a police officer requiring later production of specified documents.

hose, flexible tubing for conveying fluids.

hose clamp, hose clip.

hose clip, a device for securing a hose to a pipe or fitting.

hose coupling, a device with a screw thread to connect a hose to a rigid pipe or part.

hose fitting, hose coupling.

hot, an engine that is at its normal running temperature.

Hotchkiss drive, a simple rear suspension system comprising only a live axle affixed to a pair of leaf springs but designed to restrict the torque reactions through the longitudinal leaf springs.

hot hatch, a powerful version of a small hatchback car.

hotrod, a vehicle to which the acceleration performance has been significantly increased coupled with modified bodywork; originally for speed trials at Muroc, California in 1932, the forerunner of drag racing.

Hot Rod, a racing formula using a short oval circuit.

hot sparkplug, a sparkplug having a long insulator nose, used in low output engines where the sparkplug is designed to retain heat to burn off carbon deposits to prevent fouling and thereby assist cold starts.

hotspot, a part of the engine inlet manifold which is heated to aid the vaporisation of petrol before it enters the combustion chamber.

hot starting, a procedure for starting a hot

engine on some cars having a carburettor and where heat soak has caused enrichment: to gradually increase the accelerator pressure in 1 slow smooth movement whilst cranking the engine until it fires.

hot tube, a primitive engine ignition system whereby fuel is ignited by a small platinum pipe inserted into the top of the cylinder and maintained red hot by a small external flame at the other end.

hotwire, to connect temporary wiring to the ignition circuit in order to start the engine and drive away, performed if the ignition key is lost, or a method of stealing a vehicle.

hot wire element, the device in a hot wire airflow meter with which the microprocessor measures airflow in a vehicle having electronic fuel injection.

hours of darkness, the time between $1/2$ hour after sunset to $1/2$ hour before sunrise.

housecar, USA, a motor vehicle originally designed or permanently altered and equipped to provide facilities for living accommodation, or a vehicle to which a camper has been permanently attached.

house trailer, USA, a caravan, a mobile home drawn as a trailer.

HOV, high occupancy vehicle.

HOV lane, high occupancy vehicle lane.

hp, hire purchase.

hp, horsepower, brake horsepower, 1 bhp equals raising 550 foot-pounds per second, also equal to 745.7 watts, see also: PS.

HPC, High Performance Club UK.

HpL, rally pace note, a hairpin left bend exceeding 120°.

HpR, rally pace note, a hairpin right bend exceeding 120°.

HR, Australia, heavy rigid, a rigid lorry or bus having 3 or more axles.

HR, Croatia, international vehicle distinguishing sign, see appendices.

h/rest, head restraints.

hrw, heated rear window.

HSAWA, UK, Health and Safety at Work Act.

HSDI, high speed direct injection diesel engine.

HSE, UK, Health and Safety Executive, an organisation responsible for workplace safety including the use of vehicles.

hsea, high solar energy absorbing glass.

hsw, heated steering wheel.

ht, high tension, high voltage.

htd, heated.

hub, the innermost a part of the wheel that locates on the wheel bearing.

hubcap, spindle cap.

hubcap, an ornamental metal or plastic disc attached to the end of the axle or wheel centre.

hubodometer, a distance measuring instrument fitted to a wheel hub on a trailer which is rented or leased.

hub puller, a tool to aid the disassembly of a wheel hub.

hub reduction, a gear system at the wheel hubs enabling lower gearing at the wheels.

hub reduction gears, an extra set of gears at the wheel hubs, sometimes planetary, sometimes manually selectable to a lower range when required, typically on some specialist vehicles and older lorries.

HUD, head up display.

hump, speed hump

humpback bridge, a bridge where the road surface ascends and descends significantly over a single stone arch, usually marked with a hazard sign.

hump bridge, humpback bridge.

hundredweight, cwt, an imperial unit of weight equivalent to 50.8 kg, formerly indicating the carrying capacity of small goods vehicles, obsolete.

hung up, USA, grounded.

hunting, the condition of an engine when the idle revs fluctuate cyclically, sometime due to a weak mixture.

hv, high voltage.

hvac, heating, ventilation, air conditioning.

HVC, hired vehicle certificate.

HxCx, unburned hydrocarbons.

hybrid, a bifuel, dual fuel, or multifuel vehicle, typically powered primarily by petrol, diesel, or gas, and secondly by electricity, see: parallel hybrid, series hybrid.

hybrid, a home built car constructed with major components from several different vehicle models, or parts from different manufacturers.

hybrid, a production car having an engine or other major component different from any sold by the manufacturer for that model.

hybrid, see: parallel hybrid, series hybrid.

hybrid tyre, a tyre designed to give reasonable performance off-road and on a highway.

hyd, hydraulic.

hyd, hydraulic adjusters.

hydractive suspension, a system which automatically lowers the ride height when travelling at speed to improve stability, aerodynamics, and fuel economy, and on rough surfaces it raises ride height to increase ground clearance, developed by Citroën.

hydraulic, pertaining to a liquid, especially under pressure.

hydraulic actuator, a hydraulically operated strut which controls vehicle body movement in an active ride suspension system.

hydraulic brake, a brake in which the retarding force is transmitted from the pedal to the wheel by hydraulic pressure.

hydraulic clutch, a clutch operating system where the control is transmitted from the pedal to the clutch by hydraulic pressure.

hydraulic clutch, a fluid coupling, a fluid drive.

hydraulic drive, a mechanism for transmitting motion from 1 shaft to another by hydrostatic or hydrodynamic means.

hydraulic fluid, a liquid having good hydraulic properties, usually polyglycol, but silicone is also used in high performance vehicles.

hydraulic gear assistance, a gear selection system where movement of the gear lever is assisted by hydraulics to reduce driver effort, developed by Mercedes.

hydraulic hood, the roof of a convertible car which is raised and lowered by a hydraulic system.

hydraulic jack, a lever operated hydraulic pump acting on a piston and sometimes a series of levers in order to raise part of a vehicle from the ground to allow maintenance or repairs to be performed.

hydraulicked, the condition of a wrecked engine which has inadvertently ingested a large volume of water whilst running, *e.g.* submergence in deep water, such that a piston has tried to compress the water and caused severe internal damage to the engine.

hydraulic modulator, the device which regulates the pressure of the brake fluid in an ABS system.

hydraulic motor, a motor activated by fluid under pressure.

hydraulic pressure, pressure exerted on or through a liquid system.

hydraulic pump, an engine or electrically driven pump which supplies the pressure to a fluid to cause it to flow for a system to operate.

hydraulic retarder, a device fitted on the output of the gearbox on some lorries and buses to control the speed of the vehicle during a long descent by restricting the flow of fluid through a small orifice.

hydraulics, the use of pressurised liquid to transfer force or motion.

hydraulic steering, a power steering system using hydraulic rams.

hydraulic tappets, a system of operating the cylinder valves using pressurised lubrication oil.

hydraulic torque converter, torque converter.

hydraulic transmission, a drive system in which the engine drives a hydraulic pump which forces fluid under pressure to hydraulic motors at each wheel, used in some specialist off-road vehicles and some agricultural and industrial vehicles.

hydroactive suspension, hydropneumatic suspension.

hydrocarbon, the active constituent of fossil fuels, both the hydrogen and the carbon will react with oxygen from the air and burn.

hydrofluoric acid, an extremely corrosive acid, typically formed during a car fire when some types of synthetic rubber as in some O rings, oil seals, fuel hoses, etc, are exposed to temperatures exceeding 400 °C, at which the rubber changes to a sticky or charred substance which remains dangerous for many years; if it comes into contact with the skin it will rapidly penetrate to the bone and it may be necessary to amputate the limb to prevent death.

hydrogas suspension, hydropneumatic suspension.

hydrogen, a very explosive gas given off in small quantities by batteries, also a potential vehicle fuel.

hydrogen sulphide, H₂S, a flammable toxic gas smelling similar to bad eggs sometimes emitted with the exhaust gas especially from engines equipped with a cat and having a carburettor or when the lambda unit is not functioning such that there is no feedback to weaken the mixture; also named hydrogen disulphide.

hydrolastic suspension, a suspension system using compressible fluids as springs, typically having interconnections between each wheel for suspension levelling.

hydrometer, a measuring device to determine the rd (old term: sg) of a liquid, hence to determine the concentration of a mixture or solution, typically used for checking the rd of battery electrolyte or coolant.

hydroneck, a lowloader semitrailer which divides into 2 parts to facilitate vehicular access onto the bed, such that the front end of the bed is lowered to the ground and the neck is hydraulically demounted and removed with the tractive unit.

hydroplane, to aquaplane, a condition when the speed of the vehicle is greater than the ability of the tyre tread to remove the water from between the tyre and the road such that

the tyre rides up on a thin layer of water thereby having no direct contact with the road surface and suffering a severe loss of braking and steering performance.

hydropneumatic suspension, a suspension system using pressurised nitrogen gas as a spring and which is separated by a diaphragm from the hydraulic actuating fluid.

hydrostatic, a variable drive ratio system infinitely variable between limits, developed by Mercedes.

hygroscopic, a liquid that absorbs water from the air, *e.g.* polyglycol brake fluid.

hypereutectic, a quality of a piston to be lightweight and temperature resistant, typically having a high silicon content.

hypoglycaemic, a medical defect, the possible result of diabetes, it can lead to unconsciousness so known sufferers should not drive.

hypoid gear, a gear design that transmits drive between nonparallel nonintersecting shafts, hence the gears slide instead of roll against each other resulting in high pressure between gear teeth, *e.g.* many crownwheel and pinion gears, also worm and wheel.

hypoid oil, high pressure oil, specially formulated for hypoid gears.

hypsometric map, a geographical map showing elevation by shading or hatching, generally obsolete.

Hz, hertz.

143

I

i, injection, a common model suffix denoting fuel injection.

i, intelligent system, a suffix denoting a system is controlled by a microprocessor, or that several microprocessors are interlinked and communicate.

I, intermediate, a gear selection on some automatic transmissions that will restrict gear selection to the 2 lowest gears on a 3 speed automatic.

I, Italy, international vehicle distinguishing sign, see appendices.

I 4, an inline 4 cylinder engine.

I beam axle, a rigid non-driven axle constructed from a steel I beam, sometimes forged into a curved shape, common at the front of lorries, vintage cars, and some buses.

I head, USA, an ohv engine.

IAATM, International Association for Accident and Traffic Medicine, Copenhagen.

IACA, Independent Automotive Consultants Association, UK.

IACOA, Independent Armored Car Operators Association, USA.

iacv, idle air control valve.

IAM, Institute of Advanced Motorists, UK.

IAMA, International Abstaining Motorists Association, Sweden.

IAPCR, Association mondiale de la Route, PIARC World Road Association.

IAS, inertia active system.

iat, intake air temperature.

IATF, International Automotive Task Force, the big 3 USA vehicle manufacturers, plus CLEPA supplier representatives from France, Germany and Italy.

IATSS, International Association of Traffic and Safety Sciences, Tokyo.

IBCAM, Institute of British Carriage and Automobile Manufacturers.

ic, internal combustion engine.

ic, inflatable curtain, an airbag device which inflates downwards from the sides of the rooflining to cover the side windows to protect the head of a vehicle occupant during a side impact, developed by Volvo.

ic, inlet valve closes, a valve timing specification relating to a specific number of degrees abdc.

ICADTS, International Committee on Alcohol, Drugs and Traffic Safety, Sweden.

ICARE, Institute pour la Competitivite Automobile de la Recherche de l'Excellence.

ICC, intelligent cruise control.

ice, in car entertainment.

ice, frozen water, sometimes visually white, sometimes visually clear and giving an optical illusion of a wet road surface.

ICE, Institute of Civil Engineers, UK.

ICEI, Internal Combustion Engine Institute, USA.

ice scraper, a tool with a hard plastic or soft metal blade for removing frost and ice from vehicle windows and windscreens.

icing, see: carburettor icing.

icn, in car navigation, a system using GPS and a CD.

ICRL, Indy Car Racing League, USA.

id, inside diameter.

id, insulin dependent, a driver reliant on a medication to control diabetes.

IDBRA, International Drivers' Behaviour Research Association, Paris.

idc, inner dead centre, tdc.

idd, insulin dependent driver, a driver reliant on a medication to control diabetes.

ide, petrol direct injection.

identification lamp, a blue rotating beacon fitted to an emergency vehicle, or an amber rotating beacon fitted to an authorised vehicle; the lamp projects light through a 360° arc and must give the appearance of flashing at the rate between 1 and 4 flashes per second.

identification lights, USA, position lights.

IDGTE, The Institution of Diesel & Gas Turbine Engineers, formerly DEHA, UK.

idi, indirect injection.

idi, integrated direct ignition system.

idiot light, see: tell-tale.

idle, a specific slow engine speed when the throttle is fully closed, when the engine is running reasonably slowly but comfortably and evenly with no load on the engine.

idle air control valve, a valve in the throttle of fuel injected engines that controls idle speed by varying the amount of air bypassing the throttle valve.

idle mixture, the air-fuel mixture supplied to the engine whilst idling.

idle mixture screw, the screw adjuster to lean or enrich the air-fuel mixture.

idle port, the opening in the throttle body through which the carburettor dispenses fuel whilst idling.

144

idler gear, a small gear brought into mesh between 2 other gears to reverse the direction of rotation, a simple method of designing the reverse gear.
idler pulley, idler wheel.
idler wheel, a wheel used to guide or tension any belt or chain in an auxiliary transmission system, *e.g.* to tension a fanbelt.
idle speed, the rpm at which a hot engine is designed or set to run when the throttle is fully closed and with no load on the engine.
idle stop valve, a solenoid operated valve which cuts the carburettor idle fuel to prevent running on when the ignition is switched off.
idling, a condition when an engine is running at its idle speed with no load on the engine.
idling drag, creep.
idling jet, a jet within a carburettor that issues fuel during minimum load on the engine.
IDP, international driving permit.
IEI, integral electronic ignition.
IFP, international freight permit.
IFRSDC, International Foundation for Road Safety in Developing Countries, Luxembourg.
ifs, independent front suspension.
ignite, to start fuel burning.
igniter, the device which causes the pyrotechnic in an airbag or seatbelt pretensioner to detonate.
ignition, the keyswitch for starting the engine with the ignition key.
ignition, the start of combustion of the air-fuel mixture in the combustion chamber, in a petrol engine it is initiated by the hv spark.
ignition angle, the rotational displacement of position measured in crankshaft degrees by which the ignition is advanced or retarded.
ignition cable, the cable carrying the hv spark from the ignition coil to the distributor, and from the distributor to the sparkplugs; see also: carbon, copper.
ignition coil, a transformer that steps up from 12 volts to over 30,000 volts to fire the sparkplugs.
ignition delay, the short time lapse between the triggering of the ignition and spark production.
ignition disabler, a function of an alarm/immobiliser system in preventing the ignition system from operating.
ignition distributor, a unit that contains the switch for the primary circuit, the hv coil, and the distributor.
ignition interlock device, USA, a hand held breath testing device which is connected to the vehicle and requires the driver to take and pass a breath test for alcohol before the vehicle can be started; a mandatory fitment for some drivers having previous drink drive convictions.
ignition key, the key that operates an ignition switch.
ignition lag, the time delay in a diesel engine between fuel injection and combustion.
ignition lead, ignition cable.

ignition map, the parameters stored electronically relating to ignition timing for every operating condition of an engine.
ignition module, an electronic unit that is signalled by the ECU to operate the primary ignition circuit.
ignition resistor, an electrical resistor to reduce load on the hv coil whilst the engine is running, but allowing full power when starting the engine.
ignition stroke, power stroke.
ignition switch, the key-switch that controls power supply to the engine and many other circuits.
ignition system, the system that produces high voltage for the sparkplugs and delivers it to the correct sparkplug at the correct time.
ignition tdc, the tdc position of the crankshaft on the same part of the cycle as when ignition occurs.
ignition temperature, flashpoint, the lowest temperature at which a fuel will start to burn in air; for petrol vapour this is 49 °C.
ignition timing, the exact time of the delivery of the spark to the sparkplug, usually expressed in crankshaft degrees btdc.
ignition toolkit, a set of small tools enabling running repairs to any simple ignition system.
ignition trigger, an electronic switch which initiates the discharge of ignition energy to the ignition coil and sparkplugs.
ignition voltage, the voltage within the hv system, commonly exceeding 30,000 volts.
IGR, ignore gated roads, a rallying pace note indicating roads not to be used at that point.
ihp, indicated horsepower.
IHT, Institution of Highways and Transportation, UK.
IID, ignition interlock device.
IIHS, Insurance Institute for Highway Safety, USA.
IL, Israel, international vehicle distinguishing sign, see appendices.
illuminance, the quantity of luminous flux per unit area.
illuminated entry system, a system of lighting in the door entry and footwell area.
illuminating surface of a lighting device, the orthogonal projection of the full aperture of the reflector, or in the case of headlamps with an ellipsoidal reflector, of the projection lens, on a transverse plane, (C&U).
illumination, the quantity of light incident on a surface.
IMA, integrated motor assist.
imbalance, see: static imbalance, dynamic imbalance.
imbalance, when referring to a braking system, when 1 or more brakes operate before or after others, or with uneven brake pressure.
IME, Institution for Mechanical Engineers, UK.
IMEP, indicated mean effective pressure.
IMI, Institute of the Motor Industry, UK.

imm, immobiliser.
immediate prohibition notice, UK, a legal restriction on the use of a vehicle which prevents the vehicle from moving until a major defect has been repaired.
immobile, unable to move.
immobiliser, an electronic or mechanical device that prevents the engine from being started other than by the coded key for the vehicle.
impact, a forceful collision between 2 vehicles or between a vehicle and another object which is sufficient to cause damage to either.
impact absorber, a damper located between the bumper and the bumper mounting designed to prevent a minor collision from causing damage.
impact attenuator, a device sometimes used at the commencement of a safety barrier, typically containing sand or water in deformable or concertina containers to slow an impacting vehicle gradually, common in USA and Europe.
impact break, the rupture of a tyre caused by the shock of striking a kerb or pothole, etc. at speed.
impact damage, direct damage.
impact driver, a tool for loosening seized screws and nuts by converting an axial impact from a hammer into a turning motion.
impact safety, any system designed to reduce injury should a collision occur, *e.g.* airbags.
impact sensor, crash sensor.
impact socket, a tool designed to be used in conjunction with an impact driver to fit different nut or screw sizes.
impact wrench, a power operated tool that gives a rapid succession of sudden torques, usually operated by compressed air for removing and tightening wheel nuts.
impeller, the part of a pump that pushes a fluid ·by centrifugal force.
imperial, any measurements where the units used are not based upon the metric system.
imperial gallon, a unit of liquid capacity, 1 imperial gallon = 4.54596 litres, 20.1 % larger than a US gallon.
imperial horsepower, horsepower, a measure of power output, equal to 1.01387 metric horsepower.
imperial phaeton, a luxurious phaeton, typically having a second windscreen for the rear seat passengers.
imp gallon, imperial gallon.
import duty, a duty payable to customs on the CIF price, *i.e.* the purchase price of a vehicle plus its shipping fees and transport insurance, presently 10 %, for all vehicles imported to UK from non EC countries.
impound, the act of a government agency to seize and confiscate a vehicle for a wide range of offences ranging from non payment of parking or VED fees to other criminal or customs offences.

IMSA, International Motor Sports Association.
inappropriate speeding, driving a vehicle unsafely fast for the local conditions at that time, albeit less than the legal speed limit.
in a short, CB jargon, soon.
inboard, towards or near the centre of a vehicle.
inboard brakes, brake discs fitted at the inner end of each drive shaft, close to the differential, to reduce the unsprung weight.
incandescent, the emission of light from a hot surface, *i.e.* a typical light bulb with a tungsten filament that emits light due to the filament being heated by an electric current.
in car, anything situated, occurring, or carried in a car.
in car entertainment, any music system, radio, cassette, CD, TV or video systems.
in car navigation system, a system dependent on GPS to accurately identify the position, heading, speed, and direction to a destination.
inch, a unit of length equal to 25.4 mm.
in charge, the person having the keys to a motor vehicle, and where the circumstances may exist for the vehicle to be driven.
in charge with excess alcohol, UK, an act committed by a person who is at the time unfit to be in charge of a motor vehicle through drink or drugs, or, has consumed so much alcohol that the proportion in his breath, blood, or urine at that time exceeds the prescribed limit, or, within 18 hours after that time fails to provide a specimen.
inclined engine, an inline engine in which the cylinders are at an angle to the vertical, typically to lower the bonnet height or to lower the centre of gravity of the vehicle.
inclinometer, a surveyors instrument with which to measure the steepness of a gradient along a road.
inconsiderate driving, an act committed by a person who drives a mechanically propelled vehicle on a road or other public place without reasonable consideration for other persons using the road.
ind, indicators.
IND, India, international vehicle distinguishing sign, see appendices.
indentation, a dent that is small in area but deep.
independent endurance braking system, a retarder that is operated by a dedicated hand or foot control.
independent front suspension, a suspension system where each front wheel moves independently from all other wheels, *i.e.* the up/down movement of either front wheel has no effect on another whatsoever.
independent lamp, a device having a separate illuminating surface from another, separate light sources, and separate lamp bodies, (C&U).
independent rear suspension, a suspension system where each rear wheel moves

independently from all other wheels, *i.e.* the up/down movement of either rear wheel has no effect on another whatsoever.

independent suspension, a suspension system where all wheels move independently from each other, *i.e.* the up/down movement of one wheel has no effect on another whatsoever.

indicated horsepower, the theoretical power of an engine calculated from the mean effective pressure in the cylinders before allowing for any losses due to friction, induction and exhaust pumping, and driving auxiliaries *e.g.* the camshaft, oil pump, coolant pump, alternator, etc.

indicated mean effective pressure, the calculated average pressure in an engine cylinder throughout the complete cycle.

indicated speed, the figure a speedometer shows, which can vary between –0 % and +7 % + 2.5 mph with new tyres of specific size.

indicator, any mechanical or electrical device to make known some condition.

indicator, direction indicator.

indicator diagram, a chart showing cylinder pressure plotted throughout the complete cycle.

indicator light, tell-tale light.

indirect damage, damage caused to a vehicle in a collision by the internal impacts of occupants and luggage.

indirect injection, a diesel engine design in which the fuel is injected into a swirl chamber to start combustion with a little air before the combustion progresses to the combustion chamber, a design for quieter idling and smoother running but reduced economy; the fuel is not injected into the combustion chamber.

indivisible load, a load which cannot without undue expense or risk of damage be divided into 2 or more loads for the purpose of conveyance on a road, (C&U).

induction, the intake of air or air-fuel mixture into the engine.

induction manifold, inlet manifold.

induction noise, noise caused by the pulsed induction of air.

induction period, the period measured in degrees of crankshaft rotation during which the inlet valve is open.

induction port, the port in the cylinder wall of a 2 stroke engine where the charge enters the cylinder.

induction silencer, a device for reducing engine induction noise by a system of acoustic filtering.

induction stroke, the stroke of the piston from tdc to bdc with the inlet valve open.

induction valve, inlet valve.

inductor, a device on a steam powered vehicle that uses steam to force water into the boiler.

industrial solid tyre, a non-pneumatic tyre, either a resilient tyre or sometimes having a solid rubber core instead of an inner tube.

industrial tractor, a tractor not being an agricultural motor vehicle which has an unladen weight not exceeding 7,370 kg, and a maximum speed not exceeding 20 mph (32 km/h), and which is designed primarily for work off roads or for road construction or maintenance, (C&U).

industrial tyre, a pneumatic tyre designed for slow speed industrial vehicles, *e.g.* a fork lift truck.

Indy car, a racing car developed for Indy Racing League events.

Indy racing, USA, racing on an oval track.

Indy Racing League, a motor racing formula developed åt Indianapolis in 1911, typically having a duration of 500 miles (800 km) on an oval track.

inertia, a property of matter by which it continues in its existing state of rest or uniform motion in a straight line unless influenced by an external force.

inertia active system, a valve control system for gas dampers.

inertia drive, Bendix drive.

inertia fuel cut-off switch, a manually resettable switch activated by the inertia of a minor collision and which cuts the electric supply to the fuel pump to reduce the risk of fire.

inertia reel belt, a seatbelt having a retracting and tensioning mechanism which will lock by means of inertia acting on the internal mechanism during vehicle deceleration or during rapid belt extension.

infant seat, child safety seat.

infield, the area of land that is surrounded by the course of a racetrack, especially the margin along that side of the track.

infinitely variable transmission, constantly variable transmission.

inflatable curtain, a curtain airbag.

inflatable side curtain, an airbag derivative, it protects the head of an occupant against a side impact collision by inflating downwards from the side of the rooflining.

inflate, to add air, typically under pressure.

inflation pressure, the pressure of air inside a tyre which applies a tensile stress to the tyre cords such that the cords carry the load of the tyre.

influenced decision, a decision made due to the unpredictable actions of some other road user; see: voluntary.

InfoMax, a software system to analyse driver behaviour, developed by Renault.

information lights, USA, tell-tale lights.

information position speed gear acceleration, the principle Roadcraft hazard procedure, such that if every phase is considered or performed in sequence the driver will approach all hazards safely.

information safety, any system that forewarns the driver of a potential hazard ahead, *e.g.* an ice warning sensor.

information sign, a road traffic sign generally

rectangular and with a background in any of 8 different colours, colour coded to the type of information displayed.

infrared remote control, a system of transmitting and receiving a signal for remote operation of a device, *e.g.* garage doors.

infrared scanner, a device fitted to Puffin crossings to monitor the approach of a gap in traffic, others monitor the pedestrians.

in gear, a condition when a forward or reverse gear is selected.

inhibitor, a device to prevent a driver attempting to select a low gear at a high road speed.

injected engine, fuel injected engine.

injection, fuel injection.

injection period, the duration of time that fuel is sprayed into the combustion chamber or inlet ports by a fuel injection system, typically 1 to 10 milliseconds depending upon engine speed.

injection pump, the high pressure pump which delivers fuel to the injectors.

injector, a nozzle that sprays fuel under high pressure into the inlet air or combustion chamber.

injector nozzle, the tip of the injector which creates a single or multijet spray of fuel.

injury accident, a collision involving a motor vehicle on a public road in which a road user is injured.

inlet cam, the cam which controls the operation of the inlet valve in a dohc engine.

inlet manifold, a multipassage casting or set of tubes that conducts the air or air-fuel mixture to the cylinder head.

inlet over exhaust, a cylinder head having inlet and exhaust manifolds on the same side.

inlet port, the passageway through the cylinder head for induction air or air-fuel mixture to the valve.

inlet stroke, induction stroke.

inlet valve, a valve that is open during the induction stroke to allow air or the air-fuel mixture to enter the cylinder, then is closed for the other 3 strokes.

inline engine, a multicylinder engine design style in which all of the cylinders are in a single row.

inline linkage, a power steering linkage with control valve and actuation combined in a single assembly.

in motion, moving.

Inner Belt, the beltway encircling St. Louis, Missouri.

inner cap nut, sleeve nut, the part of a Budd mounting which holds the inner of a twin wheel to the hub.

inner dead centre, tdc.

inner headlamp, the inner of a pair of headlamps, normally for main beam.

innerliner, the innermost layer of a tubeless tyre, a layer of halobutyl rubber that prevents air from permeating through the carcass of the tyre.

inner loop, USA, the carriageway having clockwise direction of travel around a ringroad, first designated on the I495 Capital Beltway.

inner race, the smaller of the 2 races around which balls or rollers roll in a bearing.

inner ring road, any road which encircles the centre of a town, typically using existing roads following a grid or other system, sometimes constructed to motorway standard and reasonably circular.

innertube, a thin rubber toroid of a size to match a tyre, and which is inflated within a tyre to form a pneumatic chamber.

inner wheel, the inboard wheel of a pair of twin wheels.

inner wing, the panel on each side of the engine bay separating that from the suspension and wheel, and sometimes supporting the suspension.

inox, inoxidizable, stainless steel.

input shaft, the gearbox shaft transmitting power from the clutch into the gearbox.

inset wheel, a wheel having positive offset, *i.e.* the centreline of the rim is inboard of the mounting face.

inside wheels, all the wheels on that side of a vehicle which take the smaller radius when following a curved course.

inspect, to examine a part or system for correct condition or function, with tools and measuring equipment where necessary.

inspection lamp, a lamp on a long power lead for inspection of the undersides or under the bonnet.

inspection pit, a sunken walkway in the floor of a garage for access to work beneath a vehicle.

inst, instruments.

install, to affix and commission any accessory or kit to the vehicle.

instant spare, emergency inflator.

instruction, UK, verbal and/or written information that must be given to a driver of hazardous goods regarding the load to be transported each day, (DTR).

instruction permit, USA, a document held by a person learning to drive before a drivers license is obtained, if under 18 it is only issued if enrolled at an approved driver education class.

instructor, a person who teaches, usually referring to teaching learner drivers in a car or larger vehicle.

instructor training, teaching a potential instructor to teach or to improve their teaching methods, to enable qualification as a driving instructor.

instrument, each of the devices which inform the driver of speed, distance, quantity, temperature, pressure, and other operating parameters of the vehicle, usually located on a panel just below the windscreen.

instrument binnacle, instrument panel or housing.

instrument cluster, an array of various gauges in a single housing.

instrument panel, a layout of instruments, gauges, tell-tale lights, and other displays that the driver needs to safely drive the vehicle, usually located just below the windscreen.

instrument voltage regulator, an electronic circuit that controls the voltage supply to the instrument panel, usually maintaining a constant 5 volts.

insulation, material that prevents the flow of electricity or of heat.

insulator, a material that is a poor conductor of electricity or of heat.

insurance, motor insurance.

insurance excess, a sum that is not covered by the insurance policy, such that in the event of a claim the policy holder must pay this sum.

Insurance Institute for Highway Safety, USA, a safety organisation which crash tests vehicles for comparison.

insurance premium tax, a specific tax raised on the purchase of motor vehicle insurance.

intake, USA, inlet.

intake air temperature sensor, a sensor that sends a signal to the ECU so compensation can be made to ensure efficient mixture control.

intake port, USA, inlet port.

intake stroke, USA, induction stroke.

intake valve, USA, inlet valve.

integral, built in, part of a whole unit.

integrated child seat, a rear seat that can be converted into a child safety seat.

integrated circuit, a small solid-state electrical circuit, usually manufactured as a chip.

integrated endurance braking system, a retarder that operates automatically in conjunction with the service brake.

integrated motor assist, a function of a petrol-electric parallel or series hybrid such that the battery only assists the small petrol engine if necessary during acceleration.

integrated transport, a regional transport system which integrates all modes, designates a network of defined traffic corridors, emphasises connections, choices and coordination of transport services and promotes an optimal yield from the transportation resources.

intelligent cruise control, a sophisticated version of cruise control whereby the brakes can also be applied automatically if the traffic ahead stops, developed by Mercedes.

intelligent speed adaptation, a microprocessor based in-vehicle system using satellite navigation equipment to know its exact location such that it will automatically control the speed of the vehicle when approaching a controlled speed limit zone, and prevent excess speed in the zone.

intelligent traction control, a traction control system which operates by controlling the differential so when traction is poor the power is directed to the wheel with the most grip,

developed by BMW.

intensive driving course, a course based upon a full time driver training schedule, typically at least 7 hours per day through several consecutive days.

Inter-American Highway, the road from Laredo, Texas, to Panama City, Panama, totalling 5,470 km (3,400 miles), part of the Pan-American Highway.

interaxle differential, a differential on a lorry having 2 or more drive axles, fitted to each drive axle except the last and acting between each axle differential, to allow each axle to turn at different speeds when cornering etc.

interaxle diff lock, a device on a vehicle having 2 or more drive axles whereby the interaxle differential can be locked so both axles will rotate at the same speed, to increase traction on slippery surfaces.

interchange, a system of interconnecting motorways or freeways with grade separation and sliproads and link roads on 2 or more levels, designed such that traffic flows do not intersect; see also: intersection.

intercooler, a system which cools supercharged or turbocharged air before induction to the engine, to increase density and power.

intercooling, the use of an intercooler to cool the charge air for increased power.

interference, unwanted radio frequency emissions generated typically in the ignition system.

interior, the cabin, cockpit, or saloon of a vehicle.

interior light, courtesy lamp.

interior mirror, the main mirror on smaller vehicles, located centrally at the top of the windscreen.

interior safety, any aspect of vehicle design where the purpose is to minimise accelerations and forces acting upon the vehicle occupants in the event of a collision, to provide sufficient survival space and egress from the vehicle, a branch of secondary safety.

interior trim, all of the covers, lining, facing, and upholstery over each panel in a vehicle.

interleaf friction, the friction between adjacent leaves in a leaf spring.

interlock, a safety function that only allows the ignition key to be removed when the gear selector is in P position.

intermediate, USA, a size of car typically seating 5 or 6 persons.

intermediate gear, any gear which is not the lowest or highest.

intermediate hold, a facility for holding 2nd gear in a 3 speed automatic.

intermediate ring road, a road which encircles a town or city between the inner and outer ring roads, sometimes using existing roads following a grid or other system, sometimes constructed to motorway standard and reasonably circular.

intermediate time control, a checkpoint location during a regularity section in a road rally.
intermittent, a fault or condition that occurs at random intervals.
intermittent wiper control, a control that causes the windscreen wiper or rear wiper to operate at preset intervals; the front wiper control may have an adjustable timing through a wide range, e.g. 0.5 second delay to 30 seconds delay.
intermodal operation, combined road and rail operations allowing lorries to be loaded at up to 44 tonnes gross.
intermodal transport, the transport of goods by several modes from origin via 1 or more interface points to destination, where 1 carrier organises the whole of the transport.
internal brake, drum brake.
internal combustion, the generation of power by burning fuel within the cylinders of the engine, not externally as in a steam engine.
internal combustion engine, an engine in which the fuel is burned internally in the same place where power is produced, the expansion of the exhaust gas becomes the thermodynamic fluid which produces the motive force; the ic engine includes all 2 stroke, 4 stroke, rotary, and gas turbine engines regardless of fuel type, invented in 1860.
internal damage, indirect damage.
internal gear, an annular gear having teeth on the inner radius of its rim.
internal gear pump, a gear pump having a rotor with internally cut teeth meshing eccentrically with an idler and having a crescent shaped spacer to direct the oil flow.
international driving permit, a translation of a driving licence through 5 vehicle categories for English, French, Spanish, German, Italian, Greek, Arabic, Japanese, and Chinese, as per the Road Traffic Conventions of 24 April 1926 and 19 September 1949.
international freight permit, a document issued to operators running services from countries with which Britain has entered an agreement.
International Organisation of Motor Vehicle Manufacturers, OICA, Organisation Internationale des Constructeurs d'Automobiles.
international plate, see: distinguishing sign; see appendices.
interplate, an intermediate drive plate between the driven plates in a twin plate clutch.
intersection, a minor or major road junction without grade separation, typically a crossroads, but often referring to a junction of multilane roads controlled by traffic signals or sometimes a roundabout; see also: interchange.
intersection sight distance, the length of unobstructed view of an entire at grade intersection and sufficient lengths of the intersecting highway to permit control of the

vehicle to avoid collisions during through and turning movements.
interstate highway, USA, either: a road which is part of the Interstate Highway System, a US highway, or a state highway, and which maintains a route number through more than 1 state.
Interstate Highway System, USA, the national highway network of limited access roads denoted by a number on a red, white and blue shield, the numbering system is based on a national grid pattern with a logical ordering of the numbers, see appendices.
in tow, the state of being towed.
intoximeter, a device that accurately measures the proportion of alcohol in a persons breath and prints the figure.
intuition, the ability of a driver to respond to actions and reactions other road users either consciously or unconsciously.
invalid carriage, a mechanically propelled vehicle having a maximum permissible unladen weight of 254 kg, and which is specially designed and constructed but not merely adapted, for the use of a person suffering from some physical defect or disability and is used solely by such a person, (RTA), typically having 3 wheels, now obsolete.
invalid carriage class 2, a mechanically propelled vehicle having a maximum permissible unladen weight of 113.4 kg, a maximum speed of 4 mph (6.4 km/h), and which is specially designed and constructed for the use of a person suffering from some physical defect or disability, it may be used on a footpath without any driving licence, insurance, test certificate, or VEL, and has no minimum or maximum age restriction.
invalid carriage class 3, a mechanically propelled vehicle having a maximum permissible unladen weight of 150 kg, a maximum speed of 8 mph (12.8 km/h), if used on footpaths it must be fitted with a speed restrictor set at 4 mph (6.4 km/h), it must have a speedometer and horn, it may be used without any driving licence, insurance, test certificate, or VEL, but the driver must have a minimum age of 14 years.
invalid vehicle, invalid carriage.
invalid vehicle service, an obsolete system which provided a 3 wheeled vehicle with only 1 seat for physically disabled drivers.
inverted engine, an engine in which the cylinders are directly below the crankshaft, uncommon in motor vehicles.
io, inlet valve opens, a valve timing specification relating to a specific number of degrees btdc.
IO, UK, Insurance Ombudsman.
iodine, an element of the halogen series, often used as a vapour in bulbs to give increased brightness and prolong the bulb life.
ioe, inlet over exhaust.
IOMVN, see: OICA.

150

ip, ignition point, the ignition timing specification relating to a specific number of degrees btdc.
IPSGA, information, position, speed, gear, acceleration.
IR, Iran, international vehicle distinguishing sign, see appendices.
IRF, International Road Federation, Washington and Geneva.
IRL, Indy Racing League.
IRL, Ireland, international vehicle distinguishing sign, see appendices.
iron, a metallic element, relatively soft and susceptible to corrosion, normally alloyed to make various steels.
iron, USA, automobile.
iron, USA, tyre lever.
IRQ, Iraq, international vehicle distinguishing sign, see appendices.
irs, independent rear suspension.
IRSO, Institute of Road Safety Officers, UK.
IRTE, Institute of Road Transport Engineers, UK.
IRV, instant response vehicle, a police vehicle.
is, independent suspension.
IS, Iceland, international vehicle distinguishing sign, see appendices.
ISA, intelligent speed adaptation.
ISD, intersection sight distance.
island, roundabout.
island, traffic island, an area between lanes on a road to physically separate traffic flows, typically on approach to a junction, or for pedestrian refuge, but also including an outer separation.
ISO, International Organization for Standardization, Switzerland.
Isofix, a standard mounting system for child safety seats, provided by car manufacturers.
ISO metric, a marking indicating that standard metric dimensions have been used, especially for screw threads.

iso-octane, octane.
ISO symbol, each of over 160 different ISO approved graphic symbols describing the function of a switch or control, or an illuminated colour coded tell-tale symbol on the dashboard that gives information regarding the status or correct or incorrect function of circuits or systems or auxiliaries or devices, illuminating in blue, green, red, or yellow.
Issigonis, Sir Alec Issigonis, born in Turkey, designer of the Morris Minor, the Mini and others.
IT, a tyre design for industrial trucks.
ITA, Institute of Transport Administration, UK.
ITAI, Institute of Traffic Accident Investigators, UK.
Italian tuneup, the addition of a fuel cleaning additive into the fuel tank followed by 20 km (12 miles) of driving at high revs and maximum power, *e.g.* rapid hill climbing, to burn off all loose coke and soot from the injectors and exhaust, typically necessary before an exhaust emissions test of any vehicle but especially a diesel.
ITC, intelligent traction control.
ITC, intermediate time control, in road rally navigation.
ITE, Institute of Transportation Engineers, USA.
ITF, International Transport Federation.
ITS, an airbag system which provides head protection during side impacts, developed by BMW.
ivc, inlet valve closes.
ivo, inlet valve opens.
ivr, instrument voltage regulator.
IVS, invalid vehicle service.
IVU, in vehicle unit.
IVV, Internationaler Verband Fur Verkehrserziehung, International Association for Driver Education.

J

J, a designation for a shape of wheel construction where the rim, well, and offset conform to specific measurements.

J, Japan, international vehicle distinguishing sign, see appendices.

J flange, a common type of wheel rim flange, the part of the wheel rim against which the tyre locates.

J gate, an automatic transmission control where the selector moves in a J shape for manual override, developed by Jaguar.

J turn, the technique of inducing a controlled 180° spin from reverse to forwards at speed without braking whilst following a straight course, performed by: reversing at high revs in a straight line, flicking the steering to full lock either to the right with the right hand from a 7 o'clock hold or to the left with the left hand from a 5 o'clock hold and making use of negative castor to cause instability in the steering, as the front end slides around countersteer and select a forward gear and accelerate; used primarily as an anti-attack escape procedure, also used in some competitions e.g. auto tests, sometimes in spin recovery; CAUTION, if the steering is not turned rapidly or if attempted in a pickup, suv, 4x4, or similar the car may roll, i.e. only possible in a car having a low centre of gravity.

JA, Jamaica, international vehicle distinguishing sign, see appendices.

jack, a device for lifting a vehicle, see: bottle, go-jack, hi-lift, hydraulic, jib, quick lift, scissor, screw, tower, trolley.

jack and topple, a self recovery technique to extract a bogged vehicle by jacking both wheels at 1 end of the vehicle quite high then pushing the vehicle sideways until the jack falls, typically when grounded in deep ruts to raise and push the vehicle so the wheels land clear of the ruts.

jacking, the result of cornering forces on a swing axle suspension which tends to lift the car through the differential or transaxle causing the outboard wheel to tuck under the car resulting in a reduction in stability.

jacking, the theft of property from occupants within a car, typically whilst in slow moving or stationary traffic.

jacking out, a self recovery technique to extract a bogged vehicle by jacking to raise the vehicle to place boards, rocks, or ramps etc,

beneath 1 or more wheels.

jacking point, a strengthened area under a car body where a jack should be positioned, typically just ahead of a rear wheel or just behind a front wheel.

jackknife, a skid by the drive axle of an articulated lorry such that the tractive unit rotates until its side collides with the trailer, i.e. the trailer does not significantly turn; see also: trailer swing.

jackknife, any reversing manoeuvre that causes the sides of a trailer and its towing vehicle to contact each other.

jackscrew, USA, screw jack.

jack stand, axle stand.

jack up, to raise a wheel or the chassis or body of a vehicle.

JADA, Japan Automobile Dealers Association.

JAIA, Japan Automobile Importers Association.

Jake brake, a powerful secondary braking system fitted to some lorries, operation is effected by altering the valve timing of the engine so it will behave like an air compressor and absorb power, developed by Jacobs Vehicle Systems.

jalopy, an old vehicle in a poor condition.

JAMA, Japan Automobile Manufacturers Association.

jam jar, car, cockney rhyming slang.

jam nut, USA, locknut.

jam sandwich, any police car having a red stripe along the side of a white body.

JAPA, Japan Automobile Products Association.

Japanese lantern, a portion of a steering column resembling a steel net such that it will concertina during a severe impact.

JAPIA, Japan Automobile Parts Industries Association.

JARI, Japan Automobile Research Institute.

jaw jacking, CB jargon, a longwinded conversation.

jay walker, a pedestrian who unnecessarily increases personal risk or increases inconvenience to other road users whilst using a road, e.g. crossing a road against a red pedestrian crossing light, at an acute angle, not using a footway, or walking where pedestrians are prohibited.

JCB, Joseph Cyril Bamford, designer of the backhoe excavator-loader produced since 1945;

the name is commonly used as a generic term for similar vehicles.

jct, junction.

JDP, USA, judicial driving permit.

jeep, a tough off-road car having 4x4 transmission, long travel suspension, good ground clearance, and suitable tyres such that it will perform well on a variety of uneven surfaces; originally designed as a WW2 military scout vehicle and named GP from general purpose.

jeep dolly, a load carrying axle or axle set coupled between a tractive unit and a low loader semitrailer to reduce the imposed load on the tractive unit when carrying exceptional loads, and allow additional articulation, coupled to a tractive unit 5th wheel by its kingpin and carrying a 5th wheel coupling to support the trailer.

jeepney, a jeep taxi, common in many Asian countries, constructed with 8 seats but often carry up to 30 persons.

jerk pump, USA, a fuel injection pump.

jerky, a style of driving resulting in an endless series of sudden changes in the rate of longitudinal and/or transverse acceleration, which may tend to cause passenger discomfort.

jerrican, jerrycan.

jerrycan, a traditional flat sided narrow cuboid container adapted by special openings for transporting and discharging additional or reserve fuel, normally of 5 US gallon (20 litre) size, developed in Germany in WW2, now typically used for expeditions.

Jersey barrier, a design of concrete safety barrier, a concrete wall which is curved and tapered being slightly thicker at the bottom, designed to separate traffic lanes and restrain an out of control vehicle, typically placed along a median strip to prevent crossover, sometimes used on bridge parapets; developed in New Jersey USA.

Jersey curb, Jersey barrier.

jet, a small calibrated passage or nozzle in a carburettor where petrol is delivered for vaporizing.

jet needle, a tapered needle which controls the flow of fuel through a jet.

jib jack, a type of tower jack.

jiggle bars, a series of bi-level stepped rumble strips typically 10 mm and 20 mm high, 100 mm long, and at variable intervals, designed to produce physical vibration in a vehicle to attract a drivers attention to another feature.

JIS, Japanese Industrial Standard.

JJ, a designation for a shape of wheel construction where the rim, well, and offset conform to specific measurements.

JK flange, a type of wheel rim flange used on some heavy vehicles.

jlb, jointless nylon bead.

jockey pulley, a spring loaded idler wheel for maintaining tension in a timing belt or chain.

jockey wheel, the nose wheel on a light trailer or caravan for manoeuvring manually when uncoupled.

Johnson bar, a trailer hand valve.

jointless nylon bead, a type of tyre construction designed for ideal contact patch, load distribution, and comfort.

joule, a unit of work or energy expended when 1 newton is raised 1 metre, = 1J.

jounce, the bump stroke, *i.e.* upward travel of a wheel and suspension; see also: rebound.

jounce buffer, a rubber bump stop, especially at the top of a MacPherson strut.

journal, the part of a rotating shaft which turns in a friction bearing.

journey data recorder, a microprocessor based device that records all operations of a vehicle enabling later analysis of speeds and use of controls, sometimes also linked to a GPS system for location and route monitoring.

joust, to drive competitively in busy traffic, to drive assertively but not aggressively.

joyride, a pleasurable trip.

joyride, to take a car without the owners consent.

joyrider, a person who takes a car without the owners consent, typically for entertainment and causing damage to the vehicle.

joystick gearlever, a gear selector connected to the gearbox by electronics instead of by mechanical levers, allowing fingertip selection of gears, usually sequentially.

JSAE, Japanese Society of Automobile Engineers.

JSL, John Safety Lock, a device for locking bus and lorry wheelnuts.

JSR, Japanese Safety Regulations.

jubilee clip, a type of hose clip secured with a worm screw.

judder, a movement being a series of vibration-like jerks.

judicial driving permit, USA, a special permit issued by the office of the Secretary of State 31 days after a judges order to a first offender serving a statutory summary suspension following arrest for driving under the influence of alcohol and/or other drugs, and which allows driving only during specified times along specified routes for work, education, or medical reasons.

juggernaut, a large lorry.

jumper cable, USA, jump leads.

jumping the lights, the action of deliberately ignoring an amber or red traffic signal either by driving on a few moments before the green light illuminates or a few moments after the green light is extinguished when it is assumed that crossing traffic isn't moving; see also: blowing, running.

jump lead, each of a pair of heavy duty electric cables with powerful spring clamps at the ends, to briefly supply power from a good battery to a flat battery.

jump seat, an additional or temporary seat in a

– JJJ –

vehicle, sometimes in the aisle of a minibus.
jump seat, an instructors seat fitted adjacent to the driver in a bus.
jump start, to start the engine of a vehicle having a flat battery using a pair of jump leads and a good battery: before connecting the leads always start the engine of the vehicle having the good battery, firstly connect the red lead at the positive (+) of the good battery, secondly the other end of the same red lead to the positive (+) of the flat battery, thirdly connect the black lead at the negative (−) of the good battery, fourthly connect the other end of the black lead to a bare metal earth part on the stricken vehicle; after starting the engine of the stricken vehicle removal of the jump leads is the reverse of the above procedure, do not stop the engine before 30 minutes.
jump start, the action of a racing car moving forwards on the grid before the start signal, resulting in a penalty.

jump wire, a short length of wire as an additional temporary conductor in a circuit, sometimes for testing circuits.
junction, the point of intersection of 2 or more roads.
junction, see: $^1/_2$ cloverleaf, $^1/_2$ diamond, 2 bridge, 3 level, braid, cloverleaf, diamond, diverging, dumbbell, full, grade separated, hamburger, magic, restricted, roundabout, SPUI, trumpet, whirl, windmill.
junction number, the number given to a motorway junction, shown on roadsigns as white numerals on a black background.
junction offset, the alignment of opposing offside turns at a staggered crossroads.
Junkers engine, a double-opposed-piston 2-stroke internal combustion engine having intake and exhaust ports at opposite ends of the cylinder.
junkyard, scrapyard, a place where vehicles are broken for scrap.

K

k, kilo, 1,000, a suffix to any units including vehicle price and mileage.

k, kilometre, a measure of distance, spoken only.

k, kilometre per hour, a measure of speed, spoken only.

K, UK, a driving licence category for pedestrian controlled vehicles, *i.e.* where the driver is not seated but walks with the vehicle to operate it, *e.g.* some mowing machines and road rollers.

K, a designation for a shape of wheel construction where the rim and well and offset conform to specific measurements.

K, Kampuchea, international vehicle distinguishing sign, see appendices.

K band, a band of radio frequencies from 10,900 to 36,000 megahertz on which transmissions are made by some radar speed measuring equipment at speed traps.

K flange, a type of wheel rim flange on some heavy vehicles, the part of the wheel rim against which the tyre locates.

K jettronic, a mechanical fuel injection system whereby fuel is constantly injected to the inlet ports and the fuel volume is controlled by an airflow meter.

K left, a rally pace note, a sharp left bend through approximately 75°.

K nut, a high strength locknut incorporating a widened circular base and a deformed top thread for self-locking.

K rail, Jersey barrier, a design of concrete wall used to separate traffic lanes along a median strip to prevent crossover, and for bridge parapets.

K right, a rally pace note, a sharp right bend through approximately 75°.

Ka band, a radio sub band within the K band on which transmissions are made by some radar controlled cameras to detect a driver contravening a red light.

Kadenacy effect, the result of a rectangular exhaust port of a 2 stroke engine opening abruptly causing a positive pressure wave to propagate along the exhaust at the speed of sound.

KAMA, Korean Automotive Manufacturers Association.

Kamm back, Kamm tail.

Kamm tail, W. Kamm, the designer of the shape of the rear of a vehicle which tapers

down significantly over the rear window as if to reach a point about 2 metres behind the car but is then cut vertically, the design optimises weight, length, cost, and aerodynamic and surface drag.

kangaroo start, the effect caused when the clutch is released suddenly at low revs such that the engine almost stalls but recovers, repeatedly, causing a series of significant jerks reacting through the suspension; typically caused by a learner driver attempting to rush.

kart, cart.

Kassel kerb, a road edge formation that allows a bus driver to "feel" the kerb without damage to the tyre sidewall, and to enable easy access to a bus by disabled passengers, named after the German town of origin.

Kay left, a rally pace note, a sharp left bend through approximately 75°.

Kay right, a rally pace note, a sharp right bend through approximately 75°.

KBW, kerbed busway.

KdF wagon, Kraft durch Freude, German, strength through joy, the original design name for the VW Beetle as designed by Dr. Ferdinand Porsche in 1935.

keep between the ditches, CB jargon, safe driving.

keeper, the custodian responsible for the security of a vehicle whilst it is not in use.

keep it clean, CB jargon, keep your licence clean, don't gain penalty points, don't get arrested.

keep your eyes moving, scanning, to observe systematically following a predetermined sequence to ensure the driver is aware of everything which is or may happen.

kerb, a raised edge along the side of the road physically marking the limit of the road surface.

kerb, to cause the tyre to strike a kerb violently such that damage to the tyre, wheel, steering, and suspension is possible.

kerb dragging, the action of driving with the 2 wheels on the inside of a bend off and below the edge of the road so steering is assisted by the sidewall of the tyre being guided by the road edge, for additional speed and stability when rallying off public roads.

kerb drill, a series of precautions taken by a pedestrian to ensure it is safe before crossing a road.

kerb extension, a buildout.
kerb idle speed, the low idle speed of an engine specified by the manufacturer with all electrical systems switched on, in a manual transmission whilst neutral is selected, for an automatic transmission stationary whilst drive is selected.
kerbing, the action of violently striking a kerb with a tyre such that damage to the tyre, wheel, steering, and suspension is possible.
kerb marking, a kerb which may painted in a variety of colours or twin colours to describe the parking, waiting, standing, stopping, or loading restrictions, as defined and coloured differently in each country.
kerbside, the side of a road or lane nearer the kerb.
kerbstone, each of a series of stones forming a kerb.
kerbstrike, an occurrence when a tyre violently strikes a kerb such that damage may be caused to the tyre, wheel, steering, or suspension.
kerb to kerb, the definition of a turning circle or radius referring to the space a vehicle requires to make a 1 point turn without allowing for the front and rear overhangs, *i.e.* measuring the path of the tyres only.
kerb to wall, see: wall to kerb.
kerbweight, the weight of a vehicle unladen and without the driver, but including the weight of all tools, fluids, and fuel at the maximum level.
kerf, sipe.
kerosene, USA, paraffin, a fuel sometimes used in older tractors but typically in jet engines or as heating fuel.
KERR, kinetic energy recovery rope.
Kevlar, a very strong light flexible synthetic fibre sometimes used in tyres and body panels.
key, a coded instrument inserted into a lock to permit operation of a mechanism.
key, a small peg or wedge for locating and restraining a part on a shaft.
key, a spanner or tool of a specific size.
key, an explanatory list of symbols used on a map.
key fob, an accessory for a key ring to simplify visual identification.
keyless system, any security and ignition system using a transponder card instead of an ignition key.
key on engine off, a necessary or specific condition for some tests.
key on engine running, a necessary or specific condition for some tests.
kg, kilogram, a unit of mass.
kg/cm², kilogram per square centimetre, a unit of pressure, commonly the unit for lorry and bus air brake pressure gauges,
$1 \text{ kg/cm}^2 = 14.2233$ psi.
kg.m, kilogram metre, a unit of torque as used on a torque wrench, $1 \text{ kg.m} = 7.233$ foot pounds.
Khardungla Pass, the highest motorable road

in the world between Leh and Manali in Kashmir in the Indian Himalayas, reaching an altitude of 5,682 metres (18,640 feet).
Khyber pass, the road through the Himalayas joining Kabul in Afghanistan to Islamabad in Pakistan, featuring a large number of hairpin bends; part of Highway 1, GTR.
kickback, a backward thrust, *e.g.* the result of ignition and power occurring before tdc causing the crankshaft to rotate in the wrong direction as it is cranked.
kickback, the feedback felt through the steering wheel as a front wheel crosses any unevenness in the road surface.
kickdown, the shifting to a lower gear by an automatic transmission, especially when the accelerator is rapidly or fully depressed.
kickout, to initiate a rear wheel skid in a rwd car by significantly increasing the accelerator whilst negotiating a bend.
kickover, to start firing, the start of running of an internal combustion engine.
kickstart, a method of starting the engine of some vehicles, typically some motor tricycles and motor cycles, manually by rapidly and forcefully depressing a lever with the foot.
kickup, a raised section of chassis rails over the vehicle axles to provide sufficient clearance, especially on 4x4 and pickups.
kickup, the portion of a modern headlight beam that is angled upwards to the nearside above the normal cutoff, for the purpose of reading roadsigns.
killer overtake, a situation when 2 vehicles are overtaking a long vehicle, the lead vehicle delays moving back to the nearside and remains level with the front of the long vehicle until the last moment before oncoming traffic arrives, then the lead vehicle moves to the nearside and the second overtaking vehicle remains to face a head-on collision; a technique occasionally used when being followed by an attacker, the situation often occurs inadvertently.
kill switch, an emergency switch for cutting off the ignition and fuel.
kill the engine, to stop the engine.
kilogram, a unit of mass equal to 1,000 grams, and 1-thousandth of 1 tonne.
kilometrage, the distance travelled per unit of consumption with regard to fuel, oil, tyres, etc.
kilometrage, the number of kilometres between 2 points.
kilometre, a measure of distance equal to 1,000 metres, originally defined for Napoleon Bonaparte as the surface distance from the north pole through Paris to the equator divided by 10,000.
kilopascal, kPa, the metric unit of pressure, 1 psi = 6.9 kPa.
kilowatt, a measure of power equal to 1.34 bhp, 1.3596 PS.
kinematics, the branch of applied mathematics which studies the way in which velocities and

accelerations of parts of a moving system are related, without reference to the forces which cause the motion.

kinesophobia, a fear of motion.

kinetic, of or due to motion.

kinetic energy, energy possessed by a vehicle, occupant, or load by virtue of its motion and momentum, the product of mass x velocity x velocity, m.v², measured in joules, J; see also: potential.

kinetic energy recovery procedure, a method of recovering a bogged 4x4 vehicle using a KERR rope: the towing 4x4 vehicle accelerates with 2 metres (6 feet) of slack rope such that the bogged vehicle is recovered by the momentum of the towing vehicle rather than by traction, and without any significant shock to either vehicle; steel rope, chain, or other fibre ropes will cause damage and must NOT be used; also named snatch recovery.

kinetic energy recovery rope, a special type of nylon webbing typically having a 9 tonne minimum breaking strain, used as an elastic tow rope which will stretch significantly under tension especially when snatch recovering a bogged 4x4 vehicle, such that neither shock nor damage is caused to either vehicle.

kingbolt, kingpin.

king lead, the hv lead from the ignition coil to the distributor.

king of the road, a long distance driver, especially a lorry or coach driver, but also a taxi driver, or a travelling salesman.

kingpin, part of the steering mechanism, the vertical post on which the front wheel slews to vary the directional angle, not on modern cars.

kingpin, the coupling device on a semitrailer that mates with the 5th wheel, hence couples to the tractive unit.

kingpin axis, the line between the balljoints around which the steering mechanism of a modern car pivots.

kingpin inclination, the lateral angle of the kingpin axis from the vertical as viewed from the front.

kingpin offset, the lateral distance between the centreline of the wheel and a line extended from the kingpin axis, being positive if the lines intersect below ground level and negative if intersecting above ground level.

Kings highway, Queens highway.

king terminal, the central distributor terminal fed by the ignition coil.

kink, a sharp bend or a twist in a hose such that capacity is reduced.

kiss and go lane, USA, a lane outside a railway station where commuters being dropped can spend an extra few moments kissing goodbye without causing congestion.

kissing duals, the contact of a pair of tyre sidewalls at their lowest point on a twin wheel axle as they flex under load, a sign of tyre overloading.

kit, a large or small set of tools.

kit, a set of parts for a specific job.

kit car, a home built car where most or few of the parts are supplied by the kit manufacturer, often constructed with major components from several different vehicle manufacturers.

KL, a rally pace note, kay left bend through approximately 75°.

km, kilometre, a measure of distance equal to 1,000 metres.

km/h, kilometres per hour, a measure of speed.

knee bar, USA, knee bolster.

knee bolster, a padded panel beneath the dashboard which is designed to absorb energy during a crash and reduce injury to occupants legs whilst preventing the occupants from submarining.

kneeling bus, the ability of a bus to lower its air suspension to improve access for disabled passengers.

kneeling valve, an automatic device to enable a pickup or lorry with air suspension to lower to the lowest height necessary for travel, to increase stability.

knee room, the distance between the rear of the front seat and the front of the squab of the rear seat, i.e. the space available for the calves of a rear passenger; see also leg room.

knight of the road, any person giving assistance to another motorist having broken down.

knock, pinking, a condition in si engines whereby there is unwanted rapid combustion of the last part of the charge before ignition by the flamefront.

knock, a metallic rattle sound from the engine, usually from worn bearings especially the big end bearings or the crankshaft main bearings.

knock control, a system having a knock sensor to recognise knock and which retards the spark timing when detonation occurs.

knock for knock, an agreement between insurance companies whereby for most minor collisions they each pay to repair the damage to their own clients car, and do not claim from each other.

knock on nut, a spinner, a Rudge nut.

knock on wheel, a road wheel that fits to the hub on a splined shaft and which is secured with a central Rudge nut; the nut is tightened and loosened with a single hammer blow to a lug, from which the name is derived, common on some classic sports and racing cars.

knock rating, the numerical indexing of petrol according to its knock resistance.

knock resistance, a function of the octane rating of a fuel, a higher octane rating has a higher resistance to knock.

knock sensor, a detonation sensor, a system which detects high frequency vibrations that are early signs of pinging, pre-ignition, or knocking and which sends a signal to the ECU to retard the spark timing until the knock ceases.

knock suppressor, a substance added to motor

fuel to retard or prevent detonation or knock.

knock through, a gear selector system where extending the movement in the neutral position operates a switch that causes the selector mechanism to change between high and low ranges.

knowledge, The Knowledge.

knuckle, the area around the axis of a hinged object.

knuckle boom, a type of hydraulic crane with a folding boom, common as a self loading crane on lorries.

knucklepin, kingpin.

knurl, the effect of a special wheeled tool that makes indentations and leaves ridges in metal it is pressed against, applied to the handles of some tools, occasionally to some piston skirts or to valve guides.

koeo, key on, engine off.

koer, key on, engine running.

Kombi-Verkehr, German, a rail service for carrying cars and lorries long distances between cities.

kPa, kilo pascal, a unit of pressure equal to 1,000 pascal.

kph, a misnomer for kilometres per hour, see: km/h.

kpi, kingpin inclination.

KR, a rally pace note, kay right bend through approximately 75°.

krpm, 1,000 rpm, a designation to signify a tachometer is showing the revs divided by 1,000.

krypton, an inert gas used to fill most bulbs typically fitted as oe in most new vehicles to ensure a working life longer than the warranty period; see also: argon.

KS, Kyrgyzstan, international vehicle distinguishing sign, see appendices.

k's, kilometres, a measure of distance, spoken only.

k's, kilometres per hour, a measure of speed, spoken only.

KSI, killed or seriously injured, referring to accident statistics.

kW, kilowatt, a measure of the power output of an engine; 1 kW = 1.34 bhp.

KW, kerbweight.

KWT, Kuwait, international vehicle distinguishing sign, see appendices.

Kyoto Protocol, the international agreement among industrialised countries to reduce emissions of greenhouse gasses, resolved in Kyoto, Japan in 1997.

KZ, Kazakhstan, international vehicle distinguishing sign, see appendices.

L

l, litre, a measure of capacity.

L, UK, a former driving licence category for electrically propelled vehicles, an obsolete category for driving tests.

L, USA, a driving license and vehicle category: any motor driven cycle with less than 150 cc displacement.

L, laden.

L, leaded, referring to fuel type to be used, use leaded fuel, or use lrp or awa.

L, learner, a plate bearing the letter L signifying the driver has not yet passed a driving test in that category of vehicle.

L, left, a rally pace note describing a slight bend to the left through approximately 10°.

L, left, at a junction to turn in that direction in road rally navigation.

L, left hand thread, a marking on some wheel studs having a non-standard thread, typically on the left side of some lorries and buses.

L, Look, a section of the PSL mnemonic.

L, low, on an automatic gearbox a selectable position that restricts automatic selection by the gearbox to the lowest forward gear only.

L, low pressure, a cover on a valve on ac piping marking the connection to that section of the system.

L, luxe, originally a luxury model car, now denoting a rather basic model but above C.

L, Luxembourg, international vehicle distinguishing sign, see appendices.

L, the tyre speed rating code denoting a maximum design speed of 120 km/h (75 mph), moulded into the tyre sidewall.

L1, on an automatic gearbox, a selectable position that restricts automatic selection by the gearbox to the lowest forward gear only.

L1 test, a 480 hour engine test using a single cylinder diesel engine to determine the detergency of heavy duty lubricating oil.

L2, on an automatic gearbox, a selectable position that restricts automatic selection by the gearbox to the 2 lowest forward gears only.

L2 test, an engine test using a single cylinder diesel engine to determine the oiliness of lubricating oil, also named scoring test.

L3 test, an engine test using a 4 cylinder engine to determine the stability of oil at high temperatures and severe conditions.

L4, low range 4wd, a selectable gear range on a 4wd vehicle, it transmits the drive to all 4 wheels using the low range of gears.

L4 test, an engine test using a 6 cylinder si engine to evaluate lubrication oil oxidation stability, bearing corrosion, and engine deposits.

L5 test, an engine test using a diesel engine to determine detergency, corrosiveness, ring sticking, and oxidation stability properties.

l/100 km, litres per 100 kilometres, the metric form of measuring fuel consumption where the lowest number is the most desirable.

L driver, a learner driver, a person who has not yet passed a driving test in that category of vehicle.

L head, a side valve engine having an L shaped combustion chamber.

L head engine, an engine having both the inlet and exhaust valves on 1 side of the cylinder block and operated by pushrods from a single camshaft.

L plate, learner, a sign bearing the shape of a letter L, an obligatory display on a vehicle when a learner driver is under instruction, the sizes and colours of the L and background vary in different countries.

L plate syndrome, the unwarranted need by many drivers to overtake a car carrying L plates regardless of speed or if the instructor is driving.

L ring, a piston ring having an L section, whereby combustion gas increases the pressure of the ring against the cylinder wall, typically in high performance 2 stroke engines.

LA, Licensing Authority.

LAADA, Latvian Authorised Automobile Dealers Association.

labouring, the action of an engine being forced to produce power at very low revs, *e.g.* climbing a hill in the wrong gear, resulting in high engine wear.

lacquer, a clear automotive pyroxylin paint applied over some types of bodywork paint to protect the surface and enhance a visual effect.

LAD, look, assess, decide.

LADA, look, assess, decide, act.

ladder chassis, USA, ladder frame.

ladder frame, a traditional chassis with 2 structural rails from front to rear, connected by several lateral members for stiffness, the typical construction of lorries, buses and 4x4 cars.

ladder marking, a road marking formed by 2 longitudinal lines separated by many transverse lines painted along the centre of a road, typically to separate traffic flows but sometimes to narrow the lanes to reduce speeds.

laden, a vehicle at any weight above its kerbweight, up to its maximum gross weight with either goods or passengers.

LADEN, look, assess, decide, emerge, negotiate.

lading, material used to prevent a load being damaged through contact with restraining chains or lashings etc.

lading, the actual load or freight carried by a vehicle.

lag, the angle measured in degrees of crankshaft rotation after bdc or tdc until a valve opens or closes.

lag, an unwanted condition when the front wheels of a 4wd vehicle revolve slower than the rear wheels; it may occur in an awd car fitted with non-identical tyres where a front tyre is smaller or more worn than a rear tyre resulting in high tyre wear and damage to the transfer case; see also: lead.

lake pipes, imitation exhaust pipes usually chromed and typically fitted along the lower sides of a sports or custom car for aesthetic purposes.

lambda, λ, the symbol for perfect stoichiometric ratio for each specific fuel type, measured with respect to the residual oxygen in exhaust gas.

lambda sensor, an oxygen sensor made from ceramic zirconium oxide with a thin layer of platinum, it reacts to residual oxygen in the exhaust and sends a signal to the ECU.

laminated glass, a composite material formed with 2 layers of glass bonded to a plastic film sandwiched between, a type of safety glass.

lamp, any device that emits a beam of light.

lamp cluster, see: combined lamps, grouped lamps, reciprocally incorporated lamps.

lamp post, a pole which supports a public lamp at a height for efficient illumination of the road surface.

lamp socket, USA, bulb holder.

lamp standard, a post supporting a public lamp.

landau, a large veteran car having a removable top over the front seats, a roof and windows for the centre saloon, and a folding top over the rearmost pair of seats; named after the German town where it was first constructed.

landau bar, each of a pair of S shaped ornamental metal bars mounted on the C pillar, to resemble a folding hood stay on a convertible.

landaulet, a small landau having open front seats and a folding hood over the rear saloon.

landing gear, landing legs and the winding mechanism to set their height at the front end of a semitrailer.

landing legs, the retractable legs that support the front end of a semitrailer when uncoupled.

land line, CB jargon, a telephone

land transport, the movement of persons, goods, or equipment on or across land by means of any conveyance.

land vehicle, a self propelled locomotive device moving on the earth's surface, of which the propulsion and the steering are under the control of the driver aboard the vehicle.

lane, a narrow rural road, sometimes unsurfaced.

lane, a longitudinal division of a carriageway intended to accommodate a single line of moving vehicles, sometimes reserved for a specific direction of travel or a specific vehicle, *e.g.* bus lane, or having a restriction from use, *e.g.* lorries over 7.5 tonnes.

lane, see also: $^1/_2$ 1, 2, 2+, 2 way, 3, acceleration, auxiliary, buffer, bus, car pool, climbing, contraflow, crawler, cycle, deceleration, dedicated, diverging, escape, fast, filter, fire, granny, green, highway, high occupancy, HOV, kiss, main, median, mobile, multi, nearside, nearside bypass, nearside diverging, nearside passing, no-car, open, operational, overtaking, passing, pit, road, sandwich, single, slow, speed change, splitting, storage, street, suicide, through, traffic, tram, transit, turning, unlaned, with flow.

lane 1, UK, the nearside lane, the leftmost lane, sometimes named slow lane.

lane 1, USA, the offside lane, the leftmost lane, sometimes named fast lane.

lane 2, UK, the 2nd lane from the nearside, an overtaking lane unless lane 1 is dedicated as a bus lane or similar.

lane 2, USA, the 2nd lane from the offside.

lane 3, UK, the 3rd lane from the nearside, on a 3 lane road the righthand lane, an overtaking lane, although it may be restricted, *e.g.* prohibiting heavy lorries, sometimes named fast lane.

lane 3, USA, the 3rd lane from the offside, on a 3 lane road the righthand lane, sometimes named slow lane.

lane button, USA, cats eye, reflective stud.

lane closure, a section of road that is not available to be used, resulting in a reduction in the number of lanes available.

lane control signals, illuminated traffic signals in the form of arrows and crosses that inform drivers which lanes are available when a tidal flow system is operating.

lane discipline, a skill exhibited by a driver when positioning correctly on any road, requiring planning such that any necessary lane changes are performed timely and with due allowance for other road users.

lane divider, lane line.

laned road, a road having road markings to delineate the centre.

lane gain, a benefit at some motorway junctions where a joining lane does not merge but continues along the main carriageway increasing the number of lanes available.

lane hog, a driver travelling indefinitely and unnecessarily in a lane other than the nearside lane on a motorway or similar road when a lane to the nearside is freely available, especially if traffic flow in another lane is hindered.

lane line, a broken white line consisting of a short stripe and a long gap, used on wide carriageways to divide the road into lanes.

lane sharing, the use of 1 lane for traffic moving towards 2 or more routes.

lane splitting, the action of driving partly in 2 lanes, typically inconsiderate driving.

lane splitting, USA, the action of a motorcyclist riding along the white line between 2 lanes of traffic.

laning, driving along a green lane.

LAO, Laos, international vehicle distinguishing sign, see appendices.

lap, 1 complete circuit of a race course.

lap, the situation when a leading racing driver has caught up to and overtaken a slower car that is actually 1 or more laps behind.

lap, to grind an engine valve so its face makes a good metal to metal seal with its seat, performed using grinding paste and an oscillating rotary motion of the valve.

lap and diagonal, a 3 point seat belt fitted over the upper thighs and across the chest.

lapping, the action of a leading racing driver in overtaking a slower car that is actually behind.

lapse, an embarrassing situation when a driver forgets the intended destination and continues on an otherwise familiar route.

lapse, a minor fault committed by a driver unthinkingly or unknowingly, and where the action does not impinge upon the safety of others.

lap strap, a 2 point seat belt fitted over the upper thighs and round the hips.

lap time, the time taken to complete a single lap of a circuit, starting and finishing the lap at speed.

LAR, Libya, international vehicle distinguishing sign, see appendices.

LARA, Land Access and Recreation Association, an organisation for 4x4 and similar off-road users, UK.

large goods vehicle, UK, a goods vehicle exceeding 3.5 tonnes GVW, (MVDLR).

large goods vehicle, UK, an articulated vehicle; or, a motor vehicle constructed or adapted to carry or haul goods and the permissible maximum weight exceeds 7.5 tonnes, (RTA).

LARSOA, Local Authority Road Safety Officers Association, UK.

laser detector, an electronic device that may be mounted in a vehicle to sense specific infra red and radio speed trap beams and give an alarm to the driver.

laser lights, a misnomer, emitted light from an LED light source, sometimes the light source may be remote from the lens and uses fibre optic bundles to transmit the light to the lens.

lash, freeplay, clearance, a specific space between 2 moving components, *e.g.* clearance between a valve and actuator or tappet.

lashing, any type of fastening device for restraining a load on a lorry, including: cable, chain, rope, webbing, etc.

latching pillar, the B pillar.

late apexing, on a race circuit, the action of turning into a bend slightly later than the optimum, not reaching the inside edge at the apex such that full advantage is not taken of the available road width.

late apexing, on a public road, the action of turning into a bend slightly late to create an artificial apex on ones own half of the road approximately $^3/_4$ of the distance around the bend for optimum performance coupled with maximum safety.

late model, a recently dated model, or a vehicle produced towards the end of any production run.

lateral acceleration, the sideways force developed when following a curved course; the force can reach 0.8 g in some cars, depending upon the surface and the tyres.

lateral air bag, air bags at the sides of the seats to protect occupants against side collisions.

lateral force, transverse force, sideways force, centrifugal force.

lateral grip, a quality of a tyre in displaying minimal sideslip when cornering.

lateral runout, the sideways wobble of a wheel or brake disc etc.

lateral stability, the resistance of steering and suspension to react to longitudinal ridges along a road.

lateral stiffness, the resistance of a vehicle body to withstand a side impact.

lateral support, the support on the sides of a seat, restraining the persons torso during cornering.

latex, a material from which rubber gloves are made, to protect the hands from various vehicle fluids.

launch control, the control of the acceleration of the vehicle when starting from rest, either by the driver manually with respect to clutch control and wheelspin, or assisted by a traction control system.

laurel, a wreath of green foliage presented to a race winner and worn loosely around the neck.

Laurin & Klement , the original name for Skoda when production started in 1895.

lay-by, a longitudinal parking area off the side of the road but parallel to the road and contiguous to the road edge.

lay-by bus stop, a bus stop positioned off the side of the carriageway to allow the free flow of other traffic when a bus halts.

layshaft, an intermediate shaft which is gear driven from the input shaft and which gear drives the output shaft to provide the necessary gear ratios in a gearbox.

lay up, the process of manufacturing a grp fabrication in a series of layers.
lay up, to put a vehicle into long term storage.
lazy trailer, an articulated trailer on which the rear axle(s) is/are located further rearwards than normal, such that the cut in on bends is greater.
lb, libra, pound weight, equal to 0.453592 kg, generally obsolete.
LB, Liberia, international vehicle distinguishing sign, see appendices.
lb.ft, pound foot, the measurement of torque produced by an engine, now superseded by the Newton metre, Nm, 1.0 lb.ft = 1.35 Nm.
LBPN, London bus priority network.
lc, low compression.
lcd, liquid crystal display.
LCS, load compensating suspension.
LCV, light commercial vehicle.
ldc, USA, lower dead centre, bdc.
LDT, USA, light duty truck.
LDV, Leyland Daf Vehicles.
LDW, loss damage waver.
lead, a soft metallic element, used as an alloy in batteries, often used in engine bearings, poisonous if it accumulates within the body.
lead, an additive as tetraethyl lead in some types of petrol to lubricate valve seats.
lead, an electrical wire or cable, usually copper with plastic insulation.
lead, the angle measured in degrees of crankshaft rotation between a valve opening or closing and before tdc or bdc occurs.
lead, the condition when the front wheels of a part-time 4wd vehicle or tractor are designed to revolve about 2 % faster than the rear wheels; it may occur in an awd car fitted with non-identical tyres where a front tyre is larger or less worn than a rear tyre resulting in high tyre wear and damage to the transfer case; see also: lag.
lead, see: dry ballast.
lead antimony, an alloy usually used to form the negative plate in most lead acid batteries.
lead calcium, an alloy sometimes used to form the negative plate in maintenance-free lead acid batteries.
lead calcium battery, a maintenance-free battery without facility for checking the electrolyte.
leaded, petrol to which tetraethyl lead has been added to provide antiknock properties and for valve seat lubrication, typical lead content is between 0.05 g/litre and 0.4 g/litre.
lead free, a misnomer, see: unleaded petrol; unleaded petrol usually has minute natural traces of lead compounds.
lead indium, an alloy usually with tin used as a thin wall metal strip used to make plain bearings for big ends etc.
leading axle, a tag axle ahead of a driven axle.
leading shoe, a shoe in a brake drum that opens outwards against the rotation of the drum.

lead/lag, the relationship between the speed of the front wheels compared to the rear wheels, typically a lead of 2 % is designed into some part-time 4wd vehicles and some tractors, *i.e.* the front wheels revolve 2 % faster than the rear wheels; it can also occur in an awd car fitted with non-identical tyres resulting in high tyre wear and damage to the transfer case.
lead loading, a method of bodywork repair using molten lead to fill dents etc, generally obsolete.
lead memory, a coating of lead built up on the valve seats that protects against serious erosion for up to 16,000 km, (10,000 miles) or longer if driven gently.
lead peroxide, an alloy used to form the positive plate in most lead acid batteries.
lead replacement additive, an additive for unleaded petrol that contains either manganese, phosphorus, potassium, or sodium compounds instead of lead to protect the engine's exhaust valve seats from excessive wear, the various types should not be mixed.
lead replacement gasoline, USA, lead replacement petrol typically containing sodium compounds instead of lead.
lead replacement petrol, a petrol that contains potassium compounds instead of lead to protect the engine's exhaust valve seats from excessive wear, usually having a rating of 97 octane.
leadsled, a customised style of car where all seams and joints in the bodywork are filled with molten lead to achieve smooth uncluttered lines.
lead sulphate, the coating on the positive and negative plates of a discharged lead acid battery.
lead up ramps, a pair of sloping steel rails behind the 5th wheel coupling on a tractive unit enabling the tractive unit to force its way under a semitrailer by lifting the semitrailer a few centimetres when the height of the kingpin is slightly below that of the 5th wheel coupling.
lead weight, a small balance weight attached to a wheel rim.
leaf spring, a suspension spring comprising 1 or several flat strips of spring steel, typically semielliptic, designed usually as a beam but sometimes in cantilever layout, commonly fitted on older vehicles but not usually on new vehicles, becoming obsolete.
leakage, the gradual loss of air from a tyre through the carcass, rim, or valve, typically 1 psi per month.
leaker, an engine having faulty seals and which leaves several drips of oil below where the vehicle was parked; see also: gusher.
lean burn, a mode of engine management, when conditions permit the ECU will deliver less fuel such that the air-fuel ratio may rise from 14.7:1 up to 22:1 for greater economy.
lean burn engine, an engine designed to run on a weak mixture to increase economy.
lean mixture, an air-fuel mixture having less

fuel and a higher proportion of air, *i.e.* the stoichiometric ratio is increased above the usual 14.7:1 such that $\lambda > 1$.

leapfrog, to overtake a long line of vehicles individually at intervals on a single carriageway road with no significant gain unless the front of the queue is reached.

learner, a person not holding a full licence, a person learning to drive a car or larger vehicle but not yet having passed a driving test for that size of vehicle, characterised by having to display L plates.

leather bonnet strap, a positive locking device for retaining the engine cover on some classic and older cars.

leathercloth, a pvc plastic layer having a leather texture surface bonded to a fabric reinforcing material, typically used as an alternative to duck for the hood and tonneau of convertibles etc.

led, light emitting diode.

left foot braking, a rallying technique allowing a smooth clutchless gearchange using the accelerator to match the revs whilst braking, for maximum stability and control.

left foot braking, a safety technique for drying the brakes after leaving deep water, performed by selecting 2nd gear and keeping a constant speed with the accelerator whilst gently depressing the footbrake with the left foot to wipe, warm, and dry the brakes.

left foot braking, double footing, a technique used by some drivers of a vehicle having automatic transmission, typically when manoeuvring in confined spaces especially on steep or uneven surfaces, often recommended as a standard technique for elderly drivers to prevent panic freeze on the wrong pedal.

left hand drive, any vehicle where the drivers controls are on the left side of the vehicle.

left hand side, the side of the vehicle on the left as viewed from the drivers seat when facing forward.

left hand thread, a screw thread that advances when the nut or bolt is rotated counterclockwise, sometimes used on wheel nuts at the left side of buses and lorries.

left hook, left hand drive.

left hooker, a left hand drive vehicle.

leg, a part of a rally, a 1 day section.

leg, an approach/departure road to/from a junction.

legal lettering, notices that must be displayed in lories and buses, *e.g.* travelling height, seating and standing capacity, emergency exit, fuel cutoff, electrical isolator, first aid, fire extinguisher, unladen weight, engine stop, registered company name and address.

legal obligation, a requirement with which a driver must comply.

legend, an explanatory list of symbols used on a map.

leg out of bed, an engine condition when a con rod breaks and then punches a hole in the side

of the crankcase causing catastrophic damage to the engine.

legroom, the distance between the rear of the front seat and the backrest of the rear seat, *i.e.* the length available for the thigh of a rear passenger in a car; see also: knee room.

leisure battery, a battery internally designed to withstand deep discharging and recharging, which would shorten the life of an automotive battery, for use in a split charging system.

LE jettronic, a petrol fuel injection system having an injector very close to each inlet valve and having the fuel metered electronically.

LE JOG, Lands End to John O' Groats, the 2 points furthest apart in UK at a distance of 1,320 km (820 miles), used as a long distance route for a variety of speed and endurance trials.

Le Mans, a race circuit near the town of the same name in northern France since 1923, known for hosting 24 hour endurance races, originally starting each race with each driver sprinting to his car.

Le Mans start, a starting pattern where all the racing cars were parked reverse herringbone style at one side of the track and at the start flag the drivers sprinted across the track to their respective car; a style devised at Le Mans but used at many other circuits, discontinued internationally since 1970 due to the advent of seat belts; sometimes still used for motorcycle races.

lemna, a metal plate which bridges the gap in the wheel valve slot of a heavy vehicle to prevent the tube from bulging through.

lemon, a recently purchased second hand or new car having a large number of faults.

length, a physical property of a vehicle created by its design and including any towing devices, for some vehicles a physical prohibition in some places; see: overall length.

length limit, a limit imposed on a section of road that prohibits use by any vehicle exceeding that length.

lengthman, a person employed to maintain a particular section of road.

Lenoir, Jean-Joseph Etienne Lenoir, Belgium, maker of the first practical internal combustion engine in 1862, and driver of the first spark ignition petrol engined car 18 km from Paris to Joinville-le-Pont in 1863.

lens, an optical surface that is designed to refract the light from a lamp to a specific direction.

lens repair tape, a self adhesive tape specially designed for the temporary repair of a cracked lens on a lamp.

let in, to engage the clutch by release of the clutch pedal.

lev, low emission vehicle.

level, the height of a liquid in the reservoir of a fluid system.

level crossing, a place where a railway line crosses a road at the same elevation; it may have gates or full, half, or no barriers, any of which may be automatic, attendant, or user operated, see: controlled, uncontrolled, open, user operated.

level of motorisation, a mathematical ratio describing the number of vehicles per head of population in each country.

level plug, a cap sealing the filling aperture on the side of the transmission or differential where the oil level must be up to that level but its position ensures it cannot be overfilled.

lever shift, the operation of a manual gear lever to change gear as opposed to using the splitter shift on some lorries and buses.

lever shock absorber, a hydraulic damper in a cast iron body operated by a lever.

Lexan, the shatterproof heat resistant plastic used for windscreens and windows of some racing cars.

LGU, a designation on a plate on a vehicle to indicate it has been fitted with noise suppression, exhaust emission suppression, and road-friendly air suspension, a legal requirement to drive lorries into some cities in Europe.

LGV, large goods vehicle, a goods vehicle over 3.5 tonnes, in driver licensing category C or C+E.

lh, left hand.

l/h, litres per hour.

LHA, UK, Local Highways Authority, an organisation within each county council responsible for roads in that area.

lhd, left hand drive.

lhm, a mineral based brake fluid, only to be used where specified, often specified by Citroën.

LHM, liquide hydraulique mineral.

LI, load index.

licence, driving licence.

licence, vehicle excise licence.

licensing authority, UK, a local official appointed to act on behalf of the Traffic Commissioners for a Traffic Area.

license, USA, driving licence.

license plate, USA, registration plate.

licit drug, any drug that can be purchased without prescription but will degrade a drivers performance, *e.g.* cough medicine.

lick, speed, usually fast.

lickety-split, at maximum speed.

lien, mechanic's lien.

lifesaver look, a last look over the shoulder to check the offside blindspot area, especially just before turning off a main road to the offside, or before a lane change, performed by any road user but typically by motorcyclists.

lift, aerodynamic lift.

lift, the distance a poppet valve moves when opening.

lift axle, a suspension controlling device typically on a lorry or trailer enabling the road wheels of a non-driven axle using an air suspension system to be raised from the road,

to reduce costs when running empty or part loaded.

liftback, USA, hatchback.

lifter, USA, tappet.

liftgate, USA, a top hinged tailgate, as on a hatchback.

lifting bridge, a bridge at which the road surface pivots around a horizontal axis at one end whilst the other end is raised in an arc; to permit tall boats etc. to cross beneath.

lift kit, replacement and or additional parts required to give additional ground clearance to a vehicle by modifying the suspension and in some cases raising the body above the chassis.

lift off oversteer, vehicle oversteer caused by the driver lifting off the accelerator in mid-bend causing the nose to dive and the rear to rise, resulting in sudden reduced tyre friction at the rear and a potential spin.

lift out roof, a car with a removable roof panel, it may have a dedicated stowage elsewhere in the vehicle.

lift pump, fuel pump.

lift steer squeeze, an emergency avoidance procedure when faced with an imminent collision where there is space to make a lane change: lift off the brake (if ABS equipped stay hard on the brake), steer into a safe area, brake gently to stop.

lift the dot, a rapid-action disc shaped fastener for fabric car hoods and tonneau covers which is released only by lifting the marked edge.

lift throttle oversteer, USA, lift off oversteer.

light, a quality of a mechanical system, *e.g.* steering which requires little effort.

light, a visual beam of electromagnetic radiation emitted from a lamp to see or be seen in dark and other conditions, and a means of signalling to other road users.

light, lamp or bulb.

lightbar, a device fitted across the roof of an emergency vehicle housing several rotating coloured beacons.

light duty, USA, under 8,500 lbs (3.85 tonnes) GVW.

light duty truck, USA, a light truck having a LVW less than 5,750 lb (2.6 tonnes).

light emitting diode, an electronic device which emits light when a very small current passes through it, used in some instrument displays, and to show digits as in clock numbers, also used in some high level brake lights because they illuminate much faster than an incandescent lamp.

lighter, cigarette lighter, a small removable electric heater having an element that glows red hot when actuated.

lighter socket, a socket originally used to house and operate a cigarette lighter, now often used to supply electrical power for a range of temporary or mobile accessories.

lightfooted, a quality of an economic driver, feathering the accelerator.

lighting, the mandatory lamps that must be

carried and illuminated on a vehicle.

lighting up time, night, the period of darkness between sunset and sunrise.

light locomotive, a mechanically propelled vehicle not constructed itself to carry load other than equipment for propulsion, loose tools and loose equipment, unladen weight exceeding 7,320 kg, but not exceeding 11,690 kg, (RTA).

light-off temperature, the temperature at which a cat achieves a 50 % conversion rate, typically approximately 250 °C.

light pod, a bar across the front of a car on which to mount additional lights, typically for rallying.

light pressure, a turbo that is designed to give only a small boost to inlet air pressure.

lights on reminder, a pleasant chiming or similar alarm signalling to a driver that the headlamps are still illuminated when opening the drivers door or removing the key.

light source with regard to filament lamps, the filament of a bulb itself, in the case of a lamp having several filaments, each one constitutes a light source, (C&U).

light truck, typically any vehicle under 3.5 tonnes, but the figure varies from 1.5 to 8.5 tonnes in different countries.

light van, a car derived van.

light vehicle, typically any vehicle under 3.5 tonnes, but the figure varies from 1.5 to 8.5 tonnes in different countries, see also: weight.

lightweight, a space saving spare wheel.

limit, the edge of a performance envelope for a chassis, steering, suspension, engine, tyres, etc.

limited access highway, a motorway or freeway where entry and exit is only available at specific junctions and there is no direct access to/from property or places along the roadside.

limited edition, each of a small number of a production model of car, factory fitted with some parts which are different from the standard model, typically for aesthetic purposes.

limited sight distance, a restricted preview of the road ahead due to horizontal or vertical curvature of the road, or to blockage or obstruction by a roadway feature.

limited slip differential, a device that only permits a small difference in speed between left and right drive shafts, such that if a small difference in speed is exceeded the differential locks so both wheels will turn at similar speeds; to prevent a situation where 1 wheel is spinning on a poor surface resulting in no power to the other wheel.

limited speed zone, New Zealand, a sign indicating that traffic may travel at up to 100 km/h in good conditions, but must not exceed 50 km/h in poor conditions.

limited stop service, a bus service operating under stage carriage conditions but only stopping at specified points.

limited use area, USA, an area of public land on which travel by vehicle is limited to approved routes of travel, which are at least 2 feet (600 mm) wide and showing significant evidence of prior vehicle use.

limit line, USA, stop line.

limit point, the furthest point at which the driver can see continuous road surface, characterised on a bend where the left and right road edges appear to meet at an arrowhead.

limit point analysis, an advanced driving technique involving matching of vehicle speed to the speed at which the limit point appears to move, slowing as it becomes closer, and accelerating as it visually moves away.

limo, limousine.

limousine, a large luxury car, typically having a glass panel between driver and passengers and having a lengthened chassis and bodywork to create more internal space for the carriage of VIPs, typically chauffeur driven.

Lincoln Highway, USA, a route from New York to San Francisco, the first transcontinental highway specifically constructed for use by automobiles.

line, the path of a vehicle along a road.

linear route, any journey from an origin to a destination and returning to the origin, by which the return route retraces the outward route; see also: circular.

line lock, an hydraulic valve that will maintain pressure in a system, *e.g.* as a hydraulic handbrake.

liner, a thin layer of halobutyl rubber inside a tyre to contain the inflation air.

liner, cylinder liner, a thin steel cylinder used where the cylinder block is a soft material *e.g.* aluminium.

lingering, the action of travelling at speed for longer than necessary alongside a large vehicle on a multilane road, especially a car in the blindspot of a lorry, reducing the escape routes for both vehicles if an incident should occur.

lining, the friction material on a brake pad, brake shoe, or clutch drive plate.

link, a length of road between 2 junctions.

link, a section of a rally on public roads between 2 off-road sections.

link, any lever or moving part in a suspension system.

linkage, an assembly of rods or links to transmit mechanical force.

link road, a road that carries traffic between motorways where they join at an interchange, sometimes with sharp loops, motorway regulations normally apply.

liquefied natural gas, a hydrocarbon mixture, primarily methane having an equivalent octane rating exceeding 120, stored under very high pressure, sometimes used as a vehicle fuel.

liquefied petroleum gas, a hydrocarbon mixture of propane with small amounts of butane, propylene, and butylene, having a typical RON of 112 depending upon mixture; it is stored and transported under pressure as a liquid and boils at –42 °C at atmospheric pressure, sometimes used as a vehicle fuel.

liquid, any fluid above the temperature of its freezing point and below the temperature of its boiling point.

liquid ballast, a solution of calcium chloride in water used with a little air for filling the tyres of tractors when additional weight is required for traction on specific soil conditions; desirable due to its high rd and low freezing point; see also: dry.

liquid cooled, an engine or system that is cooled by liquid circulating through hot parts.

liquid cooled engine, an engine where excess heat is removed by circulation of a water based fluid through hot areas to a heat exchanger and return.

liquid crystal display, a means of displaying information to a driver, often in digital style.

liquid gasket, a gasket material typically a gel applied from a tube and which vulcanises at room temperature.

liquid traction, a liquid applied to the tyres of a dragster to increase traction.

liquimatic, a hydraulic automatic gearbox.

list price, the retail price of a car inclusive of delivery and VAT but excluding on the road charges, *e.g.* registration and road tax.

lithium, a metallic element, used as a base for some grease, especially for high temperatures, *e.g.* wheel bearings and brake parts.

lithium-ion battery, a battery having a fast recharge rate developed for vehicles, also of light weight, and which can be made in any shape.

litre, a measure of capacity, of liquids and of engine size, 1 litre = 1,000 cc.

Litronic, light electronic, a headlamp system using a xenon filled gas discharge lamp, typically operated at 20,000 volts.

little end, the small end of the con rod that is connected to the piston.

little end bearing, the bearing in the little end of the con rod that locates the gudgeon pin that locates the piston.

little wheels, CB jargon, a car or other light vehicle.

live axle, an axle assembly transmitting drive to the wheels, comprising a rigid casing containing 2 half-shafts and a differential, patented by Louis Renault in 1899.

live load, the weight of passengers in a vehicle.

livery, the specific colour scheme used by a particular company on its vehicles.

living van, a vehicle used primarily as living accommodation by 1 or more persons, and which is not used for the carriage of goods or burden excepting items needed for the purpose of residence in the vehicle, (C&U).

lkc, locking compound.

l/km, litres per kilometre, a measure of fuel consumption.

LL1, low low 1, the lowest gear in a deep

reduction range, *i.e.* 1st crawler in the transmission of some lorries.

LL2, low low 2, the second lowest gear in a deep reduction range, *i.e.* 2nd crawler in the transmission of some lorries.

LL3, low low 3, the third lowest gear in a deep reduction range, *i.e.* 3rd crawler in the transmission of some lorries.

LL4, low low 4, the fourth lowest gear in a deep reduction range, *i.e.* 4th crawler in the transmission of some lorries.

LL5, low low 5, the highest gear in a 5 speed deep reduction range, *i.e.* 5th crawler in the transmission of some lorries.

LLLL, look, lower, left, leave.

LLS, load levelling suspension.

lm, lumen, the measure of luminous flux.

LMC, lesser motorised country, typically many African, Asian, and South American countries

lmps, lamps.

LNG, liquefied natural gas.

lo, low, *e.g.* a gear range or headlamp beam.

load, the burden placed on an engine, measured in bhp, kW, or PS.

load, the power carried by an electrical circuit.

load, the weight of goods transported.

load alteration effect, torque steer.

load cells, a self weighing device within the suspension of a lorry to ensure that gross or axle weights are known and not exceeded.

load compensating suspension, a system by which the dampers are automatically adjusted according to the load carried, developed by Volvo.

load controlled power distribution, torque distribution as achieved by a Torsen differential.

loaded, bearing or carrying a load.

loaded section height, the vertical height of the section of the tyre between the bead seat and the tread measured from the lowest point on the rim bead seat to the road surface.

loader, a vehicle which loads bulk materials into a lorry.

load floor, bed.

load index, a numerical code marked on the sidewall of a tyre, ranging from 0 to 279 relating to the maximum load carrying capacity of a tyre at the speed associated with its speed symbol under service conditions specified by the tyre manufacturer; most car tyres are in the range 75 to 105; see appendices.

loading, an increase in insurance premium due to a factor that has increased the level of risk to the driver or vehicle.

loading, any action of placing or removing bulky or heavy goods or materials into/onto, or, from/off a vehicle or trailer or where more than 1 handling trip is necessary, providing the driver or another person having lawful permission to drive that vehicle remains in attendance, but shall not include any time when loading is not actively performed.

loading box, an area at the roadside delineated

with a broken coloured line on a red route, where loading may be permitted with restrictions as signs display; see: red loading box, white loading box.

loading rack, headboard.

load levelling bars, spring bars which can be used to distribute hitch weight among all axles of a tow vehicle and trailer, where a load distributing hitch is fitted.

load levelling suspension, a system that automatically responds to increased load in the rear of a vehicle and adjusts the suspension to compensate, developed by Chrysler.

load lift height, the distance from the ground to the cargo floor or to an open tailgate when the vehicle is at its kerbweight.

load limiter, force limiter.

loadlugger, an estate car or station wagon.

load overhang, the distance a load extends beyond the rear axle of a vehicle.

load proportioning valve, a device to optimise the braking effect between front and rear axles in accordance with weight and distribution of any load.

load rating, load index.

load sensing proportioning and bypass valve, a device mounted to the chassis and the rear suspension arm or rear axle which senses the weight distribution of the vehicle and automatically varies the amount of hydraulic pressure to the rear brakes based on the load, to reduce rear wheel lockup with either light or heavy loads.

load sensing valve, a valve in an air brake system that automatically adjusts to vary the brake pressure depending upon the loading of the vehicle at each axle.

load sharing axle set, an axle set having a suspension system which shares the total load in proportion to the number of tyres on each axle.

load transfer, apparent weight transfer.

load up, to place goods or materials in or on a vehicle.

lobe, a projecting part, *e.g.* the raised part of a cam on a camshaft.

lo beam, low headlamp beam, dipped beam.

local area traffic management, a traffic calming scheme.

local distributor, a road which distributes traffic within a district of a town or city, in a residential area it forms the link between district distributors and residential roads.

localizer siren, a siren on some emergency vehicles which emits a sound that causes less echo so it is easier for other road users to determine its approach direction.

local street, USA, a road for access to residential, business, or other commercial property.

lock, to clamp or fix in position.

lock, an anti theft device which restricts entry to a vehicle when the mechanism is actuated.

lock, an anti theft device which restricts

movement of the steering wheel when the key is removed.

lock, referring to manually lockable freewheeling front hubs on some 4wd vehicles, the locked position whereby the wheel is driven by the axle.

lock, see: full lock.

lock, the angle through which the front wheels slew whilst steering.

lock, to halt rotation of the wheels, to apply brake pressure such that there is greater friction exerted in the brakes than the friction present between the tyres and the road surface, such that the wheel stops rotating and slides along the road surface.

lockable differential, a differential that can be locked to increase traction when the driver selects that function, either electrically, hydraulically, or commonly pneumatically.

lock angle, the angle through which the wheels are slewed whilst steering.

lock buster, a device designed to violently withdraw the complete lock mechanism from a door by a car thief, resulting in significant damage.

locked wheel, the condition which occurs when a wheel stops rotating whilst the vehicle is moving, caused by applying greater braking force than there is friction available between the tyre and the surface, *i.e.* a brake-induced skid.

locker, a differential which can be locked by the driver, typically air operated.

locking compound, an adhesive to prevent nuts or studs from vibrating loose.

locking differential, a differential which can be locked by the driver, typically using an air operated remote control system, to lock the axle shafts together to increase traction on slippery surfaces.

locking synchromesh, a synchromesh system whereby the pressure to operate the synchromesh is proportional to the gearchange force, *i.e.* rapid movement of the gearlever will not override the synchromesh, the increased force will cause it to synchronise faster.

locking torque converter, a torque converter having a lockup clutch to prevent slipping losses between the turbine and impeller, to improve fuel efficiency and performance.

locking wheelnut, a wheelnut having a mechanism or casing requiring a special key to enable it to be turned, but typically there are very few combinations of key.

locknut, a nut having self locking properties, having a high friction component on the thread to prevent movement by vibration, *e.g.* a K nut.

locknut, a slim nut used to restrain an adjusting nut to prevent an adjustment changing, or to prevent another nut loosening.

lockout prevention, a system which prevents external locking of the drivers door if the key is still in the ignition.

lock puller, lock buster.

– LLL –

lockup, a garage for keeping a car, usually with no amenities, typically some distance from the owners home.

lockup, the condition which occurs when a wheel stops rotating whilst the vehicle is moving, caused by applying greater braking force than there is friction available between the tyre and the surface, *i.e.* a brake-induced skid.

lockup clutch, a device in some torque converters which when conditions are appropriate automatically locks the turbine to the impeller to prevent slipping losses to improve fuel efficiency and performance.

lockwire, special wire to prevent nuts from vibrating loose, or for tamperproof security during a rally.

locomotion, progressive movement of a vehicle.

locomotive, a mechanically propelled vehicle designed to pull or push very heavy loads, not constructed to carry any load itself but which may carry water or concrete ballast to assist traction, where the unladen weight exceeds 7,370 kg, (C&U).

Locomotives Act, UK, commonly named the Red Flag Act, introduced in 1865 and which introduced a 4 mph speed limit and required that each motor vehicle must be preceded by a person carrying a red flag, repealed in 1896.

Lodge, Sir Oliver Joseph Lodge, inventor of the sparkplug.

logbook, a means of recording the duty hours, driving hours, and resting hours of a lorry or coach driver, generally superseded by a tachograph, but still used in some countries.

log book, a record of the progress of a learner driver written by the driving instructor.

log book, registration document, archaic name.

lo gear, low gear range, a range of gears below another range.

logistics, the time related positioning of a resource, especially the storage, movement, and distribution of goods, facilities, or people.

logo plate, a registration plate incorporating an official logo in the border or in the space between character groups, in some countries where permitted.

lollipop lady/man, a person controlling a school crossing using a portable prohibition sign.

lollipop man, the member of a race pit crew who monitors the pit stop and other crew members and signals to the driver using a circular sign on a pole when he can restart.

London orbital motorway, the M25, the outer ringroad around London.

loneliest road, USA, highway 50 across Nevada.

long apex area, an apex area around a transitional bend such that the front wheel of the vehicle remains parallel to the road edge or centreline for some distance.

long block, an engine block complete with crankshaft, pistons, oil pump, cylinder head, camshaft, valve train, and all bearings.

long braking, the action of braking early and gently to have a very small rate of retardation, also to show the brake lights for an extended period of time; a method of reducing the risk of collisions.

long haul, a long journey.

longitudinal, any arrangement of parts, or a measurement, along the fore-aft axis of a vehicle.

longitudinal plane, a vertical plane parallel to the longitudinal axis of a vehicle, (C&U).

longitudinal tyre clearance, the fore and aft space between a tyre and the nearest fixed point, allowing for any longitudinal movement of the wheel during suspension travel, especially on trailing arm suspension

long legged, high geared.

long stroke, an engine in which the length of the piston stroke is greater than the bore diameter.

long vehicle, Australia, any combination vehicle having an overall length up to 30 metres long, and a gross combination mass up to 84 tonnes; see also: double road train, triple road train.

long wheelbase, a variant of a vehicle having a greater distance between the front and rear axles compared to some similar models, hence a longer chassis or body length.

look assess decide, the last section of a hazard approach procedure.

look assess decide act, the sequence of actions to be performed for safety when planning to join any traffic flow.

look assess decide emerge negotiate, the sequence of actions to be performed for safety when turning from a minor road onto a main road, especially for large vehicles.

look lower left leave, a system for avoiding head-on collisions: look well ahead for the hazard, lower your speed without stopping, move as far left as possible, (applies to the 73 countries that drive on the left, otherwise right), leave the road into a survivable area.

loom, the complete wiring harness for a vehicle.

loop detector, a loop of conductive wires buried in the road surface on approach to a signal controlled junction, and which signal to the microprocessor controlling the junction.

looped seat belt, a seat belt having a loop in 1 end and which is installed by passing the buckle around a structural part of the seat base then through the manufactured loop in the other end, typically used on some bus seats.

Loop Freeway, the beltway encircling Houston, Texas.

loop ramp, USA, a cloverleaf loop.

loose, a car which will readily oversteer.

loosen, to slacken, to make less tight.

lorry, a vehicle designed to carry goods or machinery.

168

lorry driver, the driver of a goods vehicle, usually a vehicle exceeding 3.5 tonnes GVM.
lorry park, a place where lorry drivers may park for the night, usually having services and a reasonable level of security.
lorry route, an advised or compulsory route to a specific location, e.g. a port, marked by black rectangular signs showing a white silhouette of a lorry, typically for vehicles exceeding 7.5 tonnes.
lose speed, to decrease speed.
loss damage waver, additional insurance to hire car insurance covering loss of, or damage to, a hire vehicle.
lot, USA, a ground level outdoor car park.
LOTS, London Omnibus Traction Society.
loud pedal, accelerator pedal.
louvre, each of a series of long thin ventilating slots cut and pressed in thin metal to form a rectangular area, typically more for aesthetic than practical reasons.
louvre, each series of flat strips across a traffic signal lens, typically the green, angled to ensure a signal is not seen by an adjacent traffic flow.
low, a gear selector control button to enable the driver to select and hold the lowest gear on some bus automatic transmission selector systems.
low, the lowest gear on a gear selector system, sometimes below the numbered gears, giving maximum torque but minimum speed, 1st gear on cars, low 1st on many 4x4 vehicles, crawler on many lorries.
lowball, the practice by a car salesman of deliberately under pricing the cost of a new car to a potential customer who is believed to be shopping around, then when they return admit a mistake in the original quote.
low battery, a battery which is almost discharged.
low beam, dipped headlights.
low bed trailer, a low deck trailer or semitrailer having small diameter wheels and a low bed height for carrying tall and/or heavy loads.
low box, the low range of gears.
low boy, a low deck trailer or semitrailer having small diameter wheels and a low bed height for carrying tall and/or heavy loads.
lowbridge bus, a double deck bus having a sunken gangway along the offside for the upper saloon, to reduce the overall height by approximately 300 mm (1 foot).
low emission, a vehicle emitting fewer pollutants than another.
lower fitting radius, a measurement of a tractive unit in a horizontal arc from the kingpin in a 5th wheel coupling to the extreme rear corner of the chassis or mudguards etc; any trailer having landing legs or side rails at a smaller arc distance from the kingpin cannot be coupled.
lowest rated horsepower, USA, the power

output of a specific engine having the lowest output from a series of related engines, e.g. where a standard block can be fitted with different cylinder heads etc. giving different power outputs.
low floor, a bus with a specially designed low floor for easy access by disabled persons.
low fuel indication, a warning light which illuminates when there is little fuel remaining, typically sufficient for only 30 km (20 miles).
low gear, the lowest gear on a selector system giving maximum torque but minimum speed.
low geared, a vehicle having a lower than usual gear or range of gears.
lowloader, a semitrailer having small diameter wheels and a low deck height for carrying tall and/or heavy loads.
low maintenance battery, a battery that is designed to endure long intervals between being topped up because it consumes little water.
low mileage, a car that has covered less than an average of 16,000 km (10,000 miles) per year of age.
low noise surface, a special type of road surface that produces less tyre noise, sometimes used on urban motorways and similar roads to reduce noise pollution.
low oil sensor, oil level sensor.
low oil warning light, oil level warning light.
low profile, a radial tyre that has a profile between 36 % and 80 % with respect to the section width.
low rider, a car with lowered suspension.
low risk, a condition or action unlikely to result in a traffic violation or a collision.
low risk area, a situation or location with a low potential for a collision, e.g. a straight rural road with good sight lines.
low risk colour, a vehicle colour that is easily seen in most lighting conditions hence is involved in fewer collisions, e.g. yellow or white.
low rolling resistance tyre, a tyre which consumes less energy as it turns, mainly by having a very supple sidewall which generates less internal heat.
low side, the low pressure section of an ac system from the expansion valve through the evaporator to the compressor.
low spec, a basic car with no or few optional extras or accessories.
low sulphur diesel, a medium quality diesel fuel having less than 0.03 % m/m (300 ppm) sulphur content, common in most countries having emissions limits, see also: ULSD.
low sulphur petrol, a medium quality unleaded petrol fuel having less than 0.02 % m/m (200 ppm) sulphur content, common in most countries having emissions limits, see also: ULSP.
low volume approval, a type approval scheme for manufacturers intending to register less than 500 cars per year, where it is not cost

effective to conduct crash testing.

lozenged, the condition of a vehicle body or chassis having suffered severe collision damage to a corner and which has become parallelepiped or rhomboid shaped.

LPG, liquefied petroleum gas, a fuel distilled from crude oil but relatively clean.

lr, lower fitting radius.

LR, Australia, light rigid, a rigid lorry or bus less than 8 tonnes GVM.

LR, Latvia, international vehicle distinguishing sign, see appendices.

LRG, lead replacement gasoline.

LRP, lead replacement petrol.

LRP additive, lead replacement petrol additive.

LRT, Light Rapid Transit, a tram system that shares a road on some of the network.

LS, luxe special, a basic model of car but having trim features common only to a small number of vehicles.

LS, Lesotho, international vehicle distinguishing sign, see appendices.

lsd, limited slip differential.

LSD, low sulphur diesel.

lsg, laminated safety glass.

LSP, low sulphur petrol.

LSP&BV, load sensing proportioning and bypass valve.

LSZ, limited speed zone.

lt, low tension, low voltage, either 6v, 12v, 24v, or 42v, the battery voltage of any vehicle.

LT, light truck, a tyre suffix that indicates a tyre has a suitable load rating for a particular type of vehicle.

LT, USA, light truck, a van or pickup or similar vehicle.

LT, Lithuania, international vehicle distinguishing sign, see appendices.

LT, London Transport.

LTC, Lady Truckers Club, UK.

lth, leather covered upholstery.

lube job, a vehicle service comprising only engine oil and filter change.

lube oil, lubricating oil.

lubricant, any material between 2 moving parts which will reduce friction, usually petroleum based *e.g.* oil or grease, but also including dry substances *e.g.* graphite.

lubricant additive, any material added to any lubricant to give the product special properties, *e.g.* resistance to extreme pressure, cold or heat, improved viscosity, and detergency.

lubricated fuel, fuel into which a lubricant has been added, *e.g.* 2 stroke petrol containing 4 % lubricating oil.

lubricating grease, a solid or semisolid lubricant consisting of a thickening agent, *e.g.* a metallic soap, in a fluid lubricant.

lubricating oil, selected fractions of refined petroleum or other oils used to reduce friction between moving surfaces.

lubricating system, a system that supplies a lubricant to reduce friction between moving

surfaces; it normally comprises: an oil pressure pump, filter, and distribution system.

lubrication point, the place at which a specific lubricant should be applied, typically to steering, suspension, and other parts on classic and older vehicles.

lubrication service, an engine oil and filter change only.

lug, a large block of tread without sipes forming the shoulder of a tyre, as in a military style bar tread.

lug, to drive at low engine revs, or to accelerate from very low engine revs, *i.e.* without downchanging to a suitable gear, potentially causing excessive engine wear.

lug, USA, wheelnut.

luggage carrier, a rack fastened to a boot lid, especially on sports cars and convertibles.

luggage net, a device to restrain articles in the boot of a car, especially in a hatchback or estate, to prevent occupant injury in a collision.

lug nut, USA, wheelnut.

lum, lumbar support.

lumbar support, a slightly protruding or firm area in the lower region of a seat backrest, and which is typically adjustable for driver comfort.

lumen, the unit of luminous flux, the measure of radiant power emitted by any vehicle lamp assessed on the basis of spectral brightness sensitivity; a main beam headlamp should have an output of typically 1,800 lumen.

luminaire, a complete lighting unit, either a vehicle lamp or a street lamp.

luminance, the luminous intensity *i.e.* brightness of a surface measured in candela per m^2, cd/m^2.

lump, engine.

lumper, USA, a person who unloads a lorry by hand.

lunar rover, each of the 3 cars sent to the moon by NASA, first for the Apollo 15 mission in 1971, the transmission was similar to a design made by Dr. Ferdinand Porsche in 1902.

lurker, a small vehicle being driven closely behind a large oncoming vehicle, hence is not seen from ahead and can increase the risk of a head on collision when overtaking others on a multilane 2 way road.

lustre, a sheen or gloss on vehicle bodywork.

Luton van, a van having the goods containing body in the form of a simple box with an extension over the cab roof, usually having an MGW under 3.5 tonnes.

LV, Latvia, international vehicle distinguishing sign, see appendices.

LVA, low volume approval.

lvl, level.

LVNTA, low volume national type approval.

LVW, USA, laden vehicle weight.

lwb, long wheelbase.

LWR, long way round, a directive at a triangle in road rally navigation.

Lysholm supercharger, a lobe type supercharger having high efficiency.

M

m, metre, a unit of length.

M, Malta, international vehicle distinguishing sign, see appendices.

M, Manoeuvre, the last phase of the MSM mnemonic.

M, manual transmission.

M, medium mode, referring to remote controlled variable dampers whereby the driver may select medium to match road surface and driving style.

M, middle, referring to a selectable range of gears.

M, Mirror, the first phase of the MSM mnemonic.

M, the tyre speed rating code denoting a maximum design speed of 130 km/h (81 mph), moulded into the tyre sidewall.

M, UK, motorway, as a prefix to a route number it identifies a specific motorway.

M, UK, as a suffix to a road number it denotes that route is of motorway standard and subject to motorway regulations.

M, USA, a driving license and vehicle category: any motorcycle or motor driven cycle.

M, a hire car size and price category for cars based upon their floor pan; luxury executive cars.

M4, manual 4 speed transmission.

M4/s, manual 4 speed transmission, having close ratio gears.

M5, manual 5 speed transmission.

M5/s, manual 5 speed transmission, having close ratio gears.

M5N, manual 5 speed transmission, having a lower range of gearing but where normal (high) range is selected.

M5NE, manual 5 speed transmission, having a lower range of gearing but in which economy (highest gear) in the normal (high) range is selected.

M5x2, manual 5 speed transmission having high and low range gearing.

M6, manual 6 speed transmission.

M6/s, manual 6 speed transmission, having close ratio gears.

M25, the orbital motorway around London, having a circumference of 195.5 km (121.5 miles).

M85, a fuel comprising a mixture of 85 % methanol with 15 % petrol.

M mode, manual mode, a manual override

selection on an automatic transmission which allows the driver to select the gear.

MA, Morocco, international vehicle distinguishing sign, see appendices.

MA, Motorcycling Australia.

MA, Motorists Association, UK.

MAA, Motor Agents Association, now RMIF, UK.

mac, multiactivity car.

MAC, UK, Ministers Approval Certificate, see also: P-MAC, sub MAC.

macadam, uniformly graded stones typically coated with tar or bitumen, consolidated by rolling to form a road surface, developed by John McAdam in 1815.

MacArthur Highway, the main north-south highway along the Philippines, passing through Manila, constructed during WW2 by General Douglas MacArthur.

machine, a power operated tool used to perform a task, sometimes referring to an engine or vehicle .

MacPherson, Earle S. MacPherson, inventor of the MacPherson strut in 1947 for GM, first developed by Ford UK in 1950.

MacPherson strut, a suspension system incorporating a helical spring concentric around a damper with a single flexible upper mounting and having the hub carrier rigidly attached to the lower end, common on the front of small and medium sized cars, sometimes at the rear.

MacPherson suspension, a suspension system incorporating MacPherson struts.

macrobus, a passenger carrying vehicle typically seating between 35 and 70 passengers.

made road, a road having a weatherproof surface of tarmac, concrete, or similar.

mad mile, a very long straight stretch of single carriageway road which encourages drivers to speed.

maf, mass airflow meter.

mag, magneto.

Magee, Carlton Magee, inventor of the parking meter in USA in 1935.

magic roundabout, a gyratory system formed by a series of closely linked mini roundabouts around a central island where traffic direction is conventional around each mini roundabout but is contra-directional around the major island, and resulting in at least 2 separate routes from every approach to every exit; see appendices.

magnesium, a metallic element, lighter and stronger than aluminium, sometimes alloyed together or used alone, typically for wheels, engine blocks, transmission housings, etc, it is explosive when powdered.

magnetic, the ability to attract iron, either naturally or when an electrical current flows through a coil of wire.

magnetic clutch, a clutch that is operated electromagnetically, usually driving auxiliaries *e.g.* ac compressor or supercharger.

magnetic drain plug, a sump drain plug containing a powerful magnet to hold any loose steel particles.

magnetic field, the space around a magnet to where the lines of force extend.

magnetic pulse generator, a stationary magnetised pick-up coil in which a small pulse of voltage is generated as each tooth or notch on a rotating reluctor disc passes creating the Hall effect.

magneto, a type of electrical generator that can directly produce hv for the ignition circuit, typically on some vintage and older vehicles.

magneto file, a small tool for cleaning contact breaker points.

mags, road wheels made from an aluminium-magnesium alloy.

main beam, the headlight beam which is directed straight ahead, necessary for safety on a dark road at speeds above 75 km/h (45 mph).

main beam tell-tale, a blue light on the dashboard informing when main beam is in use.

main bearings, the bearings that support a crankshaft at its ends and usually between each crankpin.

main bow, the principal bar supporting a hood and carrying the hinge point for the folding mechanism.

main drag, USA, main street.

main jet, the principal fuel nozzle supplying fuel in a carburettor when the throttle is open at any position.

mainlane drop, a feature at some motorway junctions where a diverging lane results in a reduction in the number of through lanes on the main carriageway.

main road, a trunk, arterial, or distributor road.

main shaft, the gearbox output shaft.

main street, the principal street of a town, typically passing through the main shopping area.

maintenance, any action taken during servicing to prolong the working life of any component.

maintenance charge, to apply a charging voltage of 13.8 volts to a 12 volt charged battery, this may be maintained indefinitely to preserve the battery in a good condition.

maintenance free, a part that is designed to remain sealed or unserviced for the duration of its working life.

maintenance free battery, a lead-calcium battery without facility for checking the electrolyte or adding water.

maintenance manual, a book detailing routine maintenance instructions.

major access road, a residential road with footways that may serve approximately 100 to 300 dwellings.

major controls, primary controls.

major street, USA, an arterial highway with intersections at grade and direct access to abutting property, and on which traffic control measures are used to expedite the safe flow of traffic.

make, the manufacturer of a specific type of vehicle.

MAL, Malaysia, international vehicle distinguishing sign, see appendices.

MAM, UK, maximum authorised mass.

MAMSF, Mongolian Automobile and Motorcycle Sports Federation.

man, manual transmission.

MAN, Maschinenfabrik Augsburg Nürnberg, a manufacturer of lorries and buses.

Mandarin road, the route from Saigon to Hanoi, 1,800 km, (1,125 miles) in Vietnam.

maneuver, USA, manoeuvre.

manganese, a metallic element used as an alloy with steel and other metals.

manganese oxide, a metallic compound commonly used in Canada in LRG and in lead replacement additives to protect valve seats from regression.

manifold, an arrangement of pipes or tubular passageways for distribution or gathering of gas or liquid.

manifold heater, a facility to heat parts of the inlet manifold to improve cold running of an engine.

manifold pressure, the pressure in the inlet manifold, it can vary from partial vacuum to high pressure in different vehicles and at different times.

manipulative coordination, the ability of a driver to use several controls collectively, *e.g.* to operate front and rear windscreen washers, wipers, direction indicators, and dipswitch etc. without confusion.

mannequin, a plastic dummy the size and weight of a person and fitted with electronics to record decelerations, used when crash testing cars.

manoeuvrability, the ease with which a vehicle can be repositioned.

manoeuvrable, a quality of a vehicle in being easy to reposition.

manoeuvre, to change the direction, position, or speed of a vehicle.

manoeuvrer, a person who repositions a vehicle.

manoeuvring, the action of repositioning a vehicle.

manual, a book describing in detail the

component parts of a vehicle and their disassembly and repair.

manual, manual transmission, manual gear selection usually by operation of a gear lever, usually also necessitating manual operation of a clutch.

manual automatic transmission, automated transmission.

manual hood, a folding roof on a convertible where it has to be manually removed and refitted when the driver desires.

manual hubs, manually selectable front wheel hubs that may be selected as lock or free, so the front transmission will not rotate when in 2wd; on some 4wd vehicles.

manual override, to be able to control a normally automatic function, especially with respect to some automatic gearboxes.

manual transmission, manual selection of each gear, usually requiring manual operation of a clutch.

map, a diagram representing the features on the surface of the earth, especially roads and towns etc.

map, manifold absolute pressure.

map controlled ignition, a microprocessor controlled ignition system based upon an electronic envelope of engine parameters.

map light, a small light on a flexible mounting for use by a navigator at night for reading a map or roadbook.

map read, to examine and decipher a map.

map reference, a set of numbers and letters which specify a location on a map.

marbles, loose gravel on a road surface.

mark, the model number of a car type, often given in Roman numerals; see also: marque.

marker lamp, side marker lamp.

marque, the make or manufacturer of a car; see also: mark.

marshal, a person assisting with the administration of each car passing an individual checkpoint on a rally.

marshal, a person stationed at each of several strategic positions around a racing circuit to assist in case of emergency.

mask, a device worn to protect the lungs when near harmful dusts or vapours, *e.g.* respraying a car.

mask, to hide from view, to prevent an area becoming exposed, *e.g.* to a paint spray.

masking tape, an adhesive tape used to cover areas of bodywork not being painted.

mass, see: base, dry, DGW, frpl, GCW, gross, GLW, GTW, GVM, GVW, GVWR, kerbweight, laden, LVW, MAM, MGW, MVW, notional, reference, RTM, TAW, unladen, wet.

mass airflow meter, a device which measures airflow into an engine and continuously sends a signal to the ECU.

mass damper, a weight fitted to a fwd drive shaft to balance undesirable vibrations.

mass produced car, a car manufactured in great numbers to a standardised pattern.

mass transit system, a system for the transportation of large numbers of persons, typically a light rail or rapid tram system.

master cylinder, the brake or clutch cylinder which is operated by the action of the pedal, and which is the initiating device that causes pressure in the fluid so the fluid moves towards the slave cylinders at the wheels or clutch.

master time control, a location at the start and end of a road rally.

matatu, an unlicenced privately owned passenger carrying vehicle in many east African countries, typically a minibus, covered truck, or pickup excessively overloaded with passengers and effects; named from Swahili for '3 shillings'.

match mounting, the action of aligning the red dot on a tyre sidewall with the wheel marking or tyre valve when fitting a tyre to minimise runout vibration.

mate, a lorry drivers assistant or trainee.

mate, to fit together.

matrix, a light unit constructed with many small bulbs which may be collectively or individually controlled, *e.g.* some high level brake lights, and some motorway signs.

matt, a dull surface, without gloss.

MAV, multiactivity vehicle.

MAVIS, Mobility Advice and Vehicle Information Service, UK.

maximum authorised mass, the maximum gross weight at which a vehicle is authorised for use.

maximum cargo capacity, the greatest volume a vehicle can accommodate with all seats except the drivers folded away.

maximum gradeability, the steepest slope a vehicle can climb in its lowest gear fully loaded, usually expressed in percentage of the slope.

maximum gross weight, UK, the design gross weight as shown on a Ministry plate, or the weight which the vehicle is designed or adapted not to exceed when the vehicle is travelling on a road, (C&U).

maximum inflation pressure, the maximum air pressure to which a cold tire may be inflated before internal structural damage may occur, the figure is usually moulded into the sidewall.

maximum permitted lateness, the time limit in road rally navigation before going OTL.

maximum speed, the speed which a vehicle is incapable of exceeding by reason of its construction, on a level surface under its own power when fully laden, (C&U).

maximum towing capacity, the maximum weight the vehicle is rated to tow, allowing for a hill start on an 18 % gradient, and based upon engine power, gearing, cooling capacity, braking performance, rear spring rates, and hitch design and quality.

m/c, motorcycle.

MC, Australia, multicombination, any vehicle having 2 or more trailers.

MC, Monaco, international vehicle distinguishing sign, see appendices.
MCI, Motor Cycle Industry Association of Great Britain.
MCP, motor carrier permit, USA.
MC(PH)R, UK, Motor Cycles (Protective Helmets) Regulations 1980.
m/cycle, motorcycle.
MD, Moldova, international vehicle distinguishing sign, see appendices.
MDC, MasterDriver Club, UK.
mdl, model.
mdu, mobile display unit.
MDV, USA, medium duty vehicle.
meals on wheels, a service which organises and delivers meals to old people and invalids, etc.
mean effective pressure, the average pressure on a piston during the power stroke.
measured mile, the exact distance of 1 mile, (1,609.344 metres).
meat in the sandwich, a vehicle in the centre of a multivehicle collision, being struck at both sides or both ends, especially a car struck by 2 lorries, or being crushed between a vehicle and a fixed object.
mechanic, motor mechanic.
mechanical efficiency, the ratio between indicated horsepower and brake horsepower.
mechanically propelled, a vehicle that is propelled by any mechanical means carried on the vehicle or on a trailer which it is drawing, including batteries, electricity received from trolley wires, internal combustion engine, external combustion engine, fuel cell, etc. but not where a vehicle is powered by muscular effort by a person or drawn by an animal.
mechanics, the study of the behaviour of physical systems under the actions of forces, the branch of physics which seeks to formulate general rules for predicting the behaviour a physical system under the influence of any type of interaction with its environment.
mechanic's lien, a claim against property permitting the seizure of a vehicle due to non-payment of work and/or parts when a customer disputes a bill or abandons the car.
mechanism, a system of related parts that form a working assembly.
mechanist, an expert mechanic.
median, USA, central reservation, the land separating the 2 opposing carriageways of a freeway or divided highway.
median barrier, a longitudinal physical barrier to prevent an out of control vehicle from crossing onto the opposing carriageway
median crossover, USA, a short loop on which to perform a U turn through the centre of a dual carriageway or divided highway.
median lane, USA, a speed change lane within the median to accommodate traffic turning across the median, i.e. a sliproad and deceleration lane within the central reservation for turns across the central reservation.

medical examination, an examination by a doctor that is a pre-requisite to gain and hold a driving licence for a LGV or PSV.
medium duty truck, USA, a truck having an LVW less than 14,000 lb (6.35 tonnes).
medium sized goods vehicle, UK, a mechanically propelled vehicle constructed or adapted to carry or haul goods and is not adapted to carry more than 9 persons including the driver; the maximum permissible weight exceeds 3.5 tonnes but not exceeding 7.5 tonnes, (RTA).
meet, a situation where traffic is approaching a point from opposite directions, e.g. to meet head-on, especially at a feature causing a width restriction.
meeting beam, dipped beam.
MEG, mono ethylene glycol, a common additive as an engine coolant.
megabus, a passenger carrying vehicle typically carrying over 70 passengers.
MEK, methyl ethyl ketone, a substance used as a reagent to cause resins to set in the production of fibreglass vehicle bodies.
MEMA, Motor Equipment Manufacturers Association, USA.
memorabilia, see: automobilia.
memory, the ability of an electronic circuit to recall previously stored information.
MeOH, methanol.
mep, mean effective pressure.
Mercedes, the Spanish name of the daughter of Emil Jellinek which was used as his pseudonym in the Nice – Magagnon – Nice rally in 1898; in 1900 he demanded that it should be the model name of the 36 cars he purchased from Gottlieb Daimler in order to Frenchify the cars of Germanic origin, and in 1902 was registered as a trademark by Daimler.
Mercier engine, a revolving block engine in which 2 opposing pistons operate in a single cylinder.
mercury, a metallic element used as a vapour in some street lights, characterised by the emission of blue-green light.
mercury switch, a device used to trigger early airbags, now superseded by a Hamlin switch.
mercury vapour lamp, a lamp in which light is produced by an electric arc between electrodes in an ionised mercury vapour, it emits uv and blue-green light, sometimes used for street lighting on minor roads.
merge, a situation where a stream of traffic converges with another with negligible difference in direction to form a single stream, e.g. joining a motorway.
merge, part of a rally route used more than once, where 2 routes converge.
mesh, the mating of the teeth of 2 gearwheels as 1 is driven by the other.
message identifier, part of a vehicle microprocessor control, the part that identifies from which component a message is sent.
metal, any substance in a class of chemical

elements, or when alloyed with other substances is or becomes a lustrous, malleable, fusible, ductile solid being a good conductor of heat and electricity.

metal, see: road metal.

metalflake, a body finish having large 0.5 mm to 5 mm coloured metallic flakes within a clear gel coat or lacquered surface.

metalled, a road with a durable surface, *e.g.* surfaced with tarmac or concrete, or paved with cobbles or similar.

metallic finish, a bodywork paint designed to sparkle when viewed closely under bright light.

metallic paint, paint containing a metal pigment usually of opaque aluminium or copper alloy flakes.

meter, a device that measures or controls the flow of a substance, *e.g.* as an injection system meters air and fuel.

meter, a test instrument that may measure voltage, current, resistance, pressure, temperature, etc.

metering rod and jet, a cone shaped rod moving within a jet in a carburettor to control fuel flow.

meter zone, an area where parking is permitted only in marked bays provided payment is made using a coin operated timing device.

methane, a hydrocarbon gas, CNG, a fuel having an equivalent octane rating exceeding 120, and stoichiometric ratio of 17.2:1 w/w.

methanol, methyl alcohol, wood alcohol, a colourless tasteless poisonous liquid which can be manufactured from natural gas, coal, wood, and other vegetable matter, a clean fuel having a RON 117, MON 92, stoichiometric ratio 6.46:1 w/w, giving a high power output compared to petrol but containing less energy per litre; occasionally mixed with water as engine coolant but corrosive.

methaqualone, a drug that should not be used by drivers, often contained in sleeping pills.

methyl alcohol, methanol.

methylamphetamine, MDMA, a drug that should not be used by drivers, often contained in sleeping pills.

methylated spirit, a mixture of ethyl and methyl alcohols plus colouring, used as a cleaning solvent, also as an antifreeze agent in windscreen washer fluid.

methyl tertiary butyl ether, a substance derived from methanol added at up to 15 % to reformed petrol as an octane booster, and to oxygenate the fuel, but believed to be a carcinogen.

metre, a unit of length, originally defined for Napoleon Bonaparte as the surface distance from the north pole through Paris to the equator divided by 10,000,000; now defined as the distance travelled by light in $^1/_{299,972,458}$ seconds (approximately equal to 39.37 inches).

metric horsepower, the power output of an engine in metric units named pferdestärke, abbreviated to PS; 1 PS = 75 m.kg/s;

1 PS = 0.75349875 kW;
1 PS = 0.98632 imperial horsepower.

metric thread, a screw or nut having dimensions based upon metric units and having either a course or fine pitch.

metric tyre, a modern sizing system for radial tyres formulated by ETRTO, where the section width is measured in millimetres but the rim diameter is measured in inches.

metro driving, USA, urban driving, town driving.

mewp, mobile elevating working platform, a cherry picker.

MEX, Mexico, international vehicle distinguishing sign, see appendices.

Mexican Highway, the motorway linking north and south Mexico, having a length of 3,485 km (2,178 miles) on which an annual road race is run; part of the Inter-American Highway.

Mexican wave, phantom jam, the effect on a congested motorway after some drivers brake and others brake more and may stop, but all then accelerate, causing a standing wave of stationary traffic with no apparent reason; the effect can persist at 1 place for several hours.

mf, multifocal.

MFA, Motor Factors Association, now ADF, UK.

MFR, Motorcycle Federation of Russia.

MG, Morris Garages, previously a car manufacturer.

MGV, medium goods vehicle, a goods vehicle in the driver licensing categories of C1 and C1+E.

MGW, UK, maximum gross weight.

mi, USA, mile.

MIAFTR, Motor Insurers Antifraud and Theft Register, UK.

MIB, Motor Insurers Bureau, UK.

mica, a natural mineral, sometimes used as an insulator between commutator copper bars on starter motors.

Michelin, André and Edouard Michelin, they commercially developed the first pneumatic car tyre in 1895.

Michelin man, the trademark of Michelin tyres, named Bibendum, registered in 1898.

Michigan left turn, USA, a pattern for turning left off a divided highway without hooking or causing congestion, performed by: following the road ahead for 200 metres, then U turning through the median crossover, merging, and turning right off the main road; traffic approaching on the minor road turn right to the median crossover to facilitate a left turn.

MICOPS, UK, Motor Industry Code of Practice.

microbus, a passenger carrying vehicle typically seating up to 12 passengers.

microcar, a lightweight car having a kerbweight not exceeding 550 kg hence classed as a B1 tricycle or quadricycle, and which may be driven using a B1 motorcycle licence.

– M M M –

micrometer, a very accurate measuring device used to to detect wear in mechanical parts, usually measuring to 10 microns, or, if imperial to 1-thousandth of 1 inch.

micron, a measurement of length, a thousandth part of one millimetre, 0.03937 thou; oil filter, fuel filter and air filter performance may be stated as the size of particle they will restrict.

micron air filter, a particulate air filtration system that removes airborne particles larger than 3 microns to prevent more than 90 % of pollens, spores, and road dust from entering the cabin, which helps those who suffer from allergies, asthma or other breathing problems.

microprocessor, an integrated circuit having chips, a central processor that receives signals from sensors and determines an output if any.

microprocessor optimised vehicle actuation, a traffic signal control system used at busy junctions, having loops on all approaches typically at 100 m and 40 m before the junction to sense all traffic approaching and maximise the flow.

micro sleep, the condition when the brain is effectively asleep with the eyes open, it may have a duration of 2 to 12 seconds.

MID, message identifier.

MID, multi-information display.

MiDAS, UK, Minibus Driver Awareness Scheme.

MIDAS, UK, Motorway Incident Detection and Automatic Signalling.

mid engine, a vehicle engine and chassis layout where the engine is significantly ahead of the rear axle and behind the driver.

mid gate, a moveable bulkhead, typically behind the rear seats.

midibus, a passenger carrying vehicle typically seating between 17 and 35 passengers.

mid lift, a feature of some 6x2 tractive units or a rigid lorry in which the centre axle can be raised when not load carrying.

midrange, mid revs.

midrange torque, the amount of torque available at mid revs.

mid revs, an engine speed approximately halfway between idle speed and red line speed.

midsize car, USA, a car size seating 5 persons in comfort.

MIG, metal inert gas, an electric welding system using a metal electrode with an inert gas shield where the electrode is also the filler metal, for some types of body/chassis repair.

mile, a measurement of distance, equivalent to 1,609.334 metres, defined about 2,000 years ago by the Romans as 1,000 left and right paces by a marching soldier.

mileage, the distance travelled per unit of consumption, with regard to fuel, oil, tyres, etc.

mileage, the number of miles between 2 points; when measured between towns the distance measured to the town hall, town square, or market cross; sometimes the number of kilometres.

mileage allowance, travelling expenses paid to an employee.

mile eater, a fast driver.

mile eater, a fast vehicle.

mile mark, milestone.

milepost, each of a series of short pillars, typically made from painted cast iron and placed at regular intervals from a town to show the name of the town and the distance, usually in whole miles or kilometres.

milestone, each of a series of carved stones typically painted and placed at regular intervals from a town to show the name of the town and the distance, usually in whole miles or kilometres.

milestone, USA and Australia, milepost.

milestone, USA, any vehicle built during the years 1946 to 1970 inclusive.

military sign, a rectangular sign with a white background and a red border showing directions to a military base.

military specification, parts on a vehicle that are designed to a high standard of durability as may be specified for military use.

military transport vehicle, a wheeled or tracklaying vehicle designed to transport personnel or equipment, except for use as a fighting vehicle.

military vehicle, a wheeled or tracklaying vehicle designed to transport personnel or equipment for any military purpose.

milk float, an electrically powered milk delivery vehicle, designed for silent milk delivery during the early morning, originally some were pedestrian controlled although most have a drivers seat.

mill, a complete engine.

Millbrook, a vehicle proving ground and test track in Bedfordshire, UK.

Mille Miglia, a former 1,000 mile (1,600 km) rally on public roads in Italy.

Miller cycle, a version of the Otto cycle where more air is forced in during induction but the inlet valve closes very late losing some of the charge, to reduce overheating and knocking.

milli, a 1-thousandth part.

milometer, odometer, a distance measuring device showing the total distance the vehicle has covered in its life.

mineral fuel, any carbonaceous fossil fuel.

mineral oil, a lubricating oil refined from crude oil.

mineral spirits, a solvent, sometimes used for cleaning or for thinning some paints.

minibus, a motor vehicle which is constructed or adapted to carry more than 8 but not more than 16 seated passengers in addition to the driver, (C&U).

minibus driver awareness scheme, a scheme to raise the quality of driving of minibuses to a safe standard, especially those driving for voluntary organisations.

minicab, a car operated similar to a taxi but where each journey must be requested by telephone as plying for hire is not permitted.

minicar, a very small saloon car seating not more than 4 persons without a high degree of comfort.

mini gridlock, a traffic jam that occurs on 1 road due to opposing traffic not leaving space at junctions for others to turn off the main road across the centre into a side road.

mini mpv, a small mpv, usually a 7 seat vehicle or having moderate load carrying capacity or a compromise.

minimum braking distance, the shortest possible distance taken for a moving vehicle to stop on a clean dry level road providing the vehicle is mechanically sound, not including reaction distance, *i.e.* it is measured from the moment the brake is applied; the actual distance increases with the square of the speed of the vehicle, and is further increased when any factor *e.g.* road surface, tyres, or suspension, etc. is not in the best condition.

minimum kerbweight, the kerbweight of a vehicle not fitted with any optional extras.

minimum required visibility distance, the distance necessary to permit observation, comprehension, decision making, response selection, and safe completion of a manoeuvre.

minimum stopping distance, the sum of the reaction distance plus the braking distance for any given speed, dependant upon the driver, the road surface, and vehicle condition.

minimum test vehicle, a specified minimum size and performance of vehicle that is acceptable for each driving test category.

minimum turning circle, the diameter of the circle described by the outermost projection of a vehicle when the vehicle is making its shortest possible turn.

minimum turning radius, the radius of the arc described by the centre of the track made by the outside front wheel of the vehicle when making its shortest possible turn, (SAE).

mini roundabout, a junction of several roads where traffic moves in one direction around a central island that is painted on the road surface, and may or may not have a raised central area.

Ministers Approval Certificate, UK, an approval certificate under SVA rules issued by a vehicle examiner if a vehicle complies with all C&U Regulations.

Ministry of Transport, UK, an official body now renamed DTLR.

Ministry plate, UK, a plate affixed to goods vehicles and trailers when first tested showing maximum vehicle and axle weights.

minivan, a small van built on the floorpan of a small car, typically having a payload between 250 kg and 500 kg.

minivan, USA, a mpv typically seating 7 passengers in comfort with space for a significant load.

minor access road, a residential road with footways that may serve up to approximately 100 dwellings.

minor controls, secondary controls.

minor fault, a fault committed by a driver which does not have the potential to impinge upon the safety of others.

mint condition, a vehicle in perfect condition.

mir, mirror.

MIRA, Motor Industry Research Association, UK.

mirage, an optical illusion that a road surface is covered with water often seen when looking along a hot road surface, occurring due to light from the sky being refracted by hot low-density air just above the surface.

MIRRC, Motor Industry Repair Research Centre, UK, sometimes named Thatcham.

mirror, a reflective safety device, either flat, convex, or multivex, to enable a driver to see an area behind with minimal effort, see: convex, interior, door, driving, multivex, vanity, wing.

mirror indicator repeaters, direction indicator repeater lamps mounted in the leading face of each door mirror housing, developed by Mercedes.

mirror signal manoeuvre, the basic procedure to be performed when approaching any hazard.

mirrors signal position brake gear, a basic sequence of actions to be considered or performed for safety when approaching any hazard.

misalignment, a condition in any part which is not aligned as it was designed.

misfire, an intermittent or continuous condition in 1 or several cylinders when the air-fuel mixture fails to ignite.

MISA, Motor Industry Safety Association, UK.

MISG, Motor Industry Study Group, UK.

missing, misfiring, an intermittent or continuous condition in 1 or several cylinders when the air-fuel mixture fails to ignite.

mist, a thin cloud of water droplets suspended in the atmosphere at ground level where visibility is reduced but exceeds 100 metres.

mist action, USA, intermittent wiper control.

mixing bowl, USA, any very complex junction between major interstates and other roads involving many link roads, originally the junction of the I395, US1, and US27, near the Pentagon, Washington DC; see also: spaghetti junction.

mixture, the air-fuel charge in a petrol engine.

mixture, the lubricated fuel consumed by a 2 stroke engine.

mixture control, a choke knob.

mixture control unit, a part of a fuel injection system which monitors the airflow and meters the fuel to the injectors.

MK, Macedonia, international vehicle distinguishing sign, see appendices.

MK, mark, a model series number, the number suffix is usually written in Roman numerals; see also: marque.

ML, motor light, a lubricating oil for engines

– M M M –

working under light loads in clean conditions, not for road vehicles.

ML, a rally pace note, a medium left bend through approximately 60°.

ML, miss a left turn, a direction in road rally navigation.

mm, millimetre, a unit of length, 1-thousandth part of 1 metre.

m/m, mass/mass, a comparison of 2 substances by weight, *e.g.* a measure of the sulphur content in fuel may be 0.003 % m/m.

MM, motor medium, a lubricating oil for engines working in moderate conditions experiencing moderate loads, occasional high speeds and average dusty conditions, not usually used for road vehicles.

MMT, methylcyclopentadienyl manganese tricarbonyl, an octane enhancing fuel additive.

MNZ, Motorcycling New Zealand.

mobile crane, a road-going lifting machine either wheeled or tracklaying.

mobile display unit, a specialist trailer used at exhibitions.

mobile home, a trailer caravan.

mobile lane closure, a convoy of vehicles painted bright yellow and displaying very large traffic signs and flashing amber warning lights for visibility, which move slowly along the closed lane to effect brief carriageway repairs and which are guarded by a block vehicle.

mobile library, a library accommodated in a van, converted bus, or articulated lorry, in order to offer a service in rural communities.

mobile shop, a shop accommodated in a van or converted bus, in order to serve customers outside their homes, especially in rural villages.

MOC, Mozambique, international vehicle distinguishing sign, see appendices.

model, a specific size and/or style of vehicle made by a manufacturer; see also: mark.

model year, the year of manufacture of a vehicle, or the year in which most of that type were manufactured; typically the next model year starts in production a few months before the end of the previous calendar year.

modify, to alter an original part.

modular trailer, a special trailer designed to carry very heavy loads, having many axles of which most or all may steer under hydraulic control of a steersman.

modulate the accelerator, to accurately control the accelerator, *e.g.* for a delicate balance of fore/aft centre of weight whilst negotiating a bend.

modulate the footbrake, to accurately control the footbrake, *e.g.* for a delicate balance of fore/aft weight distribution whilst trail braking, threshold braking, or feathering the brake.

mofa, moped.

mogas, motor gasoline, petrol, sometimes referring to leaded.

moggy minor, Morris Minor.

MOL, Moldovia, international vehicle distinguishing sign, see appendices.

molybdenum, a metallic element, used as an alloy with steel and as a lubricant in grease.

molybdenum steel, a tool steel containing up to 10 % molybdenum plus varying amounts of carbon, chromium, vanadium, tungsten, and cobalt.

momentum, the quantity of motion of a moving body, the product of mass x velocity, having units of kg.m/s.

MON, motor octane number.

Monaco, a small independent state on the Mediterranean coast, host to the annual Monaco Formula 1 street race.

Mondeo man, a typical average driver.

monkey seat, the passenger seat of a motorcycle having a significant backrest.

monkey wrench, adjustable wrench, a spanner having 1 fixed jaw and 1 movable jaw, both approximately perpendicular to the handle.

monobeam suspension, non-independent suspension using an I beam axle.

monoblock casting, a common style of engine design where a single cast block is bored to produce the cylinders, the top is machined to mate with the cylinder head, and the bottom is machined to carry the crankshaft.

monocoque, a vehicle in which the bodyshell carries all the structural strength without chassis rails.

mono ethylene glycol, a common engine coolant, but toxic.

monograde oil, a mineral oil rated to have a specific viscosity at a specific temperature, but as the temperature rises the viscosity reduces significantly, generally obsolete and superseded by multigrade, but occasionally used in some classic and older vehicles.

mono-jetronic, a single point fuel injection system developed by Bosch.

mono propylene glycol, a synthetic engine coolant protecting down to –48 °C and up to +122 °C at 70 % v/v concentration and at 7 psi; believed to be non-toxic.

monotube damper, single tube damper.

monotube shock absorber, single tube damper.

Monroney sticker, USA, an obligatory sticker on every new car sold which specifies the manufacturers suggested retail price for the vehicle and all factory installed options, delivery cost, and EPA fuel economy figures.

Monte Carlo, a town in Monaco, famous as the finishing point of the annual Monte Carlo Rally, first run in 1911.

moonroof, a specially coated glass panel in the roof of a car, specifically designed to restrict solar heating, usually opening for ventilation, usually named as such in hot countries instead of sunroof.

Mopar, a trade name used by DaimlerChrysler for its spare parts.

moped, a motorcycle having a maximum design speed not exceeding 50 km/h (30 mph), a kerbweight not exceeding 250 kg, and if propelled by an internal combustion engine an engine capacity not exceeding 50 cc, (C&U) (MVDLR), originally Swedish from motorvelociped.

moquette, a thick long pile fabric sometimes used as weatherstrip.

morphing, the action of an airbag as it rapidly fills with gas when the detonator is triggered.

MORR, management of occupational road risk.

MoT, UK, Ministry of Transport, now renamed DTLR.

MOT, UK, the system for testing vehicles to ensure roadworthiness, conducted by the VI.

motable, an early name for a garage.

motel, a motorists hotel typically near a junction of main roads, providing accommodation for travellers and parking for their vehicles

Mother Road, highway US66 from Chicago to Santa Monica, USA.

motion, the process of moving.

motionless, at rest.

motion lotion, CB jargon, petrol or fuel.

motion sickness, nausea resulting from acceleratory movement, especially by jerky movements initiated by the driver.

motive power, the driving engine.

motive unit, a rigid lorry fitted with a hitch and necessary equipment such that it may draw a trailer.

motocross, cross country racing on motorcycles.

motor, a car.

motor, to drive.

motor, a device that converts 1 type of energy into another, *e.g.* an electric motor converts electrical energy into mechanical energy.

motor, an internal combustion engine.

motor, electric motor.

motorable road, a route along which it is possible to drive a typical motor car.

motorable route, a track along which it is possible to drive a 4x4 vehicle.

motorail, a system of long distance transport for cars and other vehicles by railway between major cities.

motor ambulance, a motor vehicle which is specially designed and constructed for carrying equipment permanently fixed to the vehicle for medical, dental, or other health purposes and is used primarily for the carriage of persons suffering from illness, injury, or disability, (C&U).

motor barn, an early name for a garage.

motor benzol, a grade of benzene used in fuels for internal combustion engines.

motor bicycle, a motorcycle or moped.

motorbike, motorcycle.

motorcade, a procession of motor vehicles.

motor car, a mechanically propelled vehicle constructed to carry load or up to 7 passengers, having a maximum unladen weight of 3,050 kg; or maximum unladen weight of

2,540 kg, for other vehicles, (C&U regulations).

motor caravan, a motor vehicle which is constructed or adapted for the carriage of passengers and their effects and which contains, as permanently installed equipment, the facilities which are reasonably necessary for enabling the vehicle to provide mobile living accommodation for its users, (C&U regulations).

motor carrier permit, USA, a document required for the operation of a commercial vehicle either for hire or privately.

Motor City, Detroit, USA.

motor coach, a luxurious passenger carrying vehicle having more than 8 seats, an MGW exceeding 7.5 tonnes and a maximum speed exceeding 100 km/h (60 mph).

motorcycle, a mechanically propelled vehicle, not being an invalid carriage, with less than 4 wheels and the unladen weight does not exceed 410 kg, (C&U).

motorcycling, the action of riding a motorcycle.

motorcyclist, a person riding a motorcycle.

motor den, an early name for a garage.

motor gate, South Africa, cattle grid.

motorhome, USA, a motor vehicle typically up to 12 m long permanently fitted with a body which is fully equipped as a self contained home with living and sleeping accommodation.

motoring taxes, all of the taxes which a motorist must pay: import duty, purchase tax, registration, insurance tax, VED, fuel tax, VAT.

motor insurance, a payment made against the risk of an accident occurring, whereby the insurer pays for any claims that are covered by the policy.

motor insurers bureau, a body set up by UK motor insurers to deal with claims where there is no valid certificate of insurance.

motorisation level, a mathematical ratio describing the number of vehicles per head of population in a country, usually measured and stated as motor vehicles per 1,000 population.

motorist, the driver of any motor vehicle.

motorium, an early name for a garage.

motorize, to provide an unpowered vehicle with a motor.

motorize, to supply with transport which is motorized.

motor mechanic, a person who services or repairs vehicles.

motor octane number, an index number derived by testing the antiknock properties of a fuel using parameters different from RON.

motor oil, engine oil

motor quadricycle, a mechanically propelled vehicle, not being an invalid carriage, having 4 wheels and a design speed exceeding 50 km/h (30 mph) and the unladen weight does not exceed 550 kg, (MV(DL) regulations).

motorracing, the staging of a competition of speed capabilities between 2 or more motor vehicles over an accepted point to point course or a closed circuit, the first race was of 127 km (79 miles) from Paris to Rouen, in 1895.

motor scooter, a 2 wheeled motor cycle having an open frame, a platform for the feet, and wheels smaller than those of a conventional motorcycle.

motor shed, an early name for a garage.

motor show, an exhibition of new models for purchase, and concept and futuristic vehicle models which may or may not enter production.

motor spirit, petrol.

motorsport, any competitive event involving motor vehicles.

motor tractor, a mechanically propelled vehicle, not constructed itself to carry load other than equipment for propulsion, loose tools and loose equipment, maximum unladen weight not exceeding 7,370 kg, (RTA).

motor tricycle, a mechanically propelled vehicle, not being an invalid carriage, having 3 wheels and a design speed exceeding 50 km/h (30 mph) and the unladen weight does not exceed 550 kg, (MV(DL) regulations).

motor truck, a motor vehicle used for the transport of freight.

motor vehicle, any mechanically propelled vehicle intended or adapted for use on a road (C&U regulations); the first in Britain was a steam powered 14 seat coach in 1834.

motor vehicle safety act, USA, the legal regulations applying to the manufacture and import of motor vehicles and equipment, to reduce the risk of death, injury, and damage to property and the environment.

motorvelociped, Swedish, believed to be the origin of moped.

motorway, a particular type of special road having dedicated regulations, designed to carry a large volume of traffic at high speed, with physical segregation of opposing traffic, with grade separated junctions allowing access and exit without disrupting the traffic flow, prohibited from use by some classes of road user, and without direct access to property; the first UK motorway opened in 1958 as the Preston bypass which later became part of the M6.

motorway services, a large area at the side of a motorway for re-fuelling, refreshments, and sometimes accommodation may be available.

motorway telephone, a telephone for emergency use, usually spaced approximately 1 mile (1.6 km) apart along the edges of a motorway, and which are directly connected to the nearest police traffic control centre.

motor wheel, each of a pair of electric drive motors which are mounted in the wheel hub for propelling an electric vehicle.

motory, an early name for a garage.

Motown, Detroit, USA.

MOT test, UK, the vehicle testing system to ensure roadworthiness for vehicles, conducted by the VI.

Moulton hydragas suspension, a version of hydropneumatic suspension developed by BL.

Moulton hydrolastic suspension, a version of hydrolastic suspension developed by BL.

mound, the raised area at the centre of a roundabout.

mount, to fit a tyre to a wheel rim.

mount, to cause a wheel to climb onto a kerb.

mountable kerb, low kerbing with an angled face designed to encourage drivers not to drive on it although it may be driven over and causes no damage to a tyre or vehicle crossing it.

mounty, a fork lift truck carried on the rear of a lorry for rapid unloading at any drop.

MOVA, microprocessor optimised vehicle actuation.

moveable bridge, a bridge in which either the horizontal or the vertical alignment can be readily changed to permit the passage of traffic beneath it; see: swing, lifting, transporter.

moveable components, any body panel or other vehicle parts the position of which can be changed by tilting, rotating, or sliding without the use of tools, but excluding tiltable driver cabs of trucks, (C&U).

move in, to change lanes to the nearside.

move off, to put into motion a vehicle that has been parked at the roadside.

move off, to set a vehicle in motion.

move on, to set a vehicle in motion.

move out, to change lanes to the offside.

move over, a demand to take over the drivers seat.

moving brake test, a daily test of the footbrake system to ensure all is balanced and working correctly; at the first safe opportunity after first moving the vehicle, the footbrake pedal should be operated progressively and firmly to sense for an appropriate rate of retardation and that the vehicle or steering does not pull to 1 side.

moving contact, the component in a starter motor solenoid which switches on the circuit to the windings.

moving van, USA, a pantechnicon.

moving vehicle ram, see: fishtail.

mpg, miles per gallon, a measure of the fuel consumption of a vehicle.

MPG, mono propylene glycol, an additive as an engine coolant, believed to be non-toxic.

mph, miles per hour, a measure of speed.

mpi, multipoint fuel injection.

MPSS, Motorparc Statistics Service, UK.

mpv, multi purpose vehicle.

MR, Australia, medium rigid, a 2 axle rigid lorry or bus exceeding 8 tonnes GVM.

MR, map reference, the numerical identification of a location in road rally navigation.

MR, a rally pace note, a medium right bend through approximately 60°.

MR, miss a right turn, a direction in road rally navigation.

MRVD, minimum required visibility distance.

MS, Mauritius, international vehicle distinguishing sign, see appendices.

MS, motor severe, a lubricating oil for engines working under heavy loads at high speeds in adverse conditions, the normal grade for road vehicles.

m/s, metres per second, a measure of speed.

M+S, mud and snow, a tyre tread designation.

msa, motorway service area.

MSA, Motor Schools Association, UK.

MSA, Motor Sports Association, UK.

MSA, Motorsport South Africa.

MSAI, Motor Schools Association of Ireland.

MSF, Motor Sports Federation.

MSM, Mirror, Signal, Manoeuvre.

MSPBG, Mirrors, Signal, Position, Brake, Gear.

MSTS, microprocessor spark timing system.

mt, manual transmission.

mt, mechanical transport.

M/T, mud terrain, a tyre designed primarily for off road use in deep mud.

MTA, manual automatic transmission.

MTBE, methyl tertiary butyl ether.

mtbf, mean time between failures.

MTC, master time control, in road rally navigation.

MT(E&W)(A)R, Motorways Traffic (England &Wales) (Amendment) Regulations 1992.

MT(E&W)R, Motorways Traffic (England &Wales) Regulations 1982.

MT(S)R, Motorways Traffic (Scotland) Regulations 1995.

MTV, Europe, Minimum Test Vehicle.

mud, CB jargon, coffee.

mud and snow, winter tyre, all season tyre, a tyre having a tread and compound giving good traction in snow and mud.

mudflap, a flexible rubber or plastic guard behind a tyre to prevent dirt and stones from being thrown up.

mudguard, protection over the top and rear of a wheel to prevent dirt and stones from being thrown up.

mudplugger, a vehicle modified to be driven on a muddy surface, especially competitively.

mudplugging, driving off road or cross country.

muffler, USA, a silencer, a chamber within an exhaust system designed to reduce the noise of the exhaust by reflection and absorption of sound waves.

mule, a hybrid assembled by a vehicle manufacturer as a mobile test bed in order to evaluate changes to engineering details, *e.g.* a different engine or suspension etc.

multiactivity vehicle, a vehicle that has elements of an MPV, off-roader, and a standard car.

multicon, a 13 pin electrical connection system for trailers.

multifocal, a lamp having a multiple focus parabolic reflector.

multifocal headlamp, multiple focus headlamp, a headlamp having a multiple focus parabolic reflector.

multifunction control stalk, a lever on the steering column having many controls upon it, *e.g.* 10 wiper modes of various speeds and including windscreen, rear, and headlamp wash-wipe.

multigrade, an oil that has a low variation in viscosity rating between cold and hot engine temperatures, its range of viscosity is reasonably stable between 2 limits, *e.g.* SAE 20-50 will not have a viscosity less than SAE 20 when the engine is hot, and it will not rise above SAE 50 when the engine is cold.

multihole injector, a fuel injection nozzle with more than 1 orifice, each dispensing a jet of fuel I different directions.

multi-information display, a digital display screen on which the driver may select information from the onboard computer or from GPS navigation, etc. developed by BMW.

multilane highway, any road having more than 1 lane in each direction.

multilane totalling, USA, the number of through lanes in each direction, thus an 8 lane freeway has 4 lanes in each direction.

multileaf spring, a typical leaf spring having several individual leaves clamped together at the centre.

multilink suspension, any type of irs layout having 4 or 5 control arms, typically designed for compactness.

multimeter, a measuring instrument capable of measuring different parameters or quantities in different ranges.

multimodal transport, the carriage of goods by at least 2 different modes of transport, usually between different countries.

multipiece rim, any wheel that is not manufactured in 1 piece, having at least a demountable bead seat or rim flange to facilitate tyre removal and replacement.

multiplate clutch, a clutch assembly having 2 or more drive plates with intermediate drive plates, all controlled by 1 pressure plate.

multiple decisions, a series of driving decisions made almost simultaneously, typically because speed is too high.

multiple disc clutch, USA, multiplate clutch.

multiple pile up, a collision involving 3 or more vehicles.

multiple reduction gearing, a transmission system in which the ratio is reduced in 3 or more stages, typically having a main gearbox plus a splitter and a range change, or sometimes hub reduction.

multiple roundabout, a traffic layout at a complex junction where there may be a number of contiguous or adjoining roundabouts or mini roundabouts, see also: magic roundabout.

multiple sclerosis, a medical condition that may prevent a person holding a driving licence due to insufficient muscular control.

multiple viscosity, an oil viscosity rating

showing its range of viscosity between 2 limits, *e.g.* SAE 10-30 will not have a viscosity less than SAE 10 when the engine is hot, and it will not rise above SAE 30 when the engine is cold.

multiplex, an electrical system using a central processor and local processors to greatly reduce vehicle wiring.

multipoint fuel injection, a petrol fuel injection system in which the fuel is injected separately for each cylinder.

multiport fuel injection, multipoint fuel injection.

multipull handbrake, a handbrake lever system that is pulled and pushed several times against forward and rearward ratchets in order to apply the brake sufficiently, on some older lorries.

multipurpose vehicle, a vehicle smaller than a minibus, having up to 8 seats, some of which are removable for carrying various loads.

multispark coil, a type of ignition coil having an output directly to each sparkplug, *i.e.* the distributor is in the primary circuit.

multistorey carpark, a building constructed to house cars on several levels, each level being connected by access ramps; first constructed near Piccadilly London in 1901.

multitrailer roadtrain, a roadtrain comprising more than 2 semitrailers, all except the 1st having an A frame dolly for coupling and steering; or, comprising more than 2 full trailers.

multitronic, a CVT automatic transmission using a linkplate chain with a 6 speed paddle triggered manual override incorporating DSP and DRP, and using a multiplate wet clutch which can vary the degree of creep to suit various conditions, developed by Audi.

multivalve engine, an engine having more than the basic 1 inlet and 1 exhaust valve per cylinder, to increase the flow of air-fuel mixture into the engine and exhaust gases out of the engine.

multi V belt, polygrooved belt.

multivex mirror, a convex mirror which is uniformly curved across a horizontal plane from its inner edge to a mid point, and increasingly curved from the mid point towards its outer edge, to increase the angle of view and reduce blindspots.

multiwheel drive, any vehicle having more than 2wd.

multiwheeler, any vehicle having more than 4 wheels.

muscle car, a powerful car, typically exceeding 400 bhp.

mushroom valve, poppet valve.

MUW, may use whites, in road rally navigation you may or will use white roads as marked on as OS map.

MV, medical car.

MV, motor vehicle.

MV(AST)GO, UK, Motor Vehicles (Authorisation of Special Types) General Orders 1979.

MV(C&U)(TLV)R, UK, Motor Vehicles (Construction and Use)(Track Laying Vehicles) Regulations 1955.

MVDA, Motor Vehicle Dismantlers Association, UK.

MV(DL)(HGPSV)R, UK, Motor Vehicles (Driving Licences)(Heavy Goods and Public Service Vehicles) Regulations 1990.

MV(DL)R, UK, Motor Vehicles (Driving Licences) Regulations 1996.

MVMA, Motor Vehicle Manufacturers Association, USA, now AAMA.

MVRA, Motor Vehicle Repairers Association.

MVRIS, UK, Motor Vehicle Registration Information System.

MVSA, USA, Motor Vehicle Safety Act.

MVSA, Motor Vehicle Safety Association, USA.

MV(TA)(GB)R, Motor Vehicles (Type Approval)(Great Britain) Regulations 1984.

MVW, maximum vehicle weight.

MV(WSBCFS)R, UK, Motor Vehicles (Wearing of Seat Belts by Children in Front Seats) Regulations 1993.

MV(WSBC)R, UK, Motor Vehicles (Wearing of Seat Belts by Children) Regulations 1982.

MV(WSBCRS)R, UK, Motor Vehicles (Wearing of Seat Belts by Children in Rear Seats) Regulations 1989.

MV(WSB)R, UK, Motor Vehicles (Wearing of Seat Belts) Regulations 1993.

MV(WSBRSA)R, UK, Motor Vehicles (Wearing of Seat Belts in Rear Seats by Adults) Regulations 1991.

MW, Malawi, international vehicle distinguishing sign, see appendices.

m'way, motorway.

my, model year.

myopia, short sightedness, a medical condition such that persons suffering from this must not drive without wearing optical correction.

N

n, new bolts or studs are required for this on re-assembly, a requirement on rebuilding some parts of an engine.

N, neutral, a gear selector position.

N, neutral, marking the external emergency operating button with which a marshal can operate the clutch of some types of racing car.

N, newton, a unit of force.

N, normal mode, referring to an automatic transmission, a switch to bias gear selection to normal.

N, north.

N, Norway, international vehicle distinguishing sign, see appendices.

N, the tyre speed rating code denoting a maximum design speed of 140 km/h (87 mph), moulded into the tyre sidewall.

N, UK, a former driving licence category for duty exempt vehicles, an obsolete category for driving tests.

N$_2$, nitrogen.

N$_2$O, nitrous oxide.

na, not adjustable.

NA, Netherlands Antilles, international vehicle distinguishing sign, see appendices.

NAAMSA, National Association of Automobile Manufacturers of South Africa.

NAASRA, National Association of Australian State Road Authorities.

NACA duct, a style of air inlet ducting designed into the vehicle bodywork, especially on high performance cars, developed originally by the National Advisory Committee for Aeronautics, USA.

nacelle, bodywork shaped to direct airflow towards the engine air inlet, especially to assist ram effect.

NADA, National Automobile Dealers Association, USA.

naked light, any open flame, acetylene carriage lamp, cigarette, or match, that could cause an explosion, especially at a petrol filling station.

NAM, Namibia, international vehicle distinguishing sign, see appendices.

NAM, not as map, a rallying note cautioning that the physical layout of a junction is different from the cartographers drawing, typically due to recent road layout improvements at the junction.

Napoléon Bonaparte, the person who, whilst marching towards a battlefield on 1st December 1805 dictated his troops to change over and march on the right, then dictated that all military and other travellers in the French Empire (much of Europe) must cease travelling on the left and change over to travel along the right side of the road.

NASA, National Autograss Sports Association, UK, for grasstrack racing.

NASCAR, National Association for Stock Car Automobile Racing, USA.

national driver improvement scheme, UK, a training course for drivers who have committed serious traffic offences.

National Driver Register, USA, a database of information about drivers who have had their licences revoked.

nationality plate, see: distinguishing sign.

National Pike, the first long distance road in USA, 591 miles (950 km) in length from Cumberland, Maryland to Vandalia, Illinois, now part of US 40.

NATO hitch, a style of coupling or hitch for towing, common on military vehicles.

natural gas, CNG or LPG.

naturally aspirated, an engine without a supercharger or turbocharger.

nature strip, the longitudinal green verge between a footway and a road.

nave, the hub of a wheel.

nave plate, hub cap.

navigate, to find the selected route, usually using a road map or pace notes.

navigational scatter, a road rally event having no defined route but a graded list of locations to visit scattered over a map, such that each car may take a different route, sometimes having more than 1 navigator per car; organised under strict MSA rules.

navigator, a person who navigates to assist the driver, in rallying the person who reads the pace notes.

navvy, a person whose occupation is to repair roads.

NB, northbound, to travel towards the north.

NCAP, New Car Assessment Programme.

NCM, NO$_x$ control module.

NCP, National Car Parks, an organisation which operates car parks in many cities in UK.

NCS, noise cancellation system.

NCSR, new car security rating.

NDIS, UK, National Driver Improvement Scheme.

NDR, National Driver Register.

near miss, the occurrence of a conflict in which there was no collision, loss, or injury.

nearside, the side of the vehicle that is adjacent to the road edge when driving normally.

nearside bypass lane, a lane constructed to widen a road only to enable passing of vehicles waiting to turn into a road on their offside.

nearside diverging loop lane, an at-grade junction facilitating a turn off a main road to the offside by leaving along a sliproad to the nearside which then loops around to approach the main carriageway at 90°, typically used where a high volume of traffic turns, and it would be dangerous for traffic to wait in the centre of the road before turning; see appendices.

nearside lane, the lane closest to the road edge in the direction of travel; UK lane 1.

nearside passing lane, nearside bypass lane.

nearside to nearside, a pattern of turning off a main road in front of opposing traffic when opposing traffic is doing the same, this pattern allows a higher traffic flow but with a reduced safety margin.

NEC, National Exhibition Centre, located near Birmingham, site of the UK motor show.

neck, a portion of a shaft or tube that has a smaller diameter than the rest of the shaft.

neck bed, a type of semitrailer low loader where the area over the 5th wheel is narrower than the load carrying area.

needle, a pointer or indicator on an instrument or gauge.

needle bearing, an antifriction bearing having rollers of very small diameter.

needle valve, a small tapered needle that moves into a hole to form a valve.

negative, a numerical value less than zero, as applied to measurements of distance, angle, speed, voltage, etc.

negative acceleration, deceleration, to slow down.

negative camber, a suspension design in which wheels on the opposite ends of the same axle are angled so their tops are closer together than the track width.

negative castor, a condition that would exist if the line extending the steering pivot axis creating a longitudinal angle was to meet the road surface behind a vertical line through the wheel centre, which would result in extremely unstable steering; the effect is actually experienced when reversing especially at speed.

negative electrode, cathode, negative plate, negative terminal, the terminal of a battery or alternator etc. that has a surplus of electrons.

negative offset, a condition in steering geometry in which the transverse angle of the steering pivot axis cuts the wheel vertical centreline above ground level.

negative offset, a condition in wheel geometry in which the mounting face of the wheel is inboard of the rim centreline.

negative scrub radius, the lateral distance at ground level between a vertical line through the centre of the tyre footprint and a line extended through the swivel axis, in the case of lines which intersect above ground level.

negative terminal, an electrical terminal or electrode on a battery or other device that has an excess of electrons, and from which electrons flow to a more positive point in a circuit, marked with a – symbol.

negatory, CB jargon, no.

neon, a gaseous element that will emit red light if electrically charged.

neon lamp, a discharge lamp containing neon gas which emits red light, sometimes used for high level brake lights giving superior performance.

neoplan, a tour bus or coach having 2 decks but with limited accommodation on the lower deck, and without a rear window.

neoprene, a synthetic rubber that is not affected by most chemicals, used for gaskets and seals.

NEP, Nepal, international vehicle distinguishing sign, see appendices.

nerf bar, USA, an additional steel tube front bumper ahead of the manufacturers bumper.

nested lamps, lamps having a common housing and lens but with individual bulbs, *e.g.* headlamp with built-in position marker lamp, (C&U).

net power, engine power measured at the crankshaft with all necessary auxiliary equipment, *e.g.* camshaft, oil pump, coolant pump, alternator, etc. driven by the engine.

net torque, the turning force available from an engine whilst driving all of its normal auxiliaries.

neutral, a gear selector position in which there is no geared transmission of torque between the input shaft and the output shaft in the gearbox, *i.e.* a disconnection of the drive from the engine to the wheels.

neutral camber, a suspension design in which wheels on the opposite ends of the same axle are vertical, having neither negative nor positive camber, as on a live axle.

neutral castor, a condition that exists when the line extending the steering pivot axis creating a longitudinal angle coincides at the road surface with the vertical line through the wheel centre, resulting in steering without feedback and which does not self centre, used on some engineering plant.

neutral control, a function in some automatic transmission by which the gearbox will automatically select from drive to neutral whilst the car is stationary with the footbrake applied, then re-select drive when the footbrake is released, in order to save a small amount of fuel, developed by Vauxhall.

neutral handling, a vehicle displaying neither understeer nor oversteer characteristics, occurring in a vehicle when the front and rear slip angles have been designed to be equal.

neutral offset, a condition in steering geometry in which the transverse angle of the steering pivot axis coincides with the wheel vertical centreline at ground level.

neutral offset, a condition in wheel geometry in which the mounting face of the wheel coincides with the rim centreline.

neutral safety switch, a switch wired into the starter motor circuit to prevent the engine cranking unless the gear selector lever is in neutral or park, and unless the clutch is depressed.

neutral scrub radius, a condition in steering geometry in which a line extended through the swivel axis intersects with the centre of the tyre footprint at ground level.

neutral section, a non-competitive section in a road rally to allow the route to pass through a built-up or sensitive area, usually having an average speed requirement of 20 mph (32 km/h).

neutral start switch, neutral safety switch.

neutral steer, neutral handling.

neutral time control, a location at the end of a neutral section in a road rally.

neutral torque axis, the location of engine mountings positioned to absorb load changes, also using a torque support damper to reduce noise and vibration.

new car assessment programme, a European standard of crash testing by a consortium including: Alliance Internationale de Tourisme, FIA, ADAC, plus the Governments of UK, Netherlands, and Sweden, to directly compare crash protection by different manufacturers at speeds of 64 km/h (40 mph); also US-NCAP a parallel USA system operated by IIHS.

New Jersey barrier, see: Jersey barrier.

New Means of Transport, a customs document for notification of acquisition to be completed on arrival when importing a new vehicle having an engine exceeding 48 cc, or 7.2 kW, and which is less than 6 months old or has travelled less than 6,000 km.

new old stock part, a new spare part for an old model car especially where the original manufacturer has ceased production of those parts.

newton, a unit of force, 1 newton force will increase the velocity of a 1 kg object by 1 m/s^2.

Newtonian mechanics, the system of mechanics based upon Newton's laws of motion in which mass and energy are considered as separate, conservative, mechanical properties.

newton metre, the unit of measurement of the torque, *i.e.* rotational force, required to tighten nuts and bolts.

newton metre, the unit of measurement of torque produced by an engine.

newton metre of energy, joule.

newton metre of torque, the unit of torque produced by 1 newton force acting at a perpendicular distance of 1 metre from an axis of rotation.

Newton's equations of motion, Newton's laws of motion expressed in the form of mathematical equations.

Newton's first law of motion, every object will remain at rest or continue moving in a straight line at constant speed unless acted upon by an external force.

Newton's second law of motion, every object will accelerate at a rate inversely proportional to its mass and proportional the size of the force acting on it.

Newton's third law of motion, for every action there is an equal and opposite reaction.

new tread, USA, a retreaded tyre.

NHRA, National Hot Rod Association, USA.

NHTSA, National Highway Traffic Safety Administration, USA.

nibbling, USA, tramlining.

NIC, Nicaragua, international vehicle distinguishing sign, see appendices.

ni cad, nickel cadmium, an alloy sometimes used in the manufacture of vehicle batteries.

nicad battery, nickel cadmium battery.

NiCaSil, a nickel calcium silicon plating sometimes used on the cylinder walls of high performance engines to reduce friction.

nickel, a metallic element, often alloyed for specific purposes, sometimes used in electroplating.

nickel cadmium battery, a sealed storage battery having a nickel anode, a cadmium cathode, and an alkaline electrolyte.

nickel hydride, a battery system giving 7.2 volts per cell, used in some electric and hybrid vehicles.

night, the period of darkness between the moment of sunset and the moment of sunrise.

night blindness, nyctalopia, an eyesight defect when a drivers eyes do not function in dim light and/or cannot readily adjust from bright to dark conditions, commonly due to retinal disease, sufferers must not drive at night.

night heater, a small heater fuelled by diesel to maintain a warm temperature for drivers sleeping in a lorry cab bunk.

night panel, illumination of essential instruments only, and at reduced brightness, to reduce night driving distraction.

night trial, a navigational scatter road rally event conducted overnight when most roads are almost empty, and typically finishing with breakfast; organised under strict MSA rules.

night vision windscreen, a system using thermal imaging technology and an infra red video camera; an image from beyond the range of the headlights is projected onto the inside of the windscreen superimposing on the drivers field of view, developed by GM, introduced in Cadillac.

nimby, not in my back yard, a person who wants road improvements but not directly affecting where they live.

NiMH, nickel metal hydride, an alloy sometimes used in the manufacture of vehicle batteries.

NIP, Notice of Intent to Prosecute.

nipple, grease nipple.

nippy, a vehicle having reasonable acceleration from slow speeds.

nitrogen, a gas present in air that can react during the combustion process to form polluting compounds.

nitrogen oxides, any chemical compound of nitrogen and oxygen usually including nitric oxide and nitrogen dioxide, NO_x a series of polluting gasses.

nitromethane, a fuel typically used in drag racing.

nitrous oxide, a pollutant gas in the exhaust of diesel engined vehicles.

nitrous oxide, a gas injected under high pressure by a drivers control with the fuel, effectively it adds oxygen to the combustion so more fuel can also be added to give increased performance from an engine, it may more than double the power output from an engine, typically used for drag racing.

NL, Netherlands, international vehicle distinguishing sign, see appendices.

Nm, newton metre, a unit of torque.

N/m², newton per square metre, a unit of pressure equal to 1 Pascal.

NMA, National Motorists Association, USA.

NMAA, National Motorists Association of America.

N/mm², newton per square millimetre, a unit of pressure.

no-car lane, a lane on a road having a prohibition from use by cars.

no claim bonus, a discount given by insurance companies to policy holders who have not made a claim in the preceding year.

no cost option, a variation from a standard model car or a choice of alternative extras or facilities where any choice does not add to the cost of a new vehicle.

n-octane, octane.

Noddies, CB jargon, motorcycle police.

node, a surveyors mark, usually a pair of studs or a pair of paint spots in the centre of the road, especially at junctions.

noise, any unpleasant or unwanted sound generated inside or outside the vehicle, including banging, knocking, tapping, booming, buzzing, clunking, humming, whistling, etc.

noise cancellation system, the reduction of audible noise by means of anti-noise speakers producing an output wave that is equal and opposite to the noise wave.

noise pollution, excessive or unwanted noise from engines, exhausts, tyres, etc.

noise vibration and harshness, recognised factors which negatively affect comfort and quality feel, and which cause distraction to the

vehicle occupants.

no loading, a prohibition from loading or unloading goods or materials into or from a vehicle.

no load test, a test of a starter motor when it is operated without load but measuring voltage and current and armature speeds.

nomex, a fire resistant fabric used for the manufacture of racing clothing.

nominal capacity, the rated capacity of a battery.

nominal engine speed, rated speed.

nominal power, the maximum net power of the engine at full throttle.

nominal rim diameter, the diameter of the tyre rim at the point where the tyre bead seats, and normally given in whole numbers of inches except metric rims.

nominal voltage, rated voltage.

nonasphaltic road oil, any nonhardening petroleum distillate or residual oil having a viscosity low enough to be applied without heating, sprayed onto the surface of an unmetalled graded surface to prevent road dust.

noncombat vehicle, a military vehicle used only for the transport of persons or equipment.

non-driver, a person who does not drive a motor vehicle.

non-radial, a tyre having a carcass which is constructed either as a crossply or bias belted.

non runner, a car having an engine which cannot or will not run, or no engine, or a significant part of the engine or drive train missing.

non servo brake, a braking system in which there is no mechanical assistance by the vehicle, its engine, or its momentum.

non-stop accident, hit and run.

non-stop crash, hit and run.

non urban road, a road not in a built-up area of a town or city, usually in a rural area.

nonvolatile memory, memory of a microprocessor that is not lost when the power is disconnected.

no parking, a prohibition from leaving a vehicle unattended by anyone having lawful authority to drive it.

no passing zone, USA, an area in which overtaking is prohibited.

Nordic anticorrosion code, a quality assurance for cars developed by Scandinavian automobile and consumer associations in 1983 which requires that all cars must be free of surface corrosion for 3 years and free from perforation or weakening corrosion for 6 years.

normal condition of use of a vehicle, the situation when the vehicle is ready to move with its engine running and its movable components in their normal position, (C&U).

normally aspirated, naturally aspirated.

normal position of use of a movable component, the position of a movable component as specified by the vehicle manufacturer for the normal condition of use and the park condition of the vehicle, (C&U).

north, the direction of the north terrestrial pole, the principal cardinal point and reference direction as marked on maps and used for navigation.

North American Stock Car Auto Racing, USA's most prestigious motor racing series, having 36 cars per event, and 36 rounds per year, typically racing at speeds of 200 mph (320 km/h).

northbound, travelling towards the north.

northing, in navigation, the second half of a grid reference usually having 6 numbers in total, numbered from south to north from a reference point, enabling numerical identification of a location.

north-south layout, an engine layout having the cylinders on a longitudinal axis from front to rear.

nose, the front end of a vehicle or assembly or part.

nosebag, CB jargon, a meal.

nose bra, a nose protector.

nose protector, a shaped cover to prevent stone chipping damage to a bonnet, leaving holes for the lights and having long fastening straps.

nose to tail, a driving condition suggesting very slow speeds in congested traffic.

nose up, the condition of a breakdown truck when giving a suspended tow to a vehicle that is heavier than its normal capacity.

nose up, the condition of a goods vehicle if it is loaded with all the weight behind the rear wheels.

noseweight, the weight imposed on a towing coupling on a level road by the drawbar of a trailer; the recommended loading in UK is 7 % of the actual weight of the trailer, *i.e.* 70 kg per tonne; in USA the recommended loading is 10 % to 15 %; see: tongue.

NOS, nitrous oxide injection system.

NOS part, new old stock part.

no spin diff, limited slip differential.

no stopping, a prohibition from stopping a vehicle, including prohibition from picking up or setting down passengers, the prohibition usually extends to the verges of a road but excludes queueing in traffic.

notchback, a saloon car, 3 box style.

notchy, the quality of a gear selector system which requires uneven force at different parts of its movement.

no through road, a road having only 1 place for entrance and exit.

notice of intended prosecution, a notice given to a driver having committed a motoring offence, and which informs the driver that he/she may be summonsed to court.

notice to owner, a postal notification to the registered owner of a vehicle that a parking ticket was attached to the vehicle and the fine remains unpaid

notifiable animal, any of the domestic animals: dog, sheep, cattle, horse, goat, pig,

ass, mule.

Notification of Acquisition, UK, a customs document titled "New Means of Transport" to be completed on arrival when importing a new car.

notional gross weight, a rule of thumb accepted in law for assessing an unknown gross weight as a multiplying factor from a known unladen weight; a factor of x 2 is applied to rigid vehicles, and a factor of x 2.5 is applied to articulated lorries.

no turn on red, USA, a worded sign at traffic signals where it is not permitted to turn right at a red light, or left onto a 1 way street.

no waiting, a prohibition from remaining stationary for longer than necessary to allow passengers to alight or board.

NO_x, nitrogen oxides, any chemical compound of nitrogen and oxygen but typically nitric oxide and nitrogen dioxide, a series of polluting gasses.

no zone, USA, the blindspot areas around a vehicle, especially those around a large truck where another driver should not linger.

nozzle, an opening or jet through which any fluid passes as it is discharged.

nozzle restrictor, a narrow fuel filling neck on cars having a cat so that the larger nozzle dispensing leaded fuel will not fit.

NPA, National Playbus Association, UK.

NPR, number plate recognition.

NRMA, National Roads and Motorists Association, Australia.

NRSF, National Road Safety Foundation, USA.

NRTF, national road traffic forecast.

ns, nearside.

NSDA, National Safe Drivers Association.

NSU, Neckarsulmer Strickmaschinen Union, German, Neckarsulm Knitting machines Company, a former manufacturer of cars.

NT, nominated tester, a person employed by an AE to perform roadworthiness tests on vehicles.

nta, neutral torque axis.

NTC, national traffic census.

NTC, neutral time control, in road rally navigation.

NtO, Notice to Owner.

NTR, no through road, in road rally navigation.

NTS, national traffic survey.

NTSB, National Transportation Safety Board, USA.

nudge bar, bull bar.

nudge parking, touch parking.

nudge test, a slow-speed frontal test collision at 8 km/h (5 mph) which should result in zero damage to any part, the bumpers may deform and reform.

NUKS, not UK specification.

number plate, registration plate.

number plate lamp, rear registration plate lamp.

number plate recognition, a system that will

automatically read the registration of every approaching vehicle and interface with various databases to use the information *e.g.* to charge a toll, to identify speeding, to identify a stolen car, or to prevent fuel being served.

numeric tire, USA, an older tire sizing system which may only include the section width and rim diameter, although sometimes additional characteristics are denoted.

nursery route, a series of wide roads with little traffic and easy junctions on which a learner driver is taught during his/her first lessons.

nut, an internally threaded fastener for bolts and screws.

nu-tread, USA, a retreaded tyre.

nvh, noise vibration and harshness.

NVQ, UK, National Vocational Qualification.

NVSR, National Vehicle Security Register.

nyctalopia, night blindness, an eyesight defect when a drivers eyes do not function in dim light and/or cannot readily adjust from bright to dark conditions, commonly due to retinal disease, sufferers must not drive at night.

nyloc, a nut having a nylon insert to prevent it loosening due to vibration.

nystagmus, a rapid wobble of the eye which may preclude a person from driving.

NZ, New Zealand, international vehicle distinguishing sign, see appendices.

NZAADEF, New Zealand Automobile Association Driver Education Foundation.

NZIDI, New Zealand Institute of Driving Instructors.

O

O, Oils, a section of the POWER checks mnemonic.

O, orange, or brown roads, the colour of roads to be used at that point in road rally navigation as marked on an OS map.

O, over, in road rally navigation a requirement to cross a bridge or similar.

O licence, operators licence, a licence required to be held by a person in each organisation which operates a lorry or a bus.

O ring, a rubber ring of a specific size to produce a liquid tight seal between 2 parts.

O$_2$, oxygen.

O$_2$ sensor, the lambda sensor in the exhaust system that measures oxygen in the exhaust gas and sends a signal to the ECU for accurate control of the air-fuel ratio.

ÖAMTC, Österreichischer Automobil, Motorrad und Touring Club, Austrian Motor Federation.

oba, onboard analysis.

obd, onboard diagnostics.

obligatory sign, a road traffic sign, generally circular with a blue background, typically showing white arrows which must be followed.

oblique method, a method of parking in a car park by turning the vehicle through approximately 45° whilst moving forwards, then reversing through another 45° into the parking space; potentially the simplest and safest method of parking.

oblique parking, the action of parking by reversing into a parking space using the oblique method.

obo, or best offer, a suggestion in an advertisement that an offer of a lower sum for the purchase of a car may be accepted

observation link, a mental link formed by recognition of an observed road sign or occult sign which relates to the probability of encountering a different unseen hazard, *e.g.* an arched bridge sign suggests a tall vehicle may be approaching in the centre of the road.

observation platform, a raised area at the side of a motorway and some other roads large enough to position a car, for use by police only.

observed horsepower, USA, the engine output measured on a dynamometer before being corrected to standard conditions, *e.g.* before allowing for atmospheric pressure, temperature, humidity, etc.

observer, a person who informally assesses a

drivers performance and gives advice but does not hold an instructors licence; see also: qualified.

obw, onboard weighing.

oc, overhead camshaft.

occasional hazard, any hazard marked by a hazard warning sign but where the hazard may not actually be present for much of the time, *e.g.* the subcategories of signs showing animals or persons, but not *e.g.* a junction.

occasional seat, a folding seat in the rear of some MPV or in the aisle of some minibuses.

occult sign, a cryptic observation link, where recognition of an observed clue relates to the probability of encountering an unseen hazard, *e.g.* observation of a series of water streaks along a road suggests a slow moving road cleaning vehicle may be ahead.

occupant space sensor, an ultrasonic sensor located in each A pillar which recognises the position of each occupant and sends a signal to the ARTS system.

occupation road, a road having private rights for those with an interest in adjacent land, and which may also have public rights; see also: accommodation.

occupied, a vehicle condition when the driver is seated at the wheel.

ochophobia, a fear of vehicles.

octane, an alkane hydrocarbon, a constituent of petrol used to control its burning speed to give anti-knock properties.

octane number, an index number indicating the speed at which a sample of petrol will burn, the higher the number the slower it burns thereby allowing its use in high compression engines; it is also a measure of the fuels ability to resist autoignition hence resist engine knock.

octane rating, an index number indicating the speed at which a sample of petrol will burn, the higher the number the slower it burns thereby allowing its use in high compression engines.

octane requirement, the minimum octane rating of fuel that an engine requires to ensure it will operate without detonation.

octane scale, a series of numbers from 0 to 120.3 used to rate the octane number of petrol; n-heptane = 0 octane, isooctane = 100 octane, isooctane plus tel = 120.3 octane.

od, outside diameter.

od, overdrive.

OD, over dimension, a sign directing traffic to

and along a suitable route for oversize lorries.

O-D, origin to destination.

odc, outer dead centre, bdc.

ODC, Owner Drivers Club, UK, a club for lorry drivers.

odometer, a distance measuring device showing the total distance the vehicle has covered in its life.

oe, original equipment.

oem, original equipment manufacturer.

OFA, Oxygenated Fuels Association, USA.

off, the action of a car in leaving the surface of a race or rally track, causing delay or retirement.

offence, an illegal act, a breach of traffic law.

offer up, to bring parts close together in the process of assembly.

off-highway equipment, earthmoving vehicles or tyres etc, designed for off-highway duty in quarries and similar places.

off-highway truck, a truck of such size, weight, or dimensions that it cannot be used on public highways, typically used for quarrying being up to 400 tonnes GVW.

off-line take-off, acceleration from rest, typically from a stop line at a green traffic signal.

offload, to unload goods, materials, or passengers from a vehicle.

off ramp, USA, the deceleration lane leading off a freeway.

off-road, not on a carriageway, to drive on unmade surfaces, including unsurfaced tracks and driving cross country.

off-roader, a vehicle which has been designed to be used off-road.

off-roading, the action of driving over rough terrain.

off-road vehicle, a vehicle having 4x4 transmission, long travel suspension, good ground clearance, and suitable tyres such that it will perform well on a variety of uneven surfaces.

offset, the alignment of parts which are deliberately at an angle or displaced sideways.

offset, the lateral distance between the mounting face of the wheel and the centreline of the tyre.

offset, see: negative, positive.

offset angle, the angle between the banks of cylinders in a vee engine, which can be: 15°, 45°, 60°, 66°, 72°, 90°, 120°, or 135°.

offset cab, a cab in a vehicle where it is positioned to 1 side only, a half cab.

offset crankshaft, a crankshaft layout which is not centrally below the cylinders, it is positioned so that during the power stroke the con rod is more central with the piston to reduce sideways pressure on 1 side of the piston skirt and bore.

offset twin, a 2 cylinder motorcycle engine where the crankpins are 180° apart.

offside, the side of the vehicle that is furthest from the road edge when driving normally.

offside to offside, a pattern of turning off a main road behind opposing traffic when opposing traffic is doing the same, this pattern restricts traffic flow and causes hooking but may increase the safety margin.

off the map, to be at, or referring to, a location beyond the edge of the map.

off the pace, to drive at a speed considerably less than the speed of the race leader.

off track, to follow a vehicle ahead such that the longitudinal centreline of the trailing vehicle is significantly to the right or left of the longitudinal centreline of the leading vehicle, usually to maximise vision.

off tracking, the condition of a trailer when the longitudinal centrelines of drawing vehicle and trailer are not in line on a straight road; see also cut in, cut out.

off-wire, the status of a trolleybus which is deliberately or accidentally detached from the overhead trolley wires.

OFT, Office of Fair Trading.

OH, overall height.

ohb, owners handbook, to be referred to for specific details.

ohc, overhead camshaft.

ohm, Ω, the unit of measurement of electrical resistance R, that restricts current flow, 1 volt will force 1 ampere through a resistance of 1 ohm, $R = v/I$.

ohmmeter, an instrument that measures resistance R in units of Ω through an electrical conductor or device or circuit.

ohv, overhead valves.

OICA, Organisation Internationale des Constructeurs d'Automobiles, International Organisation of Motor Vehicle Manufacturers.

oil, a liquid lubricant usually made from crude oil, used for lubrication between moving parts and for cooling.

oil additive, any of a variety of substances which may be added to oil to improve a characteristic.

oil bath filter, a type of air filter where the air passes through an oil wetted screen.

oil breather pipe, crankcase breather pipe.

oil burner, a diesel engine.

oil burner, a vehicle having a diesel engine.

oil can, a container with a narrow nozzle for dispensing oil.

oil change, the replacement of the engine oil and usually the filter.

oil clearance, the space filled by oil between a bearing and the shaft journal.

oil consumption, the quantity of oil an engine uses, the amount burned plus the amount leaked, in a set time or distance.

oil control ring, the lower ring(s) on a piston that prevent excessive oil from entering the combustion chamber.

oil cooler, a system of cooling the lubricating oil by passing it through a dedicated radiator before recirculation.

oil dilution, contamination of the lubricating

oil by liquid fuel passing from the combustion chamber to the sump.

oil drum, a metal barrel used for the transport of oil and sometimes fuel and other fluids, typically having a capacity of 42 US gallons (160 litres).

oil filter, a device which prevents particles from recirculating in the lubrication system, it may have a typical filter size of 10 microns.

oil gallery, a main oil passage within a block, crankcase, or cylinder head, through which oil flows under pressure.

oil gauge, an oil pressure gauge, or an oil temperature gauge.

oil immersed clutch, a wet clutch.

oil level indicator, an electronic sensor that sends a signal to a gauge or illuminates a tell-tale.

oil level indicator, a dipstick.

oil life system, a system that continuously analyses the oil quantity and quality and informs the driver when an oil change is necessary.

oil pan, a receptacle into which oil is drained from an engine before disposal.

oil pan, USA, sump.

oil pressure gauge, an instrument displaying the instantaneous oil pressure in the engine primary lubrication network, typically reading in bar or psi.

oil pressure warning light, a tell-tale that illuminates when the operating pressure in the oil lubrication system is insufficient.

oil pump, the device which forces lubricating oil at high pressure to all necessary parts within the engine, or within a transmission.

oil scraper ring, the lowest ring on a piston having the purpose of removing surplus oil from the cylinder wall.

oil seal, a seal around a shaft or other part to prevent oil moving to an area where it is not wanted.

oil strainer, a course filter to prevent dirt and large particles from entering the oil pump.

oil temperature gauge, an instrument displaying the instantaneous oil temperature in the engine primary lubrication network, typically reading in °C.

oil thrash, the action of the crankshaft splashing into the oil in the sump when the oil level is too high, causing heat and consuming power.

oil viscosity, the rating of resistance to flow, the higher the number the thicker the oil, usually measured and numerated by the SAE.

oilway, an oil passage within a crankshaft, connecting rod, and other moving parts, through which oil flows under pressure.

oilway, gallery.

OL, overall length.

old damage, any damage that was caused previously before the relevant collision.

oleopneumatic suspension, hydropneumatic suspension.

oleo strut, a telescopic damper that incorporates a gas spring, such that as hydraulic fluid is forced into the gas chamber the spring rate increases.

omnibus, bus, meaning to go everywhere, its original name.

ON, octane number.

onboard analysis, a microprocessor based system often fitted to larger commercial vehicles to monitor driver efficiency.

onboard computer, a microprocessor based system for controlling various electronic circuits, or to give a display to the driver, *e.g.* fuel consumption.

onboard diagnostic system, a microprocessor based system that informs the driver when there is a fault in a system, or when the next service is due.

onboard weighing, a system fitted to some lorries which displays a readout on the dashboard to ensure that individual axle weights and gross weight are not exceeded.

on centre, the condition when the steering is angled in the straight ahead direction.

on-centre feel, the quality of the feedback and responsiveness to the driver when the steering is centred.

on channel, CB jargon, on the air.

oncoming traffic, traffic approaching towards the front.

ono, or near offer, a suggestion in an advertisement that an offer of a slightly lower sum for the purchase of a car will be accepted.

on ramp, USA, the acceleration lane leading onto a freeway.

ONS, German Motorsport Federation.

ONS, Office of National Statistics.

on street parking, marked or signed parking areas at the side of a street, sometimes restricted by vehicle category, time, or for a fee.

on the fly, to perform any function whilst the vehicle is moving, especially at speed, typically to shift on the fly, *i.e.* to change from 2wd to 4wd whilst moving.

on the peg, CB jargon, at the legal speed limit.

on the road, in the course of a journey.

on the road charges, costs additional to the list price of a new car, *e.g.* registration fee, and road tax.

on the wagon, to refrain from having an alcoholic drink; originally of drivers of horse drawn drays delivering to public houses, said because it was not appropriate to have a drink at every delivery.

on the way, in the course of a journey.

on tow, the state of a motor vehicle being towed by another.

on track, to follow a vehicle ahead such that the longitudinal centrelines of both vehicles are in line.

on tracking, the normal condition of a trailer when the longitudinal centrelines of drawing vehicle and trailer are aligned.

191

OOP, out of position, a system fed by sensors which monitors the occupants seating positions for safe operation of airbags, developed by DaimlerChrysler.

open area, USA, an area in which 4x4 vehicles may operate anywhere with no restrictions.

open bend, a bend where the sightlines give good distance visibility.

open car, a car with no roof or a removable roof, see: cabriolet, convertible, drophead, droptop, roadster.

open circuit, a break or opening in an electrical circuit that prevents current flowing.

open coil glowplug, a wire glowplug.

open corner, a corner or junction where the sightlines give good visibility in each direction.

open crossing, a railway level crossing without any traffic signal, barrier, gate, or attendant, but having only a stop or a give way sign; drivers should be extremely cautious.

open differential, the usual simple planetary differential which permits each wheel to turn at different speeds, and which directs the drive to the wheel with the least traction.

open ended spanner, a tool for turning nuts and bolts having a fixed pair of parallel open jaws at both ends of the handle.

openface helmet, a crash helmet where the lower face is not protected, typically used in closed cockpit cars.

open gate, a design of gear selector system where gate is positioned such that it is seen, common in vintage and sports cars.

open junction, a junction where the sightlines give good visibility in every direction.

open lane, an adjacent lane on either side known to have no traffic at that time and which can be used as an escape route.

open loop, in an electronic ECU a condition during warming up when the lambda sensor signal is ignored to maintain a specific air-fuel ratio for optimum performance.

open top, a car with no roof or a removable roof, see: cabriolet, convertible, drophead, droptop, roadster.

open wheel, a vehicle without bodywork over the wheels, typically a racing car.

opera light, USA, an ornamental courtesy lamp mounted on the B or C pillars of limousines and luxury cars.

operating costs, the various costs including fixed costs and variable costs incurred in operating a vehicle.

operating piston, the hydraulic piston in an automatic gearbox which causes the clutch or brake band to be applied to cause a gearchange.

operating safety, a function of vehicle design such that controls are ergonomic in order to reduce driver stress levels, a branch of primary safety.

operating tell-tale, a visual or auditory signal indicating that a device has been switched on and is operating correctly or not, (C&U).

operational lane, each of the individual lanes which carry general traffic on a multilane road.

operational parking, parking of vehicles at the premises of a business when the vehicles are essential for the operation of the business.

opposed engine, a flat engine having pistons on opposite sides of the crankshaft.

opposed pistons, an engine having a pair of crankshafts synchronised to stroke a pair of pistons in each cylinder such that as the pistons approach each other the resulting space between the piston crowns in the centre of the cylinder becomes the combustion chamber.

opposite lock, the steering input when the front wheels are steered in the opposite direction to which the vehicle is yawing, usually to counter or control oversteer during a rear wheel skid or a 4 wheel skid.

optical beam setter, a device that visually displays the headlight beam against a calibrated screen and facilitates accurate adjustment of lamp alignment.

Opticruise, a semiautomatic gear selector system, only requiring the use of the clutch for starting and stopping, developed by Scania trucks.

optimising violation, a violation performed deliberately in order to hasten a journey, typically where the risk is perceived to be low and the gain is perceived to be moderate, *e.g.* eating a snack whilst driving instead of stopping.

optimum shift control, an automatic transmission that considers many parameters before a gear change, developed by Mitsubishi.

optional equipment, parts or systems which may be supplied by the manufacturer at additional cost.

optional lamp, a lamp of which the installation is left to the discretion of the manufacturer, (C&U).

OPUS, oscillating pickup ignition system.

orange arc, a coloured area on a rev counter showing the best rev range for maximum performance of the retarder.

orange badge, a parking concession scheme for disabled persons, now replaced by the European and USA standard blue badge system.

orange peel, a condition in vehicle paintwork following a low quality respray where the finished result has a texture resembling the surface of the peel of the fruit.

orange road, a brown road, *i.e.* B class road in road rally navigation, as marked on OS maps.

ORC, Off Road Club, UK.

ORDIT, UK, Official Register of Driving Instructor Training.

Organisation Internationale des Constructeurs d'Automobiles, International Organisation of Motor Vehicle Manufacturers.

orifice, a small calibrated hole or opening in a system carrying liquid or gas.

origin, the starting point of a journey.

original condition, a car in a condition which

192

may be old or worn but which has not been resprayed, reupholstered, without significant repairs, and has not been modified or had any modern accessories fitted.

original equipment, the parts as originally provided by the vehicle manufacturer including those bought in from their suppliers, but not parts of similar specification manufactured by others.

original equipment manufacturer, the manufacturer of the parts supplied to the vehicle manufacturer in the assembly of a new vehicle.

ORPA, other routes with public access, a designation shown on OS maps to indicate some but not all UCRs.

orphan, a parallel import with a different specification to similar cars found in the country of final destination.

ort, off-road tyre, a tyre designed for use on unmade or rough surfaces, either for agriculture or construction, or for recreational vehicles.

ORTC, Off Road Trialers Club.

os, offside.

OS, Ordnance Survey, the organisation responsible for producing maps in UK and many other countries.

OSC, optimum shift control.

OSCA, Officiene Specializzate Costruzioni Automobili, Italian sports car manufacturer.

oscillating axle, each of a pair of short transverse axles aligned axially, each mounted with 2 wheels at least 0.5 metre apart, and able to oscillate, *i.e.* allowing 1 wheel of a pair to rise whilst the other falls, typically on some older trailers; also named 4 in line.

oscillating pickup ignition system, an ignition system having a timing rotor, pickup module, and amplifier, instead of contact points.

OSGR, Ordnance Survey grid reference.

OSS, occupant space sensor.

otdc, overlap tdc

otg, outside temperature gauge.

OTL, over total lateness, an arrival too late to book in to a checkpoint in road rally navigation.

otr, on the road, a statement that the advertised price of a new car includes all items necessary to legally drive away from the showroom.

OTS, Office of Traffic Safety, USA.

Otto, Count Nicholas August Otto, Germany, developer and patentee the 4 stroke internal combustion engine in 1876 from an invention by Rochas.

Otto cycle, the 4 cycles of an internal combustion engine: induction, compression, power, exhaust; patented by Count Nicholas August Otto, Germany, in 1876.

out, an engine which has stopped.

out, an escape route.

out accelerate, a comparison of vehicles in which 1 has greater acceleration performance than another.

outboard, near, at, or beyond, the sides of a vehicle.

outboard brakes, brakes fitted at the wheel hub, conventional on most vehicles.

out brake, a comparison of drivers in which 1 brakes later but more efficiently than another.

out brake, a comparison of vehicles in which 1 has greater breaking performance than another.

outdrive, to drive better than another.

outdriving the headlights, to drive above a speed such that the overall stopping distance is greater than the distance illuminated by the headlights; typical dipped headlights illuminate up to 50 metres ahead giving a safe maximum speed on dipped headlights of approximately 75 km/h (45 mph).

outer, a marking moulded into the sidewall of a directional tyre indicating the side of the tyre which must be fitted away from the vehicle.

outer cap nut, the part of a Budd mounting which secures the outer of twin wheels to the hub.

outer dead centre, bdc.

outer headlamp, the outer pair of twin headlamps, normally emitting dipped beam only, or dip and main beam.

outer loop, USA, the carriageway having anticlockwise direction of travel around a ringroad, first designated on the I495 Capital Beltway.

outer ring road, any road which encircles a town outside of the town or outside of an inner ring road, sometimes using existing roads or constructed to motorway standard.

outer separation, USA, the area of land between the main carriageway of an arterial highway and a frontage street or road.

outer sill, the strip of bodywork visible externally below the doors.

outer terminal, each of the distributor terminals feeding to a sparkplug.

outer wheel, the outboard wheel of a pair of twin wheels.

outfield, the area outside a racetrack, the verge between the track and the safety fencing.

outfit, a complete lorry having a semitrailer or trailer.

outfit, a motorcycle combination.

outlet, exhaust port.

outlet valve, exhaust valve.

outload, the primary load on a lorry as it leaves its base.

out of balance, the condition when a wheel or rotating part is not balanced, when a wheel is statically unbalanced or dynamically unbalanced, such that at a critical speed vibration is felt.

out of gear, a condition when neutral gear or park is selected.

out of true, not circular, or not lying in 1 plane, *e.g.* a wheel with an axial or radial buckle.

out of tune, an engine condition when certain parameters require adjusting, *e.g.* mixture, ignition, valve timing etc.

out pull, a comparison where a lorry has greater hauling power than another.

output shaft, the gearbox shaft transmitting power out to the propeller shaft and to the wheels.

outride, to ride better, faster, or further than another.

outrider, a motorcyclist acting as escort to a vehicle.

outrigger, a lateral chassis extension supporting the body edge or running boards, etc.

outrigger, each of a pair, or 2 pairs, of extendible legs typically hydraulically operated, on which to raise the vehicle from its wheels for stability when working, fitted on all vehicles having a crane or hydraulic platform for aerial work.

outset wheel, a wheel having negative offset, *i.e.* the centreline of the rim is outboard of the mounting face.

outside temperature gauge, a device indicating the ambient air temperature; the sensor is typically located behind the front bumper and can give an erroneous reading due to hot air from the radiator when idling in traffic.

outside wheels, all the wheels on that side of a vehicle which take a larger radius when following a curved course.

outtrack, cut out, the action of semitrailer wheels in following a wider radius than those of the tractive unit on a moderate curve at speed, due to the effect of centrifugal force on the trailer.

outturned wheel, a front wheel of a potentially active stationary vehicle at the roadside, which is significantly slewed towards the course of a vehicle approaching from behind, having the potential for the stationary vehicle to move into the path of the approaching vehicle with no other warning.

over, a premium paid above the list price of a car by a buyer who is very keen to purchase a particular model when the waiting list is long.

overall diameter, the diameter of an unloaded inflated tyre measured from crown to crown across the diameter.

overall gear ratio, the relationship between the number of engine revolutions for exactly 1 rotation of the driving wheels, expressed for each gear.

overall height, the vertical distance between the ground and the point on the vehicle which is furthest from the ground calculated when the tyres are correctly inflated, the vehicle is at its unladen weight, with any raising parts at their lowest height, and the ground under the vehicle is reasonable flat, (C&U).

overall length, the distance between the transverse planes passing through the extreme forward and rearward projecting points of the vehicle or combination, inclusive of all parts of a permanent character and which are strong enough for repeated use, but excluding any mirror, snow plough blade, customs seal, and sheeting, (C&U).

overall stopping distance, the sum of the reaction distance plus the braking distance at any given speed.

overall width, the distance between the 2 vertical planes where they meet the median longitudinal plane of the vehicle and touching at its lateral outer edge, but excluding the distortion of a tyre near the point of contact with the ground as is caused by the weight of the vehicle, connections for tyre pressure gauges, rear view mirrors, and any side direction indicator lamps, end outline marker lamps, front and rear position lamps, parking lamps, side marker lamps, or retro reflectors, (C&U).

overall width, the distance across a tyre between the outside of the 2 sidewalls, including lettering and designs.

overboost, excessive pressure created by a supercharger or turbocharger that could damage an engine.

overcharging, continued charging of a fully charged battery at a high rate which will cause gassing and will eventually shorten the life of the battery.

overdrive, an additional gear or several, usually on the highest gear of a 3 or 4 speed manual transmission where it is selected electrically, typically on large classic cars.

overdrive, any gearing system in which the speed of the propeller shaft is higher than the speed of the crankshaft.

overdriving the headlights, outdriving the headlights.

over engineered, a vehicle or part that will withstand hard use beyond normal service conditions.

overhang, the length of any part of the body of any vehicle ahead of the centreline of the front axle, or behind the centreline of the rear axle, or behind the mid point of any group of axles.

overhaul, overtake.

overhaul, to completely disassemble a unit, inspect all parts, and reassemble with new parts where necessary to produce an as-new unit.

overhead camshaft, an engine in which the camshaft is located in the cylinder head.

overhead console, a switch panel located above the drivers head, usually above the centre of the windscreen.

overhead lifter, overhead cam.

overhead spotlights, additional headlamps mounted above the windscreen of a vehicle, typically used for overland expeditions and not a lawful fitment in many countries.

overhead valve, an engine in which the camshaft is located in the cylinder block, the valves are in the cylinder head and operated by pushrods and tappet levers.

overheating, a condition when the engine coolant has exceed its maximum design temperature, typically caused by a fault or blockage in the cooling system, insufficient coolant, high ambient temperature, wrong coolant with a low boiling point, slipping fan belt, missing fanbelt, lack of engine oil, or a very lean mixture, etc.

overheight, a loaded vehicle where any part exceeds 5.25 m (17 ft 6 in) high.

overinflation, a condition when a tyre is inflated to a higher pressure than corresponds to the actual load and/or beyond the manufacturers recommended pressure, measured cold.

overland bus, a bus designed for long distance travel having a reasonable degree of comfort including highback seats, and typically having drinks and toilet facilities onboard.

overland expedition, the use of 1 or more vehicles to travel into and across places or countries not easily accessible.

overlap tdc, the tdc position of the crankshaft when the exhaust valve and inlet valve are both open because the exhaust and inlet strokes overlap some degrees.

overload, to load a vehicle such that the maximum designed or permitted load in/on that vehicle is exceeded, see: weight.

overload spring, helper spring, an additional leaf spring above a standard leaf spring to increase the spring rate and continue giving suspension when overloaded, on the rear axles of many lorries.

overpass, a grade separated road layout to carry 1 highway over another, with or without facilities for interchange, such that traffic crosses without interference to flow.

overrev, to cause an engine to run at a speed above the red line.

overrevving, the action of increasing the speed of an engine beyond the manufacturers recommendation, beyond the red line or into the red arc, by sustained use of the accelerator either in neutral or in a low gear.

overrevving, the action of increasing the speed of an engine beyond the manufacturers recommendation, beyond the red line or into the red arc by selecting a lower gear whilst travelling at a road speed that is too high for that gear.

overrider, each of a pair of short vertical extensions or posts above and/or below a vehicle bumper, designed to reduce damage by overcoming any slight mismatch in bumper heights during a minor collision, especially useful for touch parking, common until the end of the classic era.

overrider board, running board.

overrun, a condition when the driver lifts off the accelerator such that the momentum of the vehicle is turning the engine at a speed greater than idle revs, *i.e.* the wheels are driving the engine.

overrun area, a part of a road bounded by mountable kerbs creating an illusion of a

buildout as a speed reduction measure, and typically having a coloured surface but which can be driven over if necessary by larger vehicles.

overrun area, an area around the island of a roundabout which is bordered by a mountable kerb and a textured surface, to allow larger vehicles space to turn whilst not visually creating the appearance of a wide roundabout

overrun brake, a braking mechanism on a light trailer whereby inertial pressure of the drawbar against the coupling actuates the trailer braking system.

overrun braking, the retardation effect provided by the engine compression during overrun especially when the revs are just below the red line and enhanced in progressively lower gears, but operating only on the drive axle hence leading to potential instability especially on slippery surfaces.

overrun cutoff, deceleration fuel cutoff.

overrunning clutch, a freewheeling clutch that transmits torque in 1 direction but turns freely in the other, sometimes used in starter motors and automatic transmissions.

overseas registration document, the foreign equivalent of the V5 registration document.

overshoot, a type of collision in which a driver fails to stop or give way before emerging and collides with a vehicle on the priority road.

overshoot, to go beyond a desired point, especially at a junction.

oversize load, a load on any vehicle where the GTW/GCW/GVW exceeds 42 tonnes but not exceeding 150 tonnes; or exceeds 2.9 metres wide but not exceeding 6.1 metres wide; or exceeds 18.3 metres long but not exceeding 27.4 metres long.

oversize piston, a piston which is larger in diameter than an original but of a size to suit a rebored engine.

oversize valve guide, a replacement valve guide having a larger outside diameter sized to fit a bored and reamed cylinder head.

overslung, a suspension system in which the leaf spring is attached above the axle.

overspray, the remnants of a low quality respray as seen on adjacent areas that were not properly masked.

oversquare, the comparison of the bore and stroke dimensions of an engine where the bore is larger than the stroke.

oversteer, the effect when the tyre slip angle at the rear wheels increases more than it does at the front, when the rear tyres lose adhesion and the rate of yaw of the vehicle is more than anticipated with respect to steering input, a rear wheel skid; it can be caused by brake-steer overlap, by lift-off in mid bend, or by excessive power in a rwd.

oversteering, a condition when a driver turns the steering wheel more than necessary for a specific situation, *e.g.* causing minor zigzags along a straight road, or threepenny bitting around a bend.

oversteer recovery, the procedure for recovering from oversteer providing there is space available before a collision occurs: undo whatever driver input caused the skid, release the footbrake, steer rapidly so the front wheels roll along the direction of travel, clutch down or select neutral in an automatic, when moving in a straight line brake gently; see also: spin.

overtake, to catch up to and drive past another vehicle travelling in the same direction, *i.e.* to 'take-over' the relative position of another vehicle; note, it is not possible to overtake a stationary vehicle, see: pass.

overtaking distance, the distance travelled by a faster vehicle in performing an overtaking manoeuvre from first leaving the original lane until fully repositioned in the same lane, *e.g.* if the overtaking vehicle is travelling at 80 km/h (50 mph) and the overtaken vehicle is moving at 60 km/h (40 mph) the overtaking distance is 450 metres (0.3 mile) with minimal safety margin.

overtaking lane, usually the 2nd and 3rd or subsequent lanes counted from the nearside of the road, excluding bus lanes etc.

overtaking position, the safest position from which to commence overtaking a vehicle being followed: 2 seconds behind its rear and when safe over the road centreline for maximum visibility; see also: following position.

overtaking triangle, the ideal course to be followed whilst performing overtaking; moving to the offside of the road gradually on approach to increase the view, then accelerating through the overtake and gradually returning to the nearside.

overtaking visibility, the distance along a road that must be seen to be clear before starting to overtake, typically double the overtaking distance on a single carriageway road to allow for approaching traffic.

over total lateness, to arrive at a checkpoint in road rally navigation too late to book in.

over your shoulder, CB jargon, behind you.

OW, overall width.

owner, a person or organisation to whom the title of property belongs.

owner driver, a person who owns and drives his/her own lorry, finding his/her own contracts.

oxidation, the combining of a material with oxygen; rusting is slow oxidation, burning is rapid oxidation.

oxides of nitrogen, NO_x, nitrogen oxides, any chemical compound of nitrogen and oxygen but typically nitric oxide and nitrogen dioxide, a series of polluting gasses.

oxygen, the gas within air necessary for combustion of fuel, at times emitted in small quantities by a battery.

oxygenated gasoline, any fuel mixed with up to 15 % of ether, ethyl alcohol, or methyl alcohol which adds oxygen in liquid form to the fuel for cleaner emissions, and results in a weaker mixture which will prevent or remove carbon buildup especially in older engines.

oxygen sensor, a lambda sensor in the exhaust system that measures oxygen in the exhaust gas and sends a signal to the ECU for accurate control of the air-fuel ratio.

oxyhydrogen gas, a highly explosive mixture of oxygen and hydrogen gas generated within a lead acid battery during charging.

P

P, park, referring to a gear selector position on an automatic transmission.

P, parking area, sometimes having a requirement to pay a fee and/or having a time limit.

P, passenger vehicle, including cars, a tyre code prefix referring to the vehicle category for which it was designed.

P, people carrier, a car body style.

P, Petrol, a section of the POWER checks mnemonic.

P, Phuel, a section of the POWER checks mnemonic when referring to diesel.

P, Portugal, international vehicle distinguishing sign, see appendices.

P, Position, a phase of the PSL mnemonic.

P, power mode, referring to some automatic transmission, a switch to bias gear selection, *i.e.* it will accelerate to higher rev's before changing up.

P, the tyre speed rating code denoting a maximum design speed of 150 km/h (93 mph), moulded into the tyre sidewall.

P, UK, a driving licence category for mopeds.

P clip, a type of hose clip where the section resembles a letter P.

P metric, USA, a metric tyre size as used for all radial tyres; originally for passenger vehicle tyres, established in 1976.

P plate, a plate on a vehicle identifying the driver as holding a probationary licence only, as in several countries.

pa, power antenna, an electrically extending/retracting radio aerial.

pa, power assisted.

Pa, pascal, a unit of pressure, 1 Pa = 1 newton per square metre, 1 Pa = 1 n/m², 1 Pa = 0.01 bar.

PA, Panama, international vehicle distinguishing sign, see appendices.

pab, power assisted brakes.

pace car, safety car.

pace notes, a list of directions and hazards in a rallying roadbook.

pacing, the action of following other traffic at their speed.

package tray, USA, rear shelf.

packhorse bridge, an ancient bridge where the road surface ascends and descends significantly over a single stone arch, it may or may not be wide enough for a car to drive over.

packhorse route, an ancient route originally used by packhorses but which may be passable to 4x4 vehicles.

PACTS, Parliamentary Advisory Council for Transport Safety, UK.

pad, brake pad.

paddle, each of a pair of small buttons or toggle switches on the steering wheel for driver control of gear selection on many semiautomatic gear selector systems.

paddle gearshift, paddleshift.

paddleshift, a semiautomatic gearshift controlled by use of small toggle switches *i.e.* paddles on the steering wheel.

paddock, an area in which the competing cars are gathered before a race.

paddy wagon, USA, a police van.

PAG, power assisted gear selection.

pagoda roof, a car roof style having a low centre and raised sides.

pah, polyaromatic hydrocarbon.

PAI, personal accident insurance, additional insurance to hire car insurance for medical costs.

paint, a pigmented liquid applied to form a thin film and which then converts into a solid layer.

paint, the application of a liquid to a surface.

paint code, a code of letters and numbers defining the exact colour of each car bodywork, usually marked on a plate in the engine compartment.

painted channelization, a ghost island.

paintshop, a workshop or paint booth in which the various layers of primer and paint etc, are applied.

paint stick, a ball point pen that writes with quick drying paint for touching up bodywork.

paintwork, a painted surface.

PAK, Pakistan, international vehicle distinguishing sign, see appendices.

palladium, a white noble metal used as a catalyst in a catalytic converter.

pallet, a portable platform or tray, typically wooden, onto which loads are placed to enable fast loading and unloading of a lorry by fork lift truck, typically having a weight capacity of 1 tonne.

palm down thumb down, the position of either hand on the steering wheel in order to commence a J turn, either the left hand at the 5 o'clock position, or the right hand at the 7 o'clock position.

palming, a technique for turning the steering

wheel where the palm of 1 hand only is used against the face of the wheel to rotate the wheel, not as safe as other techniques but it permits rapid rotation of the wheel when manoeuvring at very slow speeds.

pan African highway, a planned route from Alexandria to Cape Town through East Africa, although the roads in Sudan and Ethiopia are unsurfaced and are passable only by 4x4 vehicles.

Panamericana Highway, the main north-south road from Barranquillita, Columbia, to Ushuaia, Tierra del Fuego, Argentina, along the west coast of South America, part of the Pan-American Highway.

Pan-American Highway, the route from Prudhoe Bay, Alaska, to Tierra del Fuego, Argentina, including the Alaska Highway, Pacific Coast Highway, Inter-American Highway, and Panamericana Highway, totalling 25,760 km (16,100 miles) although it has a 85 km (54 miles) break at the Darrian Gap on the Panama – Columbia border.

pancake engine, USA, a flat or boxer engine.

pancake engine, USA, radial engine, uncommon on road vehicles.

panda car, a police car painted white with some black panels.

panel, a part made from a flat sheet of material, *e.g.* a door skin or a door internal trim

panel beating, to hammer dents in damaged bodywork back to their original contour.

panel indicator, tell-tale, an illuminated colour coded symbol on the dashboard that gives information regarding the status or correct or incorrect function of circuits or systems or auxiliaries or devices, illuminating in blue, green, red, or yellow.

panel truck, USA, a small enclosed delivery van.

panel van, a van having a body constructed from pressed steel sheets, such that the cab and the load carrying area are without externally obvious division.

panel warning light, the illumination for a tell-tale symbol.

Panhard layout, Système Panhard.

Panhard rod, a transverse bar for lateral location of a rigid axle to the chassis, the rod is mounted at 1 end of the axle and extends to the chassis near the opposite end of the axle.

panic envelope, sealed instructions detailing the finish location of a rally, to be opened only if totally lost.

panic freeze, a driver condition on realising an impending collision ahead whereby the driver freezes hard on the footbrake only, instead of steering into an escape route and pulse braking if without ABS.

panic freeze, a driver condition in an automatic transmission vehicle when the accelerator is mistakenly pressed assuming it to be the brake, and panic causes the driver to press harder on the wrong pedal; a mistake

sometimes committed by an elderly driver which would be overcome by double footing.

panic stop, emergency stop.

panoramic mirror, a curved or segmented wide angle mirror positioned in place of the interior mirror to give a wider angle of view especially through the rear side windows.

panoramic windscreen, wraparound windscreen.

pantechnicon, a lorry in the form of a large box van having a low floor, typically used for furniture removals.

pantograph wiper, a windscreen wiper mechanism having additional linkage such that the blade maintains a constant usually vertical angle as it sweeps, typically on buses and coaches.

PAR, potential for accident reduction.

parabolic leaf, a type of leaf spring for a vehicle suspension system, using curved springs conforming to a specific mathematical shape.

parabolic reflector, a headlamp reflector having the shape of a parabola, an old style which has returned to fashion with the advent of CAD to eliminate dazzle.

parade lap, the warm-up lap directly before a race starts.

paraffin, an inflammable waxy substance.

paraffin oil, a liquid fuel used in older tractors, having a very low octane number of approximately 77, also used in gas turbine engines, for heating fuel, and as a solvent.

paraffin wax, paraffin in its solid form.

parallel diverge, an exit sliproad where the diverging lane commences with a full width auxiliary lane for a significant distance, typically where queueing on the slip road is expected.

parallel hybrid, a vehicle having both an ic engine and an electric motor(s) for motive power, switching between them to use either or both depending upon the situation and power requirements, but without an engine-driven generator to recharge the battery.

parallel import, the private import of a vehicle to the same specification as others available, because it can be purchased cheaper in another country.

parallel merge, an entry sliproad where the merging lane continues as an auxiliary lane for some distance before merging, typically where traffic is known to be heavy or the route is used by a high volume of lorries.

parallelogram door, a double hinged door.

parallelogram steering, a steering system comprising a steering gearbox on the offside and an idler box on the nearside, with a drop arm and idler arm respectively.

parallelogram suspension, double wishbone suspension.

parallel parking, to park a vehicle close and parallel to the roadside, typically in a space longitudinally between 2 other vehicles, entering the space using reverse gear for manoeuvrability.

parallel trailing link, a suspension system where each wheel is supported by a pair of trailing links such that the angles of camber, castor, and swivel axis, and the track width all remain constant as the suspension oscillates.

parallel twin, a 2 cylinder 4 stroke engine having parallel cylinders, pistons, and crankpins.

parameter identifier, part of a vehicle microprocessor control, the part that identifies the affected component or system.

parc à voitures, French, car park.

parcel shelf, rear shelf.

parc fermé, the secure area for scrutinising of rally and racing cars, or for their overnight parking with no servicing allowed.

parclo, USA, partial cloverleaf, any junction having less than a full permutation of grade separated links thereby restricting transfer from 1 highway to another.

park, referring to a gear selector position on an automatic transmission in which drive is uncoupled from the engine and the transmission is mechanically locked, normally selected before the driver exits a vehicle.

park, to bring a motor vehicle to stationary position and to leave it unattended by any person having lawful permission to drive that vehicle.

parkage, French, parking.

park and ride, system of car parking at the edge of a city with transfer buses to the city centre.

park condition of a vehicle, the situation when the vehicle is stationary and its engine is stopped and its movable components are in their normal position, (C&U).

park distance control, a system to enable safer reversing, using an ultrasonic emitter and detector to determine the distance from the rear of the vehicle to an unseen object and give an audible signal to the driver, developed by BMW.

parking abeam, a method of parking neatly alongside other cars by positioning such that the B pillars are exactly level regardless of vehicle length or the direction each are facing, typically used where spaces are not marked.

parking abreast, a style of parking such that the vehicles are facing in the same direction with the fronts level.

parking box, an area at the roadside delineated with a broken coloured line, on a red route a place where parking may be permitted with restrictions as signs display; see: red parking box, white parking box.

parking brake, a friction device with which to lock the wheels whenever stationary and before exiting a vehicle, usually operated by a hand lever but sometimes operated by foot, operating on the rear wheels of most vehicles usually by Bowden cable but by air on larger vehicles.

parking brake pedal, a pedal operated by the left foot which actuates the parking brake mechanism, typically on some larger cars having either automatic or manual transmission.

parking brake release lever, a hand lever with which to release a foot operated parking brake, typically located in the lower edge of the dashboard.

parking card, a single use card for which payment is made for parking, and on which the date and time of arrival at a parking place is irreversibly marked.

parking disc, a cardboard or plastic clock face on which a driver indicates the time of commencement of parking in a disc zone, and which is positioned visibly on the dashboard.

parking heater, night heater.

parking lamp, a lamp which is used to draw attention to the presence of a stationary vehicle, optional on vehicles less than 6 metres long and 2 metres wide, prohibited on larger vehicles, see position lamp, (C&U).

parking lights, originally named side lights, required for parking when illumination is mandatory, or to increase parking safety, they can typically be selected to just the left or right side only to conserve power by use of the direction indicator switch.

parking lock, a safety interlock whereby the gear selector cannot be moved from P with the engine stopped unless a release button is operated.

parking lot, USA, a ground level outdoor carpark.

parking meter, a coin operated timing device which measures the duration of paid time and indicates the expiry of the payment, invented by Carlton Magee in Oklahoma USA and in service on 16 July 1935, first used in UK on 10 July 1958.

parking space, a marked area where a vehicle may be parked.

parking ticket, a notice attached to a vehicle indicating a penalty is due for a parking offence.

Parkinsons disease, a medical condition that may prevent a person holding a driving licence due to insufficient muscular control.

park-neutral safety switch, start inhibitor switch.

park pilot, a system that will identify objects behind a vehicle by transmitting and receiving either ultrasound or infra red pulses, and signal an alarm to the driver.

parkway, a ring road around the outside of a city or urban area, typically landscaped and planted.

parkway, USA, a broad landscaped arterial highway not open to commercial vehicles.

part, a basic mechanical element or assembly, especially as listed in a parts catalogue of replaceable units.

part ex, part exchange.

part exchange, the purchase of a vehicle from a dealer for which another vehicle of lesser value is given as part payment.

part ex value, the worth of a car being used as part payment for another.

partial flow filter, bypass filter.

participant, the employee of an organisation who is learning advanced or defensive driving.

particle, a very small piece of metal, dirt, or impurity in the air, fuel, or oil of a vehicle.

particulate, any substance except water which is present in exhaust gas in a solid or liquid state, especially the carcinogenic fine black soot emitted from the exhaust of diesel engine vehicles.

particulate emission, the exhausting of solid particles of carbon, *i.e.* hydrocarbons which are not fully burned.

particulate emission limit, a legal restriction of the weight of particulate emissions exhausted from a vehicle measured in grams per kilometre, g/km.

particulate filter, a device in a diesel exhaust system which removes large particulates from exhaust gas to reduce pollution.

part load, operating an engine or system at any percentage below full load.

part out, USA, to break up a car for spares.

parts catalogue, a listing of all of the available spare parts.

part throttle, driving with the accelerator only partly depressed.

part time 4wd, a 4wd vehicle selectable between 2wd and 4wd without a centre differential in the transmission system; the vehicle should not be driven on dry tarmac or similar with 4wd selected.

part time signals, traffic signals which do not operate throughout 24 hours, typically they operate only during rush hour periods.

pas, power assisted steering.

pascal, a unit of pressure, Pa, 1 Pa = 1 newton per square metre, 1 Pa = 1 n/m^2, 1 Pa = 0.01 bar.

Pascal's law, the law of hydraulics which states that when a pressure is exerted on a confined liquid the pressure is transmitted undiminished; as applied to hydraulic brake systems.

pass, passenger.

pass, the action of driving past a vehicle that is stationary at the roadside; note, it is not possible to overtake a stationary vehicle.

pass, the highest point on a road as it crosses a col between 2 hills as the road continues from 1 valley to another.

pass, to successfully complete a driving test.

passable, an optimistic belief when a surface condition exists that will make driving difficult or dangerous, *e.g.* deep snow, deep mud, or soft sand, etc. but which may be overcome by equipment or technique.

passage, a small hole or gallery in an assembly or casting for the flow of a fluid.

passage control, a usually unmanned location having a code board in a road rally.

passenger, an occupant of a vehicle other than the driver or rider in control.

passenger air bag cutoff switch, a switch that can manually be set in the on or off position by turning the ignition key in the switch which is typically located in the centre console; it should always be switched on except when using a rearward facing child safety seat although for safety this seat position is not recommended.

passenger car, a motor vehicle constructed or adapted for the carriage of passengers and is not a goods vehicle; having no more than 8 seats in addition to the drivers, has 4 or more wheels, has a maximum design speed exceeding 25 km/k (16 mph) and a maximum laden weight not exceeding 3.5 tonnes (RTA).

passenger car combination, a passenger car drawing a trailer.

passenger carrying vehicle, a bus used for carrying passengers, or other vehicle except a taxi or tram.

passenger car unit, a quantifying system that identifies the capacity of a road in terms of volume of traffic by considering all vehicles in terms of cars; *i.e.* cars and light vans = 1.0 unit, medium goods vehicles = 1.5 units, buses and coaches = 2.0 units, heavy goods vehicles = 2.3 units, motorcycles = 0.4 unit, bicycle = 0.2 unit.

passenger car wheel, a 1 piece rim and disc made from alloy or pressed sheet steel, and designed for tubeless tyres.

passenger cell, the structure enclosing the passenger compartment which is designed to resist deformation by the force of a collision, thereby protecting the occupants.

passenger compartment, the saloon or cabin.

passenger road train, a bus drawing a trailer.

passenger service vehicle, a bus used for carrying passengers for hire or reward, or other vehicle except a taxi used for carrying passengers for hire or reward at separate fares in the course of a business.

passenger side, nearside.

passenger vehicle, a vehicle constructed solely for the carriage of passengers and their effects, (C&U).

passenger window lock-out switch, a drivers control switch which disables the passenger and rear windows from being operated by anyone except the driver.

passing beam, the dipped beam, a lamp used to illuminate the road ahead of the vehicle without causing undue dazzle or discomfort to oncoming drivers and other road-users, (C&U).

passing lane, USA, the overtaking lane, the offside lane, lane 1.

passing place, a small area at the side of a single track road where a vehicle can move off the road in order for an oncoming or following vehicle to pass.

passive breath test, a test conducted using a

small device held near the subjects mouth to detect the presence of alcohol without measuring quantity, used as an initial test in some countries before a breath screening test or an evidential breath test.

passive collision, a collision after which a driver makes a statement that includes "I was hit by …".

passive rear wheel steering, a system whereby the rear suspension of a vehicle permits the rear wheels to change steering angle slightly whilst subject to centrifugal force generated when cornering at speed.

passive restraint, any device which restricts the movement of a person during a collision and which operates without occupant input, *e.g.* an air bag.

passive safety equipment, safety equipment which functions continuously, *e.g.* door beams or laminated glass.

passive safety measure, see: secondary safety measure.

pass plus, a scheme for giving additional training to a person who has just passed a learner driving test.

path, the line taken by a vehicle along a road.

patience, the art of waiting for a safe opportunity to move in traffic without becoming upset or aggressive.

patrol car, a police car used in patrolling roads.

patrolette, a female roadside repair mechanic employed by a breakdown recovery organisation.

patrol wagon, USA, a police van for transporting prisoners.

pattern panel, a body panel made other than by the original manufacturer, typically because the originals have become discontinued.

paved, an area having a surface suitable for frequent all-weather use by pedestrian or vehicular traffic.

pavement, a road surface especially if made from hand-laid wooden blocks, cobbles, rectangular stones, Belgian pavé, but also from asphalt or concrete etc.

pavement, footway, a raised area along the side of a road for use by pedestrians.

pavement, USA, a firm road surface, a carriageway.

pavement crossing, a place where a private entrance from the road to property crosses a roadside footway, often characterised by an angled or lowered kerb.

pavement markings, USA, road markings.

pawl, an arm pivoted so its free end may fit into a detent or slot to hold that part stationary.

pay and display zone, an area where parking is permitted in marked places providing a pre-paid ticket is displayed in the parked vehicle.

payload, the maximum weight of goods a vehicle can legally transport, the mathematical figure when the kerbweight is subtracted from the MVW.

payload rating, USA, the maximum allowable weight, including occupants, equipment and cargo a truck can transport as determined by the manufacturer by subtracting curb weight from GVWR.

pb, power brakes.

pbc, polybutylcuprisol, a copper based grease typically used for slow moving parts, having excellent corrosion and high temperature resistance.

PC, passage control, a checkpoint in road rally navigation.

PC, USA, passenger car.

pcb, printed circuit board.

pcd, pitch circle diameter.

PCEA, UK, Police and Criminal Evidence Act 1984.

PCM, USA, power control module, ECU.

PCN, Penalty Charge Notice.

PCO, Parking Control Officer.

PCO, UK, Public Carriage Office.

PCP, personal contract purchase.

pcu, passenger car unit.

pcv, positive crankcase ventilation.

PCV, passenger carrying vehicle.

PD, an oil approved for use by CCMC in a passenger car having a diesel engine.

pd, pump düse.

pdc, park distance control.

pdi, petrol direct injection.

PDI, Police Driving Instructor.

PDI, prospective driving instructor.

pdq, pretty damn quick/pretty darned quick.

PE, Peru, international vehicle distinguishing sign, see appendices.

péage, French, a toll road.

peak hour, rush hour, the time of the most intense traffic, typically a duration up to 3 hours each morning and each afternoon.

peak power, the maximum power available when all the ideal conditions are met.

peak revs, the redline engine speed.

peaky, an engine quality whereby it only gives high power at high revs.

PEB, personal effects and baggage insurance, additional insurance to hire car insurance for loss of personal effects.

pedal, any lever operated by the foot.

pedal box, the space around the pedals in the drivers footwell.

pedal clearance, the distance between the pedal and the floor when the pedal is fully depressed.

pedal cycle, any bicycle, tandem, tricycle, or toy cycle, ridden on the carriageway and propelled by the riders legs, including bicycles and tricycles with battery assistance where the maximum design speed does not exceed 15 mph (25 km/h).

pedal freeplay, the distance a pedal moves before the system starts to operate.

pedal pulsation, a vibrational feedback to the driver through the brake pedal when the ABS is functioning.

pedal pulsation, vibration related to wheel speed felt through the brake pedal due to an out of true brake disc.

pedal to the metal, to speed up.

pedal travel, the total length of movement of a pedal.

pedestrian, a person standing, walking, or running etc, a child riding a toy cycle on a footway, a person pushing a bicycle, pushing or pulling a motor vehicle or cart etc, operating a pedestrian controlled vehicle, leading or herding animals, and occupants of prams and wheelchairs.

pedestrian controlled vehicle, a motor vehicle which is controlled by a pedestrian and is not constructed or adapted for use or used for the carriage of a driver or passenger, (C&U), *e.g.* some mowing machines or road rollers, etc.

pedestrian crossing, a footpath that crosses a road at a designated place, see: controlled, pelican, puffin, signal, staggered, toucan, zebra.

pedestrian crosswalk, crosswalk.

pedestrianised area, a former road that is prohibited to vehicular traffic, sometimes with exceptions.

pedestrian precinct, an area of town centre restricted to pedestrians.

pedestrian safety barrier, railings positioned between the road and the footway to cause physical separation between pedestrians and vehicles.

pedestrian underpass, a pedestrian subway, where a footpath crosses beneath a road.

pedestrian zone, a pedestrianised area, a road where pedestrians have priority and where all vehicles are prohibited, sometimes with exceptions.

pedway, USA, a pedestrian footway in an urban area.

PED XING, USA, pedestrian crossing.

peel off, CB jargon, to leave a motorway.

PEF, propane / hexane equivalency factor.

PE headlamp, a headlamp having a polyellipsoidal reflector.

Peking to Paris, an endurance race over 17,000 km, (10,625 miles) first run in 1907.

pel, pulley end left.

pelican crossing, a signal controlled crossing enabling pedestrians to cross a road, an acronym from pedestrian light controlled.

penalty charge notice, official notification of a parking offence.

pencil glowplug, sheathed glowplug.

pendulum effect, the effect of a continued oscillation of a fishtail caused by overcorrecting a power induced rear wheel skid.

pendulum turn, a rallying technique very similar to a Scandinavian flick; approaching a bend the car is deliberately unsettled by brake-steer overlap to cause oversteer and an increasing fishtail which is encouraged by appropriate steering until it develops into the required rear wheel skid to enable the bend to

be taken at maximum speed.

penetrating oil, a very thin oil in a solvent designed to rapidly permeate through rust to assist with loosening corroded parts.

peninsula, USA, a buildout on 1 side of the road only.

pent crown piston, a piston having an angular shaped crown to increase the swirl of the mixture to improve combustion.

people carrier, a cross between an estate car and a minibus, typically carrying 8 persons in comfort.

per, pulley end right.

perceive, to observe and interpret visual and other information.

perception distance, the distance a vehicle travels whilst a driver is analysing what is seen and before the decision is made on what action to take, *i.e.* the thinking distance before deciding to brake; at 100 km/h it will typically be at least 25 metres (at 60 mph at least 60 feet).

perception point, the first point at which a driver actually perceived that a condition exists that may give rise to an accident situation.

perception reaction distance, the distance travelled by a vehicle whilst the driver having seen a situation ahead is deciding which action to take, plus the distance travelled whilst physically reacting, *i.e.* the thinking distance plus the physical reaction distance; at 100 km/h it will typically be at least 28 metres (at 60 mph at least 70 feet).

perception reaction time, the interval between a drivers detection of a target stimulus or event and the initiation of a vehicle control movement in response to the stimulus or event, *i.e.* the thinking time plus the physical reaction time, typically at least 0.8 second for an alert healthy driver.

perception time, the time taken for a driver to analyse a hazard and decide to react, the normal minimum is 0.7 second for an alert healthy driver.

perceptive ability, the capacity to interpret visual information relative to the past experience of a driver.

perceptive overload, a driving situation where numerous events are occurring simultaneously or in rapid succession such that the driver is unable to assess the degree of risk of each event so ignores most; the condition is resolved by speed reduction.

perceptual safety, any safety measures that increase perceptibility, including vehicle and roadside lighting equipment, acoustic warning devices, and signing; a branch of primary safety.

performance, usually suggesting high acceleration performance, but it can also refer to braking performance or steering performance, in all cases high or low.

performance tuning, the modification or replacement of parts to improve the power and/

or torque from the engine, or improve the roadholding of the suspension, etc, to improve upon the original factory specifications.

performance tyre, a tyre designed to give high friction and greater feedback from the road surface, but often having a shorter life and/or lower level of comfort.

Perimeter, the beltway encircling Atlanta, Georgia.

period of operation, the interval between the start and finish times when a system is functioning, *e.g.* the hours and/or days when a part-time bus lane is restricted to use by buses only.

peripheral vision, the wide angle view out of the corner of a drivers eye, usually low in detail but valuable in recognising movement.

Périphérique, the Boulevarde Périphérique, the motorway inner ringroad around the centre of Paris, having a circumferential length of 36 km (22 miles), but not a true boulevard.

perm, permanent 4wd, as opposed to part time 4wd.

permanent 4wd, a vehicle having 3 differentials, specifically a centre differential permitting front and rear axles to turn at differing speeds when cornering, facilitating indefinite use on a dry firm surface without axle windup.

permanent hazard, any hazard marked by a hazard warning sign and which is permanent at that location, *e.g.* a junction, bend, or steep hill, but not a slippery road or wild animals.

permissive line, a longitudinal road marking consisting of a continuous line with a broken line alongside, which permits traffic originating from the side having the broken line to cross the lines but prohibits crossing by traffic from the side having the continuous line; see also: prohibitory.

permissive route, a route where the owner has indicated it may be used by a given class of traveller until further notice.

permit, a document issued to a learner driver in Australia, and some other countries whilst learning to drive, the driving licence being issued on passing a road test.

permitted makeup, the amount of time which can be regained on a section in road rally navigation to reduce lateness by a crew, using the ³/₄ rule.

personal, CB jargon, your name.

personal contract purchase, a method of purchasing a vehicle, typically through a finance deal linked to the manufacturer, the monthly payments may be lower than using other financial methods but the deal will have mileage and other condition penalties that can result in a negative equity situation at the end of the period.

personalised numberplate, a distinctive series of letters and numbers where the characters may appear to form a word, see also: cherished, vanity.

personal leasing, a method of financing the use of a vehicle, basically a long term rental subject to mileage and other condition restrictions; the vehicle remains always the property of the leasing company.

personal loan, a means of raising money from an independent source in order to finance the purchase of a vehicle, the simplest form of borrowing money.

personal protection, a central locking feature that operates when a car first reaches 30 km/h (20 mph), developed by Chrysler.

personnel carrier, an armoured military vehicle for transporting troops.

PES headlamp, polyellipsoidal system headlamp.

petal junction, braid junction.

pet-regs, the regulations applying to the transport of petroleum products.

petroil, lubricated fuel, 2 stroke petrol containing 4 % lubricating oil.

petrol, a liquid hydrocarbon fuel, refined petroleum, a fraction of crude oil having specific detergent, lubricant, and antiknock properties.

petrol coupon, a voucher issued by the Government entitling the holder to purchase a specific amount of fuel in times of rationing, *e.g.* during WWII and some other fuel crisis occasions.

petrol direct injection, a petrol engine in which the fuel is injected directly into the cylinder instead of injecting into the manifold.

petrol engine, an internal combustion engine that consumes a mixture of air and petrol vapour as fuel.

petroleum, crude oil, a complex liquid hydrocarbon comprising fuels, petrochemicals, and lubricants.

petroleum ether, a volatile liquid distilled from petroleum, consisting of a mixture of hydrocarbons.

petroleum jelly, a translucent solid mixture of hydrocarbons used as a lubricant, as a protective coating on battery terminals, and as an ointment.

petroleum spirit, petrol, a distilled fraction of refined petroleum.

petrolhead, a person having an occupation and significant knowledge or principal leisure pursuit in the field of motoring, motorsport, or vehicles, etc.

petroliana, memorabilia related to vehicle fuels and filling stations.

petrolic, relating to petroleum or petrol.

petrol pump, a machine which dispenses measured quantities of petrol or other fuels, invented by Sylvanus F Bowser in 1885, and an improved version for motor spirit in 1905.

petrol station, filling station.

petrol tank, a vessel for the storage of fuel in a vehicle, it may be metal or plastic.

petrol tanker, a specially constructed lorry for the transport of fuel.

pferdestärke, German, metric horsepower, abbreviated to PS; 1 PS = 75 kg.m/s, 1 PS = 0.75 kW, 1 PS = 0.98632 imperial horsepower.

pfi, port fuel injection.

phaeton, USA, a large luxury convertible touring car having a very large trunk or boot.

phantom diagram, a drawing or picture of a vehicle or assembly in which the internal parts are shown in detail, and the surrounding structure *e.g.* gearbox casing or bodywork is drawn as if transparent; see also: exploded, sectional.

phantom jam, a traffic holdup on a motorway caused only by high density traffic bunching, braking, causing others to brake more, others then stopping, typically resulting in a Mexican wave which may persist at a location for several hours.

phencyclidine, a drug that should not be used by drivers, often contained in sleeping pills.

phf, peak hour flow.

Phillips, a type of screwdriver with a 4 point cross forged into the tip with a specific axial angle at the centre, or a corresponding screw head.

p/hood, power hood.

phosphate, a coating sometimes applied to steel to prevent rusting.

phosphor bronze, an alloy of phosphorous, copper, and tin, a good electrical conductor with physical strength, used for many rigid electrical parts.

phosphorous oxide, a metallic compound commonly used in Australia and New Zealand in LRP and in lead replacement additives to protect valve seats from regression.

photocard, a driving licence of a similar size to a credit card and which displays the holders photograph.

photochemical smog, smog caused by hydrocarbons and nitrogen oxides reacting in the atmosphere, usually in bright sunlight under an inversion layer where part of the atmosphere is trapped causing eye and lung irritations.

physical intervention technique, the method used by USA police for halting the progress of a violator by using the fishtail technique.

physical overload, a situation generated by poor habits such that a driver attempts to use too many controls simultaneously or in rapid succession, caused by poor planning or bad technique, *e.g.* progressive gear changing when block changing is suited.

physical reaction time, the actual time taken by a driver for muscular control, *i.e.* after making a decision to operate a control and before starting to move the control, *e.g.* after deciding to brake, the time taken to lift the foot from the accelerator, move the foot sideways, and start to depress the footbrake.

physiological glare, the measurable reduction in a drivers ability to see caused by sources of glare; see also psychological, veiling.

PI-3, a booklet entitled "How to Permanently Import a Vehicle into UK", published by the DTLR.

PIA, personal injury accident.

PIA, Petroleum Industry Association, UK.

PIARC, Permanent International Association of Roads Congress, Paris.

pickup, a light goods vehicle having a load carrying area with fixed low sides and an open bed.

pickup camper, USA, a demountable mobile home designed to be transported on the bed of a dual wheel pickup truck.

pid, parameter identifier.

PIDS, a tyre pressure and temperature monitoring system, developed by Porsche.

piggyback, road trailers transported on special railway wagons.

piggyback, to carry a vehicle or trailer on the bed of a lorry or trailer.

pigtail, a short length of wire or several together permanently attached to a component, and typically having a connector at the loose end.

pig trailer, a trailer with a fixed front axle having Ackermann 2 point steering.

Pikes Peak, a 12.4 mile (20 km) hill climb in Colorado USA, comprising the top 4,918 feet (1,500 m) of the mountain to the summit at 14,147 feet (4,312 m), having a course record of approximately 11 minutes.

pile up, a crash involving a large number of vehicles.

piling, the buildup of metal on 1 of the contact breaker points, the result of erosion pitting in the other point.

pillar, a structural support for the roof between the windows.

pillarbox window, each of several very small windows resulting in poor visibility, as in some vehicles with wide roof pillars and some military vehicles with small windows of armoured glass; named from an exaggeration of looking out from a pillar box (mail box).

pillar jack, tower jack.

pillar lamp, a courtesy lamp mounted on a B or C pillar.

pillarless coupé , a coupé without a B pillar such that the door windows seal against the rear side windows.

pillarless doors, doors on the sides of a car such that behind the front door there is no B pillar, and the rear door is hinged suicide style, both latching at the roof and floor.

pillion, a passenger seat on a motorcycle behind the rider.

pillion passenger, a passenger riding on the pillion seat on a motorcycle.

pilot bearing, the small bearing within the end of the crankshaft that carries the end of the gearbox input shaft.

pilot car, a vehicle that escorts an oversize load.

pilot car, a vehicle that leads others through a

road construction or resurfacing area to enforce a speed limit, often marked Follow Me.

pilot injection, a system of injecting a small amount of fuel into the cylinder of a diesel engine to create a soft combustion before the remainder of the fuel is injected, to reduce noise levels.

pilot shaft, a dummy shaft used as a tool to align parts, *e.g.* to centralise a clutch plate on reassembly.

pilot vehicle, pilot car.

pin, kingpin.

pinchpoint, a physical feature created on both sides of a carriageway where a pair of buildouts have been constructed directly opposite each other as part of a traffic calming scheme to narrow the road, sometimes forming a crossing point for pedestrians.

ping, USA, pinking.

Pininfarina, Pinin Farina, a notable car body stylist for Ferrari, Alfa Romeo, and others.

pinion gear, any small gear that meshes with a larger gear creating a ratio reduction, either parallel or at 90°, *e.g.* mating with a crownwheel where the propeller shaft meets the rear axle.

pinking, predetonation within the cylinder, sometimes caused by carbon buildup, wrong ignition timing, or lugging, it will eventually damage the big end bearings.

pinstriping, coachlining.

pintaux nozzle, a 2 stage diesel injection nozzle which gives a small injection of fuel to start slow combustion before the main charge, to reduce diesel clatter.

pintle hook, a towing coupling in the form a G such that the top jaw closes to secure the trailer pintle ring, commonly used on military vehicles.

pintle pin, a towing coupling in the form of a vertical steel pin, typically used on light commercial vehicles.

pintle ring, a trailer coupling device in the form of a horizontal ring, typically on military and commercial trailers.

piping, a rubber or plastic flat strip with a tubular structure along 1 edge for aesthetic purposes and vibration reduction between bodywork joints on a vehicle having bolt on wings etc.

pip pin, a positive locking quick release pin, for retaining engine covers.

pirate fuel, rebated or untaxed fuel which is processed with acid to remove the identification colouring then offered for sale for use in road vehicles.

pirate instructor, a person illegally offering driving instruction when unlicenced and unqualified.

piston, in a brake cylinder or hydraulic jack a disc or closed tubular part that converts motion to pressure or pressure to motion to/from the actuating system.

piston, in an engine, a disc or closed tubular part that closely fits within the cylinder and which transmits motion to and from the crankshaft via the connecting rod; it is driven alternately by the expansion of burning gases and by the motion of the crankshaft.

piston bore, bore.

piston clearance, the distance between the piston skirt and the cylinder wall.

piston crown, the top surface of the piston closing the combustion chamber.

piston displacement, the displacement of 1 piston as it moves from bdc to tdc, equal to the area of the bore multiplied by the length of the stroke, *i.e.* π multiplied by $^1/_2$ the cylinder diameter squared; $(0.5 \pi d)^2 \times l$ for each cylinder.

piston engine, an internal or external combustion engine using reciprocating pistons.

pistonhead, a person who admires or enjoys driving fast cars.

piston head, piston crown.

piston pin, USA, gudgeon pin.

piston ring, each of several rings fitted into groves around the piston, usually made of machined cast iron, the upper rings are to seal the compressed gases in the combustion chamber, the lower rings prevent excessive oil reaching the combustion chamber.

piston ring compressor, a tool that holds the piston rings in their relative positions to facilitate easy installation of each piston into the cylinder bore.

piston ring groove, a groove around the sides of a piston between each land, in which a piston ring is located.

piston rod, connecting rod.

piston skirt, the lower edges of a piston below the pin that guide its movement within the cylinder.

piston slap, a hollow muffled bell type of sound caused by the piston skirt hitting the cylinder wall.

piston speed, the total distance travelled by a piston in a given time, commonly up to 25 m/s (80 feet/second).

pit, originally a trench at the side of a race circuit for repairing beneath a racing car, developed into a garage area for racing cars.

pit, to leave a racing circuit and stop at the pit for tyres, fuel, or maintenance.

PIT, Physical Intervention Technique.

PIT, Precision Immobilization Technique.

PIT, Pursuit Intervention Technique.

pit board, a framework displaying 4 rows of characters on which the pit crew to give information to a racing driver.

pitch, a car parking space.

pitch, a parking place for a caravan or trailer.

pitch, the effect of inertia causing the front of the vehicle to rise whilst accelerating; opposite: dive.

pitch circle diameter, the diameter of a circle around which the wheel studs or bolts are located.

205

pitch sensor, an instrument that measures imbalance between front and rear suspension with regard to apparent weight transfer during braking and acceleration.

pit garage, each of a series of contiguous buildings, in which each racing car is given final preparation for racing.

pit lane, the lane into, through, and out of the pit area on a racing circuit.

pitot tube, a tube for measuring pressure and velocity of a fluid flow, typically in a cvt.

pits, originally a trench at the side of a race circuit for repairing beneath a racing car, developed into a garage area for racing cars.

pit stop, a brief halt during a race for fuel, tyre change, or other brief repairs.

pit stop, a brief halt during a road journey for refreshments or fuel.

pitting, the electrical erosion of metal from 1 of the contact breaker points, resulting in piling on the other point.

pit wall, an elevated long narrow platform between the pit lane and the racing circuit used by some of the racing team to display information to a driver, originally for timing.

pivot, a pin or shaft around which another part rotates.

pivot axis, swivel axis.

pivot pin, kingpin.

PL, parking lock.

PL, Poland, international vehicle distinguishing sign, see appendices.

plain bearing, a friction bearing in the form of a short cylinder.

plain disc wheel, a wheel without any holes or slots in the disc.

plain wrapper, CB jargon, an unmarked police car.

planetary differential, a set of planetary gears used in a centre differential in a 4x4 vehicle, and which is designed to produce asymmetric torque distribution at fixed percentages between the front and rear axles.

planetary gears, gears within a gear train consisting of a central sun gear surrounded by 2 or more planet pinions and an outer ring gear, such that the planet gears centre follows a circular path on a revolving carrier around a centre different from their own, used in automatic transmissions, differentials and transfer boxes.

planetary gear train, an assembly of meshed gears consisting of a central sun gear and an outer ring gear having teeth on its internal face, and 2 or more intermediate planet pinions on a revolving carrier.

planetary transmission, an epicyclic gearbox of planetary gears.

planet carrier, a spider or web style disc which supports the planet gears and transmits drive through the transmission.

planing, the action of the tyres on the surface when driving across a wet, soft, or corrugated surface at a reasonably high speed such that the tyres skim or float over the surface; see: aqua, sand.

plank road, a road built from wooden planks for crossing sand dunes where a conventional road was formerly impossible to build, and which could be lifted to the surface again after being covered by blowing sand.

planning, the ability to act early when approaching hazards, avoiding late signalling, late changes of position, unnecessary braking, or unnecessary gearchanges, etc, and making good progress in traffic.

plant, construction and industrial vehicles which may sometimes use or cross public roads.

plasmatron, an experimental fuel preparation unit that turns a fuel into a very hot gas before combustion to increase burning efficiency, increase power, and reduce pollution.

plastic pig, a 3 wheeler car with a fibreglass body, common in the 1960s.

plastic pulley, a timing belt tensioner pulley made from plastic instead of metal, but unable to dissipate bearing heat and having a life only equal to that of the belt.

plate, a vehicle certification plate detailing the maximum gross weight, maximum train weight, gross axle weights, etc.

plate, an electrode in a battery.

plate, registration plate.

plated, a vehicle or trailer that is carrying a valid certification plate.

plated, electroplated, a thin layer of a metal deposited on another by electrolysis, usually on steel to prevent rusting.

platform, chassis, the floorpan of the car, often including the suspension.

platform frame, a structural floorpan where significant body strength is in the floor.

platform road train, a vehicle drawing a loaded trailing dolly.

platform tractor, an agricultural tractor having a reasonably flat floor but no cab.

platinum, a metallic element, an excellent conductor of heat, originally used for hot tube ignition, now sometimes used as the core or tip in a sparkplug, as a catalyst in an exhaust cat, and in a fuel cell.

platoon, a collective noun for a grouping of general traffic especially when accelerating together from traffic signals; also: bunch, clot, cluster.

play, free play.

play street, a road in a residential area which is restricted from use by non-residents of that road, and in which children at play have priority over vehicles.

plenum, an air chamber supplying either the engine or the saloon, but never combined.

PLG, private and light goods.

plies, the reinforcing members of a tyre composed of layers of cord fabric and rubber that provide the strength to support a load and resist deflection.

plipper, an electronic key fob that uses a radio signal to remotely lock or unlock a vehicle, also operating the immobiliser, and in some cases closing windows.

plonk, a quality of an engine in pulling smoothly from low revs.

plot and bash, any type of road rally in which the clues have to be plotted on the move and arrival registered at the next checkpoint within the time allowed to avoid penalties, typically carrying more than 1 navigator per crew.

plotlight, a navigators map light with calibrated base plates.

plough, snowplough.

plowing, USA, understeering.

PLP, personal lease product.

plug, to connect wire terminals to electrical circuits.

plug, core plug.

plug, sparkplug.

plug, a strip of foam rubber inserted with adhesive through a hole in a tyre tread as the first stage of a puncture repair before a patch is applied to the inside.

plug, a vehicle driven at a moderate speed in lane 2 when lane 1 is clear, hence causing congestion behind.

plug check, the removal and visual inspection of the portion of a sparkplug within the combustion chamber for surface deposits and colour to assess mixture, ignition and other defects, performed directly after climbing a long hill at high power then stopping the engine and coasting to a halt, or the equivalent on a dynamometer.

plug gap, sparkplug gap.

plug lead, sparkplug lead, a high voltage cable from the distributor to the sparkplug.

plug patch, a strip of special foam rubber with which to quickly effect a temporary repair to a puncture in a tubeless tyre, by pushing half of it through the hole and bonding with adhesive.

plug repair, to quickly effect a temporary repair to a puncture caused by a nail or similar in a tubeless tyre, by pushing a plug through the hole and bonding with adhesive.

plug temperature, the mean temperature of a sparkplug throughout the 4 cycles, typically 750 °C to 850 °C at full power.

plunger principle, an ABS control system using a plunger pump to give a high degree of hydraulic pressure modulation at all pressures.

plunger pump, a reciprocating hydraulic pump in a ported chamber used in many ABS systems.

plush, a fabric used for vehicle seats being a warp pile fabric with a silk or wool pile longer than that of velvet.

plus sizing, an option allowing the customising of vehicles by mounting low profile tyres on wider rims, or on rims of greater diameter to maintain the original rolling diameter, usually enhancing handling and stability.

ply, each layer of cords within the carcass of a tyre.

ply rating, a tyre index system originally based upon the actual number of plies but now used to denote the load rating or load index of a tyre.

pm, particulate matter.

P-MAC, Primary MAC, a certificate issued to the first vehicle of a series manufactured.

PMD, post mounted delineator.

P-metric, USA, a metric tyre size as used for all radial tyres; originally for passenger vehicle tyres, devised in 1976.

pn, part number.

PN, prohibition notice.

PNEG, Police National Escort Group.

pneumatic, pertaining to air, especially at pressure.

pneumatic suspension, air suspension.

pneumatic trail, the horizontal distance between the vertical line through the centre of a wheel and the centre of a tyre contact patch, at its greatest whilst suffering rollover whilst cornering.

pneumatic tyre, a tyre together with the wheel upon which it is mounted which forms a continuous closed chamber inflated to a pressure substantially exceeding atmospheric pressure when the tyre is in the condition in which it is normally used, is capable of being inflated or deflated without removal from the wheel or vehicle, and is such that when it is deflated and subject to a normal load, the sides of the tyre collapse,(C&U).

pneumocyclic, a semiautomatic gear selector system having a miniature open gate that is linked to the gearbox by pneumatic tubes where the gears are selected by pneumatic actuators; the system also incorporates a torque converter.

PNG, Papua New Guinea, international vehicle distinguishing sign, see appendices.

PNR, private non-residential parking.

pocket, turning pocket.

pocket rocket, a small but powerful car.

pod, a device to hold 1 or more instruments mounted on top of the dashboard.

podium, a staging raised at 3 levels where the winning racing driver and runners up stand to receive their trophies.

POI, point of impact.

point and squirt, a vehicle having automatic transmission, *i.e.* it only needs steering and power.

point and squirt, to steer whilst accelerating, typically referring to directional stability at speed.

point duty, the work of a police officer or traffic warden at a junction manually controlling traffic with arm signals.

point of no escape, the point at which a driver recognises that a collision is inevitable.

points, contact breaker points.

points gap, the exact distance between the contact breaker points when they are fully open, typically 0.4 mm (15 thou).

poison the cat, poisoning the catalytic converter, to use leaded fuel in an unleaded system such that the catalytic converter becomes coated internally with lead and can no-longer function.

poke, acceleration performance.

polarity, the direction of current flow in an electrical component.

pole, either of the positive or negative terminals of a battery.

pole, the first position on a racetrack starting grid.

police cruiser, USA, police car.

pollen filter, a very fine filter with which to remove dust and microscopic particles from air passing through it, typically preventing all particles exceeding 3 microns from entering the saloon.

pollutant, any substance emitted from a vehicle that is not a natural component of the environment in that place or concentration.

pollute, to cause the contamination of the environment by any unnatural substance.

polycarbonate, a plastic often used instead of glass for headlamp covers.

polyellipsoidal headlamp, a headlamp having a reflector divided into several sectors each of which conforms to that specific mathematical ellipsoidal shape.

polyellipsoidal system headlamp, a design of headlamp having a small reflector and projector optics incorporating a shield to define the cutoff.

polyester resin, a 2 part resin, sometimes liquid, paste, or putty, requiring an activator to cause it to harden, usually used with fibreglass for toughness.

polyethylene, a tough plastic from which some vehicle parts are moulded.

polyglycol, a liquid commonly used for brake fluid; it is very hygroscopic.

polygrooved belt, polygrooved V belt.

polygrooved V belt, a low wide drive belt with many small V ribs across its width, it transmits power by friction between many V ribs and the pulley and can also drive with its outer face, it is more effective and has a longer life than a V belt, typically driving the cooling fan, alternator, water pump, power steering, ac compressor, etc.

polytetrafluoroethylene, the slipperiest solid material known, used as a tape for some hose joints and as a powder in some oils and greases.

polyurethane, a plastic used to make bushings for suspension and other parts.

poly V belt, polygrooved V belt, V ribbed belt.

pontoon bridge, a bridge whereby the road surface is carried on floating supports.

pool car, a car owned by an organisation for use by its staff for business purposes.

poor fuel economy, excessive fuel consumption caused by the driving style of the driver, the vehicle, or unfavourable operating conditions.

popback, USA, backfire.

popper, a lift the dot fastener.

poppet valve, the standard valve used in modern internal combustion engines, having a circular head and seat, and a long stem.

pop rivets, a rivet which is placed and compressed from the same side, permitting riveting to closed sections *e.g.* to a tube.

pop the clutch, to let the clutch in very quickly, typically by sidestepping.

pop top, a section of vehicle roof that raises vertically or at an angle, typically to extend the accommodation in a small mobile home.

pop up headlamps, headlamps that retract within the bodywork when not in use, usually to improve aerodynamics on some sports cars.

pop up tacho, a tachograph where the charts are inserted or removed via a pop-up mechanism in the top of the dashboard.

porpoising, an uncomfortable and dangerous ride condition caused by worn dampers when the front and/or rear suspension pitch and dive alternately, *i.e.* to continually oscillate or bounce.

Porsche, Professor Ferdinand Porsche, designer of many vehicles including the VW Beetle in 1935, also vehicles for Mercedes and Auto Union.

Porsche Stability Management, a system that supervises the traction control, brake balance, ABS, and ECU, developed by Porsche.

port, the valve seat and the inlet or exhaust passage through the cylinder head, to/from a cylinder.

port bar, a guide or bridge vertically across the exhaust port of some 2 stroke engines to ensure the piston rings do not become trapped.

port fuel injection, multipoint fuel injection.

porthole window, a circular window, sometimes in the rear sides of a vehicle.

position for vision, a principle of advanced driving in which the driver varies the lateral position of the vehicle on the road to maximise forward vision.

position lamp, position marker lamp.

position lights, position marker lamps.

position marker lamp, each of a series of lamps used to indicate the presence and the width of the vehicle when viewed from the front or rear, and allow its actual or potential direction of travel to be recognised, (C&U); formerly named side lights or parking lights.

position speed look, a specific section in a hazard approach procedure.

positive, a numerical value greater than zero, as applied to measurements of distance, angle, speed, acceleration, voltage, etc.

positive camber, a suspension design in which wheels on the opposite ends of the same axle are angled so their tops are further apart than the track width.

positive castor, the normal steering geometry such that the line extending the steering pivot axis creating a longitudinal angle tilts towards the front at the lower steering pivot and meets the road surface ahead of a vertical line through the wheel centre which results in stable self centring steering; if the angle is reduced or if both sides are not equal it will cause straight line instability and steering pull.

positive clutch, a dog clutch.

positive crankcase ventilation, a system in which the inlet manifold vacuum draws crankcase vapours and blowby gases into the cylinder to be burned to reduce pollution.

positive electrode, anode, positive plate, positive terminal, the terminal of a battery or alternator etc. that has a deficit of electrons.

positive offset, a condition in steering geometry in which the transverse angle of the steering pivot axis cuts the wheel vertical centreline below ground level.

positive offset, a condition in wheel geometry in which the mounting face of the wheel is outboard of the rim centreline.

positive scrub radius, the lateral distance at ground level between a vertical line through the centre of the tyre footprint and a line extended through the swivel axis, in the case of lines which intersect below ground level.

positive steer, a semitrailer with automatic rear steering which steers in the opposite direction to the 5th wheel angle, fitted to some low loaders to assist turning around sharp corners.

positive terminal, an electrical terminal or electrode on a battery or other device that has a deficiency of electrons, and to which electrons flow from a more negative point in a circuit, marked with a + symbol.

post, the A, B, C, or D pillars which support the roof.

post, the terminal for an electrical connection.

post accident procedure, the actions required to efficiently assist at the scene of an accident.

posted speed limit, the speed limit as shown by road signs.

post heating, a glowplug system which continues to heat for a short while after a diesel engine has fired to reduce misfiring and smoke.

postillion, the rider on the rear left horse of a team drawing a coach when there is no coachman.

post mounted delineator, a hazard post, a colour coded retroreflective device located on a short post at the side of the carriageway to indicate road alignment.

postwar classic, any vehicle built on or after 12th November 1945 and more than 25 years old.

pot, a brake cylinder.

pot, a cylinder in an engine.

potassium oxide, a metallic compound commonly used in Europe in LRP and in lead replacement additives to protect valve seats from regression.

potential energy, the energy possessed by a vehicle, occupant, or load by virtue of its

position above some lower position to which it could move; see also: kinetic.

potential hazard, any situation that may cause a driver to change speed or direction.

potentially active vehicle, a parked vehicle at which an event has just occurred showing that further action is probable which could influence the course of another vehicle, *e.g.* a flash of the brake lights, a door closing, or a drivers shoulder movement suggesting handbrake or gear lever operation.

pothole, a small defect in the road surface, large enough to be felt if a tyre drives over it, sometimes large enough to cause vehicle damage.

pot joint, a type of universal joint with which to transmit power through varying angles between rotating shafts, having an internally grooved cylinder in which balls are free to move along the grooves.

pound, car pound.

pour point, the lowest temperature at which an oil can be poured, related to its ability to lubricate in cold temperatures.

pousse-pousse, push-push, a rickshaw in some Asian countries.

powdercoat, a coating for metal that is applied as a dry powder then baked to cure.

power, the rate at which work is done, measured in joules per second, J/s or watts, W.

power, see: actual, altitude, asymmetric, bhp, climbing, drag, drawbar, fhp, flat, friction, gross, hp, ihp, imperial, kW, lowest, metric, net, nominal, observed, peak, propulsive, PS, RAC, rated, road load, SAE gross, SAE net, shp, specific, volumetric.

power and brake, an inefficient driving style in congested traffic involving hard acceleration to fill a clear space in front followed immediately by braking sharply behind a stationary vehicle, resulting in jerky and uncomfortable progress.

power assisted brakes, a footbrake system having a means of mechanical assistance when the brake is operated to reduce driver effort, typically by a vacuum operated servo; see also power brakes.

power assisted gear selection, a gear selection system in which the gear lever is assisted by hydraulics to reduce driver effort, developed by Mercedes.

power assisted steering, a steering system having a means of mechanical assistance to reduce driver effort, especially when manoeuvring at slow speeds, typically hydraulic or electrohydraulic, see also: power steering.

power assisted variable assist power steering, a variable assist power steering system.

power band, the range of engine speeds within which the engine produces most of its power, typically ranging from just below the torque peak and extending to just above its power peak.

power brakes, a footbrake system where the operating fluid, typically air, performs all of the braking effort and the driver merely controls the pressure within the system using a lightly sprung pedal; see also: power assisted brakes.

power braking, a technique for descending a very steep slippery gradient in an automatic transmission 4x4: after selecting the lowest gear in the lowest range, to gently use left foot braking coupled with feathering the accelerator.

power bulge, a raised area on a bonnet to make space beneath for an enlarged engine or auxiliaries.

power change, the action of making a smooth gear change without wear to any parts by manually matching the engine speed to the road speed; to change to a lower gear: the clutch is pressed out whilst the accelerator raises the rev's as required to match the next gear to the road speed, keeping the rev's set constant the gear is selected, then the clutch is let in again still keeping the revs constant; to change to a higher gear: the clutch is pressed out whilst the accelerator reduces the rev's as required to match the next gear to the road speed, keeping the rev's set constant the gear is selected, then the clutch is let in again still keeping the revs constant.

power checks, a mnemonic to aid the systematic completion of daily checks: petrol, oils, waters, electrics, rubbers.

power closing system, a system of closing the vehicle doors using electric motors instead of inertia, developed by Mercedes, see also: automatic closing.

power control module, USA, the ECU.

power curve, a graph displaying the power output relative to engine speed that is unique to each engine design, usually an inverted U shape, the peak showing at which revs the greatest power is available.

power cutoff switch, battery cutoff.

power density, the ratio of the power output of a vehicle divided by its kerbweight, the higher the ratio the greater the acceleration performance and climbing ability, measured in W/kg, or more usually kW/tonne; a lorry must not have less than 4.4 kW/tonne and a typical loaded lorry has 10 kW/tonne, most cars are in the range 50 to 100 kW/tonne, high performance cars exceed 100 kW/tonne up to or exceeding 250 kW/tonne; the inverse of power to weight ratio.

power distribution, the distribution of torque between front and rear axles in a 4x4, it can be variable using a d-pump and wet clutch, or it can be at a specific percentage using a planetary differential, or fixed at 50-50 using a standard open differential.

power door locks, electrically operated door locks.

powered, provided with any means of power.

power hood, the roof of a convertible which is raised and lowered using an electric motor or electrohydraulics.

power hop, USA, axle tramp.

power induced skid, a skid caused by the driver operating the accelerator, such that there is greater torque applied from the engine to the wheels than the friction present between the tyres and the road surface, resulting in wheelspin.

power mass ratio, power density, a vehicle acceleration performance figure comparing engine power with vehicle weight, typically measured in kW/tonne.

power oversteer, the result when the tyre slip angle at the rear wheels increases more than it does at the front, when the rear tyres lose adhesion and the rate of yaw of the vehicle is more than anticipated with respect to steering input, a rear wheel skid caused by excessive power in a rwd whilst cornering.

powerpack, the whole engine unit, including all auxiliary systems.

power peak, the engine speed at which the maximum power output is attained, the highest point on the power curve.

powerplant, the whole engine unit, including all auxiliary systems.

power screw, an operating mechanism which pushes the pads against the disc rotor on heavy vehicles having air operated disc brakes.

power seat, seats which are adjustable electrically, and may have 20 switches and 10 motors for position selection.

powershift, a clutchless semiautomatic gearchange system allowing quick upshifts or downshifts whilst transmitting power.

powershift, USA, flatshift.

Powershift, a Government funded scheme to financially assist the conversion of petrol vehicles to bifuel/dual fuel operation.

powerslide, a power-induced controlled skid, whereby a rally or racing driver deliberately induces and controls a rear wheel skid or 4 wheel skid for maximum speed through a bend.

power steering, indirect control of a steering system which is operated hydraulically and where the drivers control only varies the pressure in the system, see also: power assisted steering.

power steering pump, a hydraulic pump which operates the power steering or assisted steering system, and which is driven by the engine or electrically.

power stroke, the stroke of the piston from tdc to bdc with both valves closed, during which the fuel is ignited and the expanding gases push the piston from tdc to bdc, hence the only stroke that drives the vehicle.

power takeoff, a transmission system addition allowing power to be taken from the engine via the gearbox to drive auxiliary equipment, *e.g.* a winch on a 4x4, a crane on a lorry, or machinery on a tractor.

power to weight ratio, the ratio of the

kerbweight of a vehicle divided by its power output, the smaller the ratio the greater the acceleration performance and climbing ability, normally measured in kg/kW, most cars being in the range 10 to 20 kg/kW, high performance cars being below 10 kg/kW, some as low as 4 kg/kW; the inverse of power density.

powertrain, all of the systems that transmit the power, *i.e.* the power pack and the drive line, the complete series from the combustion of the air-fuel mixture to the tyres.

Powertronic, an automatic gear selector system developed by Volvo.

power turn, in a fwd, the technique of turning a car in its own length by: applying the handbrake firmly, steering to full lock, significantly raising the revs and suddenly releasing the clutch causing the driving wheels to rapidly spin in either reverse or forward gear to drag the car around.

power turn, in a rwd or 4wd, the technique of turning a car in its own length by: steering to full lock, significantly raising the revs and suddenly releasing the clutch causing the driving wheels to rapidly spin in a forward gear to push the car around.

power unit, the whole engine including all auxiliary systems.

power unit, tractive unit.

power windows, electrically operated windows.

Pozidrive, a type of screwdriver with a 4 point cross forged into the tip with a specific axial angle at the centre, or a corresponding screw head.

pp, personal protection.

PPA, permitted parking area, *e.g.* a meter bay.

PPCRGD, UK, Pelican Pedestrian Crossing Regulations and General Directions 1987.

ppm, parts per million, a measurement of impurity within a substance, or of pollutants, especially of HC in exhaust gas with an exhaust gas analyser; 1 ppm = 1 drop in 60 litres (13.3 gallons).

ppm, pence per mile, a direct measure of the running cost of a vehicle, especially for comparison between vehicles.

PPMA, Petrol Pump Manufacturers Association, UK.

PPVA, UK, Public Passenger Vehicles Act 1981.

PR, ply rating, the load range classification of a tyre.

PR, public relations, an area known to have residents adversely sensitive to traffic participating in road rally navigation.

PRA, Petrol Retailers Association, UK.

practical test, a practical test of competence to drive a motor vehicle, to pass the driving test is the minimum acceptable standard of proficiency, including manoeuvring and road driving.

prechamber, precombustion chamber.

precision, a condition achieved when a driver purposefully controls the vehicle to be in exactly the right position at the right speed with respect to all hazards.

precision immobilization technique, the method used by USA police for halting the progress of a violator by using the fishtail technique.

precombustion chamber, a small extension to a combustion chamber in which combustion is started before progressing to the combustion chamber, a design for quieter idling and smoother running but reduced economy in some diesel engines.

precombustion engine, a diesel engine having a precombustion chamber for each cylinder, hence indirect injection.

pre-driver education, instruction in the theory of driving given to any person who is below the legal age to drive a motor vehicle, sometimes as part of school curriculum.

pre-driving checks, the power checks followed by the cockpit checks and static and moving brake tests.

pre-engaged starter, a starter motor having a solenoid operated engagement for the pinion such that the pinion engages with the flywheel ring gear before power is applied to the windings of the starter motor.

preheater system, a system for cold starting a diesel engine having glowplugs or an air intake heater.

pre-ignition, unwanted ignition of the air-fuel mixture before the sparkplug fires.

pre-injection, a diesel engine having a direct injection system, when immediately before the main fuel injection a minute amount of fuel is pre-injected to create exactly the specific temperature and pressure for the main combustion, to give improved performance, developed by Fiat.

preload, the amount of mechanical load on a bearing due to the design of its fitting before any operating loads are imposed.

prelubricator, a secondary electrical oil pressure pump which operates for several seconds before an engine is started to reduce bearing friction and prolong engine life.

premium, leaded petrol equivalent to 4 star rating.

pre-owned, second hand.

prescribed drug, any drug prescribed by a physician, but which will degrade a drivers performance, *e.g.* painkiller.

preselect, a gear selector system in which the driver may select the next gear some time before it is required, then later when required by the driver by operation of a foot control or hand control the gearchange is performed; typically on some buses.

pre-signal, a traffic signal some distance before a junction, typically at the end of a bus lane, which controls all traffic except buses thereby giving buses priority, especially for positioning for turning at a junction.

– PPP –

press fit, an assembly condition whereby 2 parts can only be assembled or separated by use of a hydraulic press.
pressure, the force exerted on a unit of area, newtons per square metre, N/m^2, Pa, bar, or psi.
pressure cap, radiator cap.
pressure carburettor, an old name for a fuel injection system.
pressure gauge, an instrument that measures pressure in a system and displays the reading.
pressure limiting valve, a hydraulic restriction in the rear braking system of some vehicles to reduce the pressure to the rear wheels under hard braking to reduce the risk of a rear wheel skid.
pressure plate, clutch pressure plate.
pressure regulator, a governor which controls the pressure of the fuel delivered to the injectors.
pressure relief valve, a valve that opens at a set pressure to maintain a standard pressure in a system, *e.g.* the lubricating oil.
pressure test, to pressurise a system with air or liquid to prove a system is healthy or to find a fault.
pressurise, to apply a pressure to a fluid or system.
pre-tensioner, a safety device on some seatbelts, using a pyrotechnic it will rapidly tension a seatbelt at the commencement of an impact to reduce slack in a seatbelt and hold the occupants firmly in the seats.
pre-trip information system, a PC based database and mapping system which suggests suitable routes from any given origin to any given destination, and computing for many variable parameters, *e.g.* assumed average speeds on each type of road, but without enroute updating.
pretty parking, to reverse into a parking bay and position the vehicle such that the car is symmetrical with the markings and the front wheels are straight.
prevailing torque fastener, nuts and bolts designed to have a continuous resistance to turning.
preventive maintenance, work done to a predefined schedule, to replace parts before they reach the end of their life and fail, to make any lubrication or adjustments necessary to prolong the life of components to prevent failure.
prewar classic, any vehicle built between 1st January 1930 and 2nd September 1939 inclusive.
PRI, International Road Safety Organisation, Luxembourg.
primary cell, a non-rechargeable individual cell, or a cell within a non-rechargeable battery.
primary circuit, the electrical path from the vehicle battery through the ignition coil.
primary collision, the impact of a vehicle with any other object, person, or vehicle.
primary compression, the compression

performed in the crankcase of a 2 stroke engine.
primary controls, the drivers controls for speed and direction: accelerator, footbrake, clutch, steering wheel, gear selector, and parking brake.
primary distributor, a major road which is part of the primary network within a town or city, carrying traffic between district distributor roads, and to/from the town.
primary escape route, any space ahead longer than the vehicle driven that can be entered without steering to avoid an impending collision, including the queueing distance maintained when stopping provided this is at least 5 metres (15 feet) long although a longer queueing distance is required in high risk situations.
primary key, a key which operates all of the locks on a car, including: ignition, driver and passenger doors, boot, fuel filler, glove box, etc.
primary piston, the first piston in a tandem master brake cylinder.
primary pump, an engine driven pump where an electrical secondary pump is also fitted, *e.g.* in the lube oil system, cooling system, power steering system, etc.
primary road, a road used as part of a primary route, given an A prefix to its number in UK.
primary route, a route that is designated as the most satisfactory all-purpose route for through traffic between 2 or more places of traffic importance.
primary safety measure, a device, modification, or tactic that reduces the probability of a collision occurring, *e.g.* ABS brakes, or crossview observation.
primary safety restraint, a device designed to hold a vehicle occupant securely in position during an impact to reduce risk of injury, *i.e.* any type of seatbelt.
primary shaft, first motion shaft.
primary shoe, USA, the leading shoe in a drum brake.
primary structure, any structural part of a vehicle which if damaged or corroded and collapsed would render the vehicle unsafe to drive, or seriously reduce occupant safety.
primary traffic signal, a traffic signal located approximately level with the stop line at a junction.
primary V pulley, the cvt pulley which is driven by the engine.
primary winding, the low voltage winding in an ignition coil, having a relatively small number of windings.
prime, to apply a coat of priming paint to a bare metal surface.
prime mover, a tractive unit.
prime mover, a rigid lorry when it is drawing a trailer.
prime mover, a locomotive.
primer, a type of paint designed to adhere well

212

to bare metal and provide a foundation for following coats of paint.

principal road, a non-trunk road which is classified as being sufficiently important in the national highway system to justify principal status.

priority, the situation where 1 driver has legal or conventional precedence over another.

priority junction, a junction where signs and/ or markings define which traffic has precedence over other traffic, *e.g.* a T junction on minor roads, but without signalized control.

privacy glass, deeply tinted rear and side window glass that helps keep the suns rays out of the passenger cabin and provides an added measure of occupant privacy.

privateer, a person privately entering a car in a major race or rally and competing against works teams.

private hire, a service similar to that of a taxi but where each journey must be requested by telephone because plying for hire is not permitted.

private & light goods, a class of vehicles defined for VED purposes.

private transport, any private passenger vehicle, specifically a car either owned or hired.

PRND, park, reverse, neutral, drive, the relative sequence of the gear selector positions in an automatic transmission; D is usually subdivided numerically.

proactive transmission, an automatic transmission that recognises a drivers style and changes gear to suit.

probationary licence, a driving licence issued after passing a driving test, and which restricts the holder to types of vehicles, passengers, speeds, penalty points, BAC, for a period of time, all of which vary from country to country.

Procon ten, a secondary safety system whereby the impact of a severe collision and movement of the engine rearwards causes the steering column to be drawn forwards away from the driver, developed by Audi.

producer, a HORT1 document issued by a police officer requiring later production of specified documents.

production car, a car made in significant numbers by a manufacturer.

production line, a manufacturing process to reduce the time taken to build a car, introduced by Henry Ford in 1913.

profile, the relative height of a tyre sidewall compared to the section width, see: full profile, low profile, ultra low profile.

programmable ECU, an ECU where operating parameters can be adjusted.

progress, a driver quality in travelling efficiently at safe speeds up to the speed limit where suitable.

progressive braking, a braking technique commencing with feathering on the brake, then smoothly increasing the pressure up to threshold level if necessary, then as the vehicle slows reducing the pressure and feathering off the brake.

progressive changing, the act of using every gear in numerical sequence when changing up or down, typically an unnecessary procedure on most vehicles; see: block changing.

progressive shifting, an obsolete gearchanging method in which it was assumed that each successive upchange is performed at higher revs than the previous upchange.

progressive transmission, a gearbox in which the selection of the gear ratios must be performed in sequence, *e.g.* in an automatic transmission.

prohibited user, when referring to classes of road user prohibited from using a motorway: pedestrians, vehicles driven by holders of provisional car or motorcycle licences, motorcycles under 50 cc, cyclists, horse riders, slow moving vehicles, agricultural vehicles, and invalid carriages.

prohibition, see: absolute, relative.

prohibition notice, a legal restriction on the use of a vehicle at 2 levels: immediate prohibition prevents a vehicle from moving until a major defect has been repaired; delayed prohibition allows 10 days for the repair of minor faults.

prohibitive sign, a road traffic sign, generally circular with a red border, sometimes with a pictorial representation of the prohibition.

prohibitory line, a longitudinal road marking consisting of a continuous line with a broken line alongside, which prohibits crossing by traffic from the side having the continuous line but permits traffic originating from the side having the broken line to cross the lines; see also: permissive.

projection marker, a white triangular plate having a red border and red diagonal stripes, fitted to mark the width and length of any projecting load.

projector cats eye, an active coloured road stud that incorporates solar cells, a microprocessor, and a light source, such that they can be seen from a greater distance than reflective road studs.

propane, a basic gas fuel which is the main component in LPG, having a RON of 112, MON of 97, and stoichiometric ratio of 15.7:1 w/w.

propane / hexane equivalency factor, a mathematical factor used when measuring HC in the exhaust of an LPG fuelled vehicle, by dividing the measured HC reading by 0.48 to give a result comparable to that of petrol.

propel, to move a vehicle, to drive, to pull or push a vehicle manually, to draw by an animal, or by any other mechanical means.

propeller shaft, the rotating shaft that transmits the drive from the gearbox to the axle.

proportional load synchromesh, locking

synchromesh.

proportioning valve, a hand control that allows the driver to adjust the proportion of brake pressure to the rear wheels, for competition use only.

proportioning valve, USA, pressure limiting valve.

propoxyphane, a drug that should not be used by drivers, often contained in sleeping pills.

propshaft, propeller shaft.

propulsive power, the force with which a vehicle may accelerate allowing for traction between the wheels and the surface, *i.e.* horsepower minus loss of traction.

prop up, to fix the bonnet, boot lid, or tilting cab in a raised position using a stay.

prosecute, to take legal proceedings in court against a driver.

Prospective Driving Instructor, UK, a person who has applied to become an ADI but has not completed the examinations or not registered with the DSA.

pro-street, a road legal competition car.

protected parking, a linear roadside parking area following a buildout.

protective position, the defensive position by which to use another vehicle to protect your own, *e.g.* on approach to a busy high risk crossroads on a dual carriageway to position your vehicle diagonally behind the protecting vehicle in the adjacent lane.

protocol, digital communication between vehicle components and the central processor.

prototype, the first full size functional model of a new design of vehicle.

proving ground, a test track having a variety of surfaces, but especially areas for high speed trials, used or owned by vehicle manufacturers to test versions of vehicle design before production, sometimes also used by the press for vehicle testing and for specialist driver training off the public highway.

provisional licence, a driving licence held whilst learning to drive and until passing a driving (or riding) test in the relevant category of vehicle.

prowl car, USA, a police squad car.

proximity mirror, a mirror on the nearside of a large vehicle allowing the driver to see down to the front wheel and its position in relation to the road edge.

proximity sensor, a device which transmits and/or receives a signal controlled by a microprocessor which informs the driver the closeness of an object behind when reversing.

ps, power steering.

PS, pferdestärke, German, metric horsepower, 1 PS = 0.75 kW, 1 PS = 0.98632 imperial horsepower.

PSA, Peugeot-Citroën group of companies.

PSCRI, Professional Sports Car Racing Inc, USA.

pse, passive safety equipment.

psi, pounds per square inch, a unit of pressure,

lb/in^2, generally obsolete but still used in some countries for tyre pressures, replaced by kPa.

psig, pounds per square inch gauge, a measure of pressure above that of atmospheric pressure.

PSL, position, speed, look.

PSM, Porsche Stability Management.

psr, power sun roof.

psr, primary safety restraint, *i.e.* a seatbelt.

PSV, public service vehicle, now renamed PCV, passenger carrying vehicle.

PSV(CFEUC)R, UK, Public Service Vehicle (Conditions of Fitness, Equipment, Use, and Certification) Regulations 1981.

psychoactive drug, any drug that influences the normal action of the brain, hence degrades a drivers performance.

psychological glare, an occurrence when glare causes actual discomfort but without reducing a driver's ability to see; see also physiological, veiling.

pt, personal transportation.

ptfe, polytetrafluoroethylene.

pto, power takeoff.

PTW, powered two wheeler, a motorcycle.

pu, pickup.

Public Carriage Office, the organisation that oversees black cab drivers in London.

public carriageway, a right of way having the highest status hence is open to all types of road users.

public highway, a highway maintained at public expense.

public lamp, lamp on a tall post serving to illuminate part of a public road.

public path, a right of way which is a bridleway or footpath with no higher rights, *i.e.* not available to motor vehicles.

public place, a place, other than a road, to which the public have access, including carparks that are open to the public at the time, and areas in which public events are taking place; any offence that could be committed on a road can also be held to be committed in a public place.

public road, a road maintained at public expense.

public service vehicle, a motor vehicle adapted to seat 8 or more passengers for hire or reward, excepting trams.

public transport, a means of transporting people to and from their homes to work or recreation on predetermined routes to a timetable by bus, tram, train, tube, ferry, or air, but excluding taxi and coach.

public works vehicle, a mechanically propelled vehicle which is specially designed for use on a road by or on behalf of any statutory undertaking, *e.g.* water, electricity, gas, telephone, or other utility, but excluding the carriage of persons other than crew or of goods other than goods needed for the works in respect of which the vehicle is being used, (C&U).

puddle lamp, a lamp mounted in the bottom

edge of a door and which illuminates the ground when the door is opened, see also: doorstep lights.

puffin crossing, a signal controlled crossing enabling pedestrians to cross a road, the system includes pressure pads and infra-red detectors to reduce traffic delays and increase pedestrian safety; named from pedestrian user friendly crossing.

pull, a condition when a vehicle has a tendency to be drawn to 1 side, typically caused by uneven tyre pressures, binding brakes, or faulty castor angle alignment.

pull, the situation when requested to stop by police for a traffic offence or routine check.

pull, to haul a semitrailer with a tractive unit, especially when referring to a contract between organisations.

pull ahead, to overtake.

pull apart, to dismantle.

pull away, to start a vehicle in motion from any stationary position.

pull back, to slow down slightly to increase the distance between ones vehicle and the vehicle ahead.

pulley, a wheel with a toothed or grooved rim that rotates on a shaft and carries a toothed, V belt, or multi V belt to transmit motion and energy from 1 shaft to another.

pull in, a lay-by.

pull in, a roadside café.

pull in, the action of a solenoid or relay as it operates electrically.

pull in, to arrive, especially by bus.

pull in, to change lanes to the nearside.

pull in, to slow down and stop close to the road edge.

pull in, to slow down and turn off the road, *e.g.* into a lay-by or carpark.

Pullman, G M Pullman, designer of motor coaches having extreme internal luxury.

Pullman saloon, a luxury stretch limousine typically having facilities not usual in motor vehicles, designed for the supreme comfort of a small number of passengers.

pull off, to slow down and turn off the road, *e.g.* into a lay-by or carpark.

pull on, to move from an acceleration lane onto the carriageway of a motorway or similar road.

pull out, to change lanes to the offside.

pull out, to depart, especially a bus.

pull out, to emerge.

pull out, to move off.

pull over, to slow down and stop close to the road edge.

pull push steering, an efficient style of steering which gives the driver good control of the steering wheel, the first movement being a pull down from the top of the wheel to the bottom with 1 hand, followed by a push upwards from bottom to top with the other hand on the opposite side of the wheel to continue the wheel rotation, the method can be repeated until full lock if necessary, and straightening the wheel is similar but entailing opposite movements, at all times both hands will be horizontally level with the non-griping hand sliding around the wheel, see also: handover, hand shuffle.

pull type clutch, a clutch in which the release bearing is pulled away from the flywheel to disengage the clutch.

pull up, to slow down and stop without reference to road position; originally from stopping a carriage by pulling up on the horses' reins.

pull up, USA, a forward shunt during a reverse manoeuvre.

pulse braking, rhythmic braking.

pump, a machine that adds pressure to or moves a fluid, including: engine oil, gearbox oil, coolant, fuel, fuel injection, power steering, suspension, hood, windscreen and headlamp washers, air horn, air compressor, ac compressor.

pump and run, a crime committed when a driver fills a car with fuel then drives off without paying.

pump düse, a diesel fuel injection system having an individual injector for each cylinder and which typically operates at an extremely high pressure of approximately 2,000 bar (30,000 psi) for improved efficiency, developed by Volkswagen.

pumping losses, the engine power expended during induction of charge air and expulsion of exhaust gas.

puncture, a condition when an object penetrates a tyre, usually causing air loss.

punt chassis, backbone chassis.

pup, the first trailer of a roadtrain.

pupil, a person learning to drive, usually referring to a learner driver in a car, or someone learning to drive a new category of vehicle.

purpresture, an illegal encroachment on the roadside, *e.g.* hawkers or traders stalls, deliberate cultivation of a verge, white painted stones placed along the road edge to dissuade drivers from encroaching onto a verge, etc.

pursue, for a vehicle to follow another, usually police following a suspect vehicle.

pursuit driving, the driving of a police vehicle in an urgent manner when the driver is following a violator who refuses to stop.

pursuit intervention technique, the method used by USA police for halting the progress of a violator by using the fishtail technique.

pursuit test, a test of the riding abilities of a motorcycle rider conducted on a motorcycle, where the examiner follows behind either on a motorcycle or in a car.

push, USA, understeer.

push button gearshift, a semiautomatic gear selector system using buttons on the steering wheel, usually named paddles, for fingertip gear selection by the driver.

pusher axle, front trailing axle.

pusher lift axle, a non-driven load carrying axle closely ahead of a driven axle on a tractive unit, lorry, or bus, which may be raised from the road surface to reduce costs when the vehicle is operated lightly loaded; see also: tag lift axle.

push in, to drive alongside other traffic in an attempt to join a queue at the front instead of exercising patience.

pushing, USA, understeer.

pushing big wheels, CB jargon, driving a lorry.

pushing wheels, CB jargon, driving a vehicle.

push-pull steering, pull-push steering.

push-pull suspension, a racing suspension having rising rate geometry and where the springs and dampers are inboard clear from the airflow.

pushrod, a connecting link in a mechanism to transmit linear motion, typically driven by a cam to operate a valve.

pushrod engine, an ohv engine.

push start, to start the engine of a vehicle having a flat battery by pushing the vehicle until it is moving at above 10 km/h (6 mph) then using 2nd gear the clutch is rapidly let in so inertia from the wheels turns the engine to start it; not possible with automatic transmissions.

push type clutch, a common clutch in which the release bearing is pushed towards the flywheel to disengage the clutch.

PVEC, Police Vehicle Enthusiasts Club.

pw, per wheel.

pw, power windows.

px, part exchange.

PY, Paraguay, international vehicle distinguishing sign, see appendices.

pylon, USA, cone, a hollow conical rubber or plastic shape of various heights from $1/4$ m to $1^{1}/_2$ m, usually orange with a retroreflective band and deformable if driven over, used to mark the edge of the carriageway at temporary hazards, *e.g.* construction etc.

pyramid, each of several triangular white markings painted on speed humps.

pyrometer, an electronic device with which to measure the temperature of surfaces *e.g.* brakes, tyres, radiators, hoses, bearings, etc. without contact; some operate by laser sighting.

pyrotechnic, an explosive device with which to operate some safety equipment, *e.g.* an airbag or seatbelt pretensioner, using sodium and nitroglycerine compounds.

pyroxylin paint, clear lacquer.

Q

Q, quad drive, 4wd.

Q, quiet zone, in road rally navigation a PR sensitive area, pass through slowly and quietly.

Q, Thatcham category Q, a category of device tested to ensure it performs as described by the manufacturer, but with no pass/fail, *e.g.* tracking systems or image recorders etc.

Q, a tyre speed rating code denoting a maximum design speed of 160 km/h (99 mph), moulded into the tyre sidewall.

Q plate, a registration number prefix showing that the age of the car has not been determined, either due to the car being a homebuilt hybrid or kitcar incorporating some parts that were not new, or that it was imported without documentation verifying its actual age.

Q system, an automatic gear transmission system with manual override using an electronic H gate selector.

QA, Qatar, international vehicle distinguishing sign, see appendices.

QA4, 4wd automatic 4 speed transmission.

QA5, 4wd automatic 5 speed transmission.

QM4, 4wd manual 4 speed transmission.

QM5, 4wd manual 5 speed transmission.

QM6, 4wd manual 6 speed transmission.

QM7, 4wd manual 7 speed transmission.

quad, quadricycle.

quad camshaft, 4 camshafts as fitted to a vee engine with 2 camshafts above both cylinder heads.

quadrant, the display adjacent to the selector lever in an automatic transmission showing the selected gear.

Quadra-Trac, a power sensing system on a 4x4 that will transmit the power to the wheel(s) with greatest traction, developed by Jeep.

quadrizontal engine, USA, a flat 4 engine, where the cylinders are 180° opposed.

quadricycle, a motorcycle with 4 wheels, typically steered by handlebars, having a kerbside weight not exceeding 550 kg.

qualified observer, a person having passed advanced theory and advanced practical driving tests, and who informally assesses a drivers performance and gives advice, but does not hold an instructors licence.

qualifying tyre, a tyre with a special very soft compound for additional friction, used to meet qualifying times before a race, but with a life too short for a race.

quarter bumper, a style of bumper mounted around the 4 corners of a vehicle only, leaving the centre of the front and rear unprotected, typically on some classic sports cars.

quarter elliptic spring, half of a semi-elliptic leaf spring, typically mounted longitudinally and cantilevered such that all leaves are rigidly attached to the chassis with the axle at the sprung end.

quarter floating axle, an axle drive shaft which transmits torque to a wheel, and at its outer end it also supports and restrains the wheel vertically and laterally.

quarter light, a small triangular side window sometimes abutting an A pillar, it usually swivels on a vertical axis to open, or occasionally abutting a C pillar.

quarter panel, the rear side section of a bodyshell including the C pillar.

quarter turn fastener, a button sized positive locking quick release device for retaining engine covers etc.

quarter widow, USA, quarter light.

quartz halogen, a lamp that produces an intense white light, having a bulb made from quartz glass to resist melting at high temperatures, and the envelope contains a halogen gas, usually iodine vapour to prolong the life of the filament.

quartz iodide, a lamp that produces an intense white light, having a bulb made from quartz glass to resist melting at high temperatures, and the envelope contains iodine vapour to prolong the life of the filament.

quayside, a place where boats are moored, having a paved area for vehicles with an unguarded edge and a vertical drop into deep water.

Queens highway, any public road.

quench area, in some engines, the part of a combustion chamber where the piston becomes very close to the cylinder head such that both surfaces conduct heat from the gas to reduce detonation, although it may encourage the formation of unburned hydrocarbons.

queueing distance, a recommended safety margin of 5 metres (15 feet) minimum ahead of every vehicle when stopped in a queue of traffic in order to maintain a space as a primary escape route, thereby increasing the level of one's safety by allowing for unforeseen potential occurrences.

quick lift jack, a device used during pit stops

during racing and rallying, it allows one end of a car to be rapidly raised and lowered sufficient for a tyre change.

quick rack, a high geared steering rack providing quick steering.

quick release steering wheel, a steering wheel that can be removed by operation of a push button to allow a racing driver to enter and leave the seat, also used on road cars as anti-theft protection.

quickstart, an easily ignited ether based fuel, dispensed from an aerosol into the air intake to assist a cold engine in starting, especially for diesel engines.

quick steering, high geared steering, a vehicle in which a small angular movement of the steering wheel results in a larger slew of the front wheels.

quiet road, a highway restricted to use on horseback, pedal cycle, or on foot only.

quiet running, an engine that does not exhibit high frequency audible vibrations.

quill gear, any gear mounted on a hollow shaft.

quill shaft, a hollow shaft, typically in a planetary gearbox.

quitting, an offence committed by a driver, the action of leaving a vehicle unattended on a public road with the engine running.

R

r, rear.

r, refer to the manufacturer for greater detail regarding octane rating and other parameters of fuel type to use.

R, radial construction, a designation within a tyre size coding.

R, red, the colour of roads to be used at that point in road rally navigation, as marked on OS maps.

R, reserve.

R, retread number.

R, reverse gear.

R, right, a rally pace note describing a slight curve to the right through approximately 10°.

R, right, at a junction to turn in that direction in road rally navigation.

R, rubbers, the last section of the power checks mnemonic.

R, a tyre speed rating code denoting a maximum design speed of 170 km/h (106 mph), moulded into the tyre sidewall.

R, UK, a former driving licence category for trolley buses, an obsolete category for driving tests.

R12, freon, a cfc refrigerant used in older ac systems.

R134a, a refrigerant which is cfc free, used in ac systems since 1995.

R clips, an R shaped spring clip, used to secure some hoses.

RA, Argentina, international vehicle distinguishing sign, see appendices.

RA, UK, the Roads Act 1920.

RA3, rwd automatic 3 speed transmission.

RA4, rwd automatic 4 speed transmission.

RA5, rwd automatic 5 speed transmission.

RAC, Royal Automobile Club, UK.

race, a speed event in which drivers compete directly against each other.

race, the hard metal rings on which ball or roller bearings run.

race, to run an engine at high speed, especially off-load.

race boots, footwear worn by competition drivers, usually suede with a nomex lining.

race gloves, suede gauntlets with a nomex lining.

racer, a vehicle used for racing.

race suit, fire resistant overalls made from nomex, a competition requirement.

race track, racing circuit.

RAC horse power, an obsolete and inaccurate reckoning of horsepower for the purpose of motor vehicle taxation, calculated only from the square of the bore in millimetres multiplied by the number of cylinders and divided by 1,613 and which had the unfortunate effect of creating a demand for long stroke narrow bore engines to reduce tax.

racing car, a car designed to be used in competitive events.

racing circuit, a venue comprising an enclosed private area having a wide smooth road surface with a variety of bends forming a complete loop typically approximately 5 km (3 miles) per circuit and which has been carefully designed to be suitable for racing numbers of vehicles at high speed; many circuits have been developed on former airfields.

racing driver, the driver of a racing car.

racing fuel cell, a fuel tank containing a foam so fuel will not rapidly spill after a collision, required for many types of driving competitions.

racing line, the ideal line using the full width of the race track having the greatest possible radius through a bend or series of bends, for maximum speed on a racing circuit.

racing start, to set a vehicle in motion on a street very rapidly, using maximum power in each gear to gain maximum acceleration performance but not necessarily continuing to a high speed, typically from a signal controlled junction up to the speed limit.

racing weight, the weight of a racing car in running order with all fuel tanks full and the driver aboard wearing complete racing apparel.

rack, steering rack, a linear design of gearing for converting rotation of the steering wheel into lateral movement to control the track rod ends.

rack and pinion, a linear design of gearing, especially a steering gearbox having a toothed rail driven laterally by a pinion on the lower end of the steering column.

RAC MSA, Royal Automobile Club Motor Sports Association, officially abbreviated to MSA.

rad, radiator.

radar detector, a special radio receiver in a vehicle tuned to the K and/or Ka band and which sounds an alarm when a radio signal is detected.

radial engine, an engine cylinder and

crankshaft layout in which the cylinders are arranged radially at equiangular intervals around the crankshaft, similar to an X engine but always having an odd number of cylinders in 1 or in each of several banks, uncommon in road vehicles.

radial highway, an arterial road leading to/ from an urban centre.

radial ply, a tyre having an internal construction of cords such that they are laid at 90° to the centreline, *i.e.* directly from bead to crown to bead.

radial ply tyre, a tyre construction with the cords arranged radially from bead to crown to bead under the tread resulting in flexible sidewalls for good roadholding, and having a belt of plies beneath the tread to stabilise the tread and define the tread diameter.

radial runout, a variation in the radius of the tyre tread from the wheel axis, minimised by correct match mounting.

radial shaft seal, a design of seal having a sealing lip held by a garter spring, to contain a liquid under pressure where a shaft passes through a casing, *e.g.* the crankshaft extension to the clutch.

radial tyre, radial ply tyre.

radiation fog, fog caused by a clear night sky and no wind, the surface of the earth radiates heat to space and chills the air, typically resulting in a shallow layer of morning fog.

radiator, a heat exchanger having hot coolant from the engine passing internally through tubes, and air passing over the external surfaces of the tubes to remove the heat.

radiator cap, a removable aperture seal on the radiator or cooling system fill point that causes the cooling system to operate under pressure to achieve a higher and more efficient temperature.

radiator fan, cooling fan.

radiator grille, grille.

radiator hose, see: bottom hose, top hose.

radiator shutter, a set of shutters or a roller blind which can be adjusted to reduce the air flow to the radiator when operating in very cold climates.

radiator tank, coolant expansion tank.

radio broadcast data system, a system which allows the radio to receive digital data transmitted along with the standard FM radio signal to make it easier to find traffic, emergency, and other information.

radio cab, a taxi equipped with 2 way radio.

radio static interference, the generation of interference to the reception of radio signals caused by a vehicle's electrics.

radius arm, a suspension link for controlling the horizontal location of the suspension, *e.g.* where a beam axle is suspended by coil springs.

radius seat, spherical seat.

ragtop, a car having a roof made from fabric, usually removable.

RAI, Nederlandse vereniging de Rijwiel-en-Automobiel Indusrie, Netherlands.

raid, a very tough high speed off-road rally in which the track is unmarked, *e.g.* the Dakar rally across the Sahara desert.

rail, a dragster constructed on a very long lightweight tubular framework having bodywork only around the cockpit.

rail mount, the mounting system for a car roof rack on a pair of permanently fitted roof rails.

railroad crossing, USA, a railway level crossing.

railroad grade crossing, USA, railway level crossing.

railway telephone, a telephone at some railway level crossings connected directly to the signal box controlling that section of line, and which must be used by drivers of long or slow vehicles, herders of animals, and the driver of any vehicle broken down on the crossing.

rain, visible water drops falling through the atmosphere thereby reducing visibility.

rain deflector, a strip of shaped translucent plastic fitted to the leading and upper window edges of a side window, to deflect rain to allow travel with the window open.

rain sensing wipers, windscreen wipers that will operate automatically when rain influences an infrared sensor, the system also regulates the wiper frequency.

raised junction, table junction.

raised pavement marker, USA, a retroreflective road stud, cats eye, lane button.

raised white lettering, lettering in white rubber which protrudes from the sidewall of a tyre to emphasise the trade name and model of the tyre.

Rajakaruna engine, a type of rotary engine having a revolving block.

rake, the angle of slope or tilt, as in the seat backrest, the steering wheel, or windscreen, etc.

rake adjustable, an object having an adjustable angle of tilt, *e.g.* the steering wheel where the angle of tilt may be varied to suit the driver.

raked windscreen, a windscreen with a significant angle of slope away from the direction of travel to reduce drag.

ral, rear axle maximum loading.

rally, a timed competitive event typically on private or rough roads, the competitors having individual starting times.

rallycar, a powerful competitive car designed to match the type of surface or terrain at each event.

rallycross, a form of motorracing on a closed circuit having a variety of surfaces, *e.g.* shale and tarmac, on reasonably flat terrain using rally prepared or elv cars.

rally gloves, suede gauntlets with a nomex lining.

rallyist, a crew member taking part in a rally,

usually the driver or navigator but sometimes a co-navigator, mechanic or relief driver.

rallysprint, a 2 lap race between 2 rally cars on parallel circuits with a mid-way crossover.

ram, the forward motion of a nacelle through the air such that inlet air pressure is increased.

ram, to forcibly hit a vehicle or object directly with the front of a vehicle, or sometimes with the rear, typically at speed or whilst using power; see also: double vehicle, single vehicle.

ram effect, the result of air being forced into the air intake by a well designed nacelle to aid air flow into the engine and increase power, especially at speed.

ramp, a sloping surface, usually with 1 end at ground level, to enable a vehicle to travel to a higher level, *e.g.* onto a trailer, onto a ferry, or in a multi story car park.

ramp, each of a pair of devices with which to raise 1 end of a car in a home workshop for work below the car, each having an inclined surface so the wheel may be driven up to a platform about 20 cm high on which the wheel and car are supported.

ramp, a sign at roadworks marking a temporary sudden small change in the level of the carriageway surface.

ramp, USA, a roadway connecting between a freeway and a lesser highway, road, or roadside area; see: off ramp, on ramp.

ramp angle, the angle created between a line along the surface and a line drawn from the tyre footprint upwards longitudinally to the lowest point on each of the front and rear overhangs, and which defines the maximum angle of approach to a gradient at each end of a vehicle.

ramp break-over angle, on crossing a ridge, the maximum combined angles of climb and descent whereby the underside of the vehicle will not contact the ground.

ramping, the action of a vehicle in striking at speed the angled end of a safety barrier and being carried upwards by the barrier.

ram pipe, each of the short funnel shaped induction tubes to carburettors on some high performance vehicles.

ram pipe filter cover, a simple air filter to fit over the ram pipe of a carburettor.

ramp metering, a traffic management strategy using traffic signals on a motorway entry sliproad to regulate the volume of traffic entering the motorway when it is busy, to improve the throughput of traffic on the main carriageway.

ramp metering signal, a set of traffic signals on an entry to a sliproad onto a motorway which regulate the volume of traffic entering the motorway when it is busy, to improve the throughput of traffic on the main carriageway.

ramp travel index, a measure of axle articulation, typically of a 4x4, determined by driving 1 front wheel slowly up a 20° ramp until a tyre just loses contact with the surface,

measuring the length travelled along the ramp, dividing the distance by wheelbase and multiplying by 1,000.

ram raid, to deliberately reverse a vehicle at speed into a building through a weak part of its structure in order to commit a crime especially burglary.

Randle handle, the J gate gear selector as used by Jaguar, named after former engineering director Jim Randle.

range, a group of consecutive gear ratios with a specific selector mechanism, *e.g.* low range.

range, USA, any individual gear.

range, the distance a vehicle will travel on 1 full tank of fuel.

range available, the distance a vehicle will travel on the remaining fuel in the tank.

range change, an additional set of epicyclic gears usually installed at the output of a lorry or tractor gearbox to provide 2 or more consecutive ranges of gears, such that the lowest gear in the second range is higher than the highest gear in the lower range; see also: splitter.

rapeseed methyl ester, a vegetable based fuel that has very similar characteristics to diesel fuel.

ratchet, a toothed wheel with a pawl permitting rotation in 1 direction only, typically used in a socket set to create an adaptable range of tools.

ratcheting, CB jargon, talking.

ratchet tie downs, webbing straps with a ratchet tensioning device, for securing vehicles to trailers or loads on lorries.

rated capacity, the quantity of electricity which can be drawn from a fully charged battery for 20 hours at a constant current until the voltage drops to 1.75 volts per cell.

rated engine speed, the specific rotational speed of an engine at which the rated power is produced.

rated power, the bhp, kW, or PS produced at the rated engine speed.

rated torque, the torque which is produced by an engine when running at a specific engine speed.

rated voltage, the operating voltage marked on electrical equipment and devices and which if operated at that voltage will give optimum performance.

ratio, the relative quantity of 2 or more figures in proportion, expressed as a numerical relationship, *e.g.* compression ratio 19:1 or washer fluid/water mixture 1:10.

ratione tenurae, by reason of tenure, a public carriageway which is maintained at the expense of the land owner.

rat run, a minor route that is favoured by commuter traffic as a short cut between main roads.

rav, recreational activity vehicle.

rave, a rail or framework around the upper sides of a lorry box to increase capacity.

– RRR –

RAVE valve, Rotax adjustable variable exhaust valve, a device on some 2 stroke engines which automatically varies the exhaust port size.

Ravigneaux planetary gears, an epicyclic train comprising 2 differently sized sun gears, 2 sets of planet gears, and 1 internal ring gear.

raw exhaust gas, exhaust gas before it has been treated by a cat.

RB, Botswana, international vehicle distinguishing sign, see appendices.

RB, overall width of the chassis rails.

rbh, replaceable bulb headlamp.

rc, radio cassette player.

rc, reserve capacity.

RC, China, international vehicle distinguishing sign, see appendices.

RC, Taiwan (China), international vehicle distinguishing sign, see appendices.

RCA, Central African Republic, international vehicle distinguishing sign, see appendices.

RCB, Congo, international vehicle distinguishing sign, see appendices.

RCH, Chile, international vehicle distinguishing sign, see appendices.

r/cst, radio cassette player.

rd, relative density.

Rd, Road, a street name designation.

rdl, rear differential lock.

rd lock, rear differential lock.

RdON, road octane number.

RDP, USA, restricted driving permit.

RDS, radio broadcast data system.

RDS-TMC, radio broadcast data system combined with a traffic message channel linked to satellite navigation, a system combining location with traffic flow information enabling real-time route directions and instantaneous automatic diversions when necessary.

rdstr, roadster.

RDVR, UK, Removal and Disposal of Vehicles Regulations 1986.

reach, the length of a sparkplug from the seal to the electrode, approximately the thread length.

reach, the distance from a drivers shoulders to the steering wheel, usually implied generally rather than an absolute measurement.

reach adjustable, a steering wheel having a mechanism whereby the length of reach may be varied telescopically by moving the column axially to suit the size of the driver.

reach truck, a type of forklift truck having a boom that telescopes horizontally or at an angle to give a significant reach over obstacles.

reaction distance, the distance a vehicle travels whilst the driver is mentally reacting, *i.e.* between observing a hazard and deciding to react, ignoring the time taken to physically react, *e.g.* the thinking distance before deciding to brake, *e.g.* the normal minimum at 100 km/h is at least 25 metres (at 60 mph at least 60 feet); see also perception.

reaction time, the time taken for a driver to

observe a hazard and decide to react, the normal minimum is 0.7 second for an alert healthy driver; see also perception.

reactive suspension, active suspension.

reading the mail, CB jargon, listening to a channel.

real time 4wd, automatic engagement of the transmission for changeover from 2wd to 4wd, or vice versa in any running conditions.

real total mass, the actual weight of the vehicle or vehicle combination as presented for a driving test, and which must meet or exceed a minimum weight for its category, typically requiring some load to be carried.

ream, to very accurately machine a bore to a precise diameter using a reaming tool.

rear, the back end of a vehicle.

rear axis, the rear axle, or in the case of a vehicle or trailer having 2 or more non-steering axles, a horizontal transverse line midway between the first and last axles in that group of axles.

rear axle, the axle or stub axles on which the back wheels are mounted.

rear bulkhead, a rigid panel across the width of a car behind the rear seats, typically on older saloons only, sometimes reduced to a pair of diagonal braces, not fitted in a car with folding rear seats.

rear bumper, the bumper protecting the back end of a vehicle.

rear console, a switch panel located for the rear passengers, to give control of hvac, windows, lighting etc.

rear deck, an external narrow horizontal panel below the rear window of a saloon car, sometimes including the boot lid if reasonably horizontal.

rear diff, the differential mounted in the rear axle.

rear differential lock, a control on a 2wd or 4wd vehicle that allows the driver to lock the rear differential so both wheels turn at the same speed to increase traction on slippery surfaces.

rear ended, to suffer a rear end shunt.

rear end lift, the effect of airflow over the bodywork at speed causing a reduction in air pressure above the car and causing the body to move upwards into the low pressure area, hence reducing stability, but which may be counteracted by an appropriate spoiler.

rear end shunt, a situation in which the front of a following vehicle collides longitudinally with the rear of the vehicle ahead of it, typically in busy traffic.

rear engine, a vehicle engine and chassis layout in which the engine is above or behind the rear axle.

rear fog lamp, a lamp used to make the vehicle more easily visible from the rear in dense fog, snowfall, or dust clouds, (C&U).

rear footwell, the floor volume for the rear passengers in a car below the level of the door sill.

rearguard, steel protective rails across the lower rear of a lorry or trailer to prevent a colliding car from going beneath the bed, to prevent decapitation of the car occupants.

rear head restraints, a safety feature with which to prevent whiplash occurring to rear seat passengers.

rear lift, a 6x2 tractive unit or rigid lorry of which the rear axle can be raised when not load carrying.

rear lights, all of the rear lights on a vehicle, including: position, brake, fog, reversing, direction indicators, and registration plate.

rear position lamp, each of the red lamps used to indicate the presence and the width of the vehicle when viewed from the rear, (C&U); formerly named side lights or parking lights.

rear registration plate lamp, a device used to illuminate the space reserved for the rear registration plate, (C&U), the lamp must emit a white light to illuminate the rear registration plate but without allowing any light to be directly emitted rearwards from the vehicle.

rear roll centre, the point at ground level or above on the longitudinal axis between the rear wheels around which the vehicle body rolls due to centrifugal force on the body when cornering; the actual height of the roll centre depends upon suspension design; where the rear roll centre is lower than the front the vehicle will usually oversteer.

rear screen heater, an electrical heating element either sandwiched within the layers of glass or bonded to the inner surface, for demisting the inside and deicing the outer surface; an element bonded to the inside can be irreparably damaged by contact with articles on the rear shelf.

rear seat belt, a seat belt for each person riding on the rear seat of a vehicle.

rear shelf, an interior shelf behind the top of the rear seats extending to the rear window, only for carriage of lightweight non-sharp objects due to injury they would cause in a collision.

rear shunt, to be hit from behind by the front of another vehicle, usually when in a queueing situation.

rear side window, any side window rearwards of the B pillar.

rear spoiler, an airfoil mounted on the boot lid or above the rear window of an estate, to counteract rear end lift.

rear tack strip, a bar which holds the rear of the hood in close contact with the rear deck.

rear trailing axle, a tag axle, a non-driven load carrying axle close behind a driven axle on a tractive unit, lorry, or bus, some may lift and/or steer; see also: front trailing.

rear trailing lift axle, a tag axle, a non-driven load carrying axle close behind a driven axle on a tractive unit, lorry, or bus, which may be raised from the road surface to reduce costs when the vehicle is operated lightly loaded; see

also: front trailing.

rear transaxle, a gearbox, final drive, and differential all contained in a single casing at the rear axle, typical for a rear or mid engined car; where fitted to a front engined car the propshaft turns at crankshaft speeds and gives a very well balanced chassis.

rear underride, a protective framework across the lower rear of a lorry or trailer to prevent a colliding car from going beneath the bed, to prevent decapitation of the car occupants.

rear view mirror, interior mirror.

rear wash wipe system, an electrical system for cleaning the rear window, the reservoir is typically in the boot but on some small cars the front reservoir may supply the rear washer.

rear wheel antilock brakes, an older system of antilock brakes applied to the rear wheels only of typically a pickup to prevent rear wheel skids.

rear wheel drive, a vehicle in which the engine drives the rear wheels.

rear wheel skid, the condition when the rear wheels of a vehicle lock, spin, or suffer significant sideslip, resulting in reduced braking performance, reduced acceleration performance, or oversteer; it has the potential to develop into a spin, typically caused by harsh braking, harsh acceleration, or sudden lift-off.

rear wheel steering, a function of a vehicle which is designed to steer with the rear wheels, *e.g.* fork lift or dump truck, designed for manoeuvrability, but potential risk due to the rear end swinging sideways in the opposite direction at the start of a turn.

rear window, a central window permitting the driver a direct view behind the vehicle.

rebated fuel, a fuel sold untaxed or taxed at a low rate on the condition it must not be used in road vehicles, *e.g.* red diesel.

reboard, a child restraint system which is installed such that it is rear facing on the front passenger seat, generally not recommended for safety reasons.

rebore, to increase the diameter of a cylinder by a small amount, usually to remove uneven wear found during an overhaul, it will necessitate fitting correctly matched larger pistons.

rebound stroke, the downward travel of a wheel and suspension; see also: jounce.

rebuild, to recondition, to reassemble a unit using new parts.

recall, safety recall.

recap, USA and Australia, to retread a tyre.

recce, reconnaissance, detailed observation a route, *e.g.* of a rally route for note taking.

receiver, the hitch platform fitted to the towing vehicle and which carries the hitch ball.

rechargeable battery, a series of secondary cells commonly used in vehicles to store energy to restart an engine.

reciprocally incorporated lamps, lamps

having a common housing and lens but with individual bulbs, *e.g.* headlamp with built-in position marker lamp.

reciprocate, to move in a straight line back and forth, the action of a piston.

reciprocating compressor, an air compressor having a piston that reciprocates in a cylinder, common on lorries and buses to produce compressed air for braking systems.

reciprocating engine, any engine in which pistons move back and forth in a cylinder, a piston engine.

recirculating ball, a design of steering gearbox that converts the rotary motion of the steering column into transverse movement to operate the track rods by means of steel balls between a worm gear and a nut; it gives minimal feedback to the driver.

reclassification, the process whereby RUPPs are reclassified by the highway authority as a BOAT, bridleway or footpath, but without removing any higher rights.

recognised parking space, an authorised parking space or a marked parking box.

recon, reconditioned.

reconditioned engine, a worn engine that has been dismantled, the crankshaft journals reground, the cylinders rebored, and all bearings replaced, then assembled with new parts or original parts which are in a serviceable condition, to produce an as-new engine.

reconditioning, restoration of mechanical parts to a good condition.

reconfigurable telltale, an interactive system that gives the driver real-time information about vehicle systems.

reconnaissance, the act of physically going to search for and identify a place, or checking the details of a route to a place or location, before the relevant journey to that place.

recouple, to reconnect a trailer to a towing vehicle.

recover, the removal of a crashed or broken down vehicle for repair.

recover, to extract a vehicle from a bogged down position.

recovery service, a service which recovers a crash damaged vehicle and takes it to be repaired.

recovery vehicle, a vehicle fitted with a winch and/or crane designed to tow, lift, or carry a damaged or disabled vehicle to a place of repair.

recreational vehicle, a vehicle designed primarily for driving to and carrying equipment for recreational activities.

rectangular headlamp, a headlamp shape styled to meet the shapes of the body lines, not necessarily a geometric rectangle.

rectangular ring, a piston ring having a rectangular cross section for containing the compression.

rectangular sign, a traffic sign giving directions or information, in any of 10 different colour formats, colour coded to the type of information although some colour codes vary between countries.

rectifier, a diode, a device that allows current to flow in 1 direction only, for converting ac to dc.

re-cut tyre, a tyre which has had new grooves cut into the tread, permitted on some tyres on some vehicles having an unladen weight exceeding 2,540 kg.

red arc, an area marked on a tachometer, the start of which marks the maximum speed at which that engine should be run and above which damage may be caused due to high rotational speed, and at which high rates of wear may occur.

red arrow, USA, an illuminated traffic signal prohibiting a turn in the direction of the arrow.

red circular sign, generally a mandatory traffic sign having a red border giving a negative instruction which is legally enforced.

red cross, an illuminated traffic sign showing a red diagonal cross being a mandatory signal that traffic must not proceed any further in that lane, either on a motorway or as part of a tidal flow system.

red curb, USA, a painted marking denoting a restriction from stopping, standing, parking, or unloading, except buses at a marked bus stop.

red diesel, diesel fuel which contains a red dye and on which tax is not paid so is prohibited from use in road vehicles, for agricultural and marine use only; see also: white.

red dot, a harmonic marking on a tyre sidewall that should be aligned with the wheel marking or tyre valve to minimise runout vibration.

red flag, a flag with which to communicate with racing drivers, only shown at the start-finish line, meaning the race is stopped.

Red Flag Act, UK, the Locomotives Act, introduced in 1865 and which established a 4 mph speed limit and required that each motor vehicle must be preceded by a person carrying a red flag, repealed in 1896.

red hose, the air hose controlling the emergency brake system through the coupling to a trailer.

red lead, a corrosion resisting coating for steel, based upon lead tetroxide, poisonous, obsolete.

red light, a lamp which signals traffic to stop.

red light camera, an automatic camera coupled to a device that emits a radio or laser beam and which will measure and photograph any vehicle not complying with a red traffic signal and will record the time, date, speed, registration number and the elapsed time since the signal started to show red.

redline, the red line, red spot, or start of the red arc on a tachometer, showing the maximum speed at which that engine should be run, above which damage may start to be caused to the engine due to its high rotational speed, and at which high rates of wear may occur.

red loading box, an area at the roadside delineated with a broken red line on a red route, where loading only is permitted for a short duration outside rush hours, *e.g.* from 10 am to 3 pm or as signs display.

red man, a symbol of a standing pedestrian illuminated red at some pedestrian crossings indicating to pedestrians when it is not safe to cross the road.

red mist, a self-clouding of judgement by a driver, especially when distracted by a specific objective, causing the driver to be reckless without realising it by ignoring normal risk factors.

red parking box, an area at the roadside delineated with a broken red line on a red route, allowing parking or loading outside rush hours, *e.g.* from 10 am to 3 pm or as signs display.

red road, an A class road in road rally navigation as marked on an OS map.

red route, a priority route with stopping, waiting, parking, and loading restrictions marked by red lines near the road edge, first used in June 1992.

red studs, cats eyes or reflective studs which mark the left side of motorways and some other roads.

red time, the cumulative duration of time which the amber, red, and red and amber traffic signals show to a specific traffic stream at a signal controlled junction.

reduction gearbox, a gearbox located at the stubaxles to reduce wheel speeds and increase torque whilst reducing weight and cost to other parts of the drivetrain; the gearbox may not have selectable ratios, or they may be selectable manually at the stub axle; typically primarily designed to add ground clearance.

reed valve, an automatic 1 way valve which allows the air-fuel charge to flow from the carburettor into the crankcase in a 2 stroke engine.

reefer, refrigerated, a semitrailer having an insulated box body with rear doors and incorporating a refrigeration unit for the transport of foodstuffs in a temperature controlled environment; sometimes also a refrigerated van or lorry.

reface, the process of cutting, grinding, or lapping a valve seat during reconditioning.

reference mass, the kerbweight of a vehicle plus 75 kg to allow for the weight of a driver.

referred damage, damage caused to a vehicle other than direct damage, *e.g.* the roof may distort as a result of a frontal impact.

reflective, retroreflective, a surface or coating designed to reflect light towards the direction of its origin by internal refraction and reflection regardless of the angle between the origin of the light and the surface; for increased visibility and safety at night.

reflective plate, a plate of red and amber material that reflects light back towards its origin, displayed on the rear of all lorries.

reflective stud, a reflector bonded onto or partly recessed into the road surface; a colour code system is used to denote relative positions on the road surface, the reflectors may be: red, green, white, amber, or yellow.

reflective triangle, a triangular shaped reflector with sides approximately 40 cm long and reflective edges about 4 cm wide, carriage is a legal requirement in many countries, to be displayed in case of breakdown or collision.

reflector, a silvered area behind a bulb that reflects light from the bulb to redirect it at a specific angle to the lens.

reflector, an area of plastic or glass that is designed to reflect light back towards its origin regardless of angle, by internal refraction and reflection; red to reflect red light mandatory on the rear of all vehicles, amber on the sides of some vehicles.

reformed gasoline, reformulated gasoline.

reformulated gasoline, fuel which has a highly controlled vapour pressure and evaporation rate to reduce toxicity, and which is oxygenated by addition of an ether or an alcohol to increase the RON and reduce emissions.

refrigerant, a substance that by undergoing a change from liquid to gas absorbs a large amount of latent heat in relation to its volume thus has a cooling effect, as used in ac and refrigeration systems.

refrigerated truck, reefer, a vehicle or trailer having a self contained refrigeration system for delivery of goods in a temperature controlled environment.

refuel, to replenish the petrol, diesel, or gas etc, to refill the fuel reservoir.

refuelling checks, a series of visual checks at the time of refuelling including: checking the engine oil, brake fluid, windscreen washer fluid, and a visual check of the tyres.

refuge, an island between carriageways for use by pedestrians.

refuse vehicle, a vehicle designed for use and used solely in connection with street cleansing, the collection and disposal of refuse, or the collection and disposal of the contents of gullies or cesspools, (C&U).

regenerative braking, an electromagnetic braking system in which kinetic energy is converted into electrical energy and used to recharge the battery of an electrically powered vehicle hence stored as chemical energy.

regenerative retarder, a regenerative braking system which has the capacity to perform only part of the braking performance, typically it does not function at very low speeds.

regional registration, the town in which a vehicle is registered as identified by the letters on the registration plate, see appendices.

regional trunk road network, a network of roads providing access to major centres of population and economic activity.

registered, UK, a vehicle which is registered under either: the Roads Act 1920, the Vehicles (Excise) Act 1949, 1962, or the RV(R&L)R 1971 Act.

registration, the recording of details of a vehicle by a government or their agency; first in Paris on 14 August 1893, in UK on 1 January 1904.

registration document, vehicle registration document.

registration mark, the combination of characters on a registration plate which serves to identify a vehicle.

registration plate, a plate displayed on the front and rear of vehicles bearing the letters and numbers as a registered mark for that vehicle.

registration plate lamp, rear registration plate lamp.

regrind, to machine a surface, typically to remove a thin layer from crankshaft journals to make them again circular and axially aligned.

regrooveable tyre, a tyre having a thicker layer of rubber between the carcass and the tread to allow for a new tread to be cut when the original is worn.

regrooving, the cutting of a new tread into a worn tyre surface, permitted on special tyres on some vehicles with an unladen weight over 2,540 kg, but is otherwise illegal.

regroup, a halt in a 1 day route for re-spacing of rally competitors.

regs, regulations, typically traffic regulations.

regular, leaded petrol equivalent to 3 star rating.

regularity, a road rally having sections between checkpoints which must be driven at an average speed of exactly 30 mph (48.28 km/h) and which is timed either to the minute or to the second such that early or late arrivals suffer penalties in a scoring system.

regularity section, a competitive section in a road rally normally timed to the second at exactly 30 mph (48.28 km/h) and with intermediate time controls.

regularity time control, a location at the end of a regularity section in a road rally.

regular motor oil, a lubricating oil suitable for use in si engines under normal operating conditions.

regulated proportioning valve, load proportioning valve.

regulator, a hand lever on a steam powered vehicle for driver control of engine speed.

regulator, any device which automatically controls pressure, temperature, voltage, current, fluid flow, etc.

reinforced sidewall, a sidewall of a tyre that has several external concentric scuff ribs to give physical protection with flexibility, for rallying.

relais routier, French, a roadside restaurant.

relative density, the comparison of the density of a substance with respect to water; originally named sg.

relative humidity, the ratio of water vapour in the air, usually expressed as a percentage of what the air will support at that given temperature and pressure; higher humidity will reduce engine power and increase the rate of corrosion.

relative prohibition, a difference in level of priority as marked at a give way, yield, or other sign or road marking.

relay, a remote controlled electrical switch, able to switch large currents from a small input signal.

release bearing, clutch release bearing.

release button, the button on the end of a handbrake lever which when pressed lifts the pawl from the ratchet to release the handbrake.

release lever, parking brake release lever.

releasing fluid, penetrating oil.

relevant braking requirement, a requirement that the brakes of a motor vehicle including the brakes on a trailer comply with the requirements specified in regulation, (C&U).

reliability, a quality of which a vehicle and all its components continue to perform without failure throughout the service life of the vehicle.

relief map, a map showing hills and valleys by shading.

relief road, a bypass or similar road which carries traffic around a congested area.

relief valve, a valve that operates when a preset pressure is reached to prevent excessive pressure.

reline, to replace the lining on a brake shoe, or to replace the complete shoe with a new item.

reluctor, a rotating metal disc with a series of teeth or notches that induce a voltage pulse in a pickup coil as each tooth passes.

remote locking, a central locking system operated remotely by a plipper, by which all doors are electrically locked or unlocked simultaneously.

remote starter switch, a switch sometimes on the starter motor solenoid or in the engine bay so the engine can be started by a mechanic, generally out of fashion in cars due to fitting of immobilisers.

remould tyre, a retread tyre.

removal van, a pantechnicon, a large rigid lorry with a box body and a low floor, for the transport of household furniture.

Renault, Louis Renault, France, the patentee of the live rear axle in 1899 that continues as a current design.

repair, to complete the necessary procedure to fix a damaged or worn part.

repair kit, a set of parts needed for a specific task, overhaul, or reconditioning, *e.g.* a set of joints and seals.

repair manual, a book detailing all procedures to recondition each part of a vehicle, normally specific to each make and model of vehicle.

repeater indicators, side direction indicator

lamps.

repeater signal, a series of miniature traffic signals mounted approximately 1.2 m above ground level on the pole supporting the primary signals, for the convenience of car drivers in some countries.

replace, to remove a part and install a new or different part.

replacement bulb kit, a set of bulbs containing one of each type for the vehicle; carriage is a legal requirement in some vehicles and in many countries.

replacement vehicle, courtesy car.

repmobile, commonly a medium sized car as provided by companies to their sales representatives and other staff.

request stop, a bus stop at which a bus halts only at the request of a passenger.

RES, resume earlier speed, a cruise control selection commanding the system to resume the earlier preset speed.

rescue vehicle, a motor vehicle designed or adapted solely for the purpose of rescuing persons.

research octane number, an index number which refers to the speed at which a fuel will burn.

reseat, to recut a valve seat where excessive burning has caused more erosion than can be repaired by lapping.

reserve, a marking on a fuel gauge indicating that little fuel remains, typically less than 5 litres, sometimes accompanied by a warning lamp.

reserve capacity, the volume of fuel remaining in the tank when the gauge reads zero contents.

reserve capacity, the volume of fuel remaining in a tank below the normal outlet, at which the reserve valve must be opened, an obsolete system typically on vehicles not having a fuel gauge.

reserve capacity, a battery rating based upon the number of minutes a battery at 27.6 °C (80 °F), can deliver 25 amperes of current before any cell voltage drops below 1.75 volts.

reservoir, any container designed to hold a volume of fluid, *e.g.* brake, clutch, power steering, suspension, windscreen washer, rear screen washer, headlamp washer, etc.

residential access road, residential road.

residential road, a road which links dwellings and their parking areas and common open spaces to local distributor roads.

residual value, the actual saleable price of a vehicle allowing for wear, use, and desirability.

residual value, the projected resale price of a leased vehicle quoted as a percentage of the list price, but typically misleading because all options and extras added to the list price are excluded.

resilient tyre, a non-pneumatic tyre which is of soft or elastic material, (C&U); typically made from solid hard rubber as on some road rollers, fork lift trucks, and industrial equipment;

specific low speed limits are imposed.

resin, a chemical compound, usually epoxy or polyester based, which requires an activator to cause it to harden.

resistance, the opposition to a flow of electric current through a circuit or device, measured in Ω ohms.

resistor, a device used in electrical circuits to limit current or provide a voltage drop.

resonance roll, alternate left/right body roll which increases with each alternate steering input and amplified by the suspension, which develops in large vehicles especially a double deck bus or an articulated lorry when going ahead at a roundabout at speed, leading to overturn.

resonator, a tube or chamber in the exhaust that generates sound waves that cancel-out certain exhaust noise.

response time, thinking time.

respray, to repaint a vehicle by spraying.

rest, the condition when a vehicle is stationary.

restart, a type of collision after a driver stops at a junction, then emerges and collides with a vehicle on the priority road.

rest halt, an overnight stop during a rally.

restore, to totally dismantle every part of a vehicle and rebuild it, typically including reupholstering, to the standard as it existed on leaving the factory.

restraint, a device for preventing a load from moving, including ropes, straps, or chains.

restraint system, an occupant safety system including seatbelts and airbags of various types.

restricted access, a road of which entry and exit is only available at specific junctions, not having access from premises at the roadside, *e.g.* a motorway or freeway.

restricted cloverleaf, parclo, a grade separated cloverleaf junction without a full permutation of transfer from every road to every other typically because the routes cross at an acute angle; on maps the junction number is typically coloured yellow or red; see appendices.

restricted driving permit, USA, a special permit issued by the office of the Secretary of State to some drivers whose licenses have been revoked or suspended, and which allow driving only during specified times along specified routes for work, education, or medical reasons.

restricted junction, parclo, a grade separated motorway junction without a full permutation of transfer from every road to every other typically because the routes meet at an acute angle; on maps the junction number is typically coloured yellow or red; see appendices; see also: full.

restricted licence, USA, a licence issued by a professional driving school to a learner between 15 and 18 years of age permitting driving only during professional driver training.

restricted road, a road having street lights not

more than 185 metres (200 yards) apart and which is generally subject to a speed limit of 30 mph (50 km/h).

resurface, a process by which the old surface of a road is planed off and a new surface laid.

retard, to slow or delay the occurrence of an event, especially to delay the spark at the sparkplug to cause it to occur slightly later in the cycle.

retarder, a retarding system on a heavy vehicle, a device to slow down a vehicle or reduce unwanted acceleration on a steep downhill, but it will not stop a vehicle, it is intended to prevent the brakes from overheating but acts by retarding only the drive axle(s), hence it has the potential for causing a skid on a slippery surface; 4 types are in use see: compression release, electromagnetic, exhaust brake, hydraulic.

retractable aerial, a motorised telescopic aerial which extends when the radio is switched on and retracts when switched off.

retractable headlamps, headlamps that retract within the bodywork of the vehicle when not in use, for aerodynamic purposes and for aesthetic appearance.

retractable lamp, a lamp capable of being partly or completely hidden when not in use, this result may be achieved by means of a movable cover, by displacement of the lamp or by any other suitable means, (C&U).

retractor, the device which reels in a seatbelt when it is unclipped, and which locks to prevent the belt unreeling during rapid unreeling and/or deceleration.

retread, to vulcanise or bond a new tread onto a worn tyre carcass by either the hot or cold process respectively.

retread number, a moulding in the side wall of a tyre in some countries indicating the number of times the tyre carcass has been retreaded.

retread tyre, an old but serviceable tyre carcass onto which a new tread is vulcanised or bonded, using either a hot or a cold process respectively; each process is known to be illegal in some countries, in the UK cold bonding is illegal.

retro design, a redesigned car similar to a previous production model whilst retaining attributes of body style.

retrofit, to fit updated, modified, or additional parts after manufacture.

retroreflector, a device which by internal refraction and reflection returns light back towards the direction of origin regardless of the relative angle between the face of the reflector and the origin of the light.

retro reflector, a device used to indicate the presence of a vehicle by the reflection of light emanating from a light source not connected to the vehicle, the observer being situated near the source, excepting: retro reflecting registration plates, and other retro reflecting plates and signals used to comply with national

requirements, (C&U).

returnability, USA, a quality of a steering design that it will return to its straight ahead position, controlled by the castor torque influenced primarily by the castor angle.

return load, a load carried on a lorry for a third party to a convenient location to prevent returning unloaded after dropping the primary load.

rev, revolutions.

rev, to increase the speed of the engine, or to maintain at a high engine speed.

rev counter, revolutions counter, tachometer.

reverse, to drive a vehicle backwards.

reverse 180 spin, see: J turn.

reverse clutch, a clutch within a planetary gear set which couples the gears such that the vehicle can be driven backwards.

reversed Elliot axle, a front axle design in which the ends of the beam axle terminate in an eye and where the ends of the steering knuckle axis are forked.

reverse gate, a mechanical blocking device within the gear selector system preventing inadvertent selection of reverse gear.

reverse gear, a selectable gear by which the vehicle can be driven backwards.

reverse herringbone, a style of parking bays into which vehicles reverse at an angle of approximately 45° from the access road; potentially the safest parking pattern.

reverse inhibitor valve, a valve which prevents engagement of the reverse clutch in some automatic transmissions if the forward road speed of the vehicle exceeds a set figure, typically 10 km/h (6 mph).

reverse parking, to reverse into a parking bay in a carpark to position abreast or abeam other vehicles, for maximum manoeuvrability and safety.

reverse pattern gearbox, a 4 speed gearbox in which the layout positions of 3rd and 4th gears are opposite from the conventional H pattern, on some older lorries.

reverser, a hand lever on a steam powered vehicle that controls the valve timing, the power output, and the direction of the engine hence forwards or reverse.

reverse side turn, a manoeuvre whereby the vehicle is reversed from a main road into a side road or opening then driven forwards whilst steering in the opposite direction onto the main road, potentially a safe manoeuvre; see also: forward side turn.

reverse slalom, a training or testing exercise in which a vehicle is reversed alternately left and right passing a straight line of cones or marker poles.

reverse spin, see: J turn.

reverse steer, a vehicle that has been specially modified such that the steering wheel operates in the opposite direction to the front wheels, for special competition use only.

reverse warning signal, an intermittent

bleeping sound generated by a reversing horn.

reverse warning system, a system using radar or sonar fitted to the rear of a vehicle and activated when reverse gear is selected to give an audible warning to the driver when reversing towards any object.

reversing hold, a technique for using the steering wheel in which 1 hand holds the wheel at the top centre whilst the drivers upper body is turned to look rearwards; useful only for reversing in an almost straight line.

reversing horn, a device that sounds an intermittent bleep when reverse gear is selected except when the headlamps are switched on, mandatory equipment on some lorries and buses.

reversing lamp, a lamp emitting white light used to illuminate the road to the rear of the vehicle, and to warn other road users that reverse gear is selected, (C&U).

reversing lights, white lights permitted on the rear of a vehicle, originally designed for use when reversing in a dark area, now commonly used as a signal when reversing, developed in 1921.

reversing radar, a radar system that gives information to the driver regarding the proximity of obstructions behind the vehicle.

revhead, a person who likes fast or powerful cars.

rev limit, the maximum engine speed achievable before the rev limiter inhibits further acceleration in that gear.

rev limiter, an electronic device allowing a predetermined figure to be set as the maximum rpm for that engine on acceleration, incorporated into the ECU of vehicles having fuel injection, also used by racing schools; the system dose not function to prevent mechanical overrevving on downchanging at high roadspeed.

revocation, USA, the indefinite withdrawal of a driving license as the result of a serious motoring offense.

revolution counter, an instrument which records the total cumulative engine revolutions, *e.g.* for a tractor engine the extent of operation is a more useful guide to service intervals than mileage covered.

revolutions counter, tachometer, an instrument that measures engine speed, usually in revolutions per minute, displaying in rpm x 100 or rpm x 1,000.

revolutions per kilometre, the counted number of revolutions made by a tyre travelling 1 km.

revolutions per mile, the counted number of revolutions made by a tyre travelling 1 mile.

revolutions per minute, a measure of rotational speed, especially the number of times the crankshaft revolves through 360° in 1 minute, usually abbreviated to rpm.

revolving block engine, any of various engines which combine reciprocating piston motion with rotational motion of the entire engine block, uncommon in vehicles.

revs, revolutions, a measure of crankshaft rotational speed.

rev up, to increase the speed of the engine whilst the vehicle is stationary.

rfet, rolling floor ejecting trailer.

RFG, reformulated gasoline.

RFL, road fund licence, road tax for a vehicle, also named VED.

RG, Guinea, international vehicle distinguishing sign, see appendices.

rh, relative humidity.

rh, right hand.

RH, Haiti, international vehicle distinguishing sign, see appendices.

RHA, Road Haulage Association, UK.

rhd, right hand drive.

RHDTC, Road Haulage and Distribution Training Council, UK.

rhodium, a noble metal used in a cat to reduce NO_x into nitrogen and oxygen.

rhr, rear head restraints.

rhythmic braking, an emergency braking technique whereby the brake pedal is pulsed with deliberation synchronised to the frequency of oscillation of the front suspension such that each successive pulse causes the nose to dive thereby transferring weight to the front wheels to attempt to increase braking performance on a wet road whilst allowing some steering; the technique is superseded by the operation of ABS, and must NOT be used on any vehicle fitted with ABS.

RI, Indonesia, international vehicle distinguishing sign, see appendices.

rib, a continuous band of tyre tread around its circumference between 2 grooves or between a groove and the shoulder.

rib, scuff rib.

Ricardo principle, a designed shape of combustion chamber having a very narrow wedge at 1 side such that at tdc on compression the squeezed mixture would squirt across the chamber causing a swirl and improved combustion.

rich mixture, an air-fuel mixture having a higher proportion of fuel and less air, *i.e.* the stoichiometric ratio is reduced below the usual 14.7:1 such that $\lambda<1$.

ricker, a vehicle modified to compete in 4x4 off-road events, especially at speed.

rickshaw, a 2 wheeled hooded lightweight cart for the carriage of goods or 2 passengers, drawn manually by a pedestrian between horse shafts, common in many Asian countries, named from Japanese jinrikisha.

ride, a quality of comfort experienced by vehicle occupants especially with respect to the suspension.

ride, to travel in a vehicle.

ride, to travel on a cycle or motorcycle.

ride down distance, the distance a vehicle occupant travels from moment of a vehicle

– RRR –

impact until coming to rest, *i.e.* the length the crumple zone compresses plus the distance which a seatbelt stretches during the impact, plus any vehicle movement after impact.

ride height, the distance from a level road surface to the drivers seating surface when the drivers seat is occupied by a person weighing 75 kg and the vehicle is loaded to its maximum gross weight.

ride levelling, automatic levelling system.

rider, any person travelling on a pedal cycle, a moped, a 2, 3, or 4 wheeled motor cycle, or a ridden animal.

rider, USA, a bus passenger.

ride steer, USA, bump steer.

ridgeroad, ridgeway.

ridgeway, a road or track that has been constructed longitudinally for some distance along the top of a ridge between 2 valleys.

riding the clutch, the action of keeping the foot over the clutch pedal unnecessarily, or constant light pressure on the clutch pedal, or using the clutch pedal as a footrest, between gear changes.

rig, USA, a large truck especially articulated, or with one or more trailers.

right hand drive, a vehicle in which the drivers controls are on the right hand side of the vehicle.

right hand side, the side of the vehicle on the right as viewed from the drivers seat when facing forward.

right hook, rhd.

right of way, UK, a common misnomer in the case of where 1 vehicle has precedence over another, see: priority.

right of way, UK, the legal right for any specific class of road user to travel over the land of another without permission, provided it is for a genuine journey from 1 place to another; divided into 3 categories: footpath, bridleway, or carriageway.

right of way, USA, the priority of a road user to move ahead before another at a junction, as marked by signs, road markings, or convention.

right turn on red, USA, a worded sign at traffic signals where it is permitted to turn right at a red light after first stopping at the line and giving way to any other through traffic.

rigid 8, a rigid lorry with 2 steering axles at the front and 2 load carrying axles at the rear, common as bulk tippers, also named 8 legger.

rigid axle, an axle or a pair of stub axles at which the wheels do not have independent suspension, *i.e.* a deflection at 1 wheel causes a reaction in the other, typically a change in camber angle, and/or a change in longitudinal direction, and/or lateral displacement of the track.

rigidity, resistance by a vehicle chassis or body to longitudinal twisting.

rigid vehicle, a vehicle without chassis articulation or trailer.

rim, the part of the wheel that locates and holds the bead of the tyre.

RIM, Mauritania, international vehicle distinguishing sign, see appendices.

rim bead seat, the area of the wheel rim at the base of the flange where the bead of the tyre locates.

rim diameter, the diameter of the rim at the location of the tyre bead seat, normally measured in whole numbers of inches.

rim size, the measurements between opposing rim bead seats, measured across the diameter usually giving that figure in inches, and measured across the width usually giving that figure in millimetres.

rim width, the distance between the 2 inside edges of the wheel rim flange where the bead of the tyre locates.

ring, a circular part that fits in a groove or slot, to seal a liquid or gas, or to accurately hold or locate a part, see: O ring, piston ring.

ring end gap, the gap between the ends of a piston ring when it is in the cylinder.

ringer, a vehicle which has fraudulently had its identity changed, typically a stolen vehicle which is given the identity of a crash damaged vehicle.

ring gear, a crownwheel.

ring gear, gear teeth around the flywheel on which the starter motor drives.

ringing, to falsify the registration and history of a vehicle, typically by transferring the identity of a crash damaged vehicle to a stolen vehicle.

ring job, the installation of new piston rings on a piston, a cheap temporary repair when further work is usually necessary.

ring ridge, the ridge formed by the piston rings at the limit of travel as the cylinder wall is worn.

ring road, any road which encircles the centre of a town or city, sometimes using existing roads following a grid or other system, sometimes constructed to motorway standard and reasonably circular, often described as inner, intermediate, or outer ring roads.

rising rate suspension, a suspension having variable rate springs which increase in stiffness as the suspension is compressed.

rising rate suspension, a suspension system having a linkage geometry such that the spring rate increases as the wheel and suspension rises.

rising roof, a section of vehicle roof that raises vertically or at an angle, typically to extend the accommodation in a small mobile home.

risk, a chance or possibility of being caught committing a motoring offence, or of danger or collision which may result in damage, injury, or death.

risk compensation, the action of a driver in accepting a unified level of personal risk such that a safety improvement *e.g.* driving a car with ABS results in the driver driving faster to maintain the same level of risk.

risk perception, the degree of risk of collision in any specific situation as perceived differently by individual drivers.

r/km, revolutions per kilometre.

rl, rear left.

r/l, rear light.

RL, Lebanon, international vehicle distinguishing sign, see appendices.

r/lock, remote locking.

RM, Madagascar, international vehicle distinguishing sign, see appendices.

RM, reference mass.

RM4, rwd manual 4 speed transmission.

RM5, rwd manual 5 speed transmission.

RM6, rwd manual 6 speed transmission.

RM7, rwd manual 7 speed transmission.

RMA, Rubber Manufacturers Association, UK.

rme, rapeseed methyl ester.

RMIF, Retail Motor Industry Federation,UK.

RMM, Mali, international vehicle distinguishing sign, see appendices.

RMP, Royal Military Police.

RN, Niger, international vehicle distinguishing sign, see appendices.

RNR, Zambia, international vehicle distinguishing sign, see appendices.

RO, rear overhang, the distance from the centreline of the rear axle or rear axle set to the rear-most point.

RO, Romania, international vehicle distinguishing sign, see appendices.

road, any highway and any other road to which the public has access, and includes bridges over which a road passes, regardless of surface *e.g.* a track, named from Old English rad, from ride.

road, see also: 3 lane, 3 ply, A, access, accommodation, adopted, all purpose, approach, arterial, B, bituminised, blue, branch, brick, bridle, brown, byroad, C, classified, collector, country, cross, designated, directional, dirt, distributor, divided, drift, driving, drove, entry, escape, exit, fast, frontage, gated, Grand, Great, green, haul, high, highway, inner, intermediate, king, knight, lane, laned, link, loneliest, made, main, major, Mandarin, minor, Mother, motorable, non asphaltic, non native, no through, occupation, off, on, orange, outer, plank, primary, principal, public, quiet, red, regional, relief, residential, restricted, ridge, ring, rolling, Roman, rt, rule, sealed, secondary, service, shared, side, Silk, single, slip, special, street, stretch, through, toll, track, tram, trunk, unadopted, unclassified, undivided, unlaned, unlit, urban, white, X, yellow.

RoADA, RoSPA Advanced Drivers Association, UK.

road atlas, a road map compiled into book form, representing roads, towns, and other features, some pages may be at different scales for added detail.

roadbed, the carriageway, the portion of the roadway between kerbs or between shoulders of each carriageway.

roadblock, a barricade set across a road especially by police, military, customs, or other authorities to stop and examine travellers and/or vehicles and/or their contents.

roadbook, detailed route information for rally navigators, typically spiral bound.

road capacity, the maximum traffic flow obtainable on a given road using all the available lanes, usually expressed in vehicles per hour.

road car, a car that is intended to be used on a public road, *i.e.* not for racing.

road charging, a toll system whereby a driver pays a fee to use a road or network.

road check, the exercise in a locality of the power of a police officer to stop either all vehicles, or vehicles selected by any criterion.

road code, a set of rules for road users, or a book containing such rules as an equivalent to the Highway Code in many countries.

road course, a driver training course which is taught on public roads.

roadcraft, the art of driving to a high standard, demanding skill, observation, and concentration, as a way of approaching and negotiating hazards which is methodical, safe, and leaves nothing to chance.

Roadcraft, a book published by tSO describing the best driving techniques as used by police drivers in many countries.

road debris, small items that are capable of causing damage to a tyre, but which are very difficult to see whilst driving, *e.g.* shards, glass, nails, etc.

road draft tube, USA, crankcase breather pipe, used before the advent of emission controls.

road feel, the feedback to the driver through the steering wheel as a result of differences in road surface friction and imperfections in the road surface.

road friendly suspension, an axle fitted with air suspension or equivalent where at least 75 % of the spring effect is caused by an air spring or some other compressible fluid.

road fund, a former Government tax initiated in 1909 to adapt roads to the needs of motor traffic by the construction and maintenance of roads and bridges; now renamed VED.

road fund licence, a disc displayed inside a vehicle windscreen certifying that VED has been paid.

road gradient, the level or slope of a road measured by an inclinometer along the road centreline.

road hazard, USA, road debris.

road hog, a person who drives without due care for others.

roadholding, a quality in the design of a vehicle suspension and/or tyres, such that a vehicle will accurately follow the desired line especially at speed around bends having a poor surface.

roadhouse, a roadside inn or public house.

road hump, speed hump.
road infrastructure, roads, bridges, tunnels, and road furniture.
roadkill, animals killed by moving vehicles.
road load horsepower, the quantity of power required at the driving wheels to continue to move a vehicle along a road at a constant speed, and which is dependant upon: tyre rolling resistance, tyre pressure, aerodynamic drag, speed, weight, and any gradient.
road locomotive, locomotive.
roadman, a man employed to maintain or repair roads.
roadmap, a diagram representing the features on the surface of the Earth, especially roads, towns, and features of importance to drivers.
road marking, a painted line or symbol painted on the road surface in a specific colour, or a metal or coloured retroreflective stud, first devised in Michigan USA, in 1911, first used in UK in Kent in 1914.
road metal, broken stone for making the foundation or the surface of a road.
road network, the system of roads available within a locality or area.
road noise, tyre noise.
road number, a route classification and numbering system, designating roads by importance and geographical location devised in 1921, some new roads have necessitated local changes to the original numbering system.
road octane number, a measure of the octane number of a fuel determined experimentally by use in an engine coupled to a chassis dynamometer, and which for practical purposes is typically the same as the AKI.
road pricing, a system of charging drivers a fee for the use of some roads.
road rage, a disagreement between 2 drivers resulting in a display of unfriendly gesticulation, or verbal, physical, or psychological attack, especially if prolonged for more than a few moments.
road rally, an event whereby a car must follow a precise route directed by a series of clues, on a variety of usually minor roads at an average speed of exactly 30 mph (48.28 km/h), having control points interspersed along the sections of the route, organised under strict MSA rules; see also: 12 car, navigational scatter, night trial, plot and bash, regularity, special stage, treasure hunt.
road rash, USA, gravel rash.
road roller, a vehicle with steel or hard rubber tyres, used in the construction of a road surface.
road roller tyres, very wide low profile tyres as fitted to some high performance sports cars.
road sense, the degree of understanding of safe behaviour on a road as comprehended by any individual person.
road shock, movement of the suspension as wheels pass over imperfections in the road surface which is sometimes felt by the driver as

feedback through the steering.
roadside, referring typically to an object close to the side of a road but not contiguous with the road edge, *e.g.* a roadside inn.
roadside, the strip of land contiguous beside a road.
roadside marker posts, hazard post.
road sign, a panel displaying prohibitory, obligatory, hazard, directions, or general information to road users.
road slick, a tyre of which the tread is mostly smooth but having a minimum 17 % area of channels for water dispersal, permitted for road use between competitive events.
roadspeed, the speed of a vehicle along a road, measured in km/h, mph, or m/s.
roadster, an open top 2 seat or 2+2 sports car having a simple fabric top with side-screens which the driver has to assemble, and sometimes cutaway doors.
road sweeper, a person employed to sweep roads.
road sweeper, a specially constructed type of refuse vehicle designed to clean a road surface.
road tax, VED payable on a vehicle.
road test, a test of the performance of fuels, lubricants, other fluids, or other parts tested in normal operating conditions.
road test, an evaluation drive of a car by a potential purchaser of that car or another of a similar model.
road test, an evaluation of a car as a comparison against other vehicles, typically performed by a motoring journalist.
road test, to test the operation of a vehicle after repair or modification by driving it on a road.
road traffic, the flow of traffic and interaction between pedestrians, cyclists, and drivers on the road network.
Road Traffic Act, an act of Parliament which lays the framework for creating the road traffic regulations.
road traffic quality management, the control and management of road traffic in order to effect qualitative road traffic operations resulting in order, discipline, and safety on the road network.
roadtrain, any vehicle drawing 2 or more semitrailers with A frame dollies.
roadtrain, any vehicle drawing 2 or more drawbar trailers.
roadtrain, any vehicle drawing any combination of 2 or more trailers.
roadtrain, Australia, any vehicle drawing any combination of 2 or more trailers and where the overall length exceeds 30 metres but not more than 53.5 metres long.
roadtrain, a B double.
roadtrain, a B train.
roadtrain, a B triple.
roadtrain, a dromedary.
roadtrain, see also: double, triple.
road transport, the conveyance of passengers,

232

goods, and equipment on the road network between origins and destinations by means of road transport vehicles.

road transport management, the control and management of road transport to ensure that such transport is conducted in the most efficient and economic manner to the satisfaction of all users.

road used as a public path, a byway which is not a footpath or bridleway, but which may or may not be used by motor vehicles, it may be necessary to prove some previous usage by motor vehicles in order to have the status raised in order to be used by 4x4 vehicles.

road user, any user of a highway, including a person using a road either as a pedestrian, horse rider, cyclist, motorcyclist, or driving or riding in any vehicle, it also includes animals.

roadway, UK, the carriageway, a portion of a thoroughfare over which vehicular traffic passes.

roadway, USA, the carriageway including the sidewalks, slopes, ditches, channels, waterways, and other features for drainage and erosion protection.

roadwheel, any wheel and tyre assembly which bears on the road surface.

roadworks, the construction or repair of a road, or the excavation of utilities beneath a road followed by reconstruction.

roadworthy, the condition of a vehicle when all parts are mechanically sound such that no part contravenes any regulation and it is safe for use.

robot, traffic signals.

Rochas, Alphonse Beau de Rochas, inventor of the 4 stroke cycle in 1861, later patented and developed by Count Nicholas August Otto.

rocker arm, a lever pivoted in its centre that transfers motion from a pushrod to operate a valve.

rocker box, the cover over the valve train on top of a cylinder head.

rocker box cover, rocker box.

rocker cover, rocker box.

rocker shaft, the output shaft from a steering gearbox which turns the drop arm.

rocking chair, CB jargon, riding in the middle of a convoy.

rocking out, a self recovery technique, the action of rapidly alternately engaging forward and reverse gears synchronised to small alternate movements of the vehicle in order to gain momentum when bogged down in mud, sand, snow, etc.

rock rails, tough metal tubing along the underside of the sides of an off-road vehicle to protect the door sills from damage against uneven surfaces, sometimes extended to form an entrance step.

rod, hot rod.

rode, past tense of ride.

ROF, rear overhang to frame end, the distance from the centreline of the rear axle or rear axle

set to the rear end of the chassis.

ROK, Republic of Korea, international vehicle distinguishing sign, see appendices.

roll, a sideways lean of a vehicle body during cornering.

roll, a short intentional forwards or rearwards movement of a vehicle whilst not in gear as part of a manoeuvre, typically using the gradient and footbrake.

roll, a condition if a vehicle rotates 90° or more around its longitudinal axis, from its wheels onto its side, and in some cases then onto its roof, sometimes this rotation may continue.

roll, to wind the side windows up or down.

roll axis, the longitudinal axis though the front and rear roll centres; when sloping down to the front the vehicle will usually tend to understeer, and vice versa.

roll bar, a single strong curved tube internally or externally across the roof of a vehicle and extending to the floor, to protect the occupants if the vehicle should roll over.

roll cage, a strong tubular metal fabrication around all sides of the passenger cell within a vehicle to protect the occupants of a competition car if it should crash.

roll centre, the point at ground level or above on the longitudinal axis between the front wheels and between the rear wheels around which the vehicle body rolls due to centrifugal force on the body when cornering; the actual height of the roll centre at each axle depends upon suspension design.

roll down, USA, to wind down a window.

Roller, Rolls Royce.

roller bearing, an antifriction bearing containing a row of solid cylindrical rollers caged between an inner and outer race.

roller chain, a power transmission chain having sideplates retaining free tubular rollers connected by pins, as a bicycle chain.

roller clutch, a freewheeling clutch that transmits torque in 1 direction but turns freely in the other, sometimes used in starter motors and automatic transmissions.

roller dynamometer, an instrument for measuring the braking performance of a wheel, or the power developed by an engine, interfaced to the vehicle by rollers in the floor of a rolling road.

rollerskate, CB jargon, a small car.

roller vane pump, a pump having a series of rollers which move around the pump body as the rotor rotates, such that the rollers act as the pumping vane.

roll hoop, a tubular structure having an inverted U shape extending from the floor to head height behind each seat to give rollover protection to each occupant of an open top or convertible car.

rolling chassis, a chassis framework complete with all suspension, steering mechanism, and wheels; it may or may not also have an engine and/or transmission but no bodywork.

rolling circumference, the distance travelled by 1 revolution of a tyre on an asphalt road at 100 km/h (62 mph) under standard load and pressure.

rolling floor ejecting trailer, a facility built into some bulk trailers to enable a load to be discharged in a slow controlled manner, *e.g.* for gritting roads in winter.

rolling radius, the effective distance of the wheel centre above the point of contact between the tread and the surface, *i.e.* the distance the wheel travels after 1 revolution divided by 2π when correctly inflated and carrying a normally loaded vehicle; influenced by wheel diameter, tyre width, tyre profile, and tread wear.

rolling resistance, the friction developed within a tyre, wheel bearings, and transmission, such that it causes a small retardation effect, dependant on tyre size, construction, pressure, loading, and the surface, but excluding wind resistance.

rolling road, a system of rollers set into the floor of a workshop or inspection centre and connected to a dynamometer such that the wheels of the vehicle can be driven either by the engine or via an electric motor turning the rollers whilst the vehicle body remains stationary, for the purpose of performing brake tests or power output tests.

rolling roadblock, a technique used by police to safely and significantly slow the traffic in all lanes of a motorway well before a hazard to create a clear interval in the traffic to perform a recovery or other work in the road, but without stopping traffic.

rolling start, a method of starting a race initiated whilst all of the cars are moving in formation at some speed.

roll-on roll-off, a facility of a ferry or ship in which vehicles are driven directly on and off via a ramp from the quayside.

rollover, a situation when the tyre sidewall rubs the road surface, typically when cornering at speed and affecting mostly the front wheel on the outside of the bend.

rollover bar, a tubular structure extending from the floor and across the roof of a vehicle having minimal diagonal bracing, to protect the occupants if the vehicle should roll over.

rollover curb, USA, mountable kerb, a curb designed to mark the edge of the road but which can be driven over with no risk of damage to tyre or vehicle.

rollover protection system, a system fitted to some convertible cars that will rapidly deploy an extendible roll bar to protect the occupants during a rollover collision.

rollover protective structure, a roll cage or bar or a structural cab usually fitted to agricultural tractors and construction equipment vehicles to protect the driver if the vehicle should turn over.

roll oversteer, oversteer caused by body roll around the roll centre and its effect on the suspension causing changes in the angles of camber, castor, and toe.

roll pin, a spring steel pin in the form of a tube with a longitudinal split from end to end along 1 side.

roll resistance, roll stiffness.

roll steer, the effect upon the steering caused by body roll around the roll centre causing changes in the angles of camber, castor, and toe as the suspension moves.

roll stiffness, the reluctance of a body to roll when subject to cornering forces, dependent on suspension design, spring stiffness, and antiroll bar stiffness.

roll stop, to bring a vehicle to a halt by feathering the brake.

roll understeer, understeer caused by body roll around the roll centre and its effect on the suspension causing changes in the angles of camber, castor, and toe.

roll up, USA, to wind up a window.

Roman road, a long very straight road built by Roman workers in UK and Europe for the military, the route of many are still in use after 1,900 years.

romer, a multipurpose measuring and marking device for plotting a route or map reference for use in a road rally.

RON, research octane number.

ROOA, Routemaster Operators & Owners Association, UK.

roo bar, a tubular steel or similar framework designed to reduce the damage to the front bodywork and lights of a vehicle during a collision with animals and undergrowth, originally named kangaroo bar.

roof box, an aerodynamic container for carrying additional load on a car roof, subject to the car manufacturers maximum loading.

roof brace, each of several transverse rails adding strength to a car roof and supporting the rooflining.

roof light, a courtesy lamp mounted on the inside of the cabin roof.

roof light, a rotating beacon on the roof of an emergency vehicle.

roofline airbag, a curtain airbag that inflates downwards from each side of the rooflining to protect the occupants heads during a side impact.

rooflining, the material fixed inside the roof of a car for noise suppression, safety, and aesthetic purposes.

roof rack, a framework with which to carry a load on the roof of a vehicle, fastened to the vehicle by the gutter, gulley or rail, or on a van it may be bolted, subject to the vehicle manufacturers maximum loading.

roof rails, permanently fitted rails along each side of the roof of a car to allow easy installation of a roof rack.

roof spoiler, a wedge shaped air dam on the roof of a lorry cab or a car towing a caravan, to deflect air and reduce drag.

room temperature vulcanising, a silicone rubber gasket material that cures or hardens only with air, and is designed to be used at the temperature of a warm room, *i.e.* at approximately 20 °C, it may fail if not used at such temperature.

rooster tail, a plume of water spray thrown high behind a vehicle on a wet road.

Roots supercharger, a positive displacement method of compressing induction air, having a pair of contrarotating figure 8 shaped rotary pistons.

rope rail, a steel rail under the coaming of a lorry bed in some countries for tying of rope lashings.

roping and sheeting, the act of covering a load on a lorry with 1 or more tarpaulins then fastening it neatly and tightly with ropes.

roping hooks, rope anchorages below the bed of a vehicle.

ROPS, rollover protective structure.

ro-ro, roll-on roll-off, a type of vehicle ferry.

ROSC, Road Operator's Safety Council, UK.

rosejoint, a precision spherical bearing used within the suspension of some competition cars, allowing articulation but no linear movement.

RoSPA, Royal Society for the Prevention of Accidents, UK.

rotary, the motion of a part that continuously turns on its axis.

rotary, USA, roundabout.

rotary engine, an engine in which power is produced without reciprocating pistons, *e.g.* a gas turbine.

rotary piston engine, an internal combustion positive displacement engine having a single epitrochoidal rotor and very few other moving parts, *e.g.* the Wankel engine invented by Felix Wankel in Germany in 1956.

rotary pump, a pump with rotating parts, not reciprocating.

rotary switch, a switch that is operated by rotating its shaft or its body.

rotary valve, an engine valve arrangement in which a tube closely encloses the cylinder, both of which have a hole in their sides, and where the tube rotates to line up the matched holes in order to open the valve.

rotary vibration, torsional vibration causing any part to rapidly twist and untwist.

rotate out, the method used by USA police for halting the progress of a violator by using the fishtail technique.

rotating beacon, a lamp having 1 or several rotating reflectors that emit a rotating beam of light, and having a frequency of between 2 and 5 flashes per second.

rotation, see: tyre rotation.

rotational steering, a technique for using the steering wheel where the hands cross, *i.e.* hand over hand style; not as efficient or safe as other techniques, but sometimes useful when fixed-

grip steering has been misjudged.

rotbox, a seriously corroded car.

rotocap, a device which turns a poppet valve slightly each time it opens, to reduce sticking and burning.

rotoflex coupling, a hexagonal doughnut rubber coupling.

rotor, a rotating part, *e.g.* the armature of an alternator, or the impeller in a water pump.

rotor arm, the rotating part within the distributor cap that acts as a rotating switch and distributes the high voltage current to each sparkplug cable connector.

rotor pump, a type of pump in which the rotation of 2 rotors or interlocking vanes turning around each other or 1 within the other, create a diminishing space between the rotor lobes to force a fluid through the pump, often used for diesel injection at pressures of up to 350 bar.

ROU, Uruguay, international vehicle distinguishing sign, see appendices.

rough idle, an uneven or erratic engine idle which may almost cause the engine to stall or the vehicle to shake.

roundabout, a junction of several roads where traffic moves in one direction around a typically circular central kerbed island 4 metres or greater in diameter; invented by Monsieur Henard in France in 1907; see also: 2 bridge, 3 level, double mini, false, gyratory, hamburger, helical, magic, mini, sig-nabout, spiral, square-about.

roundabout tyre syndrome, a condition which may lead to slightly increased wear to the nearside tyres if a driver makes an abnormally high number of turns to the offside at roundabouts at speed with underinflated tyres.

route, a selected way or course, a series of roads from a start location to a specific destination.

Route 1, highway US1, the Pacific Coast Highway connecting Mexico to Canada, 2,600 km, (1,625 miles) in length.

Route 66, highway US66, an old highway across USA, 3,940 km (2,448 miles) from Chicago to Santa Monica, Los Angeles, formerly one of the busiest 2 lane single carriageway roads, now an enthusiasts route.

route check, a usually unmanned location in a road rally having a code board to prove a visit.

route indicator, a panel displaying externally from a bus the route number.

Routemaster, a design of bus that remained in production for 44 years.

Route Napoléon, the RN85 (N85) from Grenoble to Cannes 320 km (200 miles) long in southern France.

routier, French, a roadside café.

routine violation, an optimising violation performed as regular behaviour, typically where the risk is perceived to be low and the gain is perceived to be moderate, *e.g.* habitually eating a snack whilst driving instead of stopping.

RoW, right of way.

Royal Automobile Club Motor Sports Association, the organisation responsible for regulating motor sport in UK.

Royal Society of Arts, UK, the accreditation body responsible for many road haulage related examinations.

RP, Philippines, international vehicle distinguishing sign, see appendices.

rpk, an incorrect form of r/km, revolutions per kilometre.

rpm, revolutions per minute, a measure of crankshaft rotational speed.

RPM, raised pavement marker.

rpm sensor, engine speed sensor.

RPO, USA, lowest rated horsepower.

rps, revolutions per second.

RPS, rollover protection system.

rr, rear right.

r & r, remove and reinstall, to service a part by removal, inspection, adjustment, lubrication, and reinstallation.

RR, reversing radar.

RR, USA, rural route.

RRPM, retroreflective raised pavement marker, a cats-eye, reflective road stud.

RSA, Royal Society of Arts.

R(S)A, Roads (Scotland) Act 1984.

RSC, regularity start control, in road rally navigation.

rsi, radio static interference.

RSM, San Marino, international vehicle distinguishing sign, see appendices.

RSO, road safety officer.

RSU, road safety unit.

RSW, rain sensing wipers.

RT, rear track width.

RTA, road traffic accident.

RTA, Road Traffic Act, in UK 1988 or 1991.

RTC, regularity time control, in road rally navigation.

RT(CP)A, UK, Road Traffic (Consequential Provisions) Act 1988.

RT(DLIS)A, UK, Road Traffic (Driver Licensing and Information Systems) Act 1989.

RTI, ramp travel index.

RTITB, Road Transport Industry Training Board, UK.

RTM, real total mass.

RT(ND)A, UK, Road Traffic (New Drivers) Act 1995.

RTOA, UK, Road Traffic Offenders Act 1988.

RTP, regularity timing point, in road rally navigation.

RTRA, UK, Road Traffic Regulation Act 1984.

rt road, ratione tenurae, by reason of tenure, a public carriageway which is maintained at the expense of the land owner.

rtt, reconfigurable telltale.

rtv, road taxed vehicle trial.

rtv, room temperature vulcanising.

rtv, rough terrain vehicle.

RU, Burundi, international vehicle

distinguishing sign, see appendices.

rubber, tyres.

rubber band transmission, a cvt transmission system.

rubber bonnet hook, a positive locking quick release device for retaining engine covers etc.

rubber bush, a tubular rubber or plastic bearing, typically with relatively thick walls, in a joint which oscillates through only a few degrees, *e.g.* in the suspension.

rubbernecking, the action of slowing to stare at the result of an accident on any road, such that the driver may not be watching where he/she is going with the potential to cause another collision.

rubber suspension, a design using compressed rubber to take the place of steel springs, on various types of vehicles.

rubbing compound, cutting compound.

rubbing strip, a strip of hard rubber or plastic along each side of a car along its widest point to protect the car from being damaged by opened doors in a car park, *i.e.* to prevent door rash.

Rubicon Trail, an extremely arduous long distance route for 4x4 vehicles along the valley of the river Rubicon in the Sierra Nevada mountains, California, normally taking about 1 week to complete.

Rudge hub, a wheel mount on which the wheel is secured onto hub splines by a quick release central Rudge nut, an early method of providing rapid wheel changes during racing.

Rudge nut, the nut that secures a knock on wheel, tightened or released by a single hammer blow to a lug.

rule of the road, the law regulating which side of the road is to be taken by vehicles meeting or passing each other.

rumble, a low frequency road noise associated with off-road tyres or a ribbed concrete surface.

rumble, an engine noise associated with bending vibration of the crankshaft, especially in high compression engines.

rumble area, rumble strips.

rumble seat, USA, dickey seat.

rumble strip, a longitudinal line along both edges of some roads especially motorways, having frequent raised portions within the line to cause the steering and suspension to vibrate if a wheel rolls along it, to wake a sleeping driver before crashing.

rumble strips, transverse corrugations across the width of a road, each typically 20 mm high and a few cm long but collectively having a typical combined length of several metres, causing a vehicle to vibrate to alert drivers to a hazard ahead, *e.g.* a junction, see also: jiggle bars.

runabout, a small car used for short journeys.

run and jump, a Le Mans start.

run around, a series of short journeys, typically around a town.

runaway, a condition when a driver has no

control over the speed of a vehicle.

run down, to collide with a pedestrian or cyclist.

run flat, a tyre that can safely be driven on whilst punctured or deflated, typically for 80 km at 80 km/h (for 50 miles at 50 mph).

run in, to treat a new or rebuilt engine very gently, driving at mid revs without harsh acceleration for the first 800 km (500 miles), an obsolete idea, with a modern engine it is best to run at moderately high power to prevent cylinder glazing.

run in, to treat new tyres gently, driving without harsh acceleration or braking or steering for the first 100 km (60 miles).

run into, to collide with a vehicle or object.

run into the ground, to use a vehicle until it ceases to be roadworthy, typically using it with inadequate maintenance.

run it fine, to arrive at a destination on time but with no safety margin when time is critical.

run low, a condition when any fluid has reached its minimum safe level, including fuel.

runner, a vehicle of dubious mechanical condition of which the engine will start but it may be deficient in roadworthiness.

running board, an external step along the sides between the front and rear wheels to ease entry and exit on some vehicles.

running gear, all of the moving parts on the underside of a vehicle, *i.e.* the suspension, steering, brakes, and drivetrain.

running in, run in.

running on, dieseling, the reluctance of a carburetted hot petrol engine to stop.

running on empty, the action of driving whilst the fuel gauge shows empty.

running order, the sequence of racing cars at any moment during a race.

running repairs, repairs performed during a journey.

running speed, the average speed of a single vehicle over a specified length of road, *i.e.* the distance divided by the running time.

running speed, the average speed of all traffic, which is the summation of distances divided by the summation of running times.

running the lights, the action of deliberately ignoring a red traffic signal and driving through the junction at any time during the red phase, typically at speed; see also: blowing, jumping.

running time, the duration of time a vehicle is in motion.

running time, when measuring traffic flow or density, the time taken for vehicles to pass between 2 points.

runoff, a clear flat area on the outside of a racing circuit bend.

run on, dieseling.

run out, a condition when a fluid is depleted, especially fuel.

runout, lateral or axial runout, a disc or wheel of which all points on the circumference have the same measured radius but do not rotate

through the same point, *i.e.* an axially buckled area.

runout, radial runout, a disc or wheel where all points on the circumference do not rotate through the same point due to a variation in radius, *i.e.* having a flattened area on the rim.

runout, see also: lateral, radial.

runout, the measure of roundness error of a tyre that will cause a vibration that cannot be balanced.

runout vibration, wheel vibration caused by a small imperfection of runout in a wheel, it may be amplified if not match mounted to the tyre.

run over, to collide with a pedestrian or cyclist.

run up ramps, a pair of sloping steel rails behind the 5th wheel coupling on a tractive unit enabling the tractive unit to force its way under a semitrailer by lifting the semitrailer a few centimetres when the height of the kingpin is slightly below that of the 5th wheel coupling.

RUPP, road used as a public path.

RUS, Russian Federation, international vehicle distinguishing sign, see appendices.

rush-hour, the periods of time of the most intense traffic, typically a duration up to 3 hours each morning and each afternoon when city roads may be congested.

rust, a dark brown layer of ferrous oxide having very little strength.

rust bucket, a seriously corroded car.

rusting, the oxidation of iron or steel, a result of electrochemical reactions with components in the environment.

rusty, a driver who is out of practice, having lost some skills from non-use.

rusty, a vehicle part that has oxidised, rusted.

rut, each of a pair of depressions along a tarmac road surface aligned with the usual track of heavy lorries, caused by the weight of lorries crushing the surface or sub surface.

rut, a depression in an unmetalled surface caused by the passage of wheels eroding or squeezing the surface.

rv, recreational vehicle.

rv, residual value.

RV, recovery vehicle.

RV(C&U)R, UK, Road Vehicles (Construction & Use) Regulations 1986.

RVLR, UK, Road Vehicle Lighting Regulations 1989.

RVR, Road Vehicle Regulations.

RV(R&L)R, UK, Road Vehicles (Registration and Licensing) Regulations 1971.

rv trailer, USA, a conventional trailer caravan having living accommodation.

RW, reference weight; see: reference mass.

RWA, Rwanda, international vehicle distinguishing sign, see appendices.

RWAL, rear wheel antilock brakes.

rwd, rear wheel drive.

rwl, raised white lettering.

rws, rear wheel steering.

Rzeppa, Hans Rzeppa, the inventor of a vibrationless and snatch-free universal joint which is able to transmit power through a relatively large angle, in Czechoslovakia in 1926.

Rzeppa uj, a constant velocity joint comprising a series of balls in slots, first used for transmitting drive through the steering angle in the Mini in 1959, now used in many fwd vehicles.

S

s, second, a unit of time, used when calculating speed and acceleration, and power.

S, saloon, a car body style.

S, signal, a phase of the MSM mnemonic.

S, snow mode, referring to some automatic transmission, a switch to bias gear selection, *i.e.* it will start in 3rd gear to reduce possibility of wheelspin.

S, soft mode, referring to remote controlled variable dampers, it allows the driver to select soft to match road surface and driving style.

S, south.

S, spark ignition, an API oil classification for oils suitable for service in si engines.

S, speed, a phase of the PSL mnemonic.

S, sport, referring to selectable traction control, sport allows a limited amount of wheelspin, developed by Ferrari.

S, sport mode, referring to ABC active suspension it allows the driver to select sport to significantly reduce body roll.

S, sport mode, referring to some automatic transmission, a switch to bias gear selection, *i.e.* it will accelerate to higher rev's before changing up.

S, Sweden, international vehicle distinguishing sign, see appendices.

S, the tyre speed rating code denoting a maximum design speed of 180 km/h (113 mph), moulded into the tyre sidewall.

S cam brakes, an operating mechanism for drum brakes whereby an S shaped cam rotates between rollers to force the shoes apart, on some heavy vehicles.

S hump, a speed hump having a sinusoidal or bell shaped cross section for increased comfort at low speeds whilst creating discomfort at high speeds.

SA, Saudi Arabia, international vehicle distinguishing sign, see appendices.

Saab, Svenska Aeroplan Aktiebolaget, Swedish Aeroplanes Ltd.

Sacco panel, a side bumper panel.

saddle tank, a fuel tank mounted over the rear axle.

SAE, Society of Automotive Engineers, USA.

SAE gross bhp, a power rating of an engine without any auxiliary drives connected, *i.e.* without alternator, cooling pump, etc, such that the figure is higher than practically attainable, an obsolete measurement.

SAE horsepower, USA, an obsolete and inaccurate reckoning of horsepower, calculated only from the square of the bore in inches multiplied by the number of cylinders and divided by 2.5, originally used for licensing purposes.

SAE net bhp, a power rating of an engine with all auxiliary drives in service and carrying a typical load as in a practical driving situation, at 15.55 °C and 982 millibars of air pressure.

safari, an expedition typically by 4x4 on unsurfaced roads, especially in Africa, named from Swahili from Arabic safara, to travel.

safe, to remain free from risk of injury or damage.

safe colour, a range of colours used for vehicles that renders them easily seen such that there is a lower risk of collision, *e.g.* yellow or white.

safe driving, driving without causing or becoming involved in a collision, conflict, or a near-miss.

safe speed, a speed determined by environment, road, and vehicle limitations, assuming the driver is alert and healthy, based upon sight distance, stopping distance, and the risk imposed by other road users.

safe stopping distance, a basic safety rule relating speed to the ability to stop and which demands that every driver must be able to stop in the distance seen to be clear, or in fog or on a single track road in $^{1}/_{2}$ the distance seen to be clear.

Safe-T camera, a digital camera acting as part of an SVDD or similar system.

safety, methods, procedures, and techniques for avoiding collisions or accidents, and for reducing danger.

safety, see: active, conditional, control, drive, exterior, impact, information, interior, operating, passive, perceptual, primary, secondary, tertiary.

safety barrier, safety fencing to separate traffic or to prevent an out of control vehicle from straying into an area of increased danger, typically made from concrete, corrugated steel, steel box section, or steel wire rope.

safety bead seat, a ridge around a wheel between the rim bead seat and the well, to prevent a deflated tyre bead from moving into the well then leaving the rim.

safety belt, seatbelt.

safety bubble, the amount of space maintained

on all sides of a moving vehicle by a defensive driver, necessary to reduce risk of collision; also named: –cell, –cushion, –zone.

safety car, a high performance saloon car used to control the speed of race competitors whilst keeping them moving in their relative positions whilst an accident is being cleared from the track.

safety catch, the secondary bonnet release mechanism which prevents the bonnet from flying up if the primary mechanism fails or is operated inadvertently.

safety cell, the amount of space maintained on all sides of a moving vehicle by a defensive driver, necessary to reduce risk of collision; also named: –bubble, –cushion, –zone.

safety chains, a pair of crossed chains near the hitch, which link some trailers with their towing vehicle as a guard against hitch failure.

safety compliance certificate, USA, a label affixed in the drivers door frame on the lower B pillar specifying the VIN and other information.

safety cushion, the amount of space maintained on all sides of a moving vehicle by a defensive driver, necessary to reduce risk of collision; also named: –bubble, –cell, –zone.

safety distance, the distance required for clearance between an overtaking vehicle and an oncoming vehicle at the instant the overtaking vehicle has returned to its own lane.

safety engineering, the testing and evaluating of equipment and procedures to prevent accidents.

safety envelope, the extent of the many limiting parameters within which the vehicle is operated safely, *e.g.* matching speed to the environment with respect to the road surface, the weather, and risk of collision with other road users.

safety equipment, equipment of either primary or secondary safety function, designed to reduce the risk of a collision or reduce the severity of injury in a collision.

safety fencing, safety barrier.

safety gap, a space ahead of a vehicle equivalent at least to the 2 second rule.

safety gap rule, the 2-second rule.

safety glass, laminated glass, or toughened glass.

safety line, the line or course followed along a road, typically approximately 1 metre from the nearside road edge when there are no significant hazards but positioning to the left or right as much as reasonable to increase safety margins wherever necessary.

safety ramp, Australia, escape lane.

safety recall, a procedure when a manufacturer suspects there may be a common defect in a type of vehicle or parts and issues a request for all relevant vehicles to be checked by an authorised dealer and have remedial work performed.

safety rim, a wheel having small ridges just

inboard of the bead seat, to retain a tyre on the rim if it should deflate especially whilst cornering.

safety roadside rest, a parking area separated from the road, provided for motorists to stop and rest for short periods, having paved areas and usually other service facilities.

safety wheel, a wheel and tyre combination specially designed to have run-flat capability.

safety wheel, a wheel having a safety rim.

safety zone, the amount of space maintained on all sides of a moving vehicle by a defensive driver, necessary to reduce risk of collision; also named: –bubble, –cell, –cushion.

safety zone, USA, a space set aside for pedestrians marked by raised lane buttons or markers, typically where there are streetcars or trolleys sharing the street with motor vehicles.

safing sensor, a sensor in an air bag system is designed to prevent inadvertent deployment.

sag, a dip in a length of road, the opposite of a crest.

sagging door, a door having a very worn hinge mechanism allowing it to drop slightly when not closed.

sai, steering axis inclination.

sail panel, an unusually wide C pillar.

sala suspension, short arm long arm suspension.

saloon, a traditional 3 box car having a fully enclosed body with a fixed roof and rear window, 2 rows of seats, 2 or 4 doors, and a half height luggage compartment and an engine bay at opposite ends.

saloon, the passenger compartment of a bus.

SAMT, semiautomated manual transmission.

sand planing, the action of driving across soft sand at a reasonably high speed to prevent the tyres from sinking into the surface.

sand tyre, a tyre designed for use on sand, having straight grooves and ribs in line with the direction of travel and without any lateral channels, for maximum traction and minimum bogging.

sandwich floor, a vehicle design in which the floor of the passenger compartment and the underfloor of the body are separated by a space containing engine, transmission or other mechanical parts.

sandwich lane, any lane where there are contiguous lanes in the same direction on both sides, *e.g.* lane 2 on a 3 lane motorway.

Sankey wheel, the first type of wheel that was easily and quickly removable to repair a puncture, developed in 1910.

sans plomb, French, without lead, unleaded petrol.

Santler, Charlie Santler, builder of the 1st car in England at Malvern, Worcestershire around 1880, later registered AB 171.

SAS, Scandinavian Automotive Suppliers.

SAT4, semiautomatic 4 speed transmission.

SAT5, semiautomatic 5 speed transmission.

SAT6, semiautomatic 6 speed transmission.

satellite, a group of minor controls for finger tip operation at the end of a control stalk.
satisfactory quality, a legal standard at the purchase of a second hand vehicle by which: it must meet the standard that a reasonable person would regard as acceptable, regarding cost, appearance, finish, safety, and durability, and be free from defects except those pointed out by the seller to the buyer and those that should have been uncovered by inspection, but excepting normal wear and tear.
satnav, satellite navigation.
Sat Nav, satellite navigation system.
saturation level, a condition in any area when the ratio of cars to population ceases to show material annual increase.
saturation level, a condition on any system of roads when no increase in the throughput of vehicles is possible without traffic movement being totally stopped.
sausaged, a dealer term for a car that has been crashed; from cockney rhyming slang sausage and mash.
sav, sports activity vehicle.
SB, rear track width.
SB, southbound, to travel towards the south.
SBC, Sensonic brake control.
SBP, small bus permit.
SBS, seat integrated seatbelt system.
SC, safety car.
SC, secret check, an undisclosed location in road rally navigation.
scale, a series of graduations on a measuring device indicating specific values.
scale, the accumulation of mineral deposits, often associated with hot water cooling systems.
scale, USA, a weighbridge for weighing lorries.
scan, to keep the eyes moving, to observe systematically following a predetermined sequence, to constantly look at different distances ahead, along both sides of the road, both sides of the vehicle, and to the rear, to ensure the driver is aware of everything which is or may happen.
Scandinavian flick, a rallying technique for inducing a rear wheel skid to create a controlled spin through 90° to 180°: approaching a bend the car is deliberately unsettled by brake-steer overlap to cause oversteer which is encouraged by appropriate steering until it develops into the required rear wheel skid to enable the bend to be taken at maximum speed under power.
scanimet, a nickel silicon carbide coating sometimes applied to cylinder walls to increase wear resistance.
scanning pattern, a system of looking at different areas according to a predefined plan.
scatter shield, a physical guard over and around some parts that may fail at high revs, typically around the bell housing to protect the driver of a high performance vehicle from flying parts.
scavenging, the displacement of remaining exhaust gas from the combustion chamber by the swirl of incoming air or air-fuel mixture.
scavenging losses, the power lost by an engine due to a small proportion of the exhaust gas from the previous cycle remaining in the cylinder during the next cycle.
scavenging pump, a pump that removes oil from the sump and returns it to the reservoir in a dry sump system.
scc, spark control computer.
SCCA, Sports Car Club of America.
SCC label, the safety compliance certificate.
scenic highway, USA, a portion of a state highway which traverses areas of outstanding scenic beauty.
scheduled time, the time an individual crew is due at a time control in road rally navigation.
schematic, a pictorial representation by line drawing or diagram showing components in their relative positions and their interconnections, especially for electrical, air, or fluid systems.
schematic diagram, a representation of electrics, hydraulics, or pneumatics, showing symbols to represent components and lines to represent wiring or tubing.
school zone, USA, an area extending to 500 feet (150 m) from a school boundary on school days between 7.00 am and 4.00 pm where a 20 mph (32 km/h) speed limit is imposed and overtaking is prohibited.
Schrader valve, a small spring loaded valve serving as the access port for filling or pressurising tyres, ac, and other pressurised systems.
scissor door, a door that opens in a vertical longitudinal arc, hinged just behind the front wheel.
scissor engine, a cat and mouse engine, a type of rotary engine typified by the Tschudi engine which is an analogue of the reciprocating piston engine, except the pistons travel in a circular motion.
scissor jack, a screw jack driven by a horizontal screw, the linkages are a parallelogram whose horizontal dimensions are lengthened or shortened by the screw; commonly provided by manufacturers as standard equipment for production cars.
scissor junction, a junction of 2 roads where they cross at a very acute angle to each other.
scissor swap, the action of 2 drivers moving in the same direction exchanging lanes simultaneously.
SCM, Schweizerischer Verband der Grosshandler und Importeure der Motorfahrzeugbranche, Switzerland.
SCMG, Specialist Car Manufacturers Group, UK.
SCOOT, split cycle offset optimisation technique.
scooter, a 2 wheeled motorcycle having an

open frame, a platform for the feet, and wheels smaller than those of a conventional motorcycle, also named motor scooter.

scorching, illegal road racing.

score, a scratch that has damaged a sliding part, especially a piston, cylinder, bearing, or brake disc.

scotch, a wedge block or chock, placed against a wheel to restrain movement.

scout car, a lightly armed and armoured military reconnaissance vehicle, usually wheeled but sometimes halftrack, adapted for high speed operation on hard roads and for cross-country missions.

scrambling, the action of tyres when alternately slipping then gripping, especially when driving uphill on a poor surface when friction beneath each tyre constantly varies.

scrap, a part or a whole vehicle that has reached the end of its life, to be discarded as waste.

scrape, to rub a surface harshly, especially for vehicle bodywork to be damaged by passing against a fixed object or another vehicle.

scrappage, USA, a vehicle which has not been registered for the current year.

scrapyard, a place containing old or crashed vehicles which are retained until any salvageable parts are removed.

screen, a fine mesh used as a course filter to prevent large particles from circulating in a fluid system, *e.g.* in lubricating oil.

screen, a visual display, *e.g.* for in-vehicle navigation.

screen, windscreen.

screen shield, a wire mesh guard across the lower part of a lorry windscreen, to reduce stone impact damage.

screenwash, a fluid comprising water with additives, usually alcohol and detergents, formulated for easy removal of dirt from the windscreen.

screw, a cylindrical body with a helical groove cut into its surface.

screw compressor, an air compressor utilising 2 shaped rotors or vanes which compress air as they rotate against or around each other.

screwdriver, a tool used for turning screws, having a wedge shaped or a fluted bit that enters the screw head.

screw jack, a bottle shaped mechanical device having concentric screwed sections driven by a pinion gear, with which to raise a vehicle by rotating a handle.

screw thread, a helical ridge formed on a cylindrical core, usually of triangular section but sometimes square section for heavy duty applications.

scrub, wear caused by undue friction, especially to a tyre tread if the wheels are not correctly aligned, or dry steering, skidding, driving with a differential locked, driving a part time 4wd on a dry paved surface, or turning sharply with a semitrailer; see also: scuff.

scrubbing in, to run in new tyres, driving without harsh acceleration or braking or steering for the first 100 km (60 miles).

scrub off speed, speed reduction caused by the friction lost when a tyre sideslips, especially by the front tyres when cornering at speed.

scrub radius, the lateral distance at ground level between a vertical line through the centre of the tyre footprint and a line extended through the swivel axis, being positive if the lines intersect below ground level and negative if intersecting above ground level.

scrutineer, a person who examines vehicles used in motor sport.

scrutineering, detailed examination of a vehicle used in motor sport.

scrutinizer, USA, scrutineer.

SCS, stop control system.

scuff, wear to a tyre sidewall, typically by frequent abrasion along a kerb, but also during tyre rollover when cornering at high speed on underinflated tyres; see also: scrub.

scuff, a type of wear where material is transferred from 1 part to another, *e.g.* where paint is deposited from 1 vehicle to another during a collision.

scuff plate, a chromed or plastic trim along a door sill to resist damage by footwear as persons enter and leave.

scuff rib, a raised rib around the sidewall of a tyre to reduce wear to the sidewall when parking close to a kerb.

scuff ribs, a series of concentric raised ribs around the sidewall of a rally tyre to give physical protection from damage by rocks, especially when kerbdragging.

scuttle, the narrow strip of bodywork between the windscreen and the bonnet.

scuttle shake, a horizontal vibration of the dashboard, the effect of loss of vehicle rigidity especially in any open top car.

SD, selective detection.

SD, Svalbard, international vehicle distinguishing sign, see appendices.

SE(ADI), UK, Supervising Examiner of ADI's, the person who conducts the ADI examinations and check tests.

seal, a device which prevents passage of fluid beyond some point, or prevents ingress of dirt.

sealant, a compound used to make a seal, or to seal a surface against corrosion.

sealed beam, a complete headlamp including the filament, reflector, and lens as 1 inseparable unit.

sealed bearing, a bearing without provision for external lubrication, the lubrication is sealed inside by the manufacturer and designed to last for the lifetime of the unit.

sealed for life battery, a lead-calcium battery without facility for checking the electrolyte.

sealed gel lead acid battery, a battery of secondary cells in which the electrolyte is a gel or paste, it does not need periodic topping up with distilled water.

sealed road, the condition of a road surface having a surface layer which renders the road weatherproof, typically surfaced with tarmac or concrete.

sealing compound, sealant.

seam bleed, rust which originates in a seam between factory joined body panels, where rust prevention has not penetrated the joint.

seasonal check, a series of vehicle checks based upon the mnemonic power, but also testing the rd of the coolant and electrolyte, and the boiling point of the brake fluid.

seasoned driver, a driver with some years driving experience but typically displaying some bad practices and habits.

seat, a structure on which the driver and occupants of a vehicle sit.

seat, the surface upon which another rests, especially where a valve seals.

seat, to deliberately cause minute wear to 2 parts to make a good fit.

Seat, Sociedad Española de Automóviles de Turismo, Spanish car manufacturer.

seatbelt, a flat broad length of webbing with which to hold a person securely in a seat, especially for protection in the event of a collision, typically having a 3 point anchorage, a secondary safety feature but a primary safety restraint, invented by Nils Bohlin in 1955 in Sweden, developed for road vehicles by Volvo.

seatbelt pretensioner, a safety device on some seatbelts which deploy a pyrotechnic to rapidly tension a seatbelt at the commencement of an impact to reduce occupant injury.

seatbelt pretensioners & force limiters, a system linked to the pretensioners such that after deployment and a preset amount of force has been reached, force limiters slowly release tension on the belt to help absorb the energy of an impact.

seatbelt warning light, a tell-tale lamp which shows red on the dashboard if a belt is not worn by a seat occupant, or sometimes it is merely time controlled.

seating capacity, the number of seated persons including the driver that a vehicle is designed to accommodate.

seat integrated seatbelt system, a seat having all seat belt anchorages within its structure to improve fit and comfort, but requiring a very strong seat subframe.

seat runner, the tracks onto which seats are usually mounted to permit fore-aft adjustment.

seat saver, a waterproof dirtproof cover fitted over a vehicle seat to protect it from damage by water, mud, oil, dirt, abrasion etc.

seat time, the accumulation of time a racing driver spends on a racing circuit, including testing, practice, and racing.

seat well, the area below a seat which is also below the bottom edge of the door.

second, a gear selector control button on some bus automatic transmission selector systems.

secondary air, a system of adding air to some exhaust emission systems to complete the oxidation of HC and CO to convert the pollutants into water vapour and carbon dioxide.

secondary brake, a retarder.

secondary braking, to brake again after the normal period of braking for a hazard, especially any braking after the gearchange, typically required because the initial braking was insufficient; considered undesirable in respect of advanced driving.

secondary braking system, any of various retarder systems, as fitted to many buses and lorries.

secondary cell, a battery in which the chemical reaction may be reversed by forcing an electric current in the opposite direction, *i.e.* it may be recharged.

secondary circuit, the high voltage path from the ignition coil through the distributor rotor arm to the sparkplugs.

secondary collision, the impact of an unrestrained vehicle occupant on striking the inside of the vehicle immediately after a primary collision, or in striking an unadjusted seatbelt; see also: tertiary.

secondary controls, the switches for the minor controls that perform safety functions: direction indicators, windscreen wipers and washer, lights, horn, heating and ventilation, etc.

secondary damage, damage caused to a vehicle after the direct damage, *e.g.* due to overturning after the primary impact.

secondary escape route, a clear area alongside a vehicle ahead which can safely be entered at speed but with some steering, to avoid an impending collision.

secondary key, a key which only operates the locks necessary for valet parking, *i.e.* driver and passenger doors, ignition switch, and fuel filler, without allowing access to boot or glovebox.

secondary pump, a lube oil pump in a gearbox driven by the output shaft at a speed relative to wheel speed.

secondary pump, any electrical pump in the same system in which there is also a mechanically driven primary pump, *e.g.* automatic aftercooling of the coolant after the engine is stopped.

secondary road, any road classed with a B prefix to its number, less important than A roads in the national road network.

secondary safety coupling, a safety device normally fitted to goods vehicle trailers to prevent inadvertent uncoupling, not usually present on agricultural trailers.

secondary safety measure, a device, modification, or tactic that reduces the degree of injury to road users after a collision occurs, *e.g.* an airbag.

secondary safety restraint, any device designed to be used in conjunction with a primary safety restraint, *e.g.* an airbag to be used in conjunction with a seatbelt.

secondary shoe, USA, a trailing shoe in a brake drum.

secondary suspension, a cab suspension system by which a lorry cab is suspended above the chassis of a lorry for additional driver comfort.

secondary traffic signal, a traffic signal located on the far side of a junction, so it may be seen by drivers who have crossed the stop line.

secondary visor, a sun visor in a dual system where the primary visor can be used to shield from the front or side, and the secondary from the front only.

secondary winding, a winding in the ignition coil having a very large number of turns, and which produces up to 65,000 volts to fire the sparkplugs.

secondhand, a vehicle that has had a previous owner.

second steer, the second axle on a vehicle having 2 or more steering axles.

second steer air dump, a system on a 6x2 tractive unit that will temporarily raise the second steering axle, thereby transferring weight to the drive axle to improve traction on a slippery surface.

section, a series of controls or stages in a rally.

sectional diagram, a drawing or picture of a vehicle or assembly in which the parts are shown as if the unit was cut along 1 or 2 planes; see also: exploded, phantom.

section height, the vertical distance from the rim bead seat to the crown in an unloaded tyre.

section repair, a bodyshell repair where a good section is taken from another seriously damaged vehicle.

section width, the maximum width of a tyre from sidewall to sidewall excluding lettering and designs, when measured inflated on a rim appropriate to its size, typically the appropriate section width is 25 % wider than the rim width, but less for low profile tyres.

sector shaft, rocker shaft.

security chauffeur, a chauffeur trained in anti-attack and anti-hijack escape techniques.

security lighting, doorstep lighting, lights mounted in the bottom of the door mirrors to illuminate the ground outside the driver and passenger doors, developed by Volvo.

security post, a device used in a private driveway to deter theft of a car, or to prevent a car entering a private area.

sedan, USA, a saloon car having 4 doors, or a 2 door car having at least 33 cubic feet (0.934 m³) of interior volume.

sedanca, a 2 door coupé in which the rear seats are covered by a fixed roof and the front seats are either open or have a removable top.

sedanca de ville, a large chauffeur-driven veteran car, typically in the style of an early taxi where the driver is exposed to the weather

and the passengers ride in a closed saloon.

see 1 think 2, a defensive driving assumption based upon mathematical probability: when seeing a vehicle emerge ahead into your path on the main road always expect another is behind and may attempt to follow it into your path.

see the whole scene, to be aware of all that is happening on all sides of the vehicle.

segment, a portion of the car retail market, based upon the size and floorpan of a car, and denoted by a letter.

segment A, a portion of the car retail market based upon the size and floor pan; a small car often designated supermini, *e.g.* Mercedes A-class, or Peugeot 206 sized.

segment B, a portion of the car retail market based upon the size and floor pan; a small car designed to seat 4 with some comfort, *e.g.* Ford Focus, or Peugeot 306 sized.

segment C, a portion of the car retail market based upon the size and floor pan; a small family car to seat 5 with some comfort, *e.g.* Audi A4, or Ford Mondeo sized.

segment D, a portion of the car retail market based upon the size and floor pan; a medium sized family car that will seat 5 with comfort, *e.g.* Audi A6, or BMW 5-series sized.

segment E, a portion of the car retail market based upon the size and floor pan; a luxury car, *e.g.* Audi A8, or BMW 7-series, and usually estate versions of cars in segment D.

segment F, a portion of the car retail market based upon the size and floor pan; executive cars and cars with automatic transmission.

segment G, a portion of the car retail market based upon the size and floor pan; mpv 8 seat capacity.

segment M, a portion of the car retail market based upon the size and floor pan; luxury executive cars.

segment sub A, a portion of the car retail market based upon the size and floor pan; a very small car, *e.g.* the Mini, or Ford Ka sized.

segment W, a portion of the car retail market based upon the size and floor pan; high power sports cars.

segregated cycle track, a cycle track adjacent to a footpath or footway, and separated from it by a feature such as a kerb, verge, or white line.

seize, a condition when a mechanical part which should normally move against another part becomes immovable, *e.g.* for a bearing to melt and weld within the engine, or for a nut to be rusted to a bolt.

seize, to legally impound a vehicle and prevent its use by the owner or operator, *e.g.* as performed by Customs Officers.

selective change, block change.

selective detection, the ability of a traffic signal control system to differentiate between different vehicles, to then give priority to some types of vehicles, *e.g.* buses.

selective section, a competitive section in a

road rally timed to the second at exactly 30 mph (48.28 km/h) including checks for route compliance and for safety.

selective transmission, a gear selector system in which the driver can select any gear at any time without progressing through a sequence, *e.g.* using a H pattern gear selector.

selective vehicle detection, a system which recognises the approach of vehicles to a junction by magnetic loops buried in the road surface, and from their magnetic footprint the system can determine if the vehicle is a car, van, lorry, artic, or bus, etc. so that the system may give priority to certain vehicles, usually buses.

selector, the mechanism between the gearlever and the gears within the gearbox that moves the required gears into mesh.

selector fork, the part of a gear selector mechanism which moves a gear in and out of mesh; 2 forks usually slide along 1 rod.

selector lever, the lever in an automatic transmission which the driver uses to select between P, R, N, D, and lower gears.

selector lever lock, a system which prevents movement of an automatic transmission selector lever from P position if the engine is running unless the footbrake is firmly operated and the selector release button is depressed.

selector release button, a button at the top of an automatic transmission selector lever which prevents some movements of the lever unless the button is depressed.

selector rod, each bar along which 2 selector forks slide for selection of each pair of gears, *i.e.* 1 rod for each fore-aft line as marked on the gear lever knob, *i.e.* 2 rods in a simple 3 speed H selector but typically 3 or 4 in most vehicles.

Selectronic, a semiautomatic gear selecting system allowing preselection of the required gear range.

Selespeed, a clutchless sequential gearchange system using paddles on the steering wheel for most changes and a central lever to select neutral and reverse; the system automatically controls a manual gearbox and manual clutch using electronics to control hydraulic actuators, and has a drive by wire accelerator to automatically perform power changes for smoothness, but it will not creep when stationary, developed by Ferrari and Alfa Romeo.

self adjusting, any mechanism which automatically compensates for wear, *e.g.* in some brake mechanisms.

self aligning head restraint, a head restraint which moves upwards and forwards to cushion the head against whiplash, developed by Saab.

self aligning torque, the self centring force created by self centring effect of the castor angle against the centrifugal force of the vehicle body.

self cancelling, a function of the direction indicator switch and mechanism such that the indicators will automatically switch off as the steering wheel returns to a straight position.

self centring, the action of a typical steering mechanism under the influence of the self aligning torque created by the castor angle, such that whilst driving forwards the steering has a tendency to return unaided to a straight alignment.

self cleaning limit, the lowest temperature at which a sparkplug will burn off carbon deposits, typically approximately 500 °C.

self cleaning tread, a tyre tread having wide tapered grooves and channels to resist picking up or packing of mud or snow etc. from the surface, thereby giving greater friction on subsequent rotation.

self contained fork lift, a fork lift truck carried permanently by a lorry on its rear, for rapid unloading of heavy or bulky goods at each drop location.

self diagnostic system, a system that monitors itself and indicates when a defect occurs.

self dipping, an automatically dipping rear view mirror.

self discharge, chemical activity causing circulating currents within a battery that causes itself to discharge when there is no external current flow, sometimes caused by foreign substances added with impure water.

self drive, a facility or condition offered when hiring the use of a vehicle where the cost does not include a driver.

self ignition, the operating requirement in a diesel engine when the air-fuel mixture ignites due to the high temperature caused by the high compression.

self levelling damper, a damper incorporating an air spring, typically used at the rear of a vehicle which frequently tows heavy trailers, to assist the standard springs.

self levelling suspension, a system that reacts to weight within a vehicle and maintains a level ride by adjusting the air or hydraulic suspension.

self loading crane, a lorry mounted crane designed for loading and unloading the lorry only.

self locking nut, locknut.

self operating clutch, centrifugal clutch.

self parking wiper, a wiper mechanism that returns the blade to its designed rest position before stopping.

self propelled, a vehicle that is propelled by any mechanical means carried on the vehicle or on a trailer which it is drawing, including batteries, electricity received from trolley wires, internal combustion engine, external combustion engine, fuel cell, solar energy, etc. but not where a vehicle is powered by muscular energy by a person or drawn by an animal.

self regulating glowplug, a sheathed glowplug having heating and regulating coils.

self shifter, an automatic gearbox.

self starter, a starter motor.

self supporting technology, a tyre having specially fabricated sidewalls to provide run flat capability for 300 km (200 miles) at 80 km/h (50 mph), developed by Dunlop.

self tapping screw, a screw with a specially hardened thread which makes it possible for the screw to form its own internal thread in sheet metals and soft materials when driven into a hole.

self tracking, a semitrailer having automatic rear steering which steers in the opposite direction to the 5th wheel angle to assist manoeuvring around sharp corners.

Selwood engine, a revolving block engine in which 2 curved pistons opposed by 180° run in toroidal tracks forcing the engine block to rotate.

semaphore indicator, an electrically controlled illuminated mechanical direction indicator that pivots to extend from the side of a vehicle to signal the drivers intention to turn, common on 1950s vehicles.

semi, USA and Australia, semitrailer.

semi, USA, a tractive unit.

semiactive suspension, a suspension system allowing manual tuning of its characteristics by adjustment of hydraulics controlled electronically by the driver.

semiautomated manual transmission, a transmission that utilises a clutch pedal for starting and stopping only, with the gear selector control on the steering column.

semiautomatic, any system that can perform some functions unaided, with some driver input for some modes.

semiautomatic gearbox, a transmission and selector system in which the driver has full control over when and which gear is selected, but typically having a torque converter or electronically controlled wet clutch so there is no clutch pedal; there are many varying systems in use by different manufacturers, typically with microprocessor enhancement.

semiconductor, a material that acts as both an insulator and a conductor during different conditions, used within the charging circuit and in all microprocessors.

semiconductor ignition, an ignition system using semiconductors for all switching operations for high reliability.

semidiesel engine, an engine resembling a diesel engine but having a low compression requiring the fuel to be sprayed onto a hot spot in the combustion chamber for ignition.

semielliptic spring, a type of leaf spring for vehicle suspension of which the spring conforms to a specific mathematical shape, commonly used on the rear axle of classic and older vehicles but on few new vehicles.

semifloating axle, an axle drive shaft which transmits torque to a wheel, its inboard end floats on splines but at its outer end it also supports and restrains the wheel vertically and laterally.

semi-independent suspension, a rear axle suspension system on a fwd car in which the wheels are located by trailing links and a torsionally flexible crossmember.

semisynthetic oil, a highly refined lubricating oil having some of the properties of a synthetic oil but at a lower price.

semitractor, USA, a tractive unit.

semitrailer, a trailer which is supported at its rear by wheels and at its front by bearing on a tractive unit or dolly, drawn as part of an articulated lorry and which is attached to the tractive unit by a kingpin locked in the centre of a 5th wheel coupling turntable located forward of the tractive rear axle; at least 20 % of the fully loaded trailer weight must be born on the turntable by the tractive unit.

semitrailing arm, a type of coil sprung irs system where the arm is set at an angle such that it generates a negative camber at the wheel as the suspension compresses.

Sensonic, a semiautomatic gear selector system using paddles on the steering wheel to select the gear, developed by Saab.

Sensonic brake control, a microprocessor assisted braking system which calculates the optimum brake pressure required at each wheel to reduce the risk of skidding, developed by Mercedes.

sensor, a device that reacts to a situation and sends a signal, *e.g.* to the ECU.

separate chassis, a vehicle in which the body and chassis are separate units which are bolted together; the construction style of all pre-war vehicles, now lorries only.

separate lubrication, a development for some 2 stroke engines where oil is not added to the fuel but is metered directly to the components to be lubricated.

separation, the result caused by air seeping between the layers of a tyre carcass and causing a blister.

separation distance, the actual space ahead of a vehicle that must comply with the 2 second rule to meet safety requirements.

seq, sequential gearbox.

sequential fuel injection, a multipoint fuel injection system timed to match induction to the cylinders.

sequential gearbox, sequential shift gearbox.

sequential shift gearbox, a gear selector system in which selection is by the linear movement of the gear lever, as in an automatic transmission selector, some rally and sports cars, or a motorcycle, *i.e.* not using the conventional H pattern.

sequentronic, a 6 speed sequential semiautomatic gear selector system having an automatic mode, developed by Mercedes.

serai, see: caravanserai.

series, a designation of the aspect ratio of a tyre; *i.e.* a tyre having an aspect ratio of 60 % is a 60 series tyre.

series hybrid, a vehicle having an ic engine

and generator to produce electricity which is stored and/or fed to an electric motor(s), and in which the electric motor(s) is the only motive source used to propel the vehicle.

series motor, a series wound commutator type motor, as in the electrical construction of an engine starter motor having the armature windings and field windings in series to give high starting torque when starting an engine.

serious accident, an accident in which at least 1 person is seriously injured but no person is killed.

serious fault, a fault committed by a driver which if committed at a different time or place has the potential to impinge upon the safety of others.

serious injury, an injury for which a person is detained in hospital as an in-patient, or a person suffering from a fracture, concussion, internal injury, crushing, severe cuts, lacerations, or severe general shock requiring hospital treatment, and injuries causing death more than 30 days after the accident.

SERNAUTO, Associacion Espanola de Fabricantes de Equipos y Componentes para Automacion.

serpentine belt, USA, a polygrooved V belt.

service, to perform routine maintenance to a vehicle.

serviceable, a part or system that can be repaired or maintained.

serviceable, a vehicle that is in a roadworthy condition, ready for service.

service area, a large area off the side of a motorway for refuelling, refreshments, and sometimes overnight accommodation.

service brake, the main braking system of a vehicle which is designed and constructed to have the highest braking efficiency of any of the braking systems with which the vehicle is equipped, (C&U), typically the footbrake and having a braking efficiency of at least 50 %; if an air system to a trailer in UK it uses the yellow hose, in USA the blue hose.

service bridge, an opening panel typically in the radiator grille, giving access only for replenishing fluids on vehicles where full access to the engine is designed to be not frequently necessary or not easily accomplished.

service bus, a bus designed or used for local stage carriage service having basic passenger equipment and usually a semiautomatic or automatic gearbox.

service car, Australia and New Zealand, service bus.

service code, diagnostic fault code.

service history, documentary proof of servicing and repairs to a vehicle.

service interval, the period of time or an accumulation of distance between services, usually demanding adherence to the shorter of the time/distance intervals.

service life, the length of time or distance a component is expected to function in a safe, correct, and reliable manner.

service park, the area where rally cars may be serviced.

service rating, a designation for lubricating oils, defining the type of engine or usage for which each is suitable.

service record book, a book containing the service history of a vehicle and which should be stamped by the dealer or workshop performing a service.

service road, a restricted road allowing only goods vehicles access to commercial property for unloading.

service road, a lesser road parallel to a main road for safe and convenient access to shops, houses, property, etc.

services, a large area off the side of a motorway for refuelling, refreshments, and sometimes accommodation may be available.

service station, a place at the side of a road where vehicles may re-fuel, refreshments may also be available.

service transport, any motor traffic of an industrial or commercial nature generated by the delivery of materials or goods.

servicing, the act of maintaining a vehicle or specific parts by adjusting, lubricating, or replacing in order that the vehicle continues to be serviceable.

servo, an actuator which provides mechanical assistance, *i.e.* to give a powerful output from minimal input.

servo assistance, a system of assisting the driver to operate some controls, typically the brake, clutch, steering, or gears, usually by using a servo powered by a vacuum, air, hydraulics, or electrically, to add safety and reduce driver fatigue.

servo brake, a brake that is assisted in its operation by using a vacuum powered servo to add safety and reduce driver fatigue.

servo brake, a drum bake in which the shoes are arranged such that drag from the drum tends to increase the pressure, and the movement of 1 shoe increases the pressure on the other and vice versa, to create a self energising effect.

servomechanism, a system that provides power to assist the operation of a control.

Servoshift, a gearbox with servo assistance to the gear lever, typically for some lorry gearboxes.

set, any group of load sharing axles, see: single, tandem, triaxle.

set, to precisely adjust to a specific figure, and for the system to be locked so the setting will not inadvertently change.

set down, to allow passengers to alight from a bus.

set forth, to begin a journey.

set in motion, to cause a vehicle to start moving.

set off, to move off, to start moving.

set out, to begin a journey.

set screw, a small headless machine screw, driven by a recessed slot, flutes, or geometric socket.

set the chassis, to control a vehicle through a bend such that all forces on the vehicle are balanced and the chassis has a constant attitude.

severe driving conditions, various conditions that impose additional stress on an engine or system, *e.g.* towing, long steep gradients, dusty conditions, severe heat or cold, extended idling, or short trips of less than 6 km (4 miles).

severity ratio, the ratio of fatal plus serious accidents as a proportion of all injury accidents occurring at a specific location or along a specific road.

sfc, specific fuel consumption.

SFEPA, Syndicat des Fabricants d'Equipments et de Pieces pour Automobile, the major part of FIEV representing automotive parts manufacturers.

sfi, sequential fuel injection.

SFTC, spark fuel traction control.

sg, specific gravity.

sgl, single.

SGP, Singapore, international vehicle distinguishing sign, see appendices.

SGV, small goods vehicle.

SGW, standing give way, a specific location in road rally navigation.

SH, spot height, in road rally navigation a reference point.

shackle, a short link between the chassis and the rear end of a leaf spring, which allows the effective length of the spring to vary as the spring deflects.

shadeband, sunshield.

shaded relief map, a map of an area whose relief is made to appear 3 dimensional by the hill shading method, generally obsolete.

shaft, a long slim bar or tubular part that revolves on its axis to transmit power from 1 part to another, *e.g.* the propshaft or $^1/_2$ shaft.

shaft balancing, the process of redistributing the mass of a rotating body in order to reduce vibrations arising from centrifugal force.

shaft horsepower, horsepower measured at the crankshaft of the engine.

shake, wobble.

shaker plates, a pair of steel plates on the floor of a vehicle testing station which may be moved back and forth and sideways to check for wear in the steering and suspension of a vehicle.

shallow bend, a curve of very wide radius which may be negotiated at a high speed where safe and legal.

shared component, an identical part which is used in different body styles of the same model, or in different models, or in some cases of badge engineering in cars from different manufacturers.

shared driveway, an unadopted paved area that may serve the driveways of up to 5 houses.

shared surface, a road which has been designated a pedestrianised area and which may have significant restrictions for vehicular use, typically the surface is paved to suit pedestrians.

shared surface, a part of a shared surface road which is intended for use by both pedestrians and vehicles.

shared surface road, a residential road without a footway that may serve up to approximately 50 houses.

shared zone, Australia, a residential area having a 10 km/h (6 mph) speed limit and where pedestrians have priority.

shareway, a lane on a multilane road restricted to use by vehicles with 2 or more occupants, especially during rush-hour periods.

sharp end, the front of a vehicle.

shave, to pass very close to the side of a parked vehicle, especially at a speed unsafe for the proximity.

sheathed glowplug, a single pole glowplug having the heating coil enclosed in a thermally conductive ceramic layer.

shed, a vehicle in poor condition, especially the bodywork.

shed, to lose all or part of a load onto the road.

sheet, a tarpaulin used to cover a load on a lorry.

sheeting, the action of covering a lorry load with a tarpaulin and roping it securely.

sheet wheel, a road wheel made from thin aluminium plate.

shell, bodyshell.

shell bearing, a plain cylindrical bearing divided into 2 halves so it may be fitted around a shaft, *e.g.* a crankshaft journal.

Shellgrip, a high friction road surface manufactured from calcined bauxite in a resin binder, often applied on the approach to traffic signals, pedestrian crossings, roundabouts, etc, to reduce brake-induced skids and rear shunt collisions, often in bright colours, developed by Shell.

sheltered parking, a roadside parking area preceded by a buildout.

shift, to change gear.

shifter, USA, gearlever, or selector lever.

shiftgate, the quadrant in which a semiautomatic gear selector lever moves when the driver selects a higher or lower gear.

shiftgate, USA, gate.

shift indicator light, a tell-tale on the instrument panel of a semiautomatic indicating to the driver when an upchange or downchange should be performed.

shifting, USA, gearchanging.

shifting spanner, wrench.

shift lever, USA, gearlever.

shift light, a tell-tale which illuminates to inform a driver the optimum time to change gear.

shiftlock, a safety function that only allows an

automatic gear selector to be moved from P or N whilst the footbrake is applied.

shift on the fly, the ability of a transmission in which selection between 2H and 4H can be performed whilst driving, with a 2wd/4wd selectable transmission.

shift point, with reference to engine speed, or roadspeed and gear selected, the optimum time at which the next gear should be selected.

shift shock, a sudden pulse of power felt from an automatic transmission into the body of a car if drive or reverse is selected whilst using the accelerator, or if D or R is selected when the vehicle is moving in the opposite direction.

shift valve, USA, gearchange valve, a controlling component in an automatic gearbox.

shim, a thin sheet of metal of a precise thickness, often in the form of a washer used as a spacer or packing to exactly meet a dimension.

shimmy, the action of a wheel wobbling from side to side.

ship, to send any load by road.

shock absorber, a suspension component, principally the spring; a common misnomer see: damper.

shocker, shock absorber, see: spring, damper.

shocks, shock absorbers, see: spring, damper.

shoe, brake shoe.

shootingbrake, estate car, a large car typically seating up to 8 persons, usually having rear seats that fold and a loading area at the rear; earlier models have a wood panelled and/or wood framed rear body; designed as a utility vehicle for country houses as motor transport for shooting parties to/from the shoot; originally an open wooden horsedrawn carriage to carry shooting parties.

shooting red, the action of running a red traffic signal at speed, *i.e.* deliberately ignoring a red traffic signal and driving through the junction at any time during the red phase.

shopping car, any small city car, typically group A size.

short, short circuit.

short apex area, an apex area on a bend having a significant kink at its apex, typical of a line taken at a 90° junction.

short arm long arm suspension, a double wishbone suspension system having wishbones of unequal length and angle, usually the upper wishbone is shorter, resulting in a variation in track and camber angle as the suspension compresses to create specific roadholding characteristics.

short block, an engine block assembled with a crankshaft, bearings, cylinders, and pistons, but without a cylinder head or auxiliaries, typically the description of a reconditioned engine or a major component of a new engine.

short circuit, a defect in an electrical circuit that causes the current to take a path other than that desired, causing malfunction of components.

short engine, an engine block assembled with a crankshaft, bearings, cylinders, pistons, and cylinder head including valves and springs, but without all auxiliaries, typically the description of a reconditioned engine or a major component of a new engine.

short gearing, a gearbox having some or all gear ratios slightly lower than comparable gearboxes.

short haul, to transport goods or materials over a short distance.

short message service, a car radio on which text can be received and viewed on a dot matrix display.

short period disqualification, a disqualification from driving for a period less than 56 days, for which the court will stamp the counterpart to a driving licence but the licence will be retained by the holder who may recommence driving the day after the SPD ends without needing to renew the licence.

short shifting, changing into a higher gear at an engine speed below the optimum revs.

short stroke, an engine in which the length of the piston stroke is shorter than the bore diameter.

short wheelbase, a variant of a vehicle having a shorter distance between the front and rear axles compared to some similar models, hence typically a shorter chassis and/or body length.

shoulder, hard shoulder.

shoulder, the portion of a roadway contiguous with the carriageway for the emergency accommodation of stopped vehicles.

shoulder, the edge of the tyre tread where it meets the sidewall.

shoulder belt, that portion of a 3 point seatbelt which passes across the chest.

showman's vehicle, a goods vehicle permanently fitted with a living van or superstructure forming part of the equipment of the show of the person in whose name the vehicle is registered.

shp, shaft horsepower.

SHPD, an oil approved for use by CCMC in a super high performance diesel engined commercial vehicle.

shred, the destruction of a tyre by delamination of the carcass, especially at speed, typically if it has become overheated at a low pressure.

shrink fit, the fitting together of some parts by extreme chilling of a male part so it contracts and lodges tightly inside another at normal and higher temperatures, typically the valve seat rings and the valve guides as they fit into the cylinder head.

shroud, a cover over an electrical terminal for physical protection or electrical insulation.

shroud, a hood positioned around a fan improve and direct air flow.

shunt, a short forwards or rearwards movement of a vehicle, often accompanied by steering as part of a manoeuvre.

shunt, a very common type of collision in which the front of a vehicle collides with the rear of the vehicle ahead.

shunter, an old tractive unit not used on the public road, used only within the yard of the haulage company for repositioning of trailers.

shunt motor, a series wound motor.

shutdown, to stop the engine.

shutdown checks, a series of checks before leaving a vehicle: handbrake on, neutral selected or P if an auto, all electrics switched off, stop the engine, secure the vehicle.

shut line, the gap between an opening panel, *e.g.* a door, and its adjacent fixed panels, and which is typically narrower on vehicles having higher quality standards of construction.

shut off point, the place before a bend where the accelerator is feathered off directly before the braking point.

si, spark ignition.

SI, Statutory Instrument, a part of a regulation.

SI, Systeme Internationale d'Unités, International System of Units, *i.e.* metric.

SIAM, Society of Indian Automobile Manufacturers.

side airbag, side impact airbag.

sidecar, a device for the carriage of goods or 1 or more persons, fastened rigidly to the side of a motorcycle and having a single wheel at its outer edge for support.

side curtain, side screen, an early name.

side direction indicator lamp, an amber lamp which supplements the front and rear direction indicator lamps and flashes in phase with all on that side of the vehicle, located within 1.8 m from the front of the vehicle.

side draught carburettor, a carburettor having a horizontal barrel.

side flasher, side direction indicator lamp.

sideguard, a head level airbag system inflating downwards from the edge of the roof headlining along the length of the side windows, to protect the occupants heads during a side impact.

sideguard, steel rails along the sides between the front and rear wheels of a goods vehicle or trailer, to reduce the risk of injury to cyclists.

side impact airbag, each of a pair of air bags which inflate forwards from the outboard sides of the seats, and which are designed to inflate only in a severe side collision; seat covers must never be fitted.

side impact bars, additional strengthening in car doors to reduce passenger injury if the vehicle is hit in its side.

side impact door beams, side impact bars, steel beams inside the door that deflect certain types of side impacts to protect passengers from intrusion in certain types of side collisions.

side impact protection system, an improved vehicle design to reduce the level of injury in a T bone collision, principally: reinforced doors, burst proof locks, tough B pillars, and side impact airbags, each of which were developed by Volvo.

sidelifter, a semitrailer specially constructed with a folding crane and an outrigger at each end to self load/unload ISO containers from/to ground level.

sidelight, obsolete name, see: position marker lamp.

sidelight pod, a small lamp holder for a parking or sidelight, mounted on a short stem above a front wing, on some pre-war and early classic cars.

side loader, a semitrailer specially constructed with a folding crane and an outrigger at each end to self load/unload ISO containers from/to ground level.

side marker lamp, an amber lamp, usually 1 of several on the sides of a vehicle, used to indicate the presence of the vehicle when viewed from the side, mandatory along the sides of lorries and trailers over 6 metres long, (C&U), not to be confused with the obsolete name sidelights.

side member, a structural beam which may extend from front to rear, or shorter, typically of box or folded section, and which reinforces the floorpan or links the subframes.

side moulding, a plastic or hard rubber strip along the side of a car body, for stiffening and protection against carpark rash.

side pipe, an exhaust pipe typically chromed and having a chromed perforated cover, fitted along the lower outside edge of a sports or custom car, sometimes for aesthetic purposes.

sidepod, bodywork external to the cockpit along the sides between the front and rear wheels, typically on a single seater, usually having openings for airflow to radiators etc.

side rail, side member.

side repeater, side direction indicator lamp.

side road, a minor road at its junction with a main road.

side scoop, a nacelle, an air intake designed into the bodywork on the sides of a rear engined or mid-engined car.

sidescreen, a flexible side window surrounded by a duck or leathercloth frame sometimes having a metal support, usually removable, fitted along the sides of classic sports and kit cars, sometimes used as the means of entry instead of doors.

side shaft, half shaft.

side shake, end play.

side skirt, additional bodywork low along the sides of a lorry to fill the gap between the wheels especially on articulated trailers, to reduce wind resistance and improve aesthetic appearance.

sideslip, a controlled rear wheel skid in a rwd or 4wd car whilst negotiating a long curve.

sideslip, the small sideways movement of the tyres without a noticeable skid across a road surface when subject to centrifugal force.

sideslope, cross slope, a surface condition

where the wheels at 1 side of a vehicle are higher than the other side, *e.g.* when following a route horizontally across a lateral gradient; if the cross slope exceeds the manufacturers recommendation the vehicle will roll over onto its side.

sideslope performance, a quality regarding the maximum angle of cross slope on which a vehicle can be driven without rolling over, *i.e.* the greatest lateral gradient which can be safely negotiated when driving horizontally around a hillside.

side step, an external step between front and rear wheels to ease entry and exit to 4x4 vehicles.

sidestep the clutch, to slide ones foot sideways off a fully depressed clutch pedal so the clutch plate bites as rapidly as possible; typically performed when stationary in a low gear with maximum revs for high acceleration, albeit with wheelspin.

side street, a minor street at its junction with a main street.

sideswipe, a collision in which the side of a vehicle strikes the side of another at a shallow angle.

sidevalve, an engine in which the camshaft is located in the cylinder block and the valves are in a projection below one side of the cylinder head, not on modern cars.

sidewalk, USA, footway, a raised area along the side of the road for pedestrians.

sidewall, the portion of a tyre between the bead and the tread shoulder, sufficiently flexible to absorb unevenness in a road surface but sufficiently stiff to limit tyre rollover.

sidewall torsion sensor, a system having sensors mounted on the suspension that respond to magnets within the tyre sidewall, such that deformation is measured and ABS and TC effectiveness is improved, developed by Continental Tyres.

sideways acceleration, a transverse movement of a vehicle as may be experienced by occupants when cornering, it should normally be proportional to speed and steering angle except when skidding.

sideways acceleration sensor, an instrument that measures the transverse acceleration of a vehicle and sends a signal to the VSC or ESP.

sidewind, the wind blowing directly on the side of a vehicle, when strong or gusting it may adversely influence the directional stability.

sidewinder, USA, a vehicle having a transversely mounted engine.

sight distance, the distance at which a driver can see a 30 cm (1 foot) cube on the surface of the road, and which is limited by horizontal and vertical curves, *i.e.* bends and crests, and by other road users.

sight glass, a small window in the ac piping, typically near the receiver drier to enable a visual check of refrigerant flow.

sight line, any direction in which the driver has unrestricted visibility, the limits of which are the edges of the observable area restricted by physical objects.

sight triangle, the area between the limits of lateral visibility, especially when emerging at a junction.

sign, a roadside panel displaying an instruction, a warning, information, or directions for road users.

sig-nabout, a roundabout at which traffic is controlled by signals.

signal, visual information or a prohibition displayed by an automatic traffic controlling device, typically by illuminating coloured lamps.

signal, visual or other information transmitted from 1 road user to others describing their intention, usually as part of a plan or sequence, including signals by: arm, brake lights, direction indicators, eye contact, hazard lights, headlights, horn, reversing lights, vehicle position, vehicle speed.

signal board, a framework displaying 4 rows of characters with which the pit crew give information to a racing driver.

signal controlled crossing, a pedestrian crossing controlled by traffic signals, see: pelican, puffin, toucan.

signal head, each cluster of at least 3 coloured traffic signal lamps.

signalised intersection, a junction controlled by traffic lights.

signal light, USA, a vehicle direction indicator.

signpost, each of a series of panels at a junction displaying the name of places along each route and usually the distances to each place.

signpost, originally, a tall post at a junction having arms pointing along each road displaying the name of places along each route and the distances to each place.

silencer, a vessel or chamber within the exhaust system containing a system of baffles and tubes to reduce the noise from the exhaust by acoustic reflection and absorption.

silencer shaft, balancer shaft.

silhouette, each external outline of a vehicle as seen from the end and from the side; the shapes a shadow would cast.

silhouette signal, a signal to a driver behind that the giver is continuing ahead, given in the same style as an ahead arm signal by positioning the hand with the palm forwards, fingers upwards, below the internal mirror.

silica, a constituent of some tyres to reduce rolling resistance, having a greater coefficient of friction than carbon black at low temperature and permitting colouring.

silicone, a polymeric organic compound of silicon and oxygen, having a high resistance to temperature, water, and electricity; in various forms it is used for parts as diverse as sparkplug leads and brake fluid.

silicone brake fluid, a hydraulic fluid having a

minimum boiling point of 260 °C, being non-hydroscopic, and rated at dot 5.

silicone rubber sealant, an rtv paste material which will seal against water and oil but not petrol.

Silk road, an ancient route from Persia through Mongolia to China, 6,000 km (3,700 miles) in length, in use since 100 BC.

sill, the lower edge of the aperture to any door or tailgate.

silver, a metallic element, occasionally alloyed for electrical purposes, used as a plating for high temperature protection against corrosion.

Simca, Société Industrielle de Mecanique et Carrosserie Automobile, a French car manufacturer taken over by Chrysler.

SIMI, Society of the Irish Motor Industry.

simple engine, an engine in which expansion occurs in a single phase and is then exhausted, *e.g.* some types of steam engine.

simple trailer, a trailer having only 1 axle set, hence does not have any steering mechanism.

simplex chain, a chain having a single row of rollers.

Simpson planetary gears, a system having a single wide sun gear and 2 sets of planetary gears of which 1 planet carrier is connected to the internal gear of the other set.

simulator, a device that attempts to imitate driving scenes and conditions and the controls of a car, sometimes used to assist the learning of basic controls and procedures, or for hazard recognition.

single acting, a piston having pressure applied to 1 side only.

single axle set, a single axle, or a pair of axles spaced less than 1 metre apart.

single bed cat, a 3 way cat which contains rhodium, platinum, and palladium in a single matrix.

single carriageway, a 2 way road without any physical separation between opposing traffic, there may be any number of lanes in each direction.

single circuit brakes, a hydraulic braking system in which a single master cylinder operates the brakes at all 4 wheels, common until the 1960s.

single coil twin ignition, a system fitted to vintage straight 8 engines whereby the distributor has 2 sets of contact points firing alternately.

single cylinder brake, a drum brake system in which 1 slave cylinder operates 2 brake shoes.

single cylinder engine, an engine having a single piston and crankpin etc, typically on smaller motorcycles.

single decker, a bus having only a lower saloon, *i.e.* no upper saloon.

single exhaust, an exhaust system having at least 1 point in the system where all exhaust gas from the engine travels through the same pipe, although it may originate from separate manifolds and/or split to separate silencers or

tailpipes; see also: twin.

single function lamp, a part of a device which performs a single lighting or light-signalling function, (C&U).

single grade oil, monograde oil.

single H, a 4 over 4 gear selector layout, the ranges are selected by a switch on the gear lever to switch between low and high ranges.

single input steering, an advanced technique for steering through a bend, the action of one smooth movement of the steering wheel to a specific angle, then holding it steady without minor inputs until it is time to smoothly turn the steering straight, often combined with fixed grip steering; see also: threepenny bitting.

single lamp, a device having one function and one apparent surface in the direction of the reference axis, and one or more light sources, (C&U).

single lane bridge, a narrow bridge having sufficient width only for traffic to flow in 1 direction, typically marked with signs stating which direction has priority.

single leaf spring, a long thin spring steel beam without any additional elements.

single line brakes, an air braking system for a trailer, having a single air connection between the vehicle and the trailer.

single overhead camshaft, an engine having a single camshaft in each cylinder head.

single piece wheel, 1 piece rim.

single pivot steering, 1 point steering.

single plate clutch, a common clutch system having 1 double-sided dry drive plate between the pressure plate and the flywheel.

single point diamond, single point urban interchange.

single point fuel injection, a fuel injection system in which the fuel is injected into the common inlet manifold.

single point urban interchange, a type of diamond junction where the sliproads are positioned very close to the main carriageway and curve in to terminate at a central single point signal controlled junction on the surface street directly above or below the main carriageway, *e.g.* the junction of US19 with the FL60 in Florida, USA; see appendices.

single red line, a red line painted along the road edge to denote a red route and prohibit stopping typically 7 am to 7 pm Monday to Saturday, or as signs display.

single roller chain, simplex chain.

single seater, a racing car having only 1 seat for the driver, normally not constructed for road use, introduced in the 1920s.

single solid white line, a road marking used in many countries denoting generally the same meaning as double white lines, but saving paint.

single spark coil, an ignition coil which is dedicated to a specific cylinder, the system having a low voltage distributor to fire each ignition coil.

single track road, a road only of sufficient width for 1 vehicle and having passing places at regular intervals to enable traffic to flow in both directions.

single vehicle approval, a certification system to ensure kit cars and personal grey imports meet safety requirements.

single vehicle ram, an emergency escape procedure used to escape from being boxed in by an attackers car which is sideways across the road, the technique involves stopping 10 metres before the attacker, selecting 1st gear and accelerating with maximum power and aiming to contact and push the rear wing of the attackers car with 1 front wing and wheel in order to spin the attackers car and cause confusion to facilitate an escape; if performed in a vehicle having airbags the speed should not exceed 25 km/h (15 mph).

single vehicle type approval, a misnomer, see SVA.

single wheel suspension, independent suspension.

single wire system, a common electrical system in which 1 conductor feeds each load, bulb, etc, and the return path is through the vehicle body.

single yellow line, a central road marking used in many countries denoting generally the same meaning as double white lines, but it typically also denotes that the road is 2 way with oncoming traffic.

single yellow line, a road edge marking showing where parking and waiting restrictions exist, typically during business hours, but sometimes with exceptions.

sipe, the transverse slots at the edge of the tyre tread for water dispersal.

SIPS, side impact protection system.

sir, supplementary inflatable restraint, usually named srs.

situational awareness, the selective attention to and perception of environmental elements within a specified space and time envelope, the comprehension of their meaning, and the projection of their status in the near future.

size marking, the first digits of a tyre marking code moulded into the sidewall showing its width in mm.

SK, Slovakia, international vehicle distinguishing sign, see appendices.

skeletal, a semitrailer chassis without any body, deck, or bed, but fitted with twistlocks for carrying ISO containers, or with posts for carrying logs.

skeleton construction, a monocoque construction style in which the frame and not the panels carry the stress.

skid, the condition when 1 or more tyres slide longitudinally or transversely on the road surface; see: 4 wheel, front wheel, rear wheel, brake induced, oversteer, power induced, speed induced, spin, steering induced, understeer.

skid avoidance, measures taken by a driver that will prevent a skid occurring, *e.g.* advance planning, smooth control, speed reduction by long braking, etc.

skid block, a piece of timber or similar material 300 mm wide and 10 mm thick fastened along the underside of an F1 racing car to limit underbody suction to limit downforce to reduce overall speeds.

SkidCar, a car specially adapted for teaching skid recovery, using 4 jockey wheels fitted as outriggers to a cradle connected under the chassis of a production car such that height of each corner of the car is electrohydraulically varied by an instructor to vary the weight on each tyre to vary the friction at each tyre to simulate a variety of driving conditions and skids.

skid control, actions performed by a driver in deliberately initiating a minor skid and regulating its progress until skid recovery.

skid correction, actions performed by a driver in attempting to regain control of a skidding vehicle; typically achieved by removing the cause of the skid plus counter steering if the vehicle is yawing.

skidlid, a crash helmet.

skid mark, a dark line on a road surface, the remains of either: rubber abraded from a sliding tyre, or rubber deposited in liquid form due to heat generated by friction, sometimes the result of the surface of the tarmac being melted by heat from the tyre.

skid pad, USA, skidpan.

skidpan, a large flat off-road driving area having a specially prepared slippery surface, facilitating a vehicle to slide at slow speeds for driver training in skid recognition, skid avoidance and skid correction, also for vehicle testing; see also: aqua.

skid plate, glide plate.

skid plate, USA, sump guard.

skid recovery, actions performed by a driver resulting in a vehicle transiting from a state of skidding to a state of normal control of the moving vehicle; typically achieved by removing the cause of the skid plus counter steering if the vehicle is yawing; see: oversteer, spin, understeer.

skid reduction, measures taken by a driver that will reduce the risk of a skid occurring, *e.g.* advance planning, reducing speed by long braking, smooth control, etc.

ski hatch, an opening panel in the centre of the rear seat of some cars connecting the boot to the passenger compartment to allow long narrow loads, *e.g.* skis to be carried.

skim, to remove a thin layer from the mating surface of a cylinder head where excessive heat has caused a slight warp.

skin, the bodywork of a vehicle.

skinny spare, a lightweight spare wheel fitted with an undersize tyre, for emergency use only and usually restricted to 80 km/h (50 mph).

skip change, see: skipshift, block change,

selective changing.

skip loader, a lorry specially adapted to deposit, lift, transport, and empty skips.

skipshift, gear changing in which intermediate gears are deliberately not selected, *e.g.* to select 2-4-6-8, also named block changing.

skirt, bodywork beneath or around a bumper, typically plastic.

skirt, see: piston, side.

skitter, a suspension condition in which the tyres patter from crest to crest on an undulating surface losing potential friction, exaggerated by poor suspension design or suspension wear especially of dampers, causing the tyres to have reduced roadholding ability.

skylight, a plastic horizontal rising window in the roof of a coach, mobile home, or caravan.

SL, slot left, in road rally navigation the next turning on the left.

sla, short arm long arm suspension.

slalom, a training or testing exercise in which a vehicle is driven alternately left and right passing a straight line of cones or marker poles.

slam, to lower the body of a vehicle on its suspension.

slant engine, USA, inclined engine.

slatted grille, a triple function aerodynamic radiator grille, preventing ingress of large objects, slowing the air passing through the radiator, and directing high speed air upwards to act as a spoiler.

slave battery, a fully charged battery either in a vehicle or unconnected, used to jump start a vehicle having a flat battery.

slave cylinder, a hydraulic cylinder at a wheel or clutch that converts fluid pressure to mechanical movement to operate the brake mechanism or clutch.

sleep apnoea, a medical condition that causes many drivers to become drowsy due to insufficient natural sleep.

sleeper box, living accommodation built on behind the cab of a long tractive unit as a separate room, usually accessed through the cab, typically in USA.

sleeper cab, a lorry with a large area behind the drivers seat fitted with 1 or 2 bunk beds.

sleeping policeman, a speed hump, a specially constructed ridge across the road, usually between 50 to 100 mm high designed to create discomfort at speed, thereby causing traffic to slow down.

sleeve, cylinder sleeve.

sleeve bearing, any tubular bush.

sleeve nut, the part of a Budd mounting which holds the inner of twin wheels to the hub; sometimes named inner cap nut.

sleeve valve, a valve in the form of a concentric tube closely fitting outside the engine cylinder such that whilst both holes in the tube and the cylinder are aligned the valve is open, typically on some larger engines in vintage cars.

slew, to horizontally swing or swivel around a point less than a full rotation; to steer to change the angle of the front wheels so the vehicle will follow a different curve.

slick, a driver who has exceptionally smooth control of a vehicle.

slick, a tyre on which the tread is smooth without channels for water dispersal, for racing use on dry surfaces only.

slick, an area of road surface that has become smooth, having reduced friction especially when wet and greasy, and resulting in increased risk of skidding; but not pertaining to ice on a road.

slick, smooth, a mechanical part which slides smoothly against another.

slide, the movement of a surface along another without rolling.

slide, to skid.

slide back, a rigid lorry fitted with a sliding bed and hydraulics, such that the bed may be partially dismounted in that the rear end touches the ground; used for vehicle recovery and plant transport.

slide carburettor, a carburettor having a slide valve which varies the venturi.

sliding 5th wheel, a 5th wheel coupling on a sliding platform such that it may be moved fore and aft to change the proportion of weight on each axle of the tractive unit.

sliding bogie, a semitrailer suspension unit that may be moved fore and aft to change the position of the rear axles with respect to the body, to change the proportion of weight on the trailer and on the tractive unit, especially on skeletals and B doubles.

sliding caliper, a disc brake system in which the caliper is free to find its central position each side of the brake disc.

sliding door, a side door of a vehicle which opens by sliding rearwards, very common on minibuses and some vans.

sliding friction, the rubbing of bodies in sliding contact with each other.

sliding joint, a shaft connected to another by splines to allow axial movement of the shaft during suspension movement whilst transmitting power, *e.g.* where the propshaft meets the gearbox.

sliding mesh gearbox, a gearbox in which the layshaft gears are directly fixed to the shaft, and where gears on the mainshaft slide axially into mesh.

sliding pillar, a design of combined steering and independent front suspension in which the stub axle carrier slides up and down on the kingpin against a coil spring, resulting in constant angles of camber, caster, and kpi, but typically having a high rate of wear.

sliding post, an intermediate side support for the roof in the body of curtainside lorries.

sliding trailer, a semitrailer having a telescopic chassis to suit the length or weight of the load or manoeuvrability requirements, *e.g.* to transport ISO containers of various length.

sliding window, a side window which slides horizontally, on some older cars and buses.

slip angle, the angular difference between the direction in which the centreline of wheel is aligned and its actual direction of travel, produced by distortion within the tyre caused by lateral forces whilst it rotates, but where the tyre is not actually slipping or skidding.

slip on head restraint, a head restraint which hooks over the top of a car seat and which is not designed as part of the seat by the seat manufacturer, having little safety value.

slipping point, the condition when the clutch pressure plate exerts insufficient pressure on the clutch drive plate such that it transmits most but not quite all the power from the engine, such that there is slight slip; created either by the drivers foot pressure on the clutch pedal, or by insufficient pressure from the pressure plate springs.

slipping the clutch, a condition when the driver operates the clutch pedal such that the clutch pressure plate exerts insufficient pressure on the clutch drive plate, such that it does not transmit all the power from the engine.

slip ramp, USA, a short diagonal sliproad or link which connects a main highway with a parallel frontage road.

sliproad, a road allowing access to or exit from a motorway or similar road, see: entry sliproad, exit sliproad.

slipstream, the air behind a vehicle that tends to move with the vehicle.

slipstreaming, the action of driving dangerously close behind a large vehicle to reduce wind resistance on the front of the following vehicle.

SLO, Slovenia, international vehicle distinguishing sign, see appendices.

sloper, an inclined engine.

slotted, a type of screw head having a single straight slot.

slotted nut, castellated nut.

sloward, a vehicle travelling significantly slower than other traffic.

slow down, to decelerate.

slow lane, a common misnomer, see: nearside lane.

slow leak, a gradual loss of air from a tyre, typically caused by a faulty valve or rust or dirt at the bead seat.

slow puncture, a condition when an object penetrates a tubeless tyre and almost seals in the hole such that air loss is minimal.

slow steering, low geared steering, a vehicle in which a relatively large angular movement of the steering wheel results in a small slew of the front wheels, typically to counter heavy steering.

sls, self levelling system.

sludge, a sediment in a liquid system, consisting of microscopic particles of impurities mixed with the liquid to form a paste, sometimes in the oil system or the cooling system.

sluggish, a condition when an engine delivers less power than expected.

slush box, an automatic transmission, as referred to by a person who prefers a manual transmission.

SMA, Society of Motor Auctions, UK.

small block, USA, a small or medium size engine, generally less than 400 cu.ins, (6,500 cc).

small bus permit, documentation required by some operators of 9 to 16 seat minibuses.

small end, little end.

small goods vehicle, a mechanically propelled vehicle other than a motorcycle or invalid carriage, constructed or adapted to carry or haul goods and is not adapted to carry more than 9 persons including the driver, and of which the maximum permissible weight does not exceed 3.5 tonnes, (RTA).

small passenger vehicle, a motor vehicle other than a motorcycle or invalid carriage, which is constructed solely to carry passengers and their effects and is adapted to carry not more than 9 persons including the driver, (RTA).

smart airbag, an airbag that will inflate at a rate to suit the severity of collision and allow for the weight of each occupant.

smash, to collide with great force or impact causing excessive destruction.

SME, Suriname, international vehicle distinguishing sign, see appendices.

SMMT, Society of Motor Manufacturers and Traders, UK.

smog, a layer in the atmosphere resembling fog but containing fumes and smoke, typically over cities especially in some weather conditions.

smoke, small airborne particles resulting from combustion or incomplete combustion, especially when emitted from a vehicle in such quantities to be visible.

smoke opacity, the hindrance to the passage of light through exhaust gas caused by visible unburned particles, measured as the absorption coefficient per linear metre.

smoker, a driver who smokes, typically having double the collision rate of a non-smoker.

smoker, a vehicle having a diesel engine.

smoky, CB jargon, the police.

smoky exhaust, a colour sometimes visible in the exhaust, see: black, blue, white smoke.

smoky on rubber, CB jargon, a moving police vehicle.

smoky report, CB jargon, location of the police.

smoky the bear, CB jargon, the police.

smooth bore tank, a tanker vehicle in which the tank vessel is not fitted with bulkheads or baffles, resulting in strong surges of liquids causing instability, typically used for food products.

smooth running, an engine that does not exhibit low frequency vibrations.

SMS, short message service.

SMTA, Scottish Motor Trade Association.

SMV, stolen motor vehicle.

SN, Senegal, international vehicle distinguishing sign, see appendices.

snail, an ultra low gear or range of gears selectable on some tractors typically denoted by a symbol of a snail, where the road speed at maximum revs may be as low as 0.36 km/h, or 100 mm/second (0.23 mph, or 4 inches per second).

snakepit exhaust, a complex exhaust manifold in which each pipe curls around others for the purpose of all cylinders having the same length of tubing, typically from an engine having a large number of cylinders.

snaking, the sideways oscillation of a trailer, especially at speed; the speed at which snaking occurs is related to the relative weights of the trailer and towing vehicle; recovery of control is by gradual deceleration.

snap fastener, USA, a lift the dot fastener.

snap ring, USA, circlip.

snarl, a small bunching of congested traffic, typically at a junction or width restriction.

snarl, to hamper the movement of traffic.

snarl up, a traffic jam.

snatch change, a gear changing technique without the use of the clutch pedal, sometimes performed when changing into a higher gear in a vehicle without synchromesh but especially if the clutch actuating mechanism is broken; to change up: lift partially off the accelerator and select neutral, then at the appropriate moment as the revs are reducing and when the revs match the roadspeed the next gear is briskly selected; to change down: lift partially off the accelerator and select neutral then raise the revs to match the roadspeed to the next gear, then when matched the next gear is briskly selected; with expertise any gearchange can be performed clutchlessly in any manual transmission vehicle.

snatch recovery, a kinetic energy technique for recovering a bogged vehicle using a KERR rope: the towing 4x4 vehicle accelerates with 2 metres (6 feet) of slack rope such that the bogged vehicle is recovered by the momentum of the towing vehicle rather than by traction, and without any significant shock to either vehicle; steel rope, chain, or other fibre ropes will cause excessive shock and damage hence must NOT be used.

sneaking, the theft of car ignition keys from the owners house where the keys are left near the door or hanging on a hook by the door.

snorkel, an arrangement of ducting to take clean air from cab roof level to the air filter, very common in dusty countries and on lorries in most countries.

snow, frozen precipitation that results in a slippery layer when accumulated on a road surface.

snow blades, special windscreen wiper blades designed for maximum cleaning performance in snow.

snow blower, a vehicle that removes a deep layer of snow from a road surface using a screw blade to draw the snow into the vehicle machinery and which then ejects it to 1 side.

snow chains, a network of steel chains that can be fitted around a tyre tread to give increased traction and steering when driving on deep or packed snow; they must be fitted to all 4 wheels regardless of fwd or rwd, if not fitted to the rear wheels a spin is likely to develop.

snowcrete, snow concrete, snow that has been compacted by vehicles passing over it, and which becomes a tough surface.

snowmobile, a tracklaying vehicle steered by skis, typically the size of a motorcycle and permitted to share snow covered roads in some countries.

snowplough, a lorry fitted with a steel blade in front designed to push snow off the road, usually the same vehicle will also spread a layer of rocksalt behind.

snow post, a pole up to 3 m tall at the sides of some roads, usually painted black and white with the appropriate hazard reflectors on top.

snow scooter, snowmobile.

snow tyre, a tyre manufactured from specially formulated rubber to stay pliable when very cold and give increased traction on ice, sometimes with a self cleaning tread, but having a high rate of wear on dry surfaces; they must only be fitted to all 4 wheels for stability.

snubber, USA, a suspension bump stop.

SO, straight on, usually at a XR but also equivalent to a ML or MR in road rally navigation.

SO, straight over, a direction at crossroads in road rally navigation.

SO, Somalia, international vehicle distinguishing sign, see appendices.

SO, sulphur dioxide.

soapstone, a finely powdered soft mineral used to prevent an innertube sticking to the inside of the tyre carcass.

Society of Automotive Engineers, an organisation in USA that sets worldwide standards, especially with regard to oil viscosity.

socket, a tool that fits over a nut, gripping all 6 faces to turn the nut.

socket cap bolt, a design of bolt having a recessed drive surface, designed to be turned by an Allen key.

socket head screw, a screw fastener with a geometric recess in the head into which an appropriate tool is inserted for turning.

socket spanner, a tool comprising a handle with interchangeable sockets to fit the heads of different sized nuts or bolts.

SOD, start of duty, a note written by hand onto a tachograph disc.

sodium, a metallic element sometimes used in exhaust valves for heat transfer, also used in street lighting characterised by yellow or pale pink gas discharge lamps.

sodium cooled valve, a hollow valve partially filled with sodium which melts at 98 °C and splashes up and down to reduce temperature by transferring heat from the seat to the stem.

sodium oxide, a metallic compound commonly used in the USA in LRG and in lead replacement additives to protect valve seats from regression.

sodium vapour lamp, a lamp using an electrical discharge across a glass tube containing sodium vapour thereby emitting a yellow light for street lighting; low pressure sodium lamps give a deep yellow, other high pressure sodium lamps give a wider spectrum of yellow-pink light.

softback, a car body style having a hard top over the front seats and a soft top over the rear, typically on some 4x4 models.

soft contact, to touch an object with a vehicle such that no damage is caused to either the vehicle or object.

soft sided caravan, a caravan having fabric walls which allow folding to reduce the height whilst being towed, to increase stability and reduce fuel consumption.

soft solder, a soft metal alloy usually containing lead and tin in various proportions , having a low melting temperature typically between 200 °C and 450 °C.

soft stop, a microprocessor assisted braking system which monitors use of the brake pedal to ensure smooth deceleration in busy traffic and create a feathered stop, developed by Mercedes.

soft top, a fabric roof that can be folded away.

soft top, a car having a fabric roof that can be folded away, a convertible.

soft trim, the upholstery, roof and door linings, carpets, and internal fitments designed for comfort and aesthetic appeal.

soft tyre, an underinflated tyre, a tyre without sufficient air resulting in insufficient pressure.

sohc, single overhead camshaft.

solar car, a lightweight car powered by an array of photovoltaic cells which directly feed the electric motor.

solar cell, a semiconductor device that converts light into electrical energy, sometimes used to trickle charge a battery when a car is parked for a long period.

solar generator, an array of photovoltaic cells covering the roof and upper body panels of an electric car such that they can partially recharge the car batteries to extend its range.

solar powered vehicle, a vehicle having no emissions, powered by energy from sunlight absorbed by solar cells and converted into an electric current.

sold as seen, a legal disclaimer that will absolve the seller of a vehicle from responsibility as to the quality of a vehicle, leaving the purchaser with no recourse if a problem develops.

solder, see: soft solder, hard solder.

solder, to join metal parts by applying a filet of molten solder between them.

soldering gun, a type of soldering iron, usually with a very fast warm up time.

soldering iron, a tool used to apply heat in order to join components by soldering, usually electrically heated.

solenoid, an electromechanical actuator having electrical input and mechanical output, *e.g.* to operate a mechanism, switch, or valve.

solenoid switch, a heavy duty electrical relay, *e.g.* for switching the starting current to the starter motor, it may also move the starter motor pinion into mesh.

solid body friction, the friction exhibited by direct contact between 2 opposing surfaces.

solid paint, bodywork paint which is of a single colour and not metallic.

solid propellant, a solid explosive material which produces the gas with which to inflate an airbag.

solids, tyres not having an air chamber, as used on industrial vehicles.

solid state, a semiconductor device that has no moving parts except electrons flowing through it.

solid tyre, a resilient tyre, non-pneumatic, made from rubber having no air voids, a specific low speed limit is imposed when used on a road.

solo, a motorcyclist not carrying a pillion passenger.

solo, a tractive unit not coupled to a semitrailer; see: bobtailing.

solo, a tractor not carrying an implement or drawing a trailer.

solo machine, a motorcycle not having a sidecar.

solvent, a liquid that can dissolve another substance to form a solution.

sonic idling, a function of a specially designed carburettor using air at the speed of sound to atomise fuel from the idling jet, developed by Ford.

sonoscope, a mechanics stethoscope, a diagnostic instrument which listens to vehicle noises to identify faults, *e.g.* sticking valves, worn gears, worn bearings, piston slap, etc.

sooted plug, a sparkplug which has become fouled by a layer of carbon.

soot filter, a device designed to remove excessive soot from the exhaust of diesel engines.

soporific, music with a strong beat that can make a driver drowsy.

SORN, statutory off road notification.

souped up, an engine or vehicle that is tuned or modified to increase performance, originally from suped, from supercharged, having fitted a supercharger a device driven by the engine to increase power.

south, the direction 180° from north.

southbound, travelling towards the south.

sov, sports off-road vehicle.

SO$_x$, sulphur oxides, a range of acids that can form in small quantities in the cat.

SOX, straight on at crossroads, a direction in road rally navigation.

sp, solar powered.

SPA, special parking area, typically marked with yellow lines.

space cushion, safety cushion, the safety zone around a vehicle.

spaceframe chassis, a chassis design typically constructed by a network of tubes forming a triangular lattice resulting in lightweight construction due to using advanced techniques and materials, used in some types of high performance vehicles.

space mean speed, the speed given by the average travel time of a group of vehicles to traverse a fixed length of road.

spacer, any device which rigidly holds any 2 items some distance apart.

spacer, wheel spacer.

space saver, a space saving spare wheel.

space saving spare wheel, an inflated spare wheel and tyre assembly having a narrow section and smaller diameter compared to a standard wheel, designed to save size and weight in the boot, and which is cheaper to replace every 5 years, for emergency use only having a speed restriction of 80 km/h (50 mph).

space wagon, a 1 or 2 box van-bodied mpv having luxury specification, seating 6 to 8 persons including the driver in 3 rows of seats, typically having a sliding side door for the rear, and rear doors or tailgate.

spacing, the distance between consecutive vehicles in a lane measured front to front, used when measuring traffic flow and density; see also: headway.

spade terminal, a male electrical connection.

Spaghetti junction, the junction of the M6, A38M, and A5127 in Birmingham; now a general term for any complex grade separated junction having many link roads; see also: mixing bowl.

span, each section of a bridge between its supports.

spanner, a tool for turning a nut, typically providing significant leverage between the handle and the head, it may grip on 2 or 6 faces.

spannerman, a mechanic.

spare, a spare wheel.

spare part, any component or sub assembly kept in reserve for repair of vehicles.

spare parts list, a listing of parts available from a manufacturer.

spares, component parts used for repair of a vehicle.

spares car, a donor car.

spare tyre, a spare wheel.

spare wheel, an inflated spare tyre and wheel assembly for use if the tyre on a roadwheel deflates.

spare wheel carrier, an external structure below the rear floor in which the spare wheel is carried on light commercial vehicles.

spare wheel carrier, an external structure on the rear door or tailgate of RVs on which the spare wheel is carried.

spare wheel well, a lowered recess in the boot floor of many cars in which the spare wheel is carried.

spark, the effect of an electrical current jumping a gap between 2 electrodes and causing the air or gas between to become heated to a very high temperature.

spark advance, to cause the ignition spark to occur slightly earlier in the cycle.

spark angle map, ignition map.

spark breakaway, the end of the spark duration.

spark coil, ignition coil.

spark control computer, a microprocessor based control unit providing electronic spark timing.

spark current, the current flowing between the electrodes at any instant.

spark duration, the length of time a spark is established across a spark gap.

spark fuel traction control, a traction control system which applies the brake to a spinning wheel and reduces power from the engine.

spark gap, the space between the electrodes of a sparkplug, the space must be adjusted accurately for maximum power and efficiency, typically a measurement in the range of 0.3 mm to 1.2 mm, (0.012 to 0.048 inch) depending upon engine type.

spark ignition, an engine in which the air-fuel mixture is ignited by the heat from an electrical spark.

sparking plug, sparkplug.

sparking rate, the number of sparks per minute, calculated as $^1/_2$ the engine revs x the number of cylinders.

spark map, ignition map.

sparkplug, the electrical device that converts the high voltage surge into a spark to ignite the air-fuel mixture in the cylinder, withstanding temperatures in excess of 1,000 °C, pressures of 100 bar, and a voltage exceeding 35,000 volts; invented by Sir Oliver Joseph Lodge.

sparkplug boot, a moulded rubber terminal on the end of the sparkplug lead which fits tightly over the sparkplug insulator as a means of keeping moisture and dirt from the system.

sparkplug brush, a small brush for removing carbon from the sparkplug electrodes.

sparkplug cable, sparkplug lead.

sparkplug electrode, either of 2 electrodes, the centre electrode, or the earth electrode at the side, between which the hv spark jumps.

sparkplug gasket, a captive ring shaped device which provides a seal between the sparkplug and cylinder head, such that the sparkplug is designed to be installed finger tight then turned $^1/_4$ turn only with a tool.

sparkplug gauge, a tool having a set of metal feeler blades with which to check and re-set the spark gap.

sparkplug heat range, see: heat range, cold sparkplug, hot sparkplug.

sparkplug insulator, the glazed ceramic insulation around the central terminal and conductor, typically made from alumina trioxide, a white glass, to withstand high mechanical, thermal, and electrical stress.

sparkplug lead, the hv cable that carries the spark voltage from the ignition coil to the distributor and from the distributor to the sparkplugs.

sparkplug marker, each of several C shaped numbered markers which identify each sparkplug cable.

sparkplug spanner, a special box spanner or socket having a rubber insert to protect the sparkplug insulator

spark retard, to cause the ignition spark to occur slightly later in the cycle.

sparks, CB jargon, a radio technician.

spark test, a test of the ignition circuit to ensure the spark is delivered to the sparkplugs.

spark timing, ignition timing.

spark voltage, ignition voltage.

spat, a wheel arch extension, typically made from plastic or hard rubber, sometimes steel, often a necessary fitment around a wheel arch over widened wheels.

spatial awareness, a quality of a driver in being fully aware of all extremities of their vehicle including bodywork and the track of the tyre footprints, and predict exactly where each extremity will move during any forwards or reverse manoeuvre, especially in relation to any other fixed point that could be contacted by the vehicle.

spd, speed, as in 5 speed transmission.

SPD, short period disqualification.

spec, special.

spec, specification.

spec ed, special edition.

special body, a vehicle having a body not built by the manufacturer of the chassis, but constructed by an independent coach builder.

special edition, each of a small number of a production model of car, factory fitted with some parts which are different from the standard model, typically for aesthetic purposes.

special mileage tyre, a regrooveable tyre having a having a thicker layer of rubber between the carcass and the tread to allow for a new tread to be cut when the original is worn.

special parking area, part of a town or district where all parking is controlled, and offenders will be clamped or towed away.

special road, a road designated by an Order which restricts its use to certain classes of traffic, *e.g.* a motorway.

special road order, a regulation which defines a specific road and which restricts its use to certain classes of traffic.

special road traffic order, a regulation which defines a specific road or network and which restricts the speed limit to *e.g.* 20 mph.

special stage rally, a rally in which each car must be specially prepared to regulations, the driver and navigator wear flame retardant overalls and crash helmets, and where speed and driver ability are paramount, conducted on roads which are closed to all other traffic.

special type, a vehicle that does not or can not conform to C&U regulations and which is permitted some exceptions from certain regulations.

special types general order, legislation for vehicles that do not or cannot comply with normal C&U regulations.

special vehicle order, a permit which allows use of a non-standard vehicle which although safe does not meet the requirements of the C&U Regulations.

specification, information provided by the manufacturer for either a vehicle, a major assembly, or a component, including details of design, material, operation, adjustments, and servicing.

specification creep, the phenomenon whereby technology or gadgets initially introduced into large expensive cars eventually appear on smaller models.

specific fuel consumption, the quantity of fuel consumed to produce a unit of power, measured at full load at a range of engine speeds, typically measured in kg/kW.hour, or, kg/PS.hour, or, kg/bhp.hour.

specific fuel consumption curve, a graph displaying the rate at which fuel is used with respect to the range of engine speeds at full throttle, typically a U shaped graph the lowest point showing the revs at which the engine is most fuel efficient.

specific gravity, the comparison of the density of a substance with respect to water; archaic name, now named relative density, rd.

specific power output, the ratio of engine power in relation to its size, *i.e.* power to swept volume, measured in kW/litre; diesel engines typically less than 30 kW/litre, turbo diesel around 35 kW/litre, petrol engines around 40 kW/litre, and high performance engines exceeding 50 kW/litre.

specified front passenger seat, the front seat furthest from the driver in a vehicle having 3 or more front seats in a row abreast with the driver.

SPECS, speed police enforcement camera system.

spectacle lift, a lifting device comprising twin rectangles *i.e.* resembling spectacles, with which to lift 2 wheels of a disabled vehicle clear of the road, fitted on the rear of a breakdown recovery vehicle.

specular finish, a highly reflective mirror-like finish.

sped, to travel fast.

speed, preceded by a number, the number of selectable forward gear ratios in a gearbox.

speed, the scalar measurement of the rate of movement of an object, the measurement of the distance travelled divided by the time taken, it may be measured in m/s, or km/h, or mph; speed in 1 specific direction is named velocity.

speed, see also: 2, 3, 4, 5, 6, 8, 9, 10, 12, 13, 14, 15, 16, 18, 32, 54, advisory, automatic, average, basic, closing, combustion, constant, critical, cruise, cruising, design, engine, entry, equivalent, excessive, exit, external, flame, free, full, gather, Godspeed, high, idle, inappropriate, indicated, information, intelligent, kerb, limited, lose, maximum, nominal, piston, position, posted, rated, road, running, safe, scrub, Selespeed, space, stall, Stepspeed, time, top, turn, variable, vehicle, wheel.

speed breaker, a speed hump.

speed bump, a speed hump.

speed camera, a device that emits a radio or laser beam to measure the speed of every vehicle, and which is linked to a camera to automatically photograph each vehicle exceeding a set speed, invented by Maurice Gatsonides in 1957.

speed category, speed rating.

speed change lane, USA, an acceleration or deceleration lane for merging onto or exiting from a freeway or similar road.

Speedcheck digital camera, a digital camera acting as part of an SVDD system.

speed control, cruise control.

speed control island, a false roundabout.

speed cushion, a small square speed hump, a raised portion of the road surface in the centre of each lane having a width less than the track of a bus but greater than that of a car such that it will cause discomfort to car drivers if crossed quickly but allowing buses to straddle it.

speed gun, a device that emits a radio or laser beam with which to measure the speed of an approaching vehicle.

speed hump, a specially constructed ridge across the road, usually between 50 to 100 mm high and of various lengths, designed to create discomfort at speed, thereby causing traffic to slow down.

speed indicator, the early name for a speedometer.

speed induced skid, a skid caused by the driver entering a bend too fast such that there is greater momentum in the inertia of the vehicle than friction present between the tyres and the road surface, *i.e.* the centrifugal force of the body of the vehicle is greater than the centripetal force generated by all the tyres; it has the potential to develop into other types of skid depending upon the drivers actions.

speeding, the action of driving faster than the posted speed limit for any particular vehicle or road, a criminal activity.

speed limit, the maximum (or minimum) speed at which all vehicles or a specific vehicle type may legally travel along a specific road; a restriction first introduced in 1865 limiting farm vehicles to 4 mph but 2 mph in towns.

speed limiter, a device fitted to some vehicles to prevent a specific speed being exceeded; UK legislation: lorries over 7.5 tonnes MGW limited to 96 km/h (60 mph), EC legislation: lorries over 12 tonnes limited to 90 km/h (56 mph), buses and coaches over 7.5 tonnes MGW are limited to 100 km/h (62 mph).

speed limiter plate, a plate affixed in a conspicuous position in the drivers cab of a lorry or coach showing the limited speed of the vehicle.

speed merchant, a motorist who habitually drives fast.

speedo, speedometer.

speedometer, an instrument displaying the instantaneous speed of a vehicle, to be accurate to within –0 % to +7 %, displaying in km/h or mph, a mandatory device in UK since 1927.

speed police enforcement camera system, a new generation of SVDD speed measuring equipment installed on motorway bridges which measures the time taken for each vehicle to travel the distance between 2 places using digitised images of the registration plates, and which will be invisible to drivers until their photos are taken by digital flash cameras and which store the images on CD.

speed rating, a tyre code designation within the size marking, ranging from A to Z excepting H which is out of sequence; the rating indicates the maximum speed at which a tyre can safely carry a load corresponding to its load index under service conditions specified by the tyre manufacturer, the lowest speed rating in general use for cars is Q; see appendices.

speed ratio, the ratio of input to output for each gear in a gearbox.

speed scatter, the condition when a number of vehicles are travelling in the same direction but at different speeds.

speed sensitive power steering, a variable assist power steering system.

speed sensitive rear wheel steering, a facility that enables the rear wheels to steer opposite to the front at slow speeds to enhance manoeuvrability, and to steer slightly in the same direction as the front at high speeds for maximum stability.

speed sensitive wipers, a system that increases the pressure of the wiper blades at higher roadspeeds.

speed shift, USA, flatshift.

speedster, a high performance sports car.

speed symbol, speed rating.

speed table, a flat topped road hump having an extended length, sometimes more than 6 metres long.

speed throttle, a straight chicane giving priority in 1 direction to slow down vehicles as part of a traffic calming system.

speed up, to travel faster.

speed variance, speed scatter.

speed violation detection deterrent, a vehicle speed measuring system using 2 digital cameras some distance *e.g.* 5 km (3 miles) apart linked to a microprocessor; the registration of every vehicle approaching both cameras is recorded and the time taken between both points is measured, hence average speed is calculated; automatic processing of prosecutions can follow for those exceeding the speed limit.

speedway, motorcycle racing on a short oval track having a cinder surface.

speedway, USA, a highway designed for fast traffic.

speedway, USA, a motorracing circuit.

speedy, moving quickly.

spent gas, exhaust gas from the previous cycle which remains in the cylinder after gas exchange.

spherical bearing, a joint created by a sphere rotating within a ball race, used within the suspension of some cars to allow precision articulation but no linear movement.

spherical combustion chamber, a combustion chamber in which the piston crown is dished and the cylinder head domed, except for the valves.

spherical seat, a curved mating face on a wheel and wheelnut, as a means of providing positive centring of a roadwheel when the wheelnut is tightened; they must not be mixed or interchanged with taper types.

spi, single point fuel injection.

Spicer clutch brake, a device linked to the full travel of the clutch pedal in some lorries, which stops the gears from continued rotation to facilitate selection of 1st or reverse gear in a constant mesh gearbox when the vehicle is stationary.

spider, a 4 arm crosspiece linking the yokes of a uj, *e.g.* in a propshaft.

spider, a roadster having luxury fittings; also named spyder.

spider, an elastic tie having many hooked legs for holding a lightweight load in place on a roof rack etc.

spider, see: 4 way, 6 way.

spider, wheel spider.

spider gear, USA, the planetary gears in a differential.

spigot, a short cylindrical peg projecting from a body, to facilitate the accurate location of another part.

spigot bearing, USA, the bearing in the centre of a flywheel and which carries the clutch shaft.

spigot mounting, the mounting of a roadwheel on a hub where the hub has an accurately

machined spigot which mates with a large hole in the centre of the wheel disc, especially where the wheel is retained by bolts.

spin, a brief drive, especially for pleasure related to either the type of vehicle and/or the type of roads used.

spin, a 4 wheel skid in which the longitudinal axis of the vehicle turns more than 90° from the course it was following, usually initiated by a rear wheel skid; in some cases the vehicle may rotate through 360° several times.

spin, the action of 1 or more drive wheels rotating when there is greater torque applied from the engine to the wheels than the friction present between the tyres and the road surface.

spindle, a thin fixed or rotating rod or shaft, sometimes tapered.

spindle cap, the small metal grease cover over a front wheel bearing.

spine back, a backbone chassis.

spinner, a Rudge nut.

spinner handle, a screwdriver style handle with a socket for rapid screwing of a nut along a thread whilst it is not tight.

spinning, the actions of groups of car dealers working together at auctions and who have agreed not to bid against each other.

spin recovery, the procedure for recovering from a spin providing there is space available before a collision occurs: release the footbrake, straighten the steering, clutch down or select neutral in an automatic, when moving in a straight line backwards brake gently; in special circumstances when moving in a straight line backwards a J turn may be performed.

spiral curve, a transition curve or bend.

spiral gear, helical gear, a gear that transmits power from 1 shaft to another when the shafts are parallel; see also: hypoid.

spiral glowplug, a glowplug having an exposed heating element.

spiral roundabout, a roundabout having lane markings which are not concentric but spiral outwards from the centre, so once ensconced in the correct lane that lane takes the driver to the required exit.

spiral transition, transition curve.

Spirit of Ecstasy, the Rolls Royce radiator mascot, affectionately named Emily.

spk, spoke.

spl, spoiler.

splash and dash, a short pit stop for fuel only.

splashed graphics, custom paintwork or stickers which resemble paint drops or splashes etc.

splash flap, USA, mudflap.

splashguard, USA, mudflap.

splash lubrication, lubrication generated by the rotating crankshaft throwing oil from the crankpins to the cylinder bores.

splash oiling, a lubricating system that depends upon the crankshaft splashing into oil in the sump to distribute oil to lubricate some parts.

splash panel, a plastic panel across the bottom

of an engine bay to prevent entry of splashed water and road dirt.

splash shield, a plate which protects a brake disc from water and dirt.

splash zone, areas of vehicle bodywork which are at higher risk of corrosion due to water splash.

spline, trapezoid shaped slots machined axially along a circular bar and internally along a tubular form to facilitate a part to transmit power to another concentrically during axial movement, *e.g.* the mounting of the clutch drive plate on the first motion shaft.

split, part of a rally route used more than once, where 2 routes diverge.

split bearing, a shaft bearing composed of 2 shell halves clamped together.

split bench seat, a front bench seat for 2 passengers which is separate from the drivers seat.

split braking system, a braking system so designed and constructed that it comprises 2 independent sections of mechanism capable of developing braking force such that a failure of any part excepting a brake shoe or a fixed member in a section will not cause a decrease in the braking force capable of being developed in the other section, (C&U).

split charging system, a system that allows 2 batteries to be charged for 2 different purposes, *e.g.* caravan lighting, such that the discharge of 1 battery does not affect the other.

split collar, collet.

split cycle offset optimisation technique, a microprocessor controlled traffic signalling system which constantly measures traffic flows, predicts stops and delays, and constantly changes the timings of red and green phases to maximise traffic flow.

split diamond, USA, a 3 level diamond junction, a volleyball junction.

split friction surface, a road surface having varying degrees of friction across its width, *e.g.* a wet road which has dried along a central area, such that left and right wheels have different stopping ability, and which in extreme conditions could lead to a spin.

split grid, a situation allowing slower vehicles in a race to start at the front of the grid, with a short time interval before faster vehicles start.

split pin, a steel pin split along its length, for locking a castellated nut by opening the pin ends.

split propshaft, divided propshaft.

split rear seats, the rear seat of a hatchback or estate car in which part of the seat can be folded to carry a longer load with 1 or 2 rear passengers, sometimes split 50-50, sometimes 30-70.

split rim, a wheel made in several sections having a rim in 2 parts to facilitate tyre replacement, typically on some agricultural and industrial vehicles and some lorries.

split screen, split windscreen.

split skirt piston, a piston having a skirt which is split below a gudgeon pin bearing to allow for expansion.

split system master cylinder, tandem master cylinder.

splitter, gear selector system such that between each gear there is a $^1/_2$ gear, thus doubling the number of gears, on many lorries.

splitter box, splitter gearbox.

splitter gearbox, an additional set of epicyclic gears usually installed at the input to the gearbox to create 2 or more additional close ratio gear ranges, the gear ratios are mathematically arranged to give a $^1/_2$ gear between each primary gear, such that an 8 speed gearbox will have 16 actual gears, *i.e.* low 8th and high 8th, on many lorries; see also: range change.

splitter island, a traffic island that separates flows of traffic not parallel to each other, *e.g.* on approach to a roundabout.

splitter shift, a gear change using the splitter gear only, for a $^1/_2$ gear change up or down.

splitting lanes, the discourteous action of straddling a lane line and driving partly in 2 lanes simultaneously.

split washer, spring lock washer.

split windscreen, a front windscreen having a central division between 2 separate flat glass panes, the left and right panes typically angled slightly from transverse, common until the 1950s.

splt, split.

spoiler, a device at the lower front of a car to restrict air from passing beneath a car, it may improve roadholding at higher speeds.

spoiler, a device on the rear of a car to deflect air to attempt to give increased down-force, it may improve roadholding at higher speeds; it may increase drag.

spoke, each of several bars or rods radiating from the hub to the rim of either a steering wheel or a road wheel.

spoke hub, a hub to which wire spokes are fitted in the construction of a wire wheel, and which is itself fastened to the axle hub.

spoke wheel, an alloy road wheel styled such that between the hub and rim are a number of ornamental spokes.

spongy brakes, a dangerous condition felt when air is trapped in the hydraulic system.

spongy lead, pure lead formed into a porous plate resulting in a very high surface area, used as the negative plate in a lead acid battery.

sponsorship hunting, a major pastime for aspiring racing drivers when attempting to find funding to continue their career.

spoon & bowl, a condition when a gear selector system is badly worn, such that there is no remaining feel of the gate.

Sportronic, a semiautomatic gear selector system, developed by Alpha Romeo.

sports car, a car having 1 or 2 seats and designed to be competitive on a race circuit.

Sportshift, a 4 speed electronically controlled transmission which allows the driver to select automatic, or shift gears clutchlessly by pressing shift buttons on the steering wheel; the downshift buttons are located on the face of the steering wheel and the upshift buttons are on the back side of the steering wheel, developed by Toyota.

sportster, a sports saloon car, a high performance saloon car.

sport ute, sport utility vehicle.

sport utility truck, a powerful recreational vehicle having a pickup bed at the rear.

sport utility vehicle, a 4x4 car with moderately high acceleration performance and reasonable off-road performance.

spot lamp, a lamp having a narrow undipped beam for long range use with main beam headlamps only, controlled by its own switch and the dipswitch.

sprag, a metal bar with prongs which was trailed behind veteran cars to prevent rolling back on an uphill gradient.

sprag, a stake used as a parking brake for a veteran vehicle by inserting it through the spokes of a wheel.

sprag clutch, a freewheeling clutch that transmits torque in 1 direction but turns freely in the other, sometimes used in starter motors and automatic transmissions.

spray, clouds of water droplets that reduce visibility, created and thrown up by the action of tyres on a wet road.

spray suppression, devices resembling brushes fitted around the wheel arches of heavy vehicles to absorb spray from tyres on a wet road, to reduce loss of visibility.

spread axle, USA, tag axle, an axle on a trailer ahead from the rear axle, sometimes having only a single wheel at each side, to allow additional load to be carried.

spring, a device that changes shape under elastic stress or force but will return to its original shape providing the elastic stress threshold is not exceeded; on a vehicle suspension it is the primary device to absorb suspension movement and shocks from the road surface.

spring, see: air, barrel, coil, gas, leaf, quarter elliptic, rubber suspension, semielliptic, torsion bar.

spring actuated brakes, fail safe air brakes whereby loss of air pressure causes springs to apply the emergency brake; the parking brake operates by releasing the air thereby causing the springs to operate the brake, on large vehicles.

spring bonnet clip, a positive locking quick release device, for retaining engine covers etc.

spring bow, the bar supporting a hood above the rear window and which is sprung to maintain the hood shape.

spring brakes, spring actuated brakes.

spring compressor, a tool used in pairs with which to restrain suspension coil springs for safe removal and replacement.

spring eye, the formation at the end of a leaf spring where a loop is formed for secure mounting.

spring fastener, a positive locking quick release device, for retaining engine covers etc.

spring hanger, a support bracket for the trailing end of a leaf spring which allows the spring to vary slightly in length as it flexes, having a rubber bush which engages in the spring eye.

spring rate, the ratio of the load on a spring to the distance it deflects, measured in newtons per millimetre.

spring seat, a circular recess which accommodates the end of a coil spring.

spring windup, S shaped deformation of a leaf spring due to torque reaction in the axle casing during acceleration and braking.

sprocket, a tooth on the periphery of a pulley wheel designed to engage with the links of a chain or a toothed belt.

sprocket wheel, a toothed wheel designed to drive or be driven by a chain or toothed belt.

sprung axle, an axle separated from the chassis by a system of sprung suspension.

sprung suspension, the means whereby the body/chassis is connected to a wheel by a springing system.

sprung weight, the proportion of the vehicle weight that is supported by the suspension, *i.e.* the weight of the vehicle minus the weight of the tyre, wheel, and a proportion of the weight of the suspension.

spts, sports.

SPUI, single point urban interchange.

spur differential, a differential in a fwd comprising spur gears.

spur gear, a simple straight cut gearwheel having teeth parallel to its axis, *i.e.* cut axially, and which meshes with another to cause a change in axial speed and torque.

spyder, a roadster having luxury fittings; also named spider.

spy in the cab, a tachograph.

SqL, a rally pace note, square left bend through 90°.

SqR, a rally pace note, square right bend through 90°.

squab, the cushion of a seat base.

squab shelf, rear shelf.

squad car, a police car.

square 4 engine, a 4 cylinder engine in which the cylinder axis are in square formation as viewed from above; effectively a pair of parallel twin engines constructed as a single unit having 2 crankshafts connected by gears or chain and having either 2 stroke or 4 stroke cycles.

square-about, a roundabout style of junction where the central island is distinctly rectangular.

squareback, USA, a station wagon.

square engine, an engine in which the bore and stroke are of equal dimension.

square thread, a screw thread having a square cross section, designed for additional strength and wear resistance especially to support heavy loads, *e.g.* in a screw jack.

square wheel, a wheel with a flat spot on its rim.

square wheels, CB jargon, a broken down vehicle.

squat, the position of the rear of the body of a car under significant acceleration, where the apparent weight transfer and torque reaction cause the nose to lift and the rear suspension to compress.

squeak, a high pitched noise of a short duration.

squeal, a continuous high pitched noise.

squeeze braking, USA, threshold braking.

squirm, tread squirm.

squirt box, a carburettor or fuel injection system.

squish, the turbulence generated within the combustion chamber caused by movement of the piston and the shape of the combustion chamber.

sr, sunroof.

SR, slot right, in road rally navigation the next turning on the right.

SR, USA, state route, followed by a number, see appendices.

SRO, special road order.

srp, system for restraint and protection.

srs, supplementary restraint system.

SRTO, special road traffic order.

SRWC, Sports Racing World Cup.

ss, sequential shift gearbox.

ss, special stage, part of a rally or cross country event.

SSC, supersonic car, the world speed record was last raised to 1227.986 km/h (763.035 mph) on 15th October 1997.

SSD, stopping sight distance.

SSGA, UK, Sale and Supply of Goods Act, (1994), pertaining to the sale of vehicles.

SSPS, speed sensitive power steering.

ssr, secondary safety restraint.

ssr, super sports roadster.

sss, sequential sports gearshift.

SST, self supporting technology.

ssv, super sports vehicle.

st, seat.

St, Street, a road name designation.

stab and steer, the actions of a driver not having finesse in use of the primary controls, typical of an experienced but untrained driver trying to drive quickly.

stab braking, USA, cadence braking.

stabiliser, a damping device fitted between car and caravan or similar combinations to reduce snaking, *i.e.* sideways oscillation of the trailer at speed.

stabiliser bar, antiroll bar.

stabiliser belt, a band of wires or cords around the circumference of a radial tyre between the plies and the tread to stabilise the tread.

stability, a quality of vehicle design such that a vehicle will maintain its attitude and resist displacement, and if displaced, to develop forces tending to restore the original condition; design especially of steering, suspension, and wheelbase, but including the aerodynamics of a bodyshell many other factors.

stability, a quality which may be achieved by driving in a style such that vehicle stability is not reduced, or to enhance or maximise the stability of any vehicle.

stability and traction control, a system that reduces engine power and applies 1 or more brakes when sensors detect instability, developed by Volvo.

stabilizer bar, USA, antiroll bar.

stable, a quality of a vehicle at some moment when all forces are balanced and are unlikely to become unbalanced.

stacked diamond junction, USA, a 3 level variant of a braid junction, but where the flyover ramps meet at a signalised intersection.

stack junction, USA, a braid junction on 4 levels; see appendices.

stage 1, a size of child car safety seat for a child up to 10 kg, birth to 9 months, rearwards facing, used in the front or rear secured by existing seat belts.

stage 1-2, a size of child car safety seat for a child up to 18 kg, birth to 4 years, forwards or rearwards facing, used in the front or rear secured by existing seat belts.

stage 2, a size of child car safety seat for a child 9 kg to 18 kg, 6 months to 4 years, forwards facing, used in the front or rear secured by existing seat belts.

stage 2-4, a size of child car safety seat for a child 9 kg to 36 kg, 6 months to 11 years, forwards facing, converts into a booster seat, used in the front or rear secured by existing seat belts.

stage 3, a size of child car safety seat for a child 9 kg to 25 kg, 6 months to 6 years, forwards facing, used in the front or rear secured by existing seat belts.

stage 4, a size of child car safety seat for a child 15 kg to 36 kg, 4 years to 11 years, forwards facing, used in the front or rear secured by existing seat belts.

stage carriage service, a local bus service operating according to a route timetable and charging fares based upon stages of the journey.

staged accident, a collision caused deliberately to fraudulently claim against the insurance company of the other driver.

staggered pedestrian crossing, any pedestrian crossing having a central refuge and where the crossings on each side are not in line.

stainless steel, an alloy of steel containing at least 10.5 % chromium, plus other elements; variations in the percentages of each metal produce alloys with different characteristics.

stainless steel exhaust, an exhaust system designed to withstand the extreme temperatures, acids, and water condensation encountered within an exhaust.

stake bed truck, USA, a truck having a series of vertical metal stakes fitted along both sides of the bed for lateral load restraint when carrying cut timber or piping etc.

stake body, USA, the body of a truck or trailer having a series of vertical metal stakes fitted along both sides of the bed for lateral load restraint when carrying cut timber or piping etc.

staked nut, a nut which is secured in its tightened or adjusted position with a metal tab or tabwasher.

stake pocket, USA, each of a series of square holes along both sides of the top of a truck bed to allow it to be easily transformed into a stake bed truck.

stalk, a lever projecting from the steering column just below the steering wheel with which to operate various secondary controls, *e.g.* direction indicators.

stall, a part which is normally active which becomes inactive due to an external change, *e.g.* the engine stops running due to an external influence, typically due to mechanical overload, insufficient fuel, or braking continued below its minimum running speed.

stall speed, the maximum speed of an engine at full throttle when connected through a torque converter to an automatic gearbox where D is selected and the vehicle is stationary with the brakes fully applied.

stall test, a test of the performance of a torque converter measured by the stall speed: the speed of the engine after 5 seconds at maximum throttle where D is selected and the vehicle is stationary.

standard equipment, all parts and systems of a vehicle which are supplied by the manufacturer within the basic price.

standard hold, to hold the steering wheel with the left hand at 9 o'clock and the right hand at 3 o'clock, the modern hold for maximum control.

standard motorcycle, any motorcycle which is not a moped, (C&U).

standard section, a normal competitive section in a road rally timed to the minute or to the second at exactly 30 mph (48.28 km/h) including checks for route compliance and for safety.

standard time control, a location at the end of a standard section in a road rally.

standard wire gauge, a system of measuring the size of wire of different diameters using an index number system; the sizes are also applied to the thickness of sheet metal.

standee line, USA, a line across a bus aisle marking the foremost limit of standing passengers.

standing, USA, stopping.

standing $1/4$ mile, USA, a means of measuring acceleration performance, quoted as the minimum time required to accelerate from rest and travel 1,320 feet (402.3 metres), also measuring the vehicle speed at that point.

standing start, an acceleration performance test or race initiated from rest.

stand on the brakes, to apply the maximum brake pressure, to brake as hard as possible.

Stane Street, an ancient Roman road from London to Chichester.

star rating, a method of indexing the octane rating of petrol into several bands, see: 1 star, 2 star, 3 star, 4 star, 5 star; obsolete.

start, to operate the ignition and starter motor to crank the engine to cause it to fire and run.

starter, starter motor.

starter guard, a mechanical latch on the ignition keyswitch that prevents re-operation of the starter motor unless the ignition switch is first turned off.

starter lockout, start inhibiter.

starter motor, a small powerful electric motor powered from the vehicle battery, having an automatic gearing system for meshing with the ring gear on the flywheel for causing the crankshaft of the engine to rotate to start the engine; first fitted to a standard production car by Dechamps in 1902.

starter ring gear, gear teeth machined around the flywheel or on an annulus gear fitted to the flywheel, on which the starter motor drives to crank the engine.

starter solenoid, an assembly which engages the starter motor drive pinion onto the starter ring gear then makes the circuit to operate the starter motor.

starter switch control cable, a mechanical cable pulled manually by the driver for the operation of the starter motor on vehicles not having a starter solenoid.

starting handle, a cranked handle for manually cranking an engine.

starting interlock, start inhibiter.

starting switch, a pushbutton on the dashboard for electrical operation of the starter motor, typically on some classic and older cars.

start inhibitor, a switch which prevents operation of the starter motor unless the clutch pedal is pressed fully to the floor, typically on USA cars.

start inhibitor, a switch which prevents operation of the starter motor unless the gear selector is in P or N positions.

start out, to begin a journey.

start up, to start an engine.

star wheel, a mechanical adjuster operated by a small lever or screwdriver, with which to adjust the shoes in a drum brake.

static balance, a tyre condition in which its weight is distributed equally around its axis, when rotated quickly it will not exhibit bounce; although it may be dynamically imbalanced

265

such that there may be lighter and heavier areas at either side of its crown such that it may exhibit wobble.

static belt, a seatbelt without a retracting or tensioning mechanism and which must be adjusted manually for length to suit the size of each occupant of the seat.

static brake test, a daily test of a footbrake system during the starting of a vehicle having a brake servo: the footbrake pedal is pumped approximately 5 to 10 times until it becomes very firm and the vacuum is depleted, then firm continuous pressure is maintained on the pedal whilst the engine is cranked and started, as the engine fires the pedal should move downwards as the servo assists.

static electricity, the accumulation of excessive electrons creating an electrical charge in an insulated body, often generated by friction when a person slides from a seat then touches a metal part; usually overcome by holding metal bodywork *e.g.* the A pillar whilst alighting; it can also damage electronic components.

static friction, stiction.

static ignition timing, a low technology procedure for adjusting the ignition timing whilst the engine is stationary, by manually aligning the timing marks and adjusting the relative position of the distributor, on older vehicles only.

static imbalance, a tyre condition caused by uneven weight distribution around the circumference of the tyre resulting in bounce.

static seal, an oil seal between 2 static parts.

stationary, not moving, at rest.

stationary traffic, traffic that has temporarily stopped due to circumstances beyond the control of each driver, excluding parked vehicles.

station on the side, CB jargon, a CB user wanting to join in the conversation.

station wagon, USA, estate car, a large car typically seating up to 8 persons, usually having rear seats that fold and a loading area at the rear; earlier models have a wood panelled and/or wood framed rear body; originally designed as a utility vehicle for hotels as courtesy transport for their guests to/from the railway station.

stator, the stationary part of a rotating machine, *e.g.* the casing and coil windings of an alternator.

stator, a static element in a torque converter between the impeller and the turbine whereby its curved blades direct the fluid flow and increase the torque applied to the turbine.

status, the rights and the level of rights applying to a route, *e.g.* public or private, and whether it includes vehicular rights as an all-purpose highway.

statute mile, mile, a distance equivalent to 1.609344 km.

statutory attendant, a drivers mate, a person required in addition to the driver for wide loads over 3.5 m (11 ft 5 in) wide, or long oversized loads.

statutory instrument, a legal rule detailing an obligation or restriction, part of an act or regulation.

statutory off road notification, a formal declaration that must be made on the appropriate form when intending to keep a vehicle off the road and untaxed.

statutory power of removal, a power conferred by or under enactment to remove a vehicle from any road or from any part of a road, (C&U).

STC, stability and traction control.

STC, standard time control, in road rally navigation.

std, standard.

stealth bra, a nose bra designed to absorb microwave emissions by radar speed measuring devices to reduce the reflected signal hence evade detection.

steam coach, a steam powered stage coach, a purpose built passenger vehicle offering a regular passenger service between many towns around Britain from 1820 onwards.

steam engine, an external combustion engine in which steam is produced at pressure to operate a piston; invented by Hero in Alexandria during the 1st century AD but was not developed for vehicles until Cugnot used the idea in 1769, some continued to be manufactured in production vehicles until the 1930s.

steam injection, a water injection system using heated water to reduce detonation, especially with a turbo.

steam roller, a road roller powered by a steam engine.

steel, an alloy of iron with up to 5 % carbon, usually a trace of manganese, and with many other metals to give various properties.

steel braced radial, a radial tyre having plies constructed from metallic wires.

steel wheel, a traditional material for vehicle wheels, typically formed by a pressed disc and a rolled rim welded together.

steer, to turn the steering wheel to follow the desired course along a road.

steer by wire, a system not having a mechanical link between the steering wheel and the front wheels; instead a sensor on the steering column signals a microprocessor which controls an actuator that operates the steering mechanism to the front wheels.

steer car, a multiaxle jeep dolly with steerable axles, the steering is usually powered by an inbuilt donkey engine and controlled by a steersman, in order for very long loads to negotiate corners.

steering, the action of turning the steering wheel to follow the desired course along a road.

steering angle, the angle between the

– sSs –

longitudinal axis of the vehicle and the angle through which a wheel is slewed.

steering angle sensor, an instrument on the steering column that measures the steering input and sends a signal to the DSC or VSC or other microprocessors.

steering arm, a short lever between the steering knuckle and a tie rod.

steering axis inclination, the transverse angle between the vertical and a line though the ball joints around which the steering mechanism pivots.

steering ball, a golfball sized knob on a spindle fixed to the face of the rim of a steering wheel to allow rapid rotation of the wheel using 1 hand only, typically for disabled drivers or for a specialist vehicle *e.g.* forklift truck.

steering box, a mechanism at the lower end of the steering column which converts rotary motion into transverse linear motion, on modern cars a rack and pinion system.

steering brake, see: brake steering.

steering brake lock, an antitheft device which links the brake or clutch pedal to the steering wheel rim whilst parked, rendering the car undriveable.

steering column, the shaft between the steering wheel and the steering box.

steering column controls, each control stalk with satellite switches.

steering column gearchange, column change.

steering damper, a telescopic damper acting horizontally on the steering system to absorb vibrations from road shock and to increase directional stability.

steering effort, the magnitude of the force required to turn the steering wheel, which increases with angle from straight ahead and increases at slow road speeds.

steering gain, the relationship between steering angle, yaw, and effort, such that all should increase smoothly and proportionally.

steering gear, the entire mechanism connecting the steering wheel to the front wheels.

steering gearbox, steering box.

steering geometry, the geometric arrangement of the pivots and linkages of a steering system.

steering induced skid, a skid caused by the driver turning the steering excessively or abruptly, such that there is greater momentum in the inertia of the vehicle than the friction present between the front tyres and the road surface, *i.e.* the centrifugal force of the vehicle body is greater than the centripetal force generated by the front tyres.

steering kickback, unwanted sudden feedback from the tyres to the steering wheel as the tyres encounter road surface irregularities.

steering knuckle, the assembly comprising the stub axle and steering arm.

steering linkage, all arms, idlers, joints, links, and rods in the steering system.

steering lock, the angle through which the front wheels slew whilst steering.

steering offset, see: scrub radius.

steering pad, an extensive flat manoeuvring area typically 30 m (100 ft) diameter painted with concentric circles such that lateral acceleration and the stability of a car may be tested in a continuous bend at varying radii and speeds.

steering performance, the comparison of the radius or diameter of the turning circle of a vehicle with other vehicles.

steering play, the angular free movement of a steering wheel due to slackness in various steering linkages.

steering pull, an effect felt at the steering wheel when the vehicle has a tendency to veer towards 1 side on a straight level road without camber, typically caused by incorrect tyre pressures, or an incorrect caster angle.

steering rack, a linear design of steering gearbox that converts the rotary motion of the steering column into transverse movement to operate the track rods.

steering ratio, the ratio of the number of turns of the steering wheel to slew the wheels from straight to full lock, where full lock is enumerated 1.

steering swivel axis, swivel axis.

steering swivel inclination, steering axis inclination.

steering wheel, a hand operated wheel for controlling the direction of the road wheels of a vehicle.

steersman, a person who steers the steer car at the rear end of a vehicle carrying a very long load.

stepframe, a semitrailer having a split bed at 2 levels, part above the 5th wheel but much of its rear section at a lower level.

stepless transmission, cvt.

step on it, to drive faster.

step on the gas, accelerate, to go faster.

stepped planetary gear, a pair of planetary gears having different diameters on a common axis and manufactured as a single unit.

stepper motor, an electric motor in which the shaft rotates in short accurate equal movements or pulses, *e.g.* $1/4$ turns, not rotating continuously.

step plate, a small step to assist entry to and exit from vehicles having a high sill.

stepside, a pickup having a narrow box with external wheel arches, and an external step ahead of the rear wheel.

Stepspeed, an updated version of Steptronic, a clutchless semiautomatic cvt gear selector system having sequential selector paddles on the steering wheel and automatic override if the driver does not change gear when necessary, developed by Rover.

step through, a scooter or moped having an open frame.

Steptronic, a clutchless semiautomatic cvt gear selector system having 6 contrived fixed ratios with sequential selector paddles on the steering wheel and electronic override, developed by BMW.

sterile area, an area where police plan to stop a vehicle to arrest the occupants, usually considering safety where there will be no members of the public nearby.

stethoscope, a listening device as used by doctors with which to listen to engine noises to identify a fault, modern versions are electronic and able to filter unwanted noise and/or give a visual display.

STGO, special types general order.

STGO 1, category 1, vehicles up to 46 tonnes MGW

STGO 2, category 2, vehicles up to 80 tonnes MGW

STGO 3, category 3, vehicles up to 150 tonnes MGW.

sticker price, the price displayed by a car dealer on a placard on a new or used car but which is typically open to negotiation.

stickshift, USA, a manual transmission car.

sticky clutch, clutch drag.

stiction, friction that tends to prevent commencement of relative motion between 2 moveable parts.

stiff gear, USA, a low gear.

stillage, substantial timbers placed on the bed of a lorry to support a load and facilitate the positioning of lifting equipment etc.

still air pocket, an area behind the windscreen of a convertible where there is little turbulence.

stinger, a spiked metal mat, deployed across a road to deflate the tyres of a vehicle passing over it, used by the police to assist arrest of criminals.

stockcar, a specially prepared old large production car that is expected to collide with others during a race.

stockcar racing, a style of racing using specially prepared old large production cars that are expected to collide with each other on an oval or sometimes figure 8 race circuit.

stoichiometric, the ratio of air and fuel to achieve full combustion, for petrol this is 14.7:1 *i.e.* 14.7 parts of air to 1 part of petrol by weight; for diesel it is 18.0:1 *i.e.* 18 parts of air to 1 part of diesel by weight.

stomp on the binders, USA, to brake very hard.

stone sets, stones of a uniform size approximately 100 mm across, originally used to surface roads, often laid in ornamental patterns of interlocking semicircles etc, sometimes slippery when wet.

stone shield, a panel cover, typically chromed or self adhesive plastic fitted ahead of each rear wheel on the leading edge of each rear wing, to protect against damage by small stones and dirt thrown up by a front wheel; sometimes also below the front bumper.

stop, a mechanical device that prevents a part moving beyond a predetermined point.

stop, an action that a driver must perform if involved in any type of accident.

stop, to halt a vehicle for any period of time.

stop control system, a mechanical antilock braking system for fwd cars having only 2 channels of operation; obsolete on modern cars.

stop dead, to stop instantly, an imaginative event which is a physical impossibility.

stop docking, an automatic guidance system for buses at some bus stops to ensure accurate stopping for wheelchair access.

stop lamp, brake lamp, a lamp used to indicate to other road users to the rear of the vehicle that its driver is applying the service brake, (C&U), it may sometimes be activated by the application of a retarder.

stop light, a red traffic signal.

stop light, the light emitted by a brake lamp.

stop light, USA, brake light.

stop line, a white line painted transversely across the road surface signifying a mandatory instruction that the wheels of every vehicle must cease movement, at least for a moment whilst the driver takes effective observation for emerging, or until a signal permits onward travel.

stop nut, lock nut.

stopoff, to break a journey.

stopover, to break a journey by staying overnight at a place.

stopping distance, the sum of the perception distance, reaction distance, braking distance, and the brake lag distance if the vehicle has air brakes, is proportional to the square of the roadspeed and dependant upon the gradient, surface, tyre, and suspension conditions.

stopping procedure, a safe sequence of events performed before stopping a vehicle: check all mirrors, consider what is seen, signal if necessary, stop in a safe place, apply the handbrake, select neutral, cancel the indicators.

stopping sight distance, the sight distance required by a driver to stop a vehicle when faced with an unexpected obstruction in the carriageway, and includes the perception distance, reaction distance, braking distance, brake lag distance if the vehicle has air brakes, and is dependant upon speed, gradient, surface, and tyre conditions.

stop sign, a red octagonal traffic sign displaying a mandatory instruction that the wheels of every vehicle must cease movement, at least for a moment, whilst the driver takes effective observation for emerging.

stop signal, a traffic signal displaying a red light giving a mandatory instruction demanding that the wheels of every vehicle must not pass the line or sign until the signal permits onward travel.

stop stick, USA, stinger, a device placed across the road containing a series of hollow spikes designed to deflate the tyres of a vehicle passing over it, used by police to stop the vehicle of a violator.

storage battery, a rechargeable battery

comprised of secondary cells.

storage lane, an area along the centre of a road where a queue of traffic may safely wait for an opportunity to turn across oncoming traffic into a road to the offside.

stored energy, energy in a braking system, excepting a spring or muscular energy from the driver, stored in a reservoir for the purpose of applying the brakes under the control of the driver, either directly or as a supplement to muscular energy, (C&U).

storm drain, a deep and usually wide gulley along the side of a road, especially in countries which experience very heavy rainfall.

stow, to neatly place and secure a load or other items.

str, steering.

straddle, to drive such that the left and right wheels pass either side of a feature, *e.g.* a pothole or a painted line along the road.

straddle carrier, a motor vehicle constructed to be on both sides of its load and lift its load centrally for the purpose of transportation.

straight 6, an engine having 6 cylinders in a single row.

straight 8, an engine having 8 cylinders in a single row.

straightaway, USA, a straight section of a race circuit.

straight cut gear, a spur gear.

straight engine, an in-line engine having a single row of cylinders, *e.g.* a straight 8.

straight leg, the central line when using the herringbone method of defining a route in road rally navigation, where all roads not taken are marked either side of a straight line which is the route to be followed.

straight line stability, directional stability.

straight lining, the action of taking the straightest possible line or the course having the widest radii allowing for safety and legality, through a series of bends or through a roundabout etc.

straight oil, monograde oil, an oil that changes viscosity in relation to temperature, thick at low temperatures and thin at high temperatures, *i.e.* without multigrade properties.

straight through silencer, an absorption silencer containing a single perforated tube surrounded by acoustic fibre, and which creates minimal backpressure thereby increasing performance.

straight truck, USA, a rigid lorry, *i.e.* non-articulated.

straight weight, USA, straight oil.

strainer, a wire mesh used as a very course filter in some lube oil systems.

stranded, to be without means of transport.

stranded, the situation when a vehicle has broken down rendering onward travel impossible.

strangler, choke, an early name.

strap, a restraint made from synthetic fabric woven to form a belt of webbing to secure a

load, used with a ratchet tensioner.

straphanger, a standing passenger in a bus.

strap wrench, a tool having a flexible belt which is locked to the length required for gripping and turning large round or irregular shaped objects, especially for unscrewing an oil filter.

stratified charge, a design characteristic of a lean burn engine in which most of the air-fuel charge is weak with a small volume of stoichiometric mixture near the sparkplug for initial ignition.

stratified charge engine, an engine in which the air and fuel are not mixed uniformly in the combustion chamber, *e.g.* a diesel engine.

streamline, the contours of a vehicle body designed to reduce its resistance to motion through the air.

street, a road in a town or city, usually lined by buildings, from Latin strata.

street, see also: 1 way, Dere, Ermine, foot, high, highway, lane, local, main, major, play, road, side, Stane, surface, through, Watling.

streetcar, USA, a tram, a non-articulated light rail vehicle.

street circuit, a racing circuit organised on temporarily closed sections of public highway, *e.g.* Spa and Monaco.

street furniture, the traffic related and non-traffic objects that are placed near the roadside, *e.g.* lamp standards, road signs, telephone poles, mail boxes.

street lamp, a public lamp.

street legal, the condition of a vehicle in complying with all legislation such that it may safely be used on a public road.

street light, a public lamp.

street lighting, the illumination emitted by public lamps.

street version, a standard production model similar to a high performance competition car, but having higher standards of comfort and lower standards of performance for road use.

stress, the force or strain suffered by an object under load.

stress, any feelings of fear, apprehension, worry, anxiety, anger, or excitement which prevent a driver from concentrating on driving; any person suffering excessively from any emotions should not drive.

stretch limousine, a large luxury saloon car having a lengthened chassis and bodywork to create more internal space for the carriage of VIPs, typically lengthened more than 1 metre (3 feet) and having up to 3 doors on each side.

stretch of road, a length of road, usually reasonably straight.

striker, the anchor for a door or bonnet latch, typically U or I shaped without any moving parts.

strip, to break off a tooth or teeth from a gear.

strip, to crush or tear off the thread from a screw or nut.

strip, to take apart a vehicle, to take apart a

scrap vehicle, or to take apart an assembly.

stripdown, to totally dismantle an engine or other part in order to rebuild it.

strobe lamp, stroboscope.

stroboscope, a lamp that emits periodic very short pulses of bright light, normally containing neon or xenon gas, used as a timing light in order to check or adjust the ignition timing.

stroboscopic ignition timing, dynamic ignition timing.

stroke, a medical condition that may prevent a person from holding a driving licence due to the risk of collapse and unconsciousness whilst driving.

stroke, the distance a piston travels between bdc and tdc.

stroke, to change the length of the stroke by fitting a different crankshaft having a longer or shorter throw.

stroke-bore ratio, the ratio of the length of a piston stroke compared with the diameter of the cylinder bore; if <1 it is named short stroke, or over square; if exactly 1 it is square; if >1 it is named long stroke, or under square.

Stromberg carburettor, a carburettor having a variable venturi.

strut, see: Chapman strut, MacPherson strut.

strut, part of a vehicle structure designed to resist compressive stress.

strut brace, a transverse bar fitted to production cars between the tops of front and/ or rear suspension to add rigidity, usually for competitive use.

STS, sidewall torsion sensor.

stub axle, a short fixed spindle forming the centre of rotation to which a wheel is fixed.

stud, a thin metal plate typically 10 centimetres square, affixed to the road surface to mark pedestrian crossings, nodes, etc, usually made of stainless steel.

stud, a retroreflective road stud, a reflector bonded onto or partly recessed into the road surface; a colour code system is used, the reflectors may be: red, green, white, amber, or yellow, often named cats eyes.

stud, a rod threaded along its full length or sometimes just threaded at both ends.

stud, a wheel stud, each of several threaded rods which locate the wheel disc on the hub.

stud, a metal peg or spike screwed into the tread of a studded tyre.

studded tyre, a tyre which is made with provision to insert small steel studs into the tread to give increased traction and steering when driving on ice or packed snow, they must be fitted to all 4 wheels regardless of fwd or rwd; in competitions rules may permit up to 216 studs per tyre.

student, a person engaged in pre-driver education.

student licence, USA, a licence to drive which is valid only whilst being taught by a qualified driving instructor or school.

stud hole, a hole in a wheel disc to facilitate securing to the stud with a wheel nut.

studless tyre, a M&S tyre which is not designed to be fitted with studs.

StVG, Straâenverkehrsgestz, German, Road Traffic Act, *i.e.* Highway Code.

StVZO, Straâenverkehrszulassungs-Ordnung, German, Road Licensing Regulations, *i.e.* vehicle construction and use regulations.

stylist, a person who creates artistically the shape of the bodywork of a vehicle; often misnamed designer.

SU, Skinners Union, a company specialising in carburettor manufacture, founded by George Skinner and his brothers in 1905.

sub A, a very small car, having a floor pan smaller than an A segment car; also named supermini.

subassembly, an assembled unit which is a component of a larger unit.

subcompact car, USA, a car which will seat 4 persons in comfort although typically a 5 seat car.

subframe, a partial chassis that may carry the front or rear suspension and sometimes the engine or transmission, it typically helps to reduce noise and vibration.

sub MAC, a certificate issued to each subsequent vehicle certified under LVNTA after the P-MAC.

submarine, to slide under the lap belt during a frontal collision.

substructure, structural members and body panels within the floor of the vehicle.

subway, a footpath crossing beneath a road.

suction dent puller, a device with which to pull out wide shallow dents in bodywork panels.

suction line, the pipe from the fuel tank to the fuel pump.

suction stroke, induction stroke.

SUD, Sudan, international vehicle distinguishing sign, see appendices.

suicide door, a side door which is hinged at its rearmost edge such that the leading edge opens, very dangerous if opened whilst the vehicle is moving; on some vintage and veteran cars.

suicide jockey, CB jargon, a lorry driver carrying a hazardous load.

suicide lane, the lane adjacent to the central reservation on a motorway or similar road, named before central crash barriers were common and crossover collisions not uncommon.

suicide lane, the central overtaking lane on a 3 lane road where priority is equal in both directions, named from the prevalence of head-on collisions on such a road; also named coroners alley.

suicide lane, USA, a 2 way left turn lane, the central lane on a road marked to facilitate traffic from both directions turning off the road to the offside.

SULEV, super ultra low emission vehicle.

sulphur dioxide, SO_2, a gas emitted by the

process of combustion in an engine.

sulphur oxides, SO_x, a range of acids that can form in small quantities in the cat.

sulphuric acid, H_2SO_4, a strong acid liquid, colourless, toxic, highly corrosive, normally used at 40 % concentration as electrolyte in batteries.

Sulzer engine, a diesel 2 stroke engine.

summer tire, highway tire, a tyre designed for wet and dry use but not suitable for use on snow and ice.

summit, the highest point on a road as it crosses a col at a pass.

sump, the lowest point in an engine, the reservoir into which expended lube oil drains before recirculation.

sump filter, oil strainer.

sump guard, a strong metal fabrication beneath a vehicle designed to protect vulnerable parts underneath against striking the ground where the surface is rough, especially at speed.

sun and planet, a gear pairing in an epicyclic system.

sun car, solar car.

Sunday driver, the driver of a vehicle travelling unusually slowly for the conditions and causing a tailback.

sun gear, the central gear in a planetary train.

sunroof, a glass panel in the roof of a vehicle to brighten the interior and for ventilation, usually opening by tilting and/or sliding.

sunroof, a metal panel in the roof of a vehicle for ventilation, usually opening by tilting and/or sliding.

sunroof deflector, an angled shield attached to the front edge of a sunroof aperture to reduce turbulence within the car.

sunroof top, a folding canvas roof.

sunshield, a strip of translucent vinyl affixed across the upper edge of the windscreen to reduce glare from the sun.

sunstrike, the dazzle created by the suns rays illuminating dirt, dust, moisture, or scratches on the inside or outside of the windscreen whenever the sun is low in the sky and almost ahead.

sun strip, a sunshield.

sunvisor, a hinged or roller flap across the top of the windscreen that can be lowered to shield the drivers and passengers eyes from bright sunlight.

sunvisor, an external horizontal strip of metal or translucent plastic extending forwards along the top of the windscreen to shield the drivers and passengers eyes from bright sunlight, a 1960s fashion accessory.

suped, an engine or vehicle that is tuned or modified to increase performance; originally named from supercharged, *i.e.* having a supercharger, usually named souped up.

super, leaded petrol having a 5 star rating.

supercar, a high performance car, generally having a maximum speed exceeding 250 km/h (150 mph).

supercharged, referring to either: the induction air, the engine, or the vehicle, operating with the benefit of a supercharger to increase power.

supercharged engine, an engine fitted with a supercharger.

supercharger, an air compressor which is belt driven by crankshaft, which compresses the induction air so a greater amount of charge can be forced into the cylinder to increase power.

supercharging, the action of increasing the quantity of induction air by boosting the pressure, so an increased quantity of fuel can be added, thereby increasing the power.

superchip, a chip which may replace the standard chip in the ECU, giving enhanced characteristics.

super duty, USA, a vehicle over 8,500 lbs (3.85 tonnes) GVW.

superelevation, a banked surface around a curve, the construction of the surface of a carriageway on a bend such that the outer radius is higher than the inner radius by several degrees, typically between 2.5 % and 15 %, to increase stability for traffic at speed by reducing lateral force on the tyres.

superhighway, USA, a broad highway, *e.g.* expressway, freeway, or turnpike, for high speed traffic.

supermini, a very small car, having a floor pan smaller than an A segment car.

super single, a single wide wheel and tyre which performs the function of a twin wheel assembly, typically fitted to the load carrying and drive wheels on a lorry for improved stability and economy, sometimes also fitted to the front wheels.

super slab, CB jargon, a motorway.

super sports roadster, a 2 seat sports car having a pickup bed at the rear.

super stacker, a vehicle designed to lift, transport, and stack containers, not for road use.

supertram, a vehicle that runs on rails within a road surface hence shares the road with other vehicles, but has its own specific road signs and traffic signals.

super ultra low emission vehicle, any vehicle that can meet or exceed the standards of vehicle emissions as demanded by the Californian state standards.

super unleaded, unleaded petrol with an octane rating of 98 RON.

supervisor, a person not qualified as an instructor but supervising a learner driver, and who must be over 21 years of age and have held a licence for the same category of vehicle for 3 years.

supplementary mirror, an additional mirror near the centreline of a windscreen for use by a co-driver, examiner, instructor, navigator, or observer.

supplementary restraint system, any device

designed to be used in conjunction with a primary safety restraint, *e.g.* airbag to be used in conjunction with a seatbelt.

suppressor, an electronic device that reduces radio interference caused by electrical charges.

surface, the road surface, or whatever material with which the footprint of the tyre is in contact, *e.g.* wet or dry tarmac or concrete, gravel, mud, snow, sand, etc, the quality and conditions of which dictate the friction available for acceleration, braking, and steering.

surface carburettor, an ancient style of carburettor in which air is passed over the surface of petrol to charge it with fuel.

surface conditions, the microstructure and macrostructure of the surface, the gradients, and any material on the road surface which has the ability to change the frictional performance of the surface, *e.g.* water, or loose gravel, which will alter the friction available on tarmac, concrete, earth, etc.

surface gap sparkplug, a sparkplug having a large diameter central electrode concentric within a ring insulator concentric within the shell electrode, such that the spark may jump radially across any point from centre to edge and without any adjustment being possible or necessary.

surface ignition, ignition of the air-fuel charge due to a hotspot in the combustion chamber before the spark fires.

surface street, USA, a road having uncontrolled access, at-grade signal controlled junctions, and where turns across opposing traffic are permitted.

surf tail, a spoiler fitted as an extension to the roof at the rear of a car, especially to a hatchback or estate.

surge, unevenness in the power output of an engine due to a fault in the air, fuel, or ignition systems.

surge brakes, overrun brakes as fitted to some light trailers.

surrender, to use a submissive speed and position to give way, to remove confusion and prevent a situation developing where drivers may have a similar priority, especially when meeting head-on at a width restriction.

survival cell, the closed structure containing the fuel tank and cockpit of a racing car.

survival kit, a kit made up of items that will make life safer and more comfortable in an emergency, including a small tool kit, a first aid kit, but other contents depend upon the type of journey: cold weather kit, desert kit, jungle kit, city kit, etc.

suspended tow, a condition when a breakdown recovery vehicle tows a broken down vehicle by lifting 1 axle from the road.

suspension, a vehicle system comprising an assembly of levers, springs, and dampers, which allow each wheel to move vertically to compensate for unevenness in a road surface and minimise transmission of road shocks to the chassis, it supports the weight of the vehicle and load, and ensures traction for acceleration, braking, and steering; it may be supported by air, rubber, or steel springs, and may have numerous types of layout.

suspension, see: 4 link, 5 link, A arm, A bracket, active, air, als, antidive, cab, CATS, De Dion, delta, double wishbone, Dubonnet, ECAS, ECS, flexarm, full air, Hotchkiss, hydro—, ifs, irs, is, LCS, LLS, MacPherson, Moulton, multilink, parallel trailing, radius arm, rising rate, road friendly, rubber, sala, sls, semiactive, semi-independent, semitrailing, sliding pillar, swing axle, trailing arm, Z axle.

suspension, USA, the temporary loss of driving privileges due to being convicted of 3 traffic violations in 12 months, DUI, or 10 or more unpaid parking violations, and other offences.

suspension bridge, a bridge on which the road surface is supported by vertical wires suspended from a pair of tensioned cables which are supported on towers and which are anchored beyond the ends of the bridge.

suspension link, any rod which connects a road wheel to the chassis.

suspension mounting, any structural fabrication within the body or chassis of a vehicle which has been designed to withstand the forces generated by the relative movement of the wheel and/or body.

suspension sphere, a sphere which is pressurised with nitrogen gas and used in hydropneumatic suspensions.

suspension strut, a single unit comprising a damper with a concentric coil spring, and a hub carrier.

suspension subframe, a partial chassis on which all suspension elements are mounted, and which insulates noise and vibration from the car body.

suspension turret, a cylindrical structural pressing within a monocoque chassis to support a suspension mounting.

sut, sport utility truck.

suv, sport utility vehicle.

suzies, the coiled air hoses and electrical line with which to connect a trailer to a lorry; the name is derived from the comparison in elasticity with suspenders as in female underwear.

sv, side valve.

SVA, single vehicle approval.

svd, selective vehicle detection.

SVDD, speed violation detection deterrent.

SVO, special vehicle order.

SVS, stolen vehicle squad.

sw, switch, as marked on the ignition coil terminal powered from the ignition switch.

SW, USA, station wagon.

swage line, a decorative groove or concave crease in the bodywork, typically along the sides of a car.

swamp buggy, a vehicle having very large diameter wheels and mud clearing tyres, designed to run on land, mud, and shallow water, used especially in swamps.

swan neck, a course followed as a result of a steering input in the opposite direction immediately before turning at a junction, the result of bad planning and bad positioning, a dangerous technique in any vehicle.

swap meet, USA, autojumble.

sway bar, USA, antiroll bar.

swb, short wheelbase.

sweeper, a type of seal used on the lower edge of wind-down windows to prevent rain from entering the door void, and which wipes water and dirt from the glass as it is lowered.

sweeper car, a course closing car.

swept area, the total friction area of the discs and drums at all wheels which is swept by brake lining material, including both sides of each disc.

swept area, swept path.

swept path, the width of road taken by a vehicle including trams, including front and rear overhangs also including any trailer, as it follows any course and which becomes increasingly wider as the radius of a turn reduces, *i.e.* a 2.5 m wide vehicle may have a swept path 6.7 m wide around a path having an inner radius of 5.3 metres.

swept volume, the volume displaced by 1 piston as it moves from bdc to tdc.

swerve, a sudden change of direction caused by an abrupt or excessive movement of the steering wheel, usually having a double input *e.g.* right then left, usually because of poor observation, bad planning, or lack of anticipation.

swg, standard wire gauge.

swing axle, a design of independent suspension of a drive axle which pivots near the centre of the vehicle but not at the wheel, thereby causing a significant variation in the camber angle and track as the suspension oscillates.

swing bridge, a bridge at which the road surface pivots horizontally around a vertical axis, *i.e.* it pivots to the left or right.

swirl, a desired turbulent movement of inlet air as it enters into the cylinder, to improve combustion efficiency.

swirl chamber, a small chamber connected directly to the top of the combustion chamber within the cylinder head, where fuel is injected to start combustion before the combustion spreads to the combustion chamber, to reduce knocking and noise in diesel engines, but leading to increased fuel consumption.

swirl pot, a small tank in a cooling or fuel system to expel air to ensure that no air travels with the liquid.

switch, a device for operating an electrical circuit by connecting or disconnecting an electrical path.

switchback, a road having alternate steep ascents and descents.

switched off, a mental condition lapsed into by many drivers for parts of a journey when they are not aware of their surroundings, often caused by complacency on a frequently travelled route and resulting in longer reaction times and an increased risk of a collision.

switchgauge, a gauge which displays the temperature or pressure etc. of a vital system, and which also incorporates a switch to show a warning light, sound an alarm, or shut down the engine when an operational parameter is exceeded.

switchgear, the switches that the driver operates to control various auxiliaries.

Switchtronic, a semiautomatic gear selector system controlled by a pair of paddles on the steering wheel, developed by Alpina for BMW.

swivel, to swing or slew around a point less than a full rotation.

swivel angle, swivel axis inclination.

swivel axis, the line between the balljoints around which the steering mechanism of a modern car pivots.

swivel axis inclination, the transverse angle between the swivel axis and a vertical line.

swivel pin, kingpin.

SWR, short way round, a direction at a triangle in road rally navigation.

SY, Seychelles, international vehicle distinguishing sign, see appendices.

symmetric rim, a wheel having a well located centrally between the rims.

synchro, synchromesh.

synchromesh, an automatic synchronising mechanism within a gearbox using cone clutches on each gear to speed up or slow down the input shaft so the selected gear moves into mesh smoothly; introduced by Cadillac in 1928.

synchrometer, a device which measures the direct airflow into twin or multiple carburettor intakes for the purpose of balancing twin choke and multibarrel carburettors.

synthetic oil, an oil manufactured from polyol ester basestocks, it has a very long working life giving excellent lubrication and resulting in reduced engine wear.

synthetic rubber, a material having properties similar to or exceeding those of natural rubber, produced by polymerization of petroleum derived olefins or similar compounds.

Syntroleum, a synthetic fuel containing no sulphur, designed for diesel engines to give cleaner emissions.

SYR, Syria, international vehicle distinguishing sign, see appendices.

syst, system.

system, 2 or more parts that work together to perform a specific function.

systematic vehicle control, the system of car control as applied to any vehicle.

system of car control, a method of approaching and negotiating hazards which is methodical, safe, and leaves nothing to chance, giving time to manipulate the vehicle controls to achieve maximum safety, having the phases: information, position, speed, gear, and acceleration.

Système Panhard, a conventional chassis layout having a front engine, central gearbox, and rwd, in general use since 1890.

system for restraint and protection, a system in which the sensors and triggers for the seatbelt pretensioners and airbags are linked enabling the pretensioners to operate first.

T

T, cabriolet, a car body style.

T, tachograph, an ISO symbol used before the graphic symbol was approved.

T, Thailand, international vehicle distinguishing sign, see appendices.

T, thousand, an incorrect suffix to an abbreviated mileage in some advertisements for secondhand cars; k is the correct abbreviation.

T, toll, as a suffix to a road number it denotes that road is subject to a toll.

T, tonne, shown on a road sign referring to the MGW.

T, the tyre speed rating code denoting a maximum design speed of 190 km/h (118 mph), moulded into the tyre sidewall.

T, turn, followed by left or right, in road rally navigation.

T1, Thatcham category 1, an approval system for a combined alarm and immobiliser.

T2, Thatcham category 2, an approval system for an electronic or electromechanical immobiliser.

T3, Thatcham category 3, an approval system for a mechanical immobiliser.

T bar, trailer bar, the drawbar of a light trailer where the drawbar is of a straight beam construction.

T bar roof, a roof having a longitudinal bar connecting the top centre of the windscreen with the roll bar or rear roof section, on some sports cars and kit cars.

T bone, a collision in which the front of a car hits another car centrally in its side at 90°.

T cab, a tractive unit in conventional configuration where the engine and bonnet are ahead of the driver.

T car, training car.

t glass, tinted glass.

T head, a double row sidevalve cylinder head, having the inlet at 1 side and the exhaust at the other.

T junction, terminating junction, an intersection of 2 roads where 1 leg is perpendicular to the other 2 legs.

T nav, a system of receiving live updated traffic information, especially of congestion, along a pre-selected and logged route via a mobile phone.

T plate, trailer plate, a reflective plate showing the letter T which must be affixed to a trailer in many African countries, a red reflective T is displayed to the rear and a white reflective T is displayed at the front offside corner.

T top, targa top.

T wrench, an Allen or Torx wrench fitted with a T handle for comfort.

T&GWU, Transport and General Workers Union, UK.

T/A, traction advantage, a combination tread on an off road tyre.

TA, traffic announcements, a selective control on an rds radio.

TA, UK, Transport Act 1985.

TA, type approval, the common term for ECWVTA.

tab, the small projection on a tab washer which ensures a secure location.

table junction, a lengthened speed hump which encompasses a complete junction whereby all roads climb onto the table a short distance before the junction starts.

tab washer, a washer having a tab internally to locate in a keyed shaft, the washer is malleable to allow folding of the rim by hammering to secure the faces of a nut.

TAC, thermostatic air cleaner.

tacho, tachograph.

tacho, tachometer.

tachograph, a device for automatically measuring and recording driving hours and rest breaks, also speed and distance and time, originally recording on paper discs now typically recording onto an electronic chip.

tachograph chart, a paper disc that records driving hours, rest periods, speed, distance, time, and other vehicle operating parameters.

tachometer, an instrument that measures engine speed, usually in revolutions per minute, displaying in rpm x 100 or rpm x 1,000, commonly named rev counter.

tacho tell-tale, an indicating pointer on a rev counter showing the peak revs since it was previously re-set, typically on sports cars driven other than by the owner; re-settable with a magnetic tool.

tack coat, a thin layer of bitumen or road tar laid on a road to enhance adhesion of the course above it.

tack rag, an anti-static lint free cloth designed to absorb dust, used just before spray painting.

tack welding, to make several isolated welds where metals join without welding the whole joint.

tactic, any of a range of skillful strategies used

in the art of defensive driving whereby the driver controls the space around his/her vehicle.

tactic, a strategy used to overcome other competitors in a race or competition.

tactile paving, a series of small raised studs which can be felt underfoot and used to advise blind persons where it is suitable to cross a road.

tag, USA, a vehicle license plate.

tag axle, rear trailing axle.

tag lift axle, a non-driven load carrying axle close behind a driven axle on a tractive unit, lorry, or bus, which may be raised from the road surface to reduce costs when the vehicle is operated lightly loaded; see also: pusher lift axle.

tail, the rear of a vehicle.

tailback, a long queue of stationary or slow moving traffic behind an obstruction.

tailboard, a panel across the rear of a dropside lorry bed, which can be hinged downwards for loading.

tail end, the rear of any part, assembly, or vehicle.

tailfin, vertical bodywork above and along a rear wing as a styling feature, typically by Cadillac in the 1950s.

tailgate, the rear door on an estate car, pickup, or 4x4, usually hinged along its lower edge.

tailgating, the action of one vehicle following closely behind another, where the interval is less than that necessary for safety.

tail happy, a car with a significant or easily induced oversteer.

tail heavy, the condition of a vehicle which is excessively loaded behind the rear axle.

tail heavy, the condition of a towing vehicle when the noseweight of the trailer is excessive.

taillamp, any lamp on the rear of a vehicle, but especially the rear position lamps.

tail lift, a condition that occurs when the rear of a vehicle rises on its suspension, occurring simultaneously with dive during significant braking due to inertia and apparent weight transfer.

tail lift, a raising/lowering platform at the rear of a lorry to enable the load to be delivered to/from ground level.

taillight, the light emitted from the red rear position lamps.

tailpipe, the pipe at the end of an exhaust system through which exhaust gas discharges to the air.

tailshaft, the gearbox output shaft.

tailspin, a rear wheel skid.

tail swing, the sideways movement of the portion of the rear body of a vehicle which is behind the rear axle in the opposite direction to which the front is turning, especially when manoeuvring on full lock and with a long rear overhang.

tailwind, a wind blowing directly on the rear of a vehicle, or in the same direction that the vehicle is travelling.

take control, the action of a driving instructor in regaining the handling of the vehicle.

take off, acceleration from rest.

take out, the method used by USA police for halting the progress of a violator by using the fishtail technique.

take over, to exchange seating positions with the driver.

take up, the status of the clutch at the biting point.

take up the drive, to engage the clutch to the biting point.

take up the drive, to engage the clutch to the driving point.

taking pictures, CB jargon, police using speed radar.

talc, a finely powdered soft mineral used to prevent an innertube sticking to the inside of the tyre carcass.

tall gearing, gear ratios that are relatively high, sometimes referring to a whole range of gears in a vehicle.

tamper, to change any correct adjustment, remove, disconnect, damage, reduce the performance, or render inoperative any device associated with safety, emission control, or performance.

tamperproof carburettor, a carburettor having all adjustments set and sealed at the factory, such that further adjustments are not possible.

tandem, any arrangement of 2 axles, pistons, seats, or wheels etc. where 1 is directly in line behind the other.

tandem axle, a trailer having 2 close-coupled axles.

tandem axle set, a pair of axles which are load sharing and where their centres are spaced not less than 1 metre apart and not more than 2 metres apart.

tandem brake cylinder, a cylinder having 2 pistons linked in line each feeding separate brake circuits.

tandem distance, the legroom distance between the front and rear seats for the comfort of rear passengers.

tandem drive, a lorry having 2 rear axles in which both drive.

tandem roller, a road roller having 2 metal wheels, 1 behind the other.

tandem seats, a 2 seat arrangement in some sports cars where the passenger sits behind the driver.

tank, a container for holding, storing, or transporting a liquid.

tanker, a lorry or trailer onto which is mounted a cylindrical horizontal tank designed for the transport of liquids or powders; in some cases the chassis runs within the tank.

tank sender unit, the part of the fuel level indicating system that is located in the fuel tank.

tank transporter, a heavy duty low loader semitrailer for the carriage of tanks and similar armoured military vehicles by road.

tank truck, tanker.

tank vehicle, USA, any commercial motor vehicle having any size of fixed tank, or portable tanks of 1,000 gallons (3,785 litres) capacity or greater, excluding tanks necessary for the operation of the vehicle.

Tanners square root law, the number of accidents at a location are related to the square root of the product of the intersecting flows of traffic.

taper, an acutely angled shape, especially a hole or shaft in which 1 end is slightly wider than the other.

taper diverge, an exit sliproad at which the diverging lane leaves the through carriageway over a relatively short distance.

tapered compression ring, a piston ring having a tapered outer edge, part of which will rapidly wear off to create a good seal.

taper frame, a semitrailer in which the chassis width is reduced over the 5th wheel, usually for tankers, bulk tippers, and some low loaders, to reduce chassis weight.

taper leaf spring, a design of parabolic leaf spring having narrower leaves at the ends.

taper merge, a short entry sliproad at which the merging lane immediately begins to reduce in width.

taper roller bearing, a bearing having races and rollers which are conical, such that the bearing will resist axial thrust in 1 direction in addition to radial thrust.

taper seat, an angled mating face on a wheel and wheelnut, as a means of providing positive centring of a roadwheel when the wheelnut is tightened; they must not be mixed or interchanged with spherical types.

tape weight, a lead balance weight designed to be fitted to an alloy wheel using an adhesive backing.

tappet, a device that causes a pushrod to operate an engine valve, and which permits accurate adjustment.

tappet noise, a regular clicking noise that indicates a tappet is not correctly adjusted.

tar, a viscous material composed of complex compounds derived from distillation of petroleum.

tare, the dry weight of a vehicle, *i.e.* the kerbweight of a vehicle minus the weight of fuel, fluids, and tools.

targa, a open top sports car having a large removable roof panel and a substantial roll bar, named from Targa Florio, an annual Sicilian race.

targa bar, a roll frame constructed as a steel panel having significant longitudinal dimensions, typically the sides may be triangular.

targa timing, an obsolete method of timing for road rallies whereby a target time was set to achieve any average speed at the organisers choosing.

targa top, a removable solid roof panel between the windscreen and targa bar.

target, a vehicle being overtaken.

target, a vehicle under observation by the police.

tarmac, tarmacadam.

tarmacadam, stone chippings bound in tar used for surfacing roads.

tautliner, curtainside.

TAW, Australia, total axle(s) weight.

tax disc, a paper disc displayed in a vehicle windscreen as proof that VED has been paid.

tax dodger, a person who uses on a road an untaxed motor vehicle.

taxed, a vehicle on which the VED has been paid.

tax exempt vehicle, any vehicle manufactured before 1 January 1972 and which is exempt from VED.

taxi, a large car which is licensed to ply for hire and to carry passengers for a fee which is usually calculated by a meter.

taxi brousse, bush taxi, a public transport system in some African countries, originally a small covered lorry with bench seating, now usually a Ford Transit sized minibus typically fitted with 28 passenger seats but normally carrying up to 50 persons plus luggage.

taxicab, taxi.

taximeter, an instrument installed in a taxi which measures time and distance and calculates the fare for the journey.

taxi rank, a place where taxis wait to be hired, typically in an area frequented by pedestrians.

taxi stand, USA, taxi rank.

tb, towbar.

TB, total width at the rear wheels.

tbe, timing belt end.

tbi, throttle body injection.

TBV, a semiautomatic gear selector system utilising a clutch pedal for every gear change, developed by Renault.

tc, torque converter.

tc, twin carburettors.

TC, traction control.

TC, traffic calming.

TC 22, Technical Committee No 22 of ISO, responsible for automobile product standards.

tce, timing chain end.

tci, transistorised coil ignition.

TCI, turbocharged diesel with intercooler.

tcih, transistorised coil ignition with Hall generator.

tcm, transmission control module.

tcs, transmission controlled spark.

tcs, transmission control system.

TCS, traction control system.

td, turbo diesel.

TD, Chad, international vehicle distinguishing sign, see appendices.

TD, a special wheel and tyre system having metric wheels and a dedicated tyre with run-flat capability.

TDA, take and drive away.

tdc, top dead centre.
TDdi, turbo diesel direct injection.
TDi, turbo diesel injection.
TDI, turbocharged diesel with intercooler.
tear off, each of a series of thin plastic covers over the crash helmet visor which may be discarded as necessary during a race to maintain good visibility.
teeth, the projections on a gearwheel that mesh between corresponding parts on another gearwheel.
tel, tetraethyl lead.
telematics, the range of electronic signals, controls, or information that make driving easier or safer, *e.g.* those that give route assistance, or advance warning of traffic congestion, either in the vehicle or at the roadside.
telescopic damper, a tubular hydraulic damper that converts kinetic energy into thermal energy, typically mounted on the suspension between the wheel and chassis to prevent unwanted chassis/wheel oscillation after a deflection of the suspension, to increase safety and comfort, commonly misnamed shock absorber.
telescopic shock absorber, telescopic damper.
telescopic steering column, a steering column designed to collapse during a severe frontal impact so as not to injure the driver.
telescoping steering wheel, reach adjustable steering wheel.
Telligent EPS, a third-generation of semiautomatic gear system advising and allowing pre-selection of gears, developed by Mercedes trucks.
tell-tale, blue, a blue illuminated symbol on the dashboard, normally only used to inform the driver the main beam headlamps are selected.
tell-tale, green, a green illuminated symbol on the dashboard that informs the driver a normal system is in service, *e.g.* the dip headlamps or direction indicators, etc.
tell-tale lamp, the source of illumination for a tell-tale symbol.
tell-tale, red, a red illuminated symbol on the dashboard that informs the driver a system is not in a driveable state, the vehicle must not be driven, *e.g.* the handbrake is on, or oil pressure is low, etc.
tell-tale symbol, each of over 160 different ISO approved illuminated colour coded graphic symbols on the dashboard that gives information regarding the status or correct or incorrect function of circuits or systems or auxiliaries or devices, illuminating in blue, green, red, or yellow.
tell-tale, yellow, a yellow illuminated symbol on the dashboard that informs the driver an auxiliary system is in service, *e.g.* the rear screen heater.
Telma, a driver controlled retarding system, an electromagnetic device fitted on the propeller shaft of lorries and buses, usually having several stages.
tempa spare, a space saving spare wheel.
temperature code, a tyre rating relating to the generation of heat within a tyre and its ability to dissipate heat in controlled conditions, grade C indicates the lowest satisfactory level accepted by FMVSS, grades B, A, and AA exceed the standard by greater margins.
temperature indicator, a gauge or display that informs the driver of the temperature of the engine coolant.
tempered glass, USA, toughened glass.
temporary spare wheel, a space saving spare wheel.
temporary use spare tyre, a pneumatic tyre which is designed for use on a motor vehicle only in the event of the failure of 1 of the tyres normally fitted to the wheel of a vehicle and at a speed lower than that for which such normally fitted tyres are designed, (C&U).
TEN's, trans-European networks.
tension, a force that tends to stretch an object, *e.g.* a bolt or a fan belt.
terminal, a connecting point in an electrical circuit, especially at an electrode, *e.g.* on a battery, alternator, or lamp fitting.
terminal, an area where liquids are loaded into tankers for road haulage, or sometimes other types of load.
terminal line, a short transverse line indicating the limit of a longitudinal road marking, *e.g.* at the end of parking restriction lines and zigzag lines.
terminal voltage, the voltage measured across the battery terminals, or across the terminals of any electrical device, *e.g.* a bulb.
terminating junction, T junction, the end of a road where it meets perpendicular with another.
terminus, a bus station.
terminus, the remote end of a bus route.
tertiary collision, the impact of a persons internal organs against each other immediately after a secondary collision.
tertiary safety, any measures which would improve the chance of survival of a casualty or reduce the effect of injuries sustained, typically dependant upon the location of the incident.
test, a driving test.
test, a vehicle examination.
testable item, an aspect of a vehicle which is tested for roadworthiness during an MOT test by an examiner.
test bed, an inspection area having a range of measuring instruments and sometimes a rolling road.
test certificate, a certificate that states that the vehicle for which it was issued had been inspected and found roadworthy at the time of inspection.
test drive, a familiarisation and acceptance drive of a vehicle by a potential purchaser, having a duration variously from a few minutes to a few days.

test drive, to drive a vehicle after maintenance or repairs to check that it feels roadworthy.

test driver, a person employed to test a racing car and advise on modifications or adjustments.

tested, a vehicle exceeding a specific age that has been examined at intervals to ensure it remains in a roadworthy condition.

testing, the process of driving, adjusting or modifying and driving again a racing car to gain maximum performance from the engine, transmission, or suspension etc, sometimes linked to the performance required to suit a particular racing circuit.

test route, an approved route used for practical driving tests having a wide range of typical road and traffic conditions.

test track, a private testing ground typically having several different high quality roads for a variety of tests, all without traffic or speed limits, where manufacturers and motoring journalists can assess the abilities of vehicles.

tetraethyl lead, a chemical formerly added to petrol to increase its octane rating, reduce the risk of detonation, and to lubricate valve seats.

tetramethyl lead, a lead compound previously added to petrol instead of tetraethyl lead on some occasions, to increase the antiknock properties of the fuel.

TFHRC, Turner-Fairbank Highway Research Centre, USA.

TG, Togo, international vehicle distinguishing sign, see appendices.

t/gate, tailgate.

tgf, timing gear front bank.

tgr, timing gear rear bank.

thank you wave, courtesy wave.

Thatcham, the common name for the Motor Industry Repair Research Centre, UK, named after its location, or a set of standards defined by that organisation.

Thatcham category 1, certification for a combined alarm and immobiliser.

Thatcham category 2, certification for an electronic or electromechanical immobiliser.

Thatcham category 3, certification for a mechanical immobiliser.

Thatcham category Q, certification for equipment tested to ensure a device performs as described by the manufacturer, but with no pass/fail, *e.g.* tracking systems or image recorders etc.

theft loss waver, a standard accessory to hire car insurance covering any situation in which the renter of the vehicle is unable to return the vehicle at the end of the rental period.

The Knowledge, the photographic memory of the geography of the City of London encompassing a 6 mile (10 km) radius from Charring Cross, that a cab driver must display in order to qualify for a black cab licence.

theory test, a test of knowledge of driving rules for the safe and correct driving of a motor vehicle, to pass the test is the minimum acceptable standard of proficiency, it may be oral, written, or performed using a computer.

thermal efficiency, the relationship between the energy in the fuel burned compared with the power output of the engine; internal combustion reciprocating engines do not generally exceed 28 %.

thermal reactor, a chamber in the exhaust manifold used in conjunction with an air injection system to prolong the gas residence time to complete the oxidation of HC and CO.

thermoplastic, plastics used in vehicle manufacture that will soften when heat is applied, allowing easy re-cycling.

thermostat, a device with which to automatically control temperature; in the cooling system by directly regulating the flow of coolant from the engine to the radiator, in ac systems by sending an electronic signal to an actuator.

thermostatic air cleaner, an air cleaner which also controls the temperature of the inlet air by mixing preheated air passing over the exhaust with ambient air to maintain a temperature typically in the range 30 °C to 45 °C.

thermostatic gauge, a gauge or display that indicates the temperature of coolant, engine oil, or transmission oil etc.

thi, transistorised Hall ignition.

thinking distance, the perception-reaction distance, the distance a vehicle travels between the driver first observing a hazard and starting to depress the brake pedal, the normal minimum at 100 km/h is 20 metres (at 60 mph is 60 feet).

thinking gearbox, an automatic gearbox that allows for load, gradient, speed etc, and sometimes the drivers style, by means of electronic sensors.

thinking time, the time taken for a driver to observe a hazard and decide to react, the normal minimum is 0.7 second for an alert healthy driver.

third party, any claimant on an insurance policy that is not the insurance company or the insured driver or vehicle owner.

thoroughfare, a road or path open to the public.

thou, thousandth, usually 1-thousandth of 1 inch, 25.4 microns.

thrash, the action of the crankshaft splashing into the oil in the sump when the oil level is too high.

thrash, to drive hard using high revs and maximum power.

thread, a helical groove cut into the shaft of a stud or bolt or screw, or into the bore of a nut or other part.

thread, to pick a winding route using lesser roads, typically to cut diagonally across an area between main roads.

threepenny bitting, the action of a driver in making many minor and unnecessary steering corrections whilst travelling around a single bend, *i.e.* not using single input steering;

named from a UK pre-decimal coin having 12 corners around its circumference.

threshold braking, a skillful technique for gaining the maximum retardation possible on any particular road surface by applying the footbrake increasingly until the driver can sense, hear, or feel, that 1 or more of the tyres are just starting to slide, then slightly reducing the brake pressure such that all wheels continue to rotate albeit very slowly; now superseded by ABS.

throaty, an exhaust note having a deep pitch.

throttle, any hand operated speed control that operates a valve that controls the airflow into an engine *e.g.* on a tractor, motorcycle, boat, aircraft, etc, a misnomer where the accelerator is operated as a foot control.

throttle, the valve which the driver controls to allow more or less air into the engine, hence controlling the engine speed or power output, usually a butterfly valve or disc and normally operated by the accelerator pedal.

throttle back, to reduce the pressure on the accelerator pedal to partially close the throttle valve, to reduce power.

throttle balance, accelerator balance.

throttle body injection, a simple design of single point fuel injection for a petrol engine.

throttle off, to release the pressure on the accelerator pedal to fully close the throttle valve, to reduce power and/or engine speed.

throttle off oversteer, lift off oversteer.

throttle position sensor, a dual switch which senses only the 2 end positions of the throttle movement, fully open and fully closed, and sends a signal to the ECU.

throttle return spring, the spring which causes the throttle valve to close as accelerator pressure is reduced.

throttle steer, the art of steering a rwd car with the accelerator, the balance of accelerator and traction regulated by a driver especially when controlling slight oversteer throughout a bend and when accelerating on exit from a bend.

throttle valve, a butterfly valve or disc that is controlled by the driver and which opens and closes to allow more or less air into the engine, hence controlling the engine speed and/or power output.

through carriageway, the main road which continues through a junction without change to its status, especially on a motorway or freeway.

through effect, a optical illusion suffered by a driver where the visual impression gained appears to be a straight road with no hazard, but where there is actually a significant hazard, *e.g.* a bend, or a crossroads junction crossing a main road; typically caused by a line of trees or poles continuing straight.

through highway, USA, a main road having traffic control measures at every junction.

through lane, a lane on a multilane road which continues through a junction without change to its status, especially on a motorway or freeway.

throughput, the number of vehicles passing a point on a road per hour.

through road, any road which does not lead to a dead end.

through street, USA, a through highway having traffic control measures at every junction.

throw, the lateral distance between the axis of the crankshaft and the axis through a big end journal, half of the length of a piston stroke.

throw, the length of movement of the gear lever.

throwout bearing, USA, clutch release bearing.

throwout lever, USA, clutch release lever.

thrust bearing, a bearing that absorbs force along the axis of rotation of a shaft.

thumb nut, wing nut.

thumbwheel, a screw having a knurled head and which is designed to be adjusted by thumb and finger only.

thump, a mini road hump for speed control measures, sometimes constructed from thermoplastic material, being shorter and lower than a standard road hump, typically 900 mm long and 40 mm high.

thyristor ignition, a version of capacitor discharge ignition in which a thyristor is the switching element for the primary circuit, developed for high-speed high-output engines for high performance and racing.

ti, transistorised ignition.

ticket, parking ticket.

ticket, USA, speeding ticket.

ticket zone, an area where parking is permitted only in marked places providing that a pre-paid ticket is displayed in the parked vehicle.

tickle, to operate a tickler for cold starting.

tickler, a small plunger in some carburettors for manually increasing the mixture for cold starting.

tickover, the condition of the engine when it is running at idle speed with the transmission in neutral and without any auxiliary loads.

tidal flow system, a system of traffic management allowing *e.g.* 4 lanes into a city and 2 lanes out during a morning rush-hour period, and vice versa during the afternoon rush-hour, usually marked with overhead signs.

tiedown, a rope anchorage on the bed of a vehicle.

tiedown hook, each of a series of rings located on the inside of the bed to make securing loads easy and convenient.

tier 0 vehicle, USA, a vehicle not meeting the requirements of a tier 1 vehicle but having exhaust emissions which meet an intermediate standard.

tier 1 vehicle, USA, a vehicle not meeting the requirements of a lev but having exhaust emissions which meet a basic standard.

tie rod, any link or bar which is under tension, although tie rods in the steering system may be alternately under tension and compression.

tifoso, Italian, speed enthusiast.

TIG, tungsten inert gas, a welding system using a tungsten electrode with an inert gas shield and a separate filler metal, for some types of body or chassis repair.

tight bend, a bend which is unusually sharp compared with others along the same road.

tight corner, a corner which is unusually sharp especially where the carriageway is narrow.

tightens, a cautioning rally pace note, indicating a spiral or transitional bend which is sharper than it initially appears.

tiller, a wooden or metal bar used by the driver to control the steering system on some veteran cars before the steering wheel came into common use.

tilt, a complete canvas hood or roof that is removable.

tilt adjustable, a steering wheel of which the angle of rake may be varied to suit the driver.

tilt cab, a lorry cab that is hinged to allow it to pivot forwards for access to the engine.

timber transporter, a flatbed or skeletal lorry or trailer constructed with steel posts for restraining logs.

time, the dimension of the physical universe which at a given place orders the sequence of events; from a designated instant in this sequence it allows measurement to be made from which calculations of speed, acceleration, power, etc. can be made.

timecard, a piece of paper/card carried by a rally crew on which to record progress through a road rally.

timed fuel injection, sequential fuel injection.

time lapse formula, the 2-second rule.

time mean speed, the average speed of all individual vehicles at a point on a road.

timing, adjusting or regulating the interval in time between related events, *e.g.* ignition timing and valve timing, usually specified in terms of degrees of rotation of the crankshaft, *i.e.* a mechanical interval not an absolute time interval.

timing belt, a toothed belt driven by a sprocket on the crankshaft and which drives a sprocket to turn the camshaft.

timing chain, a chain driven by a sprocket on the crankshaft and which drives a sprocket to turn the camshaft.

timing diagram, a pictorial representation of the engine timing, specifically the times during which the inlet and exhaust valves are open and closed.

timing gear, a gear on the crankshaft which drives a gear to turn the camshaft.

timing light, a stroboscopic lamp using either xenon or neon gas that emits light synchronised with the firing of number 1 sparkplug, allowing the ignition timing to be accurately adjusted whilst the engine is running.

timing marks, marks on gears, sprockets, and other parts that must be properly aligned when the engine is assembled.

timing marks, marks on the crankshaft pulley, flywheel, or other parts, used for reference and adjustment to indicate ignition timing and spark advance.

timing window, a small aperture through which the timing marks may be seen.

tin, a metallic element, often used in engine bearings.

tinker, to amateurishly retune or repair a vehicle, typically by trial and error.

Tin Lizzie, the model T Ford.

tinted glass, glass that has been specially coloured to reduce glare from the sun; to meet regulations it must continue to allow 90 % of light transmission.

tin top, a saloon car having a fixed roof.

tin worm, rusting of steel.

TIO, The Insurance Ombudsman, UK.

tip, a place of delivery of a load or part of a load; also named drop.

tipper, a lorry having a hydraulic mechanism with which to raise one end of the body to tip the load.

Tiptronic, an automatic gear selector system controlled electronically, having selector paddles for fingertip control on the steering wheel, developed by Porsche, Audi, and Ferrari.

TIR, Transit International Routier.

tire, USA, tyre.

tire iron, USA, tyre lever.

tire ring, a whitewall ring.

TIRF, Traffic Injury Research Foundation, USA & Canada.

TISC, Tire Industry Safety Council, USA.

titanium, a metallic element, very lightweight and strong, often alloyed for specific applications.

TJ, Tajikistan, international vehicle distinguishing sign, see appendices.

TJA, traffic jam assist.

TL, total length.

TL, tubeless, a wheel designed to be airtight hence an inner tube is not recommended.

TL, turn left, in road rally navigation.

TLA, Transport for London Authority.

tlb, tractor loader backhoe, commonly named a backhoe or JCB.

tlev, transitional low emission vehicle.

tlv, track laying vehicle.

TLW, theft loss waver.

TM, Turkmenistan, international vehicle distinguishing sign, see appendices.

tmc, traffic management channel.

TMC, traffic message channel, a system on FM radio.

tmph, tonne mile per hour.

TMS, tyre mobility system.

TN, Tunisia, international vehicle distinguishing sign, see appendices.

TOD, torque on demand.

toading, USA, the action of towing a car driverless as a trailer with all wheels on the road surface using an A frame.

toeboard, the lower edge of the bulkhead which is angled for the comfort of the passengers feet, on the drivers side it supports the pedals.

toe in, a small angular difference in the static position of the front or rear wheels, such that the leading edges of the wheel rims are closer than the trailing edges of the rims, usual on non-driven wheels.

toe out, a small angular difference in the static position of the front or rear wheels, such that the leading edges of the wheel rims are further apart than the trailing edges of the rims, usual on driven wheels except live rear axles.

tolerance, the range of allowable variation in any given dimension.

tolerance limits, the extreme upper and lower limits that are permitted by a tolerance.

toll, a fee charged for using a road, bridge, or tunnel.

tollbooth, a kiosk at which a toll is paid.

tollbridge, a bridge at which a toll is charged for crossing.

tollgate, a gate or barrier preventing passage until payment of a toll.

tollhouse, a house at a toll gate used by the toll collector.

tollplaza, a wide series of tollbooths at a toll collection point, typically on a road having a high traffic flow.

tollring, an imaginary line drawn around a city or an area of a city having a toll system for every vehicle entering that zone.

tollroad, a road on which a toll is charged for its use.

ton, the speed of 100 mph (160.93 km/h).

ton, imperial ton, a unit of weight equal to 1.016 tonnes, 1,016 kg, (2,240 lb) (20 cwt), obsolete.

tongue weight, USA, the weight imposed on a towing coupling on a level road by the drawbar of a trailer; the recommended loading in USA is 10 % to 15 % of the gross weight of the trailer, *i.e.* 224 lbs per ton; in UK the recommended loading is 7 %; see: nose.

tonne, metric tonne, a unit of weight equal to 1,000 kg, (2,205 lb) (0.984 imperial ton).

tonneau, the part of a car occupied by the rear seats, especially the rear seats in a convertible.

tonneau cover, a horizontal cover over the seating area of a convertible when the seats are not in use, at a height approximately level with the dashboard, usually having a central longitudinal zip so the front passenger seat may also remain covered whilst driving; usually made from duck, pvc, or other weatherproof fabric.

tonneau cover, a horizontal cover over a luggage area, over a folded hood, or over the bed of a pickup, usually made from pvc or other weatherproof fabric, in rare cases from metal.

tonne mile, a unit of commercial traffic.

tonne mile per hour, a measure of the working capacity of a tyre without overheating.

ton up, to achieve a speed of 100 mph (160.93 km/h).

ton up kid, a motorcyclist who frequently achieves a speed of 100 mph (160.93 km/h).

tool, any device, instrument, or machine with which to perform a task.

toolkit, any set of tools, either the basic minimum with which to change a wheel, or a comprehensive set for complex work.

toot, a short honk of the horn.

toot angle, the difference in angles through which the front wheels slew when performing Ackermann steering.

tooth, an angular projection on a tool, *e.g.* a saw.

tooth, the projection on a gearwheel that meshes between 2 corresponding parts on another gearwheel.

tootle, to drive slowly and aimlessly.

tootle, to toot gently, or gently and repeatedly.

top, the hood of a convertible.

top, top gear.

top chop, the process of cutting the roof from a saloon or similar car to turn it into a convertible.

top chop, a customising style involving removal of a steel roof, shortening all the roof pillars, cutting all the glass, then refitting the roof, resulting in severely reduced headroom.

top dead centre, the crankshaft position at 0° when a piston is exactly at the top of its stroke, between the compression stroke and power stroke, or between the exhaust stroke and inlet stroke.

top end, a range of engine speeds just below maximum revs.

top end gasket set, a kit of parts containing all necessary seals, gaskets, and O rings necessary to reassemble a cylinder head.

top fuel car, a drag racing car typically constructed on an extended rail chassis and having an ic engine running on a specially designed highly reactive fuel.

top gear, the highest numbered gear on a gear selector system, giving minimum torque but high roadspeed, usually 5th in most cars, 6th in most buses, 18th in many lorries, 32nd on some agricultural tractors, and 54th on a Fastrac tractor.

top hose, the hose carrying very hot coolant from the engine to the radiator.

top off, to add liquid to an almost filled system to replenish the system to its maximum level.

top of the range, a model of car which is the most expensive compared to similar models in that range, having the largest engine and/or the greatest degree of luxury.

top speed, the rated maximum speed of the vehicle on a level road with optimum ambient conditions.

top up, to add liquid to an almost filled system to replenish the system to its maximum level.

Torotrak, an infinitely variable transmission, a

type of cvt using a split toroid and wheels instead of cones and belts, using neither clutch nor torque converter but able to progress mechanically from zero speed to high speed, developed for transverse engined fwd large cars.

torpedo body, an early type of racing car having a streamlined body, sometimes used until the 1930s.

torque, rotational twisting force or leverage, the product of a force multiplied by its perpendicular distance from the point about which it causes rotation, previously measured in foot-pounds (ft.-lb.) or pound-foot (lb.-ft.), also in kg.m, or kg.cm, now measured in newton metres Nm; as a vector it is used to measure the output of an engine, 1 bhp = torque x rpm/5252, also a measure of the force to use to tighten a nut.

torque arm, a link that restrains torque at the rear axle casing.

torque converter, an automatic clutch and power transmission device having an impeller that drives a turbine via a stator, it acts as a hydraulic pump when the rotational speed is sufficiently high, similar in principle to a fluid flywheel but having a stator between the impeller and turbine to increase efficiency, typically used between the engine and an automatic transmission instead of a clutch.

torque converter lockup clutch, a clutch between the torque converter impeller and its turbine which automatically engages to prevent slipping losses whilst speed and torque requirements are reasonably constant.

torque curve, a graph displaying the torque produced relative to engine speed that is unique to each engine design, usually a shallow inverted U shape, the peak showing at which revs the greatest torque is available.

torque limiter, a feature of some torque wrenches, or an accessory used to tighten sparkplugs to reduce the risk of cylinder head thread damage.

torque on demand, a 4wd system using an automatic transmission that transfers power from the rear wheels to all 4 wheels using electronically controlled wet multiplate clutches when sensors detect any slippage, developed by Isuzu.

torque peak, the engine speed at which the maximum torque is attained.

torque spanner, torque wrench.

torque split, the distribution of torque between different axles, sometimes at 50-50 with a standard differential, sometimes other specific percentages using an epicyclic differential, sometimes variable using a dual pump or multiple plate wet clutch.

torque steer, the effect of transmission power influencing the feel of the steering in a fwd vehicle.

TorqueTrac4, a traction control system that will apply the brake to a non-tractive wheel when it detects slippage.

torque tube, a forward projection from a live rear axle to a spherical bearing at the gearbox through which thrust is transmitted from the axle.

torque wrench, a tool for accurately tightening any nut, bolt, or screw to an exact torque.

torquey, an engine producing significant torque at low revs.

torsen differential, a torque sensing differential having a worm and roller mechanism which balances different wheel speeds when cornering but not allowing wheel speed differences due to wheelspin, used as a limited slip differential and sometimes as the centre differential in a 4x4 or awd system.

torsion, axial twisting.

torsional stiffness, the longitudinal rotational rigidity of a vehicle body and/or chassis against variations in the road surface, *i.e.* an effect where the rear end attempts to rotate around the propshaft and which affects all vehicles but especially convertibles.

torsional vibration, rotary vibration in which a part rapidly twists and untwists.

torsional vibration damper, a small flywheel on the front end of the crankshaft to reduce rotary vibration.

torsion bar, a straight bar of spring steel at which 1 end is fixed to the chassis and the other end twists radially as the suspension oscillates; also fitted as an antiroll bar.

tortoise, usually the lowest range of gears on a tractor, although snail range if fitted is lower.

Torx, a system of turning bolts and screws using a 6 or 12 point star shaped male tool of various sizes giving a superior contact and drive between tool and screw.

tot, tyres on tarmac.

total loss lubrication, an oil lubricating system in which the oil is permanently lost after lubrication by either burning or falling to the road, as in 2 stroke engines, some veteran cars, and steam powered vehicles.

total stopping distance, the sum of the perception distance, reaction distance, braking distance, and the brake lag distance if the vehicle has air brakes, and is proportional to the square of the roadspeed and dependant upon the gradient, surface, tyre, and suspension conditions.

totting distance, a minimal queueing distance, recognised when the bottoms of the tyres of the vehicle ahead can be seen on the tarmac along a sightline over your own bonnet; named from tyres on tarmac.

toucan crossing, a signal controlled crossing for a cycle lane and footpath, at which cyclists and pedestrians can cross the road simultaneously, it is sometimes also provided for ridden horses where a bridleway crosses a road; an acronym from two can cross.

touch parking, a method of parking in a short space between a longitudinal line of parked cars along the kerbside, or when parking close to an object at the front or rear, such that the car or object is deliberately but gently touched with the bumper in order to use all of the space available; formerly common in USA as bumpers were tough, at standard heights, and had reliable overriders.

touch up, to apply a small amount of paint to repair minor damage on bodywork, *e.g.* to repair damage caused by a stone chip.

toughened glass, glass that has been heat treated, so if struck it will break into very small blunt pieces.

tour, to undertake a long journey typically on a circular route, usually for pleasure.

tour bus, a coach designed to provide a comfortable ride over medium and long distances.

tourer, touring car.

touring car, a luxury saloon car having very large luggage stowage, vintage models typically having a convertible body with 2 or 4 unglazed doors.

touring cars, a racing competition featuring high performance versions of production cars.

tow, to draw a broken down vehicle using a dolly.

tow, to draw a broken down vehicle using a rope, chain, or tow bar.

tow, to draw a trailer behind a vehicle using a recognised coupling.

towable, the condition of a collision damaged vehicle in which basic safety systems continue to function satisfactorily.

towable, the condition of a non-driveable vehicle *e.g.* for use as a donor car but where basic safety systems continue to function satisfactorily.

towaway, to remove a vehicle by towing, either by a suspended tow or by a rigid or flexible means of towing, or in the case of a towaway parking zone the vehicle may be hoisted onto the rear of a flat bed lorry.

towaway zone, a part of a city or district in which any vehicle parked other than in accordance with the parking rules will be taken away to a car pound.

towball, a 50 mm diameter spherical towing device on the rear or occasionally on the front of a vehicle enabling coupling to a suitably equipped trailer; older versions were 2 inch diameter, and an unmatched ball and coupling must not be mixed in any combination.

towbar, a rigid bar used to tow a disabled vehicle in preference to using a towrope.

towbar, a rigid framework at the rear of a vehicle with which to support a towing coupling.

towboy, a car ambulance.

tower jack, a jack comprising a vertical casing concealing a threaded rod which carries a horizontal arm which is raised and lowered by a cranked handle at the top of the tower.

towing ball, towball.

towing bracket, a rigid framework at the rear of a vehicle with which to support a coupling.

towing capacity, the maximum weight a vehicle is rated to tow, allowing for a hill start on an 18 % gradient, and based upon engine power and torque, gearing, cooling capacity, braking performance, rear spring rates, and hitch design and quality.

towing eye, a ring connected to a strong point under the front and/or rear of a car designed for the connection of a tow rope.

towing hitch, any coupling device on a trailer drawbar.

towing implement, a towing dolly, a device on wheels designed for the purpose of enabling a motor vehicle to draw another vehicle by the attachment of that device in such a manner that part of the other vehicle is secured to and either rests on or is suspended from the device and some but not all of the wheels on which that other vehicle normally runs are raised off the ground, (C&U).

towing jaws, a coupling aid on the rear of a lorry facilitating solo operation, some incorporate a trigger to automatically engage the pintle pin.

towing lug, towing eye.

towing package, optional equipment ordered to be factory fitted on a new car or pickup etc, which may include with the towbar and electrics a heavy duty rear suspension, a larger radiator and a transmission oil cooler.

town lights, dimmed light from the headlamps having been electronically reduced to $^1/_3$ brightness for driving on well illuminated roads at night, to reduce dazzle.

town plan, a large-scale map of a town naming all streets.

tow rating, the maximum weight a vehicle is rated to tow, allowing for a hill start on an 18 % gradient, and based upon engine power and torque, gearing, cooling capacity, braking performance, rear spring rates, and hitch design and quality.

towrope, a rope having sufficient strength to tow a vehicle; fastened so the vehicles are 4.5 metres apart, typically made from fibre, nylon, or polypropylene, but not steel wire.

tow start, to start the engine of a vehicle having a flat battery by towing the vehicle using another vehicle and a rope, or in some cases by pushing, then using 2nd gear or higher the clutch is rapidly let in so rotation of the wheels turns the engine to start it; not possible with automatic transmission vehicles.

toys, optional extras on a car, especially those that are controlled by the driver.

TP, a display on an RDS radio showing that the radio is tuned to a station capable of broadcasting traffic announcements.

TP, triangulation point/pillar, in road rally navigation a specific reference point.

TP, track pointer.

TPC, tyre pressure control.

tpp, tread pattern percentage.

tps, throttle position sensor, a sensor that sends a signal to the ECU.

TR, a wheel rim design having all metric dimensions and a dedicated tyre, developed by Michelin.

TR, Turkey, international vehicle distinguishing sign, see appendices.

TR, turn right, in road rally navigation.

TRA, Tire and Rim Association, USA.

track, a pair of parallel metal rails for a tramway along a road laid within the road surface, or for a railway line crossing a road.

track, a racing circuit, specifically the driving surface of the racing circuit.

track, a temporary or permanent course to be followed for a motoring event.

track, a rural road without a weatherproof surface.

track, the action of the wheels in following a desired or appropriate course.

track, to follow another vehicle.

track, the crawler mechanism on any tracklaying vehicle.

track, the transverse distance between the centres of the tyre footprints of 2 wheels on the same axle but on opposite sides of the vehicle; in the case of twin wheeled vehicles, the transverse distance between the centres of the pair of wheels on opposite sides of the vehicle.

track, see: off, on.

track arc, the curved course followed by a roadwheel when the steering is not aligned straight ahead.

track bar, Panhard rod.

track control arm, transverse link.

track day, an organised event whereby a car owner can take any road car onto a racetrack for a training and practise session under the guidance of a specialist instructor.

tracker, a radio transponder hidden in some vehicles which responds to a radio signal if the vehicle is reported stolen, and which then emits a radio signal allowing the vehicle to be located by the police using a radio homing device.

tracking, the action of a hv spark in following any unwanted course to earth in any part of the hv circuit between coil and sparkplug.

tracking, the angular measurement of alignment between the direction a wheel is angled and the longitudinal centre line of the vehicle, when travelling in a straight line.

tracking, see: off, on.

tracking angle, the angular arrangement of toe in or toe out of a pair of wheels on an axle except a rigid axle, adjusted and set in order to maintain the specifications engineered by the vehicle manufacturer for optimum performance of the steering and suspension.

tracking mark, a thin dark line on the surface of any component in the hv circuit as evidence of electrical tracking.

tracklaying, a vehicle designed and constructed that its weight is transmitted to the road surface by means of continuous tracks or by a combination of wheels and tracks whereby the weight transmitted to the road surface by the tracks is not less than $1/2$ the weight of the vehicle, (C&U).

tracklaying vehicle, a vehicle driven and steered by caterpillar tracks, *i.e.* the vehicle has an endless loadbearing series of metal strips or track on each side which is laid for its wheels to drive on, *e.g.* a bulldozer.

trackless, trolleybus.

trackless trolley, USA, trolleybus.

track pointer, a forward pointing laser on each side of a car that indicates the width of the car on the road ahead, to assist the driver to squeeze through a narrow gap between obstructions, under development by BMW.

track rod, a transverse mechanical linkage connecting the steering box to the steering arm at each wheel.

track rod end, a ball and socket joint that connects the ends of each track rod to the steering box or the steering arm.

trackway, an ancient roadway.

traction, the act of pulling.

traction, the friction between the tyre and the road surface necessary to propel, brake, or steer a vehicle.

traction code, USA, a tyre rating relating to the ability of a tyre to stop a vehicle on a wet surface under controlled conditions in a straight line, where a tyre marked A will have the best braking performance and C indicates poor braking performance.

traction contract, an agreement to pull semitrailers for another organisation, made between the owner of a tractive unit and the owner of a trailer.

traction control, a system that prevents a power-induced skid by detecting wheelspin and reducing the engine power and/or applying the brake to one or more wheels.

traction differential, a limited slip differential.

traction engine, a steam powered locomotive for hauling heavy loads.

traction tradeoff, the sharing of the tyre grip available between accelerating or braking and steering, *i.e.* if more of the available friction is used for braking less will be available for steering.

traction wheel, a drive wheel.

tractive unit, the controlling part of an articulated lorry, a motor vehicle constructed or adapted to couple with, draw, and carry at least 20 % of the weight of an articulated trailer.

tractor, an agricultural vehicle used for drawing or carrying agricultural equipment.

tractor, referring to the controlling part of an articulated lorry, a common misnomer, see: tractive unit.

tractor fuel, engine distillate, a heavy naptha-kerosine distillate fuel of low octane number, obsolete.

tractor loader backhoe, a multipurpose

industrial vehicle resembling an agricultural tractor fitted at the rear with a hydraulic arm and bucket for excavating earth, and at the front a loading bucket.

tractor trailer, USA, a tractive unit drawing a semitrailer, *i.e.* an articulated lorry.

tractor unit, tractive unit.

tractor vapouring oil, a fuel similar to paraffin oil, suitable for use in low compression engines only, typically used in some older tractors.

tractor vehicle, any vehicle towing a trailer, including a car when it is towing.

trade-in, a car given as part payment by a customer when buying a new or newer car.

trade in price, a dealer valuation of a car offered in part payment against the cost of a more expensive purchase.

trade licence, a document issued to motor traders, vehicle testers, and manufacturers allowing untaxed and/or unregistered use of a vehicle displaying trade plates, but only for purposes of delivery, demonstration or testing.

trade plates, red registration plates held by a motor dealer or repairer in conjunction with a trade licence, that can be affixed to a breakdown vehicle or any unregistered or untaxed vehicle so it may be driven for restricted purposes on a public road.

trading down, to buy a smaller car with respect to a previous model, typically with cheaper running costs.

trading up, to buy a newer, or larger, or more expensive car with respect to a previous model.

traffic, the passage or flow of vehicles along defined routes.

trafficability, the capability of a terrain to bear traffic, or the extent to which terrain will permit continued movement of traffic.

traffic announcements, an optional mode on an RDS car radio, selected in order to accept traffic announcements with priority over other broadcasts.

trafficator, an electrically controlled illuminated mechanical direction indicator which pivots laterally to extend from the side of a vehicle to signal the drivers intention to turn, common on 1950s vehicles.

traffic calming, any of various measures including speed humps or chicanes, designed to increase safety by reducing traffic density and speeds, especially in residential and commercial areas.

traffic cell, a block of streets having a specific network function.

traffic circle, USA, a very large diameter roundabout having high entry, merge, circulation, and exit speeds.

traffic circulation map, a map showing traffic routes and the measures for traffic regulation, indicating the roads for use by certain classes of traffic, the location of traffic control stations, and the directions in which traffic may move.

traffic control, the control of movement of vehicles and the regulatory mechanisms used to exert or enforce control.

traffic control device, the means enabling a highway authority to communicate with the driving public, including: road markings, road signs, traffic signals, and islands.

traffic cop, a police officer engaged in traffic patrol.

traffic cylinder, a plastic red and white reflective tube 100 mm diameter and 1 m high sometimes used instead of traffic cones especially at motorway contraflow systems to delineate traffic lanes; they are affixed into cats eye bases.

traffic density, the average number of vehicles that occupy 1 km of roadspace, expressed in vehicles per km at any instant.

traffic emergency, an occurrence when 2 vehicles are about to collide.

traffic engineering, the determination of the required capacity and layout of highway and street facilities that can safely and economically serve vehicular movement between given points.

traffic film, a thin layer of diesel and oil based residue that builds up on the outside of a windscreen and which may require chemicals for its removal.

traffic flow, the total number of vehicles passing a given point in a given time, usually expressed in vehicles per hour.

traffic island, an area between lanes on a road to physically separate traffic flows, first used in Liverpool UK in 1862.

traffic jam, a condition when traffic cannot move due to a restriction in the road network ahead.

traffic jam assist, a microprocessor controlled braking system which automatically decelerates a vehicle in busy traffic and creates a soft stop without the driver operating the brake pedal; under development by Mercedes.

traffic lane, the portion of the travelled way for the movement of a single line of vehicles.

traffic light, traffic signal.

traffic management, the organisation of efficient movement of traffic within a given road system by arranging traffic flows, controlling intersections and regulating parking.

traffic management channel, a feature of some car radios which have been programmed to operate with rds.

traffic markings, all lines, words, or symbols officially placed within the roadway to regulate, warn, or guide traffic.

traffic recorder, a mechanical or electronic counter or recorder used to determine traffic movements on an existing route, measuring either per hour or per day, using an air-impulse counter, magnetic detector, photoelectric detector, or a radar detector.

traffic regulation order, a restriction on a road, whereby any or several classes of road user or vehicles may be legally prohibited from using that route, *e.g.* a motorway prohibits cycles etc, whereas a road with a weak bridge may prohibit lorries.

traffic rotary, USA, roundabout.

traffic school, USA, driving school.

traffic segregation, the separating of different types of traffic, especially separation between pedestrians, cyclists, and vehicles.

traffic sign, a device mounted on a fixed or portable support conveying a message or symbol to regulate, warn, or guide traffic.

traffic signal, a power operated traffic control device by which traffic is regulated, warned, or directed to take specific actions, but excluding road signs; typically a system of 3 coloured lights displaying a mandatory stop instruction in sequence to road users travelling in different directions; the first were manual controlled gas lit lights in London in 1868, first successful lights were in Ohio USA in 1914, next used in Piccadilly London in 1925, first UK fully automated in Wolverhampton in 1926.

traffic temperature, a computerised forecast of traffic flow using a simple number system to represent traffic congestion; under development.

traffic volume, the number of vehicles passing a given point during a specific period of time.

traffic warden, a uniformed person having the authority to issue parking tickets and direct traffic.

trail, to drag behind.

trail, to follow the vehicle ahead.

trail, a long distance off-road route used by vehicles.

trail I, USA, a route which is at least 7 feet (2.133 m) wide, paved, and easily traversable by a 2wd family car.

trail II, USA, a route which is at least 7 feet (2.133 m) wide, not paved and may be rutted, washed out, or have washboard corrugations, passable in a 2wd with care although a 4wd is recommended.

trail III, USA, a route which is a narrow unimproved dirt road, with deep mud, rocks, and steep hills, passable only by 4wd vehicles.

trail IV, USA, a route which is passable only by off-road motorcycles and ATV's, 4wd vehicles are not permitted.

trail IV+, USA, a route which is extremely severe and only passable by a group of 4wd vehicles where all are fitted with a winch.

trail bike, a lightweight motorcycle designed for use on rough ground.

trail braking, the final 10 % of braking which overlaps with commencement of steering, the action of continuing to feather off the brake after the place where braking should have been concluded especially when entering a bend; it is sometimes acceptable when entering the early stage of a transition bend where braking causes weight shift which assists the turn-in, then the brake is feathered off and the accelerator balanced to tradeoff braking friction for cornering friction in the tyres.

trailer, a non-powered wheeled vehicle drawn behind another, either: a simple trailer having a single axle set or several axles close coupled and no in-built steering; or: a full trailer having axle sets at both the front and rear, the foremost steered by the drawbar and which may have single point turntable steering or 2 point Ackermann steering.

trailer, see: 5th wheel, A frame, A trailer, B trailer, balanced, boat, box, camp, camping, centre axle, composite, dog, drawbar, dromedary, full, gritting, house, lazy, low bed, modular, multi, pig, pup, road train, rolling floor, rv, semi, simple, sliding, travel, twin, unbalanced, unbraked, works.

trailer, USA, caravan, an unpowered mobile home.

trailerboard, a portable board affixed with all rear lights, reflectors, registration plate, and a long electrical cable, mounted horizontally at the rear of any trailer and connected to the vehicle lighting system.

trailer brake, a brake control that is manually applied and released for the operation of the parking brake on a trailer.

trailer bus, USA, an articulated bus or a trailer used for the transport of more than 10 passengers.

trailer coach, USA, a vehicle designed for commercial, industrial, or professional purposes, for carrying property on its structure, but not for human habitation or occupancy.

trailer hand valve, a small hand operated lever in the cab of a tractive unit which allows the driver to test the trailer brakes after coupling, and which should not be used for any other purpose.

trailer park, USA, caravan site.

trailer plates, a pair of triangular red retroreflective plates affixed at the rear of trailers.

trailer swing, a skid by the rear of a trailer especially a semitrailer, where it rotates sideways then has the effect of attempting to overtake the towing vehicle.

trailer vehicle hitch weight, USA, the weight imposed on a towing coupling on a level road by the drawbar of a trailer; the recommended loading in USA is 10 % or sometimes up to 15 % of the gross weight of the trailer, *i.e.* 224 lbs per ton; in UK the recommended loading is 7 %.

trailing arm, an independent suspension component consisting of a longitudinal member having a pivot axis perpendicular to the vehicles longitudinal axis at its forward end and having a wheel hub attached at the trailing end.

trailing axle, a tag axle behind a driven axle.

trailing dolly, a short trailer for supporting the rear end of a very long load, but not connected to the drawing vehicle itself, connected only to the load which effectively becomes the chassis.

trailing edge, the rear edge of a body panel or side panel.
trailing shoe, a shoe in a brake drum system designed to be most effective when the vehicle is reversing.
trailing throttle, the condition resulting in overrun, when the accelerator is released but the momentum of the vehicle causes the engine to be driven at a rotational speed greater than idle revs.
trailing throttle oversteer, USA, lift off oversteer.
trailing wheel, any wheel which is not powered.
trainee, a person learning to become a driving instructor, officially known in UK as a PDI.
trainee, the employee of an organisation receiving training in advanced or defensive techniques.
trainee licence, a temporary licence issued to some trainee driving instructors who are partly but not fully qualified.
trainer, a person who teaches, usually referring to a person teaching licensed drivers advanced or defensive techniques.
training, the formal tuition of drivers of hazardous goods, providing them with education about the hazards the dangerous substances may present, (DTR).
train weight, in relation to a motor vehicle which may draw a trailer, the maximum laden weight for the motor vehicle together with the maximum laden weight of any trailer which may be drawn by it, (C&U).
tram, a passenger carrying vehicle that runs on rails within the road surface, *i.e.* a rail vehicle that shares the road with other vehicles.
trambahn, a tramway where the track and paved swept path are raised 100 mm above the road and separated by a chamfered kerb allowing other vehicles to drive along the tracks only to avoid a parked obstruction.
tramcar, tram, or any individual carriage of an articulated tram.
tram lane, a strip of road that is reserved only for trams during its period of operation.
tramlines, railway track constructed within a road surface on which trams run, of special significance where trams share the road with other vehicles.
tramlining, the sensitivity of a tyre to respond to longitudinal ridges in the road, *e.g.* road markings or tram lines, thereby reducing directional stability.
tramp, axle tramp.
tram road, a historic road having wooden, stone, or metal paving for the wheeltracks.
tram tracks, a pair of parallel metal rails laid within the road surface where a tramway shares a road with vehicles.
tramway, the route of a pair of parallel tram rails laid flush within a road surface, either sharing the road with other vehicles or having a separate designated lane along the road.

tranny, USA, transmission.
tranny van, a Ford Transit van.
trans, USA, transmission.
transaxle, transmission-axle, a gearbox, final drive, and differential combined in 1 casing.
Trans-Canada Highway, the east-west route from Victoria, Vancouver Island, to St. Johns, Newfoundland, 7,820 km (4,860 miles) in length.
trans-European networks, the road network across Europe having been given a single numbering system to supplement the national numbering in each country; see appendices.
transfer box, transfer gearbox.
transfer case, transfer gearbox.
transfer gearbox, a part of the gearbox, usually integral sometimes additional, controlled by the transfer lever or an electrical switch, for the purpose of selecting 2wd or 4wd, hence transferring some power to the front axle, the transfer lever or switch may also be operated to select a lower range of gears.
transfer lever, a lever operated by the driver for control of a transfer gearbox where 2wd or 4wd and high or low ratios can be manually selected.
transfer passage, the duct from the crankcase to the combustion chamber in a 2 stroke engine.
transfer port, the opening into the combustion chamber from the transfer passage in a 2 stroke engine.
transfer switch, a switch operated by the driver for control of a transfer gearbox where 2wd or 4wd and high or low ratios can be electrically selected.
transistorised coil ignition, an ignition system having a transistor as a power switch.
transistorised Hall ignition, an ignition system having a transistor as a power switch controlled by a Hall generator.
transitional bend, spiral bend, a bend that is not of uniform radius, typically of a parabolic nature, *i.e.* it starts and finishes very gently and bends to an increasingly smaller radius at its mid point to allow each vehicle smooth transition from a straight to a curved course, to increase stability and safety especially for lorries.
transition curve, the curving approach to a bend which is not of constant radius, it starts gently and increases as part of a spiral, to allow each vehicle smooth transition from straight to a curved course, to increase stability and safety especially for lorries.
transition time, the time taken by a racing driver in a corner between full braking and full acceleration, including the time taken for trail braking, smooth transition from brake to accelerator, balancing the accelerator, and smoothly feeding in application of full acceleration.
transit lane, a lane in a city reserved for buses, taxis, bicycles, motorcycles, trams, and

vehicles carrying 2 or more persons.

transit plates, temporary registration plates issued in the country of purchase of a personal import; they also require the purchase of a green card.

transmission, all the mechanisms that carry the power from the engine to the wheels, primarily the clutch and gearbox, but also the differential and axles.

transmission, USA, gearbox.

transmission controlled spark, a system to reduce emission of NO_x by use of a switch in the transmission which prevents advance of the distributor in low gears at low speeds.

transmission control module, an electronic control system for an automatic transmission having input signals from the engine and other vehicle parameters to optimise all operating conditions.

transmission control system, a hydraulic or electrohydraulic system which controls gearchanges in an automatic transmission dependant upon engine load, road speed, and transmission mode selection.

transmission cover, a removable floor panel over a gearbox for maintenance access.

transmission differential, a centre differential in a 4wd transmission on the output from the gearbox that divides the drive between front and rear axles.

transmission governor, governor.

transmission oil, a lubricant specially compounded for vehicle transmissions.

transmission oil cooler, a system of cooling the transmission oil by passing it through a dedicated radiator before recirculation.

transmission oil temperature gauge, an instrument displaying the instantaneous oil temperature in the transmission, usually reading in °C.

transmission tunnel, a shape pressed into the floor of a car to cover the area of the gearbox and propeller shaft.

transmission windup, a condition on a 4x4 vehicle without a centre differential or when the centre diff is locked, caused by the front axle travelling a greater distance in a curve than the rear axle, hence stresses are developed within the transmission leading to tyre slip.

transponder, a radio device which receives a radio signal and transmits a coded reply.

transport, the conveyance of goods, equipment, or persons from 1 place to another.

transportable, capable of being transported.

transportation, the process of conveying.

transportation engineering, the branch of engineering relating to the movement of goods and people.

transport café, a catering enterprise at a roadside location to maximise business from passing drivers, typically offering cheap food and drink.

transport capacity, the tonnage of goods, or the number of persons which can be carried by a vehicle under given conditions.

transporter, car transporter.

transporter bridge, a bridge on which vehicles are carried horizontally above a surface feature on a moving platform suspended from rails above.

transport network, the complete system of the routes pertaining to all means of transport available in a particular area, made up of the network particular to each means of transport.

transport section, a non-competitive section in a road rally, to allow the route to pass between competitive sections but where there is not a built-up or sensitive area.

transport service licence, New Zealand, a goods service licence, a vehicle recovery service licence, a passenger service licence, a rental service licence, or a rail service licence.

transport service vehicle, New Zealand, a goods service vehicle, a vehicle recovery service vehicle, a passenger service vehicle, a rental service vehicle, or a rail service vehicle.

transport time control, a location at the end of a transport section in a road rally.

transport vehicle, a vehicle primarily intended to transport goods or people.

transport vehicle, USA, a cargo carrying vehicle including an automobile, van, tractor, truck, semitrailer, or tank car used for the transportation of cargo by any mode, and of which each cargo body is a separate transport vehicle.

tranship, to change the mode of transport of any load.

transverse, any part or arrangement located axially across the width of a vehicle at 90° to the longitudinal axis.

transverse acceleration, a sideways movement of a vehicle as may be experienced by occupants when cornering, it is normally proportional to speed and steering angle except when skidding.

transverse acceleration sensor, an instrument that measures the sideways acceleration of a vehicle, and sends a signal to the VSC or ESP.

transverse engine, an engine in which the crankshaft is parallel to each axle.

transverse leaf spring, a suspension system typically having a pair of leaf springs mounted transversely, 1 inverted, joined at their ends and fixed to the chassis and axle at their mid points; on some pre-war vehicles.

transverse link, any suspension member providing lateral location.

transverse plane, a vertical plane perpendicular to the median longitudinal plane of the vehicle, (C&U).

transverse rod, usually, a Panhard rod.

travel, the distance moved by a part as it operates, *e.g.* the brake pedal.

travel, to journey from origin to destination.

travelled way, the carriageway, excluding the shoulders.

traveller, a person who is travelling.

travel trailer, USA, any trailer caravan or rv trailer coupled using a ball or similar hitch.

TRB, Transportation Research Board, USA.

tread, that part of the surface of a tyre that comes into contact with the road surface, having good frictional characteristics to transmit all the forces to propel, brake and steer the vehicle.

tread, USA, track, the transverse distance between the footprints of 2 wheels on opposite sides of the same axle.

TREAD, a mnemonic to prompt a series of courtesies when driving off road: travel, respect, educate, avoid, drive.

tread bar, a transverse or angled single block of tread extending from the crown to the shoulder.

tread block, an individual section of tread separated from adjacent blocks by grooves to the left and/or right and by channels or sipes ahead and behind.

tread depth, the lowest height of a block of tread above the adjacent groove, measured at points around the circumference and across the width of the tread, excluding measurements at the twi.

tread depth gauge, a gauge that measures the amount of tread remaining on a tyre.

tread groove, the channel for water dispersal between the blocks or ribs of tread around the circumference of a tyre.

treadle valve, the service brake controlling valve directly operated by the footbrake on vehicles having a full air brake system.

tread pattern, the style of the bars, blocks, lugs, ribs, channels, grooves, and sipes on a tyre, for water dispersal, friction, heat dissipation, and minimum noise generation, to a design that has been created to suit its expected use.

tread pattern percentage, the percentage of tread void compared to the total surface area of the tread; car tyres typically have a tpp of approximately 30 %, the legal minimum is 17 % for road use.

tread profile, profile.

tread rib, a tread section composed of a single circumferential ring, or closely spaced aligned blocks around the circumference of the tyre, separated from the next rib by a groove.

tread separation, the condition when laminations in the carcass become un-bonded such that heat is generated which further compounds the problem, typically leading to catastrophic failure.

tread squirm, the flexibility of each block of tyre tread between the footprint and the carcass, especially on a new tread which is taller; off-road and snow tyres having deep tread and wide grooves and channels exhibit significant squirm, racing tyres very little.

tread void, the channels, grooves, and sipes within the tread that do not touch the road surface but permit water to drain from the footprint.

tread void ratio, the ratio of the space in all the channels, grooves, and sipes, to that of the bars, lugs, ribs, or tread blocks around a tyre tread expressed as a percentage; a high ratio is required for driving off-road *e.g.* 50 %, and a low ratio for highway use *e.g.* 30%, but not less than 17 %.

tread wear, the measure of the life of a tyre tread.

treadwear indicator, a series of raised groove bases 1.6 mm high across the width of the tread at several places around the circumference of the tyre which visually show when only 1.6 mm or less of tread remains, indicated by an arrow or triangle or the letters TWI on the sidewall of a tyre near the shoulder, also named wear bars.

tread width, the width of the contact area of the tread of a tyre at the footprint.

treasure hunt, a type of road rally which is untimed and in which a route is sought along public roads from a series of clues, permitted to be organised without strict MSA rules.

tree top tall, CB jargon, a message received loud and clear.

Tremcard, Transport Emergency Card, each of a series of individual cards for each different hazardous chemical or substance detailing: its name, nature, degree of hazard, protective devices, emergency actions, fire precautions, and first aid requirements.

trial, an off-road event conducted on rough or difficult terrain.

trialist, the driver of a vehicle taking part in a trial.

trialler, a vehicle modified for use in a trial.

trial run, a preliminary test of a vehicle.

triangle, see: warning triangle.

triangle, a wide central island where 2 roads meet at a T or Y junction, typically in a rural area where the original routes took the shortest track along each side of the triangle, and where the island is typically of grass.

triangular reflector, each of a pair of triangular red retroreflectors which are displayed at the rear of a light trailer near each side to signify that vehicle type.

triangular sign, generally a hazard warning sign, warning of an occasional or permanent potential danger.

triaxle, a group of 3 axles close-coupled.

triaxle set, a load sharing set of 3 axles where the centres of the 1st and 3rd are spaced not less than 2 metres apart and not more than 3 metres apart.

tribology, the study of the phenomena and mechanisms of friction and lubrication of surfaces in relative motion.

tricar, 3 wheeler, obsolete name.

trickle, to drive at a very slow constant speed using little power, typically at idle revs, typically performed whilst waiting for a queue ahead to clear.

trickle charge, a small charging current of less than 3 amps flowing into a fully charged battery.

trickle charger, a small mains operated battery charger typically having an output voltage of 13.8 volts when applied to a 12v charged battery.

tricycle, a 3 wheeled manually pedalled cycle.

tricycle, a 3 wheeled motor vehicle, sometimes used as an invalid carriage.

tricycle rickshaw, a hooded manually pedalled tricycle for the carriage of goods or 2 passengers, common in many Asian countries, named from Japanese jinrikisha.

tri deck, a lorry having 3 decks for carrying goods, especially car transporters.

tri drive, a rigid lorry or tractive unit having 3 drive axles, *e.g.* an 8x6.

trigger, the action of operating the gear selector paddle buttons when they are located on the steering wheel.

trigger wheel, a Hall generator rotor.

Trilex wheel, a 3 piece split wheel rim and a separate cast steel hub and spokes unit in the form of a spider to mount the rim to the hub, commonly used on lorries and buses in countries where the driver must perform his own puncture repairs at the roadside.

trim, see: hard trim, soft trim.

trim panel, a decorative interior panel.

trip, a single journey.

trip computer, a multifunction computer giving real time information, *e.g.* instantaneous time, journey elapsed time, eta, destination distance countdown, average speed, average fuel consumption, instantaneous fuel consumption, fuel range, etc.

trip counter, trip recorder.

triple bottom, a tractive unit hauling 3 trailers or semitrailers, sometimes named a B train, a type of road train.

triple road train, Australia, a combination vehicle typically comprising a tractive unit drawing 3 semitrailers using 2 dollies, or a semitrailer and 2 full trailers, having an overall length up to 53.5 metres long.

trip meter, trip recorder.

tripod joint, a common uj having 3 balls in curved grooves.

trip odometer, trip recorder.

trip recorder, a driver resettable odometer for the purpose of directly measuring the distance between 2 points, typically measuring in units of 100 metres (or 176 yards).

triptyque, a temporary import permit similar to a carnet which is used for the import of non-commercial vehicles by tourists when travelling between many countries.

trishaw, a 3 wheeled taxi, the front resembling a motorcycle, the rear like a small car, typically having a windscreen, hood, and rear, but with open sides, common in many Asian countries, often nicknamed tuk-tuk from the exhaust note.

TRL, Transport Research Laboratory, formerly TRRL, UK.

TRO, UK, Traffic Regulation Order.

trolley, USA, trolleycar, a light rail vehicle which shares the road with other vehicles, powered from an overhead trolley cable.

trolleybus, a bus propelled by electric power received from overhead trolley wires and running on pneumatic tyres on the road surface.

trolleycar, USA, each carriage of a light rail or articulated tram which shares the road with other vehicles, powered electrically from an overhead trolley cable.

trolley jack, a hydraulic jack of which the body is carried by 4 small wheels, commonly used in commercial workshops.

trolley valve, trailer hand valve.

trouble code, USA, diagnostic fault code.

TR rim, a safety wheel rim having run flat capability, developed by Michelin.

TRRL, Transport & Road Research Laboratory, now TRL, UK.

truck, USA, lorry.

truck, Australia, a lorry having dual rear wheels or a carrying capacity exceeding 2 tonnes.

truck cab, a vehicle fitted with a 2 or 3 seat cab, typically a pickup.

truck camper, USA, a demountable mobile home designed to be transported on the bed of a dual wheel pickup truck.

truck driver, lorry driver.

trucker, lorry driver.

truckie, Australia, lorry driver.

trucking, lorry driving.

trucking, USA, the conveyance of goods by lorry.

truckstop, a place typically having parking, bunkering, refreshment and accommodation for lorry drivers.

truck top, bodywork comprising roof and windows fitted as a hard top unit over the bed of a pickup to securely enclose the bed, load, or passengers.

truck tractor, USA, tractive unit.

truck trailer, Australia, a rigid lorry drawing a full trailer, having a maximum overall length of 19 metres and a gross combination mass of 42.5 tonnes.

truck trailer, USA, a rigid (straight) lorry drawing a full trailer.

truck ute, USA, a utility vehicle or mpv based upon the chassis of a pickup or similar vehicle; see also: car ute

truck zone, Australia, a zone permitting loading and unloading of trucks only, with no time limit.

true, the condition of a component when all parameters are as designed, *e.g.* a wheel having no lateral or radial runout or imbalance.

trumpet junction, a grade separated T junction with flyover or underpass to allow traffic to flow unimpeded in any direction excepting to turn back along the route of origin, *e.g.* the junction of the M5 with the M50 near

Worcester UK; the name is derived from the resulting plan shape; see appendices.

trunk, USA, the luggage carrying area at the rear of a saloon car.

trunk road, a highway which constitutes part of the national system of roads for through traffic.

TS, telematics system, a system giving route assistance by radio.

TS, Telligent Shift.

TS, twilight sentinel.

Tschudi engine, a cat and mouse engine in which the pistons which are sections of a torus travel around a toroidal cylinder; motion of the pistons is controlled by 2 cams which bear against rollers attached to the rotors.

tsg, toughened safety glass.

tSO, the Stationary Office, publishers of books with Government authority, originally named HMSO.

TSO, Thierry Sabine Organisation, the organiser of the annual Dakar rally.

TSR, UK, Traffic Signs Regulations.

TSRGD, UK, Traffic Signs Regulations and General Directions 1994.

TT, theory test, a theoretical test of a drivers knowledge administered as a separate part of a driving test.

TT, UK, Transport Tribunal, the central appellant authority for all appeals involving DVO Agencies, a body appointed by the Lord Chancellor.

TT, Trinidad and Tobago, international vehicle distinguishing sign, see appendices.

TT, tube type, a wheel designed such that it requires an inner tube to be fitted in the tyre, *e.g.* for a wire wheel.

TT4, TorqueTrac4.

TTC, transport time control, in road rally navigation.

tub, a cockpit in which the driver is closely enclosed, as in some sports and racing cars.

tubed, a tyre fitted with an inner tube.

tubeless, a tyre construction having a halobutyl rubber innerliner inside the carcass to prevent air leakage.

tubeless tyre, a tyre that is designed to form a good seal with the rim of a wheel, having an airtight inner liner such that an inner tube is not required, first developed by B F Goodrich and sold from 11 May 1947.

tuck in, the result when a fwd car suffering understeer suddenly recovers due to power reduction coupled with apparent weight shift, and the car starts to steer around the corner

tuck in arrow, deflection arrow.

tug, a tractive unit.

tug, the motorcycle of a motorcycle and sidecar combination.

tuition, the teaching of theoretical or practical driving skills or procedures, at any level including learner instruction.

tuk-tuk, a 3 wheeled taxi, the front resembling a motorcycle, the rear like a small car, typically

having a windscreen and hood, but with open sides, common in many Asian countries.

tulip symbol, each of the individual schematic diagrams, each representing a junction, used in a rally roadbook to define the direction to be taken at each junction along the route, the route being from the ball at the bottom of the diagram to the arrowhead with other relevant information, first devised for the Tulip rally in Holland in 1957.

tumblehome, the inward slope of a car body above the waistline; see also: turn under.

tune, to finely adjust an engine and its auxiliaries to achieve optimum performance.

tuned for economy, adjustment of the carburettor to give a weak air-fuel mixture.

tuned induction system, an engine air intake system in which the tubing is of a calculated volume to produce a slight ram effect as the intake valve closes, especially at high revs.

tuneup, to inspect, test, adjust, or replace components of an engine, to restore an engine to its best possible performance.

tungsten, a hard metallic element having a very high melting point, typically used in lamp filaments especially in a tungsten halogen bulb.

tunnel, a route cut beneath the earth or built under some structure for vehicular access.

tunnelling, Frenching.

tunnel vision, an eyesight defect whereby a driver has a narrow field of vision less than 120° wide, hence is not fit to drive, usually caused by glaucoma.

turbine, a rotary motor having an airscrew, blades, vanes, or paddles, and designed to be pushed by gas, air, or other fluid, and mechanically connected to a machine to perform work.

turbine wheel, the output rotor in a torque converter which is driven by the hydraulic flow to transmit the torque into the gearbox.

turbine wheel, the wheel in a turbocharger which is driven by the exhaust gas and which may rotate at speeds of up to 160,000 rpm to drive the air compressor.

turbo, turbine.

turbo, turbocharger.

turbo boost gauge, an instrument displaying the instantaneous air pressure in the inlet manifold, reading in bar or psi.

turbocharged engine, an engine fitted with a turbocharger.

turbocharger, an air compressor driven by a turbine using the energy in the exhaust gas, which compresses the induction air so a greater amount of charge can be forced into the cylinder to increase power.

turbocharging, a method of increasing the power output of an engine by using the exhaust gas to drive a turbine which drives an air compressor to compress the induction air thereby increasing the air-fuel charge in the cylinder; it increases the power output but not the efficiency.

turbo cooled, any system that is force cooled by a fan.

turbo diesel, a diesel engine fitted with a turbocharger to increase power.

turbo diesel injection, a turbocharged direct injection diesel engine.

turbo dump valve, a device that allows excess compressed air in the air intake system to be discharged when the accelerator is released so it does not stall the turbo.

turbo lag, the short time interval after pressing the accelerator but before the turbocharger boost provides the additional power.

turbulence, motion of fluids in which local velocities and pressures fluctuate irregularly in a random manner.

turbulence, the rapid swirling motion imparted to the air-fuel mixture entering the cylinder.

turbulence, the violently disturbed air at the rear and sides of a vehicle when travelling quickly, especially to unaerodynamic vehicles *e.g.* lorries.

turn, USA, bend.

turnabout, USA, a 3 point turn.

turn around, to cause a vehicle to face in the opposite direction.

turn back, to retrace the route.

turned wheel, any wheel connected to a steering mechanism.

turn in, the action of starting to steer into a corner or bend, as the steering angle is increasing.

turn in point, USA, turning point.

turning circle, the space a vehicle requires to make a 1 point turn; it may be measured wall to wall, or kerb to kerb, or wall to kerb; see also: clearance circle.

turning circle radius, the radius of the arc described by the centre of the track made by the outside front wheel of the vehicle when making its shortest possible turn, (SAE).

turning lamp, a lamp fitted low on the side of a vehicle just ahead of the front wheel to illuminate the direction of travel when the steering is turned more than $^1/_2$ lock in that direction, common on some larger USA cars.

turning lane, USA, an auxiliary lane for traffic in 1 direction which is physically separated from the intersection by a traffic island.

turning over, an engine being cranked by the starter motor in an attempt to start it.

turning pocket, a road marking which guides motorists making a turn to the offside at a wide junction, to ensure they maintain a suitable course especially if they should need to stop in the middle of the junction.

turning point, the point on a race circuit just before a bend where braking and gearchanges are completed and steering commences.

turning radius, the space a vehicle requires to make a 1 point turn; it may be measured wall to wall, or kerb to kerb, or wall to kerb.

turn into the skid, the technique for counteracting a rear wheel skid involving yaw

by turning the top of the steering wheel in the same direction to which the rear of the car is moving, with the brake and accelerator released.

turn it over, to crank an engine, either manually with a starting handle, or with the starter motor.

turn off, a junction where traffic may leave a highway.

turn off, an exit sliproad leading from a freeway or motorway.

turn off, to switch off auxiliaries, *e.g.* headlamps.

turn of speed, the ability of a vehicle to go fast when required.

turn on, to switch on auxiliaries, *e.g.* headlamps.

turn on a sixpence, said of a vehicle having a very small turning circle, named from a small UK pre-decimal coin.

turnout, USA, a layby where a driver of a slow vehicle may briefly pull off the road to allow following traffic to overtake.

turnout, USA, a passing place on a single track road where opposing vehicles can pass.

turnpike, toll gate.

turnpike, toll road.

turnpike, USA, a freeway that is subject to a toll.

turn signal lamp, USA, direction indicator lamp.

turn signals, USA, direction indicators.

turns lock to lock, the number of turns and partial turns of the steering wheel from full left lock to full right lock.

turntable, an articulation system as in a 5th wheel coupling.

turntable, a 1 point steering system as on some full trailers.

turn under, the inwards slope of a car body below the waistline; see also: tumblehome.

turret, a cylindrical structural pressing within the monocoque chassis to support a suspension mounting.

tutor, a person who teaches others to become a driving instructor.

tvo, tractor vapouring oil.

TVR, a contraction of Trevor, by the founder of Trevor Wilkinson, a UK sports car manufacturer.

TVR, Transport sur Voie Reservée, French, a GLT system.

TWA, UK, Transport and Works Act, 1982.

twc, 3 way catalyst.

tweak, to make fine adjustments to an engine.

TWI, tread wear indicator.

twilight sentinel, a system which automatically turns on the parking lights or headlights in low-light situations.

twin, 2, a matched pair.

twin A arm, double wishbone suspension.

twin a/b, twin airbags.

twin airbags, two separate airbags, 1 for the driver and 1 for the front passenger.

twin air horns, a horn system comprising 2 trumpets each emitting a different note, a non-emergency vehicle must sound both horns simultaneously; see also: 2 tone horn.

twin apex, double apex.

twin axle, tandem axle.

twin barrel carburettor, a single carburettor body having 2 chokes, each with a throttle valve, operating simultaneously or sequentially for improved performance or economy.

twin cam engine, double overhead camshaft engine.

twin carburettors, an engine having 2 separate carburettors operated from a single control and balanced to perform equally.

twin choke carburettor, a single carburettor body having 2 chokes, each with a throttle valve, operating simultaneously or sequentially for improved performance or economy.

twin exhaust system, 2 complete separate exhaust systems from cylinder head to tailpipe, regardless of a balancer pipe, typically on a V engine; samples are taken from each and mathematically averaged for emissions testing; see also: single.

twin header, a pair of header pipes from the exhaust manifold which join and feed into a single exhaust pipe.

twin headlamps, a headlamp arrangement having 2 headlamps on each side, the outer pair emit dipped beam and may emit main beam, the inner pair emit main beam only.

twin ignition, an ignition system having 2 sets of contact points, each operating its own coil which feeds alternate sparkplugs.

twin overhead camshaft, double overhead camshaft.

twin planets, an epicyclic system having meshing inner and outer sets of planet gears, in which the inner planets also mesh with the sun gear and the outer planets also mesh with the internal gear.

twin plate, a clutch system having 2 drive plates with a driven plate between.

twin point injection, a fuel injection system having 2 injectors, each feeding part of the inlet manifold.

twin pole electrics, a vehicle electrical system without any earth connection, the return path of every circuit is wired, typically on a vehicle having a fibreglass body.

twin spark, an engine having 2 sparkplugs per cylinder for greater efficiency and reliability.

twin splitter, an additional set of epicyclic gears on the input to the gearbox to create 3 additional close ratio gear ranges, such that each primary numbered gear is effectively split twice into 3 gears, i.e. having 2 splits on each gear therefore gives $^1/_3$ gears, so each primary gear has a high $^1/_3$, a middle $^1/_3$, and a low $^1/_3$; hence a 4 speed gearbox will give 12 one-third gears.

twin steer, a lorry having 2 steering axles; see also: Chinese 6.

twin steer 8, a rigid lorry with 2 steering axles at the front and 2 load carrying axles at the rear, also named 8 legger or rigid 8.

twin steer set, a tandem axle set having single tyres where both axles are connected to the same mechanism so they steer similarly.

twin swirl, a design of combustion chamber and inlet valves such that the gas flow results in 2 separate swirls for enhanced combustion.

twin tailpipes, a feature of some single exhaust systems which may branch before or after the final silencer to exit through separate tailpipes.

twin trailer roadtrain, a double roadtrain comprising 2 semitrailers, the 2nd having an A frame dolly for coupling and steering; or comprising a semitrailer drawing a full trailer.

twin tube damper, a hydraulic suspension damper formed by 2 concentric tubes, the outer tube typically at atmospheric pressure.

twin wheel, a pair of wheels on 1 stub axle, common on load carrying wheels of large vehicles.

twist axle, a rear axle suspension system on a fwd vehicle where the axle is designed to twist slightly to give in effect a semi-independent system whereby vertical movement of a wheel is partially absorbed by the twisting action.

twist beam suspension, a semi-independent suspension incorporating a twist axle.

twistlock, a device with which to secure an ISO container at each of its corners to a lorry by turning each locking device 90° before transporting by road.

TWO, UK, Transport and Works Order.

TWOC, taken without the owners consent, a car that is taken for a short period then abandoned, often damaged or having parts stolen.

TWMV, 2 wheeled motor vehicle.

tws, torque wrench setting.

type approval, a series of certification systems to ensure vehicle manufacturers, importers, or constructors meet safety requirements, see: ECWVTA, LVA, SVA, VLV.

type designation, the specification of a sparkplug regarding the thread, seat type, reach, heat range, spark position, and electrode material.

type training, a training session to teach a driver the location and operation of all primary and secondary controls in an unfamiliar vehicle and to gain a feel for its size and performances.

tyre, a precisely engineered pneumatic assembly of rubber, chemicals, fabric, and metal, it is fitted around a wheel to make contact with the road and is designed to provide traction and steering, cushion road shock, and carry a load under varying conditions using compressed air to create tension in the carcass plies; invented by Thomas Hancock in 1846, patented for cycles by John Dunlop in 1888, developed for use on cars by the André and Edouard Michelin in 1895.

tyre, see: bias belted, crossply, radial.

tyre bead, bead.

tyre body, carcass.

tyre chains, snow chains.

tyre chalk test, a trial and error method of finding the correct tyre pressure for each tyre when the figure is not known, usually due to a change of tyre size: to draw a transverse chalk line across the tread of each tyre then drive a short distance on a straight dry road then check the wear on the chalk which is a magnification of wear to the rubber, the pressure is adjusted and the test repeated until the chalk wears evenly across its width.

tyre contact, footprint.

tyre deflection, the difference between the unloaded or free radius of a tyre and the loaded radius of a tyre.

tyre designation, an alphanumeric code moulded into the sidewall of a tyre describing its width, aspect ratio, rim diameter, load index, and speed rating, typically using the P metric system.

tyre deviation angle, USA, slip angle.

tyre dressing, a special coating for the tyre sidewalls to give a gloss or matt finish to temporarily improve aesthetic appearance, but which may damage the rubber compound.

tyre fire, the spontaneous ignition of a tyre caused by continuing to drive at speed on an underinflated tyre, typically occurring at 1 tyre of a pair of twin wheels.

tyre heater, a heater within a thermal jacket for pre-heating of tyres before a race, usually heated to 80 °C, occasionally up to 130 °C.

tyre iron, tyre lever.

tyre kicker, a person looking at cars on sale but not a serious customer.

tyre lever, a flat steel bar with shaped ends used for removing and fitting tyres from/to a wheel, generally obsolete due to modern machinery.

tyre mobility system, a system comprising an onboard air compressor and a tyre sealant in lieu of a spare wheel, developed by Audi.

tyre noise, noise heard within the cabin that originates from each block of tyre tread hitting the road surface.

tyre placard, a metal, plastic or coated paper tag permanently affixed to a vehicle which indicates the appropriate tyre size and tyre inflation pressure for the vehicle, usually affixed in the aperture of the drivers door frame near the striker.

tyre pressure, the pressure of air inside a tyre pressing outwards on each unit of area, typically expressed in psi or kPa; 1 psi = 6.9 kPa.

tyre pressure control, a microprocessor controlled system that monitors each tyre pressure and warns the driver of any deflation by tell-tale lamp when minor, and by audible alarm when significant, developed by BMW.

tyre pressure gauge, an instrument designed to fit on a tyre valve and which is calibrated to accurately read the pressure in the tyre and display the figure.

tyre rating, the maximum safe speed for each tyre category, see appendices.

tyre roll off, the condition when a tyre bead unseats itself from the rim as a result of running when uninflated, or cornering when underinflated.

tyre rollover, a situation when the tyre sidewall rubs the road surface, typically when cornering at speed and affecting mostly the front wheel on the outside of the bend, and is exacerbated if the tyre is underinflated.

tyre rotation, the recurring movement of tyres from 1 axle position to another in an attempt to minimise irregular wear, now believed to transfer irregular wear from tyre to tyre hence increase wear rate, an obsolete procedure; the procedure must NOT be performed on vehicles having directional or asymmetric tyres.

tyre scrub, wear caused by undue friction, especially to a tyre tread if the wheels are not correctly aligned, or dry steering, skidding, driving with a differential locked, driving a part time 4wd on a dry paved surface, or turning sharply with a semitrailer; see also: scuff.

tyre scuff, wear to a tyre sidewall, typically by frequent abrasion along a kerb, but also during tyre rollover when cornering at high speed on underinflated tyres; see also: scrub.

tyre sealant, a liquid that may be added to new tyres to prevent air loss if punctured, or by aerosol after a puncture as an emergency repair.

tyre separation, the condition when laminations in the carcass sidewall become un-bonded such that heat is generated which further compounds the problem, typically leading to catastrophic tyre failure.

tyre size, tyre designation.

tyre slip angle, slip angle.

tyre softener, a liquid that is applied to the tread of a tyre several days before competing, to increase grip.

tyres on tarmac, an angled sightline used to ensure a minimal queueing distance when stopping in traffic: to look from the drivers seat over the bonnet or windscreen wipers and to be able to see the place where the bottom of the rear tyres of the vehicle ahead touch the tarmac.

tyre squeal, a high pitched noise made by a tyre which is suffering some slip, typically under severe acceleration, braking, or steering; in the case of steering it is often caused or aggravated by underinflation.

tyre stability, the tendency for a tyre to roll in its steered direction rather than follow road contours.

tyre tread gauge, tread depth gauge.

tyre valve, a Schrader valve mounted in a hole in the wheel with which to inflate, measure pressure, adjust pressure, or deflate a tyre.

tyrewall, a barrier of old tyres between a racetrack and wall to cushion the effect of a crash, formerly tied in bundles now usually drilled and bolted together.

tyre warmer, a heater within a thermal jacket for pre-heating of tyres before a race, usually heated to 80 °C, occasionally up to 130 °C.

tyre wear, the amount by which the tread of a tyre has worn away, or the pattern in which wear has occurred, including by feathering, scrubbing, or scuffing.

tyre width, see: section width, tread width.

tyro, Latin, learner, beginner, or novice.

tyro trial, any competitive motoring event designed for newcomers to the sport.

U

U, an engine cylinder and crankshaft layout similar to a V engine but in which the cylinder axes are parallel and offset from the crankshaft.

U, the tyre speed rating code denoting a maximum design speed of 200 km/h (124 mph), moulded into the tyre sidewall.

U, unacceptable security risk, referring to insurance sub grouping.

U, under, in road rally navigation a requirement to pass beneath a bridge, ETL, or similar.

U, unleaded fuel only, referring to fuel type to use.

U, up, on a road rally typically a higher spot height.

U bolt, a bolt in the shape of a U having both ends threaded to receive nuts.

u joint, universal joint.

U turn, to perform a 1 point turn with any vehicle, to turn a vehicle around through 180° to face in the opposite direction in 1 continuous forwards movement.

UA, Ukraine, international vehicle distinguishing sign, see appendices.

UAE, United Arab Emirates, international vehicle distinguishing sign, see appendices.

UAIB, Union of Automobile Importers in Bulgaria.

ubf, unburned fuel emissions, ubh.

ubh, unburned hydrocarbons.

ucr, unclassified county road.

ucr, unclassified road.

UDA, uninsured drivers agreement.

udc, USA, upper dead centre, tdc.

UEM, Union Europeéns de Motorcycliste, European Motorcycle Union.

UITP, Union Internationale de Transports Publique.

uj, universal joint.

UK hazard information system, a system for informing emergency services in the event of an accident involving hazardous loads, involving the Hazchem emergency action coding.

UKHIS, UK Hazard Information System.

Ukravtoprom, Association of Ukrainian Motor Vehicle Manufacturers.

UL, unladen.

UL, unleaded fuel.

ulev, ultra low emission vehicle.

ullage, the empty space above a liquid load in a tanker, the size of which determines the stability of the vehicle.

ulp, ultra low profile tyre.

ULR, uninsured loss recovery.

ULS, ultra low sulphur, petrol or diesel fuel containing less than 0.003 % m/m sulphur, *i.e.* less than 30 ppm.

ULSD, ultra low sulphur diesel.

ULSP, ultra low sulphur petrol.

ultra low profile, a radial tyre that has a profile of 35 % or less with respect to the section width.

ultra low sulphur diesel, a highly refined diesel fuel containing less than 0.003 % m/m (30 ppm) sulphur, used only in a small number of countries having strict emissions limits to give less soot particles when burnt; this may be compared with 0.03 % (300 ppm) in low sulphur diesel or 0.5 % (5,000 ppm) sulphur in basic diesel in some countries.

ultra low sulphur petrol, unleaded petrol containing less than 0.003 % m/m (30 ppm) sulphur, for the purpose of reducing the quantity of sulphur dioxide emitted from the exhaust to reduce acid rain, typically having an octane rating of 95.

ULW, unladen weight.

umbrella handbrake, a handbrake lever mounted below or within the dashboard, operated by pulling the handle horizontally rearwards, named from the shape of the handle.

unadopted road, a road which is not taken over for maintenance by a local authority.

unassisted steering, a vehicle without power assisted steering, hence the steering wheel will require a greater force to turn.

unattended, a vehicle condition when the driver is not in or near the vehicle.

unauthorised signal, any signal not published in the Highway Code, or misuse of an authorised signal.

unbalanced agricultural trailer, an agricultural trailer of which some, but not more than 35 %, of the weight is borne by the drawing vehicle and the remainder of the weight is borne by its own wheels, (C&U).

unbraked trailer, a trailer which is not equipped with a braking system, (C&U).

unburnt hydrocarbons, fuel vapour which did not burn in the combustion chamber and which is released as a pollutant within the exhaust gas.

UNC, unified national course thread.

unclassified road, a road recorded on the list

of streets by a highway authority, but not classified as M, A, or B, typically a byroad or byway, sometimes without a metalled surface.

uncontrolled crossing, a railway level crossing not controlled by traffic signals but with a full or half barrier, or sometimes gates.

uncontrolled crossing, a zebra crossing not controlled by a police officer, traffic warden, nor a school crossing patrol.

uncontrolled junction, a priority junction having signs and/or road markings but no traffic signals, and without a traffic warden or police officer directing the traffic.

uncorrected eyesight, any sight defect whereby the driver does not meet the statutory minimum requirement without optical assistance.

uncouple, to disconnect a trailer from a drawing vehicle.

underbody, the underside of a car.

underbody coating, a protective layer of plastic, wax, or bitumen based material on the underfloor of a car to protect against corrosion.

underbody protection, steel plating beneath a vehicle to protect vulnerable parts from physical damage, especially for off-road use.

underbody structure, substructure.

underbonnet area, the engine bay.

undercarriage, the suspension and wheels.

underfloor, the underside of a vehicle.

underframe, the structural members beneath or within the floor of a vehicle.

undergear, all of the running gear on the underside of a vehicle, *i.e.* the suspension, steering, brakes, and drivetrain etc.

underhead collar, any washer fitted under the head of a bolt or a screw, but not named as such when fitted under the head of a nut.

underhood, USA, under the bonnet, within the engine compartment, it may also refer to parts built into a car during manufacture.

underinflation, a condition that exists when there is insufficient air pressure within a tyre to support a specific load, resulting in the tyre exhibiting excessive deflection and rollover.

underlift, a device on the rear of a breakdown truck for performing a suspended tow with a lorry or bus by lifting under its front axle.

underpass, a grade separated road layout to carry 1 highway under another, with or without facilities for interchange, such that traffic crosses without interference to flow.

underpowered, a vehicle having an engine which provides insufficient power for the weight of the vehicle.

underseal, a bituminous coating sometimes applied to the underbody and chassis of vehicles to reduce corrosion.

undershield, a wheel house panel.

underside, the lower side of the underbody which faces the road surface.

underside panelling, smooth flat panelling along the whole underside of a car to reduce drag.

underslung, an early design for reducing the floor height of a car such that the chassis was suspended below the axles.

undersquare, the comparison of the bore and stroke dimensions of an engine where the bore is smaller than the stroke.

understeer, the effect when the tyre slip angle at the front wheels increases more than it does at the rear wheels, when the front tyres lose adhesion and the rate of yaw of a vehicle is less than anticipated with respect to steering input such that the vehicle does not follow the desired line, a front wheel skid, often caused by entering a bend too fast.

understeering, a condition when a driver turns the steering wheel less than necessary for a specific situation, sometimes exhibited by a learner.

understeer recovery, the procedure for recovering from understeer providing there is space available before a collision occurs: undo whatever driver input caused the skid, release the footbrake, straighten the steering, clutch down or select neutral in an automatic, when under control brake gently or steer, or brake and steer if ABS equipped.

undertake, to overtake on the nearside *i.e.* wrong side of a vehicle, contrary to directions in the basic rule of the road in many countries.

undertray, the cover across the bottom of the engine bay.

underway, a vehicle in motion.

undivided road, a single carriageway road carrying 2 way traffic on any number of lanes, but without physical separation between opposing traffic streams.

undriveable, a vehicle in a condition such that it cannot be driven.

unequal length wishbone suspension, a system in which the upper wishbone is slightly shorter than the lower, and typically the chassis mountings are at a greater vertical distance apart than at the hub, resulting in a high quality of roadholding due to small deliberate changes in track and camber as the suspension oscillates.

UNF, unified national fine thread.

unforgiving, the nature of a roadside verge and/or street furniture in increasing a loss of control or damage if a vehicle should run into this area.

ungated crossing, a railway level crossing without any type of gate or barrier.

unhitch, to disconnect a trailer from a drawing vehicle.

unibody, a unitary or monocoque body construction forming a single body structure comprising the floor pan, framework, chassis, and body, in which all body panels welded together.

unidirectional tire, USA, directional tyre.

unidirectional wheel, a wheel designed with spokes or slots acting as vanes to draw cooling air over the brake disc, and which will function only when fitted to the appropriate left/right side and must not be interchanged.

unified driving licence, a driving licence issued in any of the 15 countries in Europe where vehicle categories have been standardised.

unified national course thread, a screw thread based upon imperial dimensions where the spanner size is related to the AF size of the nut or bolt head, obsolete.

unified national fine thread, a screw thread based upon imperial dimensions where the spanner size is related to the AF size of the nut or bolt head, obsolete.

uniflow engine, a steam engine in which steam enters the cylinder through valves at 1 end and escapes through an opening uncovered by the piston as it completes its stroke, obsolete on road vehicles.

uniform tire quality grading, a tire quality rating system developed by the USA Department of Transportation, every tire must display: a numbered tread wear rating, a lettered traction code, and a lettered temperature rating.

uninsured drivers agreement, a function of the MIB to process claims where a claim arises against an uninsured vehicle.

uninsured loss, a sum, situation, or condition not covered by the insurance premium, typically including: the excess on a motor insurance policy, the full cost of repairs, hire of a replacement vehicle, vehicle recovery and towing, personal injury compensation, medical treatment, loss of earnings, taxis, hotels, damage to personal effects.

uninsured loss recovery, an additional insurance premium paid to insure against losses incurred as the result of a collision, including: the policy excess, the full cost of repairs, hire of a replacement vehicle, vehicle recovery and towing, personal injury compensation, medical treatment, loss of earnings, taxis, hotels, damage to personal effects.

unit, 1 unit of alcohol, approximately 250 ml ($^1/_2$ pint) of beer, 120 ml of wine, 50 ml of fortified wine, or 25 ml of spirits, and which takes approximately 1 hour to be processed by the liver and leave the body.

unit, an assembly capable of independent operation.

unit, tractive unit, the controlling part of an articulated lorry.

unitary body, a monocoque body, not having a separate chassis.

unit engine, a power plant style where the engine and gearbox are in a single housing.

unitized cargo, USA, groupage.

universal joint, a joint that allows power to be transmitted by a rotating shaft through an angle to another shaft.

unladen, a vehicle which is not loaded with either goods or passengers.

unladen weight, the weight of a vehicle when not carrying any load or passengers.

unladen weight, USA, the weight of a vehicle equipped and ready for operation on the road including 5 gallons (18.9 litres) of fuel, required equipment and permanent attachments to the vehicle, and without any load.

unlaned road, a road which does not have any road markings to delineate the centre.

unleaded, petrol which contains no lead compound additives but instead contains potassium as an additive, it may however contain natural minute traces of lead; it may be available in several octane grades and having several sulphur levels, see: LSP, ULSP.

unlicenced vehicle, a vehicle which has not been registered, or a vehicle which is not carrying a licence (registration) plate.

unlit road, a road not having street lamps.

unlit vehicle, a vehicle not displaying statutory illumination; a vehicle under 1,525 kg parked on a road subject to a 30 mph or lower speed limit at night need not be illuminated; all heavier vehicles and all vehicles parked on a road with a higher speed limit commit an offence if not showing statutory lights.

unload, to remove goods or materials from a vehicle.

unloader valve, a device on an air brake system between the compressor and air reservoirs that allows the release of excess pressure.

unloading, the action of removing goods or materials from a vehicle.

unlock, to cause locked wheels to recommence rotation by reducing the brake pressure.

unlocked, a vehicle having 2 or more drive axles which does not have the axle differentials, transmission centre differential, or wheel hubs locked.

unmarked junction, a junction at which there are no signs and no road markings, all drivers must give way.

unmetalled, a road that does not have a durable or weatherproof surface.

unnecessary signal, any signal given when there is no other road user who may benefit, typically given by habit and without thought.

unoccupied, a vehicle condition when the driver is not seated at the wheel.

unpaved, the condition of a road surface which has not been weatherproofed by a layer of cobbles or tarmac etc, *i.e.* the surface may be earth, gravel, or graded stone etc; loose gravel on top of a paved surface does not constitute an unpaved road.

unrestricted junction, a motorway junction at which there is a full permutation of transfer from every road to every other, but may or may not permit a return to the route of origin, on maps these are often coloured blue or black.

unroadworthy, a vehicle which is not safe to be used on the road.

unsafe driver behaviour, any driver action that reduces the level of vehicle control, increases the risk of collision, or breaches a law.

unsealed, the condition of a road surface which has not been weatherproofed, *e.g.* the surface may be earth, gravel, or graded stone.

unserviceable, a component designed to be assembled in such a way that repair or maintenance is not possible.

unserviceable, a component which is not in a working condition.

unserviceable, a vehicle in an unroadworthy condition.

Unsin engine, a type of rotary engine in which 1 of the circular rotors has a single gear tooth upon which the gas pressure acts, the 2nd rotor has a slot that accepts the tooth.

unsprung axle, an axle directly mounted to the chassis without springs, relying only on the tyre sidewall for suspension, typically agricultural tractors and equipment, or other equipment trailers to which a speed limit of 30 km/h (20 mph) is normally imposed.

unsprung suspension, the system by which the body/chassis is connected to a wheel by a pivot but without a spring, as the front beam axle of some tractors.

unsprung weight, the proportion of the weight of a vehicle that is not supported by the suspension, *i.e.* the weight of the tyre, wheel, and a proportion of the weight of the suspension.

unsurfaced, a road or track having an earth or stone surface that has not been prepared for use by a large volume of traffic.

untaxed, a vehicle for which the VED is due and outstanding.

unwind the steering, to straiten the steering from a significant angle.

up and over, a garage door opened by raising to roof level and sliding horizontally.

upgrade, USA, an uphill gradient.

uph, upholstery.

uphill start, hill start.

upholstery, the fabric, leather, or plastic covering the seats, headlining, and door inner panels, and the springs and padding supporting the covering.

uprate, to modify or change part of a vehicle to improve strength or performance.

uprated, a part which has been designed to have increased strength or performance.

upshift, the selection of a higher gear.

upshift brake, a brake within a constant mesh gearbox operated by full depression of the clutch pedal to enable selection of a higher gear, also for selection of a gear whilst stationary.

up split, to change up $^1/_2$ a gear using the splitter.

up stroke, the movement of a piston from bdc to tdc.

urban clearway, a major road within a town having signs but not road edge markings that prohibit stopping, waiting, parking, loading,

and setting down passengers, sometimes in force for less than 24 hours per day.

urban combat car, USA, typically a beater, a well worn car near the end of its life used for short distance commuting.

urban cycle, urban test cycle.

urban driving, stop-start driving on a variety of road types and encountering various junction styles and meeting with a range of traffic situations within a typical town.

urban motorway, a motorway that is adjacent to a built-up area, sometimes having extensive elevated sections, having grade separated junctions at closely spaced intervals, sometimes with shorter sliproads, hence usually a lower speed limit.

urban road, a road in a built-up area of a town or city.

urban test cycle, a laboratory test method of measuring fuel consumption on a rolling road, starting with a cold engine at 20 °C, simulating a series of accelerations, steady speeds, decelerations, and idling, not exceeding 50 km/h (31.07 mph) and averaging 19 km/h (12 mph) over a distance of 4 km (2.5 miles).

urban traffic control, a system of electronically linking adjacent traffic signals to maximise flow by creating platoons of traffic which ideally meet every traffic signal at green.

urea, a chemical sometimes used for deicing road surfaces on steel bridges where salt may accelerate corrosion.

urethane, a plastic sometimes used to manufacture body panels.

URTU, United Road Transport Union, UK.

US, USA, United States highway, followed by a number, see appendices.

USA, United States of America, international vehicle distinguishing sign, see appendices.

USAC, United States Automobile Club.

USCAR, United States Council for Automotive Research.

useful life, the minimum life expected from a vehicle, engine, or system before a major overhaul, normally expressed as a distance, and which should exceed 100,000 miles (160,000 km) for light vehicles, 120,000 miles (200,000 km) for medium vehicles, and 180,000 miles (300,000 km) for heavy vehicles.

user operated gates, gates or barriers at a railway level crossing which require the road user to manually open the gates, cross the railway, and close the gates again.

US gallon, a unit of capacity, 1 US gallon = 3.78531 litres, smaller than an imperial gallon.

US highway system, a network of roads having a country-wide numbering system marked on black and white shields.

US-NCAP, USA, a new car assessment programme which evaluates crashworthiness and occupant survivability, evaluated by the IIHS.

UTC, urban traffic control.

ute, utility.
utility, a pickup, typically 4x4.
utility truck, a vehicle capable of serving several functions.
utility vehicle, a vehicle capable of serving several functions.
UTMV, unlawful taking of a motor vehicle.

UTQG, USA, uniform tire quality grading.
UTQG rating, a tyre marking code showing: a numbered tread wear rating, a lettered traction code, and a lettered temperature rating.
UW, unladen weight.
UZ, Uzbekistan, international vehicle distinguishing sign, see appendices.

V

v, valves, usually preceded by the total number within the engine.

v, velocity, the measure of speed in a specific direction.

v, volt, the unit of electromotive force.

V, a tyre speed rating code denoting a maximum design speed of 240 km/h (150 mph), moulded into the tyre sidewall.

V, an engine in which the cylinders are in 2 rows at an angle to each other, the angle can be at 15°, 45°, 60°, 66°, 72°, 90°, 120°, or 135°.

V, Vatican City, international vehicle distinguishing sign, see appendices.

V, vertical grid line, in road rally navigation.

V4, a four cylinder engine having 2 pairs of cylinders in V configuration.

V4 seatbelt, a seatbelt having a centre 4 point buckle connecting both parts of the lap strap and the 2 shoulder belts, also having 4 anchorage points, typically used in various motor sports.

V5, a five cylinder engine with cylinders in V configuration having 3 cylinders in the front bank and 2 cylinders in the rear bank, originally a V6 with 1 cylinder removed, developed by Volkswagen.

V5, a registration document which carries details of a vehicle and ownership.

V6, a six cylinder engine having 3 pairs of cylinders in V configuration.

V8, an eight cylinder engine having 4 pairs of cylinders in V configuration.

V10, a ten cylinder engine having 5 pairs of cylinders in V configuration.

V12, a twelve cylinder engine having 6 pairs of cylinders in V configuration.

V belt, a drive belt that transmits power by friction between its 2 angled sides and the pulley, typically driving the cooling fan, alternator, water pump, power steering, and ac compressor; often named fan belt.

V clamp, a circular clamp split into 2 semicircles which connects the headpipe to the exhaust.

V clamp, a circular clamp split into 2 semicircles which connects a turbine to its bearing housing in a turbo.

V pulley, a pulley designed to drive or be driven by a V belt, both having tapered sides to ensure friction.

V ribbed belt, a low wide polygrooved drive belt enabling the engine to power auxiliary

systems, it transmits power by friction between many V ribs and the pulley, and can also drive with its outer face, it is more effective and has a longer life than a V belt, typically driving the cooling fan, alternator, water pump, power steering, ac compressor.

VA, front overhang, the distance from the foremost point to the centreline of the front axle.

VA, voice activated.

VAC, voice actuated control.

vacuum, the total absence of air and other matter; in vehicles usually a partial vacuum, *i.e.* a pressure less than atmospheric, negative gauge pressure in the inlet manifold, influenced by throttle opening and engine load.

vacuum advance, the advancing or retarding of ignition timing controlled by pressure changes in the inlet manifold vacuum.

vacuum brake booster, vacuum servo.

vacuum brakes, an early name for a servo brake system, where power assistance to the brakes is provided by a vacuum servo powered by a partial vacuum developed in the inlet manifold.

vacuum control unit, the device which controls the advance and retard of the ignition, having a small vacuum chamber which senses inlet manifold pressure and a mechanical linkage to control the relative timing of the ignition contact breaker.

vacuum gauge, an instrument displaying the instantaneous pressure within the inlet manifold.

vacuum hose, a pipe conducting the vacuum to the vacuum servo, or to the vacuum control unit.

vacuum pump, a device that produces a low air pressure for the operation of the servo brake system on a car having a supercharger or turbocharger, typically driven by the alternator.

vacuum retard, see: vacuum advance.

vacuum sensor, a device which responds to the pressure in the inlet manifold and sends a signal to the ECU.

vacuum servo, a device having a large sealed volume and a wide diaphragm mechanically coupled to the brake master cylinder and with a vacuum hose coupled to the inlet manifold or vacuum pump, such that when the brake pedal is operated its movement is assisted by the vacuum acting on the diaphragm.

vacuum timing, vacuum control unit.

vacuum windscreen washers, a washer system whereby the fluid is propelled by a vacuum powered pump.

vacuum windscreen wipers, a windscreen wiper system whereby the wipers are powered by a vacuum generated in the inlet manifold, typically on some postwar classic cars only.

VAG, Volkswagen Audi Group of companies.

vague steering, the inability of a vehicle to accurately follow the desired course, caused by a number of possible factors including steering design, suspension design, or tyres.

valance, a panel or skirt which conceals unsightly structure around the lower edges, especially below the front and/or rear bumpers of a car.

valet, to immaculately clean the interior of a car to as new condition.

valet parking, the parking of cars by a parking attendant.

valet trunk locking system, a locking system having two different keys, the primary key opens all locks, including those for the glove box and trunk or rear hatch and operates the ignition, the secondary key used by the valet can only open the doors and operate the ignition.

valve, a device that can be opened or closed to start, stop, or regulate the flow of a liquid or gas.

valve adjusting screw, the lockable screw in the end of a rocker arm.

valve bounce, the bouncing of a poppet valve on its seat at high revs.

valve cap, the cover for tyre valves to prevent dirt from contaminating the seal.

valve clearance, the clearance in the valve train operating mechanism when the valve is closed to allow for thermal expansion.

valve core, the central part of a tyre valve that is removable for rapid deflation.

valve cover, USA, rocker box, the cover over the valve train on top of a cylinder head.

valve crown, the valve head.

valve cutout, a deliberate control of operation whereby only 1 valve is opened per cylinder at low revs on some multivalve engines to maintain high speed of induction air to maintain swirl.

valve float, a condition when a poppet valve bounces and does not close properly.

valve follower, the linkage between the cam and pushrod or valve stem.

valve grinding, an operation to reface a valve seat by machine.

valve grinding paste, a compound containing abrasive particles, used for lapping a valve and seat to create a good seal.

valve guide, a bushing or tube which aligns the stem of a poppet valve as it moves up and down.

valve head, the disc of a poppet valve which closes on the seat.

valve hole, a hole in a wheel rim for locating a pneumatic valve.

valve in head, an overhead valve engine.

valve lapping, an operation to create a gas-tight seal at the valve seat by using grinding paste between the valve face and seat, and an oscillating rotary motion of the valve face against the seat.

valve lash, poppet valve clearance.

valve lift, the distance a poppet valve is lifted from its seat, approximately $1/4$ of its head diameter.

valve lifter, USA, tappet.

valve overlap, the number of degrees of crankshaft rotation during which the inlet and exhaust valves are open simultaneously at gas exchange.

valve principle, the original method of ABS control using an electrically operated valve to control hydraulic pressure; now superseded by the plunger principle.

valve seat, the surface against which a valve closes and forms a seal.

valve seat regression, damage caused to exhaust valve seats designed for leaded fuel when unleaded fuel is used, caused by microwelding between valve and seat resulting in metal transfer.

valve shim, a calibrated shim for adjustment of valve clearance in an ohv engine.

valve slot, a slot across the rim well on some wheels on some heavy vehicles designed for tube tyres.

valve spring, a coil spring that closes a poppet valve.

valve spring tester, a gauge used to measure valve spring tension by applying a calibrated force.

valve stem, the long thin section of a poppet valve that moves in the valve guide.

valve timing, the timing of the opening and closing of the inlet and exhaust valves with respect to crankshaft position.

valve train, the complete set of valves and operating mechanism within an engine.

Valvetronic, an engine operating system having electronic control of the inlet valve lift and timing to control the engine speed, and without a throttle butterfly valve, developed by BMW.

van, a goods vehicle having a closed body, typically less than 3,500 kg MGW.

van, caravan.

vanadium, a metallic element used as an alloy with steel and other metals, first used on the model T Ford.

van camper, USA, a mobile home having living accommodation constructed in the body of a van.

vane, a curved surface, normally 1 of several similar, that drives or is driven by a fluid, *e.g.* in a water pump or turbocharger.

vane airflow sensor, a sensor attached to a single vane to measure airflow into an engine and send a signal to the ECU.

vane switch, a Hall generator.

vanishing point, the arrowhead, the visual limit point created by a bend where the left and right road edges appear to meet.

vanity mirror, a mirror on the inside of a passengers sun visor, sometimes illuminated.

vanity plate, USA, a personalized vehicle registration plate.

vanpool, USA, a minibus for collective commuting of 10 to 15 persons.

vaporization, a change of state from liquid to vapour or gas by evaporating or boiling.

vapour, a gas or any substance in its gaseous state.

vapour canister, a carbon canister.

vapour injection, a system of injecting water into the charge passing through the carburettor to cool the charge and increase density and efficiency, to reduce the risk of detonation.

vapour lock, an unwanted condition in a fuel system when fuel vaporizes to form bubbles that slow or stop delivery of fuel to the fuel injection system or carburettor.

vapour recovery, an emission control system used by filling stations whereby the gap between the filler nozzle and car is sealed and the vapours forced from the car fuel tank by the incoming fuel are recovered by the filling station and recycled into their own tank.

variable assist power steering, power assisted steering which is automatically adjusted according to engine speed and road speed, producing assistance which is greatest at low rpm or low road speed, such as when parallel parking, and low assistance when the engine or road speed is greatest such as when cruising at highway speeds; typically electronically controlled, sometimes electrically powered.

variable belt transmission, cvt.

variable compression engine, an engine in which the cylinder block can be moved with respect to the crankshaft, typically by a hinging mechanism moving several degrees which alters the size of the combustion chamber and changes the compression ratio.

variable damper, each of a set of suspension dampers which are remote controlled to allow the driver to select soft, medium, or hard, to match the road surface and driving style.

variable limited slip diff, a limited slip differential having an electronically controlled multidisc wet clutch to restrict slip.

variable message sign, a matrix type display where a worded message may be displayed by electronic means only at certain times, or where several alternative messages may be displayed to meet differing circumstances.

variable operating costs, the vehicle operating costs that are directly related to the distance a vehicle travels, *e.g.* fuel, tyres, and servicing; see also: fixed.

variable power assisted steering, variable assist power steering.

variable rate spring, a mechanical spring which becomes stiffer as it deflects.

variable rate spring, an air spring in an air suspension system which is controlled to become stiffer as the suspension compresses.

variable ratio rack, a steering rack and pinion system which is low geared in the central straight ahead zone for maximum straight line control, and progressively higher geared to full lock to reduce the angle through which the steering wheel is turned.

variable ratio steering, a steering system having a variable ratio rack which gives an increasing gear ratio as the steering is turned to full lock.

variable shock absorbers, suspension dampers that are remote controlled to allow the driver to select soft, medium, or hard, to match the road surface and driving style.

variable speed fan, an engine driven fan that will not exceed a predetermined speed or will rotate only at such a speed to prevent the engine from overheating.

variable torque split, an electronic system which controls the centre differential to vary or balance the power between front and rear axles on a 4wd car.

variable valve control, a system of varying the valve timing by electronic control of hydraulics operating the camshafts.

variable valve timing, an engine facility in which the ECU controls oil pressure to the camshaft controller to vary the timing of the inlet valves, or inlet and exhaust valves, so they can be advanced or retarded, especially to vary the gas exchange overlap depending upon engine speed and load, to increase power and reduce NO_x emissions.

variable valve timing and lift with intelligence, a VVT-i system having a cam changeover mechanism that varies the amount of lift of the inlet and exhaust valves while the engine is operating at high speeds and enables the valve timing to be optimally set, resulting in improved fuel economy.

variable valve timing with intelligence, a system which selects the ideal inlet and exhaust valve overlap under all engine operating conditions to virtually eliminate the traditional compromises between low-end torque and high-rpm horsepower, and helps enhance fuel economy and reduces emissions such that it eliminates the need for egr.

variable venturi, a carburettor in which the size of the venturi changes according to engine speed and load.

variation factor, USA, a small tolerance allowed beyond the legal limit before a driver is prosecuted for driving an overweight vehicle, typically 100 lbs (45 kg) above the legal maximum.

variomatic, cvt, an automatic transmission system without gearwheels but using V pulleys with a variable distance between their faces, and belts, to give continuous variation in gear ratio for maximum smoothness; typically having a 6:1 ratio range.

VASCAR, visual average speed computer and recorder.

VBRA, Vehicle Builders and Repairers Association, UK.

vc, viscous coupling.

VCA, Vehicle Certification Agency, UK.

VCAR, vehicle condition alert register, UK.

VCC, Veteran Car Club, UK.

vcd, viscous coupling differential.

VCEA, Vehicle Certification Executive Agency, UK.

VD, variable dampers.

VDA, Verband der Automobilindustrie eV, German association of vehicle and component manufacturers.

VDC, vehicle dynamic control.

vde, vegetable derived ester.

VDRS, vehicle defect rectification scheme.

V(E)A, UK, Vehicles (Excise) Act 1949, or 1962.

VEB, vehicle engine brake.

veci, vehicle emission control information.

VED, vehicle excise duty, originally named RFL.

vee, an engine in which the cylinders are in 2 rows at an angle to each other, the angle can be at 15°, 45°, 60°, 66°, 72°, 90°, 120°, or 135°.

vee belt, V belt.

veer, to follow a course that is not straight, to curve left or right along a straight road.

veer in, the effect of the rear of a vehicle being pushed away from the chosen course so the vehicle self corrects towards the chosen course, the result of a crosswind when the wind pressure point is behind the centre of gravity of a vehicle, *i.e.* having good directional stability.

veering, steering a course that is not straight, *i.e.* steering a series of minor zigzags along a straight road.

veer out, the effect of the front of a vehicle being pushed increasingly away from the chosen course, the result of a crosswind when the wind pressure point is forwards of the centre of gravity of a vehicle, *i.e.* having poor directional stability.

vegetable derived ester, a methyl ester used as an additive to, or a replacement for, diesel fuel; it is derived from plants, principally rapeseed, but sometimes sunflower, palm, soya, cooking oils, also animal fats; typically added at 5 % to diesel.

vehicle, a carriage, a mobile contrivance for the land transport of people, goods, or equipment, and includes a sledge, snowmobile, bicycle, pram, wheelbarrow, sedan chair, litter, cart, car, motorcycle, bus, lorry, etc.

vehicle actuated traffic signals, traffic signals incorporating a magnetic loop sensor in each approach road surface such that timing is adjusted by a microprocessor to optimise traffic flow requirements, first used by means of a pneumatic tube in London in 1932.

Vehicle Certification Agency, the UK organisation responsible for issuing type approval in the forms of ECWVTA, LVA, SVA, VLV, and others to ensure safety and conformity of production.

vehicle condition alert register, a national listing maintained by insurance companies of all vehicles which are classed in category A, B, C, or D write-off, including satisfactorily repaired category C and D vehicles, and vehicles which have been stolen and not recovered.

vehicle defect rectification scheme, a system whereby a minor defect on a vehicle noticed by a police officer results in the vehicle owner having 14 days in which to have the vehicle repaired and presented for inspection, as an alternative to prosecution.

vehicle dynamic control, a stability control system developed by Subaru.

vehicle emergency, an occurrence when a tyre, the brakes, or some other critical part suddenly fails.

vehicle emission control information, a label affixed in the engine bay displaying information regarding the engine and emission controls.

vehicle engine brake, a powerful retarder similar to a Jake brake.

Vehicle Excise Duty, the tax paid to use a vehicle on a public road.

vehicle excise licence, a licence affixed to the windscreen of a vehicle to show that VED has been paid.

vehicle identification number, a 17 digit chassis number that individually identifies every vehicle, although repetition is possible after 30 years, positioned to be readable through the vehicle glazing where the eyepoint is located outside the vehicle close to the lower left edge of the windscreen, see appendices.

Vehicle Inspectorate, the organisation responsible for roadworthiness checks of vehicles and issue of MOT certificates.

vehicle in the service of a visiting force , a military vehicle belonging to a foreign force.

vehicle intrusion protection, a break-in alarm that flashes the headlamps and taillamps, sounds the horn, and disables the starter when a secured vehicle is forcefully entered; removing the ignition key from the ignition automatically arms the system.

vehicle lift, a mechanical hoist designed to raise a vehicle bodily by lifting at 4 points on its underside, to safely enable repairs or maintenance to be performed.

vehicle parc, the total number of motor vehicles in use in a country; see also: car.

vehicle registration document, a document which identifies a specific vehicle by its registration, lists all relevant vehicle characteristics and notes the name and address of the owner or keeper.

Vehicle Registration Office, a local office of the DVLA, part of the DTLR.

vehicle skid control, a system which electronically monitors speed and direction from ABS, yaw rate, g, and steering angle sensors, and compares the direction of travel with the drivers steering, acceleration, and braking inputs to control the ECU and operate 1 or more brakes to compensate for loss of traction.

vehicle special order, a vehicle which does not or cannot meet the relevant C&U regulations and is given specific permission to be used on a public road.

vehicle speed sensor, a sensor that sends a signal to the ECU indicating vehicle speed.

vehicle stability control, a system in which ABS, TC, steering angle, yaw rate, lateral acceleration, and other sensors feed a microprocessor that will recognise oversteer or understeer, then automatically reduce engine power and apply the brakes to just 1 or 2 wheels in order to correct the problem and inform the driver, developed by Lexus and Daihatsu.

vehicle sympathy, actions performed by a driver in being considerate to the vehicle by minimising unnecessary wear, *e.g.* by depressing the handbrake button before applying the handbrake to avoid wear to the ratchet.

vehicle tax, VED.

vehicle watch, a scheme operated by the police in which a vehicle is identified by front and rear stickers showing the normal times it is not in use, if the police see it on the road within these hours it will be stopped for a check.

veiling glare, stray light entering the eye that reduces the contrast of the target which the driver is observing.

vel, velour.

VEL, Vehicle Excise Licence.

velocity, speed measured in a specific direction, a vector quantity.

velocity stack, a curved funnel shape attached directly to a downdraft carburettor typically to each air inlet of a multi carburettor system instead of an air filter, to increase performance but at the risk of ingesting uncleaned air.

velour, a plush woven fabric resembling velvet sometimes used for car upholstery.

vent, a small opening through which air can enter or leave a closed chamber.

vent, USA, a small triangular window.

ventilated disc brake, a brake disc having passages through the rotor to allow cooling air to pass through the hot disc to reduce heat build-up and reduce the possibility of the brake fade, glazing or warping.

ventilation, the circulation of fresh air through any space to replace impure air.

ventiport, each of a series of round holes typically having a chrome surround in the sides of the bonnet or sides of the front wings,

typically on USA models in 1950s.

venturi, the narrowed passageway in a carburettor that increases air speed to produce the partial vacuum necessary to discharge and vaporize the fuel.

venturi vacuum, the partial vacuum that is created by a carburettor venturi as air flows through it.

VERA, UK, Vehicle Excise and Registration Act 1994.

verge, the strip of land that directly borders a carriageway, typically covered with grass.

vertical curve, the shape or aspect of a length of a road where it crosses a crest or dip.

vertical lift bridge, a bridge having a deck that remains horizontal whilst it is lifted vertically between towers at each end.

vertical tyre clearance, the distance between the top of the tread and the nearest fixed part when the suspension is at its most compressed position.

vertigo, a medical condition that may prevent a person holding a driving licence due to problems of balance, dizziness, giddiness, and lack of control.

very high temperature, a substance designed to withstand heat, usually referring to paint suitable for exhaust manifolds, or to special grease for brake mechanisms.

very low volume vehicle, a type approval system for a model of vehicle which is manufactured in numbers of less than 50 per year and less than 100 in 5 years.

VESA, Vehicle Security Association of South Africa.

vestibule bus, articulated bus.

veteran, any vehicle built before 31st December 1918.

veteran car run, the annual London to Brighton run for cars built before 31st December 1904.

vgc, very good condition.

vgt, variable geometry turbocharger.

vhpd, very high performance derivative, typically a modified engine.

vht, very high temperature.

VI, Vehicle Inspectorate.

VI, Viscosity Index.

viacard, Italy, a card purchased in advance before driving on an autostrada toll road.

viaduct, a long bridge usually constructed with a series of stone arches to carry a road horizontally across a valley or similar.

vibrate, rapid minor oscillation of any part, usually unwanted.

vibration damper, a small flywheel sometimes fitted at the front of a crankshaft to reduce torsional vibration; also named harmonic balancer.

victory lap, an additional lap of a racing circuit by the winner.

video scout system, a system having 2 video cameras facing left and right on the front bumper, so a driver can see out of a blind exit without risk of edging out into approaching traffic, under development by BMW.

VIEA, UK, Vehicle Inspectorate Executive Agency.

vignette, a motor insurance certificate displayed on the windscreen in the form of a disc in many countries.

vignette, a toll payment, a necessary purchase before driving any vehicle on motorways in Austria, Belgium, Holland, and Switzerland, and before driving a foreign registered goods vehicle on any road in Belgium, Denmark, Germany, Luxembourg, Sweden, and UK.

VIN, vehicle identification number.

vintage, any vehicle built between 1st January 1919 and 31st December 1929.

vintageant, any vehicle built before 31st December 1939.

violation, a deviation from practices deemed necessary to maintain a safe operation in a potentially hazardous situation, *i.e.* a breach of traffic law; see also: optimising, routine.

violation record, USA, an official record of the number of times a driver has been apprehended for breaches of traffic regulations.

VIP, vehicle intrusion protection.

VIP, very important person, a category of passenger in some vehicles.

Virmel engine, a cat and mouse engine having vane-like pistons whose motion is controlled by a gear and crank system, each set of pistons stops and restarts when a chamber reaches a sparkplug.

vis, variable geometry intake system.

vis-à-vis, a veteran coachwork style in which 2 rows of passengers sit face to face; in some cases the driver sits on the rear seat facing forwards.

visco diff, viscous coupling differential.

viscoplane, a condition similar to aquaplaning but on a road having a layer of mud, or a film of oil and grime after rainwater has dried out, where the tyre is not in direct contact with the road surface and friction for braking and steering is very low.

viscosity, a quality of resistance to flow exhibited by a liquid, sometimes defined numerically, a thick oil has a higher viscosity than a thin oil; see also multiple viscosity.

viscosity index, a number indicating how much the viscosity of an oil changes with temperature, an oil having a higher VI has a smaller change of viscosity with temperature change.

viscosity index improver, an oil additive which increases the VI of the host oil, *i.e.* it reduces the variation in viscosity with temperature change.

viscosity rating, an indicator of the viscosity of an oil, sometimes having separate ratings for summer and winter use, *e.g.* SAE 10W.

visco unit, viscous coupling.

viscous, thick, tending to resist flowing.

viscous coupling, a device that performs the function of an automatic clutch, it may transmit no power at low rotational speeds but transmits power efficiently at high rotational speeds; used in some awd vehicles typically in the transfer box to connect drive to an idling axle, smaller versions are sometimes used to drive and control the speed of cooling fans etc.

viscous coupling differential, a limited slip differential using a vc to reduce slip.

viscous damping, the typical method of preventing unwanted oscillation between wheel and suspension by forcing fluid through a small hole to convert mechanical energy into heat energy.

viscous friction, the friction against motion between layers of a liquid.

viscous transmission, an awd system in which the centre differential is a viscous coupling.

visibility, a quality of being able to see from a vehicle, including: the cleanliness of spectacles, windscreen, windows, mirrors, and various weather conditions, *e.g.* fog, mist, rain, spray, dust, smoke, falling snow, etc.

visibility splay, the area between the limits of lateral visibility, especially when emerging at junction.

vision, a quality of the performance of a drivers eyes.

vision arrowhead, the visual limit point created by a bend where the left and right road edges appear to meet.

vision blockout, a situation in which vision is obstructed by vehicles, objects, or buildings, etc, whilst driving.

vision vanishing point, the vision arrowhead.

visitor parking, short term parking at commercial, retail, residential, or tourist places.

visor, sunvisor.

vista point, USA, a paved area beyond the shoulder which permits travellers to safely exit the highway to stop and view a scenic area, sometimes having other service facilities.

visual acuity, a quality of a persons sight, measured as the reciprocal of the smallest resolvable pattern detail in minutes of arc of visual angle; to drive many vehicles the visual acuity must be at least 6/9 in the better eye and 6/12 in the other eye with optical correction if required, and an uncorrected visual acuity of 3/60 in both eyes.

visual check, a brief visual inspection, *e.g.* the vehicle daily checks.

visual clear zone, the length of the merging lane at its full width beyond the end of the acceleration zone, such that if a merge onto the main carriageway is not possible the driver has space in which to brake.

visual inspection, a detailed inspection of a vehicle but without using any tools or equipment.

VLV vehicle, very low volume vehicle.

VM, vehicle manufacturer.

vms, variable message sign.

VN, Vietnam, international vehicle

– vVv –

distinguishing sign, see appendices.

VOC, vehicle operating costs.

vocational licence, a driving licence for a category of vehicle the driving of which is the essence of employment, *e.g.* any bus or lorry licence.

voice activated control, accessories and/or controls within a vehicle which will respond to verbal commands from the driver.

voice alert, a system whereby a speech synthesizer gives an audible warning when operating parameters may be exceeded.

voice recognition, the ability of a microprocessor to recognise and respond to a verbal command for the operation of minor controls.

void ratio, tread void ratio.

voiture, French, car.

voiturette, French, a small car, applied in English to a 2 seat veteran or vintage car.

volatile, a substance that readily evaporates.

volatility, the measure of the ease with which a substance will vaporize, it is directly related to the flammability of a fuel.

volleyball junction, USA, a split diamond junction, a symmetrical grade separated junction on 3 levels where 2 freeways cross in a city centre where space is limited, having centrally a signal controlled square gyratory system connected by 8 sliproads to/from the freeways, *e.g.* the junction of the I29 with the US77; see appendices.

volt, a unit of electromotive force, electrical pressure, denoted v.

voltage drop, the lowering of voltage within a circuit, the normal effect of a power consuming device, sometimes occurring due to bad design or a fault.

voltage regulator, a device that electronically controls the alternator output to prevent excessive voltage.

voltage transformer, a system of electronics that increase or decrease the battery voltage to the voltage required for the operation of a vehicle system needing a different voltage, *e.g.* to transform 12v to 5v necessary for most instruments.

voltmeter, an instrument displaying the instantaneous electrical system voltage, reading in volts.

volume, the size of a space, measured in cubic units, *e.g.* engine size measured in cubic centimetres.

volume, traffic volume.

volume car, a mass produced car.

volume control screw, a carburettor adjusting screw controlling the amount of air-fuel mixture supplied whilst idling.

volumetric efficiency, the ratio of the pressure in the cylinder relative to the ambient pressure, a measure of how completely the cylinder fills with air-fuel mixture, measured at bdc at the end of the induction stroke; typically approximately 80 % in a normally aspirated si

engine and less in a diesel engine.

volumetric energy density, the amount of energy contained within a specific volume of fuel, different for each fuel type.

volumetric power, specific power output.

voluntary decision, a decision made by the driver because of the chosen travelling direction or by the happenings or indications of traffic directors; see: influenced.

voluntary restraint, a temporary sign requesting that drivers of rv's, landowners, and farmers should not drive beyond that point to prevent further surface damage to a track having a soft surface.

voluntary restraint order, an official recommendation issued due to a green lane or track, etc. having a poor surface condition caused by weather and/or usage, advising that the route should not be used until after surface conditions improve.

VOT, vehicle operating times, the cumulative hours of daily or weekly use related to service intervals or VOC.

voucher parking zone, an area where parking is permitted in marked places providing a pre-paid voucher is displayed in the parked vehicle.

VPAS, variable power assisted steering.

vpd, vehicles per day.

VQ, very quiet zone, in road rally navigation a very PR sensitive area, competitors must pass through very quietly and slowly.

VR, the tyre speed rating code denoting a maximum design speed exceeding 210 km/h (130 mph), moulded into the tyre sidewall.

VR, vee reduced, a V engine cylinder and crankshaft layout in which the V between opposing banks of cylinders is reduced to 15° permitting the use of a single cylinder head.

VR, voluntary restraint.

VRD, vehicle registration document.

VRO, Vehicle Registration Office.

VRO, Voluntary Restraint Order.

VSA, variable shock absorber, *i.e.* variable damper.

VSC, vehicle skid control.

VSC, vehicle stability control.

VSCC, Vintage Sports Car Club, UK.

VSE, Vehicle Standards and Engineering, a division of DoT.

VSIB, Vehicle Security Inspection Board, UK.

VSO, Vehicle Special Order.

vsr, valve seat regression.

vss, vehicle speed sensor.

VSS, video scout system.

vt, viscous transmission.

VTD, variable torque distribution.

VTS, variable torque split.

vulcanise, to heat rubber to a specific temperature in the presence of a sulphur compound to give specific characteristics, performed in the construction of tyres and to make a durable puncture repair.

VUT, USA, vehicle use tax.

vv, variable venturi.

v/v, volume/volume, a comparison of 2 substances expressed when mixed in terms of volume, *e.g.* a mixture of engine coolant may be 30 % v/v.

vvc, variable valve control.

vvt, variable valve timing.

VVT-i, variable valve timing with intelligence.

VVTL-i, variable valve timing and lift with intelligence.

VW, Volkswagen (peoples' car), a large European vehicle manufacturing group of companies.

W

W, an engine cylinder and crankshaft layout having 3 rows of cylinders hence 3 cylinder heads and a single crankshaft.
W, an engine cylinder and crankshaft layout having 4 rows of cylinders in a nested V within a V such that there are only 2 cylinder heads and a single crankshaft.
W, an engine cylinder and crankshaft layout created by mating a pair of V engines side by side, sharing a single crankshaft.
W, an engine cylinder and crankshaft layout created by mating a pair of V engines side by side, the 2 crankshafts are connected by a chain drive to a common output shaft.
W, a hire car price category for cars based upon their cost and performance; high power sports cars.
W, the tyre speed rating code denoting a maximum design speed of 270 km/h (168 mph), moulded into the tyre sidewall.
W, waters, a section of the POWER checks mnemonic.
W, watt, the unit of power, the rate that work is done, measured in joules per second, J/s, also electrically the product of amperes x volts, 1W = 1 J/s.
W, west.
W, white road, the colour of roads to be used at that point in road rally navigation, as marked on an OS map.
W, Whitworth, BSW, a screw thread based upon imperial dimensions in which the spanner size is related to the thread diameter and the width across the flats of the nut is double the thread diameter, obsolete.
W, winter, referring to a suffix for an oil viscosity rating.
W, winter mode, referring to some automatic transmission, a switch to bias gear selection, *i.e.* it will start in 3rd gear to reduce the possibility of wheelspin.
W8, an engine cylinder and crankshaft layout having 2 cylinders in each of 4 rows in a nested V within a V such that there are only 2 cylinder heads and a short single crankshaft.
W12, an engine cylinder and crankshaft layout having 3 cylinders in each of 4 rows in a nested V within a V such that there are only 2 cylinder heads and a relatively short single crankshaft.
W12, an engine cylinder and crankshaft layout having 4 cylinders in each of 3 rows having 3 cylinder heads, resulting in a relatively

short crankshaft.
W12, an engine cylinder and crankshaft layout having 3 cylinders in each of 4 rows, created by mating a pair of V6 engines side by side at 72° apart and sharing a single crankshaft, developed by Volkswagen.
W16, an engine cylinder and crankshaft layout created by mating a pair of V8 engines side by side, the 2 crankshafts are connected by a chain drive to a common output shaft.
W16, an engine cylinder and crankshaft layout created by mating a pair of V8 engines side by side at 72° apart and sharing a single crankshaft, developed by Volkswagen for Bugatti.
W link, a lateral locating system for a live axle, similar to a Panhard rod but more compact.
waddle, a sideways rocking of a vehicle body at slow speeds caused by lateral damage to a wheel or tyre.
wade, to drive through deep water; see also ford.
wading depth, the maximum depth at which a particular vehicle can operate in water; it may be briefly increased beyond the manufactures limit by disconnecting the fan.
wading plug, a plug screwed into the lowest point of the clutch bellhousing before wading, to prevent water and dirt entering the clutch but removed for normal driving.
wading sheet, a crude waterproofing method for crossing a narrow but deep river at speed, by fastening a tarpaulin or heavy polythene sheet over the bonnet, down across the radiator grille, and under the engine bay.
WAG, Gambia, international vehicle distinguishing sign, see appendices.
wagon, any lorry or truck having a removable fabric cover on a framework over the load area, a common style of military vehicle.
wagon, USA, station wagon.
wagon and drag, a lorry drawing a full trailer, where the trailer incorporates a steering mechanism within its front axle(s).
wagon undercarriage, a trailer having axles at each end of the chassis and an inbuilt steering mechanism, *i.e.* a full trailer.
waistline, an imaginary horizontal line along the sides of the passenger compartment of a car at the widest point, typically just below the door handles, sometimes emphasized by a chrome or plastic rubbing strip.

wait, to bring a motor vehicle to a stationary position and to remain stationary for a period of time greater than is reasonably necessary for passengers to alight or board, and providing the driver or another person having lawful permission to drive that vehicle remains in attendance.

WAL, Sierra Leone, international vehicle distinguishing sign, see appendices.

walk in, a box van having its floor stepped down behind the rear wheels, typically used for furniture removals.

walking bus, an organised and supervised group of schoolchildren walking to/from school along a timetabled route.

walking all over you, CB jargon, a stronger station is drowning your signal.

wallow, a condition when a vehicle rolls, dives, or squats rhythmically on its suspension.

wall to kerb, referring to turning circle or radius, the space a vehicle requires to make a 1 point turn, allowing for the front and rear overhangs at one side of the turn only.

wall to wall, CB jargon, a message received loud and clear.

wall to wall, referring to turning circle or radius, the space a vehicle requires to make a 1 point turn, allowing for the front and rear overhangs.

walnut shells, organic material used with cherry stones in small fragments which are air-blast as a mild abrasive for removing carbon deposits when rebuilding an engine, but without causing damage to metal parts.

Walter engine, a multirotor engine having 2 differently sized elliptical rotors.

WAN, Nigeria, international vehicle distinguishing sign, see appendices.

wander, a tendency for a vehicle to stray from the steered course caused by worn steering or suspension.

wander, the effect of a driver oversteering to generate a course that is not a consistent with a natural line along a road, a minor zigzag.

Wankel, Felix Wankel, the inventor of the rotary piston engine in Germany in 1956.

Wankel engine, an internal combustion positive displacement engine having a single epitrochoidal rotor which performs the 4 Otto cycles in a continuous rotary motion, invented by Felix Wankel in Germany in 1956.

w/arch, wheel arch.

Wardrop's First Principle, no driver can reduce his or her generalised cost of travel by changing route, *i.e.* all routes used by drivers from any given origin to any given destination will have equal travel costs, and all routes not used will have greater travel costs.

warm up, to start an engine and let it idle for some time to equalise engine temperatures before driving, to reduce wear.

warm up, to start an engine and let it idle for some time to produce heat to demist or deice all windows before driving, for safety.

warm up lap, a lap of a race circuit driven immediately before a race in order to raise the temperature of the engine and the tyres to high temperatures for maximum performance of both.

warning instrument, the horn.

warning light, a tell-tale.

warning triangle, a triangular shaped reflector with sides approximately 40 cm long and reflective edges approximately 5 cm wide, carriage is a legal requirement in many countries; to be displayed in case of breakdown or collision, but not on a motorway.

warranty, a guarantee of quality by a manufacturer including an agreement to repair or replace specific defects occurring during the warranty period.

warranty period, a maximum period of time or a maximum driven distance whichever occurs first, for which a new car is covered under a warranty agreement, typically 3 years and 60,000 km from many manufacturers.

washboard, USA, corrugations, a close extensive series of minor but uncomfortable transverse ridges across a track having a sand or gravel surface caused by suspension resonance.

washer, a metal disc with a concentric hole approximately $1/2$ the overall diameter, usually positioned between a nut and its bearing surface.

washer, headlamp washer.

washer, windscreen washer.

washer fluid, a solution of alcohol and detergent in water for spraying onto windscreens and headlamps.

washout, a deep gulley across or along a track, where the surface has suffered erosion by a flow of surface water.

wash wipe system, a windscreen wiper function which automatically gives 3 wipes of the windscreen just after the application of screenwash.

wastegate, a control device on a turbocharger which limits boost pressure by allowing some exhaust to bypass the turbo, to prevent turbo and engine damage.

water cooled engine, an engine in which excess heat is removed by continuous circulation of a water based fluid through hot areas and a heat exchanger.

water cooling system, a system of removing excess heat from an engine by circulation of a water based fluid by a pump through the cylinder block, cylinder head, thermostat, top hose, through the radiator where it is cooled, bottom hose, and returned again to the cylinder block.

watering hole, CB jargon, a pub.

water injection, a system for injecting a small amount of water into the inlet manifold to prevent detonation by means of the steam cooling the combustion; sometimes used with a turbocharger where the water vapour cools the charge air to increase density.

water jacket, the spaces within the cylinder block through which engine coolant flows.

water pump, a centrifugal pump driven by the fan belt or electrically, which circulates engine coolant around the engine and cooling system.

water splash, a ford where the water depth is very shallow.

water temperature gauge, an instrument displaying the instantaneous water temperature leaving the engine, usually reading in °C.

Watling Street, an ancient Roman road from London to Wrexham.

watt, W, the unit of power, the rate that work is done, measured in joules per second, J/s, also electrically the product of amperes x volts, 1W = 1J/s.

watt hour capacity, the number of watt hours which can be delivered from a storage battery under specified conditions regarding temperature, rate of discharge, and final voltage, an average size car battery may have a watt hour capacity of 400 watt hours.

Watts linkage, a 3 bar system of locating a rigid axle to restrict lateral movement, comprising horizontal linkages from the axle centre transversely to the chassis.

wave effect, the effect of a liquid in a tanker lorry causing instability when surging within the tank, often the result of erratic driver control.

wax, a corrosion inhibiting layer sprayed into vehicle body voids.

wax, a protective coating applied over paintwork.

wax, any paraffinic hydrocarbon which will precipitate from solution in diesel fuel if cooled sufficiently, the crystals may then block the fuel lines and fuel filter.

wax thermostat, a thermostat in a water cooled system which opens at a temperature related to the expansion of wax as it liquefies in an internal cylinder.

way, a road of any class open to the public.

way, a specific route from origin to destination.

waymarking, the use of standard symbols on rights of way to indicate status and direction, using colour coded signs.

waypoint, a checkpoint on a rally.

waypoint, a place of reference to confirm a route.

waypoint, a stopping place on a journey.

wayside, the margin along a roadside.

wb, wheelbase.

WB, westbound, to travel towards the west.

WCCCR, World Cup for Cross Country Rallies, a race series administered by the FIA.

WD, Dominica, international vehicle distinguishing sign, see appendices.

WDCA, without due care and attention, a general offence committed by a driver which includes a myriad of different erroneous actions.

WDS, Worldwide Diagnostic System.

weak mixture, an air-fuel mixture having less fuel and a higher proportion of air, *i.e.* the stoichiometric ratio is increased above the usual 14.7:1 such that $\lambda>1$.

wear, the progressive loss of material from the surface of a solid body caused by tribological stress.

wear bar, a treadwear indicator.

wear limit, the maximum allowable tolerance from a specification, set by a manufacturer.

wear pattern, an uneven style of wear which is visually identifiable, typically as can be seen on the tread of a tyre.

weather equipment, the hood and side screens, as used on open top cars.

weatherstrip, a soft tuboid rubber seal fitted around a door aperture to prevent water, wind, and dust from entering the cabin whist moving.

weather weight width winches, the major points in a code of conduct for 4x4 drivers, such that damage should not be caused to the surface of any road or track or to anything bordering the route.

weaving, the movement of a vehicle from any lane to another and back to the original lane, generally considered bad driving due to poor planning or inconsiderate driving if attempting to gain advantage in congested traffic.

weaving section, a designed conflict zone where traffic must change lanes within a limited distance where junctions are relatively close, *i.e.* where an entry sliproad from 1 junction is close to the exit sliproad for the next, a feature of some sections of some urban motorways.

webbing, a woven nylon flat strap, from which seatbelts are manufactured.

webbing grabber, the device in an inertia reel seatbelt mechanism which grips the belt to prevent further extension if the belt is rapidly extended.

wedge brakes, an operating mechanism for drum brakes whereby a wedge is moved between rollers to force the shoes apart, on some heavy vehicles.

wedge combustion chamber, a combustion chamber having a triangular section.

weekly check, a series of vehicle checks based upon the mnemonic power and the daily checks, but in more detail, including *e.g.* a physical test of tyre pressures rather than a visual glance.

weekly driving, when referring to EC drivers hours, a period between 0.00 on Monday and 24.00 on the following Sunday, containing a maximum of 6 daily driving periods totalling up to 56 hours, but with a maximum of only 90 hours in any fortnight.

weekly rest period, when referring to EC drivers hours, a period of 45 hours of rest that may include the last daily rest period, but it may be reduced to 36 hours if taken at the base of the driver or vehicle, or reduced to 24 hours if equivalent rest is taken before the end of

3 weeks.

weighbridge, a measuring instrument having a large platform which is set into a road surface for weighing vehicles especially lorries, typically it will give each axle weight and the total weight.

weight, a physical property of a vehicle created by its design, the total mass of a vehicle and its load, for some vehicles a physical prohibition in some places.

weight, see: base, dry, DGW, frpl, GCW, gross, GLW, GTW, GVM, GVW, GVWR, kerbside, laden, LVW, MAM, MGW, MVW, notional, reference, RTM, TAW, unladen, wet.

weight distribution, the proportioning of the weight of a vehicle and its load around its structure.

weighted steering, the feedback to a driver through the steering wheel, often referring to the degree of effort to operate the power steering, especially the effect of castor angle in causing the steering to centralise.

weight limit, a limit imposed on a section of road or a bridge that prohibits use by any vehicle exceeding that weight.

weight transfer, see: apparent weight transfer.

Weissach axle, a double wishbone rear suspension system designed to reduce the risk of oversteer, developed by Porsche.

welch plug, a core plug.

weld, a joint made between 2 materials by applying heat to partially melt the material such that they join by fusion.

welding rod, a wire or rod used as filler metal when welding.

well, a part of the wheel rim between the bead seats which is reduced in diameter to allow the opposite side of the tyre bead to pass over the rim when fitting or removing a tyre.

well, the spare wheel well, the recess in the floor of a car boot for storage of a spare wheel.

well base wheel, a 1 piece wheel having a well for fitting and removing the tyre.

Wendy house, a sleeper cab.

west, the direction 90° to the left of north.

westbound, travelling towards the west.

wet clutch, a friction clutch typically of multiplate design which is immersed in oil for smoothness of take up and for heat dissipation when slipping.

wet engine, an engine complete with oil and coolant, contained within.

wet friction, the resulting friction between 2 sliding surfaces when they are separated or lubricated by any fluid.

wet grip, the frictional characteristics of a tyre on a wet surface.

wet liner, a cylinder liner that is in direct contact with the coolant.

wet sump, the common engine style where the oil reservoir is carried in the sump beneath the crankcase or block.

wet weight, the weight of a complete rolling chassis in a condition where it may be driven

under its own power, including the weight of all fluids and fuel at maximum level, but excluding spare wheel, tools, body, or driver.

WG, Grenada, international vehicle distinguishing sign, see appendices.

WGFT, Working Group on Fuel Consumption Targets.

whale tail, a very large rear spoiler, originally developed by Porsche.

what if, a driver training scenario used to increase hazard awareness and hazard assessment.

wheel, a circular construction which rotates on an axle to facilitate linear travel and which transmits forces of acceleration, braking, and steering, and supports lateral and vertical loads, and around which is mounted the tyre for contact with the road surface; invented in 3580 BC by the Sumerians in Uruk (Iraq).

wheel, an inflated assembly consisting of a tyre, rim, and disc.

wheel, steering wheel.

wheel adaptor, a fabricated ring which enables fitting of a wheel to a hub having a different number of studs, and/or where the studs have a different pcd.

wheel alignment, relating to the angular arrangement of pairs of wheels on opposite ends of an axle that should have a definite relationship; the checking and adjusting any of the: caster angles, camber angles, or tracking angles, *i.e.* the toe in or toe out of wheels, in order to maintain the specifications engineered by the vehicle manufacturer for optimum performance of the steering and suspension.

wheel alignment gauge, a measuring instrument typically using a beam of light or laser and a system of mirrors used to measure the tracking angle, *i.e.* the degree of toe in or toe out.

wheel arch, the area of bodywork around a wheel.

wheel arch extension, a spat.

wheel balancer, a machine which measures static and dynamic imbalance in an inflated wheel and tyre assembly and calculates the size and fitting location of the balance weights which must be fitted for perfect dynamic balance.

wheelbase, the longitudinal distance between the centres of the front and rear axles; for lorries, buses, and trailers having 2 or more axles in a set the wheelbase is measured to the midpoint of the axle set.

wheelbase, USA, of a semitrailer, the distance from the centre of the last axle of the drawing vehicle to the centre of the last axle of the semitrailer.

wheel bearing, a low friction device, usually ball or roller bearings between 2 races, that allow the wheel to rotate freely on the axle.

wheel bearing lubricant, a lubricating grease having the characteristics needed to be suitable for use in antifriction wheel bearings.

wheel bolt, each of a series of bolts which secure a wheel to a hub, having a spherical or tapered seat; less common than wheel nuts.

wheelbrace, a tool for turning the wheel nuts, typically a 1 piece socket on an angled long handle, sometimes cranked.

wheel change, the action of replacing a wheel having a faulty tyre.

wheel chock, a wedge or arc shaped block or fabrication placed ahead and behind a wheel to prevent a vehicle moving during maintenance or a wheel change.

wheelclamp, a device which may be applied to the wheel of a car as a penalty for not complying with parking restrictions, it renders the car immovable until a fine has been paid, first used in Denver USA.

wheel cover, a hub cap.

wheel cutout, the aperture in the outer side of bodywork panelling where it is shaped around the wheel to facilitate a wheel change such that the wheel is visible.

wheel cylinder, the hydraulic actuator that converts hydraulic pressure to movement of the brake shoes in a brake drum.

wheel disc, the part of a wheel which connects the rim to the hub.

wheel dolly, a car ambulance.

wheeled, in relation to a vehicle, so constructed that the whole weight of the vehicle is transmitted to the road surface by means of wheels, (C&U).

wheeler, preceded by a number, a vehicle having a specified number of road wheels.

wheel fairing, a panel which covers the rear wheel aperture, removable for a wheel change, fitted mainly for aesthetic purposes but also for streamlining, on some classic cars.

wheel flutter, wheel wobble.

wheel hop, wheel patter.

wheelhouse, the area between the inner and outer wings which accommodates the suspension and wheel.

wheel hub, hub.

wheelie, the effect when a car or bike transmits excessive power such that the front wheels rise from the surface for some distance; only possible with a rwd vehicle.

wheelie bar, a rear framework having a pair of very small wheels that will trail on the surface to prevent a dragster from lifting the front wheels too high during a wheelie.

wheel imbalance, see: dynamic imbalance, static imbalance.

wheel lift, the effect when a wheel lifts from the road surface, when a vehicle reaches the limit of transverse stability often the result of brake steer overlap or cornering whilst accelerating hard, *i.e.* roll combined with dive or rise, or caused by strong crosswind, sometimes followed by a roll especially with tall vehicles.

wheel liner, a chromed or similar cylindrical band fixed around the face of the rim and well

for aesthetic purposes.

wheel load, the weight of that part of the vehicle exerted on the surface through the tyre footprint.

wheel lock, the condition which occurs when a wheel stops rotating whilst the vehicle is moving, caused by applying greater braking force than there is friction available between the tyre and the surface, *i.e.* a brake-induced skid.

wheel lock sequence, the sequence in which the front and rear wheels will lock under certain braking conditions; to meet EC safety requirements the front must lock before the rear.

wheel lockup, the condition which occurs when a wheel stops rotating whilst the vehicle is moving, caused by applying greater braking force than there is friction available between the tyre and the surface, *i.e.* a brake-induced skid.

wheelman, USA, a driver, especially of a getaway car.

wheel marking, a manufacturers mark, typically near the valve hole which details the manufacturer, wheel number, rim size and date of manufacture.

wheel motor, each of a pair of electric drive motors which are mounted in the wheel hub for propelling an electric vehicle.

wheel mounting, the style of the mating of the hub and disc.

wheelnut, each of a series of nuts which secure a wheel to a hub, having a spherical or a tapered seat.

wheel patter, vertical oscillation of a wheel at moderate speeds caused by static imbalance, sometimes aggravated by a worn damper.

wheel rim, the pair of circumferential flanges and the adjoining band, the location for the tyre bead seats.

wheel ring, a circular step on the front wheel of some older lorries to gain access to the cab.

wheel rotation, tyre rotation.

wheels, car.

wheel shimmy, wheel wobble.

wheelslip, the difference between the road speed of a vehicle and the speed of the circumference of the tyre tread, typically expressed as a percentage.

wheelslip, the sideways or angular movement of a skidding wheel.

wheelslip, wheelspin.

wheel spacer, a fabricated ring between hub and wheel for the purpose of increasing the track width.

wheel speed sensor, an instrument that measures the speed of rotation of each wheel and sends a signal to the ABS or DSC and other microprocessors.

wheel spider, a spoked fabrication which connects the wheel rim to the hub in 2 piece and 3 piece wheels.

wheelspin, a condition caused by applying

more torque from the engine than the friction available between the tyres and the road surface, a power induced skid.

wheel stud, each of a series of threaded rods projecting transversely from the hub with which to locate the wheel which is secured by wheelnuts.

wheel taxes, all of the taxes which a motorist must pay: import duty, purchase tax, registration, insurance tax, VED, fuel tax, VAT.

wheel tramp, axle tramp.

wheel tree, a stand for the secure storage of a set of summer or winter tyres when not in use.

wheel trim, hub cap.

wheel trim ring, a chromed or similar cylindrical band fixed around the face of the rim and well for aesthetic purposes.

wheel tub, the inner wheel arch where it projects into the area of the rear seats.

wheel velocity sensor, an instrument that measures the speed of rotation of each wheel and sends a signal to the ABS or DSC and other microprocessors.

wheel weights, small lead weights affixed to a wheel rim to correct any imbalance in a tyre.

wheel well, spare wheel well.

wheel wobble, slewing oscillation of the front wheels at mid speeds resulting in rapid oscillation of the steering wheel, caused by dynamic imbalance of a front wheel.

whip aerial, a very long thin flexible radio aerial.

whiplash, a neck injury caused by sudden rearwards movement of the head, common in rear shunt collisions if the head restraint is not correctly adjusted.

whiplash protection system, a feature where the seat backrest is designed to partially collapse rearwards to reduce forces on the occupant, developed by Volvo.

WHIPS, whiplash protection system.

whip signal, each of several different signals given by the driver of a horse drawn carriage by movement or pointing of his whip, the forerunner before arm signals were developed.

whirl, to travel rapidly by vehicle.

whirl junction, a symmetrical grade separated junction on 2 levels between roads at 90° to each other and which allows all vehicles to move freely from any road to any other excepting a return to the route of origin, all link roads turn through 90° and are fed from sliproads on the nearside only and where link roads providing turns to the offside weave under and over other roads and links, *e.g.* the junction of the M3 with the M25 near London; the name is derived from the spiral formed by the offside curving linkroads seen in plan view; see appendices.

white, a rallying pace note indicating the next clue lies along a road coloured white on an OS map, *i.e.* an unclassified road which may be unsurfaced.

white curb, USA, a painted marking denoting

a restriction from parking, but permitting stopping for sufficient time only to pickup or drop off passengers or to drop mail, typically at airport passenger terminals.

white diesel, diesel fuel of which the price includes tax for road vehicle use; see also: red.

white flag, a flag with which to communicate with racing drivers, held stationary means the safety car or a slow vehicle is on the track, waved means it is immediately ahead.

white grease, a lithium based grease which does not freeze or melt, used on parts which move slowly or occasionally.

white loading box, an area at the roadside delineated with a broken white line on a red route, where loading is permitted at any time but only for a short duration as signs display.

white metal, a tin based alloy originally used for plain bearings.

white panel, a white area on a larger sign of a different colour showing the direction to a specific secondary route.

white parking box, an area at the roadside delineated with a broken white line on a red route, allowing parking or loading at any time but only for a short duration as signs display.

white road, an unclassified minor road or unsurfaced track in road rally navigation, as shown on an OS map.

white sign, a rectangular sign showing directions along or to a secondary route.

white smoke, visible whitish smoke emitted from the exhaust when water vapour is present, sometimes the result of high humidity or sometimes when the cylinder head gasket is leaking.

white studs, cats eyes or reflective studs which mark the centre of a road or the division between lanes, they are widely spaced in low risk areas, have average spacing in higher risk areas, and are very closely spaced in high risk areas.

white van man, a stereotype characteristic of a significant proportion of delivery van drivers using anonymous white vans and driving in reckless haste to meet delivery deadlines without care for other road users, disregarding traffic rules and having an unfounded high opinion of their own driving ability.

whitewall, a tyre having a concentric band of white rubber moulded into the sidewall for aesthetic purposes; see also: wide.

whitewall ring, a rubber ring fitted between rim and tyre which gives the visual effect of a whitewall tyre.

whitewall topper, whitewall ring.

Whitworth, BSW, a screw thread based upon imperial dimensions where the spanner size is related to the thread diameter and the width across the flats of the nut is double the thread diameter, obsolete.

whl, wheel.

whole stick, a gear change using the gear lever for a full gear change, *i.e.* not using a splitter to change $^1/_2$ gears.

wide load, any load projecting more than 305 mm (1 foot) beyond the side of a vehicle; loads up to 3.5 m (11 ft 5 in) require side markers and police notification; loads up to 4.3 m (14 ft 1 in) also require an attendant; loads up to 5 m (16 ft 1 in) are subject to lower speed limits; loads up to 6.1 m (20 ft) also require DoT approval, see appendix.

wide open throttle, USA, full throttle.

wide rim, wide wheel.

wide tyre, a pneumatic tyre of which the area of contact with the road surface is not less than 300 mm in width when measured at right angles to the longitudinal axis of the vehicle.

wide wheel, any wheel which has a greater measurement between the rims than that fitted by the manufacturer as standard to that vehicle.

wide whitewall, a tyre sidewall having a surface layer of white rubber from the bead seat to the shoulder.

width, a physical property of a vehicle created by its design measured across its widest point but excluding lamps and mirrors and their supports, for some vehicles a physical prohibition in some places; see: overall width..

width limit, a limit imposed on a section of road that prohibits use by any vehicle exceeding that width.

wig-wag headlights, headlamps controlled to flash alternately as fitted to some emergency vehicles.

wig-wag signal, a horizontal pair of red signal lamps which flash alternately to mean stop, typically used at railway level crossings, swing bridges, airfields, fire stations, and on motorways, etc.

wilderness, USA, an area in which 4x4 and all other vehicles are prohibited.

Wilson gearbox, a preselector epicyclic gearbox used in some buses.

win, to be victorious in a race, rally, or other competition.

winch, a device used to pull a vehicle a short distance by reeling a steel rope onto a drum, either electrically or hydraulic powered.

winch, the act of recovering a vehicle by dragging it a short distance by reeling a steel rope onto a drum, sometimes to recover a crashed vehicle onto a trailer, or to extract a bogged down vehicle including self recovery.

windage, the apparent headwind caused by the speed of a vehicle through the atmosphere.

wind deflector, a strip of translucent plastic fitted over side windows into a leading and upper window channel to deflect wind to allow travel with the window open.

wind down, to open a window.

winding, wire wound around an iron core or similar, to produce a magnetic field when current flows through it.

windlace, a moquette covered tuboid rubber strip sewn along the edges of a hood for draftproofing.

windmill junction, USA, a symmetrical grade separated but signalised junction on 2 levels where 2 main streets cross in a city centre where space is scarce and both roads carry a similar volume of traffic, the junction comprises 4 exit ramps for queueing terminated by a signalised junction giving direct access without entrance ramps to the other street; see appendices.

window, an opening in the body of a vehicle to admit light and permit visibility through a transparent material, usually glass.

window etching, a permanent marking in the corner of every window of some vehicles, typically displaying the registration, the VIN, or a security code as a security feature.

window net, netting across the side windows of some competition cars, especially where regulations require removal of glass.

window winder, a cranked handle with which to manually raise or lower a side or rear window.

wind noise, sound heard within the cabin that originates from external airflow.

windscreen, a forward facing glass panel to keep the driver and passengers clean and dry, usually made from laminated glass, older vehicles may use toughened glass.

windscreen pillar, A pillar.

windscreen washer, a system with which to spray a water based cleaning solution onto the front windscreen.

windscreen washer, a person who washes car windscreens for payment whilst traffic is stopped at a red traffic signal; the quality of the wash is typically low.

windscreen wash wipe system, wash wipe system.

windscreen wiper, a long thin rubber blade sprung against the glass to wipe rain and dirt from the windscreen of a vehicle, sometimes also rear window, invented by Prince Henry of Prussia in 1911, first automated in 1916.

windshield, USA, windscreen.

wind tunnel, a duct in which the effects of airflow past a vehicle body can be determined.

wind up, see: axle wind up.

wind up, to close a window.

wind up window, a window which may be manually opened and closed with a cranked handle.

wing, a major body panel which covers a roadwheel to prevent water and mud from splashing other parts, and which serves aerodynamic and aesthetic functions.

wing arch, a smoothly flared extension to bodywork around a wheel cutout.

wing mirror, a mirror that is mounted on the front wing of a car, typically 2 metres ahead of the driver, now obsolete as they do not show sufficient detail and could not easily be adjusted, replaced by door mirrors; typically on some classic cars.

wing nut, a nut with 2 small lugs designed to

be tightened and loosened by finger pressure only.

winker, direction indicator.

winter beater, USA, an older car used during the winter period whilst a newer car remains garaged to protect the newer car against potential corrosion due to salted roads.

winter compound, a type of tyre tread rubber designed to give good friction when driving on snow and ice.

winterfront, a set of radiator shutters or a roller blind which can be adjusted to reduce the air flow to the to the radiator when operating in very cold climates.

winter tyre, mud & snow tyre, all season tyre, a tyre having a tread pattern and compound giving better traction in snow and mud.

wiper, windscreen wiper, a device to wipe rain and dirt from a windscreen, sometimes also the rear window and/or headlamps.

wiper wing, a small wind deflector on some windscreen wiper arms to increase wiper blade pressure at higher roadspeeds, *i.e.* higher windspeeds.

wire, a bare or insulated metallic conductor usually having a stranded construction designed to carry current in an electrical circuit.

wire glowplug, a double pole glowplug having an unshielded heating element.

wire rope barrier, safety fencing constructed from steel wire rope, for physical separation of opposing traffic, protection against steep embankments, and for the protection of street furniture.

wire spoke, a spoke made from high tensile steel wire, and which is used with many others to connect a spoke hub to the rim to form a wheel.

wire wheel, a wheel constructed using a large number of wire spokes to maintain the rim concentric around the spoke hub; the spokes are individually adjusted under high tension to ensure no lateral or radial runout of the rim, and the weight of the car is suspended through the vertical spokes at the top of the wheel.

wiring, the installation and utilisation of a system of electrical wires.

wiring diagram, a pictorial representation, a drawing or schematic that shows wires and components in an electrical circuit or system.

wiring harness, the complete wiring loom for a vehicle.

wiring loom, individual wires for different circuits which are bound together in a protective sheath where the wires follow a similar route, resulting in a single integrated unit.

wishbone, a triangular structure hinged longitudinally at 2 corners to the chassis of the vehicle and with the wheel hub hinged at the outer corner.

wishbone suspension, a suspension system comprising 1 or 2 wishbones to support each wheel, such that the single wishbone can support longitudinal and lateral forces and each design permits a range of control over changing camber, castor, and swivel axis angles as the suspension oscillates.

with-flow bus lane, a part of a carriageway, usually the nearside lane, reserved for buses and other specified vehicles moving in the same direction as traffic in other lanes.

WL, St. Lucia, international vehicle distinguishing sign, see appendices.

wobble, sideways oscillation, lateral wheel runout.

wobble, an effect caused by a tyre that is not dynamically balanced, *i.e.* there are heavier and lighter areas on opposite sides of the tyre crown that create an oscillating yaw felt through the steering.

wood alcohol, methanol.

wood blocks, uniformly sized blocks of wood laid with the end grain uppermost sometimes used as the road surface on lifting bridges due to light weight, but very slippery when wet.

woodie, a car having a wood panelled and/or wood framed body or rear body, typically some station wagons, shooting brakes, and classic estate cars.

woody, a car having a wood panelled and/or wood framed body or rear body, typically some station wagons, shooting brakes, and classic estate cars.

work, the transfer of energy from one system to another, *e.g.* moving a vehicle against an opposing force; the product of force x distance, measured in Joules.

workplace parking, a private parking space at the location of an employer.

workshop, a place for the servicing or repair vehicles.

workshop manual, a book specific to each model of vehicle that details repairs and servicing including full stripdown and re-assembly of all parts in text with exploded diagrams.

works team, a team in a race or rally that is fully funded by a motor manufacturer.

works trailer, a trailer so designed for use in private premises and used on a road only in delivering goods from or to such premises to or from a vehicle on a road in the immediate neighbourhood, or in passing from 1 part of such premises to another, or in connection with road works while at the immediate neighbourhood of the site of such works, (C&U).

works truck, a motor vehicle designed for use in private premises and used on a road only in delivering goods from or to such premises to or from a vehicle on a road in the immediate neighbourhood, or in passing from 1 part of such premises to another, or in connection with road works while at the immediate neighbourhood of the site of such works, (C&U).

works unit, a road maintenance compound accessed by a sliproad from a motorway, not open for public use.

world rally car, a production car that is modified to meet the standards of the FIA for competing in the WRC, with a maximum engine size of 2.0 litres.

world rally championship, a series of rallies organised to FIA rules, run over 14 events in different countries.

worldwide diagnostic system, a single system that may be fitted to all models of cars to assist a mechanic repair faults, developed by Ford.

worm, a helically cut groove on a wide cylindrical rod, the helix typically having a trapezoidal cross section.

worm and lever, a type of steering box in which a peg on a lever engages in a worm, thus turning the rocker shaft.

worm and nut, type of steering box in which a concentric nut moves along the worm as the worm rotates, thus turning the rocker shaft.

worm and peg, a type of steering box in which a conical peg on a lever engages in a worm, thus turning the rocker shaft.

worm and roller, a type of steering box in which a tapered disc or a set of discs or rollers engage in a worm, thus turning the rocker shaft.

worm and sector, type of steering box in which a sector of a toothed wheel engages in a worm, thus turning the rocker shaft.

worm and wheel, a gearing system used in steering mechanism of steam traction engines and steamrollers.

worm clamp, a hose clip which tightens in the style of a worm and wheel.

worm gear, a gear cut as a helix around a rod, usually mating at 90° with a worm wheel, allowing the drive to turn at that angle, and reducing or preventing feedback.

worm wheel, a gearwheel designed to mesh with a worm gear.

wot, wide open throttle, a condition when adjusting some engine operating parameters.

wraparound bumper, a bumper style which extends from the front or rear for some distance along the sides to give additional protection, typically to the wheel cutouts.

wraparound dash, a dashboard which curves to improve ergonomics for the driver.

wraparound windscreen, a windscreen having a significant curve, especially at the sides, resulting in severely distorted visibility.

wrapper, CB jargon, a vehicle.

wrc, world rally car.

WRC, World Rally Championship.

wreck, a seriously damaged vehicle, typically unrepairable.

wreck, an end of life vehicle left to deteriorate further.

wrecker, a recovery vehicle or tow truck, especially larger vehicles for towing lorries.

wrecker, USA, a person who breaks up damaged or old vehicles for spares.

wrench, a tool for turning nuts etc. having 1 rigid jaw and 1 sliding jaw that can be set to the nut size by turning a worm gear.

wrench, to pull or lever at an angle, typically with a disproportionate amount of force.

WRI, white roads ignored/included, to be specified before a road rally to specify roads used.

wrinkle wall tyre, a tyre having special sidewalls to give a longer footprint, used on the drive wheels of a dragster and which appear to be underinflated until power is applied.

wrist pin, USA, gudgeon pin.

write off category A, a car which is seriously damaged such that no parts are reusable and the complete vehicle must be crushed, *e.g.* when burned out.

write off category B, a car which cannot be put back on the road but can be used as a donor car to yield spare parts for other vehicles, *e.g.* when the bodyshell is severely lozenged.

write off category C, a car which is damaged and where the cost of repair exceeds 60 % of the trade value of the car, but if repaired and checked by an alignment specialist a pass will be entered on the VCAR register.

write off category D, a car in which damage is confined to windows, locks, and/or bent panels, but the car remains roadworthy, *e.g.* the state in which stolen cars are typically recovered after the insurer has paid out.

wrong siding, the action of passing on the wrong side of an island or other traffic feature in contravention of an obligatory sign.

WS, Western Samoa, international vehicle distinguishing sign, see appendices.

wsm, workshop manual, to be referred to for specific details.

wt, included with the transmission.

WUW, will use whites, confirmation of road class to be used in road rally navigation.

WV, St. Vincent and the Grenadines, international vehicle distinguishing sign, see appendices.

WVTA, see: ECWVTA.

ww, wet weight.

ww, whitewall tyre.

w/w, weight/weight, a comparison of 2 substances expressed when mixed in terms of weight, *e.g.* the stoichiometric ratio of air-fuel mixture may be 14.7:1 w/w.

WW2 classic, any vehicle built during the Second World War, mainly military vehicles, from 3rd September 1939 to 11th November 1945.

w/wipe, headlamp wash wipe.

www, wide whitewall.

X

X, an engine cylinder and crankshaft layout created by mating a pair of V engines side by side, on their sides, so they share a common crankshaft.

X4 seatbelt , a 4 point crisscross seatbelt having regular 3 point lap and diagonal belts plus an extra diagonal belt across the chest in the opposite direction.

X16, a 16 cylinder engine based upon a pair of V8 blocks mated side by side, on their sides, and sharing a common crankshaft.

X band, a radio band on which transmissions are made to electronically detect road users at some pelican crossings; in some countries it is used by some radar speed measuring equipment at speed traps.

X country, cross country.

X engine, an inline engine with the cylinder banks arranged around the crankshaft such that they resemble a letter X when viewed from the end.

X flow, crossflow cylinder head.

X frame, a vehicle chassis layout having the chassis side rails bent in to the centre resulting in a plan view resembling that of a letter X.

X frame, a vehicle chassis layout having X shaped cross members between the side rails instead of members at 90°, resulting in several X shapes in plan view.

X ing, USA, pedestrian crossing.

X junction, a junction where 2 roads cross, typically at 90°, and where 1 road may be designated priority over the other.

X roads, cross roads, an X junction.

xc, cross country, driving on dirt roads, tracks, or unmade roads.

xenon, an inert gas, when electrically charged it emits a white light, used in headlamps and ignition timing lamps.

xenon halogen headlamp, a headlamp emitting a bright white light, greater than that of a pure halogen lamp, the 2 gases are mixed in a filament lamp to improve brightness by allowing the bulb to operate at a higher temperature.

xenon headlamp, a gas discharge headlamp, not having a wire filament, it operates at 5,000 °C by creation of a 20,000 volt electrical charge giving a very bright white light, an output significantly greater than that of halogen lamps.

xenon timing lamp, a stroboscopic lamp using a xenon tube, for checking or resetting ignition timing.

XP, the UK registration designation for a vehicle which is temporarily registered before being exported.

XR, cross roads, in road rally navigation.

X/spoke, cross spoke wheels.

Y

Y, the tyre speed rating code denoting a maximum design speed of 300 km/h (186 mph), moulded into the tyre sidewall.

Y, yellow road, the colour of roads to be used at that point in road rally navigation as marked on an OS map.

Y belt, a 3 point belt design for restraining a baby in a child safety seat.

Y connector, any connector in the shape of a Y, typically the windscreen washer tubing where it forks to each nozzle.

Y junction, a junction of 3 roads, or typically a junction of 1 road at a point with another road where that road changes direction at a bend.

Y pipe, a twin header.

Yank tank, any large American car.

yard, a unit of length equal to 3 feet, (0.9144018 metre), obsolete.

yaw, the turning motion of the body of a vehicle around a vertical axis, as in steering around a corner.

yaw acceleration, an increasing rate of change of yaw rotation.

yaw angle, the angular difference between the longitudinal axis of a vehicle and its direction of motion.

yaw response, the lag between causing a steering input and the vehicle starting to change direction.

yaw sensor, an instrument in the chassis that measures the rate of turn of the chassis during cornering, and sends a signal to the DSC or VSC or other microprocessors.

yellow, a rallying pace note indicating the next clue lies along a road coloured yellow on the OS map, *i.e.* a minor classified road.

yellow bar markings, a long series of transverse yellow lines across a carriageway having a reducing distance between each to provide an illusion that a vehicle is not decelerating sufficiently, *i.e.* to encourage greater braking, typically used on approach to a roundabout on a high speed road.

yellow boot, a wheel clamp.

yellow box, an area of road surface painted with criss-cross yellow lines on which drivers must not stop, except when waiting to turn into a junction to the offside, *i.e.* drivers must not enter the box junction unless their exit is clear.

yellow broken line, a central road marking used alongside a white marking in some

countries denoting an approach to a solid yellow line which prohibits crossing of the line.

yellow curb, USA, a painted marking denoting loading or unloading is permitted for a restricted time only, as detailed on the curb or an adjacent sign, provided the driver remains with the vehicle.

yellow dots, a road marking that delineates the edge of some tramways.

yellow flag, a flag with which to communicate with racing drivers, when held static meaning a hazard on the track, no overtaking, prepare to follow an unusual line, or if waved means the hazard is immediately ahead.

yellow hose, UK, the air hose controlling the service brake system at the coupling to a trailer.

yellow hose, USA, the air hose controlling the auxiliary brake system at the coupling to a trailer.

yellow line, a road marking denoting parking restrictions marked by various yellow lines near the road edge, devised in 1956.

yellow metal, any alloy of copper including brass and bronze.

yellow/red vertical striped flag, a flag with which to communicate with racing drivers, meaning oil or water is on the track, if waved the hazard is immediately ahead.

yellow road, an unclassified minor road in road rally navigation, as shown on an OS map.

yellow sign, a rectangular diversion sign, showing either a series of hollow or solid shapes to be followed along the route of a diversion, or showing lane restrictions on a main road.

yellow studs, cats eyes or reflective studs which mark temporary left and right lane boundaries at road works, especially at a contraflow.

yield, give way, a mandatory requirement.

yoke, the forked outer parts of some types of universal joint.

YU, Yugoslavia, international vehicle distinguishing sign, see appendices.

yump, a significant crest where a rally car is likely to briefly become airborne.

yump, to drive quickly over a significant crest causing the car to become airborne.

YV, Venezuela, international vehicle distinguishing sign, see appendices.

Z

Z, the tyre speed rating code denoting a maximum design speed exceeding 240 km/h (150 mph), moulded into the tyre sidewall.

Z, Zambia, international vehicle distinguishing sign, see appendices.

Z axle, on a fwd car, a rear suspension system comprising wishbones, a trailing link and coil springs.

Z axle, on a rwd car, a rear suspension system comprising a trailing arm, an upper lateral link, a lower diagonal link, and coil springs, developed by BMW.

Z bar, an antiroll bar used typically in swing axle suspensions.

ZA, South Africa, international vehicle distinguishing sign, see appendices.

ZDK, Zentralverband Deutsches Kraftfahrzeuggewerbe, German vehicle dealers umbrella organisation for local state associations of certified dealers and workshops, and franchised dealer associations.

zebra crossing, an uncontrolled pedestrian crossing where a footpath crosses a road, introduced on 31 October 1951.

zee, the structural modification to a chassis that has been angled to mount the axle at a different height, typically so larger diameter tyres can be fitted.

zerk fitting, USA, grease nipple.

zero emission vehicle, a vehicle having no emissions, *e.g.* solar powered; a misnomer if referring to an electrical vehicle powered by batteries, *i.e.* to recharge the batteries of an electric vehicle there will be significant pollution created elsewhere at a power station.

zero offset, centre point steering, a design of steering geometry where a line extended through the swivel axis meets the road surface at the same point as a vertical line through the centre of the tyre footprint, *i.e.* neutral scrub radius.

zev, zero emission vehicle.

ZF, Zahnradfabrik Friedrichshafen, a German manufacturer of transmissions used in vehicles ranging from racing cars to articulated lorries.

zigzag lines, angled white lines painted along the centre and/or edges of a road near pedestrian crossings, they prohibit overtaking and parking on approach and prohibit parking on departure.

ZIL, Zavod Imieni Likhacheva, a Russian lorry manufacturer.

zinc, a metallic element, often used to coat steel to prevent rusting.

zinc base alloy, a range of alloys made with the metals: zinc, lead, tin, and antimony, all having a low melting point and good properties to facilitate injection moulding to make carburettors and other parts.

zinc coated, a thin layer of zinc on a steel part to prevent rusting.

zip merging, the action of 2 lanes of traffic merging alternately into 1 lane to maximise flow and minimise frustration.

zipper rule, a rule applied in many countries where 2 lanes of traffic are merging into 1 lane, *e.g.* at roadworks, where precedence to move ahead alternates equally between both queues.

zone of intrusion, safety zone.

zone of vision, the width of an angular area of view into which a driver has uninterrupted sight between lateral limits, especially with respect to emerging from a blind opening.

Zonta sandwich, the position of a driver being overtaken simultaneously on both the right and the left sides.

zoo, CB jargon, police headquarters.

ZPCR, UK, Zebra Pedestrian Crossings Regulations 1971.

ZPPPCRGD, UK, Zebra, Pelican, Puffin, Pedestrian Crossings Regulations and General Directions 1997.

ZR, the tyre speed rating code denoting a maximum design speed exceeding 240 km/h (150 mph), moulded into the tyre sidewall.

ZRE, Zaire, international vehicle distinguishing sign, see appendices.

Z's, CB jargon, sleep.

ZW, Zimbabwe, international vehicle distinguishing sign, see appendices.

ZZ, the UK registration designation for a vehicle temporarily imported from abroad where the characters on the registration plate are not based upon Roman letters and Arabic numerals.

APPENDICES

Δ, delta, triangle, on a road rally the sides used may be critical.

λ, lambda, the symbol for perfect stoichiometric ratio for each specific fuel type, measured with respect to the residual oxygen in exhaust gas.

μ, mu, the coefficient of friction, *e.g.* between tyre and road surface.

π, pi, the ratio of the circumference of a circle to its diameter, 3.141592653…

Ø, phi, luminous flux, measured in lumen, lm.

Ω, ohm, the symbol for electrical resistance.

MATHEMATICAL SYMBOLS

: ratio, the relative quantity of 2 or more figures in proportion, usually expressed as a numerical relationship, *e.g.* compression ratio 9:1 or antifreeze-water mixture 1:3

+ a cruise control operating button which will cause an increase in the set speed.

+ a gearchange control paddle which will cause selection of a higher gear in a tiptronic or semiautomated system.

+ positive terminal.

− a cruise control operating button which will cause a decrease in the set speed.

− a gearchange control paddle which will cause selection of a lower gear in a tiptronic or semiautomated system.

− negative terminal.

= a cruise control operating button which will alternately either cancel or resume the preset speed.

/ divided by.

° degree, of temperature or of rotation.

≥ greater than or equal to.

> greater than.

< less than.

≤ less than or equal to.

± plus or minus, relating to a measured tolerance.

BRITISH – AMERICAN TRANSLATIONS

British	American
2 stroke engine	2 cycle engine
2 way road	2 lane highway
3 point turn	turnabout

4 cylinder engine	4 banger
4 way spider	4 way lug wrench
8 legger	dual steer straight
A framing	dingy towing
A framing	toading
acceleration lane	on ramp
acceleration lane	ramp
acceleration lane	speed change lane
accelerator pedal	gas pedal
adjustable spanner	adjustable wrench
aerial	antenna
after bottom dead centre	after lower dead centre
after top dead centre	after upper dead centre
air shield	air deflector
aluminium	aluminum
antiroll bar	antisway bar
antiroll bar	stabilizer bar
antiroll bar	sway bar
articulated lorry	tractor trailer
articulated truck	rig
auto test	autocross
autojumble	swap meet
automobile	iron
axle casing	axle housing
axle tramp	power hop
backfire	popback
banger	beater
banger	clunker
banger	winter beater
baulk ring	balk ring
before bottom dead centre	before lower dead centre
before top dead centre	before upper dead centre
belt up	buckle up
bend	turn
blowlamp	blow torch
bodyshell	body in white
bodyshell	body tub
bonnet	hood
bonnet badge	hood badge
bonnet release	hood release
bonnet stay	hood rod
boot	trunk
boot handle	trunk handle
booted version	trunk model
bootlid	trunk lid
bottom dead centre	lower dead centre
box van	cube van
boxer engine	pancake engine

brake adjusting spanner	brake wrench	driving tyre	driver
brake disc	brake rotor	drunk driving	DUI
brake light	stop light	dual carriageway	divided highway
brake pad	brake puck	dual purpose vehicle	carryall
break for spares	part out	dumb-irons	frame horns
breaker's yard	salvage yard	dynamo	generator
buildout	choker	earth	ground
buildout	peninsula	earth strap	ground strap
bulb holder	lamp socket	earth wire	ground wire
bulkhead	firewall	electric tram	trolleycar
bull bar	brush guard	endorsement	a penalty
bump steer	ride steer	endorsement	a qualification
bumper	nerf bar	engine	motor
bush	bushing	engine capacity	engine displacement
cabin light	dome light	escape lane	escape ramp
cabin light switch	dome override	estate car	squareback
cabriolet	convertible sedan	estate car	station wagon
cadence braking	stab braking	exhaust silencer	exhaust muffler
car	automobile	exit sliproad	exit ramp
car breaker	wrecker	faulty	hooped
car cover	auto bonnet	feeler gauge	gapper
caravan	house trailer	filling station	gas station
caravan	trailer	fire appliance	fire truck
caravan site	trailer park	flat 4 engine	quadrazontal engine
carburettor	carburetor	flat engine	pancake engine
carcass	casing	flatshift	powershift
career	careen	flatshift	speed shift
carriageway	traveled way	floor mounted gear lever	floor shift
castor	caster	flyover	fly past
cats eye	lane button	freewheeling	coasting
cattle grid	cattle guard	front grille	fascia
central reservation	median	fuel injection pump	jerk pump
change down	downgear	fuel pump	gas pump
cherished registration	vanity plate	full throttle	wide open throttle
child safety seat	child restraint seat	fuse block	cut-out box
circlip	snap ring	gate	shiftgate
clutch release bearing	throwout bearing	gauge	gage
clutch release lever	throwout lever	gear	range
coachbuilder	bodybuilder	gearbox	transmission
cone	pylon	gearchange	gearshift
core plug	freeze plug	gearchange valve	shift valve
corrugations	washboard	gearchanging	shifting
covered lorry	caravan	gearlever	gearstick
crankcase breather pipe	road draft tube	gearlever	shift lever
crawler gear	bull low	gearlever	shifter
crawler gear	creeper	getaway car driver	wheelman
crocodile clip	alligator clip	Glasses Guide	blue book
crossply	diagonal	goods	cargo
deceleration lane	off ramp	grab handle	assist grip
deceleration lane	ramp	gravel rash	road rash
deceleration lane	speed change lane	grounded	high centred
demister	defogger	grounded	hung up
depart	hit the trail	groupage	unitized cargo
diagnostic fault code	diagnostic trouble code	gudgeon pin	wrist pin
		gutter	drip rail
diagnostic fault code	trouble code	handballing	lumping
dickey seat	rumble seat	hatchback	liftback
dipswitch	dimmer	hatchback tailgate	liftgate
direction indicator	signal light	headlamp beamsetter	aimer
directional tyre	unidirectional tire	hill	grade
downhill gradient	downgrade	hood	top
driving licence	driver's license	inclined engine	slant engine
driving school	traffic school	indicators	turn signals
driving test	driver's test	induction stroke	intake stroke

inlet	intake	pinking	ping
inlet port	intake port	planetary gear	spider gear
inlet valve	intake valve	police car	cruiser
intermittent wiper	mist action	police car	prowl car
glazed ice	glare ice	police prison van	patrol wagon
jump leads	jumper cable	police van	paddy wagon
kerb	curb	polygrooved V belt	serpentine belt
kerbweight	curb weight	position lights	clearance lights
kickdown	forced downshift	position lights	identification lights
knee bolster	knee bar	post war classic	milestone car
layshaft	countershaft	pothole	chuck hole
lead replacement petrol	lead replacement gasoline	power hood	electric top
		power to weight ratio	horsepower weight factor
leading shoe	primary shoe		
licence	license	pressure limiting valve	proportioning valve
lift off oversteer	lift throttle oversteer	prise	pry
lift off oversteer	throttle off oversteer	propeller shaft	drive shaft
lift off oversteer	trailing throttle oversteer	provisional licence	instruction permit
		puncture	burst
lift the dot fastener	snap fastener	quarter light	quarter widow
lightweight spare	collapsible spare tire	quarter window	vent
link road	branch connection	railway level crossing	at grade crossing
locknut	jam nut	railway level crossing	grade crossing
lorry	truck	railway level crossing	railroad crossing
low gear	stiff gear	rear engine cover	deck lid
main street	main drag	rear shelf	package tray
manoeuvre	maneuver	rear window	backlite
manual gearbox	stickshift	registration plate	license plate
manual gearlever	handshaker	registration plate	tag
methylated spirit	denatured alcohol	remould	new tread
mint condition	cherry condition	remould	nu-tread
motor caravan	motorhome	restricted junction	parclo
motorway	expressway	retread	recap
motorway	freeway	reversing horn	backup alarm
motorway	speedway	reversing lamp	backup lamp
mountable kerb	rollover curb	reversing light	backup light
mudflap	splashguard	rigid lorry	straight truck
mudflap	splash flap	ring spanner	box wrench
mudguard	fender	ringroad	beltway
multiplate clutch	multiple disc clutch	road debris	road hazard
nearside lane	driving lane	road markings	pavement markings
no overtaking	no passing	road surface	pavement
nose bra	bib	road works	construction
nose weight	tongue weight	rocker box	valve cover
notchback	bustleback	rocker shaft	cross shaft
ohv engine	I head engine	Rolls Royce quality	Duesy quality
ornamental courtesy lamp	opera light	roundabout	rotary
outdoor car park	lot	roundabout	traffic circle
outdoor carpark	parking lot	roundabout	traffic rotary
overrider	bumper horn	run in	break in
overtaking	passing	runabout	driver
overtaking lane	passing lane	runabout	urban combat car
panel van	panel truck	running in oil	bedding-in oil
pantechnicon	moving van	safety barrier	guard rail
paraffin	kerosene	saloon	sedan
passing place	turnout	screw jack	jackscrew
pavement	sidewalk	scrutineer	scrutinizer
pedestrian crossing	X ing	seized	frozen
perpendicular road	avenue	self centring	returnability
petrol	gas	service road	frontage road
petrol	gasoline	shipment	cargo
petrol tank	gas tank	shooting brake	station wagon
pillarless coupé	hardtop	shunt	pull up
pilot bearing	spigot bearing	shutdown checks	coastdown

silencer	muffler
slip angle	tyre deviation angle
slipstreaming	drafting
small car	subcompact car
small saloon	compact
soft top cover	boot
soup up	hop up
spaghetti junction	mixing bowl
spanner	wrench
spat	fender flare
starter motor	cranking motor
stinger	stop stick
stop line	limit line
stopping	standing
straight oil	straight weight
street	drag
sump	oil pan
sump guard	skid plate
suspension bump stop	snubber
swerve	careen
tappet	lifter
tappet	valve lifter
taxi rank	taxi stand
tell-tale lights	information lights
the number of tyres on a vehicle	wheeler, preceded by a number
threshold braking	squeeze braking
through bolt	anchor bolt
toll motorway	turnpike
top dead centre	upper dead centre
top up	top off
toughened glass	tempered glass
tourer	phaeton
towball	hitch ball
track	tread
tractive unit	semi
tractive unit	semitractor
tractive unit	tractor trailer
tractive unit	truck tractor
trailing shoe	secondary shoe
tram	street car
tramlining	nibbling
transfer gearbox	dropbox
transverse engine	sidewinder
tread block feathering	heel wear
trolleybus	trackless trolley
truck driver	blacktop cowboy
turning pocket	2 way turning lane
twin exhaust	dual exhaust
twin wheels	duals
tyre	tire
tyre lever	iron
tyre lever	tire iron
under bonnet	underhood
unregistered vehicle	scrappage
uphill gradient	upgrade
urban driving	metro driving
urban footway	pedway
veteran	antique
vintage	antique
vinyl top	hardtop convertible
waistline	belt line
weighbridge	scale
wheel arch	wheel well
wheel fairing	fender skirt
wheelnut	lug nut
wheelstud	lug
windscreen	windshield
wind down, a window	roll down, a window
wind up, a window	roll up, a window
wing	fender
wing	quarter panel
wishbone	A arm
wishbone	control arm

AMERICAN – BRITISH TRANSLATIONS

American	British
2 cycle engine	2 stroke engine
2 lane highway	2 way road
2 way turning lane	turning pocket
4 banger	4 cylinder engine
4 way lug wrench	4 way spider
A arm	wishbone
adjustable wrench	adjustable spanner
after lower dead centre	after bottom dead centre
after upper dead centre	after top dead centre
aimer	headlamp beamsetter
air deflector	air shield
alligator clip	crocodile clip
aluminum	aluminium
anchor bolt	through bolt
antenna	aerial
antique	veteran
antique	vintage
antisway bar	antiroll bar
assist grip	grab handle
at grade crossing	railway level crossing
auto bonnet	car cover
autocross	auto test
automobile	car
avenue	perpendicular road
axle housing	axle casing
backlite	rear window
backup alarm	reversing horn
backup lamp	reversing lamp
backup light	reversing light
balk ring	baulk ring
beater	banger
bedding-in oil	running in oil
before lower dead centre	before bottom dead centre
before upper dead centre	before top dead centre
belt line	waistline
beltway	ringroad
bib	nose bra
blacktop cowboy	truck driver
blow torch	blowlamp
blue book	Glasses Guide
body in white	bodyshell
body tub	bodyshell
bodybuilder	coachbuilder
boot	soft top cover
box wrench	ring spanner

325

brake puck	brake pad	driving lane	nearside lane
brake rotor	brake disc	dropbox	transfer gearbox
brake wrench	brake adjusting	dual exhaust	twin exhaust
	spanner	dual steer straight	8 legger
branch connection	link road	duals	twin wheels
break in	run in	Duesy quality	Rolls Royce quality
brush guard	bull bar	DUI	drunk driving
buckle up	belt up	electric top	power hood
bull low	crawler gear	endorsement	a qualification
bumper horn	overrider	endorsement	a penalty
burst	puncture	engine displacement	engine capacity
bushing	bush	escape ramp	escape lane
bustleback	notchback	exhaust muffler	exhaust silencer
caravan	covered lorry	exit ramp	exit sliproad
carburetor	carburettor	expressway	motorway
careen	career	fascia	front grille
careen	swerve	fender	mudguard
cargo	goods	fender	wing
carryall	dual purpose vehicle	fender flare	spat
casing	carcass	fender skirt	wheel fairing
caster	castor	fire truck	fire appliance
cattle guard	cattle grid	firewall	bulkhead
cherry condition	mint condition	floor shift	floor mounted gear
child restraint seat	child safety seat		lever
choker	buildout	fly past	flyover
chuck hole	pothole	forced downshift	kickdown
clearance lights	position lights	frame horns	dumb-irons
clunker	banger	freeway	motorway
coastdown	shutdown checks	freeze plug	core plug
coasting	freewheeling	frontage road	service road
collapsible spare tire	lightweight spare	frozen	seized
compact	small saloon	gage	gauge
construction	road works	gapper	feeler gauge
control arm	wishbone	gas	petrol
convertible sedan	cabriolet	gasoline	petrol
countershaft	layshaft	gas pedal	accelerator pedal
cranking motor	starter motor	gas pump	fuel pump
creeper	crawler gear	gas station	filling station
cross shaft	rocker shaft	gas tank	petrol tank
cruiser	police car	gearshift	gearchange
cube van	box van	gearstick	gearlever
curb	kerb	generator	dynamo
curb weight	kerbweight	glare ice	glazed ice
cut-out box	fuse block	grade	hill
deck lid	rear engine cover	grade crossing	railway level
defogger	demister		crossing
denatured alcohol	methylated spirit	ground	earth
diagnostic trouble code	diagnostic fault code	ground strap	earth strap
diagonal	crossply	ground wire	earth wire
dimmer	dipswitch	guard rail	safety barrier
dingy towing	A framing	handshaker	manual gearlever
divided highway	dual carriageway	hardtop	pillarless coupé
dome light	cabin light	hardtop convertible	vinyl top
dome override	cabin light switch	heel wear	tread block
downgear	change down		feathering
downgrade	downhill gradient	high centred	grounded
drafting	slipstreaming	hit the trail	depart
drag	street	hitch ball	towball
drip rail	gutter	hood	bonnet
drive shaft	propeller shaft	hood badge	bonnet badge
driver	driving tyre	hood release	bonnet release
driver	runabout	hood rod	bonnet stay
driver's license	driving licence	hooped	faulty
driver's test	driving test	hop up	soup up

horsepower weight factor	power to weight ratio	parking lot	outdoor carpark
house trailer	caravan	part out	break for spares
hung up	grounded	passing	overtaking
identification lights	position lights	passing lane	overtaking lane
I head engine	ohv engine	patrol wagon	police prison van
information lights	tell-tale lights	pavement	road surface
instruction permit	provisional licence	pavement markings	road markings
intake	inlet	pedway	urban footway
intake port	inlet port	peninsula	buildout
intake stroke	induction stroke	phaeton	tourer
intake valve	inlet valve	ping	pinking
iron	automobile	popback	backfire
iron	tyre lever	power hop	axle tramp
jackscrew	screw jack	powershift	flatshift
jam nut	locknut	primary shoe	leading shoe
jerk pump	fuel injection pump	proportioning valve	pressure limiting valve
jumper cable	jump leads	prowl car	police patrol car
kerosene	paraffin	pry	prise
knee bar	knee bolster	pull up	shunt
lamp socket	bulb holder	pylon	cone
lane button	cats eye	quadrazontal engine	flat 4 engine
lead replacement gasoline	lead replacement petrol	quarter panel	wing
		quarter widow	quarter light
license	licence	railroad crossing	railway level crossing
license plate	registration plate		
lift throttle oversteer	lift off oversteer	ramp	acceleration lane
liftback	hatchback	ramp	deceleration lane
lifter	tappet	range	gear
liftgate	hatchback tailgate	recap	retread
limit line	stop line	returnability	self centring
lot	outdoor car park	ride steer	bump steer
lower dead centre	bottom dead centre	rig	articulated truck
lug	wheelstud	road draft tube	crankcase breather pipe
lug nut	wheelnut		
lumping	handballing	road hazard	road debris
main drag	main street	road rash	gravel rash
maneuver	manoeuvre	roll down, a window	wind down, a window
median	central reservation		
metro driving	urban driving	rollover curb	mountable kerb
milestone car	post war classic	roll up, a window	wind up, a window
mist action	intermittent wiper	rotary	roundabout
mixing bowl	spaghetti junction	rumble seat	dickey seat
motor	engine	salvage yard	breaker's yard
motorhome	motor caravan	scale	weighbridge
moving van	pantechnicon	scrappage	unregistered vehicle
muffler	silencer	scrutinizer	scrutineer
multiple disc clutch	multiplate clutch	secondary shoe	trailing shoe
nerf bar	bumper	sedan	saloon
new tread	remould	semi	tractive unit
nibbling	tramlining	semitractor	tractive unit
no passing	no overtaking	serpentine belt	polygrooved V belt
nu-tread	remould	shift lever	gearlever
off ramp	deceleration lane	shift valve	gearchange valve
oil pan	sump	shifter	gearlever
on ramp	acceleration lane	shiftgate	gate
opera light	ornamental courtesy lamp	shifting	gearchanging
		sidewalk	pavement
package tray	rear shelf	sidewinder	transverse engine
paddy wagon	police van	signal light	direction indicator
pancake engine	boxer engine	skid plate	sump guard
pancake engine	flat engine	slant engine	inclined engine
panel truck	panel van	snap fastener	lift the dot fastener
parclo	restricted junction	snap ring	circlip

snubber	suspension bump stop
speed change lane	acceleration lane
speed change lane	deceleration lane
speed shift	flatshift
speedway	motorway
spider gear	planetary gear
spigot bearing	pilot bearing
splash flap	mudflap
splashguard	mudflap
squareback	estate car
squeeze braking	threshold braking
stab braking	cadence braking
stabilizer bar	antiroll bar
standing	stopping
station wagon	estate car
station wagon	shooting brake
stickshift	manual gearbox
stiff gear	low gear
stop light	brake light
stop stick	stinger
straight truck	rigid lorry
straight weight	straight oil
street car	tram
subcompact car	small car
swap meet	autojumble
sway bar	antiroll bar
tag	registration plate
taxi stand	taxi rank
tempered glass	toughened glass
throttle off oversteer	lift off oversteer
throwout bearing	clutch release bearing
throwout lever	clutch release lever
tire	tyre
tire deviation angle	slip angle
tire iron	tyre lever
toading	A framing
tongue weight	nose weight
top	hood
top off	top up
trackless trolley	trolleybus
tractor trailer	articulated lorry
tractor trailer	tractive unit
traffic circle	roundabout
traffic rotary	roundabout
traffic school	driving school
trailer	caravan
trailer park	caravan site
trailing throttle oversteer	lift off oversteer
transmission	gearbox
traveled way	carriageway
tread	track
trolleycar	electric tram
trouble code	diagnostic fault code
truck	lorry
truck tractor	tractive unit
trucking	shipment
trunk	boot
trunk handle	boot handle
trunk lid	bootlid
trunk model	booted version
turn	bend
turnabout	3 point turn
turnout	passing place
turnpike	toll motorway
turn signals	indicators
underhood	under bonnet
unidirectional tire	directional tyre
unitized cargo	groupage
upgrade	uphill gradient
upper dead centre	top dead centre
urban combat car	runabout
valve cover	rocker box
valve lifter	tappet
vanity plate	cherished registration
vent	quarter window
washboard	corrugations
wheeler, preceded by a number	the number of tyres on a vehicle
wheelman	getaway car driver
wheel well	wheel arch
wide open throttle	full throttle
windshield	windscreen
winter beater	banger
wrecker	car breaker
wrench	spanner
wrist pin	gudgeon pin
X ing	pedestrian crossing

CONVERSIONS OF MEASURES AND UNITS

Length

1 micron	=	0.001 mm
1 micron	=	0.03937 thou
1 thou	=	25.4 micron
1 thou	=	0.0254 mm
1 thou	=	0.001 inch
1 mm	=	39.37 thou
1 mm	=	0.03937 inch
1 inch	=	25.4 mm
1 inch	=	1000 thou
1 foot	=	0.3048 metre
1 metre	=	39.37 inch
1 metre	=	3.280833 feet
1 metre	=	1.093611 yard
1 yard	=	0.9144018 metre
1 statute mile	=	1760 yard
1 statute mile	=	1.609344 km
1 km	=	1000 metre
1 km	=	0.6213711 statute mile

Volume

1 cubic inch	=	16.387064 cm^3
1 cm^3	=	0.0610237 cubic inch

Capacity

1 litre	=	0.219975 imperial gallon
1 litre	=	0.264179 US gallon
1 litre	=	1.0567166 US quart
1 US quart	=	0.9463275 litre
1 imperial gallon	=	4.54596 litre

1 imperial gallon	=	1.20095 US gallon
1 US gallon	=	3.78531 litre
1 US gallon	=	0.832674 imperial gallon
1 barrel	=	158.99 litre
1 barrel	=	34.97 imperial gallon
1 barrel	=	42 US gallon

Weight

1 lb	=	0.453592 kg
1 kg	=	2.20462 lb
1 cwt	=	50.8023 kg
1 ton	=	1.01605 tonne
1 tonne	=	1000 kg
1 tonne	=	0.984207 ton

Pressure

1 psi	=	6.89476 kPa
1 psi	=	0.070307 kg/cm^2
1 bar	=	100 kPa
1 bar	=	14.5038 psi
1 kg/cm^2	=	14.2233 psi
1 kg/cm^2	=	98.0665 kPa
1 Pa	=	1 N/m^2

Velocity

1 m/s	=	2.23694 mph
1 m/s	=	3.6000 km/h
1 mph	=	0.44704 m/s
1 mph	=	1.609344 km/h
1 km/h	=	0.277777 m/s
1 km/h	=	0.62137118 mph

Torque

1 pound foot	=	0.138255 kg.m
1 kg.m	=	7.23301 lb ft
1 lb ft	=	1.35582 Nm
1 Nm	=	0.737562 lb ft

Power

1 horsepower	=	550 lb.ft /s
1 horsepower	=	76.0402 kg.m/s
1 horsepower	=	0.7457 kW
1 horsepower	=	1.01387 metric horsepower, PS
1 metric horsepower	=	75 kg.m/s
1 metric horsepower	=	0.73549875 kW
1 metric horsepower	=	0.98632 imperial horsepower
1 metric horsepower	=	1 pferdestärke, PS
1 PS	=	1 metric horsepower
1 kW	=	1.34102 imperial horsepower
1 kW	=	1.35962 metric horsepower, PS
1 W	=	1 J/s
1 W	=	1 VA (volt x ampere)

Acceleration

1 g	=	9.80665 m/s^2

Fuel efficiency

1 mpg (imperial)	=	0.832674 mpg (US)

1 mpg (US)	=	1.20095 mpg (imperial)
1 mile/gallon (imp)	=	0.354016 km/litre
1 mile/gallon (US)	=	0.425208 km/litre
1 gallon (imp) /mile	=	2.82473 litre/km
1 gallon (US) /mile	=	2.35208 litre/km
1 litre/km	=	0.354016 gallon (imperial) /mile
1 km/litre	=	2.82473 mile/gallon (imperial)
1 litre/100 km	=	282.473 (divided by) mpg (imperial)
1 litre/100 km	=	235.208 (divided by) mpg (US)
1 mpg (imperial)	=	282.473 (divided by) litre/100 km
1 mpg (US)	=	235.208 (divided by) litre/100 km

Temperature

Celsius	=	(F – 32) x 5 / 9
Fahrenheit	=	(C x 9 / 5) + 32

Fuel consumption converter -

litres / 100 km	miles / gallon (imperial)
3	100
	80
4	70
5	60
6	50
	40
8	
	30
10	25
12	
	20
15	
	15
20	
	12
25	
	10
30	
	8
40	7
	6
50	
	5

– APPENDICES –

GRADIENT CONVERSION TABLE

Gradient conversion rule: To convert from either a ratio to a percentage, or from a percentage to a ratio, in both cases divide 100 by the significant number and round off the answer.

1:3 = 33%
      30%
1:4 = 25%
1:5 = 20%
1:6 = 17%
1:7 = 14%
1:8 = 12%
1:9 = 11%
1:10 = 10%
1:12 = 8%
1:14 = 7%
1:20 = 5%

Note: Other percentage figures may sometimes be signposted, especially for steeper hills, *e.g.* 22%.

TYPICAL COEFFICIENTS OF FRICTION

	wet min	wet max	dry min	dry max
Rubber on:				
asphalt	0.25	0.75	0.5	0.8
concrete	0.45	0.75	0.6	0.85
snow	-	-	-	0.2
ice	0.05	0.1	-	-

	min	max
Brake lining on metal	0.5	0.7

MAXIMUM LENGTHS OF VEHICLES (UK)

vehicle type	max. length (metres)
rigid bus	12.0
rigid lorry	12.0
articulated lorry, including stepframe types	16.5
articulated lorry, with low loader trailer	18.0
articulated bus	18.0
lorry and trailer combination	18.0
lorry and trailer combination road train	18.35
semitrailer	14.04
composite trailer	14.04
car transporter semitrailer	16.69
drawbar trailer, drawn by a vehicle over 3.5 tonnes MGW	12.0
drawbar trailer, drawn by a vehicle up to 3.5 tonnes MGW	7.0
special types for exceptionally long indivisible load	27.4
track laying vehicle	9.2

MAXIMUM WIDTHS OF VEHICLES

vehicle type	maximum width, metres
motor car	2.5
heavy motor car	2.5
motor tractor	2.5
trailer drawn by a vehicle MGW exceeding 3.5 tonnes	2.5
refrigerated vehicle / trailer	2.6
locomotive	2.75
trailer drawn by a vehicle MGW less than 3.5 tonnes	2.3
trailer drawn by a motor cycle	1.5

VEHICLE AGE CLASSIFICATIONS

Vehicle age classifications, UK
Emancipation run car: the annual London to Brighton veteran car run, for cars built on or before 31st December 1904.
Edwardian: any vehicle built between 1st January 1905 and 6 May 1910 inclusive.
veteran: any vehicle built on or before 31st December 1918.
vintage: any vehicle built between 1st January 1919 and 31st December 1929 inclusive.
classic: any vehicle built on or after 1st January 1930 and more than 25 years old.
vintageant: any vehicle built before 1st January 1940.
pre-war classic: any vehicle built between 1st January 1930 and 2nd September 1939 inclusive.
WW2 classic: any vehicle built during the Second World War, mainly military vehicles, from 3rd September 1939 to 11th November 1945 inclusive.
post war classic: any vehicle built on or after 12th November 1945 and more than 25 years old.
historic: any vehicle built before 1st January 1960.

Vehicle age classifications, USA
antique: any vehicle constructed before 1925.
classic: certain models constructed during the years 1925 to 1948 inclusive.
milestone: certain models constructed during the years 1946 to 1970 inclusive.

INTERNATIONAL ACCIDENT RATES

country	Road deaths per 10,000 motor vehicles	Motor vehicles per 1,000 population
Iceland	0.7	551
Norway	1.1	536
Japan	1.2	669
England	1.2	469

330

Country		
Sweden	1.3	501
Switzerland	1.4	602
Netherlands	1.5	447
Wales	1.5	444
Finland	1.7	446
Italy	1.8	617
Australia	1.8	614
Canada	1.8	573
Germany	1.9	559
Scotland	1.9	395
USA	2.0	787
Lebanon	2.0	333
Northern Ireland	2.1	408
New Zealand	2.2	639
Austria	2.3	580
Denmark	2.4	430
Peru	2.5	25
France	2.6	524
Belgium	2.7	525
Luxembourg	2.8	
Spain	2.9	488
Czechoslovakia	3	457
Ireland	3	388
Bahrain	3	294
Israel	3	271
Madagascar	3	
Cambodia	3	
Mexico	3	
Greece	4	497
Bulgaria	4	297
Bhutan	4	
Paraguay	4	
Singapore	4	
Barbados	4	
Estonia	4	
Bahamas	4	
Brunei Darussalam	4	
Portugal	5	436
Hungary	5	289
Bolivia	5	
Macedonia	5	
Slovakia	5	
Slovenia	5	
Hong Kong	5	
Poland	6	291
Iran	6	81
Laos	6	
Indonesia	6	
Costa Rica	6	
Yugoslavia	7	185
Chad	7	
Croatia	7	
Lithuania	7	
Malaysia	8	
Romania	9	140
Turkey	9	122
Jamaica	9	
Thailand	9	
Brazil	10	10
Georgia	10	
Fiji	10	
Korea	11	263
Belarus	11	153
Vietnam	11	

Country		
Latvia	11	
Argentina	12	12
Chile	12	11
Saint Lucia	12	
Trinidad & Tobago	13	
Saudi Arabia	14	151
Russia	14	140
Benin	14	
Mauritius	15	12
Panama	15	
Oman	16	144
Mali	16	
South Africa	17	158
Zimbabwe	17	64
Pakistan	17	
Jordan	19	68
Bosnia	19	
Herzegovina	19	
Kazakhstan	20	82
Egypt	20	37
Cuba	20	20
India	20	
Azerbaijan	20	
Ecuador	21	21
Sierra Leone	21	
Congo	23	
Algeria	24	52
Yemen	24	34
Albania	24	
Papua New Guinea	25	
Sri Lanka	25	
China	26	
Honduras	26	
Gabon	28	
Nicaragua	28	
Mongolia	30	
El Salvador	31	12
Uruguay	33	33
Belize	34	
Syria	36	29
Myanmar	37	
Zambia	39	26
Kyrgyzstan	41	
Bangladesh	44	
Swaziland	44	
Cameroon	52	
Tonga	52	
Columbia	56	55
Venezuela	58	58
Botswana	62	
Kenya	64	14
Senegal	64	
Nigeria	65	12
Lesotho	87	
Tanzania	111	5
Cape Verde	112	
Guinea	121	
Uganda	122	7
Malawi	193	6
Ethiopia	195	1
Central Africa Republic	339	

The numbering system is based upon 6 arterial routes radiating from London and which are numbered clockwise from A1 to A6, and the A7 to A9 radiating clockwise from Edinburgh.

Roads in each sector between these arterials are numbered sequentially with the lowest number signifying the road of greatest importance (when the numbering system was defined in 1921). For example, a road in the sector between the A4 and A5 will begin with the digit 4, and may be numbered A40 to A49, A400 to A499, or A4000 to A4999.

A road passing between 2 or more sectors is numbered according to the most anticlockwise sector through which it passes.

Secondary roads are prefixed with a B and continue the same numbering system after the highest numbered A road in each sector.

Motorway numbering loosely follows that of A roads.

A 3-digit motorway number is generally referenced to a primary motorway by the first 2 digits, *e.g.* M621 is a spur from M62. (opposite from USA system)

In some cases an A road may be reconstructed and upgraded to become a motorway, sometimes for only part of its length. In these cases the motorway section may be numbered *e.g.* A1M or A58M.

Road	Route
A1	London – Edinburgh
A2	London – Dover
A3	London – Portsmouth
A4	London – Bristol
A5	London – Holyhead
A6	London – Carlisle
A7	Edinburgh – Carlisle
A8	Edinburgh – Glasgow
A9	Edinburgh – John o' Groats
M1	London – Leeds (also E13)
M2	London – Canterbury
M3	London – Southampton
M4	London – Swansea (part of E30)
M5	Birmingham – Exeter
M6	Coventry – Carlisle (part of E5)
M8	Edinburgh – Glasgow (part of E16)
M9	Edinburgh – Stirling
M10	M1 – St. Albans spur
M11	London – Cambridge
M18	Rotherham – Goole
M20	London – Folkestone
M23	London – Crawley
M25	London orbital motorway
M26	M20 – M25 Sevenoaks link
M27	Portsmouth – Southampton
M32	M4 – Bristol spur
M40	London – Birmingham
M42	Birmingham eastern ring
M45	M1 – Coventry spur
M48	M4 – Chepstow link

M49	M4 – M5 Bristol link
M50	M5 – Ross on Wye spur
M53	Liverpool – Chester
M54	Birmingham – Shrewsbury
M55	M6 – Blackpool spur
M56	Manchester – Chester
M57	Liverpool east ring
M58	Liverpool – Wigan
M60	Manchester ring
M61	Manchester – Preston
M62	Liverpool – Hull (part of E20)
M63	Manchester south ring
M65	Preston – Nelson
M66	Manchester north spur
M67	Manchester east spur
M69	Coventry – Leicester
M73	M74 – Glasgow east spur
M74	Glasgow – Carlisle
M77	Glasgow south spur
M80	Glasgow – Stirling
M85	M90 – Perth spur
M90	Edinburgh – Perth
M180	Doncaster – Grimsby (part of E22)
M181	M180 – Scunthorpe spur
M271	M27 – Southampton spur
M275	M27 – Portsmouth spur
M602	Manchester city west radial
M606	M62 – Bradford spur
M621	M62 – Leeds link
M876	M9 – M80 Falkirk link

Primary and intermediate routes have 2 digit numbers.
North–South orientated primary routes have 2 digit odd numbers ending in the figure 5, and increasing from west to east.
East–West orientated primary routes have 2 digit even numbers ending in the figure 0, and increasing from north to south.
Intermediate routes have 2 digit odd numbers for north – south routes, or 2 digit even numbers for east – west routes falling within the numbers of the primary routes between which they are located.
A sea crossing within a route is indicated by ≈ symbol.

Primary Euroroutes
West – East orientation

Road	Route
E10	Narvik – Kiruna – Luleå
E20	Shannon – Dublin ≈ Liverpool – Hull ≈ Esbjerg – Nyborg ≈ Korsør Køge – Copenhagen ≈ Malmö – Stockholm ≈ Tallinn – St. Petersburg
E30	Cork – Rosslare ≈ Fishguard – London – Felixtowe ≈ Hook of Holland – Utrecht – Hannover – Berlin – Warsaw – Minsk – Moscow
E40	Calais – Brussels – Aachen – Cologne – Dresden – Krakow – L'vov – Kiev – Rostov-na Donu

E50	Brest – Paris – Metz – Nüremberg – Prague – Mukachëvo
E60	Brest – Tours – Besançon – Basle – Innsbruck – Vienna – Budapest – Bucharest – Constanta
E70	La Coruña – Bilbao – Bordeaux – Lyon – Torino – Verona – Trieste – Zagreb – Belgrade – Bucharest – Varna
E80	Lisbon – Coimbra – Salamanca – Pau – Toulouse – Nice – Genoa – Rome – Pescara ≈ Dubrovnic – Sofia – Istanbul – Ankara – Erzurum – Tehran
E90	Lisbon – Madrid – Barcelona ≈ Mazara del Vallo – Messina ≈ Reggio di Calabria – Brindisi ≈ Igoumenitsa – Thessaloniki – Gelibolu ≈ Lapseki – Ankara – Baghdad

Intermediate Euroroutes
West – East orientation

Road	Route
E06	Olderfjord – Kirkenes
E12	Mo-i-Rana – Umeå ≈ Vaasa – Helsinki
E14	Trondheim – Sundsvall
E16	Londonderry – Belfast ≈ Glasgow – Edinburgh
E18	Craigavon – Larne ≈ Stranraer – Newcastle ≈ Stavanger – Oslo – Stockholm – Kappelskär ≈ Mariehamn ≈ Turku – Helsinki – St. Petersburg
E22	Holyhead – Manchester – Immingham ≈ Amsterdam – Hamburg – Sassnitz ≈ Trelleborg – Norrköping
E24	Birmingham – Felixtowe (A14)
E26	Hamburg – Berlin
E28	Berlin – Gdansk
E32	London – Harwich (A12)
E34	Antwerp – Bad Oeynhausen
E36	Berlin – Legnica
E42	Dunkirk – Aschaffenburg
E44	Le Havre – Luxembourg – Giessen
E46	Cherbourg – Liège
E48	Schweinfurt – Prague
E52	Strasbourg – Salzburg
E54	Paris – Basle – Munich
E56	Nüremberg – Sattledt
E58	Vienna – Bratislava
E62	Nantes – Geneva - Tortona
E64	Turin – Brescia
E66	Fortezza – Székesfehérvár
E68	Szeged – Brasov
E72	Bordeaux – Toulouse
E74	Nice – Alessandria
E76	Migliarino – Florence
E78	Grosseto – Fanto
E82	Porto – Tordesillas
E84	Kesan – Silivri
E86	Krystalopigi – Yefira
E88	Ankara – Refahiye
E92	Igoumenitsa – Volos
E94	Corinth – Athens
E96	Izmir – Sivrihisar
E98	Topbogazi – Syria

Primary Euroroutes
North – South orientation

Road	Route
E05	Greenock – Birmingham – Southampton ≈ Le Havre – Paris – Bordeaux – Madrid – Algeciras
E15	Inverness – Edinburgh – London – Dover ≈ Calais – Paris – Lyon – Barcelona – Algeciras
E25	Hook of Holland – Luxembourg – Strasbourg – Basle – Geneva – Turin – Genoa
E35	Amsterdam – Cologne – Basle – Milan – Rome
E45	Gothenburg ≈ Frederikshavn – Hamburg – Munich – Innsbruck – Bologna – Rome – Naples – Villa S Giovanni ≈ Messina – Gela
E55	Kemi – Torino – Stockholm – Helsingborg ≈ Helsinger – Copenhagen – Gedser ≈ Rostock – Berlin – Prague – Salzburg – Rimini – Brindisi ≈ Igoumenitsa – Kalamata
E65	Malamö – Ystrad – Swinoujscie – Prague – Zagreb – Dubrovnic – Bitolj – Antirrion ≈ Rion – Kalamata – Kissamos – Chania
E75	Karasjok – Helsinki ≈ Gdansk – Budapest – Belgrade – Athens ≈ Chania – Sitia
E85	Chernovtsy – Bucharest – Alexandropouli
E95	St. Petersburg – Moscow – Yalta

Intermediate Euroroutes
North – South orientation

Road	Route
E01	Larne – Dublin – Rosslare ≈ La Coruña – Lisbon – Seville
E03	Cherbourg – La Rochelle
E07	Pau – Zaragoza
E09	Orléans – Barcelona
E11	Vierzon – Montpellier
E13	Leeds – London (M1)
E17	Antwerp – Beaune
E19	Amsterdam – Brussels – Paris
E21	Metz – Geneva
E23	Metz – Lausanne
E27	Belfort – Aosta
E29	Cologne – Sarreguemines
E31	Rotterdam – Ludwigshafen
E33	Parma – La Spezia
E37	Bremen – Cologne
E39	Kristiansand – Aalborg
E41	Dortmund – Altdorf
E43	Würzburg – Bellinzona
E47	Nordkap – Oslo – Copenhagen – Rødby ≈ Puttgarden – Lübeck
E49	Magdeburg – Vienna
E51	Berlin – Nüremberg
E53	Plzeò – Munich
E57	Sattledt – Ljubljana
E59	Prague – Zagreb
E61	Klagenfurt – Rijeka

333

E63	Sodankylä – Naantali ≈ Stockholm – Gothenburg
E67	Warsaw – Prague
E69	Tromsø – Tornio
E71	Kosice – Budapest – Split
E73	Budapest – Metkovi
E77	Gdansk – Budapest
E79	Oradea – Calafat ≈ Vidin – Thessaloniki
E81	Halmeu – Piteœti
E83	Bjala – Sofia
E87	Tulcea – Eceabat ≈ Çanakkale – Antalya
E89	Gerede – Ankara
E91	Toprakkale – Syria
E93	Orel – Odessa
E97	Trabzon – Askale
E99	Dogubeyazit – S Urf

USA, INTERSTATE HIGHWAYS & US HIGHWAYS

North–South interstates have **odd** numbers ranging from 5 to 95 numbered sequentially from I5 along the west coast to I95 along the east coast (plus non-sequential I99). Major interstates end in the digit 5, *e.g.* I75, the other numbers are either regional or intrastate.

East–West interstates have **even** numbers ranging from 4 to 98 numbered sequentially from south to north; I4 is in Florida and I94 runs close to the Canadian border. Major interstates end in the digit 0, *e.g.* I80 the other numbers are either regional or intrastate.

3 digit interstates: these are subsequent to the primary interstates having a numbering system I-Xyy where X is a number between 1-9 and yy is the number of the primary interstate, *e.g.* I376 is a spur from I76 (opposite from UK system).
Where X is an odd number it signifies the route is a spur from an interstate.
Where X is an even number it signifies the route is a loop from an interstate or between interstates. Most 3 digit interstates remain in 1 state.

I 5	San Diego – Los Angeles – Sacramento – Seattle – Vancouver
I 8	San Diego – Tuscan
I 10	Los Angeles – Phoenix – San Antonio – Houston – New Orleans – Jacksonville
I 15	San Diego – Las Vegas – Salt Lake City – Great Falls
I 20	Fort Worth – Dallas – Jackson – Birmingham – Atlanta – Columbia
I 25	Albuquerque – Colorado Springs – Denver – Buffalo
I 30	Dallas – Little Rock
I 35	San Antonio – Austin – Fort Worth – Oklahoma City – Wichita – Kansas City – Des Moines – St. Paul – Duluth

I 40	Flagstaff – Albuquerque – Oklahoma City – Little Rock – Memphis – Nashville – Greensboro
I 45	Dallas – Houston
I 55	New Orleans – Jackson – Memphis – St. Louis – Chicago
I 59	New Orleans – Birmingham – Chattanooga
I 64	St. Louis – Louisville – Lexington – Charleston
I 65	Mobile – Birmingham – Nashville – Louisville – Indianapolis – Chicago
I 70	Denver – Kansas City – St. Louis – Indianapolis – Columbus – Philadel phia – Baltimore
I 71	Louisville – Cincinnati – Columbus
I 74	Davenport – Indianapolis – Cincinnati
I 75	Tampa – Atlanta – Cincinnati – Toledo – Detroit
I 78	Harrisburg – New York
I 80	San Francisco – Salt Lake City – Des Moines – Cleveland – New York
I 81	Knoxville – Roanoke – Syracuse
I 85	Montgomery – Atlanta – Greensboro – Petersburg
I 90	Seattle – Billings – Sioux Falls – Chicago – Cleveland – Boston
I 94	Billings – Bismarck – St. Paul – Madison – Milwaukee – Chicago – Detroit
I 95	Miami – Jacksonville – Richmond – Washington DC – Baltimore – New York – Boston – Augusta

North–South highways have **odd** numbers the same as interstates, but numbered from US1 along the east coast to US101 along the west coast, *i.e.* opposite to interstates. Principle routes end in the digit 1, *e.g.* US51, US61.
East–West highways have **even** numbers the same as interstates, but numbered from US2 along the Canadian border to US98 along the Gulf of Mexico coast, *i.e.* opposite to interstates. Principle routes end in the digit 0, *e.g.* US50, US60.
3 digit highways, the additional digit precedes the principle route number as interstates, *e.g.* US366 is a spur from US66.
Some highways numbers are suffixed N, S, E, or W, to show the direction of travel.

US 1	Fort Kent, Maine – Key West, Florida (Atlantic coast highway)
US 10	Seattle, Washington – Detroit, Michigan
US 11	Rouses point, New York – New Orleans, Louisiana
US 20	Newport, Oregon – Boston, Massachusetts
US 21	Cleveland, Ohio – Hunting Island, South Carolina
US 30	Astoria, Oregon – Atlantic City, New Jersey
US 31	Allenville, Michigan – Mobile, Alabama
US 40	San Francisco, California – Atlantic

US 41	City, New Jersey Fort Wilkins, Michigan – Miami Beach, Florida	**EAK**	Kenya Kiribati
US 50	San Francisco, California – Ocean City, Maryland (loneliest road)	**LS**	Lesotho Macau
US 51	Hurley, Wisconsin – New Orleans, Louisiana	**MW**	Malawi
US 60	Los Angeles, California – Virginia Beach, Virginia	**MAL**	Malaysia Maldives
US 61	Grand Portage, Minnesota – New Orleans, Louisiana	**M** **MS**	Malta Mauritius Montserrat
US 66	Santa Monica, California – Chicago, Illinois (Mother Road)	**MOC** **NAM**	Mozambique Namibia Nauru
US 70	Los Angeles, California – Atlantic, North Carolina	**NEP** **NZ**	Nepal New Zealand Norfolk Island
US 71	International Falls, Minnesota – Port Allen, Louisiana	**PAK** **PNG**	Pakistan Papua New Guinea
US 80	San Diego, California – Tybee Island, Georgia	**SY** **SGP**	Seychelles Singapore Solomon Islands
US 81	Pembina, North Dakota – Laredo, Texas	**SO**	Somalia Somaliland
US 90	Pine Springs, Texas – Jacksonville, Florida	**ZA** **CL**	South Africa Sri Lanka St. Helena St. Kitts and Nevis
US 91	Sweetgrass, Montana – Long Beach, California	**WL** **WV**	St. Lucia St. Vincent and the Grenadines
US 101	Olympia, Washington – Los Angeles, California (Pacific coast highway)	**SME** **EAT** **T**	Suriname Swaziland Tanzania Thailand Tonga

---

COUNTRIES/SOVEREIGN TERRITORIES IN WHICH THE RULE OF THE ROAD IS TO DRIVE ON THE LEFT, WITH THEIR DISTINGUISHING SIGN LETTERS

GBA	Alderney Anguilla Antigua and Barbuda
AUS	Australia
BS	Bahamas
BD	Bangladesh
BDS	Barbados Bermuda Bhutan
RB	Botswana
BRU	Brunei Cayman Islands Cook Islands
CY	Cyprus
WD	Dominica East Timor Falkland Islands
FJI	Fiji
GB	Great Britain
WG	Grenada
GBG	Guernsey
GUY	Guyana
HK	Hong Kong
IND	India
RI	Indonesia
IRL	Ireland
GBM	Isle of Man
JA	Jamaica
J	Japan
GBJ	Jersey

TT	Trinidad and Tobago Turks and Caicos Islands Tuvalu
EAU	Uganda Virgin Islands UK
BUI	Virgin Islands USA
RNR	Zambia
EAZ	Zanzibar
ZW	Zimbabwe

Note, some countries either do not have distinguishing sign letters, or use letters that are not internationally recognised; some others have changed in recent years, *e.g.* Namibia has changed from SWA (South West Africa) to NAM.

COUNTRIES/SOVEREIGN TERRITORIES IN WHICH THE RULE OF THE ROAD IS TO DRIVE ON THE RIGHT, WITH THEIR DISTINGUISHING SIGN LETTERS

AFG	Afghanistan
AL	Albania
DZ	Algeria
AND	Andorra Angola
RA	Argentina
ARM	Armenia

	Aruba		
A	Austria	IL	Israel
AZ	Azerbaijan	I	Italy
BRN	Bahrain	CI	Ivory coast
BY	Belarus	HKJ	Jordan
B	Belgium	K	Kampuchea
BH	Belize	KZ	Kazakhstan
DY	Benin		Korea, Democratic Peoples
BOL	Bolivia	ROK	Korea, Republic
BIH	Bosnia & Herzegovina	KWT	Kuwait
BR	Brazil	KS	Kyrgyzstan
BG	Bulgaria	LAO	Laos
	Burkina Faso	LV	Latvia
RU	Burundi	RL	Lebanon
CAM	Cameroon	LS	Lesotho
CDN	Canada	LB	Liberia
	Cape Verde	LAR	Libya
RCA	Central African Republic	FL	Liechtenstein
TD	Chad	LT	Lithuania
RCH	Chile	L	Luxembourg
RC	China	MK	Macedonia
SU	CIS, formerly USSR	RM	Madagascar
CO	Columbia	RMM	Mali
	Comoros		Mariana Islands
RCB	Congo		Marshal Islands
CR	Costa Rica		Martinique
HR	Croatia (Hrvatska)	RIM	Mauritania
C	Cuba	MEX	Mexico
CZ	Czech Republic		Micronesia
DK	Denmark	MD	Moldovia
	Djibouti	MC	Monaco
DOM	Dominican Republic		Mongolia
EC	Ecuador	MA	Morocco
ET	Egypt	BUR	Myanmar
ES	El Salvador	NL	Netherlands
	Equatorial Guinea	NA	Netherlands Antilles
	Eritrea		New Caledonia
EST	Estonia	NIC	Nicaragua
ETH	Ethiopia	RN	Niger
FR	Faeroe Islands	WAN	Nigeria
FIN	Finland	N	Norway
F	France and territories		Oman
F	French Guiana		Palau
F	French Polynesia	PA	Panama
GAB	Gabon	PY	Paraguay
WAG	Gambia	PE	Peru
	Gaza Strip	RP	Philippines
GE	Georgia	PL	Poland
D	Germany	P	Portugal
GH	Ghana		Puerto Rico
GBZ	Gibraltar	QA	Qatar
GR	Greece	F	Reunion
	Greenland	RO	Romania
	Guadeloupe	RUS	Russian Federation
	Guam	RWA	Rwanda
GCA	Guatemala	RSM	San Marino
RG	Guinea		Sao Tome and Principe
	Guinea Bissau	SA	Saudi Arabia
RH	Haiti	SN	Senegal
	Honduras	WAL	Sierra Leone
H	Hungary	SK	Slovakia
IS	Iceland	SLO	Slovenia
IR	Iran	E	Spain
IRQ	Iraq		St. Barthélemy
			St. Martin

SUD	Sudan
SD	Svalbard & Jan Mayen Islands
S	Sweden
CH	Switzerland
SYR	Syria
RC	Taiwan, China
TJ	Tajikistan
TG	Togo
TN	Tunisia
TR	Turkey
TM	Turkmenistan
UA	Ukraine
UAE	United Arab Emirates
USA	United States of America
ROU	Uruguay
UZ	Uzbekistan
	Vanuatu
V	Vatican City
YV	Venezuela
VN	Vietnam
	Wallis and Futuna Islands
	West Bank
	Western Sahara
WS	Western Samoa
ADN	Yemen
YU	Yugoslavia
ZRE	Zaire

15	not used
16	Norway
17	Finland
18	Denmark
19	Romania
20	Poland
21	Portugal
22	Russian Federation
23	Greece
24	Ireland
25	Croatia
26	Slovenia
27	Slovakia
28	Belarus
29	Estonia
30	not used
31	Bosnia and Herzegovina
32	not used
33	not used
34	not used
35	not used
36	not used
37	Turkey
38	not used
39	not used
40	Macedonia

Note, some countries either do not have distinguishing sign letters, or use letters that are not internationally recognised; some others have changed in recent years, *e.g.* Finland has changed from SF to FIN.

e MARK AND E MARK Approval COUNTRY IDENTIFICATION NUMBERS

The following is the suffix number to the 'e mark' or 'E mark'. The E and its country identifying number are contained in a circle, the e and its number are contained in a square, marked on all vehicle parts requiring safety approval.

1	Germany
2	France
3	Italy
4	Netherlands
5	Sweden
6	Belgium
7	Hungary
8	Czech Republic
9	Spain
10	Yugoslavia
11	UK
12	Austria
13	Luxembourg
14	Switzerland

COUNTRIES/STATES WITH NO UPPER SPEED LIMIT ON SOME ROADS

British Virgin Islands
Germany
India
Isle of Man
Madagascar
Montana, USA
Wyoming, USA

UK SPEED LIMIT CHANGES BY DATES

1865 (Red Flag Act) farm vehicles restricted to 4 mph outside towns, 2 mph within towns.
1896 Red Flag Act repealed, maximum speed 12 mph.
1903 Motor Car Act: maximum speed 20 mph.
1930 Motor Car Act: maximum speed 30 mph.
1934 maximum speed 30 mph in built-up areas, unrestricted outside built-up areas.
1940 wartime night maximum speed limit 20 mph.
1956 maximum speed reduced to 50 mph on all roads outside built-up areas.
1965 motorways and dual carriageways maximum speed 70 mph.
1974 maximum speed outside builtup areas temporarily reduced to 50 mph.
1991 20 mph zones introduced in some areas.

VEHICLE EMISSION TAX BANDS (UK)

	VED band A	VED band B	VED band C	VED band D
CO2 emissions g/km	up to 150	151 to 165	166 to 185	over 185

337

Winter braking distances at 30 km/h (20 mph)

	dry tarmac metres	wet tarmac metres	snow * metres	ice ** metres
standard tyres	6	12	24	52
snow tyres	6	12	18	36
studded tyres	10	20	12	18
snow chains	15	30	12	24

Notes:

The braking distance figures do NOT include thinking and reaction distance, for overall stopping distances add 6 metres to all figures.

* The figures for snow assume it is of large flakes, dry, and frozen, *i.e.* stopping distances will be significantly longer in powder snow and wet snow.

** The figures for ice assume it is not wet, *i.e.* stopping distances will be significantly longer on wet ice.

Braking distance is proportional to the square of the roadspeed, therefore if speeds are doubled to 60 km/h (40 mph) all above figures must be multiplied by 4.

Overall stopping distances

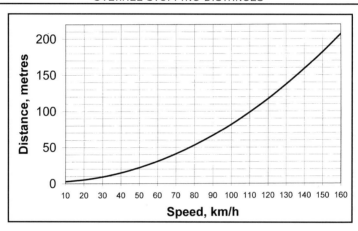

Tyre sidewall decode

European metric — 185 / 70 R 15
section width (millimetres)
aspect ratio
radial construction
rim diameter (inches)

European — 155 / 65 H R 14
section width (millimetres)
aspect ratio
speed rating
radial construction
rim diameter (inches)

European DIN — 195 / 60 R 15 91 V
section width (millimetres)
aspect ratio
radial construction
rim diameter (inches)
load rating
speed rating

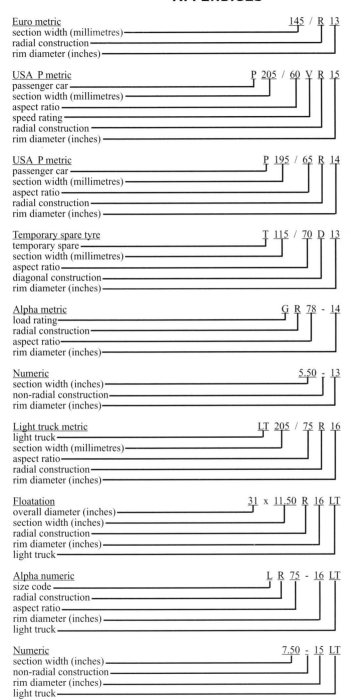

Euro metric   145 / R 13
section width (millimetres)
radial construction
rim diameter (inches)

USA P metric   P 205 / 60 V R 15
passenger car
section width (millimetres)
aspect ratio
speed rating
radial construction
rim diameter (inches)

USA P metric   P 195 / 65 R 14
passenger car
section width (millimetres)
aspect ratio
radial construction
rim diameter (inches)

Temporary spare tyre   T 115 / 70 D 13
temporary spare
section width (millimetres)
aspect ratio
diagonal construction
rim diameter (inches)

Alpha metric   G R 78 - 14
load rating
radial construction
aspect ratio
rim diameter (inches)

Numeric   5.50 - 13
section width (inches)
non-radial construction
rim diameter (inches)

Light truck metric   LT 205 / 75 R 16
light truck
section width (millimetres)
aspect ratio
radial construction
rim diameter (inches)

Floatation   31 x 11.50 R 16 LT
overall diameter (inches)
section width (inches)
radial construction
rim diameter (inches)
light truck

Alpha numeric   L R 75 - 16 LT
size code
radial construction
aspect ratio
rim diameter (inches)
light truck

Numeric   7.50 - 15 LT
section width (inches)
non-radial construction
rim diameter (inches)
light truck

– APPENDICES –

TYRE LOAD INDEX CODES

load index	kg per tyre	load index	kg per tyre	load index	kg per tyre
0	45	51	195	102	850
1	46.2	52	200	103	875
2	47.5	53	206	104	900
3	48.7	54	212	105	925
4	50	55	218	106	950
5	51.5	56	224	107	975
6	53	57	230	108	1000
7	54.5	58	236	109	1030
8	56	59	243	110	1060
9	58	60	250	111	1090
10	60	61	257	112	1120
11	61.5	62	265	113	1150
12	63	63	272	114	1180
13	65	64	280	115	1215
14	67	65	290	116	1250
15	69	66	295	117	1285
16	71	67	305	118	1320
17	73	68	315	119	1360
18	75	69	325	120	1400
19	77.5	70	335	121	1450
20	80	71	345	122	1500
21	82.5	72	355	123	1550
22	85	73	365	124	1600
23	87.5	74	375	125	1650
24	90	75	387	126	1700
25	92.5	76	400	127	1750
26	95	77	412	128	1800
27	97.5	78	425	129	1850
28	100	79	437	130	1900
29	103	80	450	131	1950
30	106	81	462	132	2000
31	109	82	475	133	2060
32	112	83	487	134	2120
33	115	84	500	135	2180
34	118	85	515	136	2240
35	121	86	530	137	2300
36	124	87	545	138	2360
37	127	88	560	139	2430
38	130	89	580	140	2500
39	133	90	600	141	2575
40	140	91	615	142	2650
41	145	92	625	143	2725
42	150	93	650	144	2800
43	155	94	670	145	2900
44	160	95	690	146	3000
45	165	96	710	147	3075
46	170	97	730	148	3150
47	175	98	750	149	3250
48	180	99	775	150	3350
49	185	100	800		
50	190	101	825		

TYRE SPEED RATING CODES

speed symbol	maximum speed capability of the car	
	up to, km/h	up to, mph
L	120	75
M	130	81
N	140	87
P	150	93
Q	160	99

R	170	106
S	180	113
T	190	118
U	200	124
H	210	130
VR	210 +	130 +
V	240	150
Z	240 +	150 +
ZR	240 +	150 +
W	270	168
Y	300	186

WIDE LOADS (UK)

width	requirements
over 305 mm beyond side of vehicle	side markers
2.9 m to 3.5 m	side markers and police notification
3.5 m to 4.3 m	side markers, police notification, statutory attendant
4.3 m to 5.0 m	side markers, police notification, statutory attendant, speed limited to 30 mph on motorways speed limited to 25 mph on dual carriageways speed limited to 20 mph on all other roads
5.0 m to 6.1 m	side markers, police notification, statutory attendant, speed limited to 30 mph on motorways speed limited to 25 mph on dual carriageways speed limited to 20 mph on all other roads Department of Transport approval

VIN NUMBER DECODE

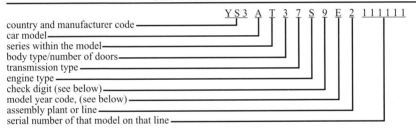

country and manufacturer code
car model
series within the model
body type/number of doors
transmission type
engine type
check digit (see below)
model year code, (see below)
assembly plant or line
serial number of that model on that line

Notes:
The 6th digit is not necessarily the actual number of doors, but is a code for the number of doors in that body type.
The check digit is calculated mathematically from an assigned value given to the letters added to the numbers and divided by 11 resulting in a number in the range $0 - 10$, but where the character X is used to represent 10.
For heavy vehicles, some of the characters have different meanings.

Model year code table

year	code	year	code	year	code
1980	A	1992	N	2004	4
1981	B	1993	P	2005	5
1982	C	1994	R	2006	6
1983	D	1995	S	2007	7
1984	E	1996	T	2008	8
1985	F	1997	V	2009	9
1986	G	1998	W	2010	A
1987	H	1999	X	2011	B
1988	J	2000	Y	2012	C
1989	K	2001	1	2013	D
1990	L	2002	2	2014	E
1991	M	2003	3	2015	F

From 1st September 2001, UK vehicle registration codes will be replaced by the following system:
The first letter denotes the region.
The second letter denotes the VRO in that region.
The 2 numbers denote the period during which the vehicle was first registered.
The last 3 letters are random.

Region code letters

code	region	code	region
A	Anglia	M	Manchester
B	Birmingham	N	North
C	Cymru	O	Oxford
D	Deeside to Shrewsbury	P	Preston
E	Essex	R	Reading
F	Forest and Fens	S	Scotland
G	Garden of England (Kent)	V	Severn Valley
H	Hampshire and Dorset	W	West Country
K	Luton	Y	Yorkshire
L	London		

code	start date	end date	code	start date	end date
			51	1 Sep 2001	28 Feb 2002
02	1 Mar 2002	31 Aug 2002	52	1 Sep 2002	28 Feb 2003
03	1 Mar 2003	31 Aug 2003	53	1 Sep 2003	29 Feb 2004
04	1 Mar 2004	31 Aug 2004	54	1 Sep 2004	28 Feb 2005
05	1 Mar 2005	31 Aug 2005	55	1 Sep 2005	28 Feb 2006
06	1 Mar 2006	31 Aug 2006	56	1 Sep 2006	28 Feb 2007
07	1 Mar 2007	31 Aug 2007	57	1 Sep 2007	29 Feb 2008
08	1 Mar 2008	31 Aug 2008	58	1 Sep 2008	28 Feb 2009
09	1 Mar 2009	31 Aug 2009	59	1 Sep 2009	28 Feb 2010
10	1 Mar 2010	31 Aug 2010	60	1 Sep 2010	28 Feb 2011
11	1 Mar 2011	31 Aug 2011	61	1 Sep 2011	29 Feb 2012
12	1 Mar 2012	31 Aug 2012	62	1 Sep 2012	28 Feb 2013
13	1 Mar 2013	31 Aug 2013	63	1 Sep 2013	28 Feb 2014
14	1 Mar 2014	31 Aug 2014	64	1 Sep 2014	28 Feb 2015

The year code numbers will follow this incremental pattern until the year 2050

For example: **AA 51 ABC**
means the vehicle was registered in the Anglia region at the Peterborough VRO,
between 1 September 2001 and 28 February 2002.

flag colour	flag movement	flag meaning
red	only shown at the start-finish line	the race is stopped.
white	stationary	the course car or a slow vehicle is on the track
	waved	the slow vehicle is immediately ahead
black	stationary, with car number in white	must stop at pit and report to clerk of the course, a stop-go penalty
black / white diagonal		warning of unsportsmanlike behaviour.
black with red spot	stationary, with car number in white	mechanical failure, must pit.
blue	stationary	a faster car is close behind, give way.
	waved	a faster car wants to overtake, urgent give way.
yellow-red vertical stripes	stationary	oil or water on the track.
	waved	the track is very slippery immediately ahead
yellow	stationary	hazard on the track, no overtaking, slow down, prepare to follow an unusual line.

	waved	imminent hazard on the track, no overtaking, slow down, possibility of stopping.
green	stationary	end of danger following yellow flags
	waved	start of warm-up lap
black / white chequered	stationary	end of race
	waved	winner, end of race

FORMULA 1 WORLD CHAMPIONS

year	driver	country	car
1950	Dr. Giuseppe Farina	Italy	Alfa Romeo
1951	Juan Manuel Fangio	Argentina	Alfa Romeo
1952	Alberto Ascari	Italy	Ferrari
1953	Alberto Ascari	Italy	Ferrari
1954	Juan Manuel Fangio	Argentina	Maserati/Mercedes-Benz
1955	Juan Manuel Fangio	Argentina	Mercedes-Benz
1956	Juan Manuel Fangio	Argentina	Ferrari
1957	Juan Manuel Fangio	Argentina	Maserati
1958	Mike Hawthorn	Great Britain	Ferrari
1959	Jack Brabham	Australia	Cooper-Climax
1960	Jack Brabham	Australia	Cooper-Climax
1961	Phil Hill	USA	Ferrari
1962	Graham Hill	Great Britain	BRM
1963	Jim Clark	Great Britain	Lotus-Climax
1964	John Surtees	Great Britain	Ferrari
1965	Jim Clark	Great Britain	Lotus-Climax
1966	Jack Brabham	Australia	Brabham-Repco
1967	Denis Hulme	New Zealand	Brabham-Repco
1968	Graham Hill	Great Britain	Lotus-Cosworth
1969	Jackie Stewart	Great Britain	Matra-Cosworth
1970	Jochen Rindt	Austria	Lotus-Cosworth
1971	Jackie Stewart	Great Britain	Tyrrell-Cosworth
1972	Emerson Fitipaldi	Brazil	Lotus-Cosworth
1973	Jackie Stewart	Great Britain	Tyrrell-Cosworth
1974	Emerson Fitipaldi	Brazil	McLaren-Cosworth
1975	Nicki Lauda	Austria	Ferrari
1976	James Hunt	Great Britain	McLaren-Cosworth
1977	Nicki Lauda	Austria	Ferrari
1978	Mario Andretti	USA	Lotus-Cosworth
1979	Jody Scheckter	South Africa	Ferrari
1980	Alan Jones	Australia	Williams-Cosworth
1981	Nelson Piquet	Brazil	Brabham-Cosworth
1982	Keke Rosberg	Finland	Williams-Cosworth
1983	Nelson Piquet	Brazil	Brabham-BMW turbo
1984	Nicki Lauda	Austria	McLaren-TAG Porsche turbo
1985	Alain Prost	France	McLaren-TAG Porsche turbo
1986	Alain Prost	France	McLaren-TAG Porsche turbo
1987	Nelson Piquet	Brazil	Williams-Honda turbo
1988	Ayrton Senna	Brazil	McLaren-Honda turbo
1989	Alain Prost	France	McLaren
1990	Ayrton Senna	Brazil	McLaren
1991	Ayrton Senna	Brazil	McLaren
1992	Nigel Mansell	Great Britain	Williams
1993	Alain Prost	France	Williams-Renault
1994	Michael Schumacher	Germany	Benetton
1995	Michael Schumacher	Germany	Benetton
1996	Damon Hill	Great Britain	Williams
1997	Jacques Villeneuve	Canada	Williams
1998	Mika Hakkinen	Finland	McLaren-Merceces
1999	Mika Hakkinen	Finland	McLaren-Merceces
2000	Michael Schumacher	Germany	Ferrari
2001	Michael Schumacher	Germany	Ferrari

RALLY PACE NOTES - BEND DESIGNATIONS

There are several methods in use for defining the sharpness of a bend. The two systems shown here are the most common.

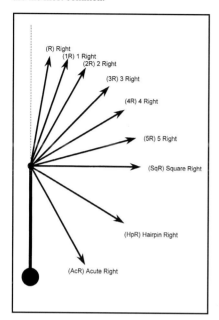

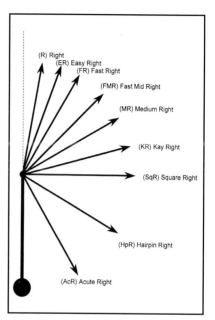

ENDORSEMENT OFFENCE CODES

Code	Offence	Penalty points
Accidents		
AC10	Failing to stop after an accident	5-10
AC20	Failing to give particulars or to report an accident	5-10
AC30	Undefined accident offences	5-10
Disqualified driver		
BA10	Driving whilst disqualified by order of a court	6
BA30	Attempting to drive whilst disqualified by order of a court	6
Careless driving		
CD10	Driving without due care and attention	3-9
CD20	Driving without reasonable consideration for other road users	3-9
CD30	Driving without due care and attention or without reasonable consideration for other road users	3-9
CD40	Causing death through careless driving when unfit through drink	3-11
CD50	Causing death through careless driving when unfit through drugs	3-11
CD60	Causing death through careless driving with alcohol level above the limit	3-11
CD70	Causing death through careless driving then failing to supply a specimen for analysis	3-11

– APPENDICES –

Construction & Use

CU10	Using a vehicle with defective brakes	3
CU20	Causing or likely to cause danger by reason of use of unsuitable vehicle or using a vehicle with parts or accessories in a dangerous condition	3
CU30	Using a vehicle with a defective tyre	3
CU40	Using a vehicle with defective steering	3
CU50	Causing or likely to cause danger by reason of load or passengers	3

Reckless/dangerous driving

DD40	Dangerous driving	3-11
DD60	Manslaughter or culpable homicide while driving a vehicle	3-11
DD80	Causing death by dangerous driving	3-11

Drink or drugs

DR10	Driving or attempting to drive with alcohol level above limit	3-11
DR20	Driving or attempting to drive while unfit through drink	3-11
DR30	Driving or attempting to drive then failing to supply a specimen for analysis	3-11
DR40	In charge of a vehicle while alcohol level above limit	10
DR50	In charge of a vehicle while unfit through drink	10
DR60	Failure to provide a specimen for analysis in circumstances other than driving or attempting to drive	10
DR70	Failure to provide a specimen for breath test	4
DR80	Driving or attempting to drive when unfit through drugs	3-11
DR90	In charge of a vehicle when unfit through drugs	10

Insurance

IN10	Using a vehicle uninsured against third party risks	6-8

Driving licence

LC20	Driving otherwise than in accordance with a licence	3-6
LC30	Driving after making a false declaration about fitness when applying for a licence	3-6
LC40	Driving a vehicle having failed to notify a disability	3-6
LC50	Driving after a licence has been revoked or refused on medical grounds	3-6

Miscellaneous

MS10	Leaving a vehicle in a dangerous position	3
MS20	Unlawful pillion riding	3
MS30	Play street offences	2
MS50	Motor racing on the highway	3-11
MS60	Offences not covered by other codes	
MS70	driving with uncorrected defective eyesight	3
MS80	Refusing to submit to an eyesight test	3
MS90	Failure to give information as to the identity of a driver	3

Motorway

MW10	Contravention of Special Roads Regulations (except speeding)	3

Pedestrian crossings

PC10	Undefined contravention of pedestrian crossing regulations	3
PC20	Contravention of pedestrian crossing regulations with a moving vehicle	3
PC30	Contravention of pedestrian crossing regulations with a stationary vehicle	3

Speed limits

SP10	Exceeding goods vehicle speed limits	3-6
SP20	Exceeding speed limit for type of vehicle (excluding goods or passenger vehicle)	3-6
SP30	Exceeding statutory speed limit on a public road	3-6
SP40	Exceeding passenger vehicle speed limit	3-6
SP50	Exceeding speed limit on a motorway	3-6
SP60	Undefined speed limit offence	3-6

Traffic direction and signs

TS10	Failing to comply with traffic light signal	3
TS20	Failing to comply with double white lines	3
TS30	Failing to comply with a stop sign	3
TS40	Failing to comply with the direction given by a police constable or traffic warden	3
TS50	Failing to comply with a traffic sign (except stop sign)	3
TS60	Failing to comply with a school crossing patrol sign	3
TS70	Undefined failure to comply with a traffic direction sign	3

Special code

TT99	To signify disqualification under the totting up procedure; when the total reaches 12 points in any 3 year period the driver is usually disqualified	

Theft

UT50	Aggravated taking of a vehicle	3-11

Note, in cases when the offence is varied by:
Aiding, abetting, counselling, or procuring:
the last digit 0 of the code is replaced by a digit 2, e.g. DR32.
Causing or permitting:
the last digit 0 of the code is replaced by a digit 4, e.g. CU14.
Inciting:
the last digit 0 of the code is replaced by a digit 6, e.g. SP36.

Visit us on the web –
veloce.co.uk
velocebooks.com

RISK OF COLLISION DUE TO BLOOD ALCOHOL LEVELS

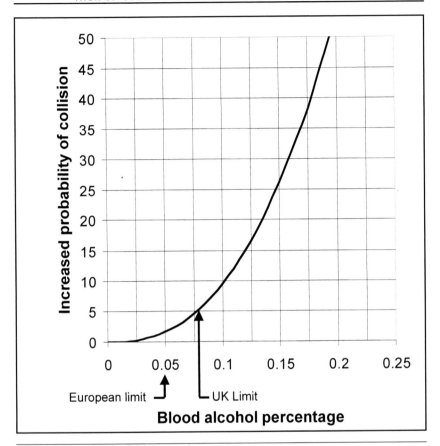

JUNCTION STYLES

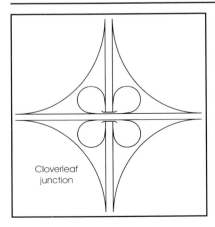

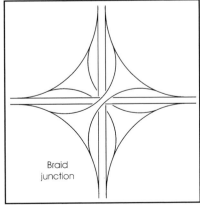

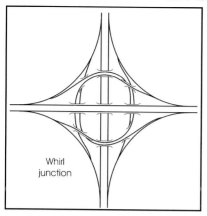

Whirl
junction

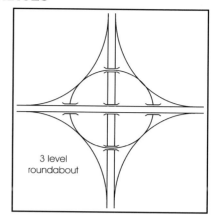

3 level
roundabout

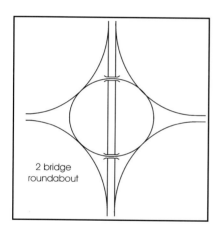

2 bridge
roundabout

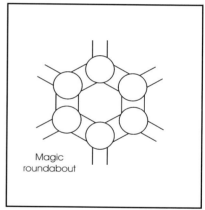

Magic
roundabout

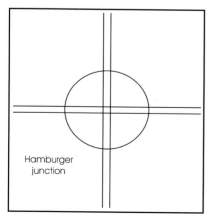

Hamburger
junction

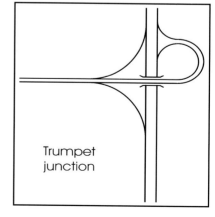

Trumpet
junction

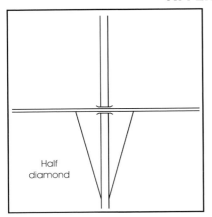

Half
diamond

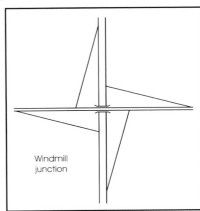

Windmill
junction

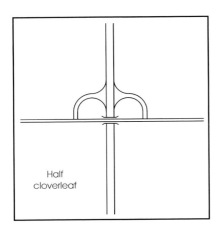

Half
cloverleaf

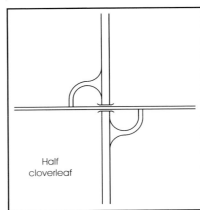

Half
cloverleaf

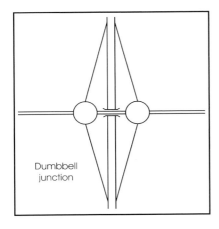

Dumbbell
junction

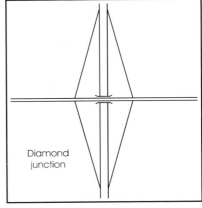

Diamond
junction

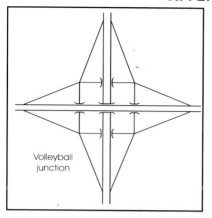

Volleyball
junction

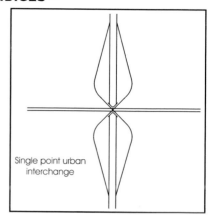

Single point urban
interchange

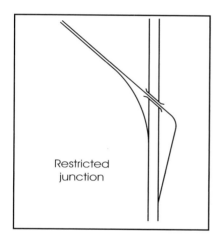

Restricted
junction

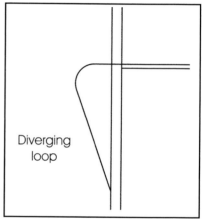

Diverging
loop

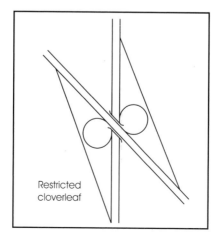

Restricted
cloverleaf

Visit us on the web –
veloce.co.uk
velocebooks.com

Visit us on the web –
veloce.co.uk
velocebooks.com